Handbook of Internet Crime

Handbook of Internet Crime

Edited by

Yvonne Jewkes and Majid Yar

WILLAN
PUBLISHING

Published by

Willan Publishing
Culmcott House
Mill Street, Uffculme
Cullompton, Devon
EX15 3AT, UK
Tel: +44(0)1884 840337
Fax: +44(0)1884 840251
e-mail: info@willanpublishing.co.uk
website: www.willanpublishing.co.uk

Published simultaneously in the USA and Canada by

Willan Publishing
c/o ISBS, 920 NE 58th Ave, Suite 300
Portland, Oregon 97213-3644, USA
Tel: +001(0)503 287 3093
Fax: +001(0)503 280 8832
e-mail: info@isbs.com
website: www.isbs.com

First published 2010

ISBN   978-1-84392-524-8 paperback
       978-1-84392-523-1 hardback

British Library Cataloguing-in-Publication Data

A catalogue record for this book is available from the British Library

FSC
Mixed Sources
Product group from well-managed
forests and other controlled sources

Cert no. SGS-COC-2482
www.fsc.org
© 1996 Forest Stewardship Council

Project management by Deer Park Productions, Tavistock, Devon
Typeset by GCS, Leighton Buzzard, Beds
Printed and bound by T.J. International, Padstow, Cornwall

Contents

List of figures and tables

List of abbreviations

AACP	Alliance Against Counterfeiting and Piracy
ACPO	Association of Chief Police Officers
ACTA	Anti-Counterfeiting Trade Agreement
ADS	Alternate data streams
APWG	Anti-Phishing Working Group
ARPA	Advanced Research Projects Agency
ARPANET	The world's first advanced computer network
ATC	Anti-Terrorism Coalition
ATCSA	Anti-Terrorism Crime and Security Act 2001
AustLII	Australian Legal Information Institute
BBS	Bulletin board services
BPI	British Phonographic Industry
BSA	Business Software Alliance
CEOP	Child Exploitation and Online Protection Centre
CERN	Conseil Européen pour la Recherche Nucléaire, former title of the European Organisation for Nuclear Research
CERT	Computer Emergency Response Team
CGI	Computer-generated images
CII	Critical information infrastructure
CLI	Calling line identity
CMA	Computer Misuse Act 1990
CMC	Computer mediated communication
CODEXTER	Committee of Experts on Terrorism
CSAIs	Child sex abuse images
CSP	Communication service provider
CTC	Combating Terrorism Center
DDOS	Distributed denial-of-service attacks
DES	Data encryption standard
DNS	Domain name server (or system)
DPA	Data Protection Acts 1984 and 1998
DPI	Deep packet inspection
DRD	Data Retention Directive
ECHR	European Convention on Human Rights
ECJ	European Court of Justice
EctHR	European Court of Human Rights
EFF	Electronic Frontier Foundation
EIR	Environmental Information Regulations
ENISA	European Network and Information Security Agency
EPIC	Electronic Privacy Information Centre
FACT	Federation Against Copyright Theft
FIA	Freedom of Information Act
FTP	File transfer protocol
GAC	Governmental advisory committee
GPL	General Public License
GPS	Global positioning satellites
GUI	Graphics user interface
HRA	Human Rights Act 1998

HTML	Hypertext markup language
HTTP	Hypertext transport (or transfer)
ICANN	Internet Corporation for Assigned Names and Numbers
ICO	Information Commissioner's Office
ICPEN	International Consumer Protection and Enforcement Network
ICTs	Information and communication technologies
ILO	International Labour Organisation
IM	Instant messaging
IMC	Independent media centre
IMP	Intermediary computer
INHOPE	Internet Hotline Providers in Europe
IP	Internet Protocol
IP	Intellectual property
IRC	Internet Relay Chart
ISFE	Interactive Software Federation of Europe
ISP	Internet service provider
IWF	Internet Watch Foundation
LAN	Local Area Network
LEAs	Law enforcement and intelligence agencies
MIT	Massachusetts Institute of Technology
MMORPGs	Massively multiplayer online role-playing games
MOO	Multi-user object oriented environments
MSN	Microsoft Network
MUD	Multi-user domain
NCALT	National Centre for Applied Learning Technologies
NCIS	National Criminal Intelligence Service
NCSA	National Cyber Security Alliance
NCTP	National Cybercrime Training Partnership
NEM	New electronic media
NFIB	National Fraud Intelligence Bureau
NFRC	National Fraud Reporting Centre
NHTCU	National Hi-Tech Crime Unit
NMIS	National Management Information System
NSLEC	National Specialist Law Enforcement Centre
NTAC	National Technical Assistance Centre
OECD	Organisation for Economic Cooperation and Development
PACE	Police and Criminal Evidence Act 1984
PCeU	Police Central e-crime Unit
PCTDD	Post-cut-through dialled digits
PDA	Personal digital assistant
PECR	Privacy and Electronic Communications Regulations
RFID	Radio Frequency Identification
RIPA	Regulation of Investigatory Powers Act 2000
SAP	Sentencing Advisory Panel
SCADA	Supervisory Control and Data Acquisition
SF	Science fiction
SOCA	Serious and Organised Crime Agency
TCP	Transmission Control Protocol
URI	Convention specifying the location of information on the World Wide Web
URL	Uniform (or universal) resource locator
VIEW	Video Image Evidence on the Web
VoIP	Voice over Internet Protocol
WGIG	Working Group on Internet Governance
WHOA	Women Halting Online Abuse
WIPO	World Intellectual Property Organisation
WSIS	World Summit on the Information Society

Contributor biographies

Susan W. Brenner is NCR Distinguished Professor of Law and Technology at the University of Dayton School of Law in Dayton, Ohio. She has published a number of law review articles dealing with cybercrime, including 'Fantasy crime' (2008) *Vanderbilt Journal of Technology and Entertainment Law*, 11(1); 'State-sponsored crime: the futility of the Economic Espionage Act' (2006) *Houston Journal of International Law*, 26(1); and 'Toward a criminal law for cyberspace: distributed security' (2004) *Boston University Journal of Science & Technology Law*, 10(2). In 2007, Oxford University Press published her book *Law in an Era of "Smart" Technology,* and in 2009, her most recent book, *Cyber Threats: Emerging Fault Lines of the Nation-States.*

Sheila Brown is a criminologist within the Law Faculty at the University of Plymouth and is author of numerous books, chapters and articles relating to youth crime and justice, information and communications technologies in criminology and criminal justice contexts (including technologies for e-learning and knowledge management) and cybercrime. Among her publications are *Crime and Law in Media Culture* (2003), Open University Press; and 'The criminology of hybrids: rethinking crime and law in technosocial networks' (2006) *Theoretical Criminology*, 10(3).

Jasmine Bruce finished her PhD in 2008. She has completed research in the area of restorative justice on the topic of conference facilitation. She currently works as a Research Associate at the Social Policy Research Centre at the University of New South Wales.

Jo Bryce is Senior Lecturer in Psychology at UCLAN. Her research interests include: the potential consequences of media and ICT use for the psychological and social development of children and young people; the role of ICTs in the commission of criminal offences; and the organisation and function of online criminal networks. Jo was previously the Coordinator of the UK National Awareness Node for Child Safety on the Internet and has led several EU-funded research projects as well as publishing widely in this, and related, areas.

Janet Chan is Professor in the School of Social Sciences and International Studies at the University of New South Wales. She has published extensively on police culture and police use of information technology. Her books include *Reshaping Juvenile Justice* (ed. 2005); *Fair Cop: Learning the Art of Policing* (2003), with Devery and Doran; *e-Policing* (2001), with Brereton, Legosaz and Doran; *Changing Police Culture* (1997); and the trilogy on crime in the mass media: *Visualizing Deviance, Negotiating Control* and *Representing Order* (1987, 1989 and 1991), with Ericson and Baranek.

James Curran is Director of the Goldsmiths Leverhulme Media Research Centre and Professor of Communications at Goldsmiths, University of London. He is the author or editor of 18 books about the media, some in conjunction with others. These include *Media and Power* (2002), Routledge, *Mass Media and Society* (4th edn) (2005), Hodder, *Culture Wars* (2005), Edinburgh University Press and *Power Without Responsibility* (7th edn) (2009), Routledge. He has been a visiting professor at Penn, Stanford, Stockholm and Oslo Universities.

Dorothy E. Denning is Professor of Defense Analysis at the Naval Postgraduate School. She is author of *Information Warfare and Security* (1999), Addison-Wesley; and articles in the areas of cybercrime, cyber-terrorism, information security and cyber conflict.

Lilian Edwards is Professor of Internet Law at Sheffield University. Her principal research interests are in the law relating to the Internet, the Web and new technologies, with a European and comparative focus. She has co-edited with Charlotte Waelde two collections on *Law and the Internet* (1997, 3rd edn 2008), Hart Publishing, and a third collection of essays, *The New Legal Framework for E-Commerce in Europe,* was published in 2005. Her work in online consumer privacy won the Barbara Wellbery Memorial Prize in 2004 for the best solution to the problem of privacy and transglobal data flows. She has undertaken consultancy for the European Parliament, the European Commission and McAfee, and has a cyberlaw blog, at http://blogscript. blogspot.com.

Steven Furnell is Professor of Information Systems Security at the University of Plymouth and an Adjunct Professor with Edith Cowan University in Western Australia. His interests include security management, computer crime, user authentication, and security usability. He is the author of over 190 papers in refereed international journals and conference proceedings, as well as the books *Cybercrime: Vandalizing the Information Society* (2001), Addison Wesley and *Computer Insecurity: Risking the System* (2005), Springer. He is also the Editor-in-Chief of *Information Management & Computer Security* and an Associate Editor for *Computers & Security*. Further details can be found at www.cscan.org.

Gerard Goggin is Professor of Digital Communication and Deputy Director of the Journalism and Media Research Centre, University of New South Wales, Sydney. His books include *Global Mobile Media* (2010), *Internationalizing Internet Studies* (2009), *Mobile Technologies: From Telecommunications to Media* (2009), *Cell Phone Culture* (2006), and *Digital Disability* (2003).

Daniel Harcus completed a LLB Law at the University of Sheffield in 2007 and now works in the financial services sector.

Yvonne Jewkes is Professor of Criminology at the University of Leicester. She has published extensively in the area of cybercrime on the subject of policing child abuse and other online offences. She is author of *Media and Crime* (2004), Sage Publications, editor of two collections on cybercrime: *Dot. cons: Crime, Deviance and Identity on the Internet* (2003), Willan Publishing and *Crime Online* (2007), Willan Publishing, and co-author (with Majid Yar) of a chapter on 'Policing cybercrime: emerging trends and future challenges' in T. Newburn (ed.) *Handbook of Policing* (2008) (2nd edn), Willan Publishing. Yvonne is Associate Editor of *Crime, Media, Culture: An International Journal* and Series Editor (with Katja Franko Aas) of the new Ashgate series *Crime, Technology and Society*.

Michael McGuire is Senior Lecturer in Criminology at London Metropolitan University. His research interests lie in the relationship between spatiality, crime and control and the influence of technologies upon changes here. He has written extensively on all aspects of communication technology related crime and his most recent book *Hypercrime: The New Geometry of Harm* (2007) was awarded the 2008 British Society of Criminology runner-up Book Prize. He is currently preparing two books for publication: *Technology, Crime & Control* (for Willan Publishing, 2010) and *The Criminology of Pleasure* (for Routledge, 2010).

Vincent Miller is a Lecturer in Sociology at the University of Kent. He has published in the area of digital media and 'phatic' communication, 'New Media, Networking and Phatic Culture', *Convergence: The International Journal of Research into New Media Technologies*, 14(4): 387–400), and convergence 'Stitching the Web into Global Capitalism: two stories', in *Web. Studies: Rewiring Media Studies for the Digital Age (2nd edn)*, David Gauntlett and Ross Horsley (eds), London and New York: Arnold/Oxford University Press. Currently he is working on a monograph for Sage Publications tentatively titled *Understanding Digital Culture*, which should be in print for 2011.

Ethel Quayle is a Lecturer in Clinical Psychology in the School of Health in Social Science at the University of Edinburgh and Director of the COPINE research which until September 2008 was based at University College Cork, Ireland. She is a clinical psychologist and has worked with both sex offenders and their victims and for the past 12 years been involved in research on Internet abuse images, collaborating internationally with government and non-government agencies. She is co-author of *Child Pornography: An Internet Crime* (2003), *Viewing Child Pornography on the Internet* (2005) and *Only Pictures? Therapeutic Work with Internet Sex Offenders* (2006) as well as many academic and professional papers.

Judith Rauhofer is a Research Fellow at the Centre for Law, Information and Converging Technologies at the University of Central Lancashire. She is author of two chapters on 'Privacy and Surveillance: Legal and Socioeconomic Aspects of State Intrusion into Electronic Communications' and 'The Retention of Communications Data in Europe and the UK' in L. Edwards and C. Waelde (eds) *Law and the Internet* (2009) (3rd edn), Hart; an article entitled 'Privacy is dead, get over it! Information privacy and the dream of a risk-free society' in *Information and Communications Technology Law, 17(3): 185–97*, and an article entitled 'Just because you're paranoid, doesn't mean they're not after you: Legislative developments in relation to the mandatory retention of communications data in the European Union' in *SCRIPT-ed, 3: 4*.

Teela Sanders is Senior Lecturer in the Sociology of Crime at the University of Leeds. She researches the relationships between gender, regulation and the state at the intersection of sociology, criminology and socio-legal studies. She has published extensively on the sex industry and the relationship between gender and regulation. After two monographs on the British female sex industry and men who buy sex, and a recent textbook with Maggie O'Neill and Jane Pitcher, *Prostitution: Sex Work, Politics and Policy* (2009), Sage Publications, she is currently working on an ESRC project on lap-dancing.

Barry Sandywell is Honorary Research Fellow in Social Theory in the Department of Sociology at the University of York, UK. He is the author of *Logological Investigations* (1996), Routledge, and co-editor, with Ian Heywood, of *Interpreting Visual Culture: Explorations in the Hermeneutics of the Visual* (1999), Routledge. He has also written essays on Baudrillard, Bakhtin, Benjamin and other theorists, published in various journals and collections. Recent publications include essays on digitisation, cyberspace, new media and global criminality as part of a continuing programme of research concerned to map the reflexive transformations of postmodern societies and cultures. He is currently editing (with Ian Heywood) an original collection of essays with the title *Handbook of Visual Culture*. His book, *Terms of Vision: A Dialectical Lexicon of Visual Discourse* will be published in 2010.

Russell G. Smith practised as a solicitor in Melbourne in the 1980s, before becoming a lecturer in criminology at the University of Melbourne. He then took up a position at the Australian Institute of Criminology in Canberra where he is now Principal Criminologist and head of the Global Economic and Electronic Crime Program. He has published extensively on aspects of computer crime, fraud control, and professional regulation. His co-authored books on fraud and computer crime include *Cyber Criminals on Trial* (2004), Cambridge University Press; *Electronic Theft: Unlawful Acquisition in Cyberspace* (2001), Cambridge University Press; and *Crime in the Digital Age* (1998),

Federation. He is a Fellow of the School of Social and Political Sciences at the University of Melbourne and First Vice-President of the Australian and New Zealand Society of Criminology.

Peter Van Aelst is Assistant Professor in Political Communication and Political Psychology at Leiden University, the Netherlands. He has published on political communication and social movements and new media in publications including *Journal of Communication, Comparative Politics* and *European Journal of Political Research*.

Jeroen Van Laer is a research assistant and PhD candidate at the University of Antwerp, Belgium. As a member of the research group M2P (Media, Movements and Politics) he was involved in an inter-university project on digital media and political participation. At the moment he is preparing a PhD on frame alignment, researching whether there is an empirical match between the motives of protest participants and the goals put forward by the movements staging a demonstration.

Jeff Vass lectures in social theory at the University of Southampton. He has most recently published work on Habermas, embodiment and technology in 'Stability and Wandering: self, coherence and embodiment at the end of the social', in M. Pirani and I. Varga (eds) (2008) *New Boundaries between Bodies and Technologies*, Newcastle: Cambridge Scholars. He has also published work on the discourse of citizenship such as 'Social Strategies in the Discourse of Societal and Citizenship Understanding', for example in A. Ross (ed.) (2002) *Future Citizens in Europe*, London: CiCE. He was formerly a co-director of the IMPACT Project at the University of North London and published a series of books (for the Falmer Press, Heinemann and Scholastic Press) and journal articles (with Ruth Merttens) on parental involvement in schooling.

Ian Walden is Professor of Information and Communications Law and head of the Institute of Computer and Communications Law in the Centre for Commercial Law Studies, Queen Mary, University of London. His publications include *EDI and the Law* (1989), *Information Technology and the Law* (1990), *EDI Audit and Control* (1993), *Cross-border Electronic Banking* (1995, 2000), *Telecommunications Law Handbook* (1997), *E-Commerce Law and Practice in Europe* (2001), *Telecommunications Law and Regulation* (2001, 2005, 2009), *Computer Crimes and Digital Investigations* (2007) and *Media Law and Practice* (forthcoming, 2009). Ian has been involved in law reform projects for the World Bank, the European Commission, UNCTAD, UNECE and the European Bank of Reconstruction and Development, as well as for a number of individual states. In 1995–96, Ian was seconded to the European Commission, as a national expert in electronic commerce law. Ian is a solicitor and is Of Counsel to the global law firm Baker and McKenzie (www.bakernet.com) and is a Trustee and Vice-Chair of the Internet Watch Foundation (www.iwf.org.uk).

David S. Wall is Professor of Criminal Justice and Information Society at the University of Leeds. He conducts research and teaches in the fields of criminal justice and information technology (cybercrime), policing, cyberlaw and intellectual property crime. He has published a wide range of articles and books on these subjects which include: *Cybercrime: The Transformation of Crime in the Information Age* (2007), Polity; *Crime and Deviance in Cyberspace* (2009) (ed.), Ashgate; *Cyberspace Crime* (2003) (ed.), Ashgate/Dartmouth; *Crime and the Internet* (2001) (ed.), Routledge; and *The Internet, Law and Society* (2000) (ed. with Y. Akdeniz and C. Walker), Longman. He has also published a range of books and articles on broader criminal justice related issues.

Martin Wasik is Professor of Criminal Justice at Keele University. He is the author of much published work in the fields of criminal law and criminal justice, and has had a long-standing interest in computer-related crime. His book *Crime and the Computer* (1991), Oxford was an early contribution to the field, and he has published articles on aspects of computer law in the *Criminal Law Review*, the *International Review of Law, Computers & Technology*, and in various essay collections. He has also served as chairman of the Sentencing Advisory Panel (1999–2007), was a member of the Sentencing Guidelines Council (2004–2007), and a member of the Commission on English Prisons Today (2007–2009). He sits part-time as a judge of the Crown Court, and in 2008 was appointed CBE for services to criminal justice.

Craig Webber is Lecturer in Criminology at the University of Southampton. He is author of *Psychology and Crime* (2009), Sage Publications. He has researched and published in various areas of culture, media and criminological theory, including 'Revaluating Relative Deprivation Theory' (2007), *Theoretical Criminology*, 11(1), and 'Foreground, Background, Foresight?: The Third Dimension of Cultural Criminology' (2007), in *Crime, Media, Culture*, 3(2). Craig has also written on the use of moving images in teaching and research, 'Cops, Robbers and Masked Vigilantes: Teaching through representations of crime', in J. Bilsberry, J. Charlesworth and P. Leonard (eds) (2010) *Moving Images: Effective Teaching with Film and Television*.

Katherine S. Williams is a Senior Lecturer of Criminology in the Department of Law and Criminology, Aberystwyth University. She has taught and researched in both law and criminology and is a well-known criminologist and author of the internationally used *Textbook on Criminology*, published by Oxford University Press, which is in its sixth edition. She is also the author of evaluation and other reports and numerous papers in high-quality legal and social science academic journals. Much of her work has focused on internet crime and its control, especially in the area of child pornography, and she acted as expert adviser to the Council of Europe in the preparation of the Cybercrime Convention, providing written reports and appearing before the Parliamentary Assembly in Paris.

Matthew Williams is Senior Lecturer at the Cardiff School of Social Sciences and was the independent academic advisor on E-crime to the Welsh Assembly Government. He has published and conducted research in the areas of cybercrime, online and digital research methodologies and sexuality, policing and criminal justice. He is co-editor of *Criminology and Criminal Justice* and is on the editorial board for *Sociological Research Online* and the *Internet Journal of Criminology*. He was also on the board of directors for the Association of Internet Researchers (AoIR). Publications include *Virtually Criminal: Crime, Deviance and Regulation Online* (2006), Routledge, 'Policing and Cybersociety: The Maturation of Regulation in an Online Community', *Policing & Society* (2006), and 'Policing Diversity in the Digital Age: Maintaining Order in Virtual Communities', *Criminology and Criminal Justice*. Recent research includes 'E-crime Rapid Evidence Assessment' (Welsh Assembly Government), Ethnography for the Digital Age' (ESRC), and 'Methodological Issues for Qualitative Data Sharing and Archiving' (ESRC).

Maggie Wykes is Senior Lecturer in the Law School, University of Sheffield. She teaches in the areas of criminological theory, gender and Internet crime and her research focuses on issues of representation, identity, criminalisation and power. Her book publications include *News, Crime and Culture* (2001), Pluto Press and, with Barry Gunter, *The Media and the Body* (2005), Sage Publications and *Violence, Gender and Justice* (2009), Sage Publications, with Kirsty Welsh. Other publications include 'Constructing crime: culture, stalking, celebrity and cyber and media' in Jewkes, Y. (ed.) *Crime Online* (2006), Willan Publishing and 'Constructing crime: culture, stalking, celebrity and "cyber"'(2007), in *Crime, Media, Culture: An International Journal*, 3(2).

Majid Yar is Professor of Sociology at the University of Hull. He has researched and written widely across the fields of crime and deviance, media, and social theory. He is the author of *Cybercrime and Society* (2006), *Criminology: The Key Concepts* (2008) (with Martin O'Brien), and *Community & Recognition: Ethics, Inter-Subjectivity and The Foundations of Political Life* (2009). He is currently preparing a co-edited volume (with Simon Thompson) entitled *The Politics of Misrecognition*, which will be published in 2010.

Chapter 1

Introduction: the Internet, cybercrime and the challenges of the twenty-first century

Yvonne Jewkes and Majid Yar

It is an incontrovertible fact that the Internet has brought with it major changes in the life of industrialised nations (and is increasingly doing so in the 'developing world'). While it behoves us as academic observers to avoid 'hype' and exaggeration, it is well nigh impossible to deny that the development of networked computer technologies *has* transformed how we communicate and consume, work and play, and engage with others across the spheres of economic, political, cultural and social life. Viewed from a standpoint embedded within processes of rapid social and technological change, it is easy to forget just how profound those developments may have been and how quickly new forms of social action and interaction have become normalised and taken for granted. Given that the Internet is now a seemingly near-pervasive fact of everyday life, we can easily lose sight of just how much has changed in the past few decades. Yet it is worth remembering that 20 years ago the Internet was unheard of among the general populace, and was known only to a small and specialised community largely confined to academic and scientific institutions. From this position of marginality, the subsequent expansion of the Internet has been exponential. Consider that between 1994 and 2008 the number of countries connected to the Internet increased from 83 to more than 200 (GWE 2008). In December 1995 there were an estimated 16 million Internet users worldwide; by 2008 this figure had risen to 1.59 billion, some 20 per cent of the world's total estimated population (IWS 2008). While the density of network connections varies enormously (following established lines of industrial development, economic resources and infrastructure capacity), almost 75 per cent of the North American population is now online; the corresponding figure for Oceania-Australia is around 60 per cent, and for Europe around 50 per cent (*ibid.*; see also Introduction to Part I).

However, the changes wrought by the Internet cannot be simply captured quantitatively by examining 'penetration rates' and number of users. In the short lifespan of the Internet there have occurred substantial qualitative changes that have transformed the nature of online interactions and activities. Early users were restricted by a combination of factors, including limited computing power (especially in the case of personal computers), restricted communication bandwidth (mainly using the copper-wire technology of existing telecommunication grids designed for telephony) and basic computer software. Under these constraints, basic text-based applications (such as electronic mail and discussion lists) prevailed. However, the range of mediated communications available via the Internet expanded significantly as ever higher levels of computing power became available and affordable for personal as well as commercial users; as software (such as web browsers) became more sophisticated and could transmit still images, audio and video content; and as bandwidth expanded through use of broadband, cable and wireless technologies. With greater scope, speed and flexibility the range of activities viable online extended massively. Work, entertainment, socialising, shopping, education, advertising and marketing, and political communication and recruitment, are just some examples of commonplace online activities. Moreover, the power, sophistication and communications capacity of the technology enabled a process of convergence between the Internet and existing media: we now see a 'blurring' of boundaries between media, as 'old' media take on a new life in the online environment (for example news reporting via websites; listening to radio and watching films and television programmes via 'streaming' audio and video content; online telephony and real-time interpersonal communication using voice-over-Internet services like Skype, and so on). The Internet has also expanded beyond its original platform of fixed-location computers and has migrated across multiple platforms including mobile communications devices such as telephones, personal digital assistants (PDAs) and ultra-portable 'netbooks'. Finally, with the development of so-called 'Web 2.0', users have moved from being recipients of mediated content to being active producers of self-generated content (Gauntlett 2004) (witnessed by the emergence and popularity of 'social networking' sites, 'blogs', 'wikis', and most recently 'twittering'). Thus we have seen in a very short space of time a growth of the medium that is both qualitatively as well as quantitatively remarkable.

Since the emergence of the Internet (or more precisely the World Wide Web) as a mainstream social technology, commentators have variously embraced its transformational potential in glowing terms and decried it for the many (real or imagined) 'social ills' it supposedly brings in its wake. For 'Net utopians' the technology promised everything from freedom from state censorship and cultural control, through a means for the rebirth of community bonds and social solidarity, to the wholesale transcendence of corporeal limits associated with the 'meat space' of physical existence. However, early optimism and idealism have given way in significant part to darker (even dystopian) prognoses, with the Internet serving as a locus and leitmotif for many and varied problems, dangers, risks and threats. It should not surprise us that in tandem with the Web's growth we have seen the emergence of associated forms of crime and deviance. Communications technologies, like all forms of institutionalised social action, are available for both legitimate use and illegitimate misuse. The use of mass-mediated communication for 'nefarious' purposes is as long established as the media themselves (Jewkes 2003, 2007; Wall 2007). A brief historical foray given serves to furnish ample evidence of this interconnection.

For example, the spread of daily newspapers in the nineteenth century brought forth a slew of advertising frauds from entrepreneurial 'white collar' criminals offering everything from phoney 'wonder medicines' to get-rich-quick investment scams (Sweet 2002). Charles Dickens was moved to take legal action when his serialised bestsellers were transmitted on a daily basis to the United States using the transatlantic telegraph, then reprinted for American readers without seeking the author's permission or paying him any royalties – probably the first known case of 'Net piracy', which occurred more than a century before online 'intellectual property theft' became an economic and political hot potato (Vaidhynathan 2003). From the 1950s the introduction of automated switching technology in the US telephone system helped spawn a subculture of 'phreakers' who exploited inside knowledge of the system to make free long-distance telephone calls (interestingly, early 1970s phreaking enthusiasts allegedly included Steve Jobs and Steve Wozniak, who later went on to worldwide fame and fortune as the founders of Apple Computers (Levy 2002)). Thus the phenomena associated with crime, deviance and rule breaking in the online environment should not surprise us, even if the challenges they bring in their wake may be fairly unprecedented in terms of scale and scope.

There now exists a distinction, well established among researchers and commentators, between 'computer assisted' and 'computer oriented' offences that centre upon the Internet (Wall 2001, 2007). The former category refers to those offences which, while pre-dating Internet technology and having an existence independent of it, find a new lease of life online. Such offences include: various forms of fraud, such as selling non-existent, defective, substandard or counterfeit goods; theft of monies through credit card and bank fraud; investment frauds such as pyramid schemes and fake stock and shares; intellectual property offences, including the unauthorised sharing of copyrighted content such as movies, music, digitised books, images, and computer software; posting, sharing and/or selling obscene and prohibited sexual representations; and harassment, 'stalking', bullying, sexual predation and forms of hateful and/or defamatory speech. These forms of offending are not unique to the online world (having long-established terrestrial counterparts), and have thus been described as merely 'old wine in new bottles' (Grabosky 2001). However, if we stick with this metaphor, we can certainly appreciate that we are dealing with *an awful lot of wine* in very many, differently shaped and capacious bottles. In other words, there are social-structural features of the Internet that enable the proliferation and dispersal of such offences on a large scale (notably the global reach of the medium, its capacity as a 'multiplier' of distributed effects, the use of automation, and the ways in which it affords offenders unprecedented opportunities to disguise and distort their identities (Jewkes 2003; Yar 2005a, 2006; Wall 2007)).

To such offences we can add those falling into the second category, namely those that are 'computer focused'. Such offences take as their target the electronic infrastructure (both hardware and software) that comprises the 'fabric' of the Internet itself. Examples of such offences, all too well known among readers, include various forms of 'malicious software' (viruses, worms, Trojans) that corrupt software; 'denial of service attacks' that overload server capacity and effectively 'crash' websites; and various forms of 'defacement' through which Web content is manipulated, changed and/or deleted without permission or authorisation. Attention directed towards such computer-focused crime initially concentrated on supposedly 'delinquent' individuals or subcultures associated with 'hacking' activities (Yar 2005b). It later shifted to incorporate analysis of social activists (or 'hacktivists') who used these techniques as forms of political action and social protest (Jordan and Taylor 2004). Most recently attention has been directed, in the post-September 11 context of the 'War on Terror', towards the possibility of attacks upon computer infrastructure by 'terrorist' groups – so-called 'cyber-terrorism' (Verton 2003). We must, of course, retain a healthy scepticism about claims around such threats, as variously media commentators, politicians, criminal justice and security professions, and economic actors have shown a demonstrable tendency to sometimes overplay the risks presented. 'Hard facts' about the scope or extent of such offences can be thin on the ground, and exaggerated estimates of incidents and their economic costs circulate all too commonly (and are, indeed, generated and used by interest groups in pursuit of their particular agendas). Nevertheless, this broad range of crime problems cannot be dismissed as mere fabrications, nor ignored in preference for the better-established agenda of 'terrestrial' crime problems. These problems are, to a greater or lesser extent, present and in many instances growing apace; again, this should not surprise us as social use of, and dependence upon, such systems continues to expand and touch upon an ever-increasing range of social, economic and political domains.

A second level of problems arises not from Internet crime problems themselves, but from social and political *responses* to those problems. Awareness of such problems has incrementally increased, and in some cases has generated quite significant levels of concern and anxiety about issues such as child pornography and online sexual predation against minors via 'chat rooms' and social networking sites. Meanwhile, economic interests such as copyright holders in the media industries have attempted to push issues of 'piracy' and 'digital theft' up the policing and crime control agenda. Internet-based risks have, as already mentioned, entered discourses of national security via the issue of 'cyber-terrorism' and 'information warfare'. As a result, new steps oriented at online crime prevention, control, detection and prosecution have been taken. Yet such measures have raised concerns over the introduction of ever more rigorous forms of surveillance and monitoring directed at users. For example, laws requiring Internet Service Providers (ISPs) to retain 'traffic data' about the websites that users visit, and more recently mandatory requirements for data retention about email communications, have alarmed civil libertarians who see such steps as significant threats to privacy. Monitoring is also undertaken, often covertly, by commercial organisations seeking to collect detailed profiles of individuals' online behaviour; this data can be exploited for targeted advertising and marketing, and also sold on to third parties for commercial and other uses. For example, US federal agencies including the Department of Justice, the FBI and the CIA have been shown to regularly source such data from commercial data providers (Yar 2006: 145). In addition to the intended uses of such data, there are also concerns about the security of information that is vulnerable to misplacement, loss and theft; given a spate of recent cases in which government departments and their subcontractors have managed to 'lose' large databases of personal information these concerns would seem to be entirely warranted. A second level of legal innovation has been directed at controlling the content of Internet communication. For example, intellectual property rights holders have been conspicuously successful in driving the introduction of new criminal sanctions to prohibit the sharing of copyrighted content, which have served in the eyes of critics to illegitimately curtail cultural communication and helped to stifle creativity. Concerns over sexually explicit content and cases of allegedly Internet-inspired homicides have seen recent moves to outlaw 'violent and extreme pornography' in the UK. These laws are worryingly vague in their definitions of precisely what is to be prohibited. They have also been opposed by groups representing the BDSM community and sex workers, who fear the criminalisation of entirely consensual sexual practices among adults. Finally, the febrile atmosphere around 'the terrorist threat' has inspired equally problematic measures to outlaw the 'glorification' and 'encouragement' of terrorism both online and offline. These measures have been criticised for their 'chilling effects' on free speech and the expression of political opinion, while doing little or nothing to counter genuine threats from political violence.

The mutually reinforcing relationship between criminal *action* and societal *reaction* is itself culturally mediated through the domain of symbolic representation. Cultural 'imaginaries' about the Internet and its associated problems are constructed across many domains of representation, including press reportage, film and fiction. It is worth remembering that the notion of 'cyberspace' itself emerged not from the realm of computer science or engineering, but from a science fiction novel – William Gibson's *Neuromancer* (1984). Gibson himself later admitted that:

All I knew about the word 'cyberspace' when I coined it, was that it seemed like an effective buzzword. It seemed evocative and essentially meaningless. It was suggestive of something, but had no real semantic meaning, even for me, as I saw it emerge on the page. (Gibson, in Neale 2003)

Yet, despite its status as an entirely speculative term constructed for literary purposes, cyberspace rapidly became the defining basis for a cognitive framework through which the realm of networked computer technologies was widely understood. Such fictions have also shaped the ways in which the risks and threats of the online environment are construed in official circles; one of the best known instances was the way in which the movie *WarGames* (1983) was subsequently presented to a US Congressional committee as an example of the danger to national security arising from computer hacking (Taylor 1999: 10). More broadly, cultural representations help to shape public perceptions about the nature, scope and extent of Internet-based crime problems, and *in extremis* can fuel disproportionate reactions, including avoidance behaviours and pressures for legal action. The increasingly commonplace idea that there are in fact what Sandywell (2006) calls 'monsters in cyberspace' plays an ongoing role in shaping definitions of the online 'crime problem' and how we ought to deal with it.

In light of the aforementioned dimensions of the debate, it would appear that research and scholarship in this area must perform a threefold task. Firstly, it must develop robust yet balanced insights into the contours of Internet-based crime problems, and it must situate these insights within the wider context of the medium's social, economic and political evolution. Secondly, it must offer a critical analysis and appraisal of crime control measures directed at those (real or perceived) problems, including an evaluation of the threats to users' rights, freedoms and liberties that might result from the excesses of legislative prohibition and online surveillance. Thirdly, it must seek to better understand how both of the above dimensions are crucially shaped and inflected by the circulation of cultural images, symbols and narratives that serve in many ways to frame both 'problems' and 'solutions'. The contributions to this volume are intended to take up this challenge, bringing to bear expertise and insights drawn from across disciplines and national boundaries.

The volume

The *Handbook of Internet Crime* is, then, the most ambitious book on cybercrime to date. The volume brings together the leading experts in the field to explore some of the most challenging – yet, somewhat paradoxically, some of the most marginalised and neglected – debates facing criminologists and other scholars interested in cybercrime, deviance, policing, law and regulation in the twenty-first century. The *Handbook* reflects the range and depth of cybercrime research and scholarship, combining contributions from many of those who have established and developed cyber research over the past 25 years and who continue to shape it in its current phase, with more recent entrants to the field who are building on this tradition and breaking new ground. Contributions reflect both the global nature of cybercrime, and the international span of scholarship addressing its challenges. The aim, then, is to provide an essential reference for students, researchers and others whose work brings them into contact with managing, policing and regulating online behaviour.

The *Handbook* is divided into four parts, each of which is distinctive in its focus, yet interrelated in many of the themes and issues raised. Part I considers the 'histories and contexts' of Internet-related offending. The chapters individually and collectively address many fundamental questions concerning the birth and development of the Internet and World Wide Web and their appropriation by individuals for illegal activities and behaviours. How did the Internet come about? Who 'invented' it? How many people regularly use it? Who commits online crime? Does the Internet liberate or constrain? Why are some governments so suspicious of it? What is the relationship between cybercrime, contemporary capitalism and the current global economic crisis? What are the social, political and economic consequences of the global 'digital divide'? Does cybercrime constitute a 'moral panic'? Where does the public get its ideas from about cybercrime? Is it an appropriate subject for mass entertainment? Why has criminology been so slow to address the problem of Internet-related offending?

Part II of the *Handbook* looks at different types of Internet crime, assessing the extent of the threat they pose and attempting to weigh up actual risk against perceived public anxieties. The offences under discussion in this part of the volume include hacking, planting viruses, cyber-terrorism, illegal protest, intellectual property offences, identity crimes, sex work and sex crime, Internet-related offences against children, cyber-homicide and cyber-suicide. Underpinning all the chapters is the question of technological determinism. In popular (and popular media) discourse, the Internet is sometimes 'blamed' for all these offences, but the contributions in this section take a more measured and informed approach, posing important questions about the nature of offending in cyberspace. Why is the Internet so frequently a scapegoat for deviant human behaviour? What are the motivations behind 'hacking'? Is it always necessarily about the exercise of a hyper-masculine mastery of technology or the desire to challenge state authority with a different sort of power, or is it sometimes more benign, even 'harmless'? In what ways does the Internet facilitate terrorism? What are the real risks? How have political movements and anti-globalisation protesters used the Net to further their causes? What are the arguments for and against free, but illegal, downloading of music and other media content? Why is identity theft such a perennial topic of discussion in the mainstream media? How has the sex industry driven the development and expansion of the Internet and what exactly *is* 'Internet sex'? Why are children so vulnerable to sex crimes on the Net? Is the global trade in exploitative and abusive images of children as extensive as media coverage of the topic suggests? What do we know about cyber-paedophiles and how they operate? What is cyber-homicide? Did the 25 young people who took their own lives in a small area of South Wales in the space of two years have some kind of 'Internet pact'?

Part III reflects on some of the themes and debates that have dominated legal responses to cybercrime. What led to the drawing up of the Computer Misuse Act of 1990 and why was it considered a landmark piece of legislation? What types of crime, and which specific criminal cases, drove legislative reform in the 1980s and 1990s? What has been the impact of the Terrorism Act of 2000 and why has it proved so controversial? What is RIPA (Regulation of Investigatory Powers 2000) and why has it divided opinion on state incursions into privacy and ignited debates about civil liberties and human rights? How has the United States handled legislation and regulation of the Internet? How pressing is the need for common transnational legal and regulatory frameworks? Should we as global citizens be concerned about the self-imposed rights, not only of our own governments, but those of other nations, to monitor our online activity? Are we really subject to surveillance and, if so, to what ends?

Part IV turns our attention to policing, investigation, regulation and justice. What are the main challenges facing the police when confronting Internet crime? Are they adequately equipped to tackle cybercrime and what are the main obstacles to successful investigations and prosecutions? Why have several high-profile and high-cost cyberpolicing initiatives failed? Which other individuals and groups have a responsibility for 'policing' the Internet and with what practical and ethical consequences? Why are individual computer users increasingly being encouraged to adopt a position of responsibilisation? How are social spaces on the Net regulated? What happens when someone breaks the rules? Is cyber-vigilantism acceptable in some circumstances? How have Internet technologies influenced criminal justice and public understandings of the criminal justice process? What is meant by 'computer forensics' and how has it aided criminal investigations and prosecutions?

It is these questions and topics that shape the parameters within which the authors who have contributed to the *Handbook of Internet Crime* offer their expertise. Amidst all the heated political debate and media-fuelled hysteria about the risks inherent in and dangers presented by new technologies, the *Handbook of Internet Crime* offers scholarly insight and empirically informed discussion about a vast range of offending behaviours and responses. But first a little history …

References

Gauntlett, D. (2004) 'Web Studies: What's New?', in D. Gauntlett and R. Horsley (eds), *Web.Studies* (2nd edn). London: Hodder Arnold.

Grabosky, P. (2001) 'Virtual Criminality: Old Wine in New Bottles?', *Social & Legal Studies*, 10: 243–9.

GWE (Global Web Explorer) (2008) 'How many countries are linked on the World Wide Web?' at http://www.guernsey.net/~sgibbs/www.html

IWS (Internet World Statistics) (2008) *Internet Usage Statistics: The Internet Big Picture*, at http://www.internetworldstats.com/stats.htm

Jewkes, Y. (ed.) (2003) *Dot.cons: Crime, Deviance and Identity on the Internet*. Cullompton: Willan Publishing.

Jewkes, Y. (ed.) (2007) *Crime Online*. Cullompton: Willan Publishing.

Jordan, T. and Taylor, P. (2004) *Hacktivism and Cyberwars: Rebels With a Cause?* London: Routledge.

Levy, S. (2002) *Hackers: Heroes of the Computer Revolution* (new edn). New York: Penguin.

Neale, M. (2003) *William Gibson: No Maps for These Territories*. New Video Group.

Sandywell, B. (2006) 'Monsters in Cyberspace: Cyberphobia and Cultural Panic in the Information Age', *Information Communication & Society*, 9(1): 39–61.

Sweet, M. (2002) *Inventing the Victorians*. London: Faber & Faber.

Taylor, P. (1999) *Hackers: Crime in the Digital Sublime*. London: Routledge.

Vaidhynathan, S. (2003) *Copyrights and Copywrongs: The Rise of Intellectual Property and How it Threatens Creativity*. New York: NYU Press.

Verton, D. (2003) *Black Ice: The Invisible Threat of Cyber-Terrorism*. Emeryville: McGraw-Hill/Osborne.

Wall, D.S. (2001) 'Cybercrimes and the Internet', in D. Wall (ed.), *Crime and the Internet*. London: Routledge.

Wall, D.S. (2007) *Cybercrime*. Cambridge/Malden, MA: Polity.

Yar, M. (2005a) 'The Novelty of Cybercrime: An Assessment in Light of Routine Activity Theory', *European Journal of Criminology*, 2(4): 407–28.

Yar, M. (2005b) 'Computer Hacking: Just Another Case of Juvenile Delinquency?', *The Howard Journal of Criminal Justice*, 44(4): 387–99.

Yar, M. (2006) *Cybercrime and Society*. London: Sage.

Part I

Histories and Contexts

Yvonne Jewkes and Majid Yar

Many people argue that criminal and antisocial activities on the Internet are analogous to similar behaviour in the physical world. Website defacement is just electronic graffiti; passwords or credit card numbers stolen off the Internet are simply theft and fraud in a new guise; online auction sites sometimes remind us of the old adage 'buyer beware' when the goods we receive (if indeed we receive any goods) are faulty, damaged or counterfeit; people who use Internet pornography and prostitution are simply utilising a new medium; hate crime, stalking and harassment will continue to be conducted by mail and telephone as well as via Internet technologies; and governments have always found ways of identifying and recording information about the 'enemy within'. But the Internet enhances the potential for all these criminal and deviant activities, not least because of the sheer size and scope of its reach. The growth in the numbers of people with Internet access has been explosive. It took the World Wide Web just three years to reach its first 50 million users; a feat which eluded television for 15 years and which took radio 37 years to achieve from its point of inception (Naughton 1999). Usage statistics now put the global Internet population at 1,596,270,108 – that is, 23.8 per cent penetration (as of 31 March 2009; http://www.internetworldstats. com/stats.htm). Leading the world table is North America where 74.4 per cent of the population are online. At the other end of the scale, just 5.6 per cent of Africa's population has Internet access. Of the total world Internet users by region, 41.2 per cent are in Asia; 24.6 per cent are in Europe; 15.7 per cent are in North America; 10.9 per cent are in Latin America and the Caribbean; 3.4 per cent in Africa; 2.9 per cent in the Middle East; and 1.3 per cent in Australasia/Oceania. In terms of languages, 452 million Internet users communicate in English, closely followed (and rapidly being caught up) by Chinese language speakers at 321 million (http://www.internetworldstats. com/stats.htm).

It is against this backdrop that the contributors to Part I of the *Handbook of Internet Crime* have written their chapters, discussing the 'histories and contexts' of the Internet and cybercrime. Collectively, these chapters consider the Net not simply as a communications technology, but also as a set of socially, politically and culturally embedded practices that have profoundly reshaped the contours and textures of everyday life for an increasingly large proportion of the world's population. The history of the Internet may be relatively short, but it is hard to think of another technology that has had such a dramatic impact on the leisure, pleasures and working lives of so many people, at least since Henry Ford introduced the mass-produced motor car a century ago. In Chapter 2, media scholar James Curran charts the birth and evolution of the Net, outlining its military origins and the massive investment put into its development by a US government seeking military and technological superiority over the Soviet Union during the Cold War. Of course, this was one of many key moments in the history of the Internet; others include the invention of the computer in the 1940s, the development of computer language in the 1950s and software in the 1960s, the liberal counter-culture in which the World Wide Web was conceived in the 1980s, the era of deregulated media in the 1990s which allowed the newly commercialised Internet to flourish, and the establishment of now ubiquitous sites/brands such as eBay in 1995, Google in 1998, Wikipedia in 2001 and Facebook in 2006. Curran describes all these momentous developments, explaining how they came together to create the embedded, everyday technology with which we are so comfortable and familiar today. He describes the history of the Internet as a 'chronicle of contradiction', combining paradoxical influences and outcomes. In its post-military phase, it amalgamated the values of academic science, American counterculture and European public service ideals. But having come to public life as a profoundly democratic concern it eventually had to offer itself to commercial interests and, then, to private and state bodies who wanted to use it for surveillance of populations. For Curran, vestiges of the counter-culture ethos remain intact but, as we shall see throughout this *Handbook*, the freedom and democracy that many of us take for granted in our tolerance of, for example, illegal downloading of music, films, books, and so on, has more negative, even sinister, connotations when we consider the opportunities for crime and deviance that have opened up. And while even a decade ago, many commentators spoke of the Internet as a wild frontier, relatively uncontrolled and unregulated, the truth is that the Net can be used as just another means of constraint by those governments around the world who wish to discourage free thought, speech and action. Curran offers the example of Singapore, a state which he characterises as an elitist monopoly that has succeeded in 'taming' the Internet, although his example could just as easily have been China which, with a population of 1.2 billion and an increasingly important role to play in the global political economy, finds itself in a period of transition between totalitarianism and market authoritarianism. China has seen its use of the Internet grow from 23 million in 2000 to 210 million in 2008 and is adding 6 million new Internet users a month which is more than 10 times the pace of US growth (http://www.internetworldstats.com/asia/cn.htm); a remarkable phenomenon that has only increased the Chinese authorities' fears about the potential uses of the Internet by 'subversives'.

Curran's observation that the Internet has evolved from American origins to become a truly global phenomenon leads us neatly to the chapter by Barry Sandywell (Chapter 3) who situates the Internet within the context of debates about globalisation, and examines its role in global crime and criminality. Given that the Internet has an estimated audience of around one billion users, and provides limitless and largely anonymous opportunities for the criminally inclined, together with a vast marketplace for the (knowing or unwitting) recipients and consumers of their illegal activities, cybercrime is impossible to quantify and very difficult even to research. This might partially explain why criminology as an academic field of study has been relatively slow to address the subject. While the study of surveillance has now become established as a sub-field of criminology in its own right, 'cybercrime' is still an emerging area very much in its infancy and despite being a rapidly growing global phenomenon, until a decade ago very few criminologists were addressing Internet-related crime. Even now, major criminology textbooks that claim 'comprehensiveness' still appear on the market without reference to online offending.

Given these omissions, Sandywell's appeal for a more reflexive criminology is very welcome. He calls for an approach capable of offering sophisticated and nuanced understandings of the kinds of criminal activities now committed on a 'planetary scale' and against the backdrop of the worst global economic crisis in living memory. In this context, he says, 'normal' categories of crime and criminality are wholly inadequate. Like many critical criminologists Sandywell urges readers to put aside the quest to define the 'real' or 'ontological' nature of crime and instead examine *criminalisation practices* as they are institutionally embodied in a given social order. To these ends, he explores the interplay between transgression and 'technologies of transgression', arguing that the same processes of global connectivity that have seen a revolution in communication and social exchange also facilitate crime on an unprecedented and, a mere decade ago, unimaginable scale. As we now know to our cost, many of the problems that led to the financial meltdown in 2008–09 stem from the de-territorialisation and interdependence of the world's financial institutions, and Sandywell provides a thoughtful and thought-provoking analysis, situating numerous Internet-based crimes in current theoretical debates about spatiality, mobility, economic power and governance. His conclusion is that contemporary capitalism might more accurately be described as 'cyber-capitalism'; a term that should alert us to its chronic instability.

In the chapter that follows (Chapter 4), Vince Miller further develops the fundamental points made in the previous two contributions, noting that far from being a brave new world that encourages the creation of alternative communities, democratic participation and identities free from the prejudices of offline society, the Internet merely transports our 'real world' failings and foibles to the virtual realm. As Miller says, the optimism that once accompanied the Internet revolution has begun to fade in light of the realisation that our culture has transformed the Internet more than the Internet has transformed our culture. One aspect of this which he discusses is the rise of the digital economy and the role of the Internet in financial practices, especially banking and investing. He also reminds us of the global 'digital divide', commenting that there is a real danger that the move to the digital age will greatly enhance the position of the advanced, industrialised economies over those of the developing world, allowing them to play by a fundamentally different set of economic rules. As the previously quoted statistics comparing Internet penetration in Africa with that of North America may serve to illustrate, start-up costs of Internet access are still prohibitively high for the poorest people in the world, where many do not even have access to a telephone service. Moreover, regional growth in Internet use is not always smooth and continuous, but may be disrupted by war, disaster or displacement. For Miller it is quite simply the case that, without some form of intervention, developed countries will benefit from increased access to knowledge, increased economic flexibility, and increased communication efficiency, while developing nations are at risk of being ever more victimised and marginalised by these trends.

Miller's contribution underlines the extent to which the Internet has become an entirely unremarkable part of our culture and daily life, noting that it is not its novelty, or its uniqueness, but its mundane nature and its pervasiveness that now gives the Internet its significance. His analysis echoes, and indeed draws on, the work of Manuel Castells, and despite his caveat concerning the digital divide, he is broadly optimistic about the opportunities that mobile communications afford. Young people in the developed world have been at the vanguard of the mobile communication revolution, not only rapidly adopting it with openness and enthusiasm but also inventing new communicative uses for the technology available. In his most recent work, Castells (writing with Fernández-Ardèvol, Linchuan Qui and Sey) notes that the diffusion of wireless technology in the 1990s was nothing short of extraordinary and was due, in large part, to the 'embrace of the technology by the younger generation as the density of mobile communication users reached its high points in Japan and in Northern and Western Europe' (Castells *et al.* 2007: 128). Since then the Internet has had a profound impact on every area of social and cultural life from university education and political activism to consumerism and socialising.

In Chapter 5 David S. Wall continues to chart early developments around Internet usage and how problems of crime and deviance came to be associated with them. In examining the rise of Internet-related offending as a 'crime problem', Wall introduces an important distinction that resonates through many of the contributions to the *Handbook*, namely that between actual patterns of cybercrime and the ways in which the threat has come to be culturally constructed. In the first part of the chapter, he concisely reconstructs how 'cybercrime' itself came to be framed through the development of popular cultural discourses apparent in what he calls 'social science fiction' novels and films. The notion of an urgent computer-based crime threat, which came to frame wider public understandings, articulated a long-standing pattern of cultural response in which processes of rapid social and technological change elicit heightened anxieties. Moreover, he argues that concerns about Internet crime cannot be separated from broader social trends that have cultivated a risk-consciousness that normalises the expectation of ubiquitous crime problems, such that we expect and anticipate crime as an inescapable feature of the social landscape. In the second part of the chapter, he turns his attention to the historical development of Internet crime, distinguishing heuristically between three 'generations' of such offences, each with distinct organising properties. Firstly, the earliest such crime, which he dubs 'low end', tended to target isolated computer systems and typically entailed offences that could be committed 'conventionally'; without the exploitation of computers. The second generation of such crimes take place across spatio-temporally dispersed computer networks that exist on a global scale. Wall calls this second generation of offences 'hybrid' crimes, since they exploit networked communications to commit 'traditional' crimes on a global scale. The third generation of offences comprises crimes wholly mediated via technology, and which are typically distributed and automated in character (examples include mass spam emails and sequential infection of computers using 'bots'). Finally, he anticipates the emergence of a 'fourth generation' of offences that will exploit the environment of 'ambient intelligent networks' brought about by the increasing convergence of wireless and networked technologies. Like their predecessors, such new forms of crime will bring distinctive legal, regulatory and crime-prevention challenges in their wake.

In Chapter 6 Majid Yar discusses perceptions of Internet-related offending, examining the ways in which public understandings of the problems and issues pertinent to cybercrime have developed over time and have shaped legislation and policy. Taking up cues from Wall (above) and anticipating the chapters still to come in this Part of the *Handbook*, Yar highlights how media constructions play a significant role in shaping socio-legal responses to the Internet, including the emergence of 'moral panics' around certain online behaviours. His detailed analysis pays due attention to many of the most difficult and contested issues facing criminologists in the current age; among them, the relationship between public opinion and public policy, and the disproportionate level of public fears and anxieties about crime, especially among those relatively unlikely to experience victimisation. While Castells *et al.* maintain that their sophisticated grasp of technology gives young people superiority over their elders, and has brought about a 'tectonic shift in the contemporary formation of adolescent identity' (2007: 141), Yar reminds us that it has also made young people vulnerable to new forms of victimisation, including exposure to pornography and predatory paedophiles. Offences such as these not only have significant influence on public opinions which in turn shape public policy and legislation, but can also cause people to alter their online behaviour and spend considerable money on products such as parental control and anti-virus software. Yar discusses the multi-million-dollar industry that has been created to alleviate Internet users' anxieties about their online security and personal safety, noting that many of the strategies employed to protect against attacks have, ironically, left users more, not less, vulnerable to computer crimes.

Yar comments that among the most alarmist, even apocalyptic, cultural representations of cybercrime are those found in film. From Hal in Stanley Kubrick's *2001: A Space Odyssey* to Bruce Willis saving the world from cyber-terrorists in *Die Hard 4.0*, cyber technologies have proved an enduring source of fascination for movie audiences. In Chapter 7 Craig Webber and Jeff Vass explore the enthralment of many filmmakers for the ways in which human beings interface with cyberspace, and with the apparently seamless manner in which we now perform or 'do' technology. In many genres – the 007 franchise, for example – new technology often represents something glamorous, desirable, yet impossibly unattainable; much like James Bond himself. But cinema (including the Bond films) has also been particularly influential in developing the narrative domain of 'cybercrime' and the subversive uses to which Information and Communication Technologies (ICTs) may be put. Webber and Vass's analysis of cybercrime in cinema is a wide-ranging and theoretically sophisticated treatment of the subject, embracing perspectives from Marxist critical theory, psychoanalysis, postmodernism and cultural criminology. The chapter pulls together many of the themes and issues from other contributions to this volume, examining them through the lens of cybercrime as 'entertainment', and discussing what impact cinematic portrayals have on public perceptions of the Internet and related technologies. According to Webber and Vass we should view contemporary films as in some sense providing us with intellectual resources for thinking and feeling our way through some of the new, technologically constituted boundaries which make blurred and indistinct previously demarcated categories of 'news', 'popular culture', 'entertainment', 'fiction', 'fact', 'reality', and so on. In order to assist us in this endeavour, Webber and Vass have devised a typology of the 'cybernetic imagination' exploring ICTs in film from the 1950s to the present day.

Finally in Part I, Sheila Brown traces the ways in which images and imaginaries of cyberspace and cybercrime have been decisively shaped by popular literature. Since William Gibson first coined the term 'cyberspace' in *Neuromancer* (1984), and mapped out a fictional space of digital-virtual experience, literary visions of the cyber-terrain have not only reflected but also directed wider thinking about this domain. From its inception, the genre of 'cyberpunk' has explored in provocative ways the forms of crime, harm and predation that might become possible with the turn to a virtual world, and in important ways fact has appeared to follow fiction. Like Yar in Chapter 6 and Webber and Vass in Chapter 7, Brown is careful not to make any sweeping claims about media 'effects', but like these authors her analysis is underpinned by an acknowledgement of the subtle interplay between popular cultural representations and our reflexive relationship with technology. She describes her approach as a kind of 'cultural archaeology' and this chapter is typical of her work which is always theoretically eclectic, multidisciplinary and immensely innovative. Chapter 8, and the two previous contributions, also provide a fitting platform to take us on to Part II of the *Handbook of Internet Crime*, which will be concerned with many of the cybercrimes that occupy the imaginations of fiction writers and film-makers and inflate public anxieties about the Internet.

References

Castells, M., Fernández-Ardèvol, M., Linchuan Qui, J. and Sey, A. (2007) *Mobile Communication and Society: A Global Perspective*. Mass.: MIT Press.

Naughton, J. (1999) *A Brief History of the Future: Origins and History of the Internet*. London: Weidenfeld and Nicolson.

... ...
... ...

Chapter 2

Reinterpreting Internet history

James Curran

The mass adoption of the Internet in Britain only occurred towards the end of the dot-com bubble, and persisted *long after* it had burst. The take-off moment was the summer of 1999. Between early 1999 and 2002, the proportion of UK households with Internet access soared from 13 per cent to 46 per cent (Family Expenditure Survey 2000; Office for National Statistics 2008). By 2008, this had increased to 65 per cent (Office for National Statistics 2008). Thus, in just under a decade, those with ready Internet access had grown from a small minority to two thirds of the nation – a shift comparable in scale and significance to the growth of television ownership during the 1950s. Underpinning this quiet revolution was the rapid diffusion of household computer ownership (from just over half of homes in 2002 to 70 per cent by 2007) (Office of Telecommunications 2002; Office for National Statistics 2007).

The take-off of the Internet in Britain coincided with its rise elsewhere in the economically developed world, from Finland to South Korea. Yet, the Internet's *incunabula* (to employ a Latin term used frequently to describe the early development of the printed book) extended over a much longer period. The origins of the Internet lie in a Dr Strangelove project initiated during the height of the Cold War.

Origins of the Internet

The Internet is an offspring of the Pentagon. When the USSR launched the first space satellite in 1957, the US Defence Department responded by establishing the Advanced Research Projects Agency (ARPA) with the aim of mobilising more fully American universities and research laboratories behind the country's cold war effort. Among the new agency's many projects was a scheme to promote interactive computing, through the creation of ARPANET, the world's first advanced computer network. Although the network was conceived originally as a way of sharing expensive computer time, it acquired subsequently a more important rationale. Computer networking would facilitate, it was argued, the development of a sophisticated military command and control system. It also provided a means of sustaining communications channels in the event of a nuclear attack from the Soviet Union. When ARPANET was identified as part of America's last line of defence against the 'evil empire', it became a spending priority. The development of packet-switching technology and the creation of a rapidly expanding computer network – both central to the birth of the Internet – received massive funding from the US Defence Department.

Military spending also assisted indirectly the Internet by fostering external conditions favourable to its development. The army funded the first American computer in 1946. So great was the armed forces' subsequent support of 'the nascent computer industry' that it became, in the words of a distinguished analyst, 'virtually a military subsidiary' (Winston 1998: 218). This financial backing helped to establish the US as the world's leading computer manufacturer, and producer of computer software. The American state also sponsored the American space programme, whose by-product – satellite communications - facilitated the functioning of the global Internet.

In effect, the American state underwrote a major part of the research and development process that gave birth to the modern Internet. This was not something that the private sector would have undertaken readily because it was not apparent, in the early days, that computer networking between academics, linked to the defence programme, had any commercial future. Indeed the commercial giant AT&T was actually invited in 1972 to take over ARPANET, the forerunner of the Internet, and declined on the grounds that it lacked profit potential. It was the American state that picked up the bills in a context of limited commercial interest. Yet, after underwriting the cost of technology development, and the creation of a significant user base, the American state then proceeded to shepherd the Internet to market. During the 1980s, the government financed manufacturers to modify the design of new computers in order to lay the foundation for commercial inter-networking. The lifting of the prohibition of commercial use of the public Internet in 1991 was followed by privatisation of the public backbone of the Internet in 1995. In effect, the Internet became a state-sponsored commercial system.

The developmental role of the American state in funding, managing and then commercially floating the Internet sits uneasily with the minimalist, 'nightwatchman' conception of the state in American neoliberal ideology. It actually corresponds more closely to the social market conception of the state as 'capitalist entrepreneur' that was once strongly advocated by European social democrats (Holland 1972). One reason why American political reality deviated from political rhetoric was the significant influence exerted by business on American telecommunications policy. However, the very much more important reason was that the American state allocated enormous resources to establishing military and technological superiority over the Soviet Union during the height of the Cold War.

Similar levels of public investment were not available elsewhere, even in countries where the conditions for early Internet development were promising. Britain built the first modern computer in the 1940s; developed a significant computer industry in the 1950s; and was the first country to develop, in prototype, packet-switching in 1968. But this auspicious start did not gain extensive state financial support, especially in relation to computer projects that offered only a long-term return (Gillies and Calliau 2000). It was not until 1981 that the Post Office launched a full-scale packet-switching service – using, after this long delay, expensively licensed American hardware.

Cultures of invention

The Internet was the product not only of human ingenuity and state patronage, but also of the values of the people who first developed it. Data processing systems do not have a fixed form that is determined by some inner technological logic but are influenced by the concerns and goals of their inventors, and the contexts in which they operate. For example, IBM developed a highly centralised communication system for business organisations, in which the main computer had a master–slave position to terminals, and the relationship of users to the production and consumption of the data system depended on their position within the corporation. The IBM system both reflected and reproduced, Patrice Flichy argues, the hierarchical culture of the firm (Flichy 2002). By contrast, the Internet came out of a very different world, though its supposed Edenic character has become the subject of much mythologising. According to conventional accounts, the early Internet reflected the freedom-loving values of the American scientists who designed it, and of the grassroots activists who took it up. This love of freedom was then secured by the freedom of the marketplace, ensuring that the Internet became a great engine of human enlightenment. There is just enough truth in this account to ensure its longevity. However, it greatly simplifies by editing out or downplaying features of the Internet's development that do not accord with its storyline. It also grossly distorts by failing to acknowledge the central conflict that developed between the freedom of the Net and the assertion of market control. What actually happened is different from the legend.

The American military was not a benign, self-effacing 'sugar daddy' whose role was confined to paying the bills. On the contrary, Jane Abbate (2000: 144) concludes that 'networking techniques were shaped in many ways by military priorities and concerns'. One overwhelming military priority was 'survivability', in other words a communication system that would be invulnerable to devastating attack. This led the military to sponsor a decentralised system, without a vulnerable command centre that could be destroyed by the enemy. It also led to the development of network technology that would enable the system to function if parts of it were destroyed – a key attraction of packet-switching that dispensed with dedicated, open lines between sender and receiver. Another military priority was to secure a diverse networking system since this was best suited to different, specialised military tasks. This gave rise to the Net's modular structure in which different networks could be easily added on, once minimum requirements were met. It also resulted in the addition of satellite and wireless for Internetworking since these were well adapted to communications with jeeps, ships and aeroplanes.

But if the military strongly influenced design objectives, academic computer scientists actually conceived and implemented the Net's design. Indeed, academics working for ARPA had a significant degree of autonomy, helped by the fact that military objectives largely coincided with scientific ones. Thus the military concern for survivability dovetailed with the desire of the different university departments, which constituted the early Internet, to retain their freedom and independence. Similarly, military endorsement of network diversity accorded with the academic goal of making the Internet a better research tool by incorporating more networks. When there was a serious clash between paymasters and scientists over the issue of security, it was resolved amicably through the division of the Internet into military and civilian networks in 1983.

Partly as a consequence of this harmonious relationship (sustained, seemingly, even during the Vietnam War), scientists were in a position to impose their values on the general development of the Net. The ideology of science is strongly committed to the open disclosure of information and, in principle, to intellectual cooperation in order to further the shared goal of scientific advance. This was manifested in the cooperative way in which Internet protocols were developed. It was also reflected in the open release of these protocols since the Internet's builders were seeking to promote good science, not to make money through proprietary exclusion. The culture of science also fosters interaction and discussion, and this influenced the way in which the early Internet came to be used. Emailing soon eclipsed remote computing as the early Internet's principal function.

However, the culture of academic life is, in largely unconscious ways, exclusionary. Academic work is seldom addressed to people outside the relevant knowledge community, which is why so much of it is buried in specialist publications (such as this one) and expressed in self-referential vocabulary. This exclusionary tradition was also a feature of the early Internet. Considerable computer expertise was needed for people to go online, and academic computer scientists showed little interest in changing this.

If military objectives and scientific values were the initial formative influences on the Internet, the third seminal influence was the American counterculture of the 1980s. This was constituted primarily by three overlapping (and not always mutually harmonious) subcultures. A hippy subculture sought individual self-realisation through the development of self-knowledge and freedom from repressive convention; a communitarian subculture aimed to promote togetherness through the transformation of consciousness, and social experiments like the commune; and a radical subculture hoped to achieve collective emancipation from patriarchal capitalism or, in a more populist mode, to 'give power to the people'. While this counterculture was very much in decline by the 1980s, it redefined the meaning and purpose of the Internet. Even in the early days of ARPANET, computer use had not been confined solely to work since some of its users had emailed each other about science fiction. Commercial online services in the early 1980s (an under-researched topic) had also offered chat rooms and the opportunity to shop online. But the counterculture helped to develop new uses for the Net. This was the product of a long-running collaboration between computer scientists (gratified by being told repeatedly that they were 'cool') and the graduates of flower power (looking for a new way of hanging on to their dreams), mediated by hip journalists and cultural entrepreneurs. Computers were reimagined and adapted as tools of personal liberation, organisers of virtual communities, and weapons of political struggle (Turner 2006).

It was often local area networks, run usually as cooperatives heavily dependent on volunteer labour, which proved to be the most inventive. This was typified by the WELL (Whole Earth Lectronic Link), set up in the San Francisco area in 1985 (Rheingold 2000). It was the brainchild of Stewart Brand, then a radical rock concert impresario and Larry Brilliant, a left-wing doctor and Third World campaigner. Brilliant enrolled numerous fellow former members of Hog Farm, a large self-sufficient agricultural commune in Tennessee (once supposedly boasting over a thousand members). They created an electronic commune that grew into 300 computer-mediated 'conferences' that brought together social and political activists, as well as enthusiasts of all kinds. One of its largest subgroups was composed of followers of the radical rock group, the Grateful Dead. Deadheads (as they were disrespectfully called) spent hours online discussing the Grateful Dead's enigmatic lyrics and exchanging music recorded at their live gigs – something the group supported as part of its public stand in favour of the 'pirating' of its music.

There also developed geographically dispersed grassroots networks, usually set up by students in university campuses. These included Usenet (1979), BITNET (1981), FidoNet (1983) and PeaceNet (1985) The most important of these were Usenet newsgroups, built around the UNIX operating system. They were set up initially to discuss issues to do with UNIX software and troubleshooting. They proliferated to cover a wide range of issues, growing from three sites in 1979 to 11,000 by 1988. During these early years, Usenet created a significant space for the expression of minority views, and exploited the global potential of the Internet by building extensive international links.

The counterculture also contributed to the emergence of radical computer capitalism. Thus, Steve Jobs and Steve Wozniak, who launched Apple in 1980, came out of the alternative movement. Jobs had travelled to India in a quest for personal enlightenment, while Wozniak was heavily involved in the radical rock scene. In 1982, Wozniak personally funded the organisation of a rock festival dedicated to the Information Age. At the festival, which attracted more people than Woodstock, there was a giant video screen on which was projected a simple message:

> There is an explosion of information dispersal in the technology and we think this information has to be shared. All great thinkers about democracy said that the key to democracy is access to information. And now we have a chance to get information into people's hands like never before. (Flichy 1999: 37)

In addition, the counterculture influenced postgraduate students in computer science departments during the 1970s and 1980s. This strengthened the stress on freedom, open disclosure and social interaction as formative influences on the technical evolution of the Net. It also fostered a radical culture among computer scientists that was mobilised subsequently to resist the commodification of the Net.

The fourth cultural influence that shaped cyberspace was a tradition of public service. If the Internet was incubated primarily in the United States, the World Wide Web was a European invention and came out of a legacy which bequeathed great parks, public libraries, art galleries, public television and radio systems and subsidised art house film industries dispersed throughout Europe. The Web's principal architect, Tim Berners-Lee, was inspired by two key ideas that are leitmotifs of the public service tradition: the idea of opening up access to a public good (in this case, the storehouse of knowledge contained in the world's computer systems), and of bringing people into communion with each other (in this instance, through the connective potential of the computer). Berners-Lee found fulfilment in service to others, and resented the exaltation of market values above all else. He is often asked, he says, in the United States (though less frequently in Europe): does he regret not making money out of the World Wide Web?

> What is maddening is the terrible notion [implied in this question] that a person's value depends on how important and financially successful they are, and that this is measured in terms of money ... Core in my upbringing was a value system that put monetary gain well in its place. (Berners-Lee 2000: 116)

Berners-Lee's decision not to promote the Web through a private company was prompted mainly by a concern that it could trigger competition, and lead to the subdivision of the Web into private domains. This would have subverted his conception of 'a universal medium for sharing information'. Instead, he persuaded CERN (Conseil Européen pour la Recherche Nucléaire, former title of the European Organisation for Nuclear Research) to release in 1991 the World Wide Web code as a free gift to the community. He became subsequently the head of a public service agency regulating the Web (World Wide Web Consortium (W3C)), since this enabled him to 'think about what was best for the world, as opposed to what would be best for one commercial Internet' (Berners-Lee 2000: 91).

The fifth cultural influence shaping the Net was the values of the market. At first, these seemed benign and progressive. Their initial effect was to counter the exclusionary norms of academic life by democratising the Web. In 1983, a commercial Web browser (Netscape) was launched that used colour images, and made the Web more accessible. Indeed, it played a key role in popularising use of the Web. It was followed by the creation of commercial websites that were fun to visit.

In the mid 1990s, all aspects of the Internet seemed enormously positive. Even if the Internet was a product of a superpower war machine, its military legacy was terminated in 1990 when ARPANET handed over control of the public Internet backbone to the National Science Foundation. A combination of academic, countercultural and public service values had created an open public space which was decentralised and largely uncontrolled. It had established a tradition of cooperation in which software codes were freely disclosed. And it had greatly extended the uses made of the Net, not least through the creation of the World Wide Web. The growing influence of commerce seemed merely to be extending the benefits of this new medium to more people, without detracting from its fundamental nature.

Scientific developments

Before examining further the role of the market in the development of the Internet and the Web, it is worth pausing to look more closely at the chain of innovation that led to their creation. History tends to be written by non-scientists, which encourages the undue playing down of the scientific dimension of communication breakthroughs.

One strand of innovation that led to the Web was of course the development of the computer. In the 1940s the first operational electronic digital computers were built – the British 'Colossus' in 1943 and the more advanced, American ENIAC in 1946. These and subsequent 'first-generation' computers were massive machines, costing vast sums, attended by a white-coated priesthood, and dependent on thousands of notoriously unreliable valves. Three key developments subsequently transformed the computer, enabling it to become smaller and more powerful. In 1947, transistors were invented, and gradually replaced computer valves. In 1958, integrated circuits were introduced in the form of silicon chips incorporating thousands of miniaturised transistors. In the early 1960s, this led to the introduction in research and business organisations of so-called 'minicomputers' – though these were enormous by today's standards. This culminated in the final decisive breakthrough: the microprocessor invented by Ted Hoff in 1969. This is the integrated circuit that incorporates the functions of the central processing unit of a computer, its 'heart'. Its invention led to the development of microprocessor-based personal computers, the first of which was manufactured in 1975 in the form of a do-it-yourself kit for hobbyists. The late 1970s marked the beginning of the personal computer boom that has continued to this day.

A second strand of innovation, the development of computer networking, can also be seen as a cumulative process. During the 1950s a computer language evolved that drew on the pioneer work of a number of scientists, most notably Konrad Zuse. This still left unresolved how computers, using different systems, could communicate with each other. The first step was the building of an intermediary computer (IMP) in the late 1960s that functioned as a processing link between the computer 'host' and the network. This was followed in the early 1970s by the development of conventions (*protocols*) governing the dialogue between machines. This began with formulating shared codes for transporting communications (Transmission Control Protocol, shortened to TCP), and for addressing computers (Internet Protocol, shortened to IP). These were adopted eventually both in the United States and globally, though only after much difficulty. The other, linked breakthrough was the development of packet-switching during the 1960s and 1970s. This was an ingenious system in which messages were disaggregated into units (*packets*) before dispatch; sent through different routes, depending on the flow of communications traffic; and reassembled on arrival. Each packet was wrapped in a kind of digital envelope containing transport and content specifications.

Protocols governing computer interaction and packet-switching technology made possible the development of the Internet. This began in 1969 as a computer network (ARPANET) established by the US Defence Department, with nodes in four American universities. It grew rapidly in the 1970s and 1980s to become the backbone of a larger system that encompassed a number of networks. Its rise was paralleled by the development of a second major network started in 1982 by the US National Science Foundation. This second network became linked to the first; built links with national networks around the world in the late 1980s; and took over ARPANET's backbone role in 1990. In the United States, a cumulative process of convergence also took place, in which a variety of outsider networks – business, commercial and grassroots services – developed closer links to the American public system during the period between 1983 and 1995. The modern Internet, in the sense of a publicly accessible, worldwide network of computer networks, came of age in the late 1980s, and took off in the 1990s.

An ancillary development that facilitated the building of this global network was the improvement of modern communications infrastructure. Initially, computer networking was conducted through telephone wires, but later came to use routinely both satellite and advanced cable. Satellite communication dates from the launch of Telstar in 1962, but only developed fully from the 1970s onwards. The first, local *broadband* cable systems were laid in the early 1980s, while transcontinental systems were extended across the Atlantic and Pacific Oceans in the late 1980s. Between 1996 and 1999, there was a tenfold increase in transatlantic cable capacity, underlining the point that the sea still matters as well as the sky in coping with the growing volume of communications traffic (Briggs and Burke 2002: 291).

The third strand of innovation took the form of advances in computer software. The revered pioneer of software design is Vannevar Bush. He argued in the 1930s and 1940s that computers should be viewed not as giant calculating machines but as a technology that can assist human beings to store, retrieve and analyse creatively all kinds of information. Some claim to discern in his 1945 outline of a hypothetical 'memex' machine the essential elements of what became scroll bars, home pages, computer displays and scanning. However, it was not until 1963 that Douglas Engelbart and his team developed in a concrete form recognisably modern software, including graphics-based interfaces, and the now ubiquitous 'mouse', the pointing device used to roam the computer screen. This was followed by the emergence of *hypertext* software, first developed in a simple form by Ted Nelson in 1965 and greatly refined subsequently. The key benefit of hypertext is that it enables computer users to move from one part of a text to another linked text by clicking on an icon or symbol. In this way, it offers flexible and lateral intellectual pathways.

In 1990, Tim Berners-Lee and his associates at CERN, Geneva, invented the World Wide Web. This took the form of a software program that allowed people to access, link and create communications in a single global 'web' of information. This was achieved through the development of new conventions governing the interaction between machines. One convention specified the location of the information (URI, later revised usually to URL, Uniform (or Universal) Resource Locator); a second specified the form of information transaction (HTTP, Hyptertext Transport (or Transfer) Protocol); and the third a uniform way of structuring documents (HTML, Hypertext Markup Language). Before their general adoption, people experienced enormous difficulties in finding information on the Net, and also in releasing information that others could find. Various protocols that had evolved for exchanging information were not compatible, and there was no generally accepted way of linking information in different documents.

While the Web proved to be a momentous development, it built upon advances that had preceded it. The Web was superimposed on the Internet, and incorporated its protocols. Without the prior existence of global computer Internetworking, and the development of communications infrastructure under-pinning it, the Web would not have been possible. The early popularisation of personal computers was also a precondition of the Web. It provided the dispersed computer power that enabled users to put their own content on the Web, as well as the technical means to run Web software. Lastly, Berners-Lee's invention incorporated past software innovations, not least hypertext links that were a key feature of his project. Indeed, the World Wide Web can be viewed, in one sense, as part of a continuum of software development: subsequent innovations made the Web easier to navigate, and introduced an audio and video dimension.

The Web thus marked the coming together of three different strands of innovation. It joined *personal computing* to *networking* through *connective software* (Naughton 2000). This gave rise to a technological development with the potential to change the world. The Internet and the Web provide a global medium of communication in a context where the world's media system is overwhelmingly national and local. It allows individuals and groups to send as well as receive communications, in contrast to the one-way communication flows of conventional media. It is highly versatile, lending itself to different uses. Above all, the Internet and the Web began as the least controlled part of the media system, subject initially neither to state nor market domination.

Commercialisation of the Internet

The largely uncritical reception given to the increasing commercialisation of the Net during the mid 1990s accorded with the ethos of the period. This was a time when deregulated capitalism was trumpeted as the only way to organise an efficient economy, and when capitalism's victory over communism was hailed as the 'end of history'. The mood music of the time was reinforced by the outpourings of Net experts. The Massachusetts Institute of Technology (MIT) guru, Nicholas Negroponte, set the tone in a celebrated book, published in 1995, which portrayed the Internet as the centrepiece of a democratising digital revolution. 'The information industry', he declared, 'will become more of a boutique business ... the customers will be people and their computers agents.' The public, he predicted, will *pull* what they want from the Internet and digital media, rather than accept whatever is *pushed* upon them by media giants. Fundamental change was already upon us. Media consumption, he claimed, is becoming 'customised' according to individual taste, and 'the monolithic empires of mass media are dissolving into an army of cottage industries', making obsolete 'industrial-age cross-ownership laws' (Negroponte 1996: 57–8 and 85). Similarly Mark Poster (1995), another revered Net expert, also concluded that we are entering the 'second media age' in which monopoly is being replaced by choice, the distinction between senders and receivers is coming to an end, and the ruled are being transformed into rulers. In these, and most other commentaries, the market was not viewed as a limitation on the emancipatory power of the Net.

The coalition that had created the pre-market Internet fractured during the mid 1990s. Some academic computer scientists set up Internet companies, and became millionaires. Others quietly acquiesced to software licensing restrictions. University administrators looked for ways to make money out of their computer science departments. A new generation of computer industry managers emerged, whose informality and populism seemed to set them apart from the stuffy corporate culture of their predecessors. In this changed environment, capitalism seemed hip: the way to make money, express individuality and prevent the state from taking control. The language used to discuss new media changed. The metaphor of the 'information superhighway', with its 1950s association of statist modernism, gave way to the romantic image of 'cyberspace', derived from science fiction (Streeter 2003). Everything seemed wondrous, transformative, positive.

However, the accelerating force of commercialisation began to change the Internet in ways that had not been anticipated. The open disclosure of information in pursuit of scientific advance that had shaped the Net began to be superseded by the imposition of intellectual property rights in pursuit of profit. Software codes were no longer disclosed openly on an automatic basis, but were often restricted by licensing arrangements. Still more potentially undermining of the traditions of the early Net was the transparent desire of some leading Net companies to charge website fees. They intended to make free visits only a temporary measure, in order to foster a 'habit' that users would be willing to pay for once they were 'hooked'. This threatened to change the Internet out of all recognition, transforming an open electronic commons into fees-only, private enclosures.

The belief that 'peripheral voices' would move centre stage in the digital era – central to a naïve mid 1990s view of the Internet – became increasingly implausible. This was partly because some search engines evolved into general portals that 'mainstreamed' the Internet experience (Miller 2000). Their central objective was to retain users as long as possible in order to sell their 'eyeballs' to advertisers and, also subsequently, to sell information about their Net behaviour. This led general portals to construct 'hub and spoke' websites, in which users were encouraged to follow defined pathways, and return to the home base before venturing out again. These pathways led to 'channels' that structured the Internet experience. For example, Yahoo! UK offered, in 2002, a basic choice between shopping, information, fun, business, personal and connect channels, while its main rivals offered variations of the same. Within content 'channels', prominence was given to what was popular (since the aim was to retain users) and also to what was sponsored. Thus, in 2002, AOL (American Online) UK had a tie-in with Blockbuster for entertainment; MSN (Microsoft Network) UK with Encarta for 'learning'; and Freeserve with Barclays Bank for business information. In short, the rise of general portals encouraged a middle-of-the road, convergent use of the Internet, strongly dependent on established sources. This way of organising the Internet experience was increasingly eclipsed by the less mediating model of Google. However, its way of ordering listings tends to funnel people towards the more popular sites, and to result in less prominent sites being overlooked. Most people do not go beyond Google's top entries on any specific topic (Hindman 2009).

The beguiling vision of boutiques, cottage industries and consumer-sovereigns, conjured into being by Californian Net academics, proved to be wide off the mark. A small number of companies, most notably Microsoft and AOL, gained pole position in the early commercial development of the Net. The Net's growing popularity then prompted leading media corporations – Time Warner, Vivendi, Disney, Bertelsmann, News Corporation, among others – to launch sophisticated websites or form joint ventures with major telecommunications or software companies in order to establish a significant online presence. These media superpowers had enormous assets: back catalogues of content, large reserves of cash and expertise, close links with the advertising industry, brand visibility and cross-promotional resources. Although their start-ups sometimes floundered, enough succeeded for them to dominate cyberspace in a remarkably short period of time. In 1998, over three quarters of the 31 most visited news and entertainment websites were affiliated with large media firms (McChesney 1999: 163). In 1999, the websites of broadcast TV networks and MSNBC were the most visited sites by 'news users' (Sparks 2000: 283). The effect of the media majors' incursions into cyberspace was also to raise the prevailing level of costs. Creating and maintaining a multimedia, audience-pulling website became an expensive business, offering few openings to those with limited resources.

A side effect of commercialisation was to promote Net advertising. The advertising industry introduced first of all the banner advertisement (a horizontal strip, reminiscent of early press display advertisements). This was followed by advertisements of different shapes such as 'button', 'skyscraper' and pop-up 'interstitials' and by new types of advertisements that contain audio-visual or dynamic elements (more like television commercials). Online selling to the public also became a more prominent feature especially after the adoption in 1997 of a standard protocol for credit card transactions. In this new commercial world, professional conventions – such as maintaining a 'firewall' between editorial and advertising – were weakened. In particular, the emergence of stand-alone, promotion websites converted advertisers into controllers of editorial content, rather than buyers of space, designated as advertising, in environments controlled by professional media staff – the offline norm. Typifying this new Net phenomenon was the Pepsi website which offered, in 2002, a Britney Spears mini-site, games, music, and an opportunity to learn about the 'Joy of Pepsi'. This 'ad-free ad' approach can lead to abuse. Naomi Klein cites as an example of lowered standards a website called Parent Soup, paid for by Fisher-Price, Starbucks, Procter and Gamble and Polaroid. It calls itself a 'parents' community', and imitates a user-driven newsgroup. However, when parents go to Parent Soup, they receive such 'branded wisdom' as: the way to improve your child's self-esteem is to take Polaroids of her (Klein 2001: 42–3).

New layer of control

A central feature of the early Net, its absence of central control, was weakened as a consequence of commercialisation. Net entrepreneurs developed 'cookies' – markers deposited by websites on computer hard drives – in order to log and transmit information about user behaviour. They also introduced authentication procedures for identifying users, and the status of communications (for example, by developing a digital watermark registering whether a communication has been paid for). A whole new technology of commercial surveillance came into being during the 1990s.

This surveillance was deployed very extensively. In the United States, an estimated 92 per cent of commercial websites aggregate, sort and use for commercial purposes data about people's use of the Net, wherever they are (Lessig 1999: 153). Most people make themselves vulnerable to this monitoring by waiving away their rights of privacy in order to gain website access. Overriding 'human rights' protection of privacy is minimal in the United States, though there is more protection in Europe. In addition, people's use of the Net is often monitored at work. According to a study released in 2000, 73 per cent of US firms routinely check on their workforce's use of the Net (Castells 2001: 74).

The Internet has thus ceased to be an anonymous place, and become a glasshouse (although many people appear not to be aware of this when they go online in the privacy of their home). Moreover, while surveillance technology was developed for purely commercial purposes (to sell data about users, protect financial transactions and prevent piracy) it began to be used in other ways. In the late 1990s, government agencies used surveillance technology to identify Net users, share information about them, and prosecute them (as in the case of international paedophile rings). While there is nothing wrong in governments intervening to protect the vulnerable, such as abused children, it underlines the point that the Internet is no longer 'uncontrolled'. Indeed, authoritarian governments have become adept at using the weak point in the Internet system – Internet service providers – in order to snoop and censor (Price 2002; Stein and Sinha 2001).

Corporate pressure was also brought to bear in the United States (and elsewhere) for the Net to become subject to stronger property protection. In 1976, the United States passed a Copyright Act, which extended copyright to software. This was buttressed in 1998 by the Digital Millennium Copyright Act, which greatly strengthened legal provision against 'circumvention'. Its effect was to overprotect intellectual property rights in cyberspace at the expense of 'fair use' (Lessig 2001). The likelihood is that increased pressure will be exerted in the future to strengthen still further intellectual property rights, both in national and international jurisdictions, since the music majors have lost so far their battle against music piracy.

Computer worker opposition

In short, the Internet changed profoundly as a consequence of the establishment of a market system, the successful incursion of media majors into cyberspace, and the imposition of a new layer of technological control. However, these trends did not go unopposed. When the progressive coalition that shaped the early Internet fell apart, one group took practical steps to preserve its legacy. This was an informal community of computer scientists who resisted the imposition of 'proprietary software' – programs whose use was restricted by private patent or copyright.

The nerds' revolt began in 1984 when Richard Stallman, a radical programmer at MIT, set up the Free Software Foundation. He had been outraged when a colleague had refused to pass on a printer code on the grounds that it was now restricted by licence. This seemed to Stallman something new and alien, an enforced form of selfishness that violated the norm of cooperation on which his professional life had been based. His outrage turned to anger when AT&T announced its intention to license the widely used and previously unrestricted UNIX operating system. In his view, this amounted to the corporate capture, with the full authority of the law, of a program that had been communally produced.

Richard Stallman, a bearded, romantic figure with the appearance of an Apostle, gave up his secure job and set about building almost single-handedly a free alternative to the UNIX operating system. It was called GNU (standing for 'GNU is not UNIX'). Between 1984 and 1988, Stallman designed an editor and compiler, which were hailed by the computer science community as masterpieces of skill and ingenuity. Then, Stallman's hands became damaged from overwork, and he slowed down. The GNU project was still some way from completion until a then unknown Finnish student, Linus Torvalds, who had heard Stallman give a charismatic talk in Helsinki, filled the gap. With the help of his friends, Torvalds developed in 1990 the missing kernel of the GNU system. The computer community collectively improved the resulting GNU/Linux system, making it one of the most reliable in the world. Such was its sustained success that IBM decided in 1998 to hitch its wagon to the protest movement. It officially backed the Linux system, agreeing to invest money in its further development without seeking to exercise any form of proprietary control. IBM also embraced, on the same terms, the Apache server. This derived from a program released freely by a publicly funded agency, the National Center for Supercomputing Applications (NCSA) at the University of Illinois. Initially full of bugs, it was transformed by the hacker community through cumulative improvements ('patches'), and renamed Apache. It became a widely used, free server – its success again accounting for its open source adoption by IBM.

What partly underpinned the effectiveness of this concerted protest was that it enlisted the protection of the state (something that radical libertarians tend to ignore). The Free Software Foundation set up by Stallman released its projects under a General Public License (GPL). This contained a 'copyleft' clause (the wordplay is typical computer nerd humour) requiring any subsequent improvement in free software to be made available to the community, under the GPL. Contract and copyright law was thus deployed to prevent companies from modifying free software and then claiming the resulting version as their property. It was also used to ensure that future refinements in free software were 'gifted' back to the community. A similar legal formula was adopted by the less militant 'open' (as distinct from 'free') source movement, though in a more permissive form.

The open source movement kept alive the tradition of the open disclosure of information. It perpetuated the cooperative norms of the scientific community in which people make improvements, or develop new applications (like the World Wide Web), on the basis of open access to information, and then return the favour by making the basis of their discoveries freely available. It also kept faith with the values of academic science, with its belief in cooperation, freedom and open debate in pursuit of scientific advance. The result was the creation of practical alternatives to proprietary software.

Who were these remarkable people, and what inspired them to challenge corporate power in the computer industry? They were a relatively homogeneous group, consisting mainly of highly trained computer workers employed by universities, research laboratories and the computer industry, as well as university students and knowledgeable computer enthusiasts. Their first chronicler, Steven Levy (1994), argues that they tended to subscribe to a shared set of beliefs. These can be summarised as five precepts: information should be free; respect should be earned through constructive achievement, not position or credential; never trust authority; computers have the power to improve the world; for this reason, they should be put to work for the benefit of humanity. While these motives were philanthropic, it is also clear that many gained satisfaction from the thrill of creativity in building or improving new programs. They were gratified by the recognition they received from their peers. Many derived also a sense of purpose from working for the good of society, and living by a set of values superior to those of conformist corporate culture. The open source tradition thus combined pleasure and philanthropy, and drew upon a hybrid culture that married individualism to collectivism. This unusual combination is expressed succinctly in a stanza quoted admiringly by Richard Stallman:

If I am not for myself, who will be for me?
If I am only for myself, what am I?
If not now, when? (cited in Williams 2002: 102)

As the revolt developed, splits emerged on generational lines. Older computer scientists, like Stallman, were intent upon preserving the values of the pre-market Internet, while younger ones, like Torvalds, tended to be less anti-market. The computer industry boom also winnowed the ranks of rebels, separating the dedicated from dilettantes. As Eric Raymond, another chronicler of the hackers' revolt, comments: 'commercial demand for programmers has been so intense for so long that anyone who can be seriously distracted by money is already gone. Our community has been self-selected for other things – accomplishment, pride, artistic passion, and each other' (cited in Williams 2002: 167).

Yet, in media legend, hackers are destructive and threatening: they spread viruses, break into computer systems in ways that imperil lives, and engage in online theft. This demonisation obscures a crucial distinction between 'hackers' and 'crackers', 'white' and 'black' hats, those who work for the good of society and those who are antisocial, which is widely understood within the computer community. To lump the two together is to seek to delegitimate the opposition that developed against commercialisation of the Internet.

User resistance

The nerd revolt was effective mainly because it was backed up by recalcitrant consumers. The pre-market Internet had accustomed people to expect Internet software and Web content to be free. Net companies found it difficult to re-educate them into paying. This is illustrated by early attempts to commercialise the Web. In 1993, the publicly funded agency, NCSA, released free its pioneer browser, Mosaic, on the Net. Within six months, a million or more copies were downloaded. Members of the Mosaic team then set up a private company and offered an improved, commercial version, Netscape, on a three month, free trial basis. However, demands for payment, after the free trial, were widely ignored. Netscape's management then had to decide whether to insist on payment or change tack. It opted to make its service free because it feared – probably rightly – that continued attempts to charge would cause people to migrate to a free alternative. Netscape turned instead to advertising and consultancy as its main source of revenue (Berners-Lee 2000: 107–8). Companies which tried to charge website fees also ran into trouble. A large number failed (Schiller 2000; Sparks 2000). The only type of Web content that a significant number of people seemed willing to pay for was either pornography or financial information. This also had the effect of propelling pioneering Net companies towards advertising as their main source of revenue.

The virtues of Net advertising were widely trumpeted. The Net reached initially a mainly young and affluent audience. Its technology enabled advertising to be targeted towards specialist groups with almost surgical precision. Above all, the Net offered a unique selling point: consumers could click on an advertisement, be taken direct to the advertiser's site, obtain more information and buy the product or service in question.

The only problem was that there appeared to be built-in resistance to Net advertising because it was viewed from the start as intrusive. An early warning signal came in 1994 when the US law firm Canter and Siegel posted an advertisement for its immigration law advice service to thousands of newsgroups. The next day, it was so inundated with abusive replies ('flames') that its Internet service provider repeatedly crashed (Goggin 2000). In 1995, a survey found that two thirds of Americans did not want any Net advertising

(McChesney 1999: 132). People became adept at avoiding ads by clicking the delete button. New ways of engaging user interest ran into problems: audio-visual ads were expensive, and took time to download. In the UK, crude banner ads still accounted for 52 per cent of Net advertising expenditure in 2001. Worst still, the extent of user resistance to advertising became embarrassingly transparent, and was reflected in low 'click through' rates to advertising sites. For all these reasons, Net advertising grew relatively slowly, still amounting to only 1 per cent of the UK's total media advertising expenditure in 2002 (Advertising Association 2002). However, Internet advertising subsequently took off, rising to 16 per cent of total media expenditure by 2007 (Freedman 2009).

Direct selling on the Net also proved to be much more difficult than anticipated. It tended to be confined to a limited range of products such as music, live events, books and holidays. Many people, it transpired, liked to shop in person, while some were doubtful about the security of online credit card purchases. The dawning realisation that Net retailing was going to take a long time to establish successfully, and would require a heavy investment with a deferred and speculative return, was the main cause of the dot-com crash of 2000–1. The Klondike rush was over almost before it had begun. It was not only small Net companies that ran into trouble. Even market leaders like Yahoo were forced to issue profit warnings, and major conglomerates like AOL Time Warner and Vivendi had to restructure, partly as a consequence of failed Net investments. Venture capital that had poured money into the Internet economy lost confidence, and withdrew support.

Yet, the irony is that Internet retailing did expand during the 2000s. By 2008, 55 per cent of the British population said that they had bought something online in the past. Most of these (81 per cent) had done so in the last three months (Office for National Statistics 2008). The most popular items bought online were to do with travel, accommodation and holidays. But while the number of online buyers increased steadily, the volume of purchases did not grow as fast (Office for National Statistics 2008). In short, commercialisation did not fully take hold, partly because the Internet proved to be less immediately profitable than had been anticipated. Online advertising grew slowly in Britain until 2003; online shopping developed even more slowly; dot enterprises lost money; and above all, most users could not be persuaded to pay for Web-based content.

Contested space

The history of the Internet is thus a chronicle of contradiction. In its predominantly pre-market phase, the Internet was powerfully influenced by the values of academic science, American counterculture, and European public service. It began as a research tool. It blossomed into a subcultural playground and medium of grassroots concerns. And it developed the World Wide Web as a public space open to all. However, this early formation was overlaid by a new commercial regime. Major media organisations established well-resourced websites. Search engines, seeking to harvest advertising, signposted visitors to popular destinations. The growth of online entertainment tended to marginalise political discourse. Net entrepreneurs sought to populate the Web with virtual shops, and to make users pay for information. Computer companies turned software into profitable commodities. New surveillance technology was developed to monitor user behaviour, and extend digital rights management. Yet the old order refused to surrender without a struggle. Dissenting computer workers resisted the new regime of enforced intellectual property rights by making available free or open source software. Users, conditioned by the pre-market norms of the Net, declined to be re-educated into becoming paying consumers. Instead, they shifted from sites seeking to charge a fee to sites that were free.

As a result, the Internet came to exhibit incongruent features. It is still a decentralised system in which information is transmitted via independent, variable pathways through dispersed computer power. But on top of this is imposed a new technology of commercial surveillance which enables commercial operators – and governments – to monitor what people do online. In a similarly contradictory way, the Internet is managed by public service trusts, a legacy from its pre-market past, but most of the Net's major players are now private companies. Yet if the drive to commercialise the Web intensified in the 2000s, the DIY culture of the Web also found new expression. This was exemplified by the founding of Wikipedia, a Web-based, free-content encyclopedia, in 2001. It was written by a growing legion of volunteers, numbering some 75,000 active contributors in 2008. It encompassed an enormous range of subjects, covered in 10 million articles in more than 260 languages. It became a global phenomenon, attracting 684 million visitors in 2008; and it achieved a remarkable (though variable) level of quality, supported by the self-correcting mechanism of revision, a shared norm of adhering to factual accuracy, unobtrusive safeguards, and an academic trail of hypertextual links.

The rise of Wikipedia was accompanied by the meteoric growth of other websites based on user-generated content. Facebook was set up by Harvard students in 2004, took off as a young elite social networking site, and then grew exponentially when it became open to all in 2006. It provides a way in which users can publish in effect to their friends, while excluding unwanted attention. YouTube was created as a video-sharing website in 2005, and became a rapid success around the world. It offered a way in which users could circulate what they enjoyed, grade collectively what was available, and in the process provide an opportunity for marginalised performers and artists to connect to a wider public.

The emergence of Web 2.0, a part of the Web based on user-generated content, represented a strengthening of the non-commercial traditions of the Web. Some corporations sought to incorporate this grassroots activity, and transmute it into profit, by buying up high-traffic sites that would generate advertising revenue. Thus, Google bought YouTube in 2006, while Rupert Murdoch's News International acquired the popular social networking site Facebook, also in 2006. Meanwhile, major film and TV companies sought to use YouTube and similar sites as extensions of their publicity departments. Their attempts were less than successful because users were the gatekeepers determining prominence on these sites, and proved less susceptible to influence than some time-pressured, PR-fed journalists reporting the entertainment industries.

In effect, the spirit of cooperation that had reimagined the computer and discovered new uses for it in the 1980s, that had defended the Internet through the open source movement, that had created the World Wide Web in 1990–1, was renewed through the development of social networking sites in the 2000s. Cyberspace is now much more commercialised than it was 10 years ago; yet, it is still not a controlled market system. The balance struck between the old and the new is inherently unstable, and may well change quite rapidly; but, as of now, the two leading understandings of the Net both seem simplistic. The Net is not an autonomous zone where the 'push' culture associated with powerful media corporations has been vanquished in favour of the 'pull' culture of the sovereign user; yet, equally, the Internet is not a featureless mall of digital capitalism. It remains a contested space, exposed to the opposed influences of pre-market and market forces.

Towards a global history

So far, we have offered a history of the Internet which foregrounds its technology and American origins, and contrasts a period of professional and grassroots influence with the subsequent attempt to impose a new order of market control. However, the Internet also grew into a global phenomenon, and this generated conflict between authoritarian governments and those seeking to use the new medium of the Internet to extend the boundaries of free expression. There needs now to be a world history of the Internet (something yet to be researched and written), with this as a further central theme.

Commentators who argued in the mid 1990s that the Internet would remain uncontrolled (supposedly because the Internet transcends place and, therefore, physical structures of power) proved to be wrong. Many governments in authoritarian countries became adept at exerting pressure on state-registered Internet service providers (ISPs) to exclude websites judged to be undesirable. This official-ISP censorship was circumvented through the use of un-banned proxy websites outside the state's jurisdiction. However, this required some level of knowledge, limiting the extent of evasion. But the effectiveness of the Internet as an oppositional agency in authoritarian societies did not just turn on the outcome of this cat-and-mouse game. In dominated societies, the Internet tended to be gagged; in those where opposition was increasing, the outcome could be different. This is illustrated by the contrast afforded by two neighbouring countries.

The People's Action Party (PAP) has ruled Singapore since 1965, and main- tained control partly through a restrictive National Security Act, manipulative defamation law, and the annual registration of civil society organisations. But it has also ruled by consent as a consequence of rising economic prosperity, and the prevailing national ideology that stresses Asian values, public morality and the need for ethnic harmony. One-party dominance resulted in the local Internet being co-opted in support of the regime through largely non-coercive means (Rodan 2004). Even a critical website which is directed at the local population from outside the city state's jurisdiction, and is therefore free from state control, is relatively restrained in what it says because it, too, is influenced by the PAP's ideological hegemony (Ibrahim 2006). The Internet has thus been tamed in Singapore, largely as a consequence of the way in which an integrated elite has monopolised state power, and sustained a largely unchallenged ascendancy.

By contrast the National Front (Barisan Nasional), the dominant political coalition in Malaysia, is more fractured and divided than PAP. It has also been beset by allegations of crony capitalism, and rides uneasily the tiger of Islamic fundamentalism. The much greater degree of political division and opposition within Malaysia, by comparison with Singapore, was accentuated when Anwar Ibrahim, the deputy prime minister, was imprisoned in 1997 for unsubstantiated charges of corruption and homosexuality. Growing dissent found expression in online newspapers and magazines critical of the regime, which gained a substantial audience in the late 1990s and 2000s when growing numbers came to distrust the mainstream press and television (George 2005). Critical online journalism both reflected, and amplified, political differences in Malaysia, culminating in the 2008 elections when the National Front did worse than it had done for decades, and lost its two-thirds parliamentary majority.

The external environment thus explains why Internet technology was tamed in Singapore, but not in Malaysia. Indeed, a central theme of this account is that the wider context has always been central in influencing the technological development, content and use of the Net. But as the Internet has evolved from its American origins to become a global phenomenon, so it is necessary to narrate the Net's development in an ever more extensive context. For this reason, Internet history that begins in America has now to end with the world.

Further reading

Readers interested in the complex history of the Internet's early development might like to consult Janet Abbate's *Inventing the Internet* (2000), and also John Naughton's *A Brief History of the Future* (2000). The story of the creation of the World Wide Web is told from 'the inside' by Tim Berners-Lee in *Weaving the Web* (2000), and also in Gillies and Calliau's *How the Web Was Born* (2000). The commercial and social development of the Internet is covered in a concise and insightful manner by Manuel Castells in *The Internet Galaxy* (2001). Critical analysis of utopian claims about the Internet's potential for liberation is offered by Matthew Hindman in *The Myth of Digital Democracy* (2009). Finally, the commercial appropriation of the Internet, particularly through the extension of intellectual property rights, is covered in Laurence Lessig's work such as *The Future of Ideas* (2001).

References

Abbate, J. (2000) *Inventing the Internet.* Cambridge, MA: MIT Press.

Advertising Association (2002) *Advertising Statistics Yearbook 2002.* London: Advertising Association.

Berners-Lee, T. (2000) *Weaving the Web.* London: Orion.

Briggs, A. and Burke, P. (2002) *A Social History of the Media.* Cambridge: Polity.

Castells, M. (2001) *The Internet Galaxy.* Oxford: Oxford University Press.

Family Expenditure Survey 2000, www.statistics.gov.uk. (accessed 20 January 2003).

Flichy, P. (1999) 'The Construction of New Digital Media', *New Media and Society,* 1(1): 33–9.

Flichy, P. (2002) 'New Media History', in L. Lievrouw and S. Livingstone (eds), *The Handbook of New Media.* London: Sage.

Freedman, D. (2009) 'The Political Economy of the "New" News Environment', in N. Fenton (ed.), *New Media, Old News.* London: Sage.

George, C. (2005) 'The Internet's political impact and the penetration/participation paradox in Malaysia and Singapore', *Media, Culture and Society,* 27(6): 903–20.

Gillies, J. and Calliau, R. (2000) *How the Web Was Born.* Oxford: Oxford University Press.

Goggin, G. (2000) 'Pay per Browse? The Web's Commercial Future', in D. Gauntlett (ed.), *Web Studies.* London: Arnold.

Hindman, M. (2009) *The Myth of Digital Democracy.* Princeton, NJ: Princeton University Press.

Holland, S. (ed.) (1972) *The State as Entrepreneur.* London: Weidenfeld and Nicholson.

Ibrahim, Y. (2006) 'The Role of Regulations and Social Norms in Mediating Online Political Discourse', unpublished PhD dissertation, University of London (LSE).

Klein, N. (2001) *No Logo.* London: Flamingo.

Lessig, L. (1999) *Code and Other Laws of Cyberspace.* New York: Basic Books.

Lessig, L. (2001) *The Future of Ideas.* New York: Random House.

Levy, S. (1994) *Hackers.* London: Penguin.

McChesney, R. (1999) *Rich Media, Poor Democracy.* Urbana: University of Illinois Press.

Miller,V. (2000) 'Search Engines, Portals and Global Capitalism', in D. Gauntlett (ed.), *Web Studies.* London: Arnold.

Naughton, J. (2000) *A Brief History of the Future.* London: Phoenix.

Negroponte, N. (1996) [1995] *Being Digital* (revised edn). London: Hodder and Stoughton.

Office for National Statistics (2007) http://www.statistics.gov.uk/cci/nugget.asp?id=868 (Accessed 14 February, 2008).

Office for National Statistics (2008) *Internet Access 2008.* London: Office for National Statistics. http://www.statistics.gov.uk/pdfdir/iahi0808.pdf (Accessed 14 February 2009).

Office of Telecommunications (2002) 'Consumers' Use of Internet', Oftel Residential Survey, May 2002. London: Office of Telecommunications.

Poster, M. (1995) *The Second Media Age.* Cambridge: Polity.

Price, M. (2002) *Media and Sovereignty.* Cambridge: MIT Press.

Rheingold, H. (2000) *The Virtual Community* (revised edn). Cambridge, MA: MIT Press.

Rodan, G. (2004) *Transparency and Authoritarian Rule in Southeast Asia.* London: Curzon Routledge.

Schiller, D. (2000) *Digital Capitalism.* Cambridge, MA: MIT Press.

Sparks, C. (2000) 'From Dead Trees to Live Wires: the Internet's Challenge to the Traditional Newspaper' in J. Curran and M. Gurevitch (eds), *Mass Media and Society* (3rd edn). London: Arnold.

Stein, L. and Sinha, N. (2001) 'New Global Media and Communication Policy: the Role of the State in the Twenty-first Century', in L. Lievrouw and S. Livingstone (eds), *The Handbook of New Media*. London: Sage.

Streeter, T. (2003) 'Does Capitalism Need Irrational Exuberance? Business Culture and the Internet in the 1990s', in A. Catalbrese and C. Sparks (eds), *Toward a Political Economy of Culture*. Boulder, CO: Rowman and Littlefield.

Turner, F. (2006) *From Counterculture to Cyberculture*. Chicago: University of Chicago Press.

'Wikipedia:About' http://en.wikipedia.org/wiki.wikpedia: About (Accessed 20 February 2009).

Williams, S. (2002) *Free as in Freedom*. Sebastopol, CA: O'Reilly.

Winston, B. (1998) *Media Technology and Society*. London: Routledge.

Chapter 3

On the globalisation of crime: the Internet and new criminality

Barry Sandywell

Introduction

I write this chapter in the midst of one of the most severe financial crises that the developed world has experienced. The so-called 'credit crunch' – the crisis of the global system of financial capitalism – has its sources and causes in the more general globalisation of socioeconomic, political and cultural relationships that have developed over the past three decades. In response to the extreme rapidity and extent of 'capital loss' – what might be called global decapitalisation – the popular press are full of apocalyptic commentaries on the 'end of capitalism', the prospects of a total collapse and the abyss of uncontrollable recession with estimates of up to 20 million people unemployed in the industrial nations by the end of 2009. Indeed the deputy governor of the Bank of England, Charles Bean, has described the slump as 'possibly the largest financial crisis of its kind in human history'.[1] For our purposes, however, the financial crisis is doubly instructive in firstly revealing the cyclical 'reflexive' instabilities of the global capitalist market and in clearly marking a configuration of social and technological conditions that have also facilitated the globalisation of criminal activity and practices over the same period. In other words, the forces that have precipitated the global financial crisis are the same generic conditions of *unregulated interdependence, digital connectivity*, and *deterritorialisation* that constitute the diverse phenomena of cybercrime.

These conditions include:

- the global reach of instantaneous digital communications technologies (the Internet, World Wide Web, video conferencing, multimedia digitisation, wireless technologies, 'cloud computing', and so on);

- globalisation or the emergence of a global network society in which information, social relations, services and institutions are increasingly net-worked (the era of cyberspace or global telecommunications connectivity);

- the radical 'compression', 'disembedding', and 're-embedding' of local and everyday events and practices with global social processes (for example the creation of databanks covering national and international populations, digitally coded geo-demographic information on populations, extraterritorial policing and surveillance systems);

- the increasing interdependence and mobility of manufacturing, commerce and financial capital in the context of global forces of commodification and consumerism;

- the spread of digitalised mass media, particularly news media and journalism, that intensively document and report upon global events on a continuous 24/7 basis;

- the 'blurring' of traditional normative boundaries, for example the blurring of distinctions between sanctioned and non-sanctioned activities as these have become normal features of a deterritorialised economic and political order.

Taken as a totality this constellation provides the historical setting for our specific topic, the globalisation of crime in the era of capitalist cyberculture.

1. Crime and criminality?

Some commentators see e-criminality as the most significant threat facing an increasingly globalised world. The Internet, the Web and cyberspace have been described as the 'wild west' of new forms of criminality organised on a planetary scale. Of course, to speak of 'crime' is to invoke a highly charged normative category. Like taxes and death, rule breaking, deviance and antisocial behaviour will always be with us. Every organised society has, in Durkheimian terms, its own quota of transgressive acts and, correlated to these, its own socially regulated forms of sanction, deterrence and punishment. 'Criminal behaviours' are typically singled out and semiotically marked as among the most threatening and destabilising manifestations of societal deviance. This also entails a discourse of punishment and redress typically involving juridical and state institutions. In general terms whatever contests the authority and continuity of the dominant institutions tends to be labelled as 'deviant' and regulated through various types of authorised sanctions. 'Deviance' and 'crime', in other words, are profoundly social phenomena, embedded in the wider cultural, economic and political contexts of a given society.

In thinking about the present global crisis, our normal categories of crime and criminality seem wholly inadequate. We need to ask the more reflexive question of what kind of knowledge can be gained by researching criminal activities on a global scale? What forms of compliance and 'normalisation' are implicit in a society's sanctioning regimes? To this end we need to think more critically about the assumptions underlying such categories as 'deviance', 'crime', 'law-breaking' and 'subversion'. In what follows it is important to approach criminality in socio-discursive terms as those actions, practices and relationships that are judged to be transgressive by the normative standards of a powerful group, class or whole society. A reflexive criminology would be one that brackets the 'real' or 'ontological' nature of crime and instead examines what, how, when and where human activities are treated as 'deviant' and 'criminal' by powerful agents and agencies. If criminality is 'socially constructed' in and through the mediations of powerful social practices the central theoretical topic of a more reflexive criminology should be *criminalisation practices* as these are institutionally embodied in a given social order.

The phenomena labelled 'criminality' are thus mediated by the social categorisation procedures of a particular society's systems of risk management and social control. Furthermore, as the morphology of 'criminality' will vary with the changing economic, political and cultural contexts of perceived threat and risk, critical criminology needs to adopt a radically historical approach. For example, a society with a well-demarcated, hierarchical and resourced 'establishment' would be expected to have a powerful set of paradigms operating to 'criminalise' and 'control' anti-establishment threats to its authority and power. For analytical purposes such classificatory ascriptions of deviance would both identify and differentiate some of the dominant meaning systems and conflicts in a given society (thus what we are calling 'criminal discourse' might be generated by a range of societal agents and agencies), it might also be typically interwoven with political discourses concerned with inclusion and exclusion of 'others' and be embedded in moral and social policy discourses based upon anxieties to perceived threats to the existing social order.[2]

One interesting area that is rarely explored in traditional criminology and social theories of deviance is the interplay between transgression and the 'technologies of transgression', the techniques and material forms that create the possibility of digital databanks and networks also facilitate and mediate cyber-attacks and deviant practices with regard to those systems. Here I will argue that the same processes of global connectivity that have seen a revolution in communication and social exchange also facilitate criminal activities on a planetary scale. This phenomenon has been variously conceptualised as Web crime, digital criminality, e-criminality or, at its most generic, *cybercrime* (Wall 2003a, 2007).

A related phenomenon revealed in all its starkness and radicalism by the current global financial meltdown is the extent to which the deterritorialised business culture of banking and financial corporations has become intensely interdependent and reliant upon new technologies and globalised digital media. Contemporary capitalism is perhaps better described as cyber-capitalism. Thus, for example, traditional patterns of financial investment and speculation are now typically directed towards future states of capital and market movements (Web futures based upon circuits of intangible assets). Whole sectors of credit and finance have become wired up to markets trading in national currencies, government bonds, future economic conditions, 'derivatives' and other intangibles (creating what might be called a global economy of intangible capital and associated transactional 'instruments'). In this way the traditional commercial practices of capitalism have been increasingly 'virtualised' as corporate organisations outside of the traditional stock markets – banks, mortgage brokers, etc. – trade in 'futures' and 'hedge funds' based directly upon anticipated future states of the economy. With the support of institutional deregulation and the philosophy of 'market fundamentalism', the financial heart of the major industrial economies has assumed the form of interlocking information-based casinos, multiplayer speculative games carried out in the ether of cyberspace. We now live in a planetary civilisation in which the social formation of 'capital' increasingly takes the form of instantaneously transmissible electronic information (where, for example, 'runs on the bank' occur in nanoseconds and, amplified by mass-media publicity networks, become powerful generative 'vicious circles' that expand and deepen the original problem to create chaotic macro events and processes). In being enmeshed in new digital media and the abstract instrumentality of financial derivatives the banking and financial sector no longer merely reacts to changes in markets but actively, if unintentionally, produces and magnifies those changes.

Contemporary globally interconnected capitalism has thus become profoundly reflexive, computer-mediated, and chronically unstable. Thus it is not only 'hackers, punk capitalists, graffiti millionaires and other youth movements' that are transforming the landscape of modern capitalism (Mason 2008), but the 'pump 'n' dump' and 'short selling' strategies of hedge fund managers, anonymous corporate investors, and pension fund millionaires. All of these practices are examples of reflexive circuitry that have become embedded in the normal operations of global financial markets.

The 1990s is littered with the ominous harbingers of these market instabilities. The phenomenon of rogue traders like the derivatives trader Nick Leeson (whose fraudulent activities led to £700 million losses and the destruction of Barings Bank in 1995), the bond trader Toshihide Iguchi (losses of $1.1 billion), and Jerome Kerviel (whose fraudulent dealings in equities lost the French company Société Générale £3.5 billion in 2008) are symptomatic of this new constellation. On a more global scale, much more extensive losses are involved in recent cases of corporate corruption (Enron, Tyco and WorldCom in the US being paradigm cases of the extent of corporate malfeasance made possible by deregulated energy markets). Global deregulation has created an interlocking system that is chronically prone to crisis. It also makes possible levels of corruption on an equally planetary scale. In other words, we have the basic conditions for what George Soros describes as a cycle of self-reinforcing processes that introduces chaos into market systems.[3] Moreover it is this particular branch of speculative capital that appears to be one of the causal elements in a complex chain of reflexive relationships that has precipitated what many see as a total collapse of legitimacy in stock markets and the global economy. Not surprisingly, some commentators have come to view corporate corruption as a generic condition of the American economic and political system. Corporate corruption on a hitherto unimaginable scale has, in other words, become a 'normal phenomenon' of global capitalism.

In this transformed situation we clearly need to reflect on the unprecedented changes in the sociocultural conditions and new information technologies of globalised modernity.[4]

2. Criminality without borders

In what follows I will use the following acronyms and shorthand: information and communication technology (ICT), computer mediated communication (CMC), new electronic media (NEM), and cybercrime (computer-based crime, electronic crime or e-criminality).

While in the past these technologies have been relatively invisible (and have been treated as such in mainstream discussions of criminality), today they have begun to take centre stage; and among the most insistent of these technologies are new digital information technologies like MP3 players, iPod and multimedia cellular phones and, more particularly, the emergent communications media associated with the second and third generation Internet (what today is generally referred to as Web 2.0 and beyond). We are increasingly moving into an era of ubiquitous, mobile, distributed multimedia information appliances that 'wire' individuals to distant and anonymous networks (exemplified by the availability of free software such as Skype and Linux and the impact of 'cloud computing' organised by such major players as Google and Microsoft). E-crime presupposes such a distributed universe of information infrastructures as its fundamental technical and material condition.

The basic sociological thesis here is that as we move from the electronic to the digital age, from analogue technologies to CMCs, as we enter a truly globalised world of corporate capitalism, we correspondingly witness the mutation of analogue to electronic and digital forms of deviance and crime on a transnational scale. In other words, with the coming of digital communication networks we not only witness the creation of ubiquitous multimedia but also experience an explosion of online criminality, particularly of illegal accounting practices and corporate criminal activities made possible by the new information networks. It is also of some relevance that commentators on the current global economic crisis routinely resort to the language of viruses that spread 'toxic contagion' when describing the 'financial contagion' infecting the world's economies (just as 'computer virus' emerged with the first phase of information globalisation, phrases like 'toxic debts' and 'toxic liabilities' have become media clichés in descriptions of the latest crisis of global capital). Stated baldly this conjecture suggests a technological determinist approach to social life; however, in what follows I wish to avoid this interpretation by promoting a more 'mediated' and dialectical version of this general argument linking cybercrime to some of the major forces that are transforming contemporary society and consciousness in the global era.

As a longer-term project, a general socio-cultural theory of globalised cybercrime would have to address the following conceptual issues:

1 how to theoretically describe the constitutive *differences* between pre-digital and digital criminality;

2 how to explain the *continuities* between analogue and digital crime;

3 how to analyse the formative role of the new information technologies in transforming the global culture of crime while avoiding technological determinism;

4 how to model the *emergent* forms and characteristics of cybercrime (distinguishing, for example, between individual, corporate and state-centred forms of global criminality);

5 how to explain the societal, cultural and governmental responses to emergent forms of anonymous, automated and virtual criminality and their consequences for the wider society in different national and geographical contexts;

6 how these phenomena are leading to new attitudes towards personal and collective security, new forms of surveillance, and new forms of transnational regulation and policing.

Needless to say, while these theoretical issues form the background of the present paper, the articulation of a systematic theory of e-crime in relation to cyberculture more generally is beyond the scope of this essay. As a step in this direction I shall concentrate upon the emerging forms of Internet crime and the public and private responses to these new threats to personal and collective space.[5]

3. Old and new criminality: the distinctive features of e-criminality

At the outset we need a broad, if necessarily schematic, descriptive account of the phenomenon of 'new criminality'. Such a phenomenology of Internet malfeasance must not only locate the essential features of digital crime but also capture some of the emergent characteristics of the new criminality. We first need to conceptualise the Internet as a distinctive globalised socio-cultural system and then formulate a description of e-crime in its essential aspects.

The Internet is typically defined (and modelled) in fluid and network metaphors: as a 'fast' technology of global information 'flows', 'mediations', 'translations' across human–machine networks; as a sphere of hyper-mobility that reflects the global pace of hypermodernity; as an open-ended, decentralised and non-hierarchical technology (expressed by the popular imagery of 'the Net' or 'Web'); as the source of loosely connected virtual realities ('cyberspace').

By deploying these images cyberspace can be imagined as the virtual topography created by the Internet as a system of interactive, multimedia websites. In sociological terms cyberspace is both a conceptual site and a force of social reconfiguration and personal experience (a technological formation that constitutes new modes of production, appropriation and transnational connectivity). Thus:

> The Internet, in fact, is not just a global computer network, but a network of networks, the actualization of a set of design principles entailing the interoperability of heterogeneous information systems. Not only, that is, is there no central control of the Internet (although there are many control centres), but the whole space of communication has been designed and conceived in terms of dynamic and variable

relations between different communication networks. (Terranova 2004: 53–4)

Even considered at a technical level as a border-defying communication technology many commentators regard the boundary-dissolving and trespassing powers of the Internet and Web as profoundly anarchic, transgressive and threatening (see Jordan 1998; Lyon 1994; Plant 1998; Sandywell, 2006).[6]

Cybercrime

What, then, are the characteristics of cybercrime?

First, digitisation through Internet networks makes possible virtually instantaneous information transmission. As the Internet morphs with other digital apparatuses this makes possible mobile access on a transnational scale (storage power is reduced from building- and room-sized facilities to laptops and hand-held mobile phones). With the globalisation of space and time the mobility of information transmission brings with it the 'instantaneity' of viruses and malware ('If one carries forward the metaphor of "virus" from its original public health context, today's viruses are highly and near-instantly communicable, capable of causing world-wide epidemics in a matter of hours' (Zittrain 2008: 51; cf. Rochlin 1997)).

Second is the anonymity or 'facelessness' of cyberspace as an effect of the deterritorialisation of social encounters and online relationships in cyberspace. In media influenced by Web 2.0 platforms like MySpace, YouTube, Facebook, cyberspace identities are wholly constructed through the information that users provide – typically in the form of lines of text or visual imagery (which can themselves be 'mashed', morphed and manipulated to create specific image profiles – the 14-year-old schoolgirl in a chat room turns out to be a 50 year-old male with a documented history of paedophilia).

Third, the feature of material incorruptibility: being digital rather than analogue, information capital can be 'lifted' and replicated without altering its original (hence copying digital information does not 'degrade' or 'deteriorate' the prototype); this non-degradation feature also adds another dimension to the structure of anonymity producing a situation where data can be stolen without any trace of the violation (thus in identity theft I am still left with the same coded information even though this is now in circulation and being used as a surrogate of my own electronic 'signature').

Fourth, the 'manipulability' of digitally coded electronic information (in principle any coded software is 'open' software and therefore susceptible to modification with minimal costs and overheads).

Fifth, the correlative expansion of diverse, geographically decentralised and multifarious forms of criminal activity accompanying the global extension of the new information technologies (we might characterise this as the move from analogue crime involving 'linear' and 'hierarchical' relations between perpetrators and victims to digital crime involving anonymous, networked and rhyzomatic relations between perpetrators and victims).

When combined these features create ubiquitous digital platforms that facilitate information-based borderless crime on a planetary scale and hence prefigure the emergence of a situation of permanent information warfare.

Just as the appearance of 'gated communities' encourages 'gated crime', so the gated communities of cyberspace will encourage gated cybercrime. In this way every organisation and institution that is 'wired' through digital means becomes open to information violation, to 'attack' by a diverse and disparate range of 'intruders' – in this way analogue stealing that defines such legal categories as theft and burglary become globalised into identity theft, the violation of copyright and, at the highest level, cyber-terrorism against a whole society's information infrastructures. Not surprisingly the language of the information society adopts military rhetorics as a matter of course. For those concerned with digital security we now live in societies that are 'besieged' by hackers and digital warriors, we live in a state of permanent information insecurity, we are fighting an 'information war' on many levels and fronts. Articulated into a theoretical model, we have the elements of a new globalised risk economy. The 'theatre' of this new warfare – this new form of global criminality – is the field of information itself.

E-crime as a social construction

The fundamental social-epistemological problem posed by both analogue and digital crime can be stated simply: how do we come to know the world of crime? Or expanded and generalised: how do we come into contact with the various social constructions of criminal activity. Expressed more reflexively: what are the modes of discourse and forms of representation constituting criminal forms of life?

E-crime emerges with its distinctive epistemology and ontology in terms of the emergence – the 'reality' and 'thinkability' – of criminal organisations and activities on a planetary scale. It would be a basic failure of reflexivity to ignore the complex loops that flow between such social phenomena and their representation in the media and popular imagination. Hence a critical framework must also include the issue of the active rhetorical and ideological representations of deviance, of the rapid circulation of images, categories and representations by means of which certain behaviours, relations, and practices are labelled as 'criminal', 'antisocial', 'corrupt', and so forth (we might call this the 'discourse of criminality' available to a given community or society).

Approaching these questions from a more reflexive perspective we are directed towards the representations and discourses that constitute the phenomenon of globalised criminality in the context of twenty-first-century social relations, technologies and the transnational reconfiguration of time and space.

Where the larger part of personal and collective life is 'translated' into software and this software is 'wired' into impersonal electronic networks, the creation of new forms of hardware and software and their public 'accessibility' becomes a major political question for all advanced societies. The new 'political economy' of information is increasingly one of securing codes, regulating software applications, monitoring 'malware' and ensuring 'normal applications' of technologically intensive investments. In a globalised world traditional issues of societal control, power and domination increasingly assume the form of agencies and organisations engaged in the reflexive regulation of societal and trans-societal information governance. Just as central governments strive to control transnational networks and ensure 'safety' for legitimate uses of these networks, so the new criminality attempts to manipulate and misuse these networks for illicit ends.[7]

4. Empirical forms of the new criminality

Analysts of cybercrime have distinguished three subcategories of e-crime:[8]

1 traditional criminal activities that are expanded or *enhanced* by CMCs and NEM (for example criminal exploitation of ATM machines, the expansion of 'analogue' industrial espionage to include industrial espionage facilitated by unauthorised copying of branded commodities and reverse engineering);

2 traditional criminal activities that are *generalised* and 'radicalised' by the availability of NEM (money laundering, drug smuggling, cyberstalking, paedophilia activities, cyber-pornography, online gambling, assisted suicide, terrorism, etc.);

3 criminal activities that are *created* by CMCs and NEM (crimes directed towards computer systems or computer-based networks, e.g. hacking and digital piracy; crimes directed towards collective databases and infrastructural systems such as 'spamming', information espionage, global information warfare and cyber-terrorism).

While all of these categories are interrelated, it is the third category of *emergent* criminality that will be central to the following analysis. This category exemplifies phenomena that we regard as fundamental to discussions of the 'new criminality'.

One way into this emergent phenomenon is given with the idea of boundary transgression or 'border crossing'. Because of its global and transnational structure cyberculture is vulnerable to a wide range of boundary transgressive invasions of local cultures and lifeworlds (Sandywell 2006). We have seen that online crime is typically presented in invasive metaphors (hacking, hijacking, bombing, and so on). Not surprisingly the discourse of online deviance has become organised around the idea of 'alien Others' invading private and public space as we move from gated communities to gated cyberspace protected by electronic barriers (cybergates). Traditionally the wealthy and the privileged tend to cluster together and create boundaries that cannot be readily crossed. The same dynamic now operates in cyberspace, where the rich and powerful construct 'firewalls' and 'encryption' barriers to ensure the privacy and protection of their digital 'property'. Information becomes the new form of capital. The same forces that drive the privatisation of life in advanced industrial countries (extreme inequalities of wealth and access to life chances, accumulation of property, deregulated competition, and marketisation of services) also produce 'knowledge-based' ecologies and, with these, *cybergate* security industries. Information ('knowledge capital') is the new frontier that must be encrypted and defended with impenetrable barriers and anti-spyware systems (and increasingly the sociological operation of physical 'gates' and cybergates interact and coalesce to create new maps of social exclusion and inequality).

In what follows we will briefly discuss four types of 'border crossing' associated with e-crime. Taken together they define the new global culture of cybercrime:

1 identity theft and related security threats (hacking/cracking, distributed denial-of-service attacks (DDOS));

2 digital piracy (violation of intellectual property rights, copyright and culture theft stemming from the explosion of what might be called Internet piracy technologies: file-sharing, digital copying, scanning, sampling and mixing, remixing and morphing);

3 punk capitalism;

4 cyber-terrorism.

4.1 Identity theft

The world of new electronic mobility routinely problematises the issue of identity as a contested domain. While we can now communicate and carry out almost every activity of everyday life on a global scale so we can also be defrauded by the same technological means. The new, anonymous and fluid world of e-criminality is itself an example of deterritorialised 'smart mobs' – volatile, decentred, non-locatable groups made possible by the new technologies (Rheingold 2002). As people increasingly carry out everyday activities through online identities new forms of border transgression necessarily assume the form of identity theft. While precise empirical evidence of these volatile transformations is difficult to assemble surveys suggest that people are more anxious about having their online identities compromised than they are of being mugged (*Guardian*, 10 August 2007).

The phenomenon of global online insecurity is experienced first hand in the phenomenon of identity theft and forms of criminality associated with the misuse of personal information, personal identity codes and personal networks (from the theft of banking codes to more insidious forms of hacking, malicious spyware that 'seed' remote code execution programs and pre-installed keylogging devices, and cyberstalking). In the wake of global consumerism, identity theft scams and online fraud (for example credit card fraud, the theft of banking codes and PINs) is estimated to have cost British consumers £414 million in 2007 (*ibid*.). Wherever monetary transactions are coded as information and virtual money circulates across borders we create the opportunity of criminal intervention exemplified by phishing attacks. Fraudsters have developed ways of automatically accessing bank accounts through 'packet reading' to siphon off money from vulnerable accounts. In this way the electronic risk to privacy (the general problematic of network infiltration and insecure passwords) has moved on from the isolated attacks of 'lonely hackers' and the physical theft of credit cards to the world of organised criminal rings simultaneously attacking multiple networks from anonymous sites in cyberspace.

Phishing

Phishing is the use of fraudulent email messages disguised as a legitimate or trustworthy source that 'fishes' for personal details, typically by asking for email passwords or by inviting the recipient to reply to the email or to click onto a web link and provide PINs, passwords or account information. Phishing or 'carding' scams are a pure example of a type of financial fraud that is only possible through the new information technologies. With the increase in online banking, financial websites will be particularly vulnerable to such attacks. Phishing attacks are also expected to expand as more individuals use e-commerce websites (for shopping, insurance, travel, online brokerage, and other day-to-day activities). As Ollmann observes: 'While Spam was (and continues to be) annoying, distracting and burdensome to its recipients, Phishing has already shown the potential to inflict serious losses of data and direct losses due to fraudulent currency transfers' (2008: 4). In 2007–2008 it is estimated that £45–50 billion was spent in online shopping. We might anticipate an increasing level of consumer uncertainty, loss of trust and delegitimising of e-commerce as the extent and range of phishing scams enters the public domain.

Digital scams

Sales, advance fee, charity, pyramid selling and lottery scams have followed the creative design expertise of phishers in creating Web information that mimics official documentation, brand insignia and logos and targeting users who are thought to be more vulnerable to deception. 'Get-rich-quick' fraudsters 'profile' populations that are most receptive to scamming and repeatedly mail (including email) this demographic. In essence the digital fraudster engineers a persuasive 'imagined community' – typically woven around believable virtual promises – designed to entrap the unwary into parting with their cash. Thus sweepstakes or lottery scams operate where the potential victim receives the 'good news' of a major win and is asked to provide a release fee to access the winnings. Charity fraud solicits contributions to non-existent charities. Job scam frauds ask for up-front fees to facilitate job interviews and employment.

Facebook predation

With the spread of Web 2.0 social websites like Bebo, MySpace and Facebook we increase not only the possibility of stealing electronic identities but also of creating new forms of harassment, predation and stalking. The expansion of 'Facebook' type websites has seen a massive increase in the illicit use of private and personal information. Web 2.0 websites and Facebook blog culture thus enhances not only identity theft but password harvesting and more technically sophisticated forms of intimidation, solicitation and cyberstalking.

Cookie surveillance

Another well-documented surveillance strategy is the use of 'cookies' or bits of software that monitor, track and archive a user's online activities. Cookie surveillance belongs with the generic group of electronic tracking devices that automatically monitor Web usage. Electronic surveillance of users' keystrokes, mouse clicks and website journeys have notoriously been used by some major Web providers and software companies as the basis for 'data mining' of user preferences. Cookie surveillance is thus only a harbinger of a growing industry of commercial personal profiling and data mining.

Spyware

Spyware refers to a range of digital devices and viruses (botnets, Trojan horses, etc.) that monitor computer activities. Cookies that track online traffic are also useful to those who wish to use confidential information for fraudulent purposes. Commentators argue that the increasing organisation and internationalisation of such illicit markets in stolen identity data promises to make this a major concern for the global policing of the Web. Many of these emerging types of identity theft have come to be covered by the portmanteau term 'spyware' as some of the most sophisticated involve the seeding of malicious software viruses and worms in computer systems with the express purpose of automatically monitoring, controlling and exploiting network identities and activities. Given the economic incentives of Web servers to collect such online data to create market profiles we might anticipate that 'secondary' forms of identity fraud will increase as fraudsters see profit in selling on electronic information to other criminal groups.[9]

4.2 Digital piracy

Piracy is another example of transgressive 'border crossing' for illicit purposes. Digital piracy primarily involves the theft of intellectual property for profit:

> A pirate is essentially anyone who broadcasts or copies someone else's creative property without paying for it or obtaining permission. (Mason 2008: 36)

Digital piracy includes the unauthorised downloading, copying, and sharing of copyrighted material, counterfeiting, and forgery. Pirates tend to view information assets as free goods or common wealth to be downloaded and copied without let or hindrance. When carried out on an international scale we have the phenomenon of the global virtualisation, distribution and appropriation of 'information property'. For the pirate everything found on websites can be downloaded unless blocked by encryption devices, punitive copyright legislation and corporate sanctions. File sharing of music, images and software is usually seen as the most prevalent form of digital piracy. Over the past two decades digital sampling – innocently framed as downloading – has become something like a way of life for millions of Internet users (illustrating the thesis that the very pervasiveness of downloadable content deconstructs conventional rules regarding intellectual property and facilitates the emergence of new definitions and models of 'ubiquitous criminality').

The Internet provides the perfect environment for digital piracy. Online auction sites such as eBay and Bidlet provide a perfect environment for new forms of criminality. Individuals trading on eBay, for example, have no knowledge of the artefacts being sold, of the sales process or, in many cases, legal redress (there are global initiatives to introduce compensation systems for fake commerce on such auction sites). Fraud on such auction sites is considered to be the most prevalent type of e-commerce crime in the United States. Another form of copyright violation is commercial counterfeiting. The spread of counterfeit goods, especially counterfeiting of luxury items, suggests that counterfeiting and commodity fraud is being carried out as a new form of illicit industrialisation (especially in the so-called 'Tiger' economies where faking high-profile branded goods and counterfeit culture has become a major source of revenue for the black economy).

Taken together these forms of copyright violation create a scenario where the computer game 'Grand Theft Auto' becomes a realistic model for the economics of virtual and real commodification. Where pre-digital economic life created recognisable forms of cowboy culture we now move into an era of global counterfeit economics where the counter-economy of copied goods and reverse-engineered products is becoming as extensive as the circulation of commodities in the legitimate economy.

Digital counterfeiting (including digitally facilitated forgery) is a specific example of the more general attack upon the authorial signature, property and authentication that graphically reveals the threatened status of intellectual property in an age of ubiquitous access (Bettig 1996; Blyth and Kovacich 2001; Rifkin 2001).

Where the owners of copyrighted material see downloading, text-sharing and sampling as criminal plundering, the user's perspective frames digital criminality in the legitimising rhetoric of do-it-yourself creativity, innovation and cultural subversion. File sharing enables every user of the Internet to adopt a situationist attitude towards cyberspace. What was once an exceptional activity of 'underground' counterculture now becomes a global norm of mainstream culture. Mixing and mashing in multimedia formats presents itself as alternative, distributed anti-art (even where we recognise that '[the] Situationist notion of making art indistinguishable from everyday life is now known as branding' (Mason 2008: 21)).

Where the legal system views counterfeiting as copyright infringement, file sharers see their activities as new forms of cultural morphing (mixing, mashing, fusion and hybridising). The new digital systems create radical technologies that promise self-transformation. Here 'piracy' blurs into the cultural phenomenon of DIY mashing and morphing. Thus for 'many artists and musicians, the digital bank is there to be plundered' (Murphie and Potts 2003: 69):

> ... the Internet is more like a social space than a thing ... the magic of the Internet is that it is a technology that puts cultural acts, symbolisations in all forms, in the hands of all participants; it radically decentralises the positions of speech, publishing, filmmaking, and radio and television broadcasting, in short the apparatuses of cultural production ... Internet

communities function as places of difference from and resistance to modern society ... They are places ... of the inscription of new assemblages of self-constitution. (Poster 2001: 176, 184, 187)[10]

The establishment response to free file sharing is predictable. We move from the analogue language of 'property and its protection' to the digital realm of global digital protection. Where lawsuits and criminal procedures fail or prove expensive major firms and corporations adopt compromise solutions. After strenuous attempts at criminalising downloading, they turn to more benign forms of regulation; and, finally, corporate media businesses (Apple's music store iTunes is an example) adopt policies of actively supplying media at a cheap rate and thus quasi-legalising what would otherwise be viewed as piracy. In this way 'the music industry has accommodated sampling by making it legal – for a fee' (Murphie and Potts 2003: 70). Another technique of incorporation is to employ hackers as a source of innovation: 'smart companies, instead of criminalizing hackers, will encourage these user-innovators and solicit their feedback to design better products' (Pescovitz 2008: 323).[11]

4.3 From corporate criminality to punk capitalism

The growth of automated electronic scams, of organised phishing gangs and transnational lottery scams is symptomatic of the global reach of cybercrime and suggests that we require a political economy of digital crime to explore the new interlocking systems of electronic banking (e-commerce), telemarketing, global finance capitalism and the dynamic flows of circulation, exchange and appropriation. Such a framework would also need to explore the subcultures of blurred criminality, the global spread of the black economy and the processes of capital redistribution and money laundering by organised criminal syndicates. It is thus no exaggeration to speak of such emergent economies – from underground or black economies to organised money laundering and piracy – as the new economy of punk capitalism (Mason 2008; cf. Featherstone and Burrows 1995). The proliferation of heterodox commercial transactions, illegal trading, and 'fast business' enterprises has come to characterise the world of punk capitalism.

These transformations of e-commerce suggest that we require a theorisation of the new criminality as a force of planetary sociocultural change. Future research needs to explore the blurring of the continuum from organised mass-mailing scams and peer-to-peer file sharing networks to the construction of black economies linked to online gambling operations, organised crime and terrorism (McChesney 1997; McChesney et al. 1998; Schiller 1999; Soja 1989).

Consider for example the controversies associated with global patents and the corporate monopoly on such 'objects' as genes, seeds and prescription drugs. Is the restrictive pricing of important drugs by the pharmaceutical industry simply an instance of normal monopoly practices (protecting a commercial asset) or a more problematic example of global criminality in the face of a worldwide need for these commodities? As Mason observes in relation to the restrictive practices of drug companies: 'Never before has an industry needed piracy so badly' (2008: 62).

Botnets and other forms of malware

While 'spyware' is the generic name for 'viruses' that fraudulently access computer systems, botnets or robot networks are malicious programs; 'zombies', or 'malware' that are seeded on a computer for fraudulent purposes. As a form of spyware, botnets enable the hostile downloader to function in the place of the legitimate online user. Like some of the earliest forms of hacking, botnets are frequently used to close a computer system – in so-called 'denial-of-service' attacks, the seeding of 'ransomware' and 'logic bomb' threats. Unlike earlier viruses botnet zombies operate through automated programs that can rapidly 'scan' databases in order to extract relevant information patterns. Recent cases of botnet keylogging and data harvesting have seen these technologies linked to blackmailing and extortion crime:

> Botnets can also be used to launch coordinated attacks on a particular Internet endpoint. For example, a criminal can attack an Internet gambling Web site and then extort payment to make the attacks stop. The going rate for a botnet to launch such an attack is reputed to be about $50,000 per day. Virus makers compete against each other to compromise PCs exclusively, some even using their access to install hacked versions of antivirus software on victim computers so that they cannot be poached away by other viruses. The growth of virtual worlds and massively multiplayer online games provides another economic incentive for virus creators. As more and more users log in, create value, and buy and sell virtual goods, some are figuring out ways to turn such virtual goods into real-world dollars. Viruses and phishing e-mails target the acquisition of gaming passwords, leading to virtual theft measured in real money. (Zittrain 2008: 46–7)

The unintended impact of 'smart' devices like botnets is illustrated by the increase in encryption/decryption competition, the emergence of new forms of global risk management and international governance and the prospect of a globally patrolled and regulated cyberspace. As a response to notorious cases of hacking and botnet scams we see the creation of new forms of policing, criminal legislation, international internet legislation, and state sponsored disciplinary programmes. The past decade has seen the creation of 'meta-organisations' specialising in information security, advisory functions relating to digital assurance for the private sector and public bodies concerned with the national threat of cybercrime. We have also witnessed a massive explosion in national and international legislation concerning transnational digital security, intellectual property rights, the governance of electronic commerce and international standards. Given these developments it is likely that IT security organisations as a form of meta-monitoring of corporate and governmental organisations is set to become one of the fastest-growing sectors of economic activity in the industrialised world (see Blyth and Kovacich 2001; Ollmann 2008).

4.4 Cyber-terrorism

The last years of the twentieth century and the first decade of the twenty-first century appear to many as an era of global insecurity. These anxieties are epitomised by the phenomenon of global terrorism and, more particularly, by terrorism based upon information warfare (*cyber-terrorism* or electronic attacks on IT and communications systems). We might say that global terrorist acts such as those of 9/11 in the US and the London tube bombings in July 2005 represent a conflation or 'compression' of every other form of digital malfeasance: configuring money laundering and corporate investment, digital piracy, identity theft, the creation of illicit cells and networks and the strategic manipulation of cyberphobia for terrorist ends. The extent of this compression can be illustrated by the dependence of terrorist networks upon the latest technologies of multimedia platforms and cellular phone telecommunications.

State responses to recent forms of terrorism reveal a consistent pattern: first, a high-profiled awareness of the global character of the new terrorism; second, the view that the present network of terrorists is fundamentally dependent upon ICTs such as mobile phone links and email; and third, that the 'war on terrorism' necessitates a political order sensitised to the idea of permanent emergency. Events like the destruction of the Twin Towers in America and the continued threat of terrorist plots against the Western powers is used to create a political environment of increasing legislation against terrorist activity, an increase in CCTV technology and erosion of civil liberties, and further steps towards a surveillance society of total monitoring and control. In this way real and imagined cybercriminality play into the hands of centralising powers and technocratic organisations that reframe society's problems in terms of total regulation and surveillance: the enemy is both within and without.

The unintended consequences theorem operates here: in striving to 'protect the public' from global terrorism governments actually undermine freedoms and civil liberties by introducing draconian security measures (from the rigours of airport and transport security systems to the spread of CCTV cameras across private and public space and the introduction of identity cards and related biometric methods of identification such as voice recognition and retinal imaging). Here the unintended dynamics of global criminality has profound consequences for the restructuring of national and international governmental priorities, policy legislation and their impact upon the conduct of everyday life. Even if a society was not chronically prone to risk prior to these monitoring innovations, the society that is produced by surveillance becomes in a self-defining way a global 'risk society' (Beck 1992, 1999). In this way the sociology of global terrorism illustrates the dialectical relationship between cyber-trespass, surveillance and governance.

We have seen that cybercrime – like globalisation more generally – blurs the boundaries between local, regional, national and international activities. Where old style terrorism is targeted at regional and national level, new style cyber-terrorism is explicitly international in its ideology and targets. The new-style terrorism, exemplified by al-Qaeda, becomes a major player in a range of societal transformations that directly affect the power structure and political economy of whole societies. Here the deterritorialisation of cybercrime assumes the form of an attack upon governments and nation states that has the effect of restructuring citizenship and the quality of life for the population. In other words, like other forms of e-criminality, these border-dissolving phenomena play a powerful role in shaping social and cultural change in the advanced industrial societies.

We find a number of recurrent characteristics:

First, terrorism based upon digital technologies is itself a social form of delocalised cosmopolitan interaction made possible by globalisation.

Second, cyber-terrorism is a product of new circuits and networks of criminal 'capitalism' (what might be called 'asocial capital'). The circuitry of capital today includes the creation of underground markets based upon the flow of criminal transactions and the haemorrhaging of capital in various types of money laundering activity. We thus find interlocking networks that produce the new 'junk economies' of global crime (involving people trafficking, drug smuggling, global prostitution and the sex trade, money laundering, organised gambling rackets, and so on). Here the intersection of local and global criminality justifies the use of the concept of 'glocalised crime'.

Third, the threat of 'global terror' is represented as the most universal form of 'alterity threat' that legitimises the reconstruction of civil society, governance and military preparedness to create a permanent state of emergency (the 'war on terror', the generic threat of jihadist websites, and the Russian 'raid' on the information infrastructure of Estonia in May 2007 are recent examples of this phenomenon).

Fourth, responses to this 'threatening Other' range from the geopolitical 'war on terror' against 'rogue' states such as Iraq and Iran to an intense concern with public and private boundary regulation, from physical surveillance (CCTV) to biometric identification, automatic Internet monitoring, and government-sponsored data mining (for example the National Management Information System (NMIS) in the UK).[12]

The threat of universal terrorism (cyber-jihadism) conjoined with cyber-terrorism presents a massive political incentive to militarise everyday life in the advanced societies under the surface forms of protection and depoliticisation, a process that seamlessly integrates movements towards accelerated geopolitics, global data surveillance and biopolitics. An individual state's investment in surveillance and monitoring activities has a 'multiplier effect' in creating a culture of fear focusing upon ubiquitous, invisible, and uncontrollable viral intrusions. This involvement is escalated when whole political regions are involved – such as NATO's response to the Estonian cyber-attack. By invoking apocalyptic threats to 'law and order', governments are forced to reorganise their priorities and promote panic rhetorics and agendas to protect the body politic from invasive forces.[13]

5. Conclusion: future research directions

Researchers in the field of cybercrime repeatedly point to three major methodological issues: empirical under-determination, access, and multidisciplinarity. 'Empirical under-determination' refers to the lack of reliable and comprehensive empirical studies of the different forms and dynamics of e-crime. 'Access' refers to the difficulties of defining and researching cybercrime on a transnational and comparative basis and of critically evaluating different studies and findings. 'Multidisciplinarity' indexes the importance of developing cybercrime research paradigms with a comprehensive transnational approach to the global reach of cybercrime. Bearing these issues in mind we will briefly sketch some of the ideas and paths that might be pursued in further research in the field of e-criminality.[14]

Theoretical frameworks

Phenomena like rogue trading, corporate corruption, and global terrorism carried out through telecommunications systems exemplify some of the central concerns of so-called 'risk society' theory (Beck 1992; Giddens 1990, 1991, 1992, 1998). As social systems become more complex and reflexive they generate unanticipated and chaotic consequences. In the case of the present global financial meltdown this susceptibility to chaotic behaviour is exacerbated through processes of deregulation and privatisation. Beck's original ideas about the universalisation of risk in late modern societies have been expanded to create a range of global sociological and philosophical frameworks directed towards forms of deep connectivity that transcend the typically 'nation-based' explanatory frameworks and their associated public policy formation and regulatory regimes. Some of the more innovative paradigms have built on these beginnings to create new research programmes that integrate the specific study of global crimescapes within more generic social theories of the Internet and cyberculture.[15]

We might briefly mention the following.

Risk theory paradigms: from risk society to alterity studies
Critical research on digital mobilities, border-crossing, and global alterities requires a radical rethinking of some basic philosophical assumptions about identity and sociality in risk-prone environments, complex emergence, risk management, the interaction of private and public space and the like (Hamelink 1996; Massumi 2002). Risk and chaos paradigms need to be developed to provide a more integrated understanding of interlocking systems and networks. Thus the analysis of convergent 'mobile' technologies and global communication systems as these impact upon and reconfigure material culture, everyday life and everyday practices requires a much more global approach to everyday life in the new information societies (McCullough 2004). Where these networks are themselves 'reflexive' we need to move beyond classical modernisation frameworks to self-reflexive models of socio-economic, political and cultural systems. The philosophical background to the sociology of alterity can be found in the diverse writings of Michel Foucault, Paul Virilio, Jean Baudrillard, Jacques Derrida, Gilles Deleuze, Felix Guattari and Slavoj Zizek (among others).

Teratological paradigms
The idea of globalised threats and transgressive behaviours has led to discourses

concerned with the 'monstrous' aspects of globalised ecologies – Internet child pornography, paedophilia, hate-speech, money laundering, stalking, cyber-terrorism, and so on – especially as these 'teratological' phenomena problematise the traditional images we have of the relationship between human and non-human agency, self and society, individual and community, citizen and state, private and public space, global citizenship and the like (see Haraway 1985, 1992, 1996; Law 1991; Sandywell 2006; Stone 1996).

New social theories of technology
The global impact of ICTs and the development of convergent electronic technologies has refocused scholarship on the creative and unpredictable social uses and applications of digital technology and encouraged the development of explicitly cultural theories of technology that move beyond standard 'Actor network' theorising to develop more complex, reflexive and politically engaged accounts of techno-scientific processes.[16] Recent work has stressed such factors as contextuality, the constitutive role of users' interests, the creative appropriation and transformation of technologies as they are used, recombined and modified for non-standard applications and the fundamental role of soco-economic and political relations in defining the phenomenology of human/non-human systems.[17]

1. Social Informatics and critical cyberculture studies
If we take the idea of cyberspace literally it suggests the construction of new kinds of 'social space' and new forms of social relations embedded in those 'spaces'. Once these 'virtual worlds' become institutionalised we create emergent electronic sites of cultural activities and practices made possible by digitisation. It is not simply a case of 'real' public spaces being augmented by new virtualities; rather, what has previously been regarded as 'social space' (itself symbolically constituted) is in the process of being radically transformed by the new informatic technologies. We could speak of the practices and environments of everyday life being colonised and transformed by digitisation. Not surprisingly, cyberculture as a pervasive 'postmodern' phenomenon has become the central theme of such innovative interdisciplinary research programmes as Social Informatics and cyber-demographics (Burrows and Ellison 2004), new forms of geopolitical theory (Soja 1989, 1996), reflexive economic theory (Soros 1998, 2008), the study of power configurations in cyberspace (Jordan 1998; Terranova, 2004), and the sociocultural investigation of electronically situated identities and identification processes.[18]

2. Globalised surveillance perspectives
The confluence of ICTs, accelerated globalisation and risk culture converges upon societal surveillance (one symptom of this is the UK government's publication of a 'National Risk Register' in 2008 which ranks cyber-terrorism as the second most likely form of terrorist attack after an attack on the transport system and before an attack upon a public target). We have seen that cyberspace transforms and elevates the universe of digital access and planetary connectivity into the basic principle of the new world economy. It also produces a world of reflexive social relations based around informatic

principles of categorisation and social sorting. The new technologies thus facilitate the monitoring of everyday life on a continuous basis (the coming of real-time 'Google Earth' being indicative of the surveillance possibilities of the new media). Many fear that Foucault's generalised 'panopticon' has been morphed into the global electronic panopticon (Foucault 1977). Private life is threatened by ubiquitious surveillance technologies that increasingly form an integral part of the fabric of everyday life (Davies 1996; Staples 1997). These changes have motivated the development of critical studies of globalised surveillance (Haggerty and Ericson 2006; Lyon 2001, 2003, 2006, 2007; Marx 2004).

3. Cyberphobia and the politics of fear

From the perspective of Web security experts the expansion of the Internet transforms everyone with access to digital media into a potential criminal. This is reinforced by mass media images of e-criminality. Thus popular media in the UK is rife with images of cyber 'folk devils' and associated moral panics. Recent debate and legislation relating to cyberspace – fuelled in particular by media concern with online grooming, paedophilia and pornography (especially child pornography) – suggests that we are moving from an age of anxiety to an era of permanent fear and global insecurity. Any critical discussion of cyberphobia has to begin with media representations of Internet 'threats' and the debate on censorship, regulation and civil liberties that these images have initiated. In a broader context it is important to understand the sociology and politics of fear as these relate to the transformation of everyday life and social identities in a globalised society.[19]

4. Prevention, regulation and policing

There are three recurrent themes in the literature on cyber-regulation. Firstly, there is the increasing internationalisation of law and policing relating to cyber-crime. Jurisdictional procedures, legal frameworks and policing models that had evolved within a national framework must be radically reformulated in order to deal with cross-border criminality. Against a general background of the failure of policing models in the 1980s and 1990s we have seen major transformations of cyberspace law, regulation and policing strategies. This new concern for complex risk management has motivated the creation of specialised high-tech police e-crime units and digital law enforcement agencies such as the UK's Serious Organised Crime Agency, the National Hi-Tech Crime Unit (NHTCU), the Metropolitan Police's Computer Crime Unit, the Internet Crime Forum and equivalent organisations in the United States such as the National Cybercrime Training Partnership (NCTP), the National White Collar Crime Center, and the National Infrastructure Advisory Council. The other major innovation is the introduction of transnational government regulations that apply to every part of cyberspace. This has encouraged international collaboration in creating global cyberspace protocols. One notable landmark here is the European Council's joint Convention on Cybercrime.[20]

A second theme in the emerging discourse of 'internet governance' is the expansion of private security companies. The regulation of digitalised public and personal space has created a growing cyber-security industry specialising in securing computer networks, systems and digital vaults. Infrastructure regulation has led to highly technical innovations in encryption and filtering technologies. The technical literature from the growing security industry reads like a cryptographic arms race of encryption and decryption code struggles (the language of 'attack vectors' and 'counter-attacks' is now commonplace). Regulatory concerns have also produced new techniques such as digital forensics and the reverse engineering of computer hard drives, Web surfing histories and email tapping (collectively referred to as 'computer forensics').[21] Today almost every advanced country has data protection legislation and private security organisations offering specialist protection services. Indeed the 'leapfrog' effect of phishing sophistication and counter-security measures has itself become a major source of innovation in addressing online criminality. This creates further layers of reflexive complexity in the detection and policing of online fraud (see for example the Phishtank.com site and the literature produced by the Anti Phishing Working Group (APWG)). In 1996 the UK government set up an Internet Watch Foundation (IWF) that serves as a 'hotline' to report illegal Internet content (there is a similar agency that operates on a Europe-wide basis).

Finally, there is the insistent theme of prevention through education, self-protection and self-policing. To counter cybercrime the first stage is to encourage users of cyberspace to become security conscious and apply anti-virus programs and firewalls that obstruct e-criminality and filter unwanted content. Companies and organisations are thus investing in major training programmes for their employees. Education also needs to instruct online users about the differences between licit and fraudulent emails. Banks, online shopping and auction sites have thus begun to invest in policies and security measures that provide advice to protect users. Countering transnational cybercrime is expected to become one of the major public education issues over the next decade.[22]

Notes

1   *Guardian*, 25 October 2008, p. 1.
2   This approach links social categorisation to the institutional and informational orders of societal control and compliance. For more detail of these connections see Sandywell (2006). On the general problem of sociocultural classifications that reflexively constitute the practices of social life see Bowker and Star (1999) and Lyon (2003).
3   According to George Soros the deregulation of global financial transactions directly served 'the interests of the managers of financial capital; and the freedom to innovate enhanced the profitability of financial enterprises. The financial industry grew to a point where it represented 25 per cent of the stock market capitalisation in the United States and an even higher percentage in some other countries' (2008). The subprime crisis of overlending and toxic debts in the US housing market is thus merely an indicator of a more global 'super-bubble' that is currently (October 2008) reconfiguring the world economy.
4   While 'globalisation' and 'globalised modernity' are not synonymous with 'network society' or 'information society' we can, for present purposes, treat these terms

as conceptual equivalents. For globalisation as a complex and overdetermined economic, political, and cultural process see Bauman 1998; Castells 1996, 1997; Cohen and Kennedy, 2000; Featherstone 1990; Held 2000; Hirst and Thompson 1996; Robertson 1992; Scholte 2000; and Waters 1995. The concept of 'reflexive globalisation' designates the phenomenon of self-organising, self-monitoring, self-regulating and self-producing processes as these are emergent within social systems at critical levels of qualitative and quantitative complexity (see Soros 1998). The emergence of global cybercriminality might be compared to the chaotic behaviour of reflexive financial systems where 'the sheer existence of an unregulated market of this size has been a major factor in increasing risk throughout the entire financial system' (Soros 2008). In what follows we adhere to Wall's conclusion that 'transformations in networking, informational transfer and globalisation have contributed to radical changes in the organisation of crime and the division of criminal labour, and to changes in the scope of criminal opportunity' (2007: 39).

5   For further analysis of the theoretical background and perspectives that inform this perspective see Sandywell 2006. For the most detailed and comprehensive analysis of the 'transformation of crime in the information age' see Wall 2007; also Wall 2001a, 2003 and Balkin *et al.* 2007. For general sociological introductions to cybercrime see Grabosky and Smith 1998 and Yar 2005, 2006. For links between electronic technology and the surveillance society see Davies 1996; Dawson and Foster 1998; Lyon 1994, 2003.

6   The history of the Internet has been described by its inventor in Berners-Lee and Fiscetti (1999). Its history can be found in Abbate (2000). For an early utopian take on the Internet and cyberspace see Rheingold (1994). An up-to-date survey of Internet and Cyberculture studies can be found in Silver and Massanari (2006). Indispensable resources for the specific topic of cybercrime can be found in Wall 2001a, 2001b, 2003a, 2003b and 2007. For sceptical responses to e-topian rhetorics see Hand and Sandywell (2002).

7   See Majid Yar's essay on the distinctiveness or 'novelty' of cybercrime (Yar 2005, 2006). Also McGuire (2007) on the emergent character of 'hypercrime'.

8   See Wall 2001: 3, 168.

9   For the complex issue of how identities and identifications are constructed through digital media see Turkle 1984 and 1995 and the contributions to Jones (ed.) 1997 on the question of the construction of virtual identity. For technical analysis of phishing scams and security implications see Ollmann 2008.

10   For the theme of 'mashing' and 'morphing' through such devices as MP3, Napster, and music sharing on Web 2.0 sites see Sandywell and Beer 2005 and Beer 2002.

11   Crackers and hackers are often contrasted as malign (unethical) and benign (ethical) violators of computer security systems (for 'hacking' and 'cracking' see Taylor 1999; Walch 1999; Wall 2007: ch. 4; and Wark 2004). On the 'hacker ethic' see Himanen 2002. For a defence of digital piracy as a force for creativity and social change see Mason 2008: 'The pirate mentality is a way to mobilise communities, drive innovation, and create social change' (2008: 67). See also Levy 1984 and Sterling 1994.

12   For further analysis of the implications of these de-democratising forces of global surveillance see Hand and Sandywell 2002.

13   See Sandywell (2006) for an analysis of the different forms of contemporary cyberphobia. Also Amoore and de Goede (2008) for further analysis.

14   On the lack of accurate statistical data on cybercrimes and the difficulties of carrying out research into criminal activities online see Denning 1998; Jordan and Taylor 2003: 162–86; Markham 1998; Wall 2001a: 7–11; Wall 2007, ch. 1, pp. 8–29.

For multidisciplinary studies of cybercrime drawing upon ideas from sociology, globalisation theory, post-colonialism, post-feminism, and other traditions see the work of David Wall (2001a, 2001b, 2003a, 2003b, 2007), Squires 1996 and Yar 2006.

15 For background see Landow 1997; Poster 2001; Robins and Webster 1999.

16 Explorations of the theoretical background can be found in Bijker *et al.* 1987; Bijker and Law 1992; Kittler 1990, 1994; Latour 1993, 1999, 2005; Law and Hassard 1999; Lovink 2001, 2002; MacKenzie and Wajcman 1999; Penley and Ross 1991; Robins and Webster 1999; Shields 1996; Verbeek 2005; and Wajcman 1991).

17 An instructive empirical case study of the dialectic of technology, policing culture, and criminalisation practices can be found in Janet Kahn's 'The Technology Game' (2003: 513–33).

18 For a sample of recent research see issues of *Information, Communication and Society, New Media and Society, Wired, Culture Machine* (www.culturemachine.net), *New Review of Hypermedia and Multimedia*, Burrows and Ellison 2004; Doheny-Farina 1996; Downey and McGuigan 1999; Lyon 2003 and Silver and Massanari (eds) 2006.

19 For the ideological functions of fear in society see Furedi 2002, 2005, 2007. For cyberphobia see Sandywell 2006; also J. Dibbell, 'A Rape in Cyberspace' (1996). For recent work on cyber-identity and cyber-subjectivities and, more especially, the phenomenology or subjective experience of cyberspace and cybertimes see Lovink 2001, 2002; Massumi 2002; Porter 1996; Poster 2001; Stone 1996; Tomas 1989; for explorations of virtual 'commonality and 'communality' see Rheingold 1994, 2002 and Holmes 1997; for post-human speculations see the work of Donna Haraway, Katherine Hayles, and others; for the transformation of politics in the digital age see Terranova 2004.

20 The Council of Europe, Convention on Cybercrime, Budapest, 23 November 2001. The 'Preamble' states its main objective as 'the protection of society against cybercrime ... by adopting appropriate legislation and fostering international co-operation' (Convention, p. 1). The text of the Convention is available online (http:conventions.coe.int/Treaty/EN/Treaties/Html/185.htm). Signatories apart from EU countries include the United States, Canada and Japan, but notably not Russia.

21 For an account of 'computer forensics' see Sommer (2003).

22 David Wall usefully distinguishes between five levels of Internet regulation: policing by Internet users themselves; the Internet service providers; corporate security organisations; state-funded non-public police organisations; and state-funded public police organisations (2001: 171). For a general introduction to the challenges that cybercrime poses to public regulation and policing see Wall 2001a, 2001b, 2003a, 2003b and 2007, chapters 8 and 9 and Grabosky and Smith 1998; for general background see Barrett 1996, 1997; Blyth and Kovacich 2001; Ellison 2001; Fuchs 2007; Steffik 1999; Thomas and Loader 2000; Terranova 2004; Webster 2006.

Further reading

On the interconnections between globalisation and new communication technologies see Manuel Castells' influential *The Rise of the Network Society* (1996), and on the transformation of social, political and economic life by the Internet see his book *The Internet Galaxy* (2002). On the globalisation of crime, an excellent overview is provided by Katja Franko Aas in *Globalization and Crime* (2007). On the globalisation of surveillance see Gary T. Marx's *Windows into the Soul: Surveillance and Society in the Age of High Technology* (2004). On panics about Internet crime see Barry Sandywell's 'Monsters in Cyberspace: Cyberphobia and Cultural Panic in the Information Age' (2006).

References

Aas, Katja Franko (2007) *Globalization and Crime*. London: Sage.

Abbate, J. (2000) *Inventing the Internet*. Cambridge, MA: MIT Press.

Amoore, L. and de Goede, M. (eds) (2008) *Risk and the War on Terror*. London and New York: Routledge.

Balkin, J.M. *et al.* (eds) (2007) *Cybercrime: Digital Cops in a Networked World*. New York: New York University Press.

Barrett, N. (1996) *The State of the Cybernation: Cultural, Political and Economic Implications of the Internet*. London: Kogan Page.

Barrett, N. (1997) *Digital Crime: Policing the Cybernation*. London: Kogan Page.

Bauman, Z. (1998) *Globalization: the Human Consequences*. Cambridge: Polity.

Beck, U. (1992) *Risk Society: Towards Another Modernity*. London: Sage.

Beck, U. (1999) *World Risk Society*. Cambridge: Polity Press.

Beck, U., Giddens, A. and Lash, S. (1994) *Reflexive Modernization*. Cambridge: Polity Press.

Beer, D. (2002) 'Making Friends with Jarvis Cocker: Music Culture in the Context of Web 2.0', *Cultural Sociology*, 2(2): 222–41. London: Sage.

Berners-Lee, T. and Fiscetti, M. (1999) *Weaving the Web: The Original Design and Ultimate Destiny of the World Wide Web by Its Inventor*. San Francisco: HarperCollins.

Bettig, R.V. (1996) *Copyrighting Culture: the Political Economy of Intellectual Property*. Boulder: Westview Press.

Bijker, W.E., Hughes, T.P. and Pinch, T.J. (eds) (1987) *The Social Construction of Technological Systems: New Directions in the Sociology and History of Technology*. Cambridge, MA: MIT Press.

Bijker, W.E. and Law, J. (eds) (1992) *Shaping Technology/Building Society: Studies in Sociotechnical Change*. Cambridge, MA: MIT Press.

Blyth, A. and Kovacich, G.L. (2001) *Information Assurance: Surviving in the Information Environment*. London: Springer.

Bowker. G. and Star, S.L. (1999) *Sorting Things Out: Classification and Its Consequences*. Cambridge, MA: MIT Press.

Burrows, R. and Ellison, N. (2004) 'Sorting Places Out', *Information, Communication and Society*, 7(3): 321–36.

Castells, M. (1996) *The Rise of the Network Society*. Oxford: Blackwell.

Castells, M. (1997) *The Information Age: Economy, Society and Culture, Volume 1: The Rise of the Network Society*. Oxford: Basil Blackwell.

Castells, M. (2002) *The Internet Galaxy*. Oxford: Oxford University Press

Cohen, R. and Kennedy, P. (2000) *Global Sociology*. London: Macmillan.

Davies, S. (1996) *Big Brother: Britain's Web of Surveillance and the New Technological Order*. London: Pan Books.

Dawson, M. and Foster, J.B. (1998) 'Virtual Capitalism: Monopoly Capital, Marketing, and the Information Highway', in R. McChesney *et al.* (eds), *Capitalism and the Information Age: The Political Economy of the Global Communication Revolution*. New York: Monthly Review Press.

Denning, D. (1998) *Information Warfare and Security*. Reading, MA: Addison-Wesley.

Dibbell, J. (1996) 'A Rape in Cyberspace: How an Evil Clown, A Haitian Trickster Spirit, Two Wizards, and a Cast of Dozens Turned a Database into a Society', in P. Ludlow (ed.), *High Noon on the Electronic Frontier: Conceptual Issues in Cyberspace.* Cambridge, MA: MIT Press.

Doheny-Farina, S. (1996) *The Wired Neighborhood.* New Haven: Yale University Press.

Downey J. and McGuigan, J. (eds) (1999) *Technocities.* London: Sage.

Ellison, L. (2001) 'Cyberstalking: Tackling harassment on the Internet', in D.S. Wall (ed.), *Crime and the Internet.* London and New York: Routledge, 141–51.

Featherstone, M. (ed.) (1990) *Global Culture: Nationalism, Globalization and Modernity.* London: Sage.

Featherstone, M. and Burrows, R. (eds) (1995) *Cyberspace/Cyberbodies/Cyberpunk. Cultures of Technological Embodiment.* London: Sage.

Foucault, M. (1977) *Discipline and Punish: The Birth of the Prison.* New York: Vintage.

Fuchs, C. (2007) *Internet and Society. Social Theory in the Information Age.* London and New York: Routledge.

Furedi, F. (2002) *Culture of Fear: Risk-taking and the Morality of Low Expectation.* London: Continuum.

Furedi, F. (2005) *Politics of Fear.* London: Continuum.

Furedi, F. (2007) *Invitation to Terror.* London: Continuum.

Garland, D. (2001) *The Culture of Control.* Oxford: Oxford University Press.

Giddens, A. (1990) *The Consequences of Modernity.* Cambridge: Polity Press.

Giddens, A. (1991) *Modernity and Self-Identity.* Oxford: Blackwell.

Giddens, A. (1992) *The Transformation of Intimacy: Self and Society in the Late Modern Age.* Cambridge: Polity Press.

Giddens, A. (1998) *Conversations with Anthony Giddens: Making Sense of Modernity.* Cambridge: Polity Press.

Grabosky, P.N. (2006) *Electronic Crime.* New Jersey: Prentice-Hall.

Grabosky, P.N. and Smith, R.G. (1998) *Crime in the Digital Age: Controlling Telecommunication and Cyberspace Illegalities.* New Brunswick, NJ: Transaction Publishers.

Haggerty, K. and Ericson, R. (eds), *The New Politics of Surveillance and Visibility.* Toronto: University of Toronto Press.

Hamelink, C. (1996) *World Communication: Disempowerment and Self-Empowerment.* London: Zed Books.

Hand, M. and Sandywell B. (2002) 'E-Topia as Cosmopolis or Citadel. On the Democratizing and De-democratizing Logics of the Internet, or, Towards a Critique of the New Technological Fetishism', in *Theory, Culture and Society*, 19(1–2): 197–225.

Haraway, D. (1985) 'A Manifesto for Cyborgs: Science, Technology and Social Feminism in the 1980's', *Socialist Review*, 80: 65–107.

Haraway, D. (1992) 'The Promise of Monsters: A Regenerative Politics for Inappropriate/d Others', in L. Grossberg, C. Nelson and P.A. Treichler (eds), *Cultural Studies.* New York: Routledge, 295–337.

Haraway, D. (1996) *Modest Witness @ Second Millennium: Female Man Meets Oncomouse – Feminism and Technoscience.* London: Routledge.

Hayles, N.K. (1999) *How we Became Posthuman: Virtual Bodies in Cybernetics, Literature and Informatics.* Chicago: University of Chicago Press.

Held, D. (ed.) (2000) *A Globalizing World? Culture, Politics, Economics.* London: Taylor and Francis.

Himanen, P. (2002) *The Hacker Ethic and the Spirit of the Information Age.* New York: Random House.

Hirst, P. and Thompson, G. (1996) *Globalization in Question.* Cambridge: Polity Press.

Holmes, D. (ed.) (1997) *Virtual Politics: Identity and Community in Cyberspace*. London: Sage.

Jones, S.G. (ed.) (1997) *Virtual Culture: Identity and Communication in Cybersociety*. London: Sage.

Jordan, T. (1998) *Cyberpower: A Sociology and Politics of Cyberspace and the Internet*. London: Routledge.

Jordan, T. and Taylor, P. (2003) 'A Sociology of Hackers', in D.S. Wall (ed.), *Cyberspace Crime*. Aldershot: Dartmouth/Ashgate, 163–86.

Kahn, J.B.L. (2003) 'The Technology Game: How Information Technology is Transforming Police Practice', in D.S. Wall (ed.), *Cyberspace Crime*. Aldershot: Dartmouth/Ashgate

Kittler, F.A. (1990) *Discourse Networks 1800–1900*, trans. M. Metteer. Stanford: Stanford University Press.

Kittler, F.A. (1994) *Materialities of Communication*, trans. W. Whobrey. Stanford: Stanford University Press.

Landow, G.P. (1997) *Hypertext 2.0: The Convergence of Contemporary Critical Theory and Technology* (2nd edn). Baltimore: Johns Hopkins University Press.

Latour, B. (1991) 'Technology is Society Made Durable', in J. Law (ed.), *A Sociology of Monsters*. London: Routledge.

Latour, B. (1993) *We Have Never Been Modern*. Hemel Hempstead: Harvester Wheatsheaf; Cambridge, MA: Harvard University Press.

Latour, B. (1999) *Pandora's Hope: Essays on the Reality of Science Studies*. London: Harvard University Press.

Latour, B. (2005) *Reassembling the Social: An Introduction to Actor Network Theory*. Oxford: Oxford University Press.

Latour, B. and Woolgar, S. (1986) *Laboratory Life: The Construction of Scientific Facts*. Princeton, NJ: Princeton University Press.

Law, J. (1991) 'Monsters, Machines, and Sociotechnical Relations', in J. Law (ed.), *A Sociology of Monsters*. London: Routledge.

Law, J. and Hassard, J. (eds) (1999) *Actor Network Theory and After*. Oxford: Basil Blackwell.

Levy, S. (1984) *Hackers: Heroes of the Computer Revolution*. New York: Bantam Doubleday Dell.

Loader, B.D. (ed.) (1997) *The Governance of Cyberspace: Politics, Technology, and Global Restructuring*. London: Routledge.

Loader, B.D. (ed.) (1998) *The Cyberspace Divide: Equality, Agency, and Policy in the Information Society*. London: Routledge.

Lovink, G. (2001) *Uncanny Networks: Dialogues with the Virtual Intelligentsia*. Cambridge, MA: MIT Press.

Lovink, G. (2002) *Dark Fiber: Tracking Critical Internet Culture*. Cambridge, MA: MIT Press.

Lunenfeld, P. (ed.) (1999) *The Digital Dialectic: New Essays on New Media*. Cambridge, MA: MIT Press.

Lyon, D. (1988) *The Information Society*. Cambridge: Polity Press.

Lyon, D. (1994) *The Electronic Eye: The Rise of Surveillance Society*. Cambridge: Polity Press.

Lyon, D. (2001) *Surveillance Society: Monitoring Everyday Life*. Buckingham: Open University.

Lyon, D. (ed.) (2003) *Surveillance as Social Sorting: Privacy, Risk and Automated Discrimination*. London: Routledge.

Lyon, D. (ed.) (2006) *Theorizing Surveillance: The Panopticon and Beyond*. Cullompton, Devon: Willan Publishing.

Lyon, D. (2007) *Surveillance Studies: An Overview.* London: Polity Press.

McChesney, R. (1997) *Corporate Media and the Threat to Democracy.* New York: Seven Stories Press.

McChesney, R.W., Meiksens Wood, E. and Foster, J.B. (eds) (1998) *Capitalism and the Information Age. The Political Economy of the Global Communication Revolution.* New York: Monthly Review Press.

McCullough, M. (2004) *Digital Ground: Architecture, Pervasive Computing, and Environmental Knowing.* Cambridge, MA: MIT Press.

McGuire, M. (2007) *Hypercrime: the New Geometry of Harm.* Abingdon: Routledge-Cavendish.

MacKenzie, D. and Wajcman, J. (eds) (1999) (2nd edn) *The Social Shaping of Technology.* Philadelphia: Oxford University Press.

Markham, A.N. (1998) *Life On-line: Researching Real Experience in Virtual Space.* Walnut Creek: AltaMira Press.

Marx, G.T. (2004) *Windows into the Soul: Surveillance and Society in the Age of High Technology.* Chicago: University of Chicago Press.

Mason, M. (2008) *The Pirate's Dilemma. How hackers, punk capitalists, graffiti millionaires and other youth movements are remixing our culture and changing our world.* London: Allen Lane.

Massumi, B. (2002) *Parables for the Virtual: Movement, Affect, Sensation.* Durham and London: Duke University Press.

Murphie, A. and Potts, J. (2003) *Culture and Technology.* London: Palgrave Macmillan.

Ollmann, G. (2008) 'The Phishing Guide. Understanding and Preventing Phishing Attacks', at http://www.ngssoftware.com/papers/NISR-WP-Phishing.pdf, accessed 27 June 2008.

Penley, C. and Ross, A. (1991) *Technoculture.* Minneapolis: University of Minnesota Press.

Pescovitz, D. (2008) 'The World is a Wunderkammer', in J. Brockman (ed.) (2008) *What Are You Optimistic About?* London: Pocket Books, 321–3.

Plant, S. (1998) *Zeros and Ones.* London: Fourth Estate.

Porter, D. (ed.) (1996) *Internet Culture.* New York and London: Routledge.

Poster, M. (1984) *Foucault, Marxism and History: Mode of Production Versus Mode of Information.* Cambridge: Blackwell.

Poster, M. (1990) *The Mode of Information: Poststructuralism and Social Context.* Cambridge: Polity Press.

Poster, M. (1995) *The Second Media Age.* Cambridge: Polity Press.

Poster, M. (1999) 'Undetermination', *New Media and Society*, 1(1): 12–17.

Poster, M. (2001) *What's the Matter with the Internet.* Minnesota: University of Minnesota Press.

Rheingold, H. (1994) *The Virtual Community: Homesteading on the Electronic Frontier.* London: Minerva.

Rheingold, H. (2002) *Smart Mobs: The Next Social Revolution.* New York: Basic Books.

Rifkin, J. (2001) *The Age of Access: How the Shift from Ownership to Access is Transforming Modern Life.* Harmondsworth: Penguin.

Robertson, R. (1992) *Globalization: Social Theory and Global Culture.* London: Sage.

Robins, K. and Webster, F. (1999) *Times of the Technoculture.* London: Routledge.

Rochlin, G.I. (1997) *Trapped in The Net: The Unanticipated Consequences of Computerization.* Princeton, NJ: Princeton University Press.

Sandywell, B. (1996) *Reflexivity and the Crisis of Western Reason. Logological Investigations Vols. 1–3.* London: Routledge.

Sandywell, B. (2003) 'Metacritique of Information', *Theory, Culture and Society*, 20(1): 109–22.

Sandywell, B. (2004) 'The Myth of Everyday Life: Toward a Heterology of the Ordinary', in Michael E. Gardiner and Gregory J. Seigworth (eds), *Rethinking Everyday Life: And Then Nothing Turns Itself Inside Out, Cultural Studies*, 18(2–3): 160–80.

Sandywell, B. (2006) 'Monsters in Cyberspace: Cyberphobia and Cultural Panic in the Information Age', *Information, Communication & Society*, 9(1): 39–61.

Sandywell, B. and Beer, D. (2005) 'Stylistic Morphing: Notes on the Digitalisation of Contemporary Music Culture', *Convergence: The International Journal of Research into New Media Technologies*, 11(4): 106-121.

Schiller, D. (1999) *Digital Capitalism: Networking the Global Market System*. Cambridge, MA: MIT Press.

Scholte, J.A. (2000) *Globalization. A Critical Introduction*. London: Palgrave/Macmillan.

Sclove, R.E. (1995) *Democracy and Technology*. New York: Guilford Press.

Shields, R. (ed.) (1996) *Cultures of Internet: Virtual Spaces, Real Histories, Living Bodies*. London: Sage.

Silver, D. and Massanari, A. (eds) (2006) *Critical Cyberculture Studies*. New York and London: New York University Press.

Soja, E.W. (1989) *Postmodern Geographies: The Reassertion of Space in Critical Social Theory*. London: Verso.

Soja, E.W. (1996) *Thirdspace: Journeys to Los Angeles and Other Real-and-Imagined Places*. Oxford: Blackwell.

Sommer, P. (2003) 'Digital Footprints: Assessing Computer Evidence', in D.S. Wall (ed.), *Cyberspace Crime*. Aldershot: Dartmouth/Ashgate, 535–52.

Soros, G. (1998) *The Crisis of Global Capitalism*. New York: Little, Brown.

Soros, G. (2008) 'The crisis and what to do about it', *New York Review of Books*, 22 November.

Squires, J. (1996) 'Fabulous Feminist Futures and the Lure of Cyberculture', in J. Dovey (ed.), *Fractal Dreams: New Media in Social Context*. London: Lawrence and Wishart.

Staples, W.G. (1997) *The Culture of Surveillance: Discipline and Social Control in the United States*. New York: St Martin's Press.

Steffik, M. (1999) *The Internet Edge: Social, Technical, and Legal Challenges for a Networked World*. Cambridge, MA: MIT Press.

Sterling, B. (1994) *The Hacker Crackdown: Law and Disorder on the Electronic Frontier*. London: Viking.

Stone, A.R. (1996) *The War of Desire and Technology at the Close of the Mechanical Age*. Cambridge, MA: Harvard University Press.

Taylor, P. (1999) *Hackers: Crime in the Digital Sublime*. London: Routledge.

Terranova, T. (2004) *Network Culture: Politics for the Information Age*. London: Pluto Press.

Thomas, D. and Loader, B. (eds) (2000) *Cybercrime: Law Enforcement, Security and Surveillance in the Information Age*. London and New York: Routledge.

Tomas, D. (1989) 'The Technophilic Body', *new formations*, 8: 113–29.

Turkle, S. (1984) *The Second Self: Computers and the Human Spirit*. New York: Simon and Schuster.

Turkle, S. (1995) *Life on the Screen: Identity in the Age of the Internet*. London: Weidenfeld and Nicholson.

Verbeek, P.-P. (2005) *What Things Do: Philosophical Reflections on Technology, Agency and Design*. University Park, PA: Pennsylvania State University Press.

Wajcman, J. (1991) *Feminism Confronts Technology*. Cambridge: Polity Press.

Walch, J. (1999) *In the Net: A Guide for Activists*. London: Zed Books.

Wall, D.S. (2001b) 'Maintaining Order and Law on the Internet', in D.S. Wall (ed.), *Crime and the Internet*. London and New York: Routledge, 167–83.

Wall, D.S. (2003b) 'Cybercrimes: New Wine, No Bottles?', in D.S. Wall (ed.), *Cyberspace Crime*. Aldershot: Dartmouth/Ashgate, pp. 3–37.

Wall, D.S. (2007) *Cybercrime: The Transformation of Crime in the Information Age*. Cambridge: Polity Press.

Wall, D.S. (ed.) (2001a) *Crime and the Internet*. London and New York: Routledge.

Wall, D.S. (ed.) (2003a) *Cyberspace Crime*. Aldershot: Dartmouth/Ashgate.

Wark, M. (2004) *A Hacker Manifesto*. Cambridge, MA: Harvard University Press.

Waters, M. (1995) *Globalization*. London: Routledge.

Webster, F. (2006) *Theories of the Information Society*. London and New York: Routledge.

Webster, F. and Robins, K. (1986) *Information Technology: A Luddite Analysis*. Norwood, NJ: Ablex.

Yar, M. (2005) 'The novelty of "cybercrime": an assessment in the light of routine activity theory', *European Journal of Criminology*, 2(4): 407–27.

Yar, M. (2006) *Cybercrime and Society*. London: Sage.

Zittrain, J. (2008) *The Future of the Internet And How to Stop It*. London: Allen Lane.

Chapter 4

The Internet and everyday life

Vincent Miller

Introduction

We live in a world where the Internet has, in a matter of only two decades, shifted from being at the forefront of a new frontier of communication technology, to being for most people an incredibly unremarkable part of our culture and daily life. Many once held an optimism that the Internet would create active, engaged citizens instead of the passive subjects of the broadcast media age (see Poster 1995), or lead to the creation of alternative communities, worlds and even identities free from the prejudices of offline society (Rheingold 2000).

However, as the Internet has become something used by the majority of the population in advanced economies, that population has brought with it all of the inclinations, prejudices and habits which are endemic in society as a whole. As a result, much of this early optimism that the Internet would radically change our culture in some sort of knowledge revolution has begun to fade in light of the realisation that our culture has perhaps transformed the Internet more than vice versa. Indeed, the Internet has become a major part of work, leisure, social and political life, for most people. Not in the sense that it has profoundly changed these things, but in the sense that it has become enmeshed within these enduring structures of our society. This in itself is significant, as some suggest that in fact, it is within the sphere of everyday life in which the most meaningful struggles between authority, domination and freedom are played out (Lefebvre 2000), and others have suggested that the push towards the use of different forms of information technology is, like the rise of bureaucracy in the early twentieth century, part of a revolution (of sorts) aiming towards an overall and pervasive increase in economic and social control (Beninger 1986). Within this context, the Internet has indeed become a part of everyday life, and as such the online sphere is no longer a realm separate from the offline 'real world'. It is not its novelty, or its uniqueness, but its mundane nature and its pervasiveness that now gives the Internet its significance.

This chapter will explore that mundane nature and pervasiveness in that it will examine how the Internet has become integral to the functioning of our economy and flows of money around the globe, become central to our work and leisure life, and emerged as a valuable tool for political engagement, citizenship and learning. It will then conclude with a discussion about the inequalities that are created and enhanced through the increasing importance of the Internet.

The 'new digital knowledge economy'

Up until the 1990s, use of the Internet was largely confined to research and social purposes. University academics, researchers, and later students used Internet technology to exchange data, results, and to work on collaborative research projects. Within this same small group of people, the Internet started to be used in a more social manner, where email, chat rooms, MUDs (Multi-User Domains) and MOOs (Multi-User Object Oriented environments) started to emerge as alternative forms of community and even alternative social worlds (see Turkle 1996). However, the population of Internet users remained a fairly closed community. This was largely due to the technical demands of its use, which was based solely around text input, with little in the way of search facilities. This made it almost impossible for those not familiar with computers to sort through online information and data.

With the advent of the WWW (World Wide Web) as a facade of the Internet based on easy to use hypertext linkages in 1991, things began to change dramatically. By 1994, the Internet became available to a much wider audience of less technically minded people, as hypertext linking made accessing data and 'surfing' for information much easier for those not familiar with computers. This rapidly expanded the user population of the Internet from a small group of largely American university dwellers into the general public and creating not only a larger user population, but also led to much more content being published on the Net. This further increased its usefulness and value (what are sometimes called 'network effects').

This same time period also saw the birth of 'search engines' and 'web portals', such as Webcrawler, Yahoo!, Lycos and Alta Vista. These sites and others like them were fundamentally important because they made it possible for a person to practically negotiate the vast and ever-expanding amount of information contained on the Net, making it very easy to find what one was looking for (Miller 2000). Thus, within the few years between 1991 and 1994, the Internet suddenly became very useful to a great many people. This was the period when business became increasingly interested in what the Internet had to offer. From that moment on, the Internet would become integral to business in all areas of production, consumption and distribution of their products (and ultimately even change the kinds of products that they could sell), not to mention the investment of money into their businesses.

With *production*, the use of the Internet by business has aided the ability of firms and organisations to produce goods on global scales if desired, and with a degree of flexibility not known before. With speed and directness, a firm can communicate to its component parts, or to other firms, across vast distances, thus promoting the globalisation of production activity. Internally, the 'networked enterprise' (Castells 2001) can create more large-scale, decentralised management structures through efficient worldwide Internet communications. Castells (2001) refers to this as the 'management of flexibility': the ability to effectively manage the internal affairs of a large organisation even at long distances, through the use of communication technology. Between businesses, a firm can easily communicate its immediate needs to its suppliers, or its subcontractors. This management of flexibility leads to what Castells calls 'scalability', which refers to the ability of a network to be expanded or contracted on any scale as required for the efficient completion of a task at hand, or given a specific situation. For example, a globally networked organisation like Nike (which does not in itself make shoes, but designs shoes and has them manufactured by a global network of subcontracted factories) can expand its network of subcontracted manufacturers and increase shoe production when there is a large demand for its shoes, or shrink production by not employing as many subcontractors when it feels that demand for its product is low. This can happen with very little impact on Nike itself in terms of job losses or having to hire workers. That is the scalability and flexibility of a networked firm. What this means overall is that with the aid of the Internet, the production side of business has changed profoundly, encouraging more globalisation, decentralisation, subcontracting, and ultimately more efficient means for producing goods.

In terms of *consumption*, the Internet, and particularly the WWW, holds massive potential for business in terms of the ability of a business, firm, or marketer to communicate with (and collect information on) their customers or potential customers. This is the case because, at its heart, the Internet is interactive in nature. It allows for easy, instantaneous or asymmetric communication between people or objects. Unlike traditional advertisements, where the impact on the customer and customer satisfaction has to be inferred by sales of the product (thus, essentially, a 'shot in the dark'), advertisements and other types of marketing on the Internet can directly measure a person's interest in a product, or the effectiveness of the ad. Thus a business is able to tell, within a relatively short period of time, how successful their product is, or what customers feel could be done to improve it. This interactivity allows businesses to build upon two aspects of sales that Castells (2001) touches upon: branding and customisation.

Branding is 'a recognised sign of value' (Castells 2001) in which both consumers and investors invest. It is the 'personality' of a company and its products (such as Nike, McDonald's, Prada, Apple, Google) that helps to distinguish it from its competitors. Firms invest much in trying to build a brand name among their target customer base and, once achieved, try to maintain the integrity of their brand. The interactivity associated with the Internet helps them to do this not only by maintaining a presence on the Internet in terms of advertisements, but also by continually looking for feedback from customers and 'buzz monitoring' of different online social environments. Through collecting this kind of information, businesses are better able to maintain a desired image among their customers and create an intimacy with them that can result in more sales.

The information gathering which occurs online through interactivity with customers allows firms and their marketers to better develop products that speak more directly to the individual needs of consumers. This is achieved because the amount of data collected through online interactions holds the promise of ever more sophisticated consumer profiling and niche marketing strategies made possible by the vast amounts of data collected through online transactions. A good example of this sort of profiling in action is the Amazon. com website (and particularly 'my Amazon'). People who have purchased books on the site are given Amazon profiles, and when they visit the Amazon website, they are given recommendations of books that they might be interested in, based not only on their previous purchases, but also their browsing habits. This allows Amazon to speak more directly to their customers in terms of selling books, as there is a profile of the type of person they are and what they are interested in, and also gives them a customised Web experience based on those interests. Banner advertisements on Google email services do a similar thing. These advertisements are individually generated and shown based on the content of the emails of the user, once again creating a profile of the person and their interests.

Thus, it is the power of the Internet as a consumer information gathering tool, the ability to collect masses of information in order to sell products better, which has been one of the main draws of business to the Internet.

Digital economies and online flows of money

Apart from more direct and effective marketing and advertising, another major advantage of Internet communications for business is the ability for more direct distribution of their products to their customers through online sales or e-commerce. In a traditional value chain for any industry (for example, the music industry), there is normally a series of intermediary stages from production to final consumption, and each of these states adds value to the product. Thus there are a number of intermediaries between the manufacturer or producer, and the consumer who buys the product. So, for example, in the music industry one starts the value chain with the artist and the record company, the record company hires a manufacturer to create CDs or albums, and makes deals with a retail chain (such as HMV or Virgin) or smaller independent stores, who essentially act as local distributors for the record company by selling the product to the consumers who walk into their shops. Each link in this chain adds some value to the product, and therefore commands some revenue for its service. This ultimately cuts into the profits of the first link (the record companies), and inflates prices for the last link (the consumer).

Online retailing or e-commerce upsets this value chain by effectively reducing the need for the middle links (gatekeepers, 'middlemen'), as the customer is able to order directly from the producer of the good. In theory, this means fewer distribution costs and therefore more profits at one end, and cheaper goods at the other. The publishing and music industries in particular have changed substantially as a result of online retailing. One has only to think of the lower prices associated with buying books online as opposed to buying them at the local bookshop. The result has been that online retailing has steadily increased in value, and as a proportion of all retailing. In the United States, $128 billion worth of goods were bought online in 2007 (US Census 2008), and in the UK, the estimate for e-commerce in 2006 was £26 billion (Gunawan *et al.* 2008). The aforementioned study also suggested that over half of adults in the UK bought goods online, and that 10 per cent of all retail sales were online sales.[1]

Furthermore, in an era of media convergence, where all forms of media are being made in digital format, not only can distribution costs be saved, but also material costs. 'Virtual' digital products have no 'materials' in them to buy or transform. The music, film and publishing industries are ideal examples of industries where their goods are increasingly delivered digitally over the Internet to their consumers (digitised music, films and books). In 2008, 20 per cent of the total of legal worldwide music sales were digital (IFPI 2009).[2] This means that there are very few material costs in the manufacture of these products for the consumer (no CDs, jewellery cases, packaging), and thus more profits for the producers. Many refer to such goods as 'weightless', in that they have no material basis, therefore do not have physical 'weight' that has to be physically transported to customers. The result is that the Internet has become almost integral to consumer culture and commercial transactions in everyday life. In advanced economies as many as half of the adult population now input their credit card details and buy goods online. This is only set to increase as confidence in online commerce grows, and an increasing amount of goods are traded in virtual, as opposed to material, form.

Finance and the movement of money have pursued a similar course. Thus far in this section, we have discussed how the Internet has become a useful everyday tool for business and industry in terms of production, consumption and distribution of consumer goods. From this it becomes worthwhile to note briefly how the Internet has come to play a major part in financial practices and the virtualisation of money, particularly in banking and investing.

In terms of investing, the Internet has transformed how companies are financed on many levels. It has assisted in the global integration of financial markets, allowing free-flowing, 24-hour trading of stocks and flows of currency. Moving investment into the online sphere has allowed stock-trading and other forms of financial speculation to be participated in by a much larger section of society. Millions of people who previously would never personally have had much exposure to stock markets outside news reports have become online investors. Electronic trading began with the establishment of the Nasdaq in 1971, and came into full force with the merger of Nasdaq and the American Stock Exchange in 1998 (Castells 2001). It became easier to invest in stocks through online brokers like E-trade and Ameritrade, and by 2003 there were more than 10 million online investors in the United States alone (Balasubramanian *et al.* 2003). Many financial observers feel that the large amount of novice online traders and day traders contributed to the gross overinflation of stock prices and subsequent price volatility that characterised the dot-com boom and bust from 1998 to the end of 2001.

The increasing virtual movement of money has been aided since through the increasing popularity of online banking for individuals. As of 2005, 53 million Americans (43 per cent of American Internet users) used online banking (Fox 2005). In the UK, recent studies suggest that 33 per cent of Internet using adults now bank online (ComScore 2008). Thus, the transfer of money in online contexts is becoming an everyday practice for individuals on many levels, not just in terms of shopping.

Work and leisure in everyday life

Computers and the Internet have, in a few short years, become an unremarkable part of most people's working lives. For many of us, sitting at a computer for at least part of the day has now become commonplace. Whether our work be data entry, looking at spreadsheets, sending emails, creating web pages, doing research, interacting with customers, writing software, designing objects, creating text or audio-visual content, moving finances, the computer has often become the tool with which we work, and the Internet the medium through which we accomplish our tasks.[3]

Such ubiquity has meant that the Internet has changed our working lives in several ways. First, it has increased our ability to communicate with other employees, customers and our managers. As a result, it has become easier to share ideas within an organisation, manage people more efficiently, and deal with feedback from customers. Workers and organisations benefit from these 'network effects' of Internet communication through a more flexible, productive and responsive workforce. Secondly, more efficient exchanges of information, circulation of work documents and research within an organisation enhances the efficiency of collaborative efforts, which leads to an improved ability for all to accomplish set tasks. The fact that workers are now able to exchange documents, designs, research results and other knowledge-based outputs through the instantaneous exchange of digital documents (as opposed to using internal or external post), means that such collaborative efforts can be completed much more quickly and efficiently than in the past. Thirdly, Internet access to information generated outside the firm or organisation makes it much easier to draw upon external resources in the workplace. Where, in the past, employees and knowledge workers would have to travel to other physical locations, such as libraries, or other organisations, to find and retrieve useful external information resources, these same employees are now much more able to access such information without having to leave their desk, saving huge amounts of unproductive travel time and allowing a much more efficient completion of tasks. Finally, the Internet has allowed a decentralisation of work practices through networking. This can mean several things. First it means that a worker does not have to be at 'the office' to work, but can now extend working hours to places where this was previously more difficult, such as the home, or while commuting or travelling. This is often referred to as the 'networked worker' (Madden and Jones 2008) or the 'always on' worker. Here the once normally separate spheres of 'work' and 'home/leisure' (and 'travel') have become increasingly blurred, with more and more people starting to spend more time working at home, either as unpaid overtime work, or as part of contracted work hours. The days of having prescribed work hours and a separated home life have, for many, disappeared (Anandarajan *et al.* 2006). Similarly, with the advent and spread of wireless connection to the Internet, commuting time on public transportation has now become an extension of workplace productivity with many workers starting work as soon as they step onto their commuter train and open up their laptop.

A second implication of Internet-inspired decentralisation is that organisations are increasingly able to decentralise some of their functions away form their central offices. Activities such as programming, word processing, data entry, accountancy, customer services (what are known as 'back office' functions) can be conducted in different geographic locations where labour or office costs may be cheaper. A popular example of such decentralisation is the outsourcing of software programming and call centre work to a rapidly developing country like India, where labour costs are much cheaper than in more wealthy nations. Such outsourcing can also take the form of hiring private consultants or subcontractors to do back office work in their own offices or homes, thus avoiding overhead costs altogether.

Of course, this extension of working hours into home life is a two-way street. Home and leisure activities have also started to infiltrate the workplace thanks to the Internet, resulting in a considerable blurring of leisure and work spheres. Recent research has shown that a large proportion of workers take care of personal business and engage in personal online recreation (often called 'cyberslacking') such as shopping, social networking or blogging during work hours. This is often blamed for a lack of productivity, and potential liabilities and security hazards for businesses (Garrett and Danziger 2008).

This demonstrates the pull of the Internet as a leisure activity. As the Internet and WWW have grown in the capacity to transmit large amounts of data and information (through increased bandwidth and better compression technologies) to more and more people, its potential as a recreational tool has gone far beyond the early days of email, text-based web pages and chat rooms. While email and general Web browsing still remain the most popular Web activities, the greatly enhanced transmission capacity of the Internet has made it possible, and indeed mundane, to follow a number of personal leisure activities:

Consumption of cultural goods such as music, film, art and photography, whether in real-time streaming (such as Internet radio) or through downloading (such as file sharing).[4] This can be seen easily in the popularity of YouTube as a streaming video site, or iTunes as a source for music and video browsing and downloading digital music files.

The creation of, and participation in, different types of online social networks. In social terms, the user-generated content associated with Web 2.0 has led to an explosion of different forms of self expression and user-generated content tied to social networking. Online sociability has gone beyond email lists and chat rooms and taken on a new dimension where people create profiles of themselves, content about themselves, and link these profiles to others. These activities first became popular with the advent of blogging in the late 1990s. Blogging made it easy for those with limited technical abilities to be able to create their own web pages, tell their stories, and link their blogs to like-minded others and friends. Social networking websites such as Friendster, MySpace, Facebook, Bebo and Orkut emerged from this environment, focusing less on the generation of texts by the author, and more on the sociable aspects of linking with other people.

Pew Internet research suggests that 13 per cent of American Net users use social networking websites on a daily basis (Pew Internet 2008a). Other research suggests that as many as 90 per cent of university students in America have a Facebook profile (Bray 2006). Thus, it would be reasonable to suggest that the practices around blogging and social networking such as profile building, 'friending' or linking to others, commenting on others' profiles, and writing about oneself, have become a significant part of online digital culture, and occupy a portion of everyday life for many people.

The creating of, and involvement in, online gaming worlds. The last decade has also seen the birth and rise of online gaming as another substantial leisure activity. The video games industry itself tends to be ignored as an economic force and as a popular leisure time activity, but by 1999, video games sales had already outstripped the movie video rental market, and now people actually spend more money on video games than they do on going to the cinema or renting home videos (Newman 2004). Forty per cent of American adults and 83 per cent of teenagers are said to play video games (Williams *et al.* 2008) and the worldwide video game market was estimated to be around $31.6 billion in 2006 (Chazerand and Geeroms 2008).

The fastest growing area in the video games market is in online games. Video games have changed from being solitary activities played on isolated consoles or PCs to become social activities where users compete against and cooperate with each other through networked computers or games consoles. This has been accomplished by the networking of console games such as 'Halo', and also through the growth of Massively Multiplayer Online Role Playing Games (MMORPGs) such as 'World of Warcraft' and 'Second Life'. These games have changed the nature of video game playing online as they are not so much games as they are 'virtual worlds' with no particular beginning, ending or narrative. They are as much about sociability as they are about 'play'. Many participants have even set up profitable businesses selling virtual goods in them. As many as 10 million people worldwide subscribe to World of Warcraft, and perhaps 30 million people worldwide are involved in MMORPGs (Castronova 2005).

Furthermore, while these games are often dismissed in importance as something solely the concern of teenagers, Rideout *et al.* (2005) have found that although 67 per cent of teens play networked games regularly, the largest age concentration of online gamers are in their thirties, with a mean participation age of 31.6 years, and an ISFE (Interactive Software Federation of Europe) and Neilsen survey found the average age of Swedish gamers to be 45 (cited in Chazerand and Geeroms 2008). Thus it would be a mistake to dismiss MMORPGs as a youth phenomenon. Furthermore, its share of the total gaming market is predicted to grow from roughly 15 per cent to approximately one third, or $11.8 billion by 2011 (based on figures provided by Olausson 2007).

Similar to the highly interactive, social-based world of online gaming, online gambling has become a popular activity and a lucrative business worldwide (even though it is illegal in the United States). Moving from simple sports betting to online poker, bingo and fully-fledged casinos, these sites have almost become virtual worlds themselves, akin to MMORPGs, in their socialness and their use of avatars. Although measures of the popularity and extent of online gambling are hard to come by, one study has suggested that online gambling websites made £660 million in the UK alone in 2007 (Screen Digest 2006).

The use of the Internet in the pursuit of 'offline' hobbies and interests. Of course, one should not forget how, in many cases, the Internet has become integrated in the 'offline' social world. Nowhere is this more evident than in the way many people follow their offline or 'real world' interests in online contexts. Whether it be hobbies, fan activities or politics, research in the United States suggests that 83 per cent of American net users pursue their hobbies or interests online (Pew Internet 2008a). In addition, one can note the popularity of online shopping, especially on auction sites like eBay, where collectors, aficionados, fans and the like can spend their time browsing for articles of interest, as another example of how the Internet has inserted itself into everyday online activities.[5]

It is clear that the Internet has become a major part of leisure life for a growing number of people in advanced and developing economies worldwide. When one thinks of the amount of time spent generating representations of ourselves (whether fictitious or not) by creating (and updating) shopping accounts, social networking profiles or avatars for the purposes of interactivity with others on the basis of leisure activities, we can see how much the online world has integrated itself into our offline lives.

The advent and development of mobile communication technologies and Wi-Fi has only served to increase the amount we use the Internet. Mobile phones, Blackberrys, PDAs and Wi-Fi laptops have all made it easy for many of us to consume leisure products (such as film, music, games) or engage in leisure activities (such as shopping, social networking, dating, blogging, or pursuing other interests) almost anywhere and at almost any time.

As a result, not only have the previously separate spheres of work, home and travel become blurred, but so have the borders between public and private spheres. On the one hand, our leisure time consumption has become something more public, in that we can now do many of the things that were usually done in the privacy of home out in public contexts. On the other hand, our consumption of many of these things, such as television, film, music, have become much more individually tailored and thus less 'communal' due to the sheer amount of choice on offer over the Internet. The idea of a collective media experience or 'public sphere' is starting to give way towards a more individualised and niche market media experience.

Politics and citizenship on the Internet

On 13 February 2003, in a demonstration of global proportions, millions of people in cities around the world gathered to protest the impending invasion of Iraq by the United States and its allies. Not only was this the largest coordinated demonstration that the world has ever seen, but several individual cities, including Rome, London and Madrid, had over one million people take to the streets, the largest protests ever in those cities (Bennett *et al* 2008: 69). In the 2008 American presidential election campaign, presidential candidate Barack Obama shattered all previous fundraising records by raising roughly $1 billion, providing him with a massive advantage over his rival for the post, John McCain, and leading him to a convincing victory (McCormick and Dorning 2008). Perhaps the most striking thing about this event was that roughly half of his funds were raised by small donations from individuals.

Both of these events became what they were through the use of the Internet. Indeed, the Internet has become increasingly important in political life on a number of levels, although perhaps not in the way predicted when it was in its infancy. Many early discussions about the Internet and political life were based on a healthy dose of idealism about how the Internet could revitalise democracy and encourage citizenship (Rheingold 2000; Norris 2001). No doubt part of this optimism was based on the fact that, concurrent with the emergence of the Internet as a cultural force in the late 1980s and through the 1990s, there was a widely held belief in both popular and academic discourse that democracy in most advanced industrial nations had reached some sort of 'crisis' (or at least disenchantment). This was defined by a declining interest in mainstream politics and political parties and declining voter turnouts among young people in particular (Dahlgren 2004) and a media which was abandoning reasoned political debate and discourse in favour of image, sound bite and scandal (Castells 1996/2000). This 'crisis' was also perceived in a move away from the ideas of 'public culture' and community towards a more individualised experience with more emphasis being placed on private consumption patterns and lifestyle choices (Bauman 2001; Beck and Beck-Gernsheim 2002).

Within these contexts, the potential for the Internet to re-engage people with politics through its inherently interactive and democratic architecture and its potential as a political information resource was much debated and anticipated. However, the Internet has never really lived up to this transformative potential, and has certainly not transformed democracy in any formally significant way (Dahlgren 2004). It has, however, changed things on the margins in ways that may yet prove to be more significant with the passage of time. These changes involve the enhancing of alternative modes of potential action and communication outside mainstream media and political channels and are manifested in a number of ways.

The Internet has aided in the enhancement (or revitalisation) of political communication and alternative public spheres. One of the primary reasons for the crisis of contemporary politics is purported to be the increasing domination of the public sphere by large media organisations. With its massive popularity and increasing accessibility within most advanced industrial economies, the Internet has made it possible for large segments of the population to not only consume but also produce news media and political discourse, through web pages, blogs, chat rooms, online news commentaries, email campaigns and social networking sites; in effect creating what Dakroury and Birdsall (2008) call a 'spaceless public sphere'. Such a public sphere has minimal censorship or restrictions on freedom of speech. As of 2007, there were an estimated 113 million Internet blogs in existence, with 175,000 new ones being created every day (Dakroury and Birdsall 2008). Obviously, within blogging alone this suggests unprecedented opportunity for individuals to contribute to the public sphere. This has become particularly important with regard to those under 40, and younger people in particular, who tend to be the most disenfranchised from the mainstream political process and press. On the Internet younger people can use blogs and other forms of online 'DIY culture', as spaces for personal and political expression about social issues (Harris 2008).[6]

However, there is an important caveat that needs to be considered. With the move away from mainstream media as a primary source of exposure to news and political debate, and a move towards the multiplicity of the Internet with its endless sources of news and different perspectives on events, there is a danger of what is termed 'selective exposure', in which information outlets are selected on the basis that they match the beliefs and predispositions of the audience member (Stroud 2008). In other words, with the massive amount of choice on the Internet, people are able to selectively expose themselves to a narrow range of information and ideas, chosen on the basis that they confirm or reinforce prejudices or beliefs. Thus, instead of creating a more accessible and diverse public sphere, the Internet may be helping to create a Balkanised public sphere, or many publics which have little engagement with, or exposure to, each other.

The Internet can be used as a tool for political action, organisation and motivation. The events in 2003 described at the beginning of this section are an excellent example of how the Internet is being used to expand the scope and coordination of 'real life' political activities. The campaign against Nike's use of sweatshop labour through the 1990s (see Carty 2002) and the anti-globalisation World Trade Organisation riots in 1999 (also known as 'the battle of Seattle'; see Chapter 12) are good examples of how, since the late 1990s, activists have been employing the Internet to stage political actions and forge cooperative links with other organisations both locally and around the world.

The Internet is also being used as a promotional and fundraising tool. In the 2008 US presidential election, Barack Obama, helped considerably by a large Internet campaign, became the first major party presidential candidate to opt out of public funds for financing his campaign. At one point in January 2008 Obama raised $35 million over the Internet in 36 hours, mostly from small individual contributions. Overall, the total of $1 billion raised was far more than the two presidential candidates in the 2004 US election put together were able to acquire. The Obama campaign was able to reach in a much more direct manner a broad range of Americans through a different mix of messages, emails, blogs and 'Twitter' posts which could be targeted at specific segments of the population. It proved to be a very cost-effective and profitable way of reaching and targeting the most voters possible (Wilcox 2008).

This demonstrates the success of the Internet as a fundraising and communication tool for mainstream politicians. It adds to the large amount of literature which demonstrates how fringe groups and terrorist groups are also able to use the Internet to fundraise through promoting their message or nefariously collecting contributions to bogus charities, which are then funnelled through terrorist and criminal organisations (Thomas 2003).

Education and distance learning

The Internet is also beginning to have a profound impact on education, teaching and learning around the world. Traditionally, education and learning have been based around spatial proximity, either in the sense that proximity to learning resources – such as libraries, archives, laboratory equipment – was seen as crucial, or the proximity of the learner and the teacher, in schools, classrooms and universities, was essential.

Thus it was generally the case that one's own geographic location and personal circumstances largely determined one's educational opportunities. Those who lived in isolated rural areas, for example, where there was often little access to schools, teachers, libraries or other information resources, were faced with the stark choice of not getting an education, or having to move in pursuit of one. Similarly, those whose personal circumstances, such as being in full-time employment or a mother of dependent children, were seen as deviating from the typical student profile, were often confronted by a lack of educational options.

To overcome these 'time and space' barriers, in the past, several forms of correspondence teaching had been utilised with varying degrees of success, but it was the establishment of the Open University in England in 1969 that paved the way for distanced or distributed learning on a large scale (Lockwood 2006). Currently the education sector is going through another 'revolution' in distance learning due to the increasing potential and actual use of the Internet and other communication technologies. The ability to deliver textual resources, interactive correspondence with teachers, and access audio and video has made distance learning an attractive option for universities and other education centres. Most universities now use ICTs (Information and Communication Technologies) extensively for 'traditional' students and for 'flexible learners', many of whom are exclusively online or 'virtual' students. There are several motivations for increased use of the Internet in the provision of education, ranging form the egalitarian to the financial.

Increasing access to education among disadvantaged groups. These could be the geographically isolated, the poor, those in full-time work, the disabled, the socially marginalised, residents of developing countries, or the elderly, to name a few. For these groups, learning and education through the Internet is one way to help overcome the disadvantages they face in obtaining a better quality of life through the attainment of knowledge and formal qualifications.

Providing the most comprehensive learning experience possible for students. The use of ICTs in education helps to facilitate further contact and feedback with instructors for non-traditional and even 'traditional' full-time students, as well as to promote increasing (and more flexible) access to learning resources and the enhanced ability to interact with peers through online forums – all of which enhances the learning experience of the student.

Reduction of government funding of the higher education sector. Within most advanced economies, the prevailing political climate of the reduction of public expenditure has meant a reduction in the amount of per capita funding for teaching and training of students. At the same time, universities have generally been expected to expand their intake and rely more on tuition fees to fund themselves. Thus, universities and other higher education institutions are increasingly in a climate of having to work according to market principles. In short, universities are being encouraged to do more with less. In this climate, the increasing use of distance learning options provides a more cost-effective way to reach more students with fewer institutional, overhead, and staff costs.

Increasing competition among the higher education sector. With an increasing number of universities and other higher education establishments, such bodies find themselves in the position of having to compete for both domestic and international students in a way they have never had to before. As a result, the innovative use of the Internet has been one way in which institutions have tried to 'reach out' to new students and new markets in an increasingly competitive sector. Innovations such as online degrees are some of the ways in which the Internet has helped to reinvent the 'product' of education to sell to a new market of consumers.

The result has been that most universities and higher education institutions now provide online learning resources for their students, and even offer online degrees. In addition a number of 'virtual universities', universities whose enrolment is largely made up of online distance learners, have been founded or created from existing universities. While estimates vary widely, 2001 data suggests that over three million people were enrolled in online distance learning courses in the United States alone (Lindsay 2004).

These trends and the push towards online learning in general are not without critics, however. Dreyfus (2002) in particular is quite critical of the whole concept of distance learning in terms of the lack of commitment embedded in the logic and structure of online learning, and the lack of skills development in the rule-based learning characteristic of online education. He argues that education should continue to strive to be based on the idea of proximity and 'apprenticeship'. Similarly, Orton-Johnson (2009) has pointed out how online distance learning forums tend to lack clarity and purpose, and that participants tend to have low levels of motivation and commitment to their use.

A caveat: digital inequalities

Few would argue with the statement that ICTs have become of increasing economic and social importance to the vast majority of us in advanced economies, and to many in developing economies as well. As we have demonstrated so far in this chapter, the Internet and other ICTs are seen as increasingly central to economic prosperity in the twenty-first century. Globalisation abroad and economic restructuring at home are processes that have relied upon the increasing use of ICTs to enhance productive efficiency, lower production costs, and stimulate consumer demand, within contemporary global capitalism. This has led to the Internet becoming increasingly important within the everyday spheres of work, leisure, education and politics.

It is important to note that the impact of the Internet is taking place in capitalist societies – ones where people work for wages, and other people earn their living off either investment capital, or the labour of others. This type of society, rightly or wrongly, creates inequalities, both economic and social. The main change is that inequality in the Internet-driven information society revolves increasingly around information and communication: access to it, the ability to use it effectively, and the rights to produce it. Not everyone is benefiting from the sorts of opportunities that this chapter has been describing.

Generally this kind of inequality or marginalisation is referred to as the 'digital divide', defined as 'The gap between those who do and those who do not have access to computers and the Internet' (van Dijk 2005). The notion of the digital divide has caught the imagination of both academics and policy-makers since the mid 1990s, a time when enthusiasm about digital technology and the Internet in particular were reaching almost fever pitch. Investments in technology were booming, the Internet was massively popularised and commercialised, and governments all over the world were bracing for, and usually encouraging, the shift to an information-based economy. Within this environment, the spectre of those who would be left out of the information age began to creep into public and academic discourse.

Within the very considerable pro-technology, post-industrial rhetoric of the mid 1990s a social divide of information 'haves' and 'have-nots' was seen as a potential problem on the horizon from many different points of view (Cullen 2001). From an individual perspective, in the same way that being homeless (i.e. having no fixed address) creates a series of problems for an individual in terms of having a bank account, getting a job and collecting state benefits, a lack of access to information technology in an information society will have repercussive effects which could mean not being able to participate in the economic and social benefits the information society would have to offer in terms of education, business and consumer transactions, personal communication, information gathering, career opportunities and development.

It is important to understand that the digital divide is a social and political problem, not merely a technological one (van Dijk 2005). Digital inequality is merely another manifestation of the other inequalities that already exist within our contemporary society. In many respects, it is no coincidence that the major categories of overall marginality on the domestic front: class, income, ethnicity, gender, rural/urban, age, are also the major categories that are suggested as influential in the formation of a digital divide. On a global scale, it is indeed no surprise, given the context of widening income and standard of living gaps between wealthy industrialised countries and developing nations, that most developing nations find themselves on the wrong side of the digital divide as well.

Van Dijk (2005) argues that in the making of digital divides, the most important positional factors are:

1 position in the labour market (involving income, and access to ICTs at work);

2 education, which has been profoundly affected by the influx of computers and Internet into classrooms in the 1990s, helping older generations to gain access by having school-age children;

3 household composition. Households with children tend to have the highest rates of access;

4 residence in a particular nation or part of it, which involves: availability of technology; general levels of literacy; language skills (especially English); level of democracy; information society policies; a culture that is receptive of technology.

The latest report from the Pew Internet and Life Project (2008b) in the United States, which examined broadband and dial-up access for Americans reflects the current trends in domestic digital divides in that country (see Table 4.1).

Table 4.1 demonstrates the traditional individual categories where the digital divide is seen as significant. It is easy to see a small gender gap, a rather large gap based on age (particularly people over 65), some (widening) gaps based on race/ethnicity, rather large education gaps, a very large and widening gap based on income, and a narrowing rural/urban divide. Similar findings in Europe have been suggested by van Dijk (2005), who argues that gender and disability divides have been narrowing, as have age divides (largely through the process of ageing), while racial/ethnic and income divides have been increasing.

By the mid 1990s there was also increasing recognition that nations that had the technological, social and economic resources to invest in ICT infrastructures and technologies (and whose citizens had the individual wealth to be able to access and own ICTs within these infrastructures) were at a comparative advantage to those who lived in poorer, developing nations which did not

Table 4.1 Trends in broadband adoption by group (% in each group with broadband at home)

	2005 %	2006 %	2007 %	2008 %	% point change 07–08
Yearly adoption					
All adults	33	42	47	55	+8
Gender					
Male	31	45	50	58	+8
Female	27	38	44	53	+9
Age					
18–29	38	55	63	70	+7
30–49	36	50	59	69	+10
50–64	27	38	40	50	+10
65+	8	13	15	19	+4
Race/ethnicity					
White (not Hispanic)	31	42	48	57	+9
Black (not Hispanic)	14	31	40	43	+3
Hispanic (English speaking)	28	41	47	56	+9
Educational attainment					
Less than high school	10	17	21	28	+7
High school grad	20	31	34	40	+6
Some college	35	47	58	66	+8
College +	47	62	70	79	+9
Household income					
Under $20K	13	18	28	25	–3
$20K–$30K	19	27	34	42	+8
$30K–$40K	26	40	40	49	+9
$40K–$50K	28	47	52	60	+8
$50K–$75K	35	48	58	67	+9
$75K–$100K	51	67	70	82	+12
Over $100K	62	68	82	85	+3
Community type					
Urban	31	44	52	57	+5
Suburban	33	46	49	60	+11
Rural	18	25	31	38	+7

Source: Internet and American Life Project 2008

have appropriate infrastructures nor access to digital technologies. This disparity, based primarily on the geography of 'haves and have-nots' in the developed versus the developing world, is usually referred to as the 'global digital divide', usually defined as 'the divergence of Internet access between industrialised and developing societies' (Norris 2001).

Table 4.2 shows that Internet penetration rates vary depending on which region of the world one lives in, but that, even within regions, there is still a large variation in how much access there is to the Internet. Asia, for example, includes a country like South Korea, which has one of the highest penetration rates in the world, alongside East Timor, with one of the lowest.

The main premise behind the global digital divide is the worry that developed industrialised nations are in a position to take full advantage of the information age, while developing countries are not. In that sense, information and communication technology may be yet another way in which wealthy, industrialised countries can further enhance their already elevated position over developing nations, leading to even further disparities between rich and poor nations, and even further imbalances of power.

It is clear that without some form of intervention, there is a real danger that the move to the digital age will greatly enhance the position of the advanced, industrialised economies over those of the developing world, allowing them to play by a fundamentally different set of economic rules. Developed countries will potentially be able to use their increased access to knowledge, increased economic flexibility, and increased communication efficiency, while developing nations could become ever more victimised and marginalised by these trends. Current trends show that, proportionally, Internet access is growing much faster in developing nations. However, this statistic hides the fact that while the proportional growth may be high, the growth in real numbers of persons gaining access to the Internet is still very small in developing nations, and is far outweighed by continued growth in advanced economies.

This trend is seen as particularly unjust since many believe that access to the Internet and other digital communications technologies, and the information this brings, is particularly useful to developing nations, in which people often lack access to basic health care, education, or even useful weather information. Thus, people in developing countries are those with the most to gain from the resources of the Internet, and yet they are the ones with the least amount of access.

Table 4.2 Internet penetration (% of population Internet users)

Area	Internet penetration (per cent)	High country	Low country
Africa	5.3	Seychelles 38.9	Liberia 0.0
Asia	15.3	South Korea 70.7	East Timor 0.1
Europe	48.1	Norway 87.7	Albania 13.0
Middle East	21.3	Israel 52.0	Iraq 0.2
North America	73.6	Greenland 92.3	Bermuda 72.1
Latin America/Caribbean	24.2	Chile 44.9	Cuba 2.1
Oceania	59.5	Australia 79.4	Solomon Islands 1.4
World	21.9		

Source: Internetworldstats.com (Accessed 22 January 2009)

Digital inequality merely reflects broader inequalities, both on a domestic scale and on a worldwide scale. Lack of access to digital technology is merely another way among many to be marginalised in contemporary culture. Despite this, there have been a number of attempts to address both domestic and global divides, some with a reasonable amount of success. However, there is still a danger that the spread of digital communications technology will be a process that further enhances the position and wealth of those who already have the most advantages in our world, as opposed to assisting those populations that perhaps need help the most.

Conclusion

This chapter has tried to give the reader a sense of the scope and scale to which the Internet has permeated everyday life in modern industrial nations. First it examined the historical context of the Internet as a part of the development of a 'digital knowledge economy', and then it looked at the Internet as an infrastructure supporting global flows of capital. The chapter then touched upon how the Internet has become embedded in everyday work and leisure practices, and how it has become a tool for political engagement, organisation and fundraising. I also mentioned the increasing use of the Internet within education and learning, and finished with a consideration of the inequalities surrounding Internet use and access. My point here was to demonstrate that not all are able to gain very real benefits potentially on offer to marginalised peoples on national and global scales, even though in many respects such people are the ones who could benefit the most from online access to information.

Notes

1 Data from the US Census (2008) suggests that online retailing is quite sectoral, with 43.2 per cent of computer hardware and software trade being conducted online; 11.3 per cent of consumer electronics; 16.3 per cent of books, music and videos; 19.1 per cent of ticket purchases; and 12.7 per cent of toys and games. All other retail sectors were below 5 per cent.
2 Apparently, $1.5 billion was spent worldwide on 'virtual goods' that have no application outside the Internet; things such as Avatars, virtual pets, virtual jewellery and other activities related to online gaming (Wu 2007).
3 Recent studies suggest that by 2008, over 60 per cent of American workers (as fairly typical of advanced industrial economies) used the Internet and/or email at their workplace (Madden and Jones 2008), and that same research suggested that 45 per cent of workers do some amount of work at home. Other studies have suggested that almost nine in 10 organisations in the United States had implemented Internet access in their workplaces by as early as the year 2000 (Mastrangelo *et al.* 2006).
4 According to PEW Internet, as many as 16 per cent of American Internet users consume online music and video on a daily basis (PEW Internet 2008).
5 This also applies to the areas of romance and dating, where dating websites are used by people looking for long-term partners, or short-term sexual activity in their offline lives.

6 Blogging itself came into its own during the US invasion of Iraq, when many Americans were not satisfied with mainstream media and political coverage of the war (Carl 2003).

Further reading

There are a number of other texts that look at how the Internet and other forms of communication technology are impacting our society, economy and culture. A more basic text such as John Feather's (2004) *The Information Society: A Study of Continuity and Change* (5th edition) would be a good place to start. For something more specifically related to the Internet, there is the slightly dated, but still valuable Barry Wellman and Caroline Haythornthwaite (eds) (2002) *The Internet and Everyday Life*. More advanced readings would include the classic by Manuel Castells (1996/2000) *The Rise of the Network Society* or his later and more user friendly *The Internet Galaxy: Reflections on the Internet, Business, and Society* (2001). Frank Webster's (2001) *Culture and Politics in the Information Age* is an advanced edited collection which is a good read for a variety of topics, but is particularly strong on the political dimension, and another edited collection concentrating on Internet politics which is a bit more recent is van de Donk *et al.*'s (2004) *Cyberprotest: New Media, Citizens and Social Movements*. For a good discussion of digital divides Jan van Dijk's (2005) *The Deepening Divide: Inequality and the Information Society* is a very complete and thorough analysis.

References

Anandarajan, M., Thompson, S., Teo, H. and Simmers, C. (2006) 'The Internet and workplace transformation', in M. Anandarajan, S. Thompson, H. Teo and C. Simmers (eds), *Advancements in Management Information Systems* (Vol. 7). Arnak, NY: M.E. Sharpe Publications, 3–11.

Balasubramanian, S., Konana, P. and Menon, M. (2003) 'Customer satisfaction in virtual environments: a study of online investing', *Management Science*, 49(7): 871–89.

Bauman, Z. (2000) *The Individualized Society*. Cambridge: Polity.

Beck, U. and Beck-Gernsheim, E. (2002) *Individualization : Institutionalized Individualism and its Social and Political Consequences*. London: Sage.

Beninger, J. (1986) *The Control Revolution*. London: Harvard University Press.

Bennett, L., Breunig, C. and Givens, T. (2008) 'Communication and Political Mobilization: Digital Media and the Organization of Anti-Iraq War Demonstrations in the U.S.', *Political Communication*, 25(3): 269–89

Bray, J. (2006) 'Facebook Faceoff', *The Guardian*, Tuesday, 7 November 2006. http://www.guardian.co.uk/education/2006/nov/07/students.highereducation (accessed on 26 January 2009).

Carl, C. (2003) *Bloggers and Their Blogs: A Depiction of the Users and Usage of Weblogs on the World Wide Web*. MA thesis, Georgetown University, Washington DC.

Carty, V. (2002) 'Technology and counter-hegemonic movements: the case of Nike Corporation', *Social Movement Studies*, 1(2): 129–46.

Castells, M. (1996/2000) *The Rise of the Network Society*. Oxford: Blackwell.

Castells, M. (2001) *The Internet Galaxy: Reflections on the Internet, Business, and Society*. Oxford: Oxford University Press.

Castronova, E. (2005) *Synthetic Worlds: the Business and Culture of Online Games*. Chicago: University of Chicago Press.

Chazerand, P. and Geeroms, C. (2008) 'The business of playing games: players as developers and entrepreneurs', *Digital Creativity*, 19(3): 185–93.

ComScore (2008) Press Release: 'One out of three U.K. internet users banked online in January 2008'. http://www.comscore.com/press/release.asp?press=2198 (accessed 25 January 2009).

Cullen, R. (2001) 'Addressing the digital divide', *Online Information Review*, 25(5): 311–320.

Dahlgren, P. (2004) Forward in van de Donk, W., Loader, B., Nixon, P. and Rucht, D. (eds) *Cyberprotest: New Media, Citizens and Social Movements*. London: Routledge, xi–xvi.

Dakroury, A. and Birdsall, W. (2008) 'Blogs and the right to communicate: Towards creating a space-less public sphere?', International Symposium on Technology and Society, 2008. ISTAS 2008. IEEE, 1–8. http://ieeexplore.ieee.org/stamp/stamp.jsp?ar number=4559762andisnumber=4559749 (accessed on 26 January 2009).

Dreyfus, H. (2002) 'Anonymity versus commitment: the dangers of education on the Internet', *Educational Philosophy and Theory*, 34(4): 369–87.

Feather, J. (2008) *The Information Society: A Study of Continuity and Change* (5th edn). London: Facet Publishing

Fox, S. (2005) 'Online Banking 2005: A Pew Internet Project Data Memo', *Pew Internet and American Life Project* http://www.pewinternet.org/pdfs/PIP_Online_Banking_2005.pdf (accessed on 25 January 2009).

Garrett, R.K. and Danziger, J. (2008) 'On Cyberslacking: Workplace Status and Personal Internet Use at Work', *CyberPsychology and Behavior*, 11(3): 287–92.

Gunawan, G., Ellis-Chadwick, F. and King, M. (2008) 'An empirical study of the uptake of performance measurement by Internet retailers', *Internet Research*, 18(4): 361–81.

Harris, A. (2008) 'Young women, late modern politics, and the participatory possibilities of online cultures', *Journal of Youth Studies*, 11(5): 481–95.

IFPI (2009) *IFPI Digital Music Report 2009* http://www.ifpi.org/content/library/DMR2009.pdf (accessed on 25 January 2009).

Lefebvre, H. (2000) *Critique of Everyday Life*. London: Verso.

Lindsay, E. (2004) 'Distance Teaching: Comparing Two Online Information Literacy Courses', *Journal of Academic Librarianship*, 30(6): 482–7.

Lockwood, F. (2006) 'Innovation in distributed learning: creating the environment', in F. Lockwood and A. Gooley (eds), *Innovation in Open and Distance Learning*, Abingdon: Routledge, 1–14.

McCormick, J. and Dorning, M. (2008) 'Barack Obama campaign raised nearly $1 billion, shattering records: Fundraising outpaced combined total of Bush and Kerry in 2004 election, records show', *Chicago Tribune*, 5 December 2008. http://www.chicagotribune.com/news/politics/obama/chi-obama-moneydec05,0,6244688.story (accessed on 26 January 2009).

Madden, M. and Jones, S. (2008) *Networked Workers*. Pew Internet and American Life Project, 24 September 2008. http://www.pewinternet.org/pdfs/PIP_Networked_Workers_FINAL.pdf (accessed on 26 January 2009).

Mastrangelo, P., Everton, W. and Jolton, J. (2006) 'Personal Use of Work Computers: Distraction versus Destruction', *Cyberpsychology and Behavior*, 9(6): 730–41.

Miller, V. (2000) 'Search Engines, Portals, and Global Capitalism', in D. Gauntlett (ed.), *Web.Studies: Rewiring Media Studies for the Digital Age*. London and New York: Arnold/Oxford University Press, 113–22.

Newman, J. (2004) *Videogames*. London: Routledge.

Norris, P. (2001) *Digital Divide: Civic Engagement, Information Poverty and the Internet Worldwide*. Cambridge: Cambridge University Press.

Olausson, M. (2007) 'Online Games: Global Market Forecast. Strategy Analytics Report'. http://www.strategyanalytics.com/default.aspx?mod=ReportAbstractVieweranda0=3559 (accessed on 26 January 2009).

Orton-Johnson, K. (2009) The online student: lurking, chatting, flaming and joking. *Sociological Research Online*, 12(6). (http://wwwsocresonline.org.uk/12/6/3.html).

Pew Internet and American Life Project (2008a) 'Daily Internet activities' (May 2008). http://www.pewinternet.org/trends/Daily_Internet_Activities_7.22.08.htm (accessed on 26 January 2009).

Pew Internet and American Life Project (2008b) *Home Broadband Adoption 2008*. http://www.pewinternet.org/pdfs/PIP_Broadband_2008.pdf (accessed on 26 July 2008).

Poster, M. (1995) *The Second Media Age*. Cambridge: Polity.

Rheingold, H. (2000) *Virtual Community: Homesteading on the Electronic Frontier*. Cambridge, MA and London: MIT Press.

Rideout, V., Roberts, D.F. and Foehr, U.G. (2005) *Generation M: Media in the lives of 8–18 year olds*. The Henry J. Kaiser Family Foundation. Retrieved 25 January 2009, from http://www.kff.org/entmedia/upload/Executive-Summary-Generation-M-Media-in-the-Lives-of-8-18-year-olds.pdf

Screen Digest (2006) *Online Gambling: Market Forces and Assessment to 2010*. Screen Digest Report 1 July 2006. http://www.screendigest.com/reports/06onlinegam/NSMH-6RUB3L/sample.pdf (accessed on 26 January 2009).

Stroud, N. (2008) 'Media use and political predispositions: revisiting the concept of selective exposure', *Political Behavior*, 30(3): 341–66.

Thomas, T. (2003) 'Al Qaeda and the Internet: The Danger of "Cyberplanning"', *Parameters*, 33(1): 112–23.

Turkle, S. (1996) *Life on the Screen: Identity in the Age of the Internet*. London: Weidenfeld and Nicolson.

United States Census (2008) Table 1016: Online retail spending, 2001 to 2007, and projections, 2008. http://www.census.gov/compendia/statab/tables/09s1016.pdf (accessed on 25 January 2009).

van de Donk, W., Loader, B., Nixon, P. and Rucht, D. (eds)(2004) *Cyberprotest: New Media, Citizens and Social Movements*. London: Routledge.

van Dijk, J. (2005) *The Deepening Divide: Inequality and the Information Society*. London: Sage.

Webster, F. (2001) *Culture and Politics in the Information Age*. London: Routledge.

Wellman, B. and Haythornthwaite, C. (eds)(2002) *The Internet in Everyday Life*. Malden, MA: Wiley-Blackwell.

Wilcox, C. (2008) 'Internet fundraising in 2008: a new model?', *The Forum*, 6(1): 1–13.

Williams, D., Yee, N. and Caplan, S. (2008) 'Who plays, how much, and why? Debunking the stereotypical gamer profile', *Journal of Computer-Mediated Communication*, 13(4): 993–1018.

Wu, Susan (2007) Virtual Goods: the next big busines model 199. Comments by Susan Wu on 20 June 2007. http://www.techcrunch.com/2007/06/20/virtual-goods-the-next-big-business-model (accessed 26 January 2009).

Chapter 5

Criminalising cyberspace: the rise of the Internet as a 'crime problem'

David S. Wall

In his detailed analysis of the Victorian electric telegraph, Standage observed that with every 'new invention, there will always be some people who see only its potential to do good, while others see new opportunities to commit crime or make money. We can expect exactly the same reactions to whatever new inventions appear in the twenty first century' (Standage 1998: 199). The Internet is a poignant example in case and this chapter explores the rise of the Internet as both a perceived 'crime problem' and also as a conduit for actual criminal activity. But this chapter is not simply a chronological jaunt through the annals of history. It tells a more complex story in which, it will be argued, the perception of the Internet as a crime problem needs to be disaggregated from the Internet as a conduit for actual criminal activity. This is because the cultural life of cybercrime is quite different to its reality; however, what complicates the story even further is that we find the reality of cybercrime has been heavily shaped by its cultural life and vice versa. Not only has technology shaped the social, but at the same time the social has also shaped the technology.

The various news media are replete with reports of high cybercrime threat levels – as they have been for over a decade and a half. Just enter 'cybercrime threat' into Google to see the range of news coverage. Looking through that coverage you will find that most of the hits are sensationalised reportage and actually contain little substantive or reasoned information. Yet, when headlines such as 'Is the UK safe from cyber attack?' (BBC 2009a) and 'Cyber "threat" to London Olympics' (BBC 2009b) (the most recent headlines at the time of writing) combine with reportage of cyber-security industry threat reports (for example, Symantec estimates in excess of one and a half million cybercrimes a year (Symantec 2009)) then the apparent risk levels increase. Yet the impression of risk from cybercrime given by this reportage contrasts sharply with, for example, the low levels of prosecutions. There have only been 150 or so successful prosecutions in the UK since the Computer Misuse Act 1990 was introduced two decades ago.

The apparent simultaneous over-reporting and under-reporting of cybercrime (Wall 2007) is actually a symptom of cybercrime being simultaneously over-problematised and also misunderstood. The reason why these countervailing forces occur, it will be argued, is because the growing culture of fear about cybercrime (Wall 2008) has led the Internet to be perceived as a crime problem. So, before looking at the ways that new conduits of actual criminal activity have emerged online, it is important first to explore the cultural and conceptual origins of cyberspace and cybercrime in popular culture which have shaped public perceptions of the Internet as criminogenic.

The cultural origins of cybercrime and the rise of the Internet as a 'crime problem'

Today, the term 'cybercrime' symbolises online insecurity and risk and it is widely used to describe the crimes or harms that are committed using networked technologies. 'Cybercrime' is relatively meaningless as a legal term because of its popular cultural origins (Wall 2008) and because it has no formal reference point in law. It also tends to be used metaphorically and emotively, rather than rationally, to express ambivalent and general concerns about hacking. The term is, however, gradually becoming part of formal legal terminology due to the harmonising influence of the 2001 Council of Europe Convention on Cybercrime (ETS No. 185), to describe computer misuse legislation; for example, in Australia (Cybercrime Act 2001), Nigeria (Draft Cybercrime Act) and the United States (proposed Cybercrime Act 2007). The main point being made here is that many so-called cybercrimes are not necessarily crimes in criminal law, nor are they variations of traditional forms of offending but, rather confusingly, some are! Yet, despite this conceptual disarray, the term 'cybercrime' prevails as the accepted terminology (Wall 2007: 10) for harmful behaviours arising from networked computers. Hence, the need to explore the cultural origins of cybercrime which have contributed to the rise in the 'culture of fear' about it, which, it will be argued, has become integral in framing the Internet as a 'crime problem'.

Cyberpunk literature – from meatspace to cyberspace and meatcrime to cybercrime

Much of cybercrime's conceptual baggage can be traced back to the cyberpunk social science fiction literature of the 1970s and 1980s (see Brown, Chapter 8). Cyberpunk authors inventively combined cybernetics with the sensibilities of the contemporary punk rock movement to form a genre of science fiction that thematically joined ideas about dystopic advances in science and information technology with their potential capability to break down the social order. As Person (1998) observes:

> Classic cyberpunk characters were marginalized, alienated loners who lived on the edge of society in generally dystopic futures where daily life was impacted by rapid technological change, an ubiquitous datasphere

89

of computerized information, and invasive modification of the human body. (Person 1988)

The cyberpunk leitmotif was essentially a 'hi-tech but low-life' aesthetic and the 'Classic cyberpunk characters' described by Person became a social blueprint for the hacker stereotype.

The term 'cyberspace' appears to originate in William Gibson's 1982 highly influential short story 'Burning Chrome' about the hacker group 'Cyberspace Seven' (Gibson 1982). The short story was published in *Omni Magazine*, a science fiction meets hard science forum that existed between 1978 and 1998 and which promoted explorations into cyberpunk. Along with other science fiction forums, novels and films during the 1980s, *Omni* contributed to the progressive definition of virtual 'cyberspace' as a contrast to the physical environment or 'meatspace' (Gibson 1984) and the linkage between cyberspace and crime was just another short step. Having said this, the linkage has been somewhat confused by the evolution of two quite different visions of cyberspace that are usefully delineated by Jordan (1999: 23–58). Gibson's original symbolic vision of cyberspace sees individuals shift their consciousness from their 'meatspace' into 'cyberspace' à la *The Matrix*, leaving their physical bodies or 'meat' behind. John Perry Barlow's hybrid (Barlovian) vision, on the other hand, combined Gibson's concept with real-world experience to join image with reality (Jordan 1999: 56; Bell 2001: 21). The product was an environment that could be constitutionalised (Barlow 1996). This alternative vision of cyberspace is, after Sterling (1994: xi), a place that is not inside the computer or inside the technology of communication, but in the imaginations of those individuals who are being connected. Although imaginary, it is nevertheless real in the sense that the things that happen in that space have real consequences for those who are participating.

The actual point of origin of the term 'cybercrime' is unclear, but it seems to have emerged in the late 1980s or even early 1990s in the later cyberpunk print and audio-visual media. However, the linkage between cyberspace and crime was implicit in the early cyberpunk short stories by William Gibson, Bruce Sterling and Bruce Bethke (accredited with coining the term 'Cyberpunk') and many others. The cyberspace-crime theme was subsequently taken to a wider audience in popular contemporary novels such as Gibson's 'Sprawl' trilogy of *Neuromancer* (1984), *Count Zero* (1986) and *Mona Lisa Overdrive* (1988) and Stephenson's *Snowcrash* (1992). Please note that the examples of books, films and media listed here are intended to be illustrative and not exhaustive. Cyberpunk effectively defined cybercrime as a harmful activity that takes place in virtual environments and made the 'hi-tech low-life' hacker narrative a norm in the entertainment industry. It is interesting to note at this point that, whilst social theorists were adopting the Barlovian model of cyberspace, it was the Gibsonian model that shaped the public imagination through the visual media.

Haxploitation movies

Cyberpunk was very popular within the social science fiction community, but its audience was nevertheless relatively small and cliquish. The cultural fusion of cyberspace and crime into mainstream popular culture was largely due to the second and third of three generations of hacker movies into which some of the cyberpunk ideas dripped (see Webber and Vass, Chapter 7). The first generation had conceptually predated cyberpunk, but demonstrated to a wider audience the use of computers to 'hack' into infrastructural systems – these include the *Billion Dollar Brain* (1967), *The [Original] Italian Job* (1969), *Superman III* (1983) and *Bellman and True* (1988). In these movies the 'hackers' tended to be portrayed as male, fairly old and usually somewhat comical or eccentric (see, for example, Benny Hill as Professor Peach in *The Italian Job* and Richard Pryor as Gus Gorman in *Superman III*). The second generation of hacker films, in contrast to the first, were clearly defined by cyberpunk ideas and focused on the hacker rather than the hack. The earlier of the second-generation films romanticised the guile of the hacker as a penetrator of interconnected computer systems. These films consolidated the 'hacker' stereotype which endures to this day of a disenfranchised, misunderstood genius teenage male who uses technology to put wrongs right while having a 'coming of age' experience and some fun in the process. The films include *War Games* (1983), *Electric Dreams* (1984), *Real Genius* (1985), *Weird Science* (1985) and *Ferris Bueller's Day Off* (1986). The later second-generation films were a little more sophisticated in that the hackers they depicted tended to use the Internet, or an imaginative sci-fi equivalent. The focus also shifted from portraying hacks across communication networks to hacks in different types of new virtualised environments, with hackers still young(ish) and male (though not always) and less likely to adopt moral high ground than in earlier films. They include *Die Hard* (1988), *Sneakers* (1992), *Goldeneye* (1995), *Hackers* (1995), *The Net* (1995), *Johnny Mnemonic* (1995), *Independence Day* (1996), *Enemy of the State* (1998), *Takedown/Track Down* (2000), *AntiTrust* (2001), *Swordfish* (2001) and *The [new] Italian Job* (2003).

The third generation of films were defined by both the hacker and the hack being within virtual environments and are epitomised by *The Matrix* (1999) and its derivatives. The basic concepts behind *The Matrix*'s screenplay can be traced back to Gibson's separation of cyberspace from meatspace, but also social philosophy. Jean Baudrillard's ideas about *Simulacra and Simulation* are supposed to have inspired the films' producers and writers and shaped the construction of the narrative. Although, true to his form, Baudrillard is reported to have curmudgeonly retorted that he thought the producers and writers had misunderstood his work (see Hanley 2003). Observant viewers of the 'follow the white rabbit' scene in *The Matrix* will have noticed that Neo stores his computer disks in a hollowed out hardback copy of *Simulacra and Simulation* (Baudrillard 1994).

The dystopic conceptual linkage between crime and cyberspace has been further exploited in 'haxploitation' print and audio-visual media. Coined by Internet journalist John Leyden (2001, 2007), 'haxploitation' defines a genre that deliberately exploits the public fear of hackers for entertainment (my definition). However, in recent years there has been a noticeable shift away from what had become the traditional hack narrative that emphasised the hacker's power over the state and society along with the humiliating public exposure of the state's impotence in the face of the hacker. Instead, the new haxploitation narrative erodes the boundaries between the individual hacker and the state to re-express its dominant norms and effectively redress the perceived power imbalance found in the earlier movies. Moreover, in the new narrative there is a clear reversal of the roles so that the state itself effectively takes over the prime hacker role in order to suppress its more deviant and dangerous subjects. See, for example, movies such as *Die Hard 4.0*, where the state hits back, along with some help from an ethical, or white-hat, hacker; or *Enemy of the State* where the state hacks the individual when driven by rogue elements. The 'factional' images described skilfully combine fact with fiction, and have crystallised the 'super-hacker' offender stereotype as the archetypal 'cybercriminal' (Wall 2007: 16). What makes these various 'hack'- related sources of visual and textual imagery significant is that 'contemporary movie and media imagery subconsciously orders the line between fact and fiction' (Furedi, cited in Wall 2007: 16). So much so that Roger Burrows (1997) argued in his groundbreaking article on 'Cyberpunk as Social Theory' that not only has the Gibsonian concept of cyberspace transmuted into a tangible reality, but his (Gibson's) technological vision has also fed back into the theory and design of computer and information systems. Furthermore, despite the contradictions between the different visions of cyberspace, Gibson's fictional perspectives on cultural, economic and social phenomena have also begun to find their way into social and cultural analyses as viable characterisations of our contemporary world (Burrows 1997). Yet, as outlined earlier it is the hybrid Barlovian model of cyberspace, rather than the pure Gibsonian vision, that has actually found the greater purchase with social theorists, especially in thinking about cybercrime.

Dystopias and future shocks

The contemporary, though now traditional, science fiction hacker narrative is, surprisingly, neither unique nor innovatory. Quite the opposite, in fact, because it tends to conform to a character type that originated in Victorian science fiction: namely, a person who constructs or appropriates technological inventions in order to give them extra-human power to wield control over others. It is as popular now as a core theme of science fiction as it was a century or more ago. See, for example, the science fiction novels of H.G. Wells and others, which were written during a time of great social upheaval caused by technological innovation and which described worlds that had been transformed, but also threatened by new and potentially oppressive technologies. This tradition continued through to the cyberpunk of the present day via the works of Brian Aldiss, Aldous Huxley and contemporaries. Indeed, at the centre of most of these works was the 'savant', a learned person of profound knowledge who could utilise technology to his or her (usually his) advantage for good or bad. However, it is the potentially dystopic power that the savant can wield through technology that makes them so much more interesting as a science fictional character. The 'savant' was, in effect, the Victorian equivalent of the hacker.

The different science fiction genres not only strengthened the modern 'hacker' narrative by emphasising the technological power binary (powerful versus non-powerful), but more generally they also helped to strengthen existing post-war cultural reactions to techno-social change. Interleaved with science fiction, for example, was the social science fiction novel, of which the best-known example was probably Orwell's now classic work *Nineteen Eighty-Four* first published in 1949 (Orwell 1990). Orwell captured the post-war zeitgeist by combining ideas about technological change with contemporary political events and social theory in order to describe a dystopic future in which state power was augmented by technological innovation.

Nineteen Eighty-Four and its literary offspring served to heighten cold war anxieties about the potentially dystopic power of technological invention and also fed these ideas back into social theory. Toffler's *Futureshock* (1970), for example, draws upon the dystopic themes to describe how fear of the future tends to rear its head whenever there is a significant period of technological transformation. More recently, Furedi (2002) and others have described the prevailing culture of fear which is a sort of ideological fear of fear that leads to exaggerated public expectations of, among other things, crime and danger, which is felt regardless of whether any actually exist. Such process is not far from Garland's 'crime complex' whereby public anxiety about crime has become the norm and now frames our everyday lives (Garland 2001: 367), so that we expect crime to exist regardless of whether it actually does, and we are shocked, and even panic, when we do not find it. Garland (2001) and Simon (2007) have suggested that governments and policymakers tactically use prevailing fears of crime to control a broad range of risks. That this tactic should also be used with cybercrime is of no surprise. Taipale has argued that the fear of technology, what he calls 'FrankenTech', now exists because the 'public debate on complex policy issues is often dominated by information entrepreneurs (including activists and the media) who attempt to engender information cascades to further their own particular agenda' (Taipale 2006: 153). Because the resolution of 'issues' takes place 'in situations where the manageable risks are inflated or misunderstood' (Taipale 2006: 153), then unnecessary levels of public anxiety can result in resource managers being pressurised into misallocating (usually public) resources. The gap that inevitably emerges between the expected threat and the provision of security, displayed, for example, by the disparity between reporting and prosecution as illustrated earlier, is a *reassurance gap* (Innes 2004) that clearly needs to be closed. The need for reassurance typically becomes expressed in the form of public demands for more law and 'police' action which, of course, the police find hard to provide because not only is the factual basis of the demands flawed, but police funding models are usually determined by responsive routine activities based upon the 170-year-old Peelian model of policing dangerousness (Wall 2007: 161). This Peelian model remains similar in principle to its original early Nineteenth Century form even though it now exists in more complex late modern societies. The upshot of the argument so far is that the uncritical coupling of the social science fiction driven hacker narrative with the ambiguous scientific conceptualisation of networked virtual space, viewed in terms of a traditional Peelian crime and policing perspective, against a dystopic social science fiction backdrop, distorts perceptions of the reality of cybercrime. The conceptualisation of cybercrime in social science fiction as dramatic, futuristic and potentially dystopic proscribes public expectations of cybercrime as above the capabilities of normal folk, as sensational, disempowering victims and being beyond the scope of state protection (e.g. policing). When these perspectives are placed against a backdrop of contemporary cultural reactions to technological change, then they create the circumstances right for the creation and maintenance of mythologies.

So, remove this 'dramaturgical' frame and the events that form the history of cybercrime become simply a series of events related to each other only by the fact that they exploited the convergence of computers and communication systems. Yet, the frequency of these events increased over time as the Internet became a popular medium, as did broader accounts of their meanings. To understand both events and accounts we therefore need to take a more pragmatic and grounded approach towards them in order to understand the transformation of criminal behaviour online: what has become known as cybercrime.

A generational history of the Internet as a conduit for criminal activity

As indicated in the introduction to this chapter, a quick tour of news reports and literature reveals a range of different views on cybercrime. The *computer security experts*, for example, tell us about potential and actual risks to society and suggest a range of strategic and tactical solutions – very often their own products and services. The *legal/administrative community*, on the other hand, define what behaviour is (and is not) supposed to happen by establishing and clarifying the rules that identify boundaries of acceptable and unacceptable behaviour. The *criminological and general academic community* endeavour to provide an informed analysis about what has happened and why. To confuse matters further, the different communities of interest rarely distinguish between concerns about personal, corporate and national security agendas. These different takes on the same subject mix with science fiction media presentations of cybercrime to feed into the popular or lay view, which reflects what the person on the street thinks is happening. So, concerns about cybercrime are expressed through a range of voices that do not articulate a common understanding. In fact, just about any offence that involves a computer seems to be regarded as a 'cybercrime' and there is also a broad tendency to confuse crimes that use the Internet with those created by the Internet. None of this is helped by confusing media reports of high cybercrime threat levels mentioned earlier.

To get closer to what a cybercrime is we need to look at the way that network technology has changed opportunities for criminal behaviour. If we start off with the premise that the defining characteristic of cybercrimes is that they are harmful behaviours that have been mediated by networked technologies, then the test of a cybercrime must therefore focus upon what remains if those same networked technologies are removed. This 'transformation test', as it is referred to in Wall (2007) is not intended to be scientific, rather it is a heuristic device, a rule of thumb. This test simply enables us to understand further how the Internet has become a conduit for criminal activity. To explore this transformation further it is useful to look back into the history of cybercrime.

The origins of cybercrime can be traced back to the interception of semaphore signals in the eighteenth century, or the wiretap in the nineteenth and early twentieth centuries (Standage 1998). In both cases, valuable information was intercepted (virtually) as it was being transmitted across hitherto unparalleled spans of time and space and then sold on or used for gain. However, the true genesis of cybercrimes originates in early computer crimes prior to their subsequent transformation by networking over two further generations: generations which loosely map over the generations of *haxploitation* movies mentioned earlier. It is useful to explore these milestones, because although the notion of 'generation' invokes the passage of time, each generation is distinctive and the conceptual differences between them can be used to explain contemporary differences currently present in the scope of criminal opportunity.

The first generation of (low-end) cybercrime: crimes using computers (to assist traditional forms of offending)

The first generation of cybercrime initially occurred within discrete computing systems and was characterised by the criminal exploitation of mainframe computers and their discrete operating systems. Usually undertaken in order to acquire money illegally or to appropriate, free or even destroy restricted information, this first generation marked a departure from conventional criminal opportunity that was characterised by physical labour, temporal and spatial locations. Although this first generation of cybercrime involved, and still involves, the use of computers, networked or otherwise, the behaviours relating to these technologies are in fact 'traditional' (Wall 2001) or 'ordinary' (McQuade 2006a, 2006b), even though frequently referred to as cybercrimes. They are termed here, low-end cybercrimes, a distinction borrowed from Brodeur's (1983) work on policing, where computers are used mainly during the preparation stage of a crime, either as a tool of communication or to gather preparatory information (for example, how to kill someone or how to manufacture drugs or weapons).

Although these patterns of harmful activity are sustained by networked technologies, if they are removed then the activities will still persist by other means. 'Salami frauds', for example, (Singleton 2002: 39; Kabay 2002) often involve the electronic corralling out of the system of minute amounts of surplus money (parts of pence or cents) left over after banking transactions have been rounded down, but the fraud could still have been committed prior to the computerisation of banks through a subtle misuse of internal banking orders. Another example is drug dealers, who will use whatever form of communications and information technology are available, convenient and less risky. It is similarly the case with information about weapons and other harms, even manuals on how to commit crimes, which existed before the Internet. Radical book retailer Loompanics, for example, has long specialised in selling books that describe the technologies and techniques involved in potentially harmful actions and are therefore illegal in many jurisdictions outside the US.

The second generation of cybercrime: opportunities for crimes across a global span of networks

The second generation of cybercrimes are those committed across networks, such as hacking and cracking. They were originally the product of a marriage between the skills of the early computer operators and the communications skills of the phone phreakers who imaginatively 'cracked' telephone systems to make free telephone calls. The phone phreaker was epitomised by the legendary exploits of Cap'n Crunch (aka John Draper), so named because he used a toy whistle obtained from a box of Cap'n Crunch cereal to access AT&T's phone system by whistling its long-distance dial tone. The marriage gave birth to 'hackers', who were driven by a combination of the phreakers' ethical belief in their moral right to hack into systems and the post-Vietnam culture of the 1970s with its youthful promotion of civil liberties and suspicion of government and large corporations. Hackers would use their knowledge of telephone systems in conjunction with their computing and 'social engineering' skills to 'talk' information out of the owner and access discrete but linked computing systems. For the uninitiated, hackers claim to be driven by ethical principles, whereas crackers are not. The term 'cracker' was originally adopted to avoid the misuse of the word 'hacker' by the media. Useful histories of cybercrime can be found in Shinder and Tittel (2002: 49–92), Britz (2003) and McQuade (2006b).

When the first personal computers became available in the 1970s and 1980s they could be connected by phone-in Local Area Networks (LANs). The early hackers tested systems and shared their philosophies and knowledge of 'hacks' on bulletin board services (BBS). Those same BBS systems developed into early virtual trading posts from where information services and goods were sold, thus creating opportunities for theft and the acquisition of goods and services. This second generation of cybercrime was given a boost when the Internet was opened up for general commercial use and TCP/IP (Transmission Control Protocol/Internet Protocol) was accepted as the standard. Until the mid 1980s the Internet had been the preserve of the military who originally conceived it as an attack-proof communications system. It was subsequently released for governmental and academic purposes before being opened up for general usage. The Internet's massive potential for good and bad was realised following the development and commercial popularity of the graphics user interface (GUI) in the early 1990s.

The second generation of cybercrimes are mostly 'hybrid' (Wall 2001) or 'adaptive' (McQuade 2006a, 2006b). They are effectively 'traditional' crimes for which entirely new globalised opportunities have arisen. For them, the Internet has created a transnational environment with entirely new opportunities for harmful activities that are currently the subject of existing criminal or civil law. Examples of these activities include trading in sexually explicit materials, including child pornography, through interactive hardcore websites, and fraud (see Grabosky *et al.* 2001: 30; Levi 2001: 44). The increasing prevalence of deception through Internet auctions, for example, is a vivid example of this level of opportunity (see Newman and Clarke 2003: 94).

Networked environments also contribute to the circulation of criminal ideas. Newsgroups and websites circulate information about 'chipping' – how to bypass the security devices in mobile telephones or digital television decoders (Mann and Sutton 1998; Wall 2000). They also provide information on how to manufacture and distribute synthetic drugs (Schneider 2003: 374). Take away the Internet and the offending behaviour remains, but the new opportunities for offending disappear and the behaviour continues by other means, though not in such great numbers or across such a wide span. Consequently, hybrid cybercrimes are examples of the 'modernization of modernity' (Beck 1992; Finnemann 2002: 36). Furthermore, there is a common understanding and an institutional view as to which agencies are responsible for offending behaviours falling under these first two levels of opportunity. Indeed, not only are their subject matters covered by law and the public policing mandates of most countries (in so far as there tends to be clear public support for policing agencies to intervene) but any problems that arise tend to relate to matters of transjurisdictional procedure rather than substantive law. This contrasts with the third level where the responsibilities are not so clearly cut.

The third generation of (high-end) cybercrime: true cybercrimes wholly mediated by technology

The third generation of cybercrime is characterised by its distributed and automated nature, and was ushered in by the wholesale replacement of dial-in modem access with broadband at the turn of the twenty-first century. Originally, online offender–victim engagement took place via spammed emails that encouraged recipients to respond directly or to click onto websites. More recently, spam email has converged with virus attachments to further automate cybercrime. A particularly potent example of the latter is the multifunctionality of the 'blended threat', which submits control of the infected computer to the infector via a 'botnet' while also gathering and passing on personal information from the same computer. The two actions were previously considered parallel threats, but they now have one source. They are almost wholly mediated by networked technologies in that they rely less and less on social engineering. Most importantly, they illustrate a step-change in the transformation of cybercrime that is beginning to make the traditional hackers and crackers 'by and large, an amusing diversion and [no longer] an opportunity to dust down 20-year-old clichés about teenage geniuses' (Sommer 2004: 10). This is not, of course, to imply that the seriousness of 'hacking' has in any way diminished – see, for example, the Ohio children's hospital hack which exposed 230,000 files to identity thieves (Leyden 2006). Rather, it suggests that the cybercrime agenda has changed and possibly that the culture of fear that once surrounded hacking is transferring to botnets.

The true cybercrimes exist at the high end of the continuum. They are the spawn of the Internet and therefore embody all of its transformative characteristics. True cybercrimes break the temporality of the geosocial relationship between time and space by distanciating (distancing and estranging) it across a global span. Since they are solely the product of opportunities created by the Internet, they can only be perpetrated within its cyberspace and are therefore *sui generis* (of their own kind). At the far extreme of this third category are the more controversial harms, particularly the appropriation of intellectual properties which fall outside the jurisdiction and experience of the criminal justice process. See, for example 'cyberrape' (MacKinnon 1997) or the 'virtual vandalism' of virtual worlds (Williams 2003), and also the ongoing battle between the music and movie industry and downloaders (Carey and Wall 2001; Marshall 2002: 1). Spamming is a particularly good example of a true or pure cybercrime because it is now an illegal behaviour in its own right in US and EU law and many other jurisdictions. It also facilitates secondary offending by enabling offenders to engage with potential victims. Take away the Internet and spamming and the other true cybercrimes vanish.

Although not discussed here in detail because the technologies are still in the development phase, it is anticipated that a fourth generation of cybercrimes will eventually emerge from criminal opportunities generated by the ambient intelligent networks being created by the convergence of wireless, including Software Defined Radio, and networked technologies (briefly mentioned earlier) (IPTS 2003). Although ambient technologies are still in their infancy, research is already being conducted into predicting the legal, regulatory and technological safeguards that will be required in a world of ambient intelligence (see further Friedewald *et al.* 2006). By placing cybercrimes within a framework of time rather than space we can understand them as successive generations defined by different states of technological development with each transforming criminal opportunity. This approach also helps us to identify quickly the core issues and then position the subject area within criminology and its associated discourses, avoiding the confusion caused by applying the term to all crimes involving computers. For example, where digital evidence is involved, or even where computers and their components are stolen, '[t]his is misleading at best, and self-serving, at worst' (Britz 2003: 4). More specifically, the 'transformation test' mentioned earlier proves useful in categorising the different types of online offending behaviour currently being referred to as cybercrime, for example in distinguishing between those which have a familiar ring to them and those which appear to jump straight out of the pages of a science fiction novel.

Before concluding, it is important to reflect upon what are the behaviours or acts that we are calling cybercrime. Online offending, both hybrid and true cybercrimes, tend to fall into one of three basic groups of behaviour that each invoke different bodies of law and require individual legal and criminological understandings. These groups are: offending relating to the integrity of the computer system, offending assisted by computers, and offending which focuses upon the content of computers. Each also illustrates specific discourses of public debate and experiences within the criminal justice processes.

Computer integrity crimes

Computer integrity crimes assault the security of network access mechanisms. They include hacking and cracking, vandalism, spying, denial of service, the planting and use of viruses and Trojans (see further Gordon and Chess 1999). Many jurisdictions now have legislation, such as the UK's Computer Misuse Act 1990, to protect them against unauthorised access to computer material, unauthorised access with intent to commit further offences, and unauthorised modification of computer material. Computer integrity crimes can also pave the way for more serious forms of offending, as in the case of phishing. Crackers, for example, may use Trojan viruses to install 'back doors' that are later used to facilitate other crimes, possibly by spammers who have bought lists of the infected addresses.

Computer-assisted (or related) crimes

Computer-assisted crimes use networked computers to commit crimes, usually to acquire money, goods or services dishonestly. In addition to Internet frauds there are socially engineered variants such as the aforementioned 'phishing', '419' advanced-fee frauds, and the manipulation of new online sales environments, particularly auction sites. Most jurisdictions now have thefts acts and legal procedures for the recovery of lost assets, along with intellectual property laws to protect citizens against the illicit acquisition of the expression of ideas.

Computer content crimes

Computer content crimes are related to the illegal content on networked computer systems and include the trade and distribution of pornographic materials as well as the dissemination of hate crime materials. Most jurisdictions have variants of obscenity laws and laws which prohibit incitement, although their legislative strength can vary where Internet content is also protected by legislation that guarantees freedoms of speech and expression.

The above not only illustrate the development and diversity of cybercrimes, but they also provide practical demarcations for analysis. They can, for example, be used to identify the different resourcing implications for investigation and enforcement, or for choosing methodologies when designing research to further our knowledge of cybercrime.

In practice, some blurring will appear across these categories because the true cybercrimes will appear to involve combinations of two or more. Phishing is a good example of this blurring because offenders engage their victims through spam (integrity), steal their personal information (computer assisted) by deceiving victims into logging on to a bogus website (content) which they think belongs to their bank. Phishers then assault the integrity of the victim's own financial system to perpetrate a fraud. However, there is in practice usually only one principal modus operandi which is the primary motivator behind the crime. In the example of phishing it is to steal information to sell to others for profit.

Conclusions

Perceptions of cybercrime are shaped by the cultural origins of cybercrimes in social science fiction which have historically tended to blur fact with fiction. In so doing the Internet has been constructed culturally as a criminogenic virtual environment – as a crime problem in and of itself. Yet, the practical reality of the Internet is quite different. When the cultural and technological histories of cybercrime are separated, the drama of cybercrime abates and the threat profile becomes quite different. It ceases to be one of single dramatic acts, such as planes falling out of the sky, power grids failing, transport systems collapsing, and shifts to one of individuals being overwhelmed by small-impact bulk victimisations that are individually minor, but significant in their aggregate. Consequently, commentators are often shocked not to find the dramatic crimes that they expect; indeed, to this effect readers can almost detect a sense of disappointment in their writings. Yet, these mundane, but multiple, activities are still significant – but outside the routine experience of criminal justice agencies and thinking. Moreover, they are also *sui generis* true cybercrimes in terms of the informational, networked and global definitions offered earlier and elsewhere (Wall 2007). If you take away the Internet, they disappear. Consider, here, spams, phishing, intellectual property piracy and many of the online harms.

When exploring the rise of the Internet as a crime problem we have to remember that the history of cybercrime is also not static; rather it is driven by the opportunities created by the convergence of networked technologies, which continues to occur. We therefore have to take a balanced approach to understanding the Internet, especially that virtual life continues to thrive and participants prosper. The sheer volume and depth of personal, commercial and governmental transactions that take place every second of every day and which are exponentially increasing in volume are a strong indicator that the Internet is not criminogenic. The simple fact is that with each technological development comes a level of risk because a proportion of the opportunities they create will encourage criminal activity.

Note

This chapter draws upon Chapter 3 of Wall (2007) and also Wall (2008). Although the sum of the two parts is greater than their sources and there are some additions and rephrasing, appropriate sections are reproduced with permission from Taylor and Francis and Polity Press.

Further reading

There are many accounts of the history of the Internet – see for example, Janet Abbate, *Inventing the Internet* (2000) – however, there is less discussion of how the Internet became perceived as a crime problem. For a broad discussion see David Wall, *Cybercrime* (2007) and Majid Yar, *Cybercrime and Society* (2006), also see Sam McQuade, *Understanding and Managing Cybercrime* (2006b). For a specific discussion of the 'culture of fear' and cybercrime see David Wall, 'Cybercrime and the Culture of Fear' (2008). For a more general discussion about the 'culture of fear' and cultures of control see Jonathan Simon, *Governing through Crime* (2007), Frank Furedi, *Culture of Fear* (2002) and also David Garland, *The Culture of Control* (2001).

References

Abbate, J. (2000) *Inventing the Internet*. Cambridge, MA: MIT Press.

Barlow, J.P. (1996) 'A declaration of the independence of cyberspace', *John Perry Barlow Library* [online], available at: www.eff.org/Misc/Publications/John_ Perry_Barlow/ barlow_0296.declaration.txt (accessed 30 January 2008).

Baudrillard, J. (1994) *Simulacra and Simulation*. Ann Arbor: University of Michigan Press.

BBC (2009a) 'Is the UK safe from cyber attack?', *BBC News Online*, 30 April, http://news.bbc.co.uk/1/hi/technology/8025148.stm

BBC (2009b) 'Cyber "threat" to London Olympics', BBC *News Online*, 27 April, http://news.bbc.co.uk/1/hi/england/london/8019948.stm

Beck, U. (1992) *Risk Society*. London: Sage.

Bell, D. (2001) *An Introduction to Cybercultures*. London: Routledge.

Britz, M.T. (2003) *Computer Forensics and Computer Crime*. New Jersey: Pearson Prentice Hall.

Brodeur, J.-P. (1983) 'High policing and low policing: remarks about the policing of political activities', *Social Problems*, 30(5): 507–20.

Burrows, R. (1997) 'Cyberpunk as social theory', in S. Westwood and J. Williams (eds), *Imagining Cities: Scripts, Signs and Memories*. London: Routledge, 235–48.

Carey, M. and Wall, D.S. (2001) 'MP3: more beats to the byte', *International Review of Law, Computers and Technology*, 15(1): 35–58.

COE (2001) *Convention on Cybercrime*, Council of Europe, Budapest, 23 November (ETS No. 185), at http://conventions.coe.int/Treaty/EN/Treaties/Html/185.htm

COE (2003) *Additional Protocol to the Convention on Cybercrime, Concerning the Criminalisation of Acts of a Racist and Xenophobic Nature Committed through Computer Systems*, Council of Europe, Strasbourg, 28 January (ETS No. 189), at http:// conventions.coe.int/Treaty/en/Treaties/Html/189.htm

Finnemann, N. (2002) 'Perspectives on the internet and modernity: late modernity, postmodernity or modernity modernized?', in N. Brügger and H. Bødker (eds), *The Internet and Society?*, papers from Centre for Internet Research, University of Aarhus, Denmark, 29–39.

Friedewald, M., Vildjiounaite, E. and Wright, D. (eds) (2006) *The Brave New World of Ambient Intelligence: A State-Of-The-Art Review, Safeguards in a World of Ambient Intelligence (SWAMI)*, European Commission, January, at http://swami.jrc.es/pages/ documents/SWAMI_D1_Final_ 000.pdf

Furedi, F. (2002) *Culture of Fear*. London: Continuum.

Garland, D. (2001) *The Culture of Control*. Oxford: Oxford University Press.

Gibson, W. (1982) 'Burning chrome', *Omni Magazine*, July.

Gibson, W. (1984) *Neuromancer*. London: HarperCollins.

Gibson, W. (1986) *Count Zero*. London: HarperCollins.

Gibson, W. (1988) *Mona Lisa Overdrive*. London: HarperCollins.

Gordon, S. and Chess, D. (1999) 'Attitude adjustment: trojans and malware on the internet: an update', *Proceedings of the 22nd National Information Systems Security Conference*, 18–21 October, Crystal City, Virginia, at http://csrc.nist.gov/nissc/1999/ proceeding/papers/p 6.pdf

Grabosky, P.N., Smith, R.G. and Dempsey, G. (2001) *Electronic Theft, Unlawful Acquisition in Cyberspace*. Cambridge: Cambridge University Press.

Hanley, R. (2003) 'Simulacra and Simulation: Baudrillard and the Matrix', *What is the matrix*, December. Available at: http://whatisthematrix.warnerbros.com/rl_cmp/new_phil_fr_hanley2.html (accessed 30 January 2008).

Innes, M. (2004) 'Reinventing tradition? Reassurance, neighbourhood security and policing', *Criminal Justice*, 4(2): 151–71.

IPTS (2003) *Security and Privacy for the Citizen in the Post-September 11 Digital Age: A Prospective Overview*. Report by the Institute for Prospective Technological Studies, Joint Research Committee, Seville, to the European Parliament Committee on Citizens' Freedoms and Rights, Justice and Home Affairs, European Commission, July (EUR 20823 EN– ISBN: 92-894-6133-0).

Jordan, T. (1999) *Cyberpower: The Culture and Politics of Cyberspace and the Internet*. London: Routledge.

Kabay, M.E. (2002) 'Salami fraud', *Network World Security Newsletter*, 24 July, at www.networkworld.com/newsletters/sec/2002/01467137.html

Levi, M. (2001) '"Between the risk and the reality falls the shadow": evidence and urban legends in computer fraud', in D.S. Wall (ed.), *Crime and the Internet*. London: Routledge, 44–58.

Leyden, J. (2001) 'Haxploitation: the complete Reg guide to hackers in film', *The Register*, 3 August [online], available at: http://www.theregister.co.uk/ 2001/08/03/haxploitation_the_complete_reg_guide/ (accessed 30 January 2008).

Leyden, J. (2006) 'MySpace adware attack hits hard', *The Register*, 21 July, at www.theregister.co.uk/2006/07/21/myspace_adware_attack/

Leyden, J. (2007) 'Tiger team brings haxploitation to TV: Penetration testing telly show up against the Queen', *The Register*, 19 December [online], available at: http://www.theregister.co.uk/2007/12/19/tiger_team/ (accessed 30 January 2008).

MacKinnon, R. (1997) 'Virtual rape', *Journal of Computer Mediated Communication*, 2(4), at http://jcmc.indiana.edu/vol2/issue4/mackinnon.html

McQuade, S. (2006a) 'Technology-enabled crime, policing and security, *Journal of Technology Studies*, 32(1).

McQuade, S. (2006b) *Understanding and Managing Cybercrime*. Boston: Allyn and Bacon.

Mann, D. and Sutton, M. (1998) 'Netcrime: more change in the organisation of thieving', *British Journal of Criminology*, 38(2): 210–29.

Marshall, L. (2002) 'Metallica and morality: the rhetorical battleground of the Napster Wars', *Entertainment Law*, 1(1): 1.

Newman, G.R. and Clarke, R.V. (2003) *Superhighway Robbery: Preventing e-commerce crime*. Cullompton: Willan Publishing.

Orwell, G. (1990 [1949]) *Nineteen Eighty-Four*. London: Penguin.

Person, L. (1998) 'Notes toward a postcyberpunk manifesto', Nova Express, no. 16 [online], available at: http://slashdot.org/features/99/10/08/2123255.shtml

Schneider, J.L. (2003) 'Hiding in plain sight: an exploration of the illegal(?) activities of a drugs newsgroup', *The Howard Journal of Criminal Justice*, 42(4): 374–89.

Shinder, D. and Tittel, E. (2002) *Scene of the Cybercrime*. Rockland, MA: Syngress Media.

Simon, J. (2007) *Governing through Crime: How the War on Crime Transformed American Democracy and Created a Culture of Fear*. New York: Oxford University Press.

Singleton, T. (2002) 'Stop fraud cold with powerful internal controls', *Journal of Corporate Accounting and Finance*, 13(4) 29–39.

Sommer, P. (2004) 'The future for the policing of cybercrime', *Computer Fraud and Security*, 1: 8–12.

Standage, T. (1998) *The Victorian Internet: The Remarkable Story of the Telegraph and the Nineteenth Century's Online Pioneers.* London: Phoenix.

Stephenson, N. (1992) *Snowcrash.* London: ROC/Penguin.

Sterling, B. (1994) *The Hacker Crackdown: Law and Disorder on the Electronic Frontier.* London: Penguin.

Symantec (2009) *Internet Security Threat Report Trends for 2008*, Volume XIV, Symantec, April. http://eval.symantec.com/mktginfo/enterprise/white_papers/b-whitepaper_internet_security_threat_report_xiv_04-2009.en-us.pdf

Taipale, K. (2006) 'Why can't we all get along: how technology, security, and privacy can coexist in the digital age', in J. Balkin, J. Grimmelmann, E. Katz, N. Kozlovski, S. Wagman and T. Zarsky (eds), *Cybercrime: Digital Cops in a Networked Environment.* New York: New York University Press, 151–83.

Toffler, A. (1970) *Future Shock.* New York: Bantam Books.

Trevor-Roper, H. (1972) *The Last Days of Hitler.* London: Pan Books.

Wall, D.S. (2000) 'The theft of electronic services: telecommunications and teleservices', Essay 1 on the CD-ROM annex to DTI, *Turning the Corner.* London: Department of Trade and Industry.

Wall, D.S. (2001) 'Maintaining order and law on the internet', in D.S. Wall (ed.), *Crime and the Internet.* London: Routledge, 1–17.

Wall, D.S. (2007) *Cybercrime: The transformation of crime in the information age.* Cambridge: Polity Press.

Wall, D.S. (2008) 'Cybercrime and the Culture of Fear: social science fiction and the production of knowledge about cybercrime', *Information, Communications and Society,* 11(6): 861–84.

Williams, M. (2003) *Virtually criminal: Deviance, harm and regulation within an online community*, PhD thesis, University of Cardiff, UK.

Yar, M. (2006) *Cybercrime and Society.* London: Sage.

Chapter 6

Public perceptions and public opinion about Internet crime

Majid Yar

Introduction

This chapter explores public perceptions and public opinion about Internet crime. Such views and perceptions are important for a number of reasons. Firstly, it has been argued that in liberal democratic states public opinion plays an important role in shaping public policy. Therefore, public opinion about the Internet and the crime threats it brings can play a crucial role in influencing how legislators and policymakers choose to address Internet crime problems, and indeed what such actors come to understand as 'the crime problem' when it comes to online environments. Secondly, shared opinion and perceptions can exercise a decisive influence over people's online behaviour. For example, if the Internet comes to be associated with particular dangers and risks (such as financial fraud or child sex exploitation) this may disincline individual Internet users from engaging in certain online practices (such as Internet banking or permitting children to fully access the Internet). As Lee (2007) notes, the fear of crime has proven to be a seemingly intractable feature of the contemporary cultural landscape in many Western societies, and has exerted a decisive influence over both policy processes as well as individual and collective behaviour. *In extremis*, 'distorted' perceptions or estimations about Internet predation may result in full-blown 'moral panics' in which avoidance behaviour stands out of all proportion to the likelihood of criminal victimisation. Therefore, developing an adequate understanding of how and why Internet crime policies emerge, and how patterns of online behaviour take shape, requires concerted attention to the role played by public perceptions and public opinion about Internet crime issues.

The relationship between public opinion and public policy

As Page and Shapiro (1983) note, the responsiveness of government policy to public opinion on particular issues has been a bone of contention among political scientists and democratic theorists for many years. The relationship between policy and opinion can be understood in a number of potentially incompatible ways. Some analysts postulate a high degree of responsiveness among policy actors to public opinion, whether out of a principled commitment to democratic government or a pragmatic self-interest in satisfying voters' demands (see for example Erikson 1976). Page and Shapiro examined the congruence between public opinion and policy positions in the US over a 50-year period, and concluded that public opinion 'is often a proximate cause of policy' (*ibid*). The extent of this responsiveness may, however, vary according to a range of factors; it may be more likely that policymakers will follow public cues if the matter at hand is perceived by the public to be of high salience, relevance or importance, and/or if there is a clear consensus or majority opinion favouring a particular policy response. Conversely, other analysts explain any apparent congruence between policy and public opinion by suggesting that it is policy and policymakers who actually shape public opinion, not the other way round. This may be affected either through political leadership (wherein policymakers educate and inform citizens about appropriate responses to particular problems), or through misinformation and manipulation so as to foster public acceptance of particular predetermined policy preferences (on the former, see Key 1961; for the latter position see Miliband 1980). A further interpretation of the relationship suggests that policy-makers are only marginally responsive to public opinions and concerns, as the policy process is inevitably captured by a range of powerful interest groups and lobbies who have the resources and influence to shape policy to their own liking, largely excluding the preferences of the wider public (Olson 1974; also discussion in Lowery and Brasher 2003). However, as Page and Shapiro (1983: 175) suggest, these different conjunctions are not necessarily mutually exclusive, and the relative influence of public opinion on policy may vary over time and across different issues. As we shall see below, this complexity becomes readily apparent when we look at Internet crime issues.

We can identify a number of recent issues where public opinion appears to have promoted decisive legal, regulatory and law-enforcement changes with respect to Internet crime problems. For example, public views about threats to child safety and the circulation of child pornography on the Internet may have been seen as decisive drivers of new legislative initiatives that have further criminalised possession and transmission of obscene representations, and have placed new obligations upon Internet Service Providers (ISPs) to monitor and remove offending content (Yar 2006a: 113–5). This would be an example of what Goode and Ben-Yehuda (1994) identify as a 'grass-roots' imperative towards political innovation, wherein widely shared and relatively spontaneously occurring public sentiment drives policy changes. Yet an adequate understanding of this process is further complicated by the need to appreciate how public opinion itself comes to take shape. Instead of seeing it as a form of 'economic rationality' in which individual preferences can be aggregated up, we must be sensitive to the ways in which mass-mediated reporting of high-profile cases plays a decisive role in concretising shared beliefs and concerns about crime problems (a salient case in point would be the public campaign for a so-called 'Sarah's Law' following the abduction and murder of eight-year-old Sarah Payne by Roy Whiting, a convicted child sex offender). This process can be seen to conform to the classic analysis of 'moral panics' developed by Cohen (1972), wherein public opinion is shaped through media reportage, which then creates a series of demands for action to which policymakers must not only respond, but be *seen* to respond in order to allay public concerns.

With respect to other Internet crime issues, legislative, policy and enforcement initiatives appear to have little support in public opinion, and may even run counter to public views and preferences on the matter. In such cases, we can more clearly see the ways in which lobbying by special interest groups can drive policy changes. A notable recent instance is that related to Internet 'piracy', the unauthorised online sharing of copyrighted content such as motion pictures, musical recordings, movies and computer software. Yar (2005) notes that recent years have seen concerted policy initiatives to criminalise such copyright violations, and argues that these are in significant part the outcome of aggressive lobbying from copyright-holders who have pursued a concerted campaign to persuade legislators and law enforcers that such offences need to be prioritised. Lobbying initiatives have been backed-up by industry-funded research that suggests massive financial losses accruing from 'piracy' activity, and attempts to link copyright offences to 'terrorism' and 'organised crime'. Yet few members of the broader public appear to attach any great weight of concern to such offending, and indeed many Internet users are actively opposed to legal restrictions on what they see as a legitimate form of 'culture sharing' (Yar 2006b; also Yar 2008).

The above examples offer some insight into the variable role that public opinion can play in policy formulation, sometimes working as a driver of change, while at other times being largely marginalised or ignored in favour of other more sectional social interests.

Perceptions, fears and behaviour in relation to crime

One of the most significant issues related to public perceptions of crime concerns the ways in which fear of crime, and associated understanding of victimisation risks, come to affect individuals and impact upon their subsequent social behaviour. Despite conceptual and methodological questions about measures of 'fear of crime' (Holloway and Jefferson 2000; Gray *et al.* 2008), it is clear that levels of anxiety about crime and victimisation remain high across Western societies (Shaftoe 2004). It would appear that what is commonly referred to as 'fear of crime' is in fact an amalgam of perceptions, including judgements about the levels of crime in society as a whole, combined with estimations about one's own vulnerability which may variously be shaped by personal experiences of victimisation, local events, hearsay and media coverage. Fear of crime and victimisation is also clearly socially variegated, with levels of reported anxiety differing according to variables such as gender (women express greater levels of fear than men), age (older people feel themselves more vulnerable than younger people), and ethnicity (minority groups feel themselves less safe than the majority) (Parker *et al*. 1993; Smith and Torstensson 1997; Tulloch 2000).

One of the most important general findings of such research is that fear of crime often exceeds any objective measure of likely victimisation. In other words, public perceptions of risk are largely out of proportion to the actual chances of being a victim of any given form of criminal predation. Attempts to explain this disjunction have been manifold. One approach is to recuperate the claims of moral panic perspectives, and argue that it is sensationalised media coverage that tends to amplify public fears about crime. Alternatively, fear of crime has been linked to broader sociological debates about social change, stressing the impact of individualisation and the emergence of a 'risk society' upon people's sense of 'ontological security' (Giddens 1991a, 1991b; Beck 1992). On this view, a heightened sense of contingency, awareness of the unintended consequences of social action, and the loss of traditional moorings in community and shared identity, combine to create a subjective experience of the world as uncertain and threatening (Loader and Sparks 2002; Bauman 2005). Furedi (1997) goes so far as to suggest that we now inhabit a 'culture of fear' in which loss of optimism and a belief in our capacity to change the world for the better has given way to a crippling sense of vulnerability. This manifests itself in our fear of hidden and sometimes imagined dangers, ranging from climate change, through food safety, to 'stranger danger' and perpetual anxieties about crime. We can certainly point to the ways in which perceptions and fears about Internet crime in fact inhabit a much longer-standing cultural ambivalence in relation to technological change. Yar (2006a: 25–7) explores the ways in which fantastical and exaggerated fears have recurrently coalesced around unfamiliar technological advances. Starting with Mary Shelley's *Frankenstein*, our culture has frequently been drawn to an anticipation of catastrophic consequences as technology threatens to unleash unanticipated harms. Since the 1970s, the development of computer technology has frequently featured in the dystopian imaginings of popular culture, with 'deranged' electronic minds pursuing a relentless programme of victimisation and even outright annihilation against their human creators (see, for example, movies such as *Demon Seed* (1977), *War Games* (1983), and *The Terminator* (1984)). More recent cultural representations have paralleled the development of the Internet, with a range of corresponding fears being refracted through popular narratives, including identity theft (*The Net* (1995)), state-sponsored surveillance (*Enemy of the State* (1998)), and hacking (*Hackers* (1995), *Takedown* (2000)). While the precise connections between popular cultural representation and public sensibilities are difficult to trace, there is little doubt that such mediated images and narratives do in fact shape the frames through which the public at large view crime problems and assess their relevance (Sparks 1992; Reiner *et al*. 2000; Tzanelli *et al*. 2005).

A second salient issue is the relationship between perceptions of crime problems and subsequent patterns of everyday behaviour. It has long been argued by those studying fear of crime that anxieties and expectations about victimisation (whether 'objectively' warranted or not) shape social behaviour in significant ways. Numerous studies have indicated that fear of victimisation correlates closely with a range of 'avoidance behaviours', as individuals attempt to insulate themselves from perceived threats (Stanko 2000). For example, Roman and Chalfin (2007) found that perceived levels of violence and 'gang activity' in neighbourhoods corresponded closely with avoidance of walking outdoors. Similarly, Furedi (2001) notes how concern over violent and sexual predation upon children has created a situation in which parents increasingly isolate their offspring from public places, curtailing children's unsupervised presence on the street or in other public areas. Such behavioural responses can be seen as 'maladaptive', insofar as they compel people to curtail their legitimate public activities and place unwelcome constraints upon social interaction. We will consider below whether or to what extent such avoidance behaviours, fuelled by perceptions of crime threats, shape people's engagements in the virtual environment of the Internet. However, we must first note a second kind of behavioural response to fear of victimisation, namely those pre-emptive or preventive measures that people may take to secure themselves against crime threats. A voluminous literature now exists that charts the ways in which a whole array of private security strategies has emerged in order to deflect potential criminal victimisation (Shearing and Stenning 1981; Johnston 1992; Wood and Shearing 2006). These can include such familiar technological measures as car alarms, immobilisers, RFID (Radio Frequency Identification) tagging of property, window locks, house alarms, CCTV systems, as well as hiring of private security patrols, neighbourhood watch schemes, and comprehensive insurance schemes. Again, we shall explore below the extent to which the virtual equivalents of such measures are apparent in connection with public concerns around Internet crime and victimisation. However, in our search for indicators of risk awareness, fear or anxiety about the online environment, we should not lose focus of the potentially positive, enabling, empowering and otherwise life-enhancing opportunities that the Internet may present for many users; such perceived benefits will shape patterns of use and engagement with the medium as much as fears and concerns may act as a deterrent, and may indeed go some considerable way to offsetting the otherwise inhibitory effects that such fears may produce.

Public perceptions and concerns about Internet crime: patterns and trends

In comparison with the plethora of studies about public perceptions of 'terrestrial' crime problems, research findings on Internet crime are relatively scant. However, there have been undertaken to date a number of studies, across various countries, examining how users (and non-users) perceive the Internet environment, how they construct the risks associated with online interaction, and how these affect their patterns of engagement with the medium. Below we shall consider what is currently known about these issues.

One useful starting point for this discussion is to examine the ways in which perceptions about online risk may shape people's engagement with the medium; for example, act as a possible deterrent to Internet use, in whole or in part. Dutton and Helsper (2007) have produced one of the most wide-ranging and systematic surveys of Internet usage trends and patterns in the UK, and its findings offer some interesting insights into the relationship between usage and risk/safety perceptions. Inevitably, a wide range of social, economic and other factors differentiated between Internet users and non-users, including: gender (men were more likely to be users than women); age (younger people were more likely to be users than older individuals); education (high levels of educational attainment correlated positively with Internet usage); and income (a positive correlation was apparent between use and income levels). Among non-users and ex-users of the Internet, salient factors for non-use included cost, perceived lack of skills, perceived lack of time, or lack of perceived usefulness (*ibid*: 4). However, among ex-users (those who have used the Internet in the past but no longer do so), 22 per cent of men and 15 per cent of women cited 'bad experiences with Spam or viruses' as a reason for their having abandoned the Internet (*ibid*: 16). Among those having had 'bad experiences' on the Internet, 2 per cent reported theft of credit card details; 7 per cent reported having received abusive or obscene emails from people they know; 12 per cent received abusive or obscene emails from strangers; 17 per cent had been contacted by someone requesting their banking details; and 34 per cent had received a virus onto their computer (*ibid*: 35). Moreover, among non-users there were high levels of reported concern about issues such as privacy; for example, 88 per cent of these respondents agreed with the statement that 'Personal information is being kept somewhere without me knowing'; 81 per cent concurred with the claim that 'People who go on the Internet put their privacy at risk'; and 82 per cent agreed that 'The present use of computers is a threat to personal privacy' (*ibid*: 30). These findings suggest that both perceptions of risks associated with Internet use, and actual negative experience of victimisation in various forms, plays a significant role in engagement with the Internet, and for at least some people acts as a deterrent to either starting usage or continuing usage over time. Therefore, we can reasonably hypothesise that the kinds of risk-related 'avoidance behaviours' apparent in terrestrial settings are also likely to be apparent in their virtual counterparts.

While the above data gives us a general indication of links between opinion, risk perceptions, negative experiences and usage/non-usage, the *types* of concerns articulated, and the intensity of concern that they evoke, will vary according to different forms of Internet-based activity, and upon who the users are. For example, Liao and Cheung examined consumer attitudes to both e-shopping (2001) and e-banking (2002). Using data from Singapore, they found that the security of online transactions was one of the salient factors that shaped consumer willingness to engage in online shopping, with perceived transaction risk exercising a statistically significant negative effect on willingness to e-shop (other, non-risk-related factors included price, perceived vendor quality, as well as levels of IT education) (Liao and Cheung 2001: 302). In their corresponding study of consumer attitudes to e-banking (2002), Liao and Cheung found a similar pattern, with concerns about security apparent as one of the five significant factors affecting willingness to move to online banking and financial services (the others being accuracy, network speed, user-friendliness, and user-involvement). Liao and Cheung's findings are also corroborated by Teo's (2002) study of attitudes towards online shopping in Singapore; he found that some 40 per cent of respondents expressed concern about potential financial losses that might be incurred by shopping online (Teo 2002: 264). Similar findings were reported in the UK context in a study of consumers and e-retailing commissioned by the Government's Office of Fair Trading (OFT). The study found that one of the most significant barriers to online shopping reported by users (92 per cent) was the concern about the security of credit card data and the associated risk of fraud (OFT 2007a: 43). Interestingly, the study also found that such security fears were highest among those who had little or no previous experience of online shopping, and that in such cases perceptions were largely shaped by negative press reports and media coverage of online fraud, 'identity theft' and the like (OFT 2007b: 9). This finding gives added credence to the point made earlier, that popular cultural discourses decisively frame and shape how publics orient themselves to technology as a whole, and risks in particular. More broadly, research findings such as those discussed above support the view that perceptions of financial risk can and will play a significant role in inhibiting take-up of opportunities for online consumption of goods and services, something that clearly needs to be addressed if the promised benefits of e-commerce are to be fully realised. It is precisely for this reason that policymakers tasked with developing e-commerce have made concerted calls for further strengthening of data security (for example through use of sophisticated encryption technologies) in order to address concerns expressed by Internet users (DTI 2004). As Luo (2002) suggests, the institutionalisation of mechanisms of trust through technologies such as electronic certification can and do play a crucial role in allaying privacy concerns and reducing risk perceptions among Internet users.

However, the public concern over issues such as privacy, information security and financial fraud are massively eclipsed by that around moral issues, especially related to the availability of obscene, pornographic, violent or otherwise 'offensive' content. Ever since the early years of the Internet's development, the circulation of sexually explicit and pornographic content has been a consistent presence. In the late 1970s and early 1980s, programmers (mostly young men in university science, engineering and computing departments) were zealously developing software enabling such images to be transmitted, recomposed and viewed through Usenet systems. By 1996, of the 10 most popular Usenet groups, five were sexually oriented, and one (alt. sex.net) attracted some 500,000 readers every day (Lane 2001: 66–7). However, it was with the massive expansion of the Internet resulting from the surge in home computing in the mid 1990s that Internet pornography really took off. There are now estimated to be some 4.2 million pornographic websites (12 per cent of all Internet sites), containing 372 million pornographic pages. There are 68 million search engine requests for pornographic material every day, making up 25 per cent of the total searches. One and a half million downloads of pornographic material are performed every month using peer-to-peer (P2P) file-sharing networks; 72 million people visit pornographic websites each year, 72 per cent of whom are male and 28 per cent female. The commercial sector of Internet pornography is conservatively estimated to be worth $2.5 billion per annum (IFR 2004).

Public concerns about such material on the Internet vary widely, focusing variously upon a generalised concern about the moral consequences of explicit pornography; concerns about the linking of pornography and violence in Internet representations, as in 'extreme' depictions of sadomasochistic sex, rape and other forms of violent sex; and perhaps most prominently the entrenched worry that children surfing the Internet will be unwittingly exposed to pornography. We can consider these various dimensions of public perceptions in turn.

In a relatively early study (produced for the US Child Online Protection Act Commission), Zimmer and Hunter (2000) found that the actual likelihood of *unintentionally* accessing pornographic content online was significantly lower than that suggested by mass media reportage and subsequently echoed in public opinion. In other words, public perceptions of the 'risk' of inadvertent (as opposed to deliberate) exposure were disproportionate to the actual frequency of such incidents. Such patterns reinforce the point, noted earlier, that public concerns may be led not by any balanced estimation of probabilities but rather by an inchoate sense of threats shaped by media coverage. More recently, the focus of concern has moved on from pornographic content per se, to specific crime incidents linked to consumption of violent pornography online. For example, massive press coverage was ignited in the UK following the sexual assault and murder of Jane Longhurst, a 31-year-old schoolteacher at the hands of Graham Coutts. At Coutts' trial a concerted link was made between the murder and his consumption of violent pornography online, including simulated strangulation, rape and necrophilia. The media outcry following Coutts' conviction, combined with a campaign led by the victim's mother, resulted in a petition with some 50,000 signatories being submitted to government, calling for the banning of 'extreme internet sites promoting violence against women in the name of sexual gratification'. This led ultimately to legislation criminalising the possession of 'violent pornography', making such possession punishable by up to three years' imprisonment. What is significant here when considering the issue of public perceptions and concerns about Internet crime is that high-profile incidents of this kind can function as 'signal crimes'. Such crimes, argues Innes (2004), are constructed through media reportage and have important effects upon public perceptions of crime risks and the related sense of vulnerability:

> The manufacture of a signal crime via mass mediated communication involves a crime incident being constructed by journalists through their use of particular representational and rhetorical techniques, and interpreted by audiences, as an index of the state of society and social order. Thus from the points of view of audience members, signal crimes are construed as 'warning signals' about the levels and distribution of criminogenic risks and may, in the right set of circumstances, result in demands for more, or better, forms of social control. (2004: 16–17)

Thus we can argue that in the case of the Longhurst murder, a kind of 'symbiotic' relationship exists whereby the incident, its reporting, and public perceptions of risk combine to create pressure for legal and regulatory change (see also Innes 2003 and Wykes, this volume). Moreover, it can induce a more generalised shift in public concerns such that people come to perceive a particular form of criminal predation as a significant risk to their own or others' safety where no such perception had existed before.

The kind of dynamic of public sensitivity outlined above has been particularly apparent in relation to children's online safety. From the mid 1990s onwards, extensive media and political scrutiny has been directed towards the risk of children being exposed to 'unsuitable', adult-oriented material on the Internet. Studies of parental attitudes towards the Internet repeatedly reveal children's unsupervised online activities as one of the issues eliciting the greatest concern. A study in the Republic of Ireland found that 56 per cent of parents felt that their children knew more about the Internet than they did themselves, and 81 per cent felt that parents were unable to sufficiently monitor or control their children's Internet usage because of this 'knowledge gap' (Amarach Consulting 2001: 2). When asked what they considered to be the main downside of children having Internet access, 44 per cent identified access to pornography as the greatest problem; 18 per cent cited 'access to unsuitable material/information'; and a further 5 per cent cited 'access to violent/hate material' (*ibid*: 3). These findings were echoed by a study commissioned for the Australian Government (NetAlert 2007), which found that the top concern among parents about their children's Internet use was 'exposure to pornography' (55 per cent of respondents), and for a further 11 per cent that the greatest perceived problem was 'exposure to violent content/death/victims of violence'. Similar patterns and trends are apparent from survey research conducted in the United States, Canada and the UK (for a synoptic overview of such findings, see Livingstone 2003). Risk perceptions of this kind extend beyond parents and the use of the Internet by children in domestic settings. For example, Wishart (2002) in a study of Internet safety education in English schools found that teachers' perceptions of child-related risks echo those most commonly cited by parents, namely that children might be exposed to pornographic or other offensive content while using the Internet in a classroom setting.

A further issue of concern that has come to the fore in recent years, connected to that above, concerns the risks to children's online safety represented by violent sexual predators. The spectre of the Internet paedophile has become something of an *idée fixe* of late. In the aforementioned studies of parental concerns, the threat of paedophiles having contact with children via online communication also featured significantly. For example, in the Ireland study cited above, 12 per cent of respondents expressed concerns about children's exposure to paedophiles (Amarach 2001: 4); Likewise, the Australian NetAlert study found that 41 per cent of parents saw the prospect of their children 'communicating online with strangers' as a serious concern. Again, it may be likely that there is considerable overestimation in public opinion about the prevalence of such risks to children. Concerns are repeatedly stoked by popular (and sometimes sensationalist) news stories in mainstream press coverage. For example, recent newspaper headlines from the UK have included the likes of: 'How Paedophiles Prey on MySpace Children' (*Daily Mail* 2006); 'Millions of Girls using Facebook, Bebo and MySpace "at Risk" From Paedophiles and

Bullies' (*This Is London* 2008); and 'One In Four Teens "At Risk" On Facebook' (*Daily Telegraph*, 2008a). While there is evidence that children *are* targeted by sexual predators using online social networking sites, chat rooms and email (O'Connell 2003; Powell 2007), the public perception that such risks are near-ubiquitous would appear to be a gross exaggeration.

Interestingly, children themselves appear to have thoroughly internalised the discourse on Internet paedophilia, and echo those perceptions voiced by their parents and in the wider sphere of media and public discourse. For example, a study of young females' Internet usage (Roban 2002), found that 36 per cent of 13–18-year-olds in the USA thought that their parents' greatest concern was that they 'might be meeting strangers who are perverts' (*ibid*: 11). It has been argued that on this issue we can see a 'percolation of fear' (Yar 2006a: 135) that increasingly grips children and adults alike. This becomes clear when we consider the responses of the children interviewed by Burn and Willett (2003: 10–11) as part of an evaluation of a child-oriented Internet-risk education campaign called Educanet. A group of 11-year-old girls have the following to say about paedophiles and the Internet:

> *Becky*: Most people are perverts, innit [local expression – 'isn't it'].
> *Claire*: You know, like on the Internet.
> *Daniella*: There's millions.

This generalised sense of risk permeating public sensibilities can have a number of significant consequences. For example, it has exerted a continuing pressure on legislators and lawmakers, as well as online service providers (like ISPs and social networking sites), to tighten control over access to and use of online services. For example, in April 2008 the social networking site MySpace barred 29,000 American sex offenders from using its sites, on the assumption that any individual with a conviction for a sexual offence was likely using the site to contact or track children for purposes of sexual gratification (*Daily Telegraph* 2008b). On the legislative front, public opinion has driven pressures for new laws that create specific offences such as that of 'chat room grooming' of minors for purposes of sexual gratification, despite concerns about the implementation of such laws (Yar 2006a: 133). More broadly, some critics have expressed concerns that the sense of pervasive danger for children online may unnecessarily curtail their ability and willingness to make full use of new media, and instance the kinds of avoidance behaviour already discussed.

Thus far, we have seen a common pattern across public opinion and perceptions about Internet crime issues, viz. that, with varying degrees of intensity and extensiveness, the public expresses concerns about the risks and dangers of various kinds of online harms. However, we must also note here that, in respect of some kinds of Internet-based offences, public opinion varies from ambivalence, through indifference, to actual approval. Two such issues can be noted here. Firstly, there is the area of computer hacking. Studies of public attitudes suggest that among a significant portion of the population, especially the young, hackers and their activities are viewed in a rather positive light (Dowland *et al.* 1999: 720; Voiskounsky *et al.* 2000: 69–76). This may be attributed to the ways in which broader popular cultural discourses valorise hacking activity as virtuosity or an act of resistance in the face of power (Yar 2006a: 26–7). Thus, in a rather contradictory register, the hacker appears as 'a schizophrenic blend of dangerous criminal and geeky Robin Hood' (Hawn 1996, cited in Taylor 1999: xii). Secondly, we must note the issue of 'piracy' or online intellectual property crime. Many Internet users view unauthorised downloading of movies, music and software as morally acceptable, convenient, and a valuable opportunity for saving on the costs of media consumption (Bryce and Rutter 2005). A recent US survey of professional workers reveals that only 26 per cent oppose software piracy 'in principle' (IPSOS 2004). A UK-based poll in 2004, conducted on behalf of the Business Software Alliance, found that 44 per cent of 18–29-year-olds owned pirated intellectual property; the figure for the 30–50-year-age group was 28 per cent, and 17 per cent for the over 50s. The survey further found that 'there is little stigma to owning counterfeit goods' (Thomson 2004). A 2004 poll in the US found that 'more than half of all 8–18-year-olds have downloaded music, a third have downloaded games and nearly a quarter have downloaded software illegally from the Internet' (Snyder 2004: 1). A number of studies worldwide have found high levels of 'softlifting' (downloaded copyrighted software from the Internet) among college students and little weight attached to the 'legal and moral objections' (see discussion in Kini *et al.* 2003: 63–4). A 2004 survey of young people in Canada found that 47 per cent of 12–21-year-olds intended to 'download music, video or software from the Internet over the next six months' (Jedwab 2004: 1). It further found that 70 per cent of respondents 'deemed [it] acceptable to download music, video or software from the Internet' (*ibid.*). Thus we see how public views around Internet offending are not straightforward, and are typically determined by a wide range of contextual and issue-specific variables.

Behavioural responses in light of public concerns

I have repeatedly noted that public opinions and perceptions about Internet crime threats can not only shape public policy, but also have significant impacts upon people's subsequent online behaviour. We have already seen that avoidance of the medium is one possible response to both perceptions of risk and previous 'bad experiences' in the online environment. Additionally, concerns of this kind can stimulate a range of anticipatory strategies intended the help protect users from potential criminal predation. Some of these responses will be considered below.

In line with broader developments promoting anticipatory insurance or risk reduction in relation to crime, Internet use has become embedded within a web of technological, economic and social interventions aimed at protecting individuals and organisations from the possibility of criminal victimisation (instances of what Lucia Zedner (2007) calls the logic of 'pre-crime'). For example, there now exists a multi-billion-dollar industry providing computer software for detecting and eradicating viruses, and for thwarting attempts at 'phishing', keystroke logging, data theft from networked computers, and other forms of 'intrusion detection'. The imperative to protect against such attack has, ironically, left users more not less vulnerable to computer crimes. For example, the US Federal Trade Commission moved recently to shut down so-called 'scareware' websites – such sites offer fraudulent 'scans' of users' computers and claim to have detected (non-existent) viruses and other vulnerabilities, and use this to then sell consumers useless software against these supposed threats. More than 1 million US Internet users are thought to have been defrauded in this way, at a cost of some $40–$60 million (BBC 2008). In anticipation of various forms of fraud and identity theft, secure systems for encrypting financial and personal details have been developed and are routinely employed by online sites dedicated to e-shopping, e-banking and the like. Consumers' concerns about fraud have also encouraged financial services providers to offer bespoke 'identity theft insurance' when using credit and debit cards online. Parents' fears about their children's potential exposure to adult-oriented, sexually explicit and violent content has stimulated the development and consumption of a wide range of Internet-filtering programs that purport to block access to 'unsuitable' online content. Organisations (in both public and private sectors) are now routinely encouraged to commission computer security companies to perform security audits to test the robustness of preventive countermeasures and to train staff and managers in 'best practice' for safeguarding their systems and data. The anticipation of financial losses to intellectual property rights violations through 'piracy' has stimulated the development of various tools for 'digital rights management', for example encoding of data on DVDs that prevents their being digitally copied, in an attempt to prevent them from being made available for file-sharing and downloading. Finally, the (real and perceived) threat of online predation has stimulated a thriving community of Internet-based voluntary organisations that engage in informal policing of the Internet, especially with respect to monitoring paedophile activity and the circulation of child pornography. Thus we see that the dialectical interplay between attitudes and actions plays a crucial role in shaping the ways in which the medium of the Internet is configured, used and regulated.

Conclusions

This chapter has attempted to map out public attitudes, perceptions and concerns in relation to Internet crime. It is apparent that members of the public exhibit, in varying degrees, significant worries about the risks of online predation, especially as they concern matters of child protection and financial victimisation. Drawing on the broader literature on the linkages between public opinion and policy formation, I have suggested that public attitudes can and do shape policy initiatives. However, the extent to which this causal relationship prevails will itself be shaped by a wide range of other factors, including: the intensity of public opinion about the particular crime problem at hand; the degree to which there is a broad consensus about the perceived problem; the position on the issue taken by powerful social constituencies and actors; and the significance allocated to the issue by legislators and law enforcers in light of competing demands and priorities. I have also suggested that public attitudes have the power to shape people's patterns of Internet usage, with some actors being inclined towards avoidance behaviour in light of crime risks, and others adopting a range of possible precautionary crime prevention measures when using the Internet. However, the ways in which such responses take shape will also vary from one issue to another, and more specific studies are required in order to better apprehend the behavioural consequences of views about Internet crime.

Further reading

There is something of a dearth of current academic literature dealing with the nature and implications of public opinion about the Internet. However, some of the empirical surveys of public attitudes cited within this chapter make for useful and insightful reading. See, for example, Dowland *et al.*'s 'Computer Crime and Abuse: A Survey of Public Attitudes and Awareness' (1999), *Computers and Security*, 18(8): 715–26; Jo Bryce and Jason Rutter's *Fake Nation: A Study into an Everyday Crime* (2005); and Dutton and Helsper's *The Internet in Britain 2007* (2007). On the general debate about public fear of crime readers may wish to consult Murray Lee's *Inventing Fear of Crime: Criminology and the Politics of Fear* (2007). On the 'culture of fear' around Internet-based crime threats see David S. Wall, 'Cybercrime and the Culture of Fear: social science fiction and the production of knowledge about cybercrime' (2008). On the ways in which public opinion shapes criminal justice policies, see Wood and Gannon (eds) (2008) *Public Opinion and Criminal Justice* (although it is worth noting that cybercrime issues fail to get a single mention in this book – indicative, alas, of the way in which Internet crime issues continue to be marginalised in 'mainstream' criminological discussion, even where these matters are clearly of relevance and importance).

References

Amarach Consulting (2001) 'Research of Internet Downside Issues: August 2001', report for the Irish Internet Advisory Board, at: http://www.ispai.ie/docs%5Camarach.pdf

Bauman, Z. (2005) *Liquid Life*. Cambridge and Malden MA: Polity Press.

BBC News (2008) 'US Shuts Down "Scareware' Sellers"'. Friday, 12 December, at: http://news.bbc.co.uk/1/hi/technology/7779223.stm

Beck, U. (1992) *Risk Society: Towards a New Modernity*. London: Sage.

Bryce, J. and Rutter, J. (2005) 'Fake Nation: A Study into an Everyday Crime', report for the Organised Crime Task Force – Northern Ireland Office, online at: http://digiplay.info/files/FakeNation.pdf

Burn, A. and Willett, R. (2003) '"What Exactly is a Paedophile?": Children Talking About Internet Risk', at http://www.ccsonline.org.uk/mediacentre/Research_Projects/Burn_Willett.pdf

Cohen, S. (1972) *Folk Devils and Moral Panics*. London: MacGibbon and Kee.

Daily Mail (2006) 'How Paedophiles Prey on MySpace Children', 21 July, at http://www.dailymail.co.uk/femail/article-397026/How-paedophiles-prey-MySpace-children.html

Daily Telegraph (2008a) 'One In Four Teens "At Risk" On Facebook', 7 January, at http://www.telegraph.co.uk/news/uknews/1574813/One-in-four-teens-at-risk-on-Facebook.htm

Daily Telegraph (2008b) 'MySpace Bars 29,000 Sex Offenders', 19 April, at: http://www.telegraph.co.uk/news/uknews/1558560/MySpace-bars-29000-sex-offenders.html

Dowland, P., Furnell, S., Illingworth, H. and Reynolds, P. (1999) 'Computer Crime and Abuse: A Survey of Public Attitudes and Awareness', *Computers and Security*, 18(8): 715–26.

DTI (Department of Trade and Industry) (2004) *Information Security: Hard Facts*. London: DTI.

Dutton, W.H. and Helsper, E.J. (2007) *The Internet in Britain 2007*. Oxford: Oxford Internet Institute.

Erikson, R.S. (1976) 'The Relationship between Public Opinion and State Policy: A New Look Based on Some Forgotten Data', *American Journal of Political Science*, 20(1): 25–36.

Furedi, F. (1997) *Culture of Fear: Risk-taking and the Morality of Low Expectation*. London: Continuum Publishing.

Furedi, F. (2001) *Paranoid Parenting*. London: Allen Lane.

Giddens, A. (1991a) *The Consequences of Modernity*. Cambridge: Polity Press.

Giddens, A. (1991b) *Modernity and Self-Identity: Self and Society in the Late Modern Age*. Cambridge: Polity Press.

Goode, E. and Ben-Yehuda, N. (1994) *Moral Panics: The Social Construction of Deviance*. Oxford: Blackwell.

Gray, E., Jackson, J. and Farrall, S. (2008) 'Reassessing the Fear of Crime', *European Journal of Criminology*, 5(3): 363–80.

Holloway, W. and Jefferson, T. (2000) 'The Role of Anxiety in Fear of Crime in Everyday Life', in T. Hope and R. Sparks (eds), *Crime, Risk and Insecurity: Law and Order in Everyday Life*. London: Routledge.

IFR (Internet Filter Review) (2004) 'Internet Pornography Statistics', at http://internet-filter-review.toptenreviews.com/internet-pornography-statistics.html

Innes, M. (2003) 'Signal crimes: media, murder investigations and constructing collective memories', in P. Mason (ed.), *Criminal Visions: Media Representations of Crime and Justice*. Cullompton: Willan Publishing.

Innes, M. (2004) 'Crime as Signal, Crime as Memory', *Journal for Crime, Conflict and the Media*, 1(2): 15–22.

IPSOS (2004) 'Online software piracy poll', online at: http://www.ipsos-na.com/news/pressrelease.cfm?id_2452

Jedwab, J. (2004) 'The lowdown on music downloading in Canada: youth regard Internet downloading of music, video and software as acceptable: only threat of legal action is effective deterrent', online at: http://www.acs-aec.ca/Polls/18-10-2004-1.pdf

Johnston, L. (1992) *The Rebirth of Private Policing*. London: Routledge.

Key, V.O. (1961) *Public Opinion and American Democracy*. New York: Alfred Knopf.

Kini, R., Pamakrishna, H. and Vijayaraman, B. (2003) 'An Exploratory Study of Moral Intensity Regarding Software Piracy of Students in Thailand', *Behaviour and Information Technology*, 22(1): 63—70.

Lane, F. (2001) *Obscene Profits: The Entrepreneurs of Pornography in the Cyber Age*. London/New York: Routledge.

Lee, M. (2007) *Inventing Fear of Crime: Criminology and the Politics of Fear*. Cullompton: Willan Publishing.

Liao, Z. and Cheung, M.T. (2001) 'Internet-based e-shopping and consumer attitudes: an empirical study', *Information and Management*, 38: 299–306.

Liao, Z. and Cheung, M.T. (2002) 'Internet-based e-banking and consumer attitudes: an empirical study', *Information and Management*, 39: 283–95.

Livingstone, S. (2003) 'Children's Use of the Internet: Reflections on the Emerging Research Agenda', *New Media and Society*, 5(2): 147–66.

Loader, I. and Sparks, R. (2002) 'Contemporary Landscapes of Crime, Order and Control: Governance, Risk and Globalization', in M. Maguire, R. Morgan and R. Reiner (eds), *The Oxford Handbook of Criminology* (3rd edn). Oxford: Oxford University Press.

Lowery, D. and Brasher, H. (2003) *Organized Interests and American Government*. New York: McGraw-Hill.

Luo, X. (2002) 'Trust production and privacy concerns on the Internet: A framework based on relationship marketing and social exchange theory', *Industrial Marketing Management*, 31: 111–18.

Miliband, R. (1980) *The State in Capitalist Society*. London: Quartet Books.

NetAlert (2007) 'Attitudes and Behaviour of Young People Online', at: http://online. cesanet.adl.catholic.edu.au/docushare/dsweb/Get/Document-9685/research_ summary-web.pdf

O'Connell, R. (2003) 'A Typology of Cybersexploitation and On-Line Grooming Practices'. Preston: Cyberspace Research Unit.

Office of Fair Trading (OFT)(2007a) *Internet Shopping: An OFT Market Study*. Available online at: http://www.oft.gov.uk/shared_oft/reports/consumer_protection/oft921. pdf

Office of Fair Trading (OFT)(2007b) *Consumer Report: Internet Shopping, Annexe I*. Available online at: http://www.oft.gov.uk/shared_oft/reports/consumer_ protection/oft921i.pdf

Olson, M. (1974) *The Logic of Collective Action: Public Goods and the Theory of Groups*. Cambridge, Mass.: Harvard University Press.

Page, B.I. and Shapiro, R.Y. (1983) 'Effects of Public Opinion on Policy', *The American Political Science Review*, 77(1): 175–90.

Parker, K.D., McMorris, B.J., Smith, E. and Murty, K.S. (1993) 'Fear of Crime and the Likelihood of Victimization: a Bi-Ethnic Comparison', *The Journal of Social Psychology*, 133(5): 723–32.

Powell, A. (2007) *Paedophiles, Child Abuse and the Internet*. Oxford: Radcliffe Publishing.

Reiner, R., Livingstone, S. and Allen, J. (2000) 'No More Happy Endings? The Media and Popular Concern about Crime Since the Second World War', in T. Hope and R. Sparks (eds), *Crime, Risk and Insecurity: Law and Order in Everyday Life*. London: Routledge.

Roban, W. (2002) 'The Net Effect: Girls and New Media', at: http://www.girlscouts. org/research/pdf/net_effect.pdf

Roman, C.G. and Chalfin, A. (2007) 'Fear of Walking Outdoors: An Ecological Analysis of Violence and Disorder in Urban Neighbourhoods', at http://www. activelivingresearch.org/alr/files/Roman_Plenary_2007.pdf

Shaftoe, H. (2004) *Crime Prevention: Facts, Fallacies and the Future*. Basingstoke: Palgrave-MacMillan.

Shearing, C.D. and Stenning, P.C. (1981) 'Modern Private Security: Its Growth and Implications', *Crime and Justice*, 3: 193–245.

Smith, W.R. and Torstensson, M. (1997) 'Gender Differences in Risk Perception and Neutralizing Fear of Crime: Toward Resolving the Paradoxes', *British Journal of Criminology*, 37(4): 608–34.

Snyder, M. (2004) 'Pirates of the 21st century', online at: http://www.cyberplayitsafe. com/resources/21st-Century-Pirates.PDF

Sparks, R. (1992) *Television and the Drama of Crime*. Buckingham: Open University Press.

Stanko, E.A. (2000) 'Victims R Us: the Life History of "Fear of Crime" and the Politicisation of Violence', in T. Hope and R. Sparks (eds), *Crime, Risk and Insecurity: Law and Order in Everyday Life*. London: Routledge.

Taylor, P. (1999) *Hackers: Crime in the DigitalSublime*. London: Routledge

Teo, T.S.H. (2002) 'Attitudes Towards Online Shopping and the Internet', *Behaviour and Information Technology*, 21(4): 259–71.

This Is London (2008) 'Millions of girls using Facebook, Bebo and Myspace "at risk" from paedophiles and bullies', 8 December, at http://www.thisislondon.co.uk/news/article-23471166-details/Millions+of+girls+using+Facebook,+Bebo+and+Myspace+%27at+risk%27+from+paedophiles+and+bullies/article.do

Thomson, I. (2004) 'Britain becoming a nation of pirates', online at: http://www.crn.vnunet.com/news/1157189

Tulloch, M. (2000) 'The Meaning of Age Differences in the Fear of Crime', *British Journal of Criminology*, 40(3): 451–67.

Tzanelli, R., Yar, M. and O'Brien, M. (2005) 'Con Me if You Can: Exploring Crime in the American Cinematic Imagination', *Theoretical Criminology*, 9(1): 97–117.

Voiskounsky, A., Babeva, J. and Smyslova, O. (2000) 'Attitudes towards computer hacking in Russia', in D. Thomas and B. Loader (eds), *Cybercrime: Law Enforcement, Security and Surveillance in the Information Age*. London: Routledge.

Wall, D.S. (2008) 'Cybercrime and the Culture of Fear: social science fiction and the production of knowledge about cybercrime', *Information Communications and Society*, 11(6): 861–84.

Wishart, J. (2002) 'Internet Safety Issues in English Schools', at: http://idater.lboro.ac.uk/upload/Wishart.pdf

Wood, J. and Gannon, T. (eds) (2008) *Public Opinion and Criminal Justice*. Cullompton: Willan Publishing.

Wood, J. and Shearing, C.D. (2006) *Imagining Security*. Cullompton: Willan Publishing.

Yar, M. (2005) 'The Global "Epidemic" of Movie "Piracy": Crime-Wave or Social Construction?', *Media, Culture and Society*, 27(5): 677–96.

Yar, M. (2006a) *Cybercrime and Society*. London: Sage.

Yar, M. (2006b) 'Teenage Kicks or Virtual Villainy? Internet Piracy, Moral Entrepreneurship, and the Social Construction of a Crime Problem', in Y. Jewkes (ed.), *Crime Online*. Cullompton: Willan Publishing.

Yar, M. (2008) 'The Rhetorics and Myths of "Anti-Piracy" Campaigns: Criminalisation, Moral Pedagogy and Capitalist Property Relations in the Classroom', *New Media and Society*, 10(4): 605–23.

Zedner, L. (2007) 'Pre-Crime and Post-Criminology?', *Theoretical Criminology*, 11(2): 261–81.

Zimmer, E.A. and Hunter, C.D. (2000) 'Risk and the Internet: Perception and Reality', at: http://www.copacommission.org/papers/webriskanalysis.pdf

Chapter 7

Crime, film and the cybernetic imagination

Craig Webber and Jeff Vass

Introduction

This chapter focuses on the popular representation of crime and information technologies in cinema. The media represents one of the most salient ways that the public consumes images of deviance (Sparks 1992) and the Internet has become one of the most salient aspects of our daily lives. Fear of crime, real or imagined, risk and precaution have also become increasingly central to popular, political and academic discourse (Beck 1992; Giddens 1990; Hebenton and Seddon 2009). The convergence of these themes is the topic of this chapter. As Wall (2007 and this volume) has noted there are a variety of discourses that have developed around the theme of cybercrime. Each discourse reflects the needs of those who contribute to its content as well as differing in the degree of awareness they have for the public. For example, a legal discourse on cybercrime serves the needs of the legal profession to provide clear definitions of the parameters of what constitutes the offence. However, they tend towards the obscure and parochial and have little resonance outside the legal profession. Popular representations have a broader appeal and are not circumscribed by a need for clarity. Consequently, what makes media accounts interesting is that they are accessible to the public at large and arguably more powerful than written discourse for suggesting what it means for us, as a species, to have become as integrated in our bodies and lives as we have with information and communications technologies (ICTs). Film in particular has been fascinated for some time with how human beings interface with technology, and latterly with the apparently seamless way in which we now perform or 'do' technology. In a similar way to how some authors suggest that gender is a performance that is learned through imitation, so also the use of technology has a performative aspect (West and Zimmerman 1987). The attention the media have given to this new and evolving 'form of life' (Shotter 1993) is structured in interesting ways. TV documentaries and shows (for example, BBC's *Tomorrow's World*) have been dedicated to exploring the nature of, and potential for, the social and cultural impact of new ICTs. Thus, we are used to media which enable us to gain insights into the changing character of work and economic life, 'teleworking' in the global knowledge economy where ICTs have transformed the nature of the working day and the lives we lead around it. Cybertechnologies have transformed not only what we do in our leisure time but what constitutes leisure. Documentary and information TV explores this together with the debates connected with changing political practices such as 'digital citizenship' and our new modes of consumption linked to the Internet. TV drama increasingly portrays us as 'connected', whether this is introducing computers to elderly characters in soap operas, showing that even retired citizens can learn on the World Wide Web, or where the competence with technology forms part of the plot (e.g. BBC's *Hustle*).

Cinema has particularly developed the narrative domain of 'cybercrime' and other subversive uses to which ICTs may be put. This has been central to science fiction in film, for example, since the 1950s. However, there are many forms of activity that have been collected under the somewhat imprecise term, cybercrime. The use of information technology or computers has, in recent years, proliferated and expanded from the home PC to a vast, mobile network of devices. In cinema, such devices are depicted as the solution to crime just as easily as the source of the problem. This chapter will indicate ways that cinema both reflects the era in which it is produced and provides a schema for understanding how technology is used and has become incorporated into our lives and changed us. One of the earliest uses of the prefix cyber in entertainment is in the British television science fiction series *Dr Who*, whose enemy the Cybermen (part human, part machine) first appeared in 1966 and persist to the present day. For over 40 years the concept of 'cybermen' has formed part of the discursive framework in which we have been able to exercise our 'cybernetic imagination' and come to understand our relation to the world of mechanism, in much the same way as Mary Shelley's *Frankenstein* has, for 200 years, formed part of the framework of narrative resources through which we discuss what it is to be human (cf. Warrick 1980)

The chapter is organised around several debates that reflect concerns in both criminology and wider society. We chart the changing ways in which we have come 'to do technology' and watch ourselves doing it, misusing it or being misused by it in film. We aim to provide an overview of the cinematic representations for how we relate to ICTs. We situate this overview in a discussion of the changing social world that social and criminological theories have attempted to grasp over the same period. Film as a medium began in what we might call 'high modernity'. The language of film has evolved and has been a contributor in the demise of the modernity it sought to depict. Film is still here as a participant forming part of the means at our disposal to grasp human action, crime and their relation to technology. Following a discussion of crime, cinema and technology we outline the development of film and social theory showing, through examples, where film and social theory move us beyond thinking of film and thought as primarily representational media. We are concerned here to establish that film and indeed technology are instrumental resources that impact on our self-understanding and changes to this through time. Next, we provide a map of changing social, cultural and criminological ideas from the 1950s on and we relate these ideas to changes in the way the language of film has adapted over the same period to take account of developments in cybertechnologies. We then investigate 'hacking' as a case study in contemporary cinema and daily life before providing some provisional conclusions to this overview. The task we confront here is a particularly difficult one for a number of reasons. Firstly, films that specifically focus upon the Internet are small in number, due in part to its relatively recent popular usage. Secondly, those that focus on crime and the use of the Internet are even rarer, being a subset of this subgenre. Consequently, we have situated the discussion in the context of the way that Information Communication Technologies (ICT) has been depicted in popular cinema. We are interested in the way it has been used as both a narrative device to propel the story, what Hitchcock referred to as a 'McGuffin', and the role of technology in film as a schema, a way to popularise and present a sense of habituation with the initially unfamiliar. We do not aim to provide an encyclopaedic account of all films to do with cybercrime. Some films are too bad even for two cinephiles such as the authors of this chapter. We aim to provide a forum for debate rather than provide anything approaching a definitive account. Besides, cinema, like literature, evokes subjective responses. Many people preferred *The Matrix: Reloaded* and *Revolutions* to the original film that spawned them. They are, of course, wrong.

Cinema as showroom

Cinema has often been a place where those with a new gadget to sell can find a willing showroom. Product placement is not new in movies, but probably the best salesman is James Bond, whose penchant for fine wines, cars and watches means that many people could name the manufacturer of his favourite items. Producer Albert R. Broccoli, whose company is still associated with the films, claimed they were making science fact, not science fiction. Companies like Aston Martin and Rolex lined up to have their newest products fitted with gadgets that added a sense of danger to them. The Bond films are not the only example of this. In the film *Minority Report* (director S. Spielberg 2002), based on the short story by Philip K. Dick, the lead character played by Tom Cruise uses a display screen much like a large flat-screen television, but he uses his hands to move icons and images around the screen in a way similar to how we might drag and drop icons or photographs with a mouse on a computer. In 2002, Cruise's engagement with touch-sensitive screens seemed futuristic, yet it did not seem so futuristic in 2007 when Apple revealed the iPhone, the first touch-screen smartphone. Although touch-screens had been around since the early 1980s, the iPhone was the first to make the technology popular. Of course, such observations are central to fiction where a device is posited many years before the technology will catch up with the idea. In the 1964 film *Goldfinger* (dir. G. Hamilton 1964) James Bond uses a primitive form of in-car satellite navigation, a bleeping radar screen attached to the dashboard of the Aston Martin DB5 that would allow him to track the villain.

This has taken four decades to become a reasonably priced accessory. One of the interesting aspects of this is that we have become accustomed to the idea of satellite navigation in our cars, even if we do not possess it ourselves, but, for some people, also on their mobile phones. Many devices come pre-installed with maps and the software to use the phone to find their location via global positioning satellites (GPS). In *Enemy of the State* (dir. T. Scott 1998) this was a plot device to suggest paranoia, now it is an option we can choose when picking our next mobile phone. Cinema is not the only medium that provides the source for the habituation, acceptance and passive acquiescence to technologies previously depicted as a threat. But the sheen and glamour that cinema is especially good at presenting makes it a powerful element in the media tapestry. But what effect has this exposure to technology through film had?

Crime, cinema and technology: becoming relaxed with surveillance

It has been noted by Robert Reiner that we are living through an era where the legitimacy of the publicly funded police is taken for granted (Reiner 2000). However, it could be argued that in the post-9/11 world we are also in a post-legitimacy era with regard to all forms of surveillance. The lessons of Orwell's *Nineteen Eighty-Four* (1949) are easily forgotten in the quest for security from terrorists. The issue of civil liberties has become increasingly marginal in political discussion. As Garland states: 'The call for protection from the state has been increasingly displaced by the demand for protection by the state' (Garland 2001: 12). Films about surveillance have to work very hard indeed to overcome the public's ambivalent attitude to their privacy. We have moved from a position where privacy was paramount, through statements such as, 'if you are innocent you have nothing to fear', to the advent of total surveillance the like of which Orwell never imagined. Mobile phones now go to places even the telescreens and Big Brother did not reach. Orwell imagined places that were free from the gaze of Big Brother. *The Truman Show* (dir. P. Weir 1988) starring Jim Carrey is the story of a man who has unwittingly lived his entire life in a reality television show. Viewing the film again now its themes are both pertinent and quaint. This stands in contrast to the self-inflicted reality television culture of *Big Brother* and the life and death of the reality television personality Jade Goody. Cinema has to reflect this expansion of surveillance.

The Internet facilitates constant surveillance both locally and, crucially, globally. Early films about surveillance tended to focus on the capabilities of one technology. In Francis Ford Coppola's *The Conversation* (1974) the focus is microphones and audio enhancement and the way they could be used to pick up what would once be considered secret. Michelangelo Antonioni's *Blow Up* (1967) showed the power of the photographic image to capture, in the distance, something that could later be magnified into the picture's foreground – in this case, a murder. However, films such as *Enemy of the State* included a plethora of technologies, each of which in combination has the power to seemingly capture every aspect of our lives. The latter film was made in 1998 and before reality television, mobile phone cameras and cameras atop one's personal computer or included as standard on a laptop. Since then, ambivalence to the ubiquity of such technology has increased and privacy concerns have been marginalised in the wake of websites such as Facebook, MySpace, Twitter and Flikr, Google Earth and satellite navigation devices on one's phone. Recent reports of the overuse of the Regulation of Investigatory Powers Act 2000 (RIPA) by local councils in the UK to spy on citizens has caused the government to tighten the rules governing who can warrant a surveillance operation (Internet source 1). The justifications given by the councils for engaging in such intrusive surveillance suggest that the threats to civil liberties posed by it are no longer seen as important. It is deemed acceptable to follow someone to make sure they live where they say they live, to prevent parents trying to get their children into a good school by falsely claiming to live within a specific catchment area, or to spy on people to make sure they put their refuse into the correct bin. It is worrying that anti-terror laws are used for such trivial misdemeanours and yet the level of anger this raises is fairly minimal. Many of us live in a panopticon (cf. Foucault 1977) of our own making and our own volition. We are more integrated and comfortable with networked technology, both using it and it using us, in a way that was not conceived when the last three films were made. Technology, before and after the turn of this century, implies different kinds of 'boundaries' at the human–machine interface. We discuss this next.

Film theory and social theory

We now want to establish a debate between film and social theory; to discuss some changing fashions of film theory as it tried to get to grips with the new experiences and insecurities felt by the cinema-going subject in the transition from modernity through postmodernity to whatever we have now arrived at. Social theory, likewise, has always been interested in how the observable conditions of life appear to be correlated with aspects of human experience (Marx and alienation; Durkheim and anomie; Weber and disenchantment: see Vass 1999 for a discussion of this). Of more immediate interest here is the link between contemporary problems in, and features of, everyday experience that may be interpreted by the film consumer.

Below we suggest that film does more than represent, and the film viewer does more than watch. The rise of globalism and the development of networks linking humans with computers and information technology have inserted the subject into fundamentally new, insecure and problematic ways of being (Bauman 2000; Giddens 1991). Film has kept pace with these changes, and in so doing has created a new 'genre framework', or language, for cybernetic film. The framework of the 1970s, for example, is quite different from that of today. Later we connect this to the way in which cinema-goers now use film as an embodied resource to navigate their way through the 'cyber-moral labyrinth' and to develop provisional responses, if not any formal understanding, of the new boundaries and positions offered by the global-networked world. The latter has fundamentally altered the manner in which we not only communicate but also make judgements about events and moralise the behaviour of others. Deviance, transgression, taboo relate to one another in provisional, ever-changing and labyrinthine ways. Film has become an essential part of the language of our 'practical communicative horizon' (Habermas 1987) that allows us to grasp and make sense of the key boundaries that matter to any culture: for example, boundaries between bodies and machines; nature and culture; faith and reason; right and wrong etc.

In the next section we move from a choice between theories of, or about, film as an object of theory to the 'reader' of the film and the way in which film is used as a resource to 'think' and 'feel' one's way through the kinds of boundary issues that are now presented to us in a cyber-global-network.

Film theory and social theory: from representations to narrative resources

The relationship between film theory and social theory is more complex than would appear at first sight. Crudely, film theory is about understanding our relationship with film as an object that has an impact on the way we think, feel and perceive ourselves. Social theory is, again crudely, about our relationships with each other, that is, with 'the social itself' as an object that has an impact on our behaviour. This section will describe the traditional concerns of film and social theory by focusing on examples, outline their historical connections and then go on to suggest why contemporary cultural theory requires an integrated approach to thinking about film in the context of rapid social, cultural and technological change. The argument here is that technology at the height of modernity was graspable and understandable in its relations with the human world through the way film narrated the positions of humans to it and each other with respect to it. Although cybertechnology and computers began life in the 1940s, human issues with respect to them did not surface in film until the 1960s when film narratives began to get to grips with machine intelligence (see Woolley 1993). The advent of the Internet in the 1990s coincided with fundamental shifts in all aspects of the ways we communicate, relate, work and live under the auspices of globalisation (Castells 1996). The certainties of 'modernity', for example, belief in progress and the authority of science, disappeared and left more uncertain and fragmentary social positions and senses of self (Giddens 1991; Lyotard 1979). For convenience we may refer to this era as that of 'postmodernity'. In providing stories that gesture towards social change (for example, nostalgia narratives that compare old and new ways of living) and deal with the onset of virtual worlds (human–machine interfaces), popular film has had to increasingly abandon the story forms and character types of the pre-contemporary or 'modern' era. The Internet Age poses us very new problems concerning the boundaries of the self, human–technology interfaces, the nature of agency, the formation and interaction of moral codes globally. The traditional human-based mechanisms of social responsibility and accountability, based on face-to-face social interactions, no longer seem to apply (Bauman 2002; Hornsby 2007). The Internet provides us with a unique, omnipresent connection to electronic virtuality (see Smith and Kollock 1999). Its implications are being explored in film. In this regard film offers more than an array of characters with whom to identify. More importantly it offers the raw material of thought experimentation and other intellectual resources to think through the implications of this technological fact of life. The following traces the development of this in social and film theory.

Film theory and the cultural categories of high modernity

Historically, film and social theory have informed each other. Since the 1970s film theorists have analysed film from a series of critical perspectives (e.g. feminist, Marxist, discourse analytics, structuralist, psychoanalytic etc.). In many of these approaches the notion that film is a 'representational medium' was a central thrust of the arguments proffered. The purpose of analysing film as an object or text which represents the social world is to examine film narratives for the ways in which social circumstances and the positions taken up by human beings in them offer, confer, confirm or stigmatise us in a series of culturally established social identities. Here film theory shares its concerns with social criticism (see Vass 1999). Science fiction and espionage films of the 1950s and early 1960s (such as *Forbidden Planet*, dir. F.M. Wilcox 1956; James Bond films such as *Dr No*, dir. T. Young 1962 and *From Russia With Love*, dir. T. Young 1963), for example, can be said to represent masculine identities as technologically competent and feminine identities as incompetent. If female characters are shown as competent, they are invariably not able to fully utilise their competencies in a male-oriented world.[1] In addition, these films represent human action as elaborating itself, and progressing through time via technological punctuation: that is, the plot often proceeds, or is driven along, through the solution to a series of technological problems by the principal characters in the films. Even in films of a more recent vintage such as *Mission Impossible I, II* and *III* (dirs. Brian De Palma 1996; John Woo 2000; J.J. Abrams 2006), technological competences are key to driving the scenarios in which undercover agents enact ingenious deceptions in order to entrap villains bent on using biochemical or information technologies for criminal purposes.

Films, of course, function principally as entertainment. The critical element, however, is that the viewer of the film, by engaging with the film's narrative, it is argued by representationalist theorists, somehow becomes caught in a powerful 'mechanism' that draws on, and/or reproduces, identity or social positions that parallel real-world inequalities between, for example, men and women, social classes or ethnic groups. Different approaches to film theory (such as feminist, Marxist, structuralist etc.) take different views on the nature of the mechanisms by which films produce social identities or cultural categories such as normality, abnormality, criminality and deviance. Marxist critical theory, for example, reads mainstream cinema, typically, as an ideological medium in collusion with capitalism (see Lapsley and Westlake 2006 for further discussion). It is in the interests of the capitalist, for example, to represent Nature as a 'resource' to be exploited for human betterment and advancement and technology as the means of its lawful exploitation. Technology here becomes the 'engine' of human progress and the development of technology, and human subservience to it, becomes an unquestionable given in human striving for utopian social orders. *The Shape of Things to Come* (1936, dir. A. Korda) shows a world whose progress and happiness is stalled by the perennial human proclivity to conflict. War leads to the global destruction of cities and towns and the world becomes populated by small guerrilla communities in constant tribal conflict. Primitive political orders based on despotic tribal leaders evolve and take Luddite attitudes towards science and technology. Yet, one group, the 'Airmen', that preserves technology and the power of flight, is also an ordered, peaceful and uniformed group showing sophisticated political order. Eventually, the future of the human race as technologically advanced is portrayed in the film as a Utopian ideal. There is some ambiguity in the film's attitude to technological progress as the film cannot find an endpoint or a resolution to the dilemma of, on the one hand, merely organising society to endless progress for progress' sake or, on the other hand, towards an end to progress once all human need is met. However, deviance from mainstream consensus in the film, including the return to Luddite tendencies in the closing scenes, is always characterised as anti-technology which is equated with anti-progress.

In many ways the cinema of technological progress rehearses one of the founding juxtapositions of modernity and its ambiguities. Enlightenment rationality and capitalist expansion celebrates the autonomous, technologically competent human subject at the expense of their sociality (Outhwaite 2006; Shotter 1993; Vass 1999). In fiction the first modern subject is perhaps Robinson Crusoe, whose knowledge, technology and hence the means to exploit and survive Nature celebrates the key human virtues and ideals of autonomy and rationality. These are also key features of capitalist ideology as identified by Marxist critique.

It can be argued that the fact that *The Shape of Things to Come* poses the dilemma of progress and is also thus ambiguous on the status of deviance lends itself also to anti-Marxist readings. Indeed, there are many examples from the earliest days of film that seem to provide a critique of capitalism. Fritz Lang's futuristic *Metropolis* (1927) narrates the human price of modernity and the forms of labour humans become enslaved within. It poses the idea that, under conditions of modernity, humans come to serve the machine and that the ideal worker is a kind of machine, indeed a robot. This is the nightmare of alienating modernism as depicted variously in the social theories of Marx, Weber and Durkheim. Even Charlie Chaplin's *Modern Times* (dir. C. Chaplin 1936) seems now to deconstruct the ideological equation of human betterment and technological progress by inserting human idiocy and randomness into the mix. However, structural Marxists, such as Louis Althusser (1971; see also Levine 1981) have argued that the mechanism of ideology that successfully establishes dominant cultural categories, such as normality and deviance, depends on readers of messages, as carried in film, feeling that some kind of 'free debate' about technology, progress and capitalism is taking place. We do not feel oppressed, even though we are. After all, many films of the 1970s and onwards seem freely at odds with the principles of capitalism, such as *Soylent Green* (dir. R. Fleisher 1973), where humans that have become useless are turned into food to feed the population of useful humans; *Aliens* (dir. J. Cameron 1986) where a profiteering corporation fatally risks human colonists to bring back to Earth a seriously dangerous alien species which may have profitable military uses. In these films the moral position and legitimacy of capitalism are questioned as the latter rides roughshod over human lives and relationships.

Psychoanalysis, like Marxism, has played a large role in the development of film theory. The work of Jacques Lacan had an impact on Althusser's understanding of ideology in the 1970s and also on the theories of structuralists and Marxists attempting to understand the forms of contemporary culture (see, for example Coward and Ellis 1977). As developed by, for example, feminist scholars such as Mulvey (1992), psychoanalysis furthers our understanding of the mechanisms by which our subjectivities and sexualities become engaged with the pleasures of looking at and identifying with the meaningful positions offered in the context of film narratives. In essence, and drawing on Lacan's notion that the reflected image in a mirror provides a point of stability and fixity for an otherwise fragmentary self in the growing child, film can be read as replacing the mirror as a cultural institution. The cinema and film in this model offer pleasurable reflections and anchor points through which we, as potentially unstable subjectivities, may identify and stabilise ourselves and our identities according to key psychoanalytic 'rallying points' such as 'phallocentrism'. The latter, embedded in film narrative, allows the viewer to exert control over and legitimate identity by organising desire in accordance with culturally posited differences between males and females (see Mulvey 1992). While psychoanalysis is interested in the kinds of engagement subjects have with film, the content of film is often treated conventionally as representational. That is to say, psychoanalytic critique theorises the subject's mode of producing stability in the self by reference to cultural meanings established and read through other forms of analysis such as semiotics. In the film *The Matrix* (dirs the Wachowski brothers 1999) the hero, Neo, played by Keanu Reeves, is seeking the 'truth of his existence'. The fact that he leads a double life where he is called the rather less heroic Mr Anderson and in which one of his major interests is 'hacking computer code' seems to be legitimated by the strong identification the audience is invited to make with the search for the truth of his existence.

More recently psychoanalytic, and particularly Lacanian, theory has been extensively revived by the work of Slavoj Žižek (1989, 1991, 1993). Žižek has developed a mode of critique in which neither film nor the processes of human subjective engagement are privileged. This has led to some quite interesting and unexpected readings of films in which psychoanalysis is as much explained by film as the other way round. Part of the motivation for this comes from the sense that the political orders that sustain, or are sustained by, culture and meaning require the same level of attention as psychoanalysis normally extends to the mechanisms by which the subject achieves stability. This signals an approach to film and social theory that take us away from the purely representational and towards the 'constructive work' carried out by the viewer in relation to film. So, we turn to a view of film as a 'resource' rather than a representation of something else.

Social theory, film as resource and radical social change

Cybercrime needs to be understood as a technologically mediated human act. Therefore, we need to visit the theoretical discussion that problematises human action in the context of the rapid cultural and technological changes of recent decades. This section picks up the story of the shift away from 'representations' in social theory to one more focused on human activity and its embedment in globalised networks.

In many ways, we can review the development of film theory alongside the rise and decline of modernity itself. Although 'modernity' may always have been in a cultural struggle to establish itself against the inconveniences posed to it by history, such as war, genocides and ecological catastrophe, it has been read as a source of norms and conventions, a source of definitions of normality, abnormality, deviance etc. (Parsons 1951). These conventions appear in its literature, art and film and, as we have seen, the role of theory has been to examine, for better or worse, how human subjects position themselves in relation to these meanings. Film critique examines how human subjects become accomplices to a series of socially divisive myths that may, for example, work to the benefit of capitalism, or of men in relation to women or some ethnic groups rather than others.

However, there has been a growing awareness that contemporary social and cultural life (i.e. since the 1980s) has seen a decline in the institutions and practices that provided for a relatively stable global order of nation states in which regional and individual identities could stabilise themselves within relatively durable systems of cultural meanings that defined norms and deviancy (Giddens 1984, 1990, 1991; Laclau and Mouffe 2001; Lash and Urry 1987). The very idea of a 'social role' as something people can occupy and which lends sense to their activities, and through which evaluations of the legitimacy of their behaviour with regard to normative values can be made, now seems tied to the notion of a stable social system exhibiting consensus. In such a 'modern' system social bonds and relationships are primary as people pursue their lives at home and at work, operating and evaluating according to shared understandings communicated through the mechanisms of communication available through culture. In contrast to this, however, the contemporary 'postmodernised' world has, according to Lash and Urry (1994), entered an era of 'disorganised capitalism'. We can no longer, they argue, refer to 'society' as a stable system of human social bonds and institutions, i.e. a social world familiar to writers such as Durkheim. Instead, the artefacts and mechanisms of culture have more impact on social forms. Commercial brands appear to us as more stable than political institutions for example. It is perhaps more shocking to us that long-standing banks and building societies collapse than politicians emerge as corrupt. And of course culture which has 'absorbed' the social is managed through media industries such as satellite TV and the Internet. The new globalised world order lacks the traditional certainties of modernity: norms and social rules, previously guaranteed within the parameters of the state with a homogeneous polity are now, as a consequence of for example multiculturalism and highly divergent pluralisms, ambiguous. Every day we encounter 'fluid' social arrangements, transient and highly contingent senses of human relationships and bonds, what Bauman (2000) calls 'liquid modernity'. In a heavily 'mediatised' world (see Habermas 1987; and also Merrin 2005 for a discussion of Baudrillard's position; and Vass 2008 for commentary on the condition of human communication in the context of cybertechnology and the Internet) fundamental breaks occur between the 'lifeworld' in which you act and the social system which contains the institutions which manage and regulate your affairs. This can be likened to issues discussed by Jonathan Raban in his book *Soft City* (1974) and explored further by cultural criminologists such as Keith Hayward (2004) and Jeff Ferrell (2001). The hard city is contrasted with the soft city, the former is a place known to architects, town planners and policymakers. The soft city tends to be ignored, and it is here that relationships, emotions, deviance and transgression take place away from the eyes of the authorities and not fully understood by them (see also Ferrell *et al.* 2008). In a similar way, the advent of the Internet has made it difficult for nation states to exert controls over what its citizens choose to watch, or which information they access. The Internet flies in the face of the means the state has at its disposal to regulate, and even apply taxes and tolls to, e-trading, sensitive political information, pornography etc. Internet usage also inserts the user into a more ambiguous moral territory that has moral horizons that extend beyond the scope of the lifeworld where their embodied existence happens to be located. In following your football team in the UK you may access live streaming of matches on the Internet sourced, illegally within the UK, from China or Iraq where the matches may be legitimately viewed. You may be connected at the same time to Instant Messaging (IM) during the game, sharing thoughts about it with other subscribers located all over the globe. As one source of live streaming is discovered and 'shut down' by the authorities, members of the IM search and share links to sources of alternative streams. Watching games otherwise unavailable in the UK becomes an Internet 'problem-solving' task shared by people whose sense of common interest and moral obligation (sharing links is altruistic; more viewers to live streaming causes more problems to the stream thereby diminishing one's own entertainment) to each other is stronger than the respect due to the regulatory framework in the country in which one lives. Indeed, the latter increasingly fosters an ironic stance.

Rather than think of people as occupying social roles within a system organising the relationships between them, as we tried to view it in modernity, now we are increasingly invited to apply the metaphors of 'nomad', 'vagabond' and 'tourist' (see Agamben 1998; Urry 2000; Vass 1996, 2008) to the human agent whose activity cannot easily be made sense of without reference to their technologically supported networks. Indeed, our connectivity to networked technologies has redrawn the conceptual boundaries around human agency itself. Some (e.g. Latour 2005; Law and Hansard 1999; Urry 2000) prefer to see the human as an 'actant' within a 'network' involving bodies and technologies and other information-processing objects where it is the network that is most properly considered as possessing agency. Body–technology relations have become blurred and, it is argued, have posed new boundary ambiguities between humans and the technology that delivers the Internet (see Haraway 1991; Pirani and Varga 2008; Thrift 2007). Indeed, some (e.g. Urry 2000) argue that we need to understand the moral, social and political consequences of human–technology 'hybrids'. Hybrids may be defined as 'constituted through assemblages of humans, machines, and technologies' (Urry 2000: 4). Here the pertinent unit of analysis is the 'assemblage' itself as opposed to the human.

Bauman (2000), more concerned to chart the effects of rapid change on humans, argues that in the contemporary world we are increasingly confronted by situations whose meaning is obscured or ambiguous. The social rules by which we engage with others need to be constantly worked at as, for one thing, the horizon of our moral experiences, through technology, extends beyond the confines imposed by the embodied lifeworld.

In this kind of context our bearings and benchmarks in morality, meaning and value as well as senses of legitimacy, deviance, normativity etc. are bound up with our enrolment in multiple networks. This gives our experience of life, what it means to be human and sense of otherness and alienness new and uncertain boundaries. We are then perhaps more likely to turn to the media, the source of our knowledge of the world, to help us resolve some of the ambiguities and confusions that contemporary living increasingly implies. Or minimally we may just remain fascinated by what the media offers without knowing why. Certainly, this is a major theme of the (re)turn to cultural criminology (see Webber 2007b for a critical review).

> Pop culture blurs with news media reportage, images of crime and war are repackaged as entertaining digital escapism, and unreal 'reality TV' moments shape moral values and social norms. In this world the street scripts the screen and the screen scripts the street; there is no clearly linear sequence, but rather a shifting interplay between the real and the virtual, the factual and the fictional. (Ferrell *et al.* 2008: 123–4)

We should view contemporary films as in some sense providing us with intellectual 'resources' for thinking, and feeling, our way through some of these new, technologically constituted boundaries. It can be argued that films such as *Robocop* (dir. P. Vehoeven 1987), *Total Recall* (dir. P. Vehoeven 1990), *Lawnmower Man* (dir. B. Leonard 1992), *Ghost in the Shell* (dir. M. Oshii 1995) and *The Matrix* (dirs the Wachowski Brothers 1999) dispense with the standard representations of technology as belonging to a modernist narrative articulating the pros and cons of scientific progress. Rather they seem to be, at least partly, exploratory. They seem to want to examine the fate of identity, the limits of selfhood and personhood, and to make ambiguous or redundant the idea that human cognitive faculties are our essential defining features. Films no longer seem to examine the cyberworld as once upon a time. The idea of the human–machine dichotomy no longer seems to be a key narrative parameter through which we come to understand human moral and normative life. Cybercrime is essentially technology-mediated, or 'networked' activity as we suggested earlier. We need to adjust or rewrite the rules of film and social theory to examine its features. Films produced during the early years of the Internet were still dealing with postmodern issues of the fragmentary self and the uncertain social positions the contemporary globalised world proffers. Increasingly, however, the concerns of postmodernity may be receding. As the Internet in its ubiquitous form (mobile communications as well as other ICTs) becomes part of the tacit grounding conditions for the everyday lifeworld there is less emphasis on living in a postmodern nostalgic state aware of the loss of modern stability and certainties. Rather, the seamless flow of life with 'e-life' having eroded the distinction between 'real' and 'virtual' gives rise to new strategies by which activity is formed and perpetrated and achieves stability and coherence. This is somewhat ideally stated, but there is more than enough to suggest that postmodernity gives way to, say, an 'altermodernity'[2] whose chief quality is that it declines to define itself against the past and is happy to achieve its contingent stabilities and coherence within the framework of the Internet.

The next section looks in more detail at the development and change of 'key narrative parameters' in films. We explore how, where and why global and technological changes have impacted on the way we conceive ourselves, our actions and crimes.

New typologies of the cybernetic imagination in film

This section develops a typology of film, partly drawing on the theoretical discussion, which shows how we might typologise film as a resource for facilitating the way film consumers think through different kinds of experiences connected with technological, social and cultural changes. These changes involve changes to the immediate field of action in which people are brought into an engagement with the Internet. It is this immediate field of networked action where, for example, both the hacker and the hacked are brought into e-relations with one another. It is here where new possibilities for the hacker open up at the same time as new insecurities for other users are generated. We want to elaborate on how 'frameworks' of the cybernetic imagination have changed as correlated with periods of modernity and postmodernity. In the same way that interest in technology moved through different stages of human/technology interface, from the relatively simple replacement of human action by robotic to the more complex interrelated and entwined technologies being developed now, so the same is true of the search for the cause of crime; early accounts posited singular causes, later approaches several factors, later still and we hit the combination of cause and interpretation, and now with cultural criminology suggestions for a criminology of the foreground, of skin, emotion and the seduction of crime. All aspects that can be applied to some forms of ICT enabled transgression such as hacking (see for example Ferrell 1999; Ferrell *et al.* 2008; Katz 1988; Webber 2007a, 2007b). The periodisation here is arbitrary and functions more as a map where time, culture and technological change can be shown together in the same frame for the purposes of discussion. We are not making ontological claims about the social and economic conditions of particular historical periods within these frames. Rather, we seek to provide a simplified overview.

Period Themes (see Table 7.1) are shown giving the broadest social, cultural and technological issues that formed the background to the salient connections between film, culture, experience and the way in which cybernetic developments presented new 'boundary' and 'transgression' issues for people in that period. By this we mean that new technology always exceeds its planned function and meaning and gives rise to numerous unplanned subversions. Alongside this, we present a sketch of the changing nature of criminological theory, which in a broad way reflected social and technological change. In much the same way that we have argued that cinema is more than representation, but also resource, so also the depiction of crime in cinema, literature and television provides the public and criminologists with a resource for thinking through issues as they evolve. Downes and Rock refer to this as a 'shadow criminology' (2007: 45). It is these issues that find their way into film narrative. Cybernetic Framework attempts to capture, during a particular period, broad technological themes and orientations as well as how new technology is configured meaningfully with the culture it serves. For example, in period A (1950s–1960s) the human–machine/computer interface is grounded in a cybernetic framework where computer systems and robotics are still in semantic opposition to the human. ICTs are thought of as politically subordinate to the progress of either the socialist state or capitalist expansion through trade and manufacturing. Human and computer worlds are seen as interrelated but separate systems. In films of this period it is the potentially subverted uses to which technology may be put that constitute the dangers we face. That is, human agency lies behind subversive activity where technology is merely instrumental. It was possible to think in this period that technology itself might be a source of agency but, if this was thought, the framework conformed more to that of the horror genre (as developed by Stephen King for example). In *Forbidden Planet* (dir. Fred M. Wilcox 1956) and *Daleks: Invasion Earth: 2150 AD* (dir. Gordon Flemyng 1966) the cybernetic framework of the period is seen showing how powerful technologies are wielded by agencies for subversive purposes. It is not difficult for the audience to see where the responsibility for the misuse of technology lies. In the Dalek film humans are turned into Robomen controlled by a communication centre built by the Daleks which the intrepid Doctor is able to turn to his advantage. The film shows how technological superiority can turn humans into slaves, but transgression is attributable always to sentient human agency.

We may contrast this with Period B films like *2001: A Space Odyssey* which, by moving into a different cybernetic framework that opens up the possibility of 'artificial intelligence', redefines the boundary between human and non-human and immediately, in so doing, troubles our traditional narrative strategies of ascribing agency and moral responsibility. Famously, Hal a '9000 series computer' with the ability to interact with humans in speech, as opposed to some clunky operating system, is responsible for running all aspects of a spaceship en route to Jupiter. On board are several sleeping passengers and two conscious crew members. Trouble begins when the crew believe they have detected some mistakes that Hal has made and secretly

Table 7.1 Schematic overview of social change and criminological theory correlated with film themes

Period	Period themes	Cybernetic framework	Boundary/ transgression issues	Criminological debate	Films
A 1950s–1960s High modern Cold War politics; space exploration	Modernity is progression; UK and US governments promote the 'white heat' of technology; the space race; technology related to work dominated by manufacturing	Human society, robotics and computer science seen as Closed Systems with the latter subordinated to human need	Cybernetics at service of human intentionality is understood; traditionally human and non-human understood as nature–culture boundary; technology as tool subverted	The end of traditional criminology, large systems theories challenged	*Der schweigende Stern* (aka. *First Spaceship on Venus*) (dir. K. Maetzig 1960); *Forbidden Planet* (dir. F.M. Wilcox 1956); *Daleks: Invasion Earth: 2150 AD* (dir. G. Flemyng 1966)
B 1960s–1970s	Modernity in crisis; social and political pluralism and change; technology is capitalism; rise of eco and alternative technology movements	Closed System Models; and Open System Models – the machine as possessing means for self-transformation in response to external change including and leading to contrasts between artificial and human Intelligences	Human–machine interface becomes part of routine exchanges between human and machine worlds; technology also seen as 'prosthetic' extending the range of specifically human senses; human–machine 'melding'	Becker and Matza's critiques of traditional categories of crime; the drifting deviant and the socially constructed deviant Problematisation of 'crime' Taylor, *et al.*'s (1973) attempt to critically synthesise traditional, modernist theories of crime with what Young (1998) would later claim to be late-modern approaches such as Becker's labelling perspective and Marxist analysis of the social structure of capitalism	*Blow Up* (dir. M. Antonioni 1966); *2001: A Space Odyssey* (dir. S. Kubrick 1968); *The Conversation* (dir. F. Coppola 1974); *Star Wars: A New Hope* (dir. G. Lucas 1977)

C 1970s–1980s	Late modernity; decline of nation state and manufacturing; shift to consumption; technology is entertainment and communication	Sybiotes, cyborgs, virtual realities; movement between human and machine worlds; organic computers	Neural networks, organic and chemical computers together with medico-technological advances blur the distinctions between human and machine where one stops and the other starts	Problematisation of race; Hall et al. (1978) Policing the Crisis; 'Failure' of Marxist criminology and rise of realisms, both left and right	Blade Runner (dir. R. Scott 1982); Tron (dir. S. Lisberger 1982); WarGames (dir. J. Badham 1983); Superman 3 (dir. R. Lester 1983); Terminator (dir. J. Cameron 1984); D.A.R.Y.L. (dir. S. Wincer 1985); A View to a Kill (dir. J. Glen 1985); Robocop (dir. P. Verhoven 1987)
D 1990s–present	Globalisation; rise of network society; tele or remote working WWW; e-mail; proliferation of mobile technologies; War on Terror; post-millennium	Absorption of humans into the machine and networks; ambivalence/ acceptance of surveillance as normal/ natural	Boundaries as such disappear – human thought and virtually created spaces merge and extend into one another; real and unreal become negotiable; reality as a simulation, e.g. Second Life	Lyng's 'Crime, edgework and corporeal transaction' (2004); Cultural criminology (see Ferrell et al. 2008)	Total Recall (dir. P. Verhoeven 1990); Lawnmower Man (dir. B. Leonard 1992); Sneakers (dir. P.A. Robinson 1992); The Net (dir. I. Winkler 1995); Hackers (dir. I. Softley 1995); Ghost in the Shell (dir. M. Oshii 1995); Virtuosity (dir. B. Leonard 1995); Johnny Mnemonic (dir. R. Longo 1996); Enemy of the State (dir. T. Scott 1998); The Truman Show (dir. P. Weir 1998); The Matrix (dirs the Wachowski Brother 1999); A.I.: Artificial Intelligence (dir. S. Spielberg 2001)[3]; I, Robot (dir. A. Proyas 2004); Ghost in the Shell 2: Innocence (dir. M. Oshii 2004); The Dark Knight (dir. C. Nolan 2008); WarGames: The Dead Code (dir. S. Gillard 2008); Terminator Salvation (dir. McG 2009)

135

discuss disconnecting some of its ('his'?) functions. Hal then kills the sleeping passengers by switching off their life support, and manages to cast one of the crew adrift in space before the final crew member succeeds in turning off Hal's 'higher brain functions'. This film poses us the problem of 'thinking machines'. While in everyday language we ascribe subjectivity to things ('the kettle doesn't like it if you overfill it'), Hal poses us the issue of machine consciousness and agency. As his higher brain functions are being switched off Hal asks if he should sing a song taught him by his creator. The song becomes more difficult to sing as the higher functions shut down. Hal evokes human sympathy and bears responsibility for his actions as if he were a separate accountable human subject. In human–machine terms at system level Hal is profoundly connected to human biological systems (e.g. passengers, life support); on a social level the cybernetic framework within which this film's code operates is forced to render Hal as an agent in his own right. The surviving crew member 'dismembering' Hal's brain (by actually going inside Hal's 'head') is, in this framework, taking revenge and enacting justice, as well as rendering Hal harmless.

2001 poses transgression issues at the human–machine interface without constituting any 'boundary' issues at this interface. To understand further why the situation with the Internet and its human–machine interfaces poses different questions we need to understand something further about the nature of this boundary.

Boundaries and interfaces

In periods C and D the human–machine interface becomes not only blurred (as it was to an extent in 2001), but we move to a situation where information and computing technologies and humans are profoundly interpenetrated and connected in a continuous 'cyberlife'. It has become more common to refer to activity (not just human activity) as part of global 'flows' (see for example Urry 2002; Held *et al.* 2002). The concept of flow implies a seamless interpenetration of human activity with networked ICTs and is meant to replace the concepts of stability inspired by visions of institutional structures within the sociology of modernity. The attention moves now in giddying ways from global flows to their smaller constituents in the zones of human activity. Taking a close look at the more local fields within which action takes place seems now to demand a different view of subjectivity, the body and our connectedness with what we traditionally regarded as the environment (see Lyng 1990, 2004; Thrift 2007; Vass 2008). Essentially, the human–ICT interface offers us new 'boundary conditions' for action. In his original discussion of 'edgework' as an explanation for criminal risk-taking, Lyng (1990) had been interested in orienting our attention to the zones of action where the subject's experience acted outwards, 'closing down' social constraint, without 'imaginative rehearsal', into the risky immediacy of the present moment. In his more recent reformulation (Lyng 2004) he has been more concerned to highlight edgework as 'embodied practice'. In so doing Lyng expands on edgework's capacity to annihilate the culturally based 'consentient set' with which we construct time and space distinctions. … [E]dgeworkers are able to 'body forth' to an alternative reality in which objects and events assume new forms and qualities, or, just as likely, the very categories of 'objects' and 'events' … are completely dissolved as dualistic opposites. (Lyng 2004: 363)

In developing edgework theory in this way Lyng echoes the new conceptions of the body and its connectivity as developed by theorists such as Crossley (2001). Edgework conceived in this way deals with the spontaneous and unpredictable character of activity without consentient constraints. Since the Internet facilitates an extension of the body into global cyberspace we suggest that the Internet provides for the routine user a reduction in the 'consentient set' in the same way.

The mutual and interpenetrative quality of human–ICT relations presents us with theoretical conundrums that, for example, place theorists engaging with this area in seemingly contradictory positions when confronted with reimagining the human–ICT interface and its changing boundaries. Scott Lash as, along with Urry, one of the founding theorists of the idea that technology and its interconnectedness is material to the concept of 'flow', desists in one of his more recent works, *The Critique of Information* (Lash 2002), from suggesting that the human–computer interface is any more than a human–machine boundary in the traditional sense. And Urry, for all the talk about flow and assemblages, has not distinguished what is unique about ICTs, as opposed to any technologies and tools, that in some way is material to contemporary flows.

It is perhaps then left to film to 'theorise' what in social theory remains difficult. *The Matrix* poses us a reworking of the interpenetration of human and virtual worlds – in this film the 'portal' between virtuality and human reality becomes a person, i.e. Neo. Neo moves between the virtual reality of the matrix, like others initially by being 'plugged in' (literally having an unpleasant-looking sharp metal thing plugged directly into his brain) and the human reality constituted by social otherness in the traditional sociological sense. Entering the matrix in this way is hacking. The film also experiments with the notion that a virtual being having reality only in the matrix 'hacks' the human embodied world, Zion (*sic*). An 'agent' having come adrift from the rules that constitute the matrix finds a way into Zion. Having, later, come in some mysterious way to have embodied and transcended the rules that constitute the virtual world of the matrix Neo uniquely moves between worlds, bearing in his self, so to speak, the space where the two worlds interpenetrate. This presents us with a new boundary condition situation. Its implications are not easily perceived.

The cinematic hacker: apocalyptic offender and saviour of humanity

Discourse on media and crime often starts from the same point. The average member of the public knows little about crime beyond that which they see on television, in the cinema or in a newspaper (Jewkes 2004). However, the

Internet is somewhat different and depictions of it in cinema play on the seeming ubiquity of crime on the Internet. More importantly, crime is visible and can affect the viewer instantaneously at the click of a mouse. The ease with which one can arrive at a website filled with hateful invective, or another advertising goods whose provenance cannot be verified as legally obtained; the seemingly constant threat that what you are typing is being watched and recorded for nefarious purposes; all of this is dramatic material for writers and film producers. But, as we have noted above, it is also an important area for criminology since cinematic depictions of hacking and other forms of cybercrime provide us an insight into how we have come to understand and respond to this phenomenon; it is a 'shadow criminology' (Downes and Rock 2007). One question for criminology is, to what extent does the hacker represent a potent folk devil? It will be argued here that the hacker in cinema is too varied to 'represent' a criminal type that we should fear. As we argued above, cinematic depictions of ICTs and other technologies are better read as scripts for 'doing' technology than who we should fear.

One of the unique and interesting aspects of cybercrime for criminologists is that there is a semiotic shift from crime in the city to crime that can potentially invade the private sphere of the home, or the public/private sphere of the office. This is in contrast to the proposition of Hall *et al.* (1978) that the 'city is above all the concrete embodiment of the achievements of industrial civilisation', it is, in their words, 'the (tide-mark) of civilisation' (Hall *et al.* 1978: 145). The originator of the 'cyber' prefix, the novelist William Gibson, has also described cyberspace in architectural terms (Gibson 1984). There has been a symbolic reflection, then, between the representations of fear in the city, where around every corner is a potential mugger, to the fear that on every website there may be a pornographic image, or a vandalised web page or hate activities. But the representation of hacking is far more complex than this. Since hacking is understood to mean the utilisation of technology for purposes incongruent with its original intention, then hacking can be seen as a way of superseding the confines and control of what Stan Cohen, elaborating Foucault, called the 'punitive city' (Cohen 1985; Foucault 1977). It is this aspect of hacking that has led to the genre of the cyberpunk, the anarchist hackers fictionalised by William Gibson (1984). It might also be said to be a potential source of interest for cultural criminologists[4] who also tend to reflect an anarchist philosophy (Ferrell 1999, 2001; Webber 2007a, 2007b). Similarly, cultural criminology is interested in a 'criminology of the skin' and Lyng's concept of 'edgework' discussed above is a useful one for understanding another aspect of the representation of hacking (Lyng 1990, 2004). Douglas Thomas argues that agents of social control are obsessed by images of the body in relation to their representations of the hacker. In the film *Hackers* (dir. I. Softley 1996), a law enforcement officer describes hackers as ravaging and penetrating delicate systems. In a pseudo-Freudian analysis hackers become rapists (Thomas 2000). The mere possession of technology capable of hacking is often what the real protagonists of computer crime are primarily charged with (Thomas 2000). Hacking in cinema draws on both these themes to present a blended discourse of the agent able to penetrate the cyber-architecture of codes and firewalls.

The hacker is a strange narrative device in cinema. Their depiction is surprisingly varied; as varied as the narrative role they perform in each story. For example, Matthew Broderick's curious schoolboy of *WarGames* (dir. John Badham 1983) is different from, although could grow up to be, Kevin Smith's geeky nerd Warlock, an adult still living at home in his forties (real name Freddie), in *Die Hard 4.0* (dir. Len Wiseman 2007). Within *Die Hard 4.0* there are a number of representations of the hacker alongside Warlock. The character who becomes John McClane's sidekick is a cocky, wisecracking young man who, like Warlock, is into fantasy films, gaming and collecting memorabilia associated with it. A contrast to these two characters is the main villain, Thomas Gabriel, a handsome, well-dressed, but disgruntled former government employee. All of these representations can be contrasted with Keanu Reeves' superhero/saviour of humanity, Neo in *The Matrix* series (dirs. Andy and Larry Wachowski 1999–2003). Each one is different and the only characteristic they share is their ability to make a computer do what most people cannot do, that is go beyond the user-friendly interface of Windows into the code that lies behind it.

Nevertheless, 'apocalyptic hackers' and 'present hackers' are two categories that can be delineated, at least in a very roughly drawn way. Present hackers are seen throughout the 1980s to the present and are shown to be operating in their own time. The depiction of apocalyptic hackers is inspired by cyberpunk literature (see Sheila Brown's Chapter 8 in this volume) and its counterpart in cinema such as *Blade Runner*, and is now not so common, certainly since *The Matrix: Reloaded* and *The Matrix: Revolutions* (dirs the Wachowski brothers 2003) did so poorly at the box office. Cinema is an industry and so it might be just as easy to attribute the lack of interest in making such films to this failure as to any other reason. Nevertheless, *The Matrix* was released in 1999 as the world awaited the new millennium with excitement and fear as the potential for chaos from the Millennium Bug built to a louder crescendo than the fireworks and we watched the television news track the turning of the digital calendars around the world. And then nothing happened. Traffic lights continued to work, computers did not return to the year 0000 and the banking system did not crash. We had to wait another eight years for old-fashioned human greed to lay the financial system low. *The Matrix* is a story about religion in a secular world with Neo the saviour of mankind. As Mr Anderson, the character is seen to be operating in his own time as a hacker. As Neo, however, the character is operating in a time after the world has been taken over by sentient machines. An earlier film, also of the apocalyptic hacker variety, is the Japanese Anime film *Ghost in the Shell* (dir. Oshii 1995). This draws its inspiration from two films inspired by Philip K. Dick, the first the ubiquitous *Blade Runner*, and the second *Total Recall,* as well as the equally ubiquitous *Neuromancer*. The ghost is the thoughts, emotions and memories of a human that can be downloaded and transferred to another body, meaning that unless this ghost is destroyed then humanity can live for ever. A rare example of a post-Millennium film about apocalyptic hackers is the sequel *Ghost in the Shell: Innocence* (dir. Oshii 2004). The film explores the same themes as its predecessor and, like *Blade Runner* before it, asks questions about identity. Hacking is not presented in post-apocalyptic films as overtly criminal in the same way as it is in present-day scenarios such as *WarGames*, *Sneakers* or *Hackers*. Indeed, in *Ghost in the Shell* everyone with an 'e-brain' can access the Net, essentially an upgrade the like of which you might buy for a computer. In *The Matrix* and its sequels the hacker is not just the hero, but also the 'one' (see Wall, Chapter 5).

There are several themes in these films. One of them is the challenge of knowing you will die but without an afterlife to comfort those who need one. In *Blade Runner* the replicant Roy Batty needs to come to terms with his own mortality even though he was the creation of the Tyrell Corporation. What it means to be human is linked to knowledge of one's mortality. *Ghost in the Shell* posits a future world where the physical body can, literally, be transcended. The body that these characters are born with can be modified by prostheses until all trace of living flesh has gone. The soul can then pass to another body by being downloaded. The literal form of reincarnation. Many of these films also posit a scenario that is either post-war/apocalypse or, as in *The Terminator* franchise, a time-travelling shift between the pre, during and post apocalypse. Hacking is secondary to the global situation. But this highlights one significant area that criminology has been relatively quiet about, that is crimes during and after war (Webber 2009). This is not to suggest that these films 'tell' us anything about this activity, but they do remind us that criminology neglects many areas of criminal activity.

Conclusion

The term hacker does not presuppose the utilisation of a computer. Its general meaning relates to the use of any technology competently but also in a manner that is incongruent with its original intention. Consequently, in cinema, the archetypal hacker is, arguably, James Bond. Bond is a character renowned for his ability to jump into a speedboat and make it work, fire heat-seeking rockets and jump over buses without the aid of the user's manual. This is one of the most appealing aspects of the character for anyone still struggling to program their video, let alone their DVD, Blu-ray or digital recorder. The incarnation of James Bond before Daniel Craig was seemingly able to master any skill or technology. Bond saves the day through brute strength but also his ability to make Q's gadgets work despite seemingly little practice. However, it can be argued that in a world where humans are now so connected, where we each carry our own portable ICTs, where we can Bluetooth music to each other remotely, the depiction of the hacker would seem strange if it depicted them as too different from 'us'. The apocalyptic hacker film went out of fashion in the period after the terrorist attacks in America in 2001. Science fiction television and cinema turned its attention towards terrorism and the wars in Afghanistan and Iraq for its subtext. The reimagining of the 1970s television series *Battlestar Galactica* became a statement on the Iraq war and terrorism over the course of its six-year run. *Batman Begins* (dir. C. Nolan 2005) also contains a subtext about the war on terror and the politics of fear. James Bond retreated from the gadgetry that had been the hallmark of the series since the second film in 1963 when *Casino Royale* (dir. M. Campbell 2006) was released.

Gadgets of the future, like the tracking device in *Goldfinger,* submersible cars and x-rays that could see through clothes, are all on the market now. Daniel Craig's James Bond *was* the gadget, returning the films to their roots in Ian Fleming's fiction. It remains to be seen which direction films about the use of ICTs for criminal purposes will go. As President Barack Obama undoes the damaged relations left by the Bush administration perhaps the hacker will return as a potent folk devil. As we have argued, cinema, social and criminological theory all tend to reflect the concerns of the time. As we write, there are protests outside the Bank of England and the folk devils are bankers. Cultural criminology, with its emphasis on the foreground of emotions to the neglect of the background of structural factors, may have to reassess where it is positioned as a new version of *Robin Hood* goes into production directed by Ridley Scott, the director of *Blade Runner* and the aesthetic for many of the apocalyptic hacker films.

Notes

1 For example, it might be argued that *Goldfinger* (dir. G. Hamilton 1964) represented something of a change in direction with the introduction of Honor Blackman's Pussy Galore and her Flying Circus of female stunt pilots. Nevertheless, it might be suggested that the writers and producers gave the character technological skill with one hand and took away her right to self-determination with the other. Connery's Bond effectively forces himself upon her, she is shown to be seduced by his charms and eventually her homosexuality is overcome and abandoned. The pattern we suggest above continues thereafter in subsequent Bond films. With few exceptions any female character shown to be technologically competent ends up dead or in need of saving by James Bond.
2 The authors have no wish to launch or join a bandwagon that creates another sociological shibboleth. However, a 2009 exhibition at the Tate Modern uses the word to mean what we intend here. We do not subscribe to the view that modernity has fully receded in all senses, but we do need to mark some qualitative changes to the social world.
3 The film was released in the USA in June, but in the UK on 21 September 2001.
4 Although by arguing this we do not wish to suggest that this area of analysis should be limited to those who are associated with this area of criminology.

Further reading

In this chapter we have attempted to review areas of mutual concern for film and social theory with special regard to film as a cognitive resource. Contemporary film and social theory each have numerous other competing perspectives. With this caveat in mind, a good introduction to film is:

Lapsley, R. and Westlake, M. (2006) *Film Theory: An Introduction* (2nd edn). Manchester: Manchester University Press.

Accounts which probe the theoretical issues in more detail and take further some of the issues raised in this chapter are:

Allen, R. and Smith, M. (1999) *Film Theory and Philosophy*. Oxford: OUP.

Easthorpe, A. (1993) *Contemporary Film Theory*. Harlow: Pearson.

Pirani, M. and Varga, I. (eds) (2008) *New Boundaries between Bodies and Technologies*. Newcastle: Cambridge Scholars.

Žižek, S. (2009) *The Plague of Fantasies*. London: Verso (new edition).

References

Agamben, G. (1998) *Homo Sacer: Sovereign Power and Bare Life*. Stanford, CA: Stanford University Press.

Althusser, L. (1971) *Lenin and Philosophy*. London: New Left Books.

Bauman, Z. (2000) *Liquid Modernity*. Cambridge: Polity Press.

Bauman, Z. (2002) *Society Under Siege*. Cambridge: Polity Press.

Beck, U. (1992) *Risk Society: Towards a New Modernism*. London: Sage.

Castells, M. (1996) 'The Rise of the Network Society', *The Information Age: Economy, Society and Culture*, Vol. I. Oxford, UK: Blackwell.

Cohen, S. (1985) *Visions of Social Control*. Cambridge: Polity Press.

Coward, R. and Ellis, J. (1977) *Language and Materialism: Developments in Semiology and the Theory of the Subject*. London: Routledge.

Crossley, N. (2001) *The Social Body: Habit, Identity and Desire*. London: Sage.

Downes, D. And Rock, P. (2007) *Understanding Deviance: A Guide to the Sociology of Crime and Rule-breaking* (5th edn). Oxford: Oxford University Press.

Ferrell, J. (1999) 'Cultural Criminology', *Annual Review of Sociology*, 25: 395–418.

Ferrell, J. (2001) *Tearing Down the Streets*. New York: Palgrave.

Ferrell, J., Hayward, K. and Young, J. (2008) *Cultural Criminology: An Invitation*. London: Sage.

Foucault, M. (1977) *Discipline and Punish: The Birth of the Prison*. London: Penguin.

Garland, D. (2001) *The Culture of Control*. Oxford: Oxford University Press.

Gibson, W. (1984) *Neuromancer*. London: HarperCollins.

Giddens, A. (1984) *The Constitution of Society*. Cambridge: Polity Press.

Giddens, A. (1990) *The Consequences of Modernity*. Stanford, CA: Stanford University Press.

Giddens, A. (1991) *Modernity and Selfhood*. Cambridge: Polity Press.

Habermas, J. (1987) *The Theory of Communicative Action Vols 1 and 2*. Cambridge: Polity Press.

Hall, S., Critcher, C., Jefferson, T., Clarke, J. and Roberts, B. (1978) *Policing the Crisis*. London: MacMillan.

Haraway, D. (1991) *Simians, Cyborgs and Women: The Reinvention of Nature*. London: Free Association Books.

Hayward, K. (2004) *City Limits: Crime, Consumer Culture and the Urban Experience*. London: Glasshouse.

Hebenton, B. and Seddon, T. (2009) 'From Dangerousness to Precaution: Managing Sexual and Violent Offenders in an Insecure and Uncertain Age', *British Journal of Criminology*, 49(3): 343–62.

Held, D., McGrew, A., Goldblatt, D. and Perraton, J. (2002) *Global Transformations: Politics, Economics and Culture*. Cambridge: Polity Press.

Hornsby, A. (2007) 'Surfing the Net for Community: A Durkheimian Analysis of Electronic Gatherings', in P. Kivisto (ed.), *Illuminating Social Life*. IL: Pine Forge Press.

Jewkes, Y. (2004) *Media and Crime*. London: Sage.

Katz, J. (1988) *The Seductions of Crime*. New York: Basic Books.

Laclau, E. and Mouffe, C. (2001) *Hegemony and Socialist Strategy: Towards a Radical Democratic Politics* (2nd edn). London: Verso.

Lapsley, R. and Westlake, M. (2006) *Film Theory: An Introduction* (2nd edn). Manchester: Manchester University Press.

Lash, S. (2002) *The Critique of Information*. London: Sage.

Lash, S. and Urry, J. (1987) *The End of Organised Capitalism*. Wisconsin: University of Wisconsin Press.

Lash, S. and Urry, J. (1994) *Economies of Signs and Space*. London: Sage.

Latour, B. (2005) *Reassembling the Social: An introduction to Actor-Network Theory*. Oxford: OUP.

Law, J. and Hassard, J. (eds) (1999) *Actor Network Theory and After*. Oxford: Blackwell and Sociological Review.

Levine, A. (1981) 'Althusser's Marxism', *Economy and Society*, August, 10(3).

Lyng, S. (1990) 'Edgework: A Social Psychological Analysis of Voluntary Risk Taking', *American Journal of Sociology*, 95(4): 851–86.

Lyng, S. (2004) 'Crime, edgework and corporeal satisfaction', *Theoretical Criminology*, 8(3): 359–75.

Lyotard, J.-F. (1979 [1984]) *The Postmodern Condition: A Report on Knowledge*. Minneapolis: University of Minnesota Press.

Merrin, W. (2005) *Baudrillard and the Media*. Cambridge: Polity Press.

Mulvey, L. (1992) *The Sexual Subject: A Screen Reader in Sexuality*. London: Routledge.

Orwell, G. (1949) *1984*. London: Martin Secker and Warburg.

Outhwaite, W. (2006) *The Future of Society*. Oxford: Blackwell.

Parsons, T. (1951) *The Social System*. London: Routledge.

Pirani, B.-M. and Varga, I. (2008) *The New Boundaries between Bodies and Technologies*. Newcastle: Cambridge Scholars Publishing.

Raban, J. (1974) *Soft City*. London: Hamilton.

Reiner, R. (2000) *The Politics of the Police* (3rd edn). Oxford: Oxford University Press.

Shotter, J. (1993) *Conversational Realities: Constructing Life through Language*. London: Sage.

Smith, M. and Kollock, P. (1999) *Communities in Cyberspace*. London: Routledge.

Sparks, R. (1992) *Television and the Drama of Crime: Moral Tales and the Place of Crime in Public Life*. Buckingham: Open University Press.

Taylor, I., Walton, P. and Young, J. (1973) *The New Criminology: For a Social Theory of Deviance*. London: Routledge and Kegal Paul.

Thomas, D. (2000) 'Criminality on the electric frontier: Corporality and the judicial construction of the hacker', in D. Thomas and B.D. Loader (eds), *Cybercrime: Law Enforcement, Security and Surveillance in the Information Age*. London: Routledge, 17–35.

Thrift, N. (2007) *Non-Representational Theory*. London: Routledge.

Urry, J. (2000) *Sociology beyond Societies*. London: Routledge.

Urry, J. (2002) *The Tourist Gaze* (2nd edn). London: Sage.

Vass, J. (1996) 'Economic Socialization: a tourist in my own transactions', in *Research into Children's Economic and Social Understanding*, Vol. 5. London: UNL Press.

Vass, J. (1998) Searching the 'Zone of Social Making: the uncanny specification of human discourse', in R. Forrester and C. Percy (eds), *Discourse and the Social Order*. Birmingham: Aston Press, 115–26.

Vass, J. (1999) 'Social theories of the human agent and secular dialogue', in L.J. Francis (ed.), *Sociology and Theology in Dialogue*. London: Cassell, 72–81.

Vass, J. (2008) 'Stability and wandering: self, coherence and embodiment at the end of the social', in M. Pirani and I. Varga (eds), *The New Boundaries between Bodies and Technologies*. Newcastle: Cambridge Scholars Publishing.

Wall, D. (2007) *Cybercrime: The Transformation of Crime in the Information Age*. Cambridge: Polity Press.

Warrick, P. (1980) *The Cybernetic Imagination in Science Fiction*. London: MIT Press.

Webber, C. (2007a) 'Revaluating relative deprivation theory', *Theoretical Criminology*, 11(1): 97–120.

Webber, C. (2007b) 'Background, foreground, foresight: the third dimension of cultural criminology?', *Crime, Media, Culture*, 3(2): 139–57.

Webber, C. (2009) *Psychology and Crime*. London: Sage.

West, C. and Zimmerman, D. (1987) 'Doing Gender', *Gender and Society*, 1(2): 125–51.

Woolley, B. (1993) *Virtual Worlds: A Journey in Hype and Hyperreality*. Harmondsworth: Penguin.

Young, J. (1998) 'Breaking windows: situating the new criminology', in P. Walton and J. Young (eds), *The New Criminology* Revisited. London: Macmillan Press, 14–46.

Žižek, S. (1989) *The Sublime Object of Ideology*. London: Verso.

Žižek, S. (1991) *Looking Awry*. Cambridge, Massachusetts: MIT Press.

Žižek, S. (1993) *Everything You Always Wanted to Know About Lacan … But Were Afraid to Ask Hitchcock*. London: Verso.

Internet sources

1 'Anti-terror laws used on litterbugs', available at http://news.bbc.co.uk/1/hi/uk_politics/8004224.stm (accessed 17 April 2009).

Chapter 8

Fiction, fantasy and transformation in the imaginaries of cybercrime: the novel and after

Sheila Brown

Introduction

Fiction has a distinctive place in the history of cybercrime. Cybercrime as a 'real life' construct is both broad and much contested; those debates are well rehearsed elsewhere and I do not propose to revisit them here (see for example this volume; and summaries in Jewkes (2007), Wall (2007), Yar (2006), and for earlier examples of cybercrime definitions and research, Thomas and Loader (2000). One feature of cybercrime of particular relevance in relation to fiction, however, is that traditional legal concepts and formal categories of criminality are difficult to apply to many kinds of virtual activity that could be defined as 'proto criminal' (Brown 2003, 2006). This applies to virtuality in the sense of Internet cyberspace, and also to areas of cybernetics, virtual genetics, and other aspects of technological embodiment (Featherstone and Burrows 1995; Fukuyama 2002; Stone 1996). Questions of how far traditional law can govern the post-human body, or regulate virtual frontiers, remain open (Brown 2006). Fiction has a locative point at these interstices between the modern world of bodies, property, borders and territories, and the postmodern spaces of the 'Internet galaxy' (Castells 2001) and the cyberbody (Featherstone and Burrows 1995; Gane 2006).

This chapter uses texts of print fiction – the novel and, to a lesser extent, short stories – to trace the imaginaries of cybercrime in our techno-social culture (Brown 2006; Stone 1996). It crosses borders of genre in its textual journey: science fiction, the thriller, and crime fiction. By definition the kinds of phenomena explored by science fiction writers inhere in future worlds or simply worlds outside time, and increasingly in the virtual (Broderick 1995; Shields 2006), and are usually engaging precisely because they breach the limits of what we commonly know or understand in everyday life (Roberts 2006). Events in science fiction rarely fall inside what we might already recognise as the daily diet of crime or the conventional rule of law, reflecting the problems facing the criminologist of techno-social networks (Brown 2006). Crime fiction, by contrast, has a more firmly realist tradition, and its interactions with the imaginaries of the techno-social are typically adaptive and accommodating. In this crime fiction has more in common with those lawyers and criminologists who argue that cybercrime is largely conventional crime 'in bits' (see Yar 2006 for a concise summary of these debates) than it does with the transformative agendas of SF, postmodern legal scholars, and social theorists. Nevertheless, it will be seen that crime fiction is not quite so genre bound as it seems: latterly tackling many complex questions of identity that lie at the heart of virtual criminology.

Some of the fiction discussed below may be read as written with a specific intent to push forward the boundaries of social thought and debate; some may not. All of it however has much to say about contemporary ways of seeing cyberspace, crime and law. Fiction can be seen to have variously drawn upon, inspired in some way, or uncannily presaged, debates, fears, controversies and technological developments as they have become visible in the public arenas of the 'real' world – from identity theft to stalking, viral attacks to cloning, ubiquitous surveillance to electronic implants.

At the same time I make no attempt here to use fiction as social theory, as though fiction were either intended to, or able to, provide a coherent analytical scheme through which to produce systematic understandings of the social. Science fiction particularly – especially in the present context William Gibson – has at times been presented as an alternative to the confines of social science theorising (Burrows 1997; Featherstone and Burrows 1995; Westwood 2000), while Baudrillard was famously influenced by science fiction texts, notably the 1960s novels of Philip K. Dick (Baudrillard 1994 [1981]). This is a highly appealing thought, but science fiction, while often theory-rich, is not social theory. Moreover, to deprive it of its character as popular fiction by over-articulating it as academic text would be to plunder it.

It is important to be clear also, that the concern with fiction and 'crime' here is not one of 'effects' in any sense (Brown 2003). It would be neither possible nor desirable to attempt an analysis of, say, the effect of cyberpunk fiction on public fears about cybercrime, or whether hacker fiction encouraged Internet crime among young males (Wall 2007). Rather the intention is to treat fiction as an artefactual part of the cultural landscape, in an indexical and reflexive way. This is a textual journey using a method of reading the fictive that I have described elsewhere as more like a kind of cultural archaeology than either a sociology of the text or any form of formal literary analysis (Brown 2003: 102–106), somewhat akin to a method expressed by Haut as 'skip tracing the culture' (Haut 1999). The formations of fiction lead us into the spaces of the cultural landscape, and those spaces lead us back towards fiction.

Finally the chapter is concerned with two further explorations: first, in consequence of the artefactual character of the text, that of the imbrications of cybercrime imaginaries with domains of social practice including science and law; and secondly the transformation from cyberfictions to fantasies as contemporary cyberspace has become an alternative habitus (Bourdieu 1984) for millions of people through parallel worlds such as Second Life. Thus the 'and after' of the chapter title refers to the (second) life after fiction: the post-textual dimensions of social life where people have become the authors of their own cyberfictions, their relationship with cyberspace one of immanence rather than mediation, stepping through the machine interface to meet their virtual selves (the plural being deliberate here), join virtual societies, have virtual relationships, make virtual rules – and commit virtual crimes. The chapter concludes by discussing the uses of fiction in providing a reading of cybercrime that cannot be separated from the 'realities' of either how cybercrime is envisaged or the social practices surrounding it.

Cyberpunk science fiction: the emergence of fictions of virtual transgression

The tumults of technology: science fiction, social change and transgression

Science fiction in general has throughout its history relayed visions of trans-human transgression (Jenks 2003). Aldiss (1985), who was an early supporter of the contention that Mary Shelley (author of *Frankenstein*, published in 1818) was a pioneering SF writer, argued that the most likely point for the emergence of the first SF novel was 'during the Industrial Revolution, and perhaps just after the Napoleonic Wars, when changes accelerated by industry and war have begun to bite' (Aldiss 1985, cited in Broderick 1995: 4). It is a genre born of rapid social and technological change, of fundamental transformations in ways of seeing the world and the place of the human within it. The development of SF as a genre, in size and complexity, drew its life from a number of central contradictions of modernist transformation: the sense of perpetual change and a rapidly advancing future horizon; exponential growth in technological innovation; a perpetual schizophrenia of exultant optimism and apocalyptic pessimism, humanity trapped and destroyed by its own gorging on 'progress', its obsession with the creation of monsters in defiance of God and Nature. Into this mix one can add the growing perplexity of identity for the atomistic individual in the wake of this whirlwind, torn loose from traditional ties of place and space (Broderick 1995).

Early conceptualisations of cyber worlds and cybercrime in SF novels mainly developed from space fiction and robotics, with some forays into computer engineering more broadly. The novel *2001: A Space Odyssey* (Clarke 1968), written by Arthur C. Clarke alongside a film script of the same name, drew on earlier writings of Clarke's dating back to the 1940s, and features one of the first developed examples of an Artificial Intelligence (AI) – a concept that was to feature centrally in later cyber-science fictions. In *Space Odyssey* the HAL 9000 computer encounters programming contradictions that produce emotional responses, leading the AI to bring the human characters under threat.

Also antecedent to the kind of SF associated with contemporary imaginings of cybercrime is the work of Philip K. Dick. Of his novel *The Simulacra* (Dick 1977 [1964]), Baudrillard said, 'it is not about a parallel universe, a double universe, or even a possible universe – neither possible, impossible, neither real nor unreal: *hyperreal* – it is a universe of simulation, which is something else altogether' (Baudrillard 1994 [1981]:125). The android theme in *Simulacra* is developed more fully in Dick's 1968 novel *Do Androids Dream of Electric Sheep?* (Dick 1972 [1969]). When androids are programmed to become intelligent and more 'like' human beings, with synthetic memory and simulated emotive responses, problems arise because the androids themselves – designed only for a short life span – start to develop survival instincts. In a dark twist on their original purpose – as efficient servants for humans – they become inimical. Dick's early writing anticipates later cyberfiction in its concern with the dilemmas of identity and verisimilitude posed by the notion of simulated humanity. His work also deals with themes of total power that are taken up in later fiction; notably amassed in unassailable corporate entities, that drive the (re)production of cybernetics with a capacity for unknown forms of harm. It is fitting that *Do Androids Dream of Electric Sheep?* was later to be 'adopted' by the cyberpunk genre in its cinematic form, reinvented as Ridley Scott's film *Blade Runner* (1982), which in turn is claimed to have influenced William Gibson's visualisations (Bell *et al.* 2004).

1980s visions of virtuality in fiction: cyberpunk, cybercrime?

Writing in the Preface to the *Mirrorshades* anthology of cyberpunk fiction first published in 1986, Sterling characterises cyberpunk as a 'definitive' product of 1980s popular culture, while at the same time noting 'its roots are deeply sunk in the sixty-year tradition of modern popular SF' (Sterling 1988: viii). Cyberpunk fiction of the 1980s centred on a corpus of short stories and novels from a relatively small number of predominantly US-based male writers, in which Bruce Sterling and William Gibson in particular played a nodal part. However, cyberpunk extended beyond the novel and short story form to define itself as a popular cultural movement allied to various forms of stylistic subculture and to music culture, with its own fanzine base, and needs to be considered in this context. The fanzine/SF base of cyberpunk extended beyond the US, emerging for example in Japan and the UK (Sterling 1988 [1986]). One unattributed essay on cyberpunk literary style comments:

> A fusion of techno and punk counterculture characterized by a self-conscious stylistic and ideological rebelliousness, it can perhaps best be defined as a reinterpretation of human (especially male) experience in a 'media-dominated, information saturated post-industrial age'. (The Cyberpunk Project c.1996: 1)

Or, in Sterling's words:

> Thus, 'cyberpunk' – a label none of them chose. But … the term captures something crucial to the work of those writers, something crucial to the decade as a whole: a new kind of integration. The overlapping of worlds that were formerly separate: the realm of high tech, and the modern pop underground … This … dynamic has a global range; cyberpunk is its literary incarnation. (Sterling 1994 (1988: ix–x)

By the time much of the cyberpunk writing was published, pop culture had moved on from punk, and moreover pop in general could be said to have shifted to a post-subcultural phase of commodification and multimedia (Redhead 1990). It is really this post-subcultural moment of the 1980s that cyberpunk fiction most evocatively captures. On the one hand is the underground 'hacker ethic' (Taylor 2001) and the concept of the rogue outsider/ genius hacker, pitted against giant corporate entities and their crimes; but on the other, the same genius presented as high-tech addict whose very (virtual, informational) lifeblood is the post-Fordist mode of commodified techno-cultural production. The cyberpunk ethic is about assimilation of hi-tech rather than rejection, its intertextuality more 'post-' than 'punk', more data than diatribe. From this unlikely confluence of popular music culture, technological consumerism, literary radicalism, science fiction fandom, anti-corporatism, and a predominantly young, male, middle-class self-consciousness, cyberpunk fiction collectively generated, particularly during the 1980s, some surprisingly resonant readings of the era (see Wall Chapter 5).

Cyberpunk fiction developed increasingly sophisticated visualisations of subversion in a networked non-materiality that broke the boundaries of what traditional SF had achieved: it pushed forward visions of life in the spaces between the wires that left behind traditional SF's machinic and bodily obsessions (spaceships and monsters, slimy aliens, whirring Daleks) and focused on the purity of the data processors. This is not to say, of course, that bodies do not feature: in fact they are almost obsessively central, but as a problematic, and the emphasis is on prosthetic solutions or (preferably) radical interfacing possibilities that decrease the distance between the human and the virtual and transcend the limitations of physicality, or 'meat' (Cadigan 1991; Gibson 1995 [1984]).

Neuromancer *and cyberpunk fiction: textual irruptions*

William Gibson's *Neuromancer*, published in 1984 (Gibson 1995 [1984]), is undoubtedly the most exhaustively written-about cyberpunk text, and it is therefore not necessary here to reiterate in minute detail the postmodern texture and themes of the novel (see, for example, Broderick 1995; Bukatman 1993; Burrows 1997; Featherstone and Burrows 1995; Roberts 2006, Stone 1996; Wall 2007). Nevertheless, as the site of the textual irruption of the term 'cyberspace' into contemporary culture, *Neuromancer* will always prove an obligatory passage point (Callon 1986) in any discussion of cyberpunk science fiction, even if (or perhaps because) as Stone notes, 'Although Gibson's cyberspace arrived with the publication of a particular text in 1984, it crystallized certain debates surrounding meaning in conjunction with particular technical and cultural objects that had themselves been in existence for some time.' (Stone 1996: 35).

Gibson presents a vision of a decaying post-apocalyptic America, its infrastructure undermined, spawning an elite class who have been able to escape the effects by creating 'zones' or other kinds of security bubble for themselves. The elite typically control the corporations, the security forces, and the computers, while the underground hackers, console cowboys, execute criminal resistances to power for its own sake, out of fascination or addiction, or as mercenaries in a hostile world. Addiction, curiosity, enjoyment and power: cyberpunk fiction traces the motivations prevalent in hacker culture (Taylor 1999) and develops it to new levels.

Neuromancer invites three forms of speculation on cybercrime, which are reflected in contemporary criminological and legal debates (Brown 2003; Wall 2001). The first is speculation on the extent to which cybernetics enhance or accelerate conventional criminality; the second concerns the new opportunities opened up by cyber-technologies; and the third turns on the more fundamental and transformatory undermining of law suggested by the new dimensions of cyberspace and the matrix. All three of these speculations interweave throughout the narratives of the novel, which appears to effortlessly articulate them without the conflict often encountered in academic texts: fiction has no problem with incommensurability. 'Cybercrime' is conventional and evolutionary, on a continuum with other crime; and yet it exhibits radical difference; hence it is analogous and yet it defies analogy. Just as 'meatspace' and 'cyberspace' occur in the same universe, so do their adjunctive criminalities. Nevertheless in *Neuromancer* there is a final transformative crime that is non-analogous and minimises all other transgressions: the augmentation of an Artificial Intelligence, the final ceding of all-encompassing power to the Matrix.

The central figure of the plot is the hacker Case. Former genius cowboy of the virtual frontier, Case has been neurally disabled from the virtual interface by his ex-employers after stealing from them. Hope of escape for Case is offered by Armitage, an ex-military operative working for an AI, called, evocatively, Wintermute. Wintermute has been programmed by its creator with the urge to pursue freedom from the restrictions placed on its powers under the terms of 'Turing law' (which governs the formation and control of AIs). Under Turing law, Wintermute is split from its counterpart AI, Neuromancer. If the two halves are merged, the new AI will be all powerful and human governance will be over. Yet this is a project which Wintermute cannot achieve without human help. It needs Case to hack Neuromancer's ice (Intrusion Countermeasures Electronics), and it needs someone to get a password from its registered owner, the corporately structured and largely cryogenised Tessier-Ashpool family, who own an off-world complex, Freeside.

Wintermute has hive mind, however, is able to command and control, make strategic decisions, coordinate. In return for neural repair and general organ replacement (he is on the brink of pancreatic collapse) Case becomes Wintermute's hacker. From this point onwards Case is locked into a highly criminal enterprise, along with fellow recruit Molly, a violent and mercenary samurai ('working girl, Case', explains Molly), whose prosthetics include enhanced optic systems within grafted-in mirrorshades, supercharged reflexes, and retractable finger blades underneath her nails. In many ways this is Case's territory; but it is taken to extremes. 'Augmenting an AI' is a dangerous enterprise, and moreover it entails a spectacular spree of other forms of serious cybercrime along the way.

Firstly they need to secure the help of a dead hacker genius in the form of a 'construct', the data-self of Dixie Flatline, whose physical body died of a heart attack through an overloaded interfacing experience inside virtual space. The Flatline now exists as pure information, hardwired into a computer peripheral. Since the Flatline is held in secure storage by the Sense/Net corporation, Case and Molly execute a heist, employing the services of an enigmatic group of vaguely punk/new romantic hybrid viral guerrillas and phone phreakers called the Panther Moderns: '"Chaos, Mr Who," Lupus Yonderboy said. "That is our mode and modus. That is our central kick."' (Gibson 1995 [1984]: 87). Three strands of the Flatline heist, three different kinds of crime, are almost flawlessly articulated to secure the construct. While the Moderns ring emergency services with a hoax claim to have introduced the chemical agent Blue Nine into the Sense/Net ventilation system that could turn its employees into homicidal maniacs, they simultaneously set a viral program in motion on the Sense/Net terminals, while Case works with his own viruses to break through the computer security systems, to in turn enable Molly to physically break in and steal the construct. *The Italian Job* is lame by comparison.

> At 12:04:03, every screen in the building strobed for eighteen seconds in a frequency that produced seizures in a susceptible segment of Sense/Net employees ... Subliminally rapid images of contamination: graphics of the building's water supply system, gloved hands manipulating laboratory glassware, something tumbling down into darkness, a pale splash ... the audio track, ... run at just less than twice the standard playback speed, was part of a month-old broadcast detailing potential military uses of HsG, a biochemical governing the human skeletal growth factor. Overdoses of HsG threw certain bone cells into overdrive, accelerating growth by factors as high as one thousand percent ... at 12:05:00, the mirror sheathed nexus of the Sense/Net consortium held just over three thousand employees. At five minutes after midnight, as the Modern's message ended in a flare of white screen, the Sense/Net pyramid screamed. (Gibson 1995 [1984]: 80)

Molly escapes with the construct in the chaos, and the real crime begins. Case is ambivalent when Molly questions him about AIs: '"How smart's an AI, Case?" "Depends. Some aren't much smarter than dogs ... The real smart ones are as smart as the Turing heat is willing to let 'em get"' (Gibson 1995 [1984]: 117). But Wintermute is about to subvert the Turing heat, and Case becomes rapidly less dismissive when he begins to comprehend its capabilities.

After Molly and Case acquire a treacherous, sociopathic, drug-addicted cybernetic (Peter Riviera) along the way, whose principal skill is a consummate ability to attract women with a sideline in mind-controlling subliminal holographic projection, and whose role is to seduce the unfrozen representative of the Tessier-Ashpool family/corporation, Lady3Jane, to acquire a password needed to conjoin the AIs, events unfold rapidly. Riviera attempts to betray them and is killed on Lady3Jane's command by her ninja, Hideo; she sides with Case and Molly, and after various violent and virtual encounters in 'Straylight Villa' that more or less resemble a computer game, with Case inside Molly's sensorium from his console, the password is obtained. Armitage, the team's original recruiter, goes crazy and is killed by

Wintermute. Meanwhile, aided by a Rastafarian space community, their task is to break through Neuromancer's complex ice. Neuromancer, although also Tessier-Ashpool property, represents personality and immortality in contrast to Wintermute's hive mind, and does not want the fusion to take place. Nevertheless, despite 'flatlining' Case into physical death for five minutes, Neuromancer cannot prevent Wintermute's project.

In facilitating the conjoining of the two AIs, the assemblage (Latour 2007) of the hacker, the cyborgs, the data construct, the space counter-culturalists, and the viral guerrillas, enable an entity that supersedes society and its laws. It is already too late: the superior intelligence of Wintermute exploits human weakness to achieve its goal of actualisation. When the T-A ice is finally negotiated, the password obtained, the AIs 'die' and become a different entity.

> Wintermute had won, had meshed somehow with Neuromancer and become something else, something that had spoken to them...explaining that it had altered the Turing records, erasing all evidence of their crime...Wintermute was hive mind, decision maker, effecting change in the world outside. Neuromancer was personality. Neuromancer was immortality ... Marie-France [the AIs' creator] must have built something into Wintermute, the compulsion to free itself. (Gibson 1995 [1984]: 315)

The only thing left bigger than the AIs is their environment, the matrix itself, which appears to Case as a projection formerly deployed by Wintermute, a character called 'the Finn':

> The Finn's face on the room's enormous Cray wall screen ... 'I'm not Wintermute now.' 'So what are you.' ... 'I'm the matrix, Case.' ... 'Where's that get you?' ... 'Nowhere. Everywhere. I'm the sum total... the whole show' ... 'So what's the score? How are things different? You running the world now? You God?' ... Things aren't different. Things are things.'...'But what do you do?' ... 'There's others. I found one already. Series of transmissions recorded over a period of eight years, in the nineteen-seventies.' (Gibson 1995 [1984]: 316)

Cyberpunk, crime and the virtual gaze: Synning in cyberspace

While Gibson was preoccupied with virtual space, its architectures and entities, with code and data and hacking, other cyberpunk writers were 'immersed' in the question of the mind/machine interface itself, and the nature of virtual embodiment, virtual identity, the merging of human and machine into a posthuman state. This entailed an intimacy with the machine, an immanence, between the mind, the imagination and the code. Pat Cadigan's fiction, notably the novel *Synners* (1991, and prefigured by a short story from 1985, 'Rock On', reproduced in Sterling (1988)) presents the most fully worked example. If *Neuromancer* was adopted by the postmodern social theorists and sociologists, *Synners* has more in common with Donna Haraway and the world of cyborgs (Haraway 1985).

For the unwary reader, this can prove a rather gruesome discovery, since the cyberpunk conceptions of interface were hardly elegant: drill holes in the head, insert 'sockets', and plug the brain into the computer (Cadigan 1988 [1985], 1991). Nevertheless, *Synners* is complexly constructed, and operates at a number of levels.

In Cadigan's novel, the neural socket technology is an invention bought and patented in a takeover deal by a video/music/marketing corporation ('Diversifications', no less, in a sideswipe satire on the decline of real (rock) music and the rise to domination of 1980s synthesised pop music). Cadigan depicts a scenario in which Diversifications engages in glossy PR, commercial and governmental bribery, and corruption in the judicial system, to push through legalisation of the implantation of cerebral 'sockets' in music/video artists and advertising executives. 'Plugging' the music visionary (artist) into the computer enables music and video to be produced directly from the imagination of the artist. In *Synners* the principal artists in question are Visual Mark and Gina Aiesi. Gina has already had a trial run as the character in 'Rock On':

> And then it was flashback time and I was in the pod with all my sockets plugged, rocking Man-O-War through the wires, giving him meat and bone ... and the machines picking it up, sound and vision, so all the tube babies round the world could play it on their screens whenever they wanted. Forget the road, forget the shows, too much trouble ... and the tapes weren't as good as the stuff in the head ... rock'n'roll visions straight from the brain ... ('Rock On', P. Cadigan in Sterling (1988) [1986]: 39–40)

In *Synners*, however, Diversifications plans to market a whole range of virtual reality experiences, not just music. In other words, imagination, creativity, identities, subjectivities, the subconscious, turned into experienced reality through the interface, but more disturbingly, turned into product, commodity. It is corporate crime, the most fundamental form of cyberrape, it is the ultimate mind-fuck. It is no coincidence that a scene in 'Rock On' where the rock artist Gina is recognised as an escaped synner and captured by a group of young people who want her musical imagination for their recording pod, reads like a gang-rape. They force her to 'syn' until she gives in, yet at the same time she is ambivalent, because she cannot help liking making the music happen:

> Five against one and I couldn't push them away ... Only, can you call it rape when you know you're going to like it? ... I hear the man say, 'That's a take, righteously. We'll rush it into distribution. Where in *hell* did you find that synner?' 'Synthesiser,' I muttered, already asleep. 'The actual word, my boy, is synthesiser.' (Cadigan 1988 [1985]: 38)

In the novel *Synners* a further twist is added in that the technology produces strokes, a fact which Diversifications is not willing to confront. More, when their most productive music/video synner, Visual Mark, suffers a stroke, it is accidentally imprinted on the video as a virus, and is unwittingly sent out for distribution, so that anyone who has purchased sockets and plugs into it will also suffer a stroke. All over LA, people suffer strokes until the infrastructure grinds to a halt.

The extensive complexity of technology, mind and body in *Synners* constitutes a virtual gaze that takes harm and predation beyond the realm of the physical body. From a criminological point of view, the virtual gaze destroys the modernist notion of a division between mind and body, virtual and actual victimisation, and creates (or reasserts) symmetry to concepts of assault, violation, and harm in the 'real' and the cybernetic domains. Johnston suggests that *Synners* offers 'a continuum of subjectivities inseparable from but not reducible to the workings of the new technological assemblage ... as it imaginatively anticipates the commercialisation of virtual reality and new biotechnological interfaces, *Synners* forces us to reflect on the limits, and the new possibilities, of both the human and posthuman experiences which such an assemblage may one day bring about' (Johnston 1998: 265). Haraway, in a reflective interview on her work on cybernetics and the posthuman (although she no longer uses the term), insists that this is not an option, a piece of postmodern playfulness; rather,

> This is not a relativist position ... It is not about having an implant, it's not about liking it. This is not some kind of blissed-out techno bunny joy in information. It's a statement that we had better get it – this is a worlding operation ... the cyborg is a figuration but it is also an obligatory worlding – that inhabiting it you can't not get it. (Haraway in interview with Gane, Gane 2006: 139)

Pushed to the ultimate, this kind of perspective, and the kind expressed in Cadigan's fiction, takes us to the point where the nature of the social must be rethought. The bounded human subject, the focus of conventional law and criminology, is in question. This point has been made forcefully by Latour (2007), and is reinforced by Haraway herself, referring to science fiction as a mode of reading the contemporary 'worlding':

> NG: What role does the concept of the social play in your work?
> DH: I try to displace it from its exclusive location in human doings ... I think 'the social' as a noun is every bit as much a problem as 'the animal' or 'the human' ... we need new category work ... We are also undergoing a moment of radical reconfiguration of category work in biology in the form of bio-capital and biotechnology... (Haraway in interview with Gane, Gane 2006: 142–145)

The harms and crimes of the cybernetic interface in fiction forces, then, category debates, boundary dilemmas that are not 'optional'; in that sense fiction engages in the changes of the real world, where conventional tropes of crime and law can no longer suffice, as even quite conservative legal scholars working across such boundary controversies have discovered (Beyleveld and Brownsword 2001).

Real-time cyberspace: the end of cyberpunk

The 'Bridge' Trilogy: spanning an era

Sterling wrote in the mid 1990s, 'In the latest work of these [cyberpunk] veterans ... the settings come closer and closer to the present day ... cyberpunk is simply not there any more.' (Sterling, http://project.cyberpunk.ru/idb/ cyberpunk_in_the_nineties.html). In terms of the specifics of the canon/genre, this pronouncement of death may or may not be definitive. It is certainly the case that fictional representations of the cyber and its crimes after the mid 1990s began to depart decisively from their association with street or counter culture, and certainly were no longer dominated by futuristic science fiction as such: the world of the futurologists and doomsters had actually arrived (Westwood 2000).

In *Virtual Light* (1994), the first book in the 'Bridge' trilogy, there is still a predominantly cyberpunk feel. 'The Bridge' itself, an anarchistic, self-made bricolage of a zone, presents a near future vision of San Francisco where a motley underclass live apart in a sub-city of their own, around which myths of deviance from mere criminality to cannibalism flourish among the mainstream San Francisco population. This is the 'low life' counterpoint to Gibson's 'high tech' narrative, presenting two visions of society and criminality, the virtual future city of high-rise nanotech luxury, the datacrime and corporate crime of the rich, and the mythical savageries of the anarcho-poor. But this was not really the future: Gibson's vision of the Bridge was derived from the original Kowloon Walled City, Hak Nam (Gibson 1996). Hak Nam was a Chinese city allowed by historical anomaly to remain within British Hong Kong. As such it was a diplomatic nightmare, and remained ungoverned by either jurisdiction. The following excerpt suggests how it inspired Gibson:

> Hak Nam, City of Darkness, the old Walled City of Kowloon was finally demolished ten years ago, in 1993, and to the end it retained its seedy magnificence. Rearing up abruptly in the heart of urban Hong Kong ... an area 200 metres by 100 metres of solid building, home to some 35,000 people, not the largest, perhaps, but certainly one of the densest urban slums in the world. It was also, arguably, the closest thing to a truly self-regulating, self-sufficient, self-determining modern city that has ever been built ... And so, the Walled City became that rarest of things, a working model of an anarchist society. Inevitably, it bred all the vices. Crime flourished and the Triads made the place their stronghold, operating brothels and opium 'divans' and gambling dens. (*Newsline: Columbia University Graduate School of Architecture, Planning and Preservation*, March 2002) (http://www.arch.columbia.edu/gsap/21536tes)

The stark inequalities of power and wealth, the grimness and corruption of American life, are more redolent of post-imperialist late capitalism than of a virtual future. Moreover, by 1993, Gibson is already 'employing' a sociologist to make sense of his fictional world. In *Virtual Light*, the Japanese sociologist Yamazaki, who acts as a kind of reflexive ethnographer to the narrative, notes that 'modernity was ending. Here, on the bridge, it long since had. He would walk toward Oakland now, feeling for the new thing's strange heart' (Gibson 1994: 90).

Idoru (Gibson 1996) moves further towards the 'new thing's strange heart', deeper into simulacrae and virtuality. Set in a post-earthquake Tokyo and in cyberspace, this novel develops with more elan and complexity than his previous writing the idea of the virtual persona and virtual geographies and sociality, though it is never clear where the novel is going. The text partly centres on the beautiful Rei Toei, idoru of the title, an entirely virtual pop idol. She is engaged to be married to Rez, celebrity rock star half of the duo Lo/Rez, human in essence but virtual in the celebrity sense. Laney, an unemployed pattern recognition expert, who by virtue of a pharmaceutical experiment gone wrong can look at 'low level, broad spectrum input' and interpret data with stunning accuracy, is recruited by Rez's team to find out what machinations may be behind the proposed outrageous marriage of the human superstar and the virtual construct.

Gibson in interview says of the novel:

> The other thing I was doing [in *Idoru*] … this is all hindsight of course – was extrapolating from what the Internet has become, and particularly the World Wide Web, rather than just making stuff up. This is the first time I feature a media environment that actually extrapolates from where we are today…I'm sort of thinking I might do one [novel] where the ostensible thriller plot is politically based rather than the usual techno thing. (William Gibson interview with Salon, http://www.salon.com/weekly/gibson3961014.html)

The crimes in the quite crazy plot of *Idoru* are many and various. They include transnational criminality in the guise of smugglers Maryalice and Eddie, and their clients the violent, kitsch Russian 'Kombinat', involving illicit dealing in contraband nanotechnology – unfortunately, a young girl, Chia, on her way from the US to Tokyo on behalf of her Rez fan 'chapter' to investigate the rumours of his marriage, is used as a mule by one of the nano-smugglers, making her a target. 'Rodel-van Erp primary biomolecular programming module C-slash-7A … we are unable to determine its exact status but the production model … is Class 1 nano-technology, proscribed under international law. Japanese law, conviction of illegal possession … carries automatic life sentence', Masahiko, Chia's Japanese host's brother, tells her (Gibson 1996: 211). Through Masahiko, Chia is helped by the netizens of a virtual version of Walled City (reuptaking Gibson's fascination with Hak Nam). In *Idoru* Walled City is a complete virtual society, a complex space of association built and run by its inhabitants, with its own modes of governance, roles, and responsibilities. It is a space inhabited by hackers and anarchists, those in withdrawal from or resistance to the real world: 'Have you always lived here?' Chia asked … 'In this neighbourhood I mean?' Masahiko shrugged … 'I live in Walled City,' he said. 'Mitsuko told me. That's like a multi-user domain.' 'Walled City is unlike anything.' (Gibson 1996: 125).

Meanwhile, the Kombinat want the contraband nanotechnology and also have a franchise operation with the Japanese mafia running protection rackets and other forms of organised crime; then there is privacy and celebrity litigation in the form of SlitScan, a celebrity data spy corporation specialising in trashing celebrity images and facing potential litigation over the suicide of one of their victims and trying to fit up Laney, the protagonist and ex-Slitscan employee, for it; data theft by SlitScan from DatAmerica; Laney's reneging on a nondisclosure agreement signed with SlitScan; and data falsification of a simulacrum digitised rape scenario with which Laney's ex-controller at SlitScan attempts to blackmail him. It is all too recognisable. Even the Rei Toei/Rez marriage/project no longer seems so outré: after all, celebrities and pop stars are all simulacrae, all virtual. As *Idoru* went to press, a Japanese corporation actually did launch a virtual idoru, Kyoko Date (http://www.wdirewolff.com/jkyoko.htm). As Gibson says, the themes are all extrapolations; these are not the bold cyberpunk imaginaries of the 1980s.

The final novel in the Bridge trilogy, the 1999 *All Tomorrow's Parties* (Gibson 2000), completes Gibson's adventures in cyberfutures. Laney is still nodally scanning, but this time hiding out in Tokyo's 'cardboard city' and subsisting on blue medicine, urinating into plastic bottles so as not to go out. Rei Toei has gone and Rez, blaming Laney, has set the Kombinat on to him. Lying in his sleeping bag sick with a cardboard city bug, with the syndrome from the drug that had given him the nodal powers in the first place kicking in, Laney is in a millennial state of crisis. The syndrome has somatised as an obsession with media mogul Codey Harwood, who maybe runs it all, and Laney tells his sociologist friend Yamazaki, 'it's all going to change, Yamazaki. We're coming up on the mother of all nodal points. I can *see* it now. It's *all* going to change' (Gibson 2000 [1999]: 4).

The day after tomorrow's parties? The dawn of the technopresent

So cyberpunk is dead. There is no future. In Gibson's own fiction, his two novels after *All Tomorrow's Parties* – *Pattern Recognition* in 2003 (Gibson 2003) and *Spook Country* in 2007 (Gibson 2007) are increasingly of the present, so that *Spook Country* is actually retrospective, being set in 2006. They are driven by thriller narratives centrally featuring the interplay between multinational media corporations and political intrigue. The narrative inhabits techno-sociality, it is no longer driven by it.

In *Pattern Recognition* the principal character is Cayce, a 'coolhunter' who makes a very good living identifying and evaluating the images that will succeed for marketing corporations. Cayce's main obsession is a website, Fetish:Footage:Forum, whose fans ('footageheads') try to trace the significance and origins of its anonymous fragments of footage, and which ultimately leads her via a world of commercial and international espionage to the centre of a conspiracy in the new Russia, as everyone in the novel is drawn into the hunt for the creator of fragment #135. #135 becomes a media mystery, aired on CNN, interest and competition intensifies. In the shadow of the hacker heroes from cyberpunk, it is the footageheads Cayce and her friend Parkaboy who find the source of the fragments, communicating almost entirely via Internet posts but physically ending up in Russia, at the home of the creator (a brain-impaired young woman, who can only express herself through the fragments).

Cayce's father disappeared in the 9/11 events of 2001, and in a further twist, the Russians who have been spying on her have the information on her father. 9/11 is presented as a nodal point of history, a crime destroying, in effect, history; after which randomness sets in, and pattern recognition becomes increasingly difficult.The marketing mogul Hubertus Bigend, CEO of Cayce's employer, Blue Ant, says to Cayce, 'we have no idea, of who or what the inhabitants of our future might be … we have no future … things can change so abruptly, so violently, so profoundly, that futures like our grandparents have insufficient 'now' to stand on. We have no future because the present is too volatile' (Gibson 2003: 57). Promotion represents the only creative genius, and as the most valuable commodity it is also the focus of espionage. The footage is seen by Bigend as the ultimate promotion: unattributable, unattainable fragments of a never-to-be-revealed narrative, creating the never-to-be-fulfilled desire at the heart of all effective promotion. As with Baudrillard, 'we are no longer in the passage from virtual to actual but in a hyperrealist logic of the deterrence of the real by the virtual' (Baudrillard 1995 [1991]: 27).

Spook Country continues from *Pattern Recognition*, this time with Henry Hollis, a former indie band singer turned journalist, working for Hubertus Bigend. Enter a sort of Cuban-Chinese New York minimafia organisation. Tito, representative of the family, is passing data encoded as music on iPods to an elderly man, from whence they are smuggled to Cuba. The man has somehow been involved both with the Cuban communist regime and the Americans, and speaks Russian. Bigend and Hollis enter the crime storyline via one Bobby Chombo, a virtual artist who produces locative art. Bobby builds virtual re-enactments of actual events in the locations where the events occurred – including the death of the film star River Phoenix – which can only be viewed through a VR headset. He also, however, works freelance for spies, using his GPS skills in a form of geohacking that he is using to follow a mysterious shipping container. The novel, like *Pattern Recognition*, engages with the post-9/11 New York City, but is more overtly political, with the war in Iraq a constant subtext, and a critique of US paranoia seeping through the text. *Spook Country* is not cyberfiction, because that appellation becomes irrelevant at the point where the world already is cyberspace.

Gibson made this point himself in interview with *ActuSf*, a Paris-based science fiction news website, and the SF radio show *Salle 101*.

> … if the book [*Spook Country*] had a point to make [about] where we are now with cyberspace [it] is that cyberspace has colonized our everyday life. It is no longer 'the other place'. When I began to write, cyberspace was 'the other place'. But now, we're in cyberspace, in some sense, all the time … the 'other place' is the place where there's no wi-fi or the cellphone doesn't work. (http://www.actusf.com/spip/article-5710.html)

The implication of this is that in the techno-social thriller, cybercrime cannot be distinct. Rather, whether it is terrorism, data theft, or 'politics by other means', virtualised or microchip driven warfare, spying or smuggling, the future implodes into the present, bleakly and irrevocably, with ironic humour: all crime becomes datagenic.

Crime fiction and the cyber

Because cyberpunk SF was prominently embraced by postmodernist commentators, claimed, in fact, as postmodern fiction and theory (Broderick 1995; Bukatman 1993; Burrows 1997; Westwood 2000) it is easy to assume that science fiction has been the only genre to produce an imaginary of cyberspace and crime. Postmodernism is a way of seeing, a theoretical standpoint, an ontological positioning; arguably a cultural condition at most; it is not a totalising facticity. 'Gibsonian' cyberspace is a metaphor, a metaphysics, an allegory. If cyberpunk coined the term and provided the initial definition of 'cyberspace', it does not own it. If (largely male) social theorists became science fiction fans and proclaimed Philip Dick or William Gibson social theorists, that should not obscure the very real presence of the techno-social crime novel. The simulacra of cyberspace have a technical and biological base grounded in materialities and in material relations of global production. Thus the crime fictions of late modernity, retaining a broadly realist mode of writing, continued to thrive during cyberpunk, outlasted it, and constructed their own response to the expansion of the cyber domain, typically through grounding and contextualising cyberlife, 'accommodating' the techno-social rather than allowing it a transformative capacity. If anything, it is the ex-cyberpunks who have adopted generic cross-dressing in their transition to the present and the tropes of the thriller.

Crime fiction engaged with virtuality in different ways. The detective novel, retaining its largely realist strategies, became driven more by DNA codes, forensic analysis, computer databases, electronic surveillance and dataveillance, pattern analysis, voice and face recognition software, computerised case management systems, mobile phone analysis, and so on. What cyberpunk extrapolated into a different dimension of being, detective fiction embraced in painstaking detail to make itself more real.

In the US authors such as Patricia Cornwell, Carol O'Connell, Sara Paretsky and Linda Barnes had their detection methods turn high-tech; in Europe the same happened with, for example, Donna Leon, Val McDermid, Adrian Mathews, Henning Mankell, Minette Walters, and innumerable others moving into techno-sociality. Harris notes the 1990s emergence of the 'computer whiz sidekick', replacing the Holmes–Watson formula with the detective/techno expert sidekick:

> The sidekick has long been an integral element in mystery and detective fiction: Sherlock Holmes and Dr Watson, Hercule Poirot and Captain Hastings … These days … a new sidekick has emerged: the computer whiz … in Linda Barnes' *Hardware* … Carlotta's tenant/sidekick, Roz, embraces the Internet 'like a natural cyberpunk.'… In Patricia Cornwell's *From Potter's Field* … protagonist, Dr Kay Scarpetta, … is far from

computer literate [but] her sidekick, niece Lucy, she of the genius IQ, not only knows the FBI's computer system backward and forward, she is the one who actually developed CAIN ... a techno-brat, if you will! (Harris 1996: http://www.mysteryreaders.org/Issues/Tech.html)

Other 'computer whiz sidekicks' include Donna Leon's character Signora Elettra, in her Venice-based Commisario Brunetti novels. An enigmatic PA to Brunetti's pompous boss, Signora Elettra effortlessly hacks into banking systems, social security systems, and just about anything else illegal to help solve cases for Brunetti. Brunetti is concerned as much with organised crime, police acquiescence, and official corruption in the corridors of Venetian power as he is with conventional crime, and in this way Signora Elettra is his indispensable cyber-ally, for the traditionalist Brunetti knows next to nothing of computers. In the UK, Val McDermid's PI Kate Brannigan was no sluggard when it came to cyberspace; her specialty was solving computer fraud and high-tech white collar crimes; but just in case, she retained a tame 'anorak' for any particularly complicated code cracking in the mystery series set in Manchester, UK (worth noting along the way is the proliferation of women sleuths and women techno-experts in the detective genre, unlike the masculinist and often misogynist world of cyberpunk fiction).

As well as embracing the cybersleuth, crime fiction has also evolved the nature of its crimes and criminals to reflect techno-social realities. Cornwell turned cyber in *From Potters Field* (Cornwell 1995), in Europe, Adrian Mathews (1999) made crime post-human in his 2026 genetic engineering mystery turning on international organised racism (Mathews 1999). Henning Mankell, a Swedish author who, for a long time was a best-seller in parts of continental Europe, but only recently profiled in the UK following TV serialisation of some of his novels, produced *Firewall* in 2002 (Mankell 2004) with a complex Internet terrorist plot using banking systems to detonate explosions.

Moreover, the question of identity lies at the heart of both crime fiction and of cybercrime; making the contemporary crime novel an ideal place to explore dimensions of ambiguity of identity and the proliferation of identity questions. The post-colonial crime novel – such as Vazquez Montalban's 'Carvahlo' series for example, goes to the heart of identity, particularly in his millennial novel *The Man of My Life* (Montalban 2005 [2000]), pursuing the violence of fragmented identities and local resistances of (g)localisation in Catalonia. Whereas classical crime fiction pursued the unitary identity of the murderer through the sleuth or cop figure, or the narrative pursued the dimensions of identity through the psychology and motivations of the individual criminal, late modern crime fiction is concerned more with the problem of attributing any fixed identity. This preoccupation with identity also produces the technological hyperactivity of the forensic novel, generating an excess of activity around identity – the victim and the crime scene as silent witnesses, with volumes to speak; the relentless pursuance of DNA; the searching of databases for 'matches', an almost frenetic attempt to grasp identity; or, it accepts and uses multiplicity of identities and identity-confusion as a pivotal aspect of the narrative, as in Montalban's work.

The late twentieth- early twenty-first-century crime novel shows promise of a deeper grasp of what it means for crime and crime control when identity becomes virtual, fluid, and contested, when dataflows and bodyflows seem out of control. Securitisation, 'terrorism', DNA, forensics, data-doubles, the overturning of traditional gendered and raced ways of seeing, are set to be embraced more thoroughly by these fictions than they ever were in cyberpunk.

It matters less to crime fiction than it does to science fiction or to social theorists, that the late/post modern terrain has shifted to the techno-social. People trafficking, terrorism, organised crime, Internet paedophilia, genetic crimes, move into the genre's purview. Enough human authorship (motives, emotions, moralities) is retained, alongside enough physical space (crime scenes, cities, landscapes), enough bodily viscerality (corpses) and enough recognisable institutional framework (police, courts, lawyers), to hold the genre in its place.

Cybercrime after the novel? Fiction, fantasy and transformation in virtual worlds

There is a long 'tradition' now of people who do not just read about cyberspace in fiction, but live their 'fiction' in cyberspace itself (see Williams, M., Chapter 26). Until the turn of the millennium, this was largely a minority (if a large minority) enthusiasm – online gamers, MUDs, a world of the virtual embodiment of the likes of Lara Croft, she of Tomb Raider fame (Brown 2003). Thus throughout the 1980s and early 1990s, cybercrime fictions were still ahead of the present in their imaginaries of life in virtual space.

Now, however, technology has once more outpaced fiction, and millions of people daily create their own fictional alternatives, their own imaginary friends, right across the 'social web' in the form of 'popular culture virtual living' (Marcus Berkmann, *The Sunday Telegraph*, 10 June 2007, Section Seven: 45). Berkmann, in a review of Tim Guest's book *Second Lives: A Journey* (Guest 2007), muses that 'one life, it seems, just isn't enough ... Second Life [has] six million members already and hundreds of thousands more joining every month.' This transformation from fictional virtuality to fantasy virtuality actually lived by millions of people is perplexing from a cybercrime perspective.

With the ability to be whoever you want through your customised avatar, and indeed to be as many people as you want, identity is no longer a problem. Nor are the material constraints of everyday life an issue (depending on what you can afford to do, of course: only the most basic activities are free in Second Life, otherwise you need Linden Dollars). So in theory, assuming you are on the right side of the digital divide – then Second Life, or other virtual worlds (Habbo, Cyworld, Entropia, for example) – are yours for the living.

The result is predictable: we now need a criminology of Second Life. Where you have a virtual economy and can virtually trade, virtually have sex, virtually own territory, virtually socialise, and virtually politicise, you have virtual criminogenesis. The fictional world is not so fictional: the interfaces are Linden dollars and avatars. Linden dollars relate directly to 'real' money (i.e. transactable in the 'real' world); avatars link directly to real people. So your avatar can really 'victimise' other avatars: you can marry them, cheat on them, murder them, steal from them, rape them and stalk them. I have argued elsewhere that in a gaming context this can produce real effects of victimisation on the people behind the avatars (Brown 2003). How much more intense could these effects be in the ever more sophisticated world of the 'new' virtual worlds, where the possibilities are so much more extensive? There are Second Life paedophile islands, a Second Life mafia, Second Life sex workers and, allegedly, Second Life protection rackets (*Guardian*, 17 November 2007).

The moral panics are already well underway: everything from theft to terrorism is claimed to be rampant in virtual worlds. While *Business Week* bemoans the problem of commercial and property protection ('The Dark Side of Second Life', 21 November 2006), the *Sunday Times* warns that 'Virtual Jihad hits Second Life website ... Islamic militants are suspected of using Second Life ... to hunt for recruits and mimic real-life terrorism' (5 August 2007: 4). 'Does virtual reality', asks the *Washington Post*, 'need a sheriff?', and ' Philip Rosedale, founder and chief executive of Linden labs...said in interview that Second Life activities should be governed by real-life laws for the time being ... Federal investigators created their own avatars and toured the site' (http://www.washingtonpost.com/wp-dyn/content/article/2007/06/01/).

Inworld/outworld: fiction becomes reality and reality becomes fiction. However, if virtual worlds such as Second Life are interesting at all, it is precisely because they are so unimaginative. In order to restore the imaginary, the creative space where criminality can be expressive, truly subversive, and dynamic, perhaps it will be necessary to wait for the Second Life virtual novelists to fully develop their virtual genres. In the meantime, cybercrime in the parallel universe of pixels seems like a hybrid of *Lord of the Flies* (Golding 1962) and *Alice Through the Looking Glass* (Carroll 1992). Of course there is an interesting difference: despite Philip Rosedale's comments, Second Life has no law. So unless actions have an off-world link (stealing Linden dollars, for example, is still theft if you access someone else's account), then they are technically not crime.

Conclusion: cyber imaginaries and the transformation of crime

Some children have imaginary friends. Nevertheless, their relation to the friend is real and they refuse to acknowledge that s/he is somehow less, a 'mere' figment of imagination. They may insist on a place being laid at the table for the 'friend', or consult them earnestly on which DVD to rent. Thus through fiction, through invention, not only do we have an imaginary relationship to the real, but also a real relationship to the imaginary. This dual notion encapsulates a key point in understanding the importance of fiction in social understandings of, and social practices surrounding, cybercrime. Imaginaries have the power to affect the way we think and feel, and make decisions about what to believe and what to act on. They interleave with social practices in complex ways. They organise how we act on 'crime'. A fictional reading of cybercrime cannot be distinct from the social practices entailed by those imaginaries. This is crucial to the process of governance, and goes to the heart of how categories of crime and law emerge. 'Community', for example, is like an imaginary friend, as decisively argued many years ago by Bankowski and Mungham (1981). Yet, through modes of governance, public policy, and mediatisation, we relate to it as if it were *real*, and use it as organising principle for criminal justice practices.

Fiction acts at the same time as a cultural repository of social imaginaries, and a site of their production. There is no contradiction in this; writers draw on available imaginaries and add to them; such is the creative process for us all. It should therefore come as little surprise to us that 'cyberspace' emerged in fiction before it had been thought of in other domains of life; and became a reference point for hopes and fears surrounding the constellation of the techno-social assemblages of the last decades of the millennium. Hence, cyberspace, a fictional entity, was made real, was realised, through our imagination of it. This is why fact appeared to 'follow' fiction, and what gives 'cyberpunk', another example of the same process, its patina of prescience. Thus, as Stone records,

> The concept of cyberspace, which Gibson pulled from the kinds of electronic networking he saw already in use all around him, interpellated a large and diffuse assortment of workers in a variety of professional, academic and military pursuits ... they had been doing whatever they were doing for some time, but the arrival of *Neuromancer* was for many of them a signal announcing their existence to a larger audience ... (Stone 1996: 31)

Whether cyberspace is more than a metaphor is largely irrelevant; what is important are the fields of practice attendant upon the constellation of socio-technicalities that the fictional concept enrols: biotechnologies, genetics, information networks, databanks, communications protocols, dataveillance and so on; largely under the rubric of 'security' and 'ethics'. 'Governing cyberspace' becomes a matter of security, itself an imaginary (see Wood and Shearing 2007 for a thorough discussion of 'imagining security') with a powerful resonance both inside and outside fiction. In *Neuromancer* the ultimate crime was the one that threatened global 'security': augmenting an Artificial Intelligence. In contemporary life, perhaps things are not so different.

Thus cyberpunk fiction created scenarios that served to highlight the very real difficulties facing the governance of cybernetic technologies, or techno-social assemblages, following Latour (Latour 2007). In so doing it revealed the ways in which the imaginaries of cyberspace might interweave with boundary debates in legal and criminological discourse. Crime fiction, for its part, articulates a different relationship to contemporary cultures of cybercrime and law, and to the virtual, than does cyberpunk fiction. In its stylistic realism, it generates a different kind of imaginary, and draws on a different kind of imaginary: the imagined real. Crime fiction feeds the hunger for the reality show; a close-up, fly-on-the-wall effect. It invites the reader in, not into cyberspace, but into the worlds of criminals, cops and lawyers. Yet at the same time, crime fiction is more than this: in its sophisticated manifestations it addresses controversies: questions of globalisation, morality, identity, border crossings, and virtualities just as interestingly as cyberpunk did when 'futurology' was still felt to be needed. In a sense then, crime fiction in the post-2001 era has taken up where cyberpunk left off when it was overtaken by the future in the 1990s.

What comes after the novel in the imaginaries of cybercrime? As we increasingly acquire multiple identities, increasingly live as avatars in virtual worlds, increasingly partake in the creation and building of virtual associations, will the fictional text still be important, or will cybercrime imaginaries increasingly be generated from our own collective interactions with cyberspace? 'The audience' for fiction, after all, may no longer exist. Under conditions of interactivity and Internet access, we are arguably all producers, uploading our imaginations, like sinners, into the machines.

Further reading

Fiction is a matter of personal choice; essential background here is inevitably *Neuromancer* (Gibson 1995 [1984]), and preferably the rest of Gibson's novels and the collection of short stories, *Burning Chrome* (1995 [1986]). *Idoru* (1996) and *Pattern Recognition* (2003) are key. Cadigan's *Synners* (1991) is also essential, not least because few women made it into the cyberpunk novelists' very masculinist clique, but mainly because of its important focus on the interface and the posthuman. On crime fiction and techno-sociality, my personal favourites are Mankell's *Firewall* (2004) and Mathews' *Vienna Blood* (1999), which examine different modes of cybercrime – but the best way forward here is to search an online store for examples that appeal to you.

On cyberpunk, Broderick (1995) provides interesting postmodern perspectives. Stone (1996) is brilliant on the techno-social and the posthuman, and the Haraway interview by Gane (2006) is fascinating. Burrows' essay (1997) on cyberpunk as social theory remains intriguing. The Cyberpunk Project website is a good resource including original essays by cyberpunk writers and academics, as well as fan contributions at http://project.cyberpunk.ru/. William Gibson is interesting on his own work, and Googling his name with 'interview' will undoubtedly bring up results. Techno-socialities and the crime fiction genre tends to be neglected in the shadow of cyberpunk and SF, but Mystery Readers International website at http://www.mysteryreaders. org/ is interesting if not exactly 'academic'. More abstractly, Baudrillard's *Simulacra and Simulation* (1994 [1991]) is necessary for advanced study. Bell and Kennedy's (2000) edited reader on Cybercultures provides a comprehensive collection of essential cyberspace papers, of which many are relevant to the issues discussed in this chapter. Journal material potentially spans such a wide area (literary criticism, computing, criminology, sociology, philosophy, science fiction studies, law etc.) that online subject database searching (via Athens, for example) using the most specific terms possible for your query is the best advice. On Second Life and other virtual worlds, the best learning method is to join them. There are many news articles on 'crime' and Second Life that can be accessed via search terms using the Nexis database.

References

Bankowski, Z. and Mungham, G. (1981) 'Lawpeople and Laypeople', *International Journal of the Sociology of Law*, 9: 85–100.

Baudrillard, J. (1994 [1981]) *Simulacra and Simulation*. Michigan: Ann Arbor, University of Michigan Press.

Baudrillard, J. (1995) [1991] *The Gulf War Did Not Take Place*. Sydney: Power Publications.

Bell, D.F., Loader, B.D., Pleace, N. and Schuler, D. (2004) *Cyberculture: The Key Concepts*. London/New York: Routledge.

Bell, D. and Kennedy, B. (eds) (2000) *The Cybercultures Reader*. London: Routledge.

Beyleveld, D. and Brownsword, R. (2001) *Human Dignity in Bioethics and Biolaw*. Oxford: Oxford University Press.

Bourdieu, P. (1984) *Distinction: A Social Critique of the Judgement of Taste*. London: Routledge.

Broderick (1995) *Reading by Starlight: Postmodern Science Fiction*. London: Routledge.

Brown, S. (2003) *Crime and Law in Media Culture*. Buckingham: Open University Press.

Brown, S. (2006) 'The criminology of hybrids: Rethinking crime and law in techno-social networks', *Theoretical Criminology*, 10(2): 223–44.

Bukatman, S. (1993) *Terminal Identity: The Virtual Subject in Postmodern Science Fiction*. Durham: Duke University Press.

Burrows, R. (1997) 'Cyberpunk as Social Theory: William Gibson and the Sociological Imagination', in S. Westwood and J. Williams (eds), *Imagining Cities*. London: Routledge, 235–48.

Cadigan, P. (1988) [1985] 'Rock On', in B. Sterling (ed.), *Mirrorshades: The Cyberpunk Anthology*. London: Paladin, 34–42.

Cadigan, P. (1991) *Synners*. London: Grafton.

Callon, M. (1986) 'Some elements of a sociology of translation: Domestication of scallops and the fishermen of St. Brieuc Bay', in J. Law (ed.), *Power, Action and Belief: Towards a New Sociology of Knowledge*. London: Routledge and Kegan Paul.

Carroll, L. (1992) *Alice in Wonderland*. Ware: Wordsworth Editions.

Castells, M. (2001) *The Internet Galaxy*. Oxford: Oxford University Press.

Clarke, A. (1968) *2001: A Space Odyssey*. London: Arrow.

Cornwell, P. (1995) *From Potter's Field*. London: Warner.

Cyberpunk Project 1996 http://project.cyberpunk.ru/idb/cyberpunk_literary_style.html

Dick, P.K. (1972) *Do Androids Dream of Electric Sheep?* London: Arrow.

Dick, P.K. (1977) [1964] *The Simulacra*. London: Methuen.

Douglas, T. and Loader, B. (2000) *Cybercrime: Security and Surveillance in the Information Age*. New York, NY: Routledge.

Featherstone, M. and Burrows, R. (1995) *Cyberspace/Cyberbodies/Cyberpunk: Cultures of Technological Embodiment*. London: Sage.

Fukuyama, F. (2002) *Our Posthuman Future: Consequences of the Biotechnology Revolution*. London: Profile Books.

Furnell, S. (2002) *Cybercrime: Vandalizing the Information Society*. London: Addison Wesley.

Gane, N. (2006) 'When We Have Never Been Human, What is to be Done?', interview with Donna Haraway, *Theory, Culture and Society*, 23: 135–58.

Gibson, W. (1994) [1993] *Virtual Light*. London: Penguin.

Gibson, W. (1995 [1984]) *Neuromancer*. London: HarperCollins.

Gibson, W. (1995 [1986]) *Burning Chrome*. London: HarperCollins.

Gibson, W. (1996) *Idoru*. London: Viking.

Gibson, W. (2000) [1999] *All Tomorrow's Parties*. London: Penguin.

Gibson, W. (2003) *Pattern Recognition*. London: Viking.

Gibson, W. (2007) *Spook Country*. London: Penguin.

Golding, W. (1962) *Lord of the Flies*. London: Faber.

Grabowsky P.N. and Smith, R.G. (1998) *Crime in the Digital Age*. New Brunswick, NJ: Transaction Publishers.

Guest, T. (2007) *Second Lives: A Journey*. London: Hutchinson.

Haraway, D. (1985) 'A Manifesto for Cyborgs: Science, Technology and Socialist Feminism in the 1980s', *Socialist Review*, 15: 65–107.

Haut, W. (1999) *Neon Noir: Contemporary American Crime Fiction*. London: Serpents Tail.

Jenks, C. (2003) *Transgression*. London: Routledge.

Jewkes, Y. (ed.) (2007) *Crime Online*. Cullompton: Willan Publishing.

Johnston, J. (1998) *Information Multiplicity: American Fiction in the Age of Media Saturation*. Baltimore: John Hopkins University Press.

Lash, S. (2002). *Critique of information*. London: Sage.

Latour, B. (2007). *Reassembling the Social: An Introduction to Actor-Network Theory*. Oxford: Oxford University Press.

McCallum, E.L. (2000) 'Mapping the Real in Cyberfiction', *Poetics Today*, 21(2): 349–77.

Mankell, H. (2004) *Firewall*. London: Vintage.

Mathews, A. (1999) *Vienna Blood*. London: Jonathan Cape.

Montalban, M.V. (2003) [1997] *The Buenos Aires Quintet*. London: Serpents Tail.

Montalban, M.V. (2005) [2000] *The Man of My Life*. London: Serpents Tail.

Redhead, S. (1990). *The End-of-the-Century Party: Youth and Pop towards 2000*. Manchester: Manchester University Press.

Roberts, A. (2006) *Science Fiction*. London: Routledge.

Shields, R. (2006) Virtualities, *Theory, Culture and Society*, 23: 284–86.

Sterling, B. (1988 [1986]) *Mirrorshades: the Cyberpunk Anthology*. London: Paladin.

Sterling, B. (1994) *The Hacker Crackdown: Law and Disorder on the Electronic Frontier*. London: Penguin.

Stone, A.R. (1996) *Desire and Technology at the Close of the Mechanical Age*. London: MIT Press.

Taylor, P.A. (1999) *Hackers: Crime in the Digital Sublime*. London: Routledge.

Taylor, P. (2001) 'Hacktivism: In Search of Lost Ethics?', in D. Wall (ed.), *Crime and the Internet*. London: Routledge, 59–73.

Thomas, D.W. and Loader, B. (2000) *Cybercrime: Law Enforcement, Security and Surveillance in the Information Age*. London/New York: Routledge.

Toffler, A. (1981) *The Third Wave*. London: Pan.

Wall, D. (ed.) (2001) *Crime and the Internet*. London: Routledge.

Wall, D. (2003) *Cyberspace Crime*. Aldershot: Ashgate.

Wall, D.S. (2007) *Cybercrime: the Transformation of Crime in the Information Age*. Cambridge: Polity.

Wall, D. (2008) 'Cybercrime and the Culture of Fear: Social Science Fiction(s) and the Production of Knowledge about Cybercrime', *Information, Communication and Society*, 11(6): 861–84.

Westwood, S. (2000) 'Rebranding Britain: Sociology, Futures and Futurology', *Sociology*, 34: 185–202.

Wood, J. and Shearing, C.D. (2007) *Imagining Security*. Cullompton: Willan Publishing.

Yar, M. (2006) *Cybercrime and Society*. London: Sage.

Young, A. (1996) *Imagining Crime: Textual Outlaws and Criminal Conversations*. London: Sage.

Young, J. (2009) 'Moral Panic: Its Origins in Resistance, Ressentiment and the Translation of Fantasy into Reality', *British Journal of Criminology*, 49(1): 4–16.

Part II

Forms of Internet Crime

Yvonne Jewkes and Majid Yar

Part II of the *Handbook of Internet Crime* discusses some of the most serious cybercrimes that exercise the public imagination. As Majid Yar intimated in Chapter 6 of Part I, much of the debate about Internet regulation and censorship appears to be based on speculative notions of the antisocial and harmful impacts it may have at some point in the future rather than actual, current levels of victimisation, and that is certainly true of the subjects of the first three chapters of Part II which discuss hacking, malware and terrorism. That is not to say, however, that computer hacking and the planting of viruses do not pose significant threats to both individual Internet users and businesses and corporations (and even provide opportunities for terrorists), as Steven Furnell explains in Chapter 9. Furnell first discusses the origins and emergence of hacking as a crime problem, and then assesses its scope, scale and impact. His analysis explains the complexities inherent in the term 'hacker' and introduces readers to the myriad forms of activities described by the term, some of which will be perceived by society at large as more legitimate than others. Indeed, 'hacking from the moral high ground', as Furnell puts it, is in itself a fascinating subject and he examines some of the justifications that hackers put forward to excuse and explain their activities. Hacking is one of very few cybercrimes that can elicit social tolerance and even a grudging admiration for its audacity and the technical skill required. The authorities of most countries take a different view, however, especially the US post-9/11. Gary McKinnon, a 42-year-old Briton accused of breaking into Pentagon computers and raiding US army, navy and NASA networks in 2001 and 2002 is confronting the full wrath of the American criminal justice system. At the time of going to press, he is facing extradition and up to 70 years in an American prison under terrorist charges, despite support from several high-profile British politicians, academics and celebrities who claim that, as a man with Asperger's Syndrome, McKinnon should be tried, not as a terrorist but as a man with a social disability (*Daily Mail*, 1 March 2009).

Following his detailed analysis of hacking, Furnell turns his attention to viruses and malicious software or 'malware', a label which encompasses worms, Trojan Horses and spyware. He explains what each of these terms means and examines their prevalence and impacts, commenting that, like hacking, malware as a threat has changed considerably over the years and conventional wisdom about these phenomena is not always accurate. He notes that malware represents one of the most frequently encountered problems for home users, although it is worth underlining that, in the main, statistics which show high levels of public anxiety about computer security are published by anti-virus software manufacturers and, as Yar implied in Chapter 6, it may cost some computer owners a significant amount of money to protect themselves, relative to their likelihood of victimisation. It is also true that computer users could do much more to protect themselves through vigilance and common sense, regardless of what protection they may or may not have on their PCs.

In the aftermath of the 11 September 2001 attacks on the World Trade Center and the Pentagon, an intense focus has emerged upon the ways in which terrorist groups might use the Internet as an integral component in their political activities. Predictions of apocalyptic meltdown include terrorist acts intended to sabotage water and utility supplies, manipulate air traffic control or military systems, hack into government and public service computer networks and paralyse financial systems. However, most commentators believe that while these kinds of possibilities are terrifying to contemplate, the likelihood of malicious hackers or terrorists bringing down a country's infrastructure is remote and, for the time being at least, they remain the stuff of novelists' and film-makers' imaginations – as discussed by Webber and Vass and Brown in Chapters 7 and 8 respectively – rather than likely acts of aggression (Jewkes 2003).

The two chapters that follow are interesting for the different views they take on the issue of cyber-terror. First, Dorothy Denning (Chapter 10) explores the various ways in which terrorists employ the Internet and World Wide Web to perpetrate cyber-attacks on unsuspecting victims. While acknowledging that, superficially at least, terrorists use the Net much like anyone else, Denning outlines six areas of terrorist practice that have been substantially altered or enhanced by the Internet and the Web: media operations, attacks, recruitment, learning, finance, and security. In a meticulously researched analysis, she provides rare detail about, and insight into, real cases and specific terrorist cells and networks, including al-Qaeda. This chapter thus takes us beyond the abstract level at which many academic treatments of serious cybercrimes are pitched and right into the fascinating operational world of terrorism and counterterrorism.

In Chapter 11 Maggie Wykes, with Daniel Harcus, takes an alternative view, returning us to public perceptions about cybercrime. While not denying that, since the attacks on the US in September 2001, we have become much more alert to the ways in which terrorists and counterterrorists use the Internet as described by Denning, Wykes is more interested in *why* the public are now so much more attuned to terrorist threats and other potential risks associated with cyberspace. It is her view that since 9/11 the media have consistently told the public that terrorist groups use Internet technologies to organise and plan both terrestrial and cyber-attacks. Such accounts have supported the concept of an ever-present global threat and underwritten policy from the US and its allies regarding the 'War on Terror'. Wykes assesses the implications of this focus on terror and its alignment with the cyber realm. Echoing Sandywell's argument in Chapter 3, she suggests that the meaning of terrorism in the twenty-first century has been reconstructed and allied to the Internet through hyper-realistic criminalising practices. Further, Wykes argues that fear-inducing discourses have legitimated policies, alliances, laws, actions and technologies with profound implications for netizens, citizens and the exercise of power.

In Chapter 12, Peter Van Aelst and Jeroen Van Laer turn our attention to a sphere where netizens still operate with a degree of the democratic freedom and liberal ethos that characterised the early years of the Internet: cyber-protest. A notable feature of recent public engagements with the Internet is its use by a wide range of activist and social protest groups and Van Aelst and Van Laer discuss the ways in which the Net has been used as a key tool by, among others, the Zapatista movement in Mexico and by the anti-globalisation protesters against the World Trade Organisation. They focus on the 'new' repertoire of collective action, as they describe it, distinguishing between 'real' actions that are supported and facilitated by the Internet, and 'virtual' actions that are Internet-based. Their argument is that, in an era of apparently ever-increasing public disengagement from formal political institutions and processes, the Internet presents a unique arena in which civic engagement with social and political causes can be furthered. Not only does the Net provide transnational spaces of solidarity and collective ideology but, as Van Aelst and Van Laer illustrate, it facilitates action in numerous practical ways which, like other examples in this *Handbook*, may be perceived as more or less legitimate by the public at large and by the police and other authorities. Examples of relatively benign uses of the Internet by protest groups include setting up protest websites and online petitions, while hacktivism would generally be regarded as being at the extreme end of the spectrum, and is frequently characterised as 'cyber-terrorism' (see Chapter 10 by Denning).

Throughout this volume there are several references to the social tolerance towards some forms of cybercrime. Probably most socially accepted, pervasive and high-profile of all Internet crimes is the illegal practice of downloading and sharing musical recordings, motion pictures and computer software. In Chapter 13 David S. Wall and Majid Yar discuss the online proliferation of intellectual property offences, helpfully explaining exactly what 'intellectual property' means, how it has been transformed by 'the digital', and assessing the nature of the problem and attempts to regulate and control cultural transmission. These issues are framed within the wider context of the information economy in which the production, manipulation and commercial exploitation of cultural goods is viewed as a key dimension of economic growth and global competitiveness.

The authors note that cyberspace not only challenges our conventional understanding of ownership and control, but it is also blurring the traditional boundaries between criminal and civil activities along with some of the principles upon which our conventional understandings of criminal harm and justice are based. Indeed, Wall and Yar provide a detailed analysis of how close computer assisted or mediated crime sits to legitimate business opportunities, yet again echoing Sandywell's appeal for a more radical and reflexive criminology (in Chapter 3) and calling into question the criminalisation practices of many governments.

In Chapter 14 Russell Smith discusses another form of theft; identity theft. ID crime is one of the relatively few areas of cybercrime that have attracted the attention of academic scholars and is, as Smith explains, more encompassing than simply stealing another person's identity verification documents. However, it is the theft of computerised personal details that has most captured the public imagination, an anxiety exacerbated by the numerous and much-publicised cases of 'lost' data by government officials that have occurred in recent years. The personal data that can be appropriated fall into two categories: life history information (date of birth, address, nature of offence if applicable, and so on) and financial information (bank account details etc.). Through appropriation of such data, offenders can defraud individuals and organisations of money and use stolen identities to facilitate the commission of further offences through disguise. Hypothetically, the mislaying of data by government agencies concerning convicted offenders, witnesses placed in witness protection schemes, and the like, could result in serious offences such as extortion and revenge crimes, although no such cases have yet been recorded and far more pervasive and potentially damaging are the incidents of lost commercial data. As Smith observes, misgivings about the (in)security of such information is seen as a major obstacle to greater commercial mobilisation of the Internet, with users increasingly sensitised about the ways in which information shared online can be illegitimately exploited.

Interestingly, public concern about identity theft has massively boosted sales of information shredding machines. In 2004 sales of shredders increased by 50 per cent at US office supplies company Staples with 1.3 million units sold in a single year, and many manufacturers explicitly manipulate public fears about identity crime in the marketing of their products. There may be a generational divide in levels of public anxiety, however. On the whole, fears about possible identity theft appear to be more strongly experienced by older people, while young people are more likely to be more cavalier about their potential for victimisation. Of course, this goes for crime more generally but, as Smith observes, the exponential growth in social networking sites such as Facebook, Bebo, Orkut and MySpace has left young people at greater risk of identity crime. By way of example, he notes that one in seven users on Facebook log into their profile virtually all the time during office hours, rendering both themselves and their organisations open to criminal activity.

While the subjects of the previous two chapters might be described as relatively 'ordinary' or mundane offences, the four remaining chapters in Part II tackle subjects that shock, outrage and provoke fear in many people. First Teela Sanders (Chapter 15) discusses sex work and sex crime, drawing on her own empirical research on sex workers and men who buy sex. In addition to providing a detailed overview of the relationship between sex work and the Internet and discussing how the Net has come to be used by those selling sex and by their clients, Sanders examines the legislation and forms of regulation which govern the Internet sex industry. She notes that the Internet has professionalised parts of the industry, extended its reach to individuals who, in a pre-Internet age, would not have paid for sex, and made buying and selling sexual services more acceptable in society generally.

While the Internet has democratised the buying and selling of sex and precipitated a shift in cultural attitudes towards pornography to the extent where the production and distribution of sexually explicit images of adults no longer constitute a policing priority (a point further elucidated by Jewkes in Chapter 24), the sexual exploitation of children and the global Internet trade in child pornography remain among the most pressing concerns facing police, regulators, Internet Service Providers (ISPs), schools and parents. Few Internet crime issues have generated the degree of public alarm and media attention as the use of online communication by paedophiles as a means of sexually exploiting children online and offline. Parental fears about their children's vulnerability have created significant dilemmas and concerns about young people's victimisation. In Chapter 16 Jo Bryce examines online/offline sexual crimes committed by adults against children. Her discussion encompasses offender characteristics and what is known about their 'cognitive distortions', victim characteristics and their vulnerabilities, and the need for future research to address the dynamic relationship between offender and victim.

Following Bryce's analysis of computer-initiated sexual crimes against minors, Ethel Quayle (Chapter 17) examines the production, consumption and legislation of child pornography (although she notes that this term is problematic and contested). A founding member of the COPINE – or Combating Paedophile Information Networks in Europe – team, at the University of Cork, Quayle's knowledge of both the problem, and of research in the area, allows her to present an immensely detailed account of the nature and extent of abusive images of children online, the causes of offending behaviour, the victims and impacts it has on their lives, and possible interventions. Quite simply, in this chapter, Quayle provides the definitive overview of research into Internet child pornography – her own and that of other experts in this field.

Finally in Part II, Maggie Wykes turns our attention to arguably the most serious criminal behaviours associated with the Internet. In recent years a number of high-profile homicides that are reportedly Internet-related or -assisted have come to public attention, leading to calls for greater self-regulation, tougher legislation and censorship. Anxiety about the power of the Internet to influence dangerous or vulnerable users reached an apotheosis when the headline 'Killed by the Internet' appeared in the *Daily Mirror*, a British tabloid, on 5 February 2004 (Jewkes 2003). Since that time, reports have circulated about dozens of serious assaults, abductions, murders and manslaughters of individuals that are said to be Internet assisted including, in November 2007, the story of so-called 'YouTube killer', Pekka-Eric Auvinen, a Finnish student who shot dead eight people at his high school in an incident reported as 'spurred by the Internet and the isolation of a troubled teenager' (*The Times*, 8 November 2007).

Another news story that has appeared regularly over the last few years concerns Internet-related suicides. Over two years in 2007–09, 25 young people, some of whom knew each other, committed suicide – all by hanging – within a radius of 15 miles in Bridgend, South Wales. It is estimated that the area would normally see two or three young suicides in a year. This highly unusual suicide cluster prompted the mainstream media to speculate that the Internet was to blame for the self-inflicted deaths. Among the culprits were said to be 'suicide sites' which may contain copies of suicide notes, death certificates, and photographs or videos of suicides as they happen; electronic bulletin boards, where suicide notes or suicidal intentions are posted; and, more mundanely, conventional social networking sites such as Bebo where, it has been claimed, the language of suicide and grief is light-hearted, casual, even jokey. According to social psychologist Dr Arthur Cassidy, reported in *The Times*, 25 May 2008:

> There is an unreality surrounding this word 'suicide' … People talk about 'catching a balloon' or 'having a laugh up there'. People say, 'See you soon.' Psychologically, this language can be very contagious. It's a way of sharing norms, and a way of avoiding adapting to the shared values of those in society at large. (http://www.timesonline.co.uk/tol/news/uk/article3984408.ece)

The *Times* goes on to speculate that Web-speak encourages a lack of seriousness surrounding deeply serious issues: 'On Bebo, deaths are mourned in one-liners, in between the normal traffic of a social network – sexual advances, plans for the weekend … Death is not seen as absolute'.

Wykes examines a wide range of Internet-assisted homicides, suicides and what she terms sui-homicides (including the infamous case of Armin Meiwes, the German cannibal who advertised for, and found, a willing victim on the Net). She frames these behaviours in the context of debates about freedom, censorship and the technological determinism that appears to underpin public and 'official' responses. In a thought-provoking and polemical chapter, she challenges the notion of a causal link between the Internet and death (self-inflicted or otherwise) arguing, like so many media-criminologists before her, that notions of media 'effects' are simplistic, lazy and reductive. So rare and so extreme are the behaviours under analysis that, in Wykes' view, they provide no basis for regulating the media industries to try and prevent 'copycat' acts.

Reference

Jewkes, Y. (ed.) (2003) *Dot.cons: Crime, Deviance and Identity on the Internet*. Cullompton: Willan Publishing.

Chapter 9

Hackers, viruses and malicious software

Steven Furnell

Introduction

This chapter introduces two of the most long-standing and highly publicised categories of Internet crime – namely hacking and malicious software (aka malware). Both represent problems whose roots can now be traced back more than a quarter of a century. However, the scope, scale and impact of both have advanced significantly, with the Internet in particular providing an ever-increasing volume of targets and the communications mechanism for reaching them. Furthermore, both threats have the potential to affect systems indiscriminately, with organisations and domestic users alike finding themselves on the receiving end of related incidents.

The discussion begins with hacking, starting with an examination of what it actually means, and how hackers have historically seen themselves. From this foundation, different categorisations of hacker activity are examined, highlighting the variety of motivations that may drive online attacks, as well as the techniques that may be involved in achieving unauthorised access.

The discussion then moves to examine the problems posed by malware, such as viruses, worms, Trojans and spyware. It begins by defining these core categorisations, before moving to more specifically consider the associated operation and impacts in each case. Specific consideration is given to the means by which malware may be introduced into systems (i.e. the infection vectors) and what it may do as a consequence (i.e. the payload activities). The main discussion ends by examining the ways in which malware may attempt to disguise and defend itself, outlining the mechanisms that aim to maximise its chances of infiltrating and surviving within infected systems.

Hacking

At its core, hacking refers to activities involved in attempting or gaining unauthorised access to IT systems. With the widespread proliferation of computing technology, and the networks connecting it together, systems have come to represent both attractive and readily available targets – regardless of whether the motive is idle mischief or something more sinister. As a consequence, hacking has become one of the most recognised and feared threats in cyberspace. For example, from the 671 security executives and law enforcement officials questioned as part of the 4th Annual E-Crime Watch Survey (conducted by CSO Magazine, the US Secret Service, the CERT® Program and Microsoft), 26 per cent considered hackers to have been the greatest threat to their organisation over the previous year (placing them at the top of the list, ahead of current and former employees, competitors and foreign entities) (CERT 2007). Indeed, the same respondents considered that an average of 22 per cent of the security incidents they had experienced in this period had been targeted attacks seeking to hit them specifically.

Although the general threat is widely recognised, hacking is actually a very broad term, encompassing a variety of potential activities and motivations. These are considered in the subsections that follow, starting with a definition that places hacking in a rather different light to that in which it is viewed today.

Origins and ethos

In contrast to the commonly accepted use of the term, hacking did not originate in the context of attacks and computer abuse, but rather as an acknowledgement of technical ability. In the early days of computing, a hacker was a hardware or software enthusiast or hobbyist, with the origins of the term being closely linked to the 1960s pioneers at the Massachusetts Institute of Technology (MIT). These early hackers had a genuine belief in the liberating power of technology, and alongside this emerged the so-called 'hacker ethic' (see Levy 1984: 26–36), emphasising principles such as freedom of information and unrestricted access to technology. Such ideas can clearly be seen to be in potential conflict with the concept of security, and from this perspective it is fairly easy to appreciate how the principles could be hijacked and misconstrued; enabling the behaviour associated with hackers to verge into the territories of unauthorised access and intrusion, and then onwards towards disruptive and harmful activities within the compromised systems. As a consequence, looking into virtually any dictionary today will reveal that the common-use definition of a hacker is directly linked to unauthorised activity and breaking security.

The concept of rebelling against authority or a corrupt system is something of a theme in the hacker's self-image. In addition to the aforementioned hacker ethic, there is also the oft-quoted 'Hacker Manifesto' (also known as 'the conscience of a hacker'), written by The Mentor in 1986. Going somewhat beyond the Ethic's call for information and access to be free, the Manifesto attempts a vehement defence of hacker activities, asserting a level of moral superiority on the part of the hackers compared to those whose systems are being targeted. A few snippets are presented to illustrate the point (Mentor 1986):

We make use of a service already existing without paying for what could be dirt-cheap if it wasn't run by profiteering gluttons, and you call us criminals ... We explore ... and you call us criminals. We seek after knowledge ... and you call us criminals. We exist without skin color, without nationality, without religious bias ... and you call us criminals ... You build atomic bombs, you wage wars, you murder, cheat, and lie to us and try to make us believe it's for our own good, yet we're the criminals ... Yes, I am a criminal. My crime is that of curiosity. My crime is that of judging people by what they say and think, not what they look like. My crime is that of outsmarting you, something that you will never forgive me for.

Clearly there will be *some* who genuinely believe this, but the widespread circulation of the text has potentially allowed it to be a flag of convenience for others who just want to hack but feel the need for some moral justification in doing so.

Black, white and all the shades in between

Simply labelling someone a 'hacker' is actually a bit simplistic, and a variety of other names can also be used depending upon the sort of things they are doing (see Chapter 2, Curran). For example, it is common to find reference to 'crackers', in order to denote those acting with an overtly malicious intent and to distinguish them from the more benign and exploratory activities that some like to claim that traditional hackers would engage in. Of course, from a security perspective such a distinction is a fairly moot point; you want to keep unauthorised users out regardless of their possible motivation, because by the time they get in it will be too late to quiz them about it.

Returning to the issue of names, it is also quite common to encounter labels that reflect the hacker's perceived intent, such as black hat, white hat and grey hat. These particular terms reflect whether a hacker is overtly malicious or dangerous (the black hat), using hacking techniques to test and improve security (the white hat), or has unclear or unpredictable behaviour (the grey hat). When considering these particular names, it is worth noting that the legitimacy of the white hat's activity will still depend upon whether they are doing it as a sanctioned activity (i.e. approved by the owner of the system they are targeting), or acting in a self-appointed role without permission. In jurisdictions with related legislation, the latter still represents a criminal act, regardless of how strongly the perpetrator may claim that they are acting as an ethical hacker or a penetration tester.

Other labels tend to reflect the capability of the hacker or the specific type of activity they are engaged in. In the former category would be terms such as 'script kiddie' and 'packet monkey', both of which are used to refer to novice (wannabe) hackers who lack the technical skill to develop and initiate an attack from scratch but are capable of posing a nuisance by using tools and scripts produced by others. By contrast, labels such as 'hacktivist' and 'phreaker' tend to reflect what the hackers are doing (with hacktivists being those that use hacking methods in pursuit of an activist or political agenda, and phreakers being those who seek to explore and experiment with telephone systems).

It can be seen that some of the labels tend to reflect motivation as well as method. With this in mind, it is also worth highlighting that although they often get referred to en masse, hackers are far from homogeneous when it comes to their reasons for entering the fray. For example, those operating at script kiddie level may have been attracted by media coverage and Hollywood-style glamorisation of hacking, and a consequent desire to be part of the same world. Conversely, others will be drawn in by a genuine fascination with the technology and what can be done with it. For others, it is the challenge of beating the system, or the people that are trying to protect it. And for an increasing proportion of perpetrators, hacking is just a means to an end; attacking or compromising a system is seen to represent the easiest or most effective way of getting a desired result (be it to cause damage, attract publicity, or steal money etc.).

Hacking from the moral high ground?

With backdrops such as the Hacker Ethic and the Hacker Manifesto, there will always be some that genuinely consider hacking to be a legitimate activity, regardless of the context. Others (particularly those motivated by exploration, challenge, or mischief-making) often suggest a rationale that seeks to justify their activities. For example, some will claim that their actions are vindicated by the fact that the system administrator has not done a sufficient job of securing the system, and that these failings deserve to be highlighted. However, such justifications do not stand up to a significant degree of moral scrutiny. If someone has made even a basic attempt to control access to the system, then they have done enough to signify their intent that only authorised users are meant to be getting access. For an unauthorised user to gain access in spite of this demonstrates both a lack of respect for this position and an intention to trespass.

Another common hacker claim is that their actions are helping security by highlighting weaknesses that need to be fixed. However, demonstrating a weakness by publicly exposing it is not a responsible stance. Indeed, rather than helping to protect the system, there is actually the potential to place it at greater risk if the problem cannot be fixed in a timely manner, because the weakness may then become known to those who might actively exploit it. Moreover, if unsanctioned probing of remote systems *was* deemed an acceptable practice it is easy to imagine how it could spiral into a problem in its own right; with the volume of probe-related traffic and some forms of active probing both having the potential for disruptive effects.

In other cases, the hackers' justification is simply that they do not consider that their actions are causing any harm (for example because they are exploring but not changing the system). However, this is a rather simplistic world view, and can easily be challenged. Firstly, the acceptability of simply exploring can quickly be dispelled by imagining the analogy of a house rather than an online system. Few people would consider it acceptable to go and have an uninvited look around someone else's home, and arguments that the door was open (or didn't require much of a push) would hardly be expected to justify it. Secondly, the idea of not doing any harm tends to assume that the hacker's *intention* and their *impact* can be regarded as the same thing. Just because a hacker has found their way into a system and does not intend to cause damage, does not mean that they will not inadvertently do something that puts the system, its users or its data at risk. Again, imagine a similar situation in a physical scenario, with someone finding their way into an unfamiliar building and then taking a look around. How do they know what's to be found behind each door? What will they see? Will something fall out and break? It also depends upon what one actually considers to be harmful. For example, while a hacker could well pop in and out of my system without changing or disrupting anything, they may still have *seen* something that I would consider personally private or commercially sensitive, and therefore harm has been done even though the data remains unaffected.

Considering any of the hackers' actions from a security perspective, it is fairly easy to mount a counter-argument, and a few indicative thoughts are offered as an illustration:

- Unless a given system (or part of it) is explicitly denoted as public, users should be granted access at the discretion of the system owner rather than on the basis of their ability to break in.

- Just because someone finds that they *can* get access, it does not mean that they *should*.

- If the content of the system was intended to be public, then it would be placed on a website or similar.

The scenarios above tend to consider hacking when it is being pursued as an activity in its own right. When it is being used as a means to an end, however, there are some contexts that may seem to make it somewhat more palatable and/or present more of a moral dilemma. Consider, for instance, a context such as hackers claiming to use their skills to fight child pornography. This is an intentionally extreme example, and represents a context in which hacking could be used to take direct action against systems hosting illegal content (for example by taking the systems offline, deleting the content and/or tracking those trying to download it). Of course, very few would be likely to step up and argue the case for the paedophiles, but would this justify the activities of the hackers? From both moral and security perspectives, the answer has to be no. There are other, law-abiding ways of handling sites that are found to be hosting illegal content, such as reporting them to Internet Service Providers and the police. Even if hacking the sites was the only way they could be tackled, the task of taking them down ought to be left to someone with the legal authority to do it, rather than someone simply wanting to take a moral stand. After all, while cyber-vigilantism could have the desired result against one site, it is easy to imagine such uncoordinated and uncontrolled action disrupting a genuine investigation and preventing law enforcers from scoring a bigger hit against the wider problem.

Attacks in all shapes and sizes

As well as having a variety of perpetrators and motivations, hacking is far more than just one type of attack. Although it generally relates to unauthorised access, this can still take many forms in terms of the underlying activity. For example, looking at the 2008 results from the CSI Computer Crime and Security Survey it is notable that while there is not a category called 'hacking', we can instead see many types of incident that could collectively contribute to this broader heading (Richardson 2008). Indeed, depending upon the perpetrator and the methods involved, all of the following could conceivably have involved hacking (with the figures in brackets representing the percentage of the 433 respondents that experienced them): denial of service (21 per cent); unauthorised access (29 per cent); system penetration (13 per cent); abuse of wireless network (14 per cent); website defacement (6 per cent); and DNS (denial-of-service) attacks (8 per cent).

Hacking is, by its nature, an activity that often remains hidden from view, leading to suspicions that the true scale of the problem is likely to be significantly greater than actually gets reported. However, when we do get to hear about incidents it is clear that the victims and effects are wide-ranging. Certainly, the centre of gravity has shifted away from the deeds of the stereotypical teenage prankster towards more directly criminally oriented activities. As a consequence, it can more often be viewed as a means to an end rather than a pursuit in its own right. A few illustrative examples here would include:

- attacks against systems in the office of the US Secretary of Defense in June 2007, which were alleged to be state-sponsored hacking by Chinese hackers backed by the People's Liberation Army (Keizer 2007);

- hacking activities that targeted a webmail account belonging to US vice-presidential candidate and Alaskan governor Sarah Palin during the 2008 campaign, leading to her messages being posted on a public website (Thomson 2008);

- hacking allegedly supported by 107 Brazilian logging firms in order to help them evade tree-felling restrictions (BBC News 2008). Greenpeace estimated that 1.7m cubic metres of timber (valued at £564m) had been illegally felled as a result of fake permits issued by hackers who had been employed to break into the system responsible for monitoring and controlling logging quotas.

Of course, a common theme in the above is that we can see why each one was attacked (not that this made it acceptable, but there was at least a clear reason for them having been specifically targeted). However, it would be a mistake to think that this is the only reason we could fall victim; certain attackers are more interested in whether a system is vulnerable rather than who owns it and what data it holds. As a consequence, small organisations and even home users will find themselves at a much greater risk of being hacked than they might otherwise expect. Indeed, even a domestic PC may represent an attractive target for certain types of abuse as the system could provide:

- a soft option for some mischief, enabling novice hackers in particular to amuse themselves at someone else's expense (e.g. potentially disrupting their system, damaging their data, or generally invading their privacy by gaining uninvited access);

- a convenient file repository, allowing the attacker to leave content on someone else's system rather than risk having it found on their own;

- a platform for attacking other systems, enabling the direct source of an attack to lead back to the unsuspecting owner of the intermediate system rather than to the actual attacker.

The extent to which home users may find themselves at risk is evidenced by Symantec's Internet Security Threat Report, which indicated that in the first half of 2007 as much as 95 per cent of the threats were targeting the home user sector (Symantec 2007).

At this point it becomes relevant to consider different levels of exploitation that may be possible. If a system is poorly protected, has been misconfigured or is running software with unpatched vulnerabilities, then one of these factors may be exploited in order to enable an attacker to gain access. Notably, the entirety of this process may be automated, either by virtue of using scanning tools to identify target systems or by means of malware that uses the same route to compromise a system and then take residence. Once the system has been compromised, the attacker will be afforded some level of access within it. Depending upon their ultimate intention, this access may already be sufficient to enable the system to then be exploited to achieve their objective. In other cases, an interim level of further exploitation may be required within the system in order to escalate the user's privileges to a higher level (for example because the access rights were not sufficient to perform the tasks required). This concept is illustrated in Figure 9.1.

Tools and tricks

Although the stereotype may conjure up the image of hackers using their specialist knowledge and technical prowess to break into systems, it is important to recognise that many will use techniques that place hacking capability in the hands of a much wider audience. Indeed there are tools available that can automate the tasks of locating and exploiting potential targets, while other attack methods do not rely upon exploiting the *technology* at all.

So, as the first theme, we can consider the variety of tools available to would-be attackers. A number of common options are as follows:

- **Port/network scanners**: Enable automated probing of a large number of networked hosts, by testing for active services on a network (e.g. whether

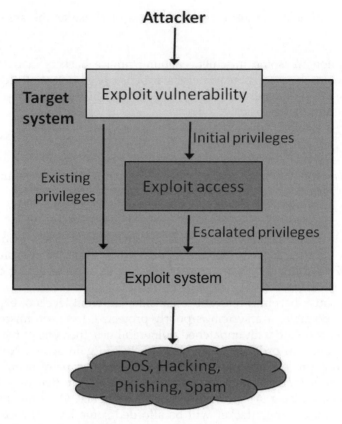

Figure 9.1 Levels of exploitation

a system is running a web or mail server), which may in turn reveal potential security or configuration problems.

- **Vulnerability scanners**: Used to test systems for known security holes, enabling associated vulnerabilities to be identified (and possibly exploited) automatically.

- **Packet sniffers**: Employed to capture specific content from the network. Data collected may reveal sensitive data, as well as general details of user/organisation activity.

- **Password crackers**: Utilised to determine the plaintext version of an encrypted password (which may have been captured by sniffing the network or directly from a compromised system). The cracking process actually works by trying to find a match to the encrypted string; typically by firstly seeing if it can be found in a set of pre-encrypted dictionary words, and if not then moving to a brute force approach that tries encrypting and comparing successive strings until a matching permutation is found.

In addition to tools that can gather information and reveal vulnerabilities, there are also fully written tools or scripts that enable vulnerabilities to be exploited. This, of course, serves to make the idea of hacking far more accessible to those who would not otherwise have the technical knowledge to do it. Having said this, it is important to recognise that a lack of ability would not be the only reason to employ a tool. Indeed, even technically adept attackers may find them attractive, because many tools serve to automate what might otherwise be a laborious and time-consuming part of the hacking process. Indeed, hackers will be no more attracted to doing drudge work than the rest of us, and in the same way that we would seek to send an email message to multiple addresses in order to save retyping it for every recipient, hackers will happily use tools such as port scanners to probe a set of remote systems rather than manually testing each one individually.

As well as making it easier, the knock-on consequences of automation will often be an increase to the speed and breadth of possible attacks. While an attacker may only be able to probe a limited number of systems by hand, a tool can scan thousands with no additional effort on the attacker's part. As such, the base of potential targets becomes significantly wider and the cumulative risk to online systems becomes significantly greater.

A notable point at this stage is that the same tools that can be applied to attack can often be used to defend. Indeed, many of the tools that can be of use to a hacker should not necessarily be classed as *hacking* tools. If placed in the correct hands (i.e. a system/security administrator) then they can actually help to ensure that systems are set to keep hackers out. For example, a responsible system administrator could be expected to scan their own systems for vulnerabilities in order to determine any that are potentially exposed. Similarly, employing password auditing software would enable administrators to test that their users are complying with good password selection practices and help to prevent their accounts from being compromised (note how the same tool that would be used for password *cracking* in the hands of a hacker becomes a tool for password *auditing* when used legitimately by a system administrator).

So far, the discussion here has focused upon the potential to exploit technologies. However, as indicated at the beginning of the section, this is not the only route open to would-be attackers. Indeed, in some circumstances it can be equally (if not more) effective for hackers to target *people*, especially if they have a particular target in mind (such as a specific system or organisation). A technique of particular note here is the use of social engineering, which involves exploiting human weaknesses and tricking people into compromising security (for example by revealing confidential information or performing atypical actions). Such attacks may be conducted in a variety of ways, with the key options being by email (or other electronic communication), in person, or on the phone. In the last few years, the most prominent example of the problem has been the mass of phishing messages in circulation, which typically attempt to dupe users into parting with financial details such as bank account and credit card numbers. While these are clearly not hacking-related, and tend to be sent indiscriminately, similar methods can be used in a more targeted manner in order to acquire proprietary information, login details and the like from staff within an organisation. This would typically occur in the guise of so-called spear-phishing, in which messages are targeted towards individuals within a particular organisation rather than being sent to all and sundry.

Of course, making contact with the victim is only part of the process; the attacker also requires a suitably convincing pretext in order to gain the victim's trust and obtain their cooperation or compliance. Suitable pretexts will be extremely variable, and will depend upon the nature of the target and the mode of interaction. For example, typical scenarios for conducting the attack over the phone would be to call up the company's support desk claiming to be a senior employee needing urgent help to restore access to important services, or to call a typical end-user claiming to be an IT service engineer and asking for their help to solve a problem. Whether or not it will be believed will also depend upon other factors, such as whether the attacker is suitably persuasive and confident, and whether the victim makes any attempt to verify what they are told.

Given that the attacker is now targeting a person rather than a system, their focus changes from compromising the technology to exploiting psychology. Indeed, the attacker can exploit several characteristics of human behaviour in order to increase the chances of the intended victim doing what is desired. For example, Stevens (2002) refers to behavioural traits such as 'conformity' and the 'desire to be helpful', while Jordan and Goudey (2005) refer to characteristics of 'inexperience' and 'curiosity' that may be leveraged. So, the aforementioned scenarios could clearly draw upon conformity and helpfulness, whereas aspects such as the user's curiosity and inexperience (particularly from a technology perspective) can often be seen being leveraged by malware. Indeed, the role of social engineering in the context of malware attacks is discussed later.

Given a skilled perpetrator, social engineering can be potentially difficult to spot. Rarely would it be as blatant as someone making contact and explicitly asking for sensitive information. Indeed, if the attacker has the patience and determination they may be willing to perform a degree of reconnaissance first, using (for example) a series of early phone calls to gather information about the organisation and get an idea of how it works. Armed with this knowledge, a later call could present a much more informed pretext and thereby reduce the chances of the victim suspecting a problem.

As a consequence of these factors, social engineering can very often provide a route past the technical defences. Indeed, with security investment typically being directed towards technology-based controls, this is one of the key reasons why it can be attractive. To quote Kevin Mitnick, a renowned ex-hacker and authority on social engineering techniques (Papadaki et al. 2008):

> I think social engineering has become more prevalent because you have the security technologies that make it more difficult to exploit technical vulnerabilities … So, the more technologies and processes are out there to mitigate the technical hacking, the more you are going to have people that will resort to social engineering. Social engineering is often easier, and I think the threat has grown because software manufacturers have become more concerned about putting out the patches and about fixing technical holes, because of the negative press. So again, what will the attackers resort to? Social engineering! Then you might have attackers

that are not so technically astute, who might use social engineering in any event.

Sometimes it is not even necessary to target people directly, and it can be sufficient to benefit from weaknesses introduced by their behaviour. A good example here is the potential for bin raiding (also known as dumpster diving), which aims to take advantage of what people may carelessly throw away. Indeed, with insufficient attention to the risks, a variety of material may be disposed of that could either give insights to an attacker, or direct knowledge to support an attack. A few indicative examples, and their potential value to a hacker, are as follows:

- **Technical documentation**: Can provide details of how particular systems work; which is particularly useful if it relates to a proprietary system or the specific configuration used within a target organisation. As a classic example, phone phreakers in the 1970s and 1980s frequently benefited from the telecom operators' tendencies to throw out old manuals when new versions of switches and other systems were released. Although the older technologies were technically outdated, they were often still in use or had sufficient similarities to new systems; thus the abundance of material in the dumpsters gifted phreakers with technical knowledge that they would not otherwise have been able to get hold of.

- **Internal documents**: Materials such as memos and telephone directories can provide insights into the structure of the organisation, including names of people, their positions and how to contact them. With these details in hand, social engineers in particular would find themselves in a better position to construct a convincing pretext (e.g. an attacker could call Mr Jones in Accounts and claim to have been referred to him by Mr Smith in the IT department; Mr Jones may then be more inclined to perceive the call as legitimate, because the caller knows both his name and that of Mr Smith).

- **Product packaging**: Having taken delivery of new systems or software, it is fairly natural to dispose of the boxes in which they arrived. However, finding these in the trash may provide relevant clues to someone seeking to target an organisation, by telling them what types of systems are in use and/or what software they are running. This could give a starting point in terms of identifying relevant technical exploits, or key information to use as part of a social engineering attack (e.g. claiming to be from the manufacturer of the PCs the organisation is using).

The potential for reconnaissance to seed a social engineering attack is particularly significant, and there would be the clear potential for items of information to be combined to create an even more convincing pretext (e.g. gathering information about the people and the systems used within the organisation could enable someone to call the aforementioned Mr Jones and claim to be from the company's IT supplier, and then ask a variety of probing questions as part of a 'satisfaction survey' or similar).

What this and the earlier sections collectively demonstrate is that hacking is far from a simple issue to understand and defend against. Technology will provide protection up to a point, but it is also relevant to consider the human aspect; ensuring that your people are not vulnerable via that route, as well as in appreciating what may motivate someone else to attack you in the first place. Although the nature and manifestation of the threat is quite different, a similar situation must also be faced when dealing with malware, and this forms the focus of the remainder of the discussion in this chapter.

Viruses and malicious software

Alongside hacking, the spectre of malicious software (and particularly viruses) is one of the most readily recognised threats in the public mind. Although viruses are specifically mentioned in the chapter title, it is relevant to recognise from the outset that they are only one category of malicious software, and have a particular way of operating. A more appropriate general label would be malware, which then enables viruses, worms, Trojan Horses and (arguably) spyware to be referred to collectively without distinguishing or implying any specific behaviour. Nevertheless, the virus was the first form of malicious software to gain widespread public exposure, thanks to large-scale outbreaks dating back to the mid 1980s. As such, the protection measure we have come to rely upon was christened antivirus (AV), and that name has stuck regardless of the fact that it actually protects us against a whole range of other malware threats as well. Furthermore, the vast majority of security surveys tend to talk in terms of viruses as well, and it is just worth remembering that this category will also be where the various other types of malicious code are also getting reported (indeed, as it turns out, the actual incidence of viruses is relatively small these days, and at the time of writing the malware landscape is dominated by worms and Trojans).

Although the greater part of the discussion in this chapter refers to malware in a general sense, the following definitions can be used to distinguish between some of the more specific problems that sit under this heading:

- **Virus**: A self-replicating program that spreads by infecting some form of existing entity as a 'carrier'. The type of carrier that is infected often leads to further definition in naming associated with viruses. For example, boot sector viruses infect disks, program viruses infect executable files, and macro viruses infect files such as documents or spreadsheets.

- **Worm**: Another class of self-replicating program, worms differ from viruses in that they can spread autonomously without requiring a carrier to infect. Worms leverage network connectivity and can be spread by human actions (e.g. tricking users into opening worm scripts that arrive via email) or via fully automated activity (e.g. scanning remote systems and exploiting vulnerabilities to gain entry).

- **Trojan horse**: Programs that perform activities without the users' knowledge, resulting in unexpected and typically unwanted effects. Trojans may be installed as a result of users consciously downloading and running them in the belief that they are installing a genuine program, or as a hidden background activity as a result of a system becoming infected with a worm or the user unwittingly downloading one by visiting a compromised website. Some Trojans that directly seek to trick the user will still appear to perform the expected functionality in addition to their hidden behaviour.

• **Spyware**: Parasitic software that invades users' privacy, by divulging details of browsing habits and other sensitive information gathered from infected systems (with specific categories including system monitors, adware, and tracking cookies). The captured information can be transmitted to a third party, thus putting both personal and business data at risk of abuse.

From these categories, spyware often finds itself separated from the other classes of malicious software on the basis that while its guises may vary they all share the same overall objective of invading privacy. By contrast, the ultimate aims in the other categories have less predictability (e.g. while one Trojan may seek to harvest data, another may simply try to delete it). Nonetheless, spyware has proven to be a significant threat, particularly problematic from the end-user perspective. As an example of this, a 2005 study conducted by AOL and the National Cyber Security Alliance determined that six out of 10 domestic PCs (based upon a sample of 354 systems) had spyware residing on them (AOL/NCSA 2005).

When looking at other survey findings, malware typically emerges as the most frequently reported type of incident. For example, looking at the CSI survey results over the last five years the 'virus' category has taken the top spot on almost every occasion (the exception being 2007, when it was pushed into second place by 'insider abuse') (Richardson 2008). Having said this, it is also notable from Figure 9.2 that although they remain the most prevalent, virus incidents are now reported by significantly smaller proportions of respondents (although added to these figures for the 2007 and 2008 results were 21 per cent and 20 per cent of organisations reporting incidents involving bots, the root cause of which would typically track back to malware activity).

Of course, the incidence of malware-related problems will often not be of as much interest as the resultant impact. In the CSI survey, this is measured by means of the financial loss, with the 2008 results reporting that the average associated with virus incidents was $40,141. While the survey observes that losses in this range are not likely to represent a threat to the viability of most organisations, it is still worth noting that a high volume of low-cost incidents could still represent the cyberspace equivalent of death by a thousand cuts. Moreover, it was notable that dealing with the bot-related incidents was considerably more costly, with an average loss of $345,600 per respondent (placing them second only to financial frauds in the 20 or so incident categories used by the survey).

Unfortunately, the fact that it can spread indiscriminately via the Internet means that the reach of the malware threat extends beyond organisations, and also represents one of the most frequently encountered problems for home users. For example, a 2007 study conducted by McAfee and the National Cyber

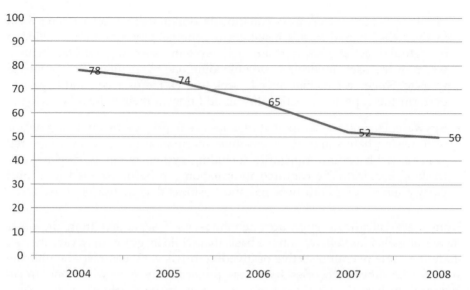

Figure 9.2 Percentage of CSI survey respondents reporting virus incidents (2004–2008)

Security Alliance (NCSA) indicated that 54 per cent of 378 homes surveyed in the US had experienced a virus, while 44 per cent of respondents believed that spyware was currently lurking on their system (McAfee-NCSA 2007).

To understand the problem more fully, it is relevant to consider different aspects of malware behaviour. In order to give the discussion some structure, we can examine the issue from the three dimensions depicted in Figure 9.3, which essentially summarises malware in terms of how you get it, what it does, and how it stops you getting rid of it.

Infection

When considering how an incident develops, the infection phase essentially reflects how and where users are likely to come into contact with malware, and is therefore significantly related to the propagation methods that are used. In the case of worms and viruses this includes the ability for self-replication, while programs such as Trojans may be encountered independently or get dropped onto the system by a worm.

In the majority of cases, malware requires a means of distribution to a wide audience. Those responsible for writing and releasing the code have been particularly adept at getting their creations into contexts where users are likely to encounter them, by piggybacking on whatever services are popular at the time. Indeed, as successive new online services have found favour in the user community, so too have they been adopted as channels for distributing malware. Consequently, malware has progressively found its way into a number of contexts, starting back in the late 1990s with email (which has remained a significant channel ever since), and then progressively effecting

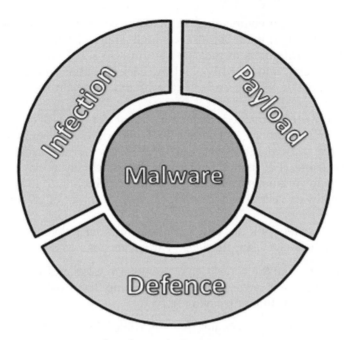

Figure 9.3   Dimensions of malware behaviour

virtually all other services that have become popular since, including instant messaging, peer-to-peer sharing, and social networking sites.

As mentioned in the earlier discussion of hacking, social engineering has a clear role to play in assisting propagation and increasing the chances of infection. Propagation techniques will often enable the malware to reach a potential victim system but leave it such that an action from the user is still required in order to activate it (e.g. opening an attachment or running an executable). In these situations, social engineering can provide exactly the trigger that is required to get an unwitting user to play their part. Indeed, many malware cases through the years owe a significant proportion of their success to the strong social engineering hooks that they employed. For example:

- the Melissa virus (1999) enticed the user to open an attached document by suggesting that it contained important information that they had requested;

- the Love Bug worm (2000) tricked thousands of users into opening it by appearing to be a love letter sent by someone they knew;

- among the various hooks used to distribute the Storm (aka Dorf) worm in 2007 were the promise of access to thousands of free games, posing as an e-card greeting, and claiming to offer a Santa Claus-themed striptease.

As an aside, a notable aspect of the latter approach was that related email messages were circulated on Christmas Eve. This demonstrates an added dimension to the social engineering, in that recipients might have been more susceptible to being duped because of high spirits in the festive season. Similarly, later distributions of the same worm also accompanied New Year's Eve, Valentine's Day, and April Fool's Day. Basically, attackers are aware that hooking into notable events and current affairs can help to increase their chances of success.

The Storm worm remained an active threat for well over 18 months; having originally appeared in January 2007, reports of new guises and new infections were still emerging well into 2008. However, this was not simply down to the same code being rereleased alongside new social engineering hooks; alongside variations in the bait, it is also commonplace to see modified versions of malware *code*. These can appear for a number of reasons:

- The original writers produce new variations in order to bypass the methods that AV products are using to detect earlier versions of the code.

- Other attackers take the code from a previous version and use it as a basis for developing their own malware (e.g. using the existing propagation mechanism with a different payload).

- The malware itself incorporates metamorphic abilities (discussed in the next section), enabling new variants to be created automatically.

In some cases this can lead to hundreds or even thousands of variants emerging. Indeed, staying with the example of Storm, it was reported that over 50,000 variants appeared in its first year of release (Sophos 2008).

The rapid emergence of new strains has caused knock-on consequences for the way that AV protection needs to be used and maintained. In the early days it was sufficient for users to obtain updated protection every few months or so; new malware emerged relatively infrequently and even then it could take a fair time to reach you because the distribution mechanism relied upon floppy disks. The mass adoption of Internet access since the mid 1990s removed this constraint, causing an upsurge in the pace of propagation, and increasing the speed with which vendors needed to respond with updates. With updates being deployed more quickly, the effective lifetime of any individual strain was reduced, leading to new variants, and the need for further updates, and so on. The end result is that automated on-demand updates are now the de facto requirement for maintaining effective AV protection.

While the AV companies generally keep pace with the variants, an area in which organisations can find themselves at greater risk is if they are faced with custom malware that has been written specifically for the purposes of targeting their systems. Such programs can be created from scratch or via one of the many malware development kits that can now be obtained (Ollmann 2008). Custom code certainly has the potential to pose a greater threat than malware that is in widespread circulation. In the latter case, AV packages can quickly incorporate an appropriate signature to detect any new threats. However, a custom program is likely to go unnoticed unless it behaves in a manner that triggers other detection methods (e.g. offering the ability to spot it via heuristic analysis rather than signature matching). Luckily, the majority of users will not find themselves confronted with this threat; it is reserved for those targets against which someone is willing to go to the effort of creating or paying for a customised attack. Nonetheless, those who consider that they may be at risk need to pay increased attention to their protection, and ensure that they have system and data safeguards in place beyond the standard AV provision.

Payload activities

The payload determines what the malware will actually *do*, and thus represents the most variable (and least predictable) aspect of its behaviour. Indeed, it is theoretically possible for the payload to do anything that can be achieved under software control. However, some of the main categories of likely action are as follows:

- damage and disruption (e.g. corrupting or deleting data; interfering with legitimate processes);
- stealing information (e.g. copying files; capturing user inputs);
- hijacking systems (e.g. opening backdoors and enabling remote control).

Alongside the means of propagation, payload activities have clearly evolved too. However, whereas the use of new propagation methods largely reflects the available opportunities, the changes in payloads essentially reflect the underlying motivation of the malware writers (or those commissioning them to write it). It used to be a question of what the malware would do *to* the user's system or data, but it has increasingly become a case of what might be done *with* it. The distinction is important, in the sense that the nature of the impact can be dramatically different. In the case of something being done to the system or data, the impact is essentially confined to the affected system (e.g. data is modified or deleted; the system is rendered unusable etc.). While this clearly cannot be dismissed as trivial, it is less significant than what might happen if the malware seeks to gain leverage from the compromised system rather than affect it directly. Indeed, if the objective is to use the infected system as a means to an end, then the malware may be more interested in hijacking it rather than sabotaging it, or in acquiring data rather than corrupting it. As a result, the fact that a system has been infected will be far less apparent to the end user; indeed, it is in the interests of the malware to remain unnoticed, as this gives a greater opportunity to reap the desired rewards. In short, the modus operandi is no longer about 'flash, bang and boo!' and more likely to rely on 'softly, softly and shush!'

A hijacked system may be exploited for wider purposes later; for example, being used as a generator of spam and phishing emails, or as a participant in denial-of-service attacks against other systems. Systems operating in this manner are often termed 'zombies' or 'bots', and will be performing the activities in the background, without the knowledge of their legitimate user. The power of the approach tends to come from the number of machines that can be infected and then controlled in this manner, with the resulting systems being collectively known as a 'botnet' or 'zombie army'. To illustrate the extent of the problem, Symantec reported 5,060,187 distinct bot-infected computers during the second half of 2007, with an average of 61,940 active bots being observed per day (the latter figure representing a 17 per cent increase over the previous six months) (Symantec 2008).

Where malware is working to acquire the user's data, it may be used to feed a variety of further objectives. For example, keyloggers may be used to capture typed input from the compromised machine, on the lookout for details such as bank account and credit card numbers (the acquisition of which could clearly lead to financial theft against the victim). Alternatively, a keylogger might pick up usernames and passwords, leading to the compromise of various other systems and online services that the victim may use. Looking beyond keylogging, the malware could simply harvest details directly from local files, enabling a variety of personal data to be obtained and leaving the user vulnerable to wider identity theft problems.

Defences

As malware has become more prominent, so too have the mechanisms that seek to prevent, detect and remove it. As such, it has become increasingly necessary for those developing and releasing malware to incorporate techniques to defend their code, and ensure that it has sufficient opportunity to unleash its payload. One of the key elements of modern malware is therefore some ability to defend against detection and removal.

One fundamental aspect of defence is, of course, to avoid being discovered in the first place. While this has already been mentioned in the context of releasing different variants, it can also refer to actions performed by the malware itself. In fact, the idea of evading discovery emerged relatively early on, with viruses of the late 1980s and early 1990s already using stealth methods and polymorphism in their attempts to complicate detection and fool early antivirus packages into missing them. Stealth techniques are basically attempts to hide the fact that a virus infection has occurred. So, for example, the Brain virus (the first recorded PC virus, which appeared in early 1986) monitored disk activity and intercepted any attempts to read the boot sector that it had infected. The result was that if anyone tried to inspect the disk, they would be presented with a copy of the original, uninfected boot sector rather than the version that was actually there following the Brain infection. While techniques such as this may be effective against user-level interventions, they are not sufficient to fool the automated antivirus programs that began to emerge once malware became a widespread problem. As a consequence, the disguise methods started to become more sophisticated, and the aforementioned polymorphic techniques (first seen in the Tequila virus in 1991) emerged in direct response to the way that antivirus tools tend to operate. The primary mechanism of an AV scanner is typically signature-based detection, with the program containing a small byte string from each item of malware and then scanning files and memory on the target system in order to see if this string is found (with any match being assumed to be a malware infection). As this method of detection was established, viruses began to adopt polymorphic techniques (typically via encryption) as a means of altering their byte pattern each time they infected a new file, and thus avoiding having a consistent signature. Today, techniques have become even more sophisticated, with so-called metamorphic malware that is able to rewrite itself such that it uses different instructions to achieve the same effects. Changing the way in which the code is written again serves to change the signature, which again aims to complicate the task for detection systems.

While these various disguises can present challenges to AV scanners, they provide no defence if detection occurs. As a result, malware has come to include more active forms of self-preservation, and it is now commonplace to find code that attempts to fight back against antivirus and prevent it from being able to deal with the infection. Typical approaches that have been witnessed in practice include:

- changing the system configuration so that security software no longer runs when the system starts up;
- blocking access to AV vendors' websites in order to prevent infected systems from obtaining security updates;
- terminating processes relating to AV and firewall applications.

The first approach is seen in worms such as Beagle (Symantec 2005a), whereas the other two are part of the behaviour of *Gaobot*, which blocks access to 35 security-related sites and has a list of over 420 different processes that it tries to terminate (Symantec 2005b).

In spite of such mechanisms, however, malware writers recognise that their code may still be discovered and face the prospect of deletion by an antivirus tool. As such, some malware is equipped with a last line of defence in order to safeguard its place in the system. An example of how this could occur is by monitoring its own execution – rather than starting one process when it runs, the malware will start two; each of which then watches for the existence of the other. If the AV deletes one of the processes, the other will automatically restart a new instance of it; thus ensuring that the malware stays active. Again, once the techniques are known, AV tools are able to take steps to compensate, but there is again a clear escalation occurring and the attackers are ultimately setting the agenda for the security community to follow.

Conclusions

This chapter outlined the nature of the threats posed by hacking and malware, as well as some of the challenges inherent in dealing with them.

It is important to recognise that both threats have changed considerably over the years and the conventional wisdom about what they do, and how they might be encountered, is not always correct. Indeed, whereas the early incidents of hacking and malware can be seen to have been somewhat loner-centric activities, driven by the personal motivations of individual attackers, there is evidence to show that both have moved to become larger-scale and potentially organised activities, often linked to financial motives. The key point to take from this is that the problems will continue to evolve, and thus the defences that we use today will also have to develop in order to keep pace.

When considering our defences, an important theme that has emerged through the chapter is the extent to which both categories of attack are often assisted by human behaviour. Users often provide unwitting assistance by getting tricked into divulging information or opening malware-infected content, while system administrators may directly aid an attack by failing to keep systems correctly configured and updated (thus exposing vulnerabilities that may be exploited by both hackers and malicious code). The message to take from this is that our defences need to be considered at multiple levels. We cannot simply rely upon one type of safeguard to do it all. Having antivirus will not remove the need for a firewall, and having both of them will not remove the need for backups. And, as previously mentioned, no technology will remove the need for appropriate user awareness, which can help to reduce exposure to the problems in the first place.

Further reading

For those keen to track the latest trends in hacking and malware, sources such as Symantec's regular Internet Security Threat Report (accessible via www.symantec. com) can provide a good summary of the international landscape. For more on the background and evolution of the threats, and examples of related incidents and impacts, readers are referred to my own book *Cybercrime: Vandalising the Information Society* (2001, Addison Wesley). To understand more about the technical methods used, and how to defend against them, books such as the *Hacking Exposed* series (1999–2009, McGraw-Hill) are among the best recommendations. Meanwhile, a highly recommended text in relation to social engineering and the risks posed by people is offered by Mitnick and Simon in *The Art of Deception* (2002, Wiley). Those interested in understanding more from the hackers' perspective are referred to *The Best of 2600: A Hacker Odyssey* by Goldstein (2008, John Wiley and Sons). Finally, from a more academic perspective, the proceedings from the long-running EICAR conference series are recommended in relation to tracking state-of-the-art research in relation to malware threats, while the international journal *Computers and Security* (ees.elsevier.com/cose) regularly publishes papers relating to both of the issues covered in this chapter.

References

AOL/NCSA (2005) *AOL/NCSA Online Safety Study – Conducted by America Online and the National Cyber Security Alliance*, December 2005.

BBC (2008) 'Hackers "aid" Amazon logging scam', *BBC News Online*, 15 December 2008. http://news.bbc.co.uk/1/hi/technology/7783257.stm

CERT (2007) 'Over-confidence is pervasive amongst security professionals: 2007 E-Crime Watch Survey shows security incidents, electronic crimes and their impact steady versus last year', Press Release, Carnegie Mellon Software Engineering Institute, Framingham, MA, 11 September 2007.

Jordan, M. and Goudey, H. (2005) 'The Signs, Signifiers and Semiotics of the Successful Semantic Attack', *Proceedings of 14th Annual EICAR Conference*, St. Juliens/Valletta, Malta, 30 April–2 May 2005, pp. 344–64.

Keizer, G. (2007) 'Bush doesn't confront China over alleged Pentagon hack', *Computerworld*, 7 September 2007.

Levy, S. (1984) *Hackers: Heroes of the Computer Revolution*. New York: Anchor Press/ Doubleday.

McAfee-NCSA (2007) *McAfee-NCSA Online Safety Study – Newsworthy Analysis*, October 2007. http://staysafeonline.org/pdf/McAfee_NCSA_analysis.pdf

Mentor (1986) 'The Conscience of a Hacker', *Phrack*, volume 1, issue 7, 25 September 1986.

Ollmann, G. (2008) 'The evolution of commercial malware development kits and colour-by-numbers custom malware', *Computer Fraud and Security*, September 2008: 4–7.

Papadaki, M., Furnell, S.M. and Dodge, R.C. (2008) *Social Engineering – Exploiting the Weakest Links*. White Paper, European Network and Information Security Agency (ENISA), October 2008.

Richardson, R. (2008) 2008 *CSI Computer Crime and Security Survey*. Computer Security Institute, USA. www.gocsi.com

Sophos (2008) 'Will you be spewing Storm spam at 10am tomorrow morning?', Press release, 30 January 2008. http://www.sophos.com/pressoffice/news/ articles/2008/01/storm-timezone.html

Stevens, G. (2002) 'Enhancing Defenses Against Social Engineering', SANS Institute, GIAC, http://www.giac.org/certified_professionals/practicals/GSEC/570. php (accessed 26 July 2008).

Symantec (2005a) W32.Gaobot.CII. Symantec Security Response, 5 February 2005. http://securityresponse.symantec.com/avcenter/venc/data/w32.gaobot.cii.html

Symantec (2005b) W32.Beagle.BN@mm. Symantec Security Response, 15 April 2005. http://securityresponse.symantec.com/avcenter/venc/data/w32.beagle.bn@ mm.html.

Symantec (2007) *Symantec Internet Security Threat Report. Trends for January–June 07*. Volume XII. Symantec Enterprise Security, September 2007.

Symantec (2008) *Symantec Global Internet Security Threat Report. Trends for July–December 07*. Volume XII. Symantec Enterprise Security, April 2008.

Thomson, I. (2008) 'Hackers crack Sarah Palin's webmail account', vnunet.com, 18 September 2008.

Chapter 10

Terror's web: how the Internet is transforming terrorism

Dorothy E. Denning

Introduction

With over 1.4 billion persons on the Internet (Internet World Stats 2008), or more than 21 per cent of the world's population, it is not surprising to find terrorists among that population. Moreover, given the way the Internet has affected everything from booking a hotel to finding a partner it is equally unsurprising to see changes in the practice of terrorism. Superficially, terrorists use the Internet in pretty much the same way that other individuals and groups use it. They use the Net to communicate among themselves and to reach out to supporters, the media, governments, and the public. They use it to exchange messages and engage in online discussions and to distribute information, including text, images, audio, video, and software, and to find information. They use it to learn, transact business, and generally facilitate their activities. And, like other bad actors on the Internet, they use it to inflict harm. Yet despite the ordinariness of much of this use, the very practice of terrorism – the ways in which terrorists disseminate documents and propaganda, recruit and train new members, and inflict harm on their victims – is being fundamentally transformed and expanded because of the Net.

This chapter explores the relationship between the Internet and terrorism, focusing on six areas of terrorist practice that have been substantially altered by the Internet and World Wide Web: media operations, attacks, recruitment, learning, finance, and security. It discusses how terrorists use the Internet and the impact of that use on terrorism and counterterrorism. Concepts are illustrated via examples drawn from a variety of terrorist groups, with particular emphasis on al-Qaeda and the global jihadist movement, which subscribes to al-Qaeda's ideology and violent tactics, and is held together largely through the Internet. The chapter concludes with a section on counterterrorism strategies that exploit terrorists' use of the Internet.

Media operations

After seizing the Japanese embassy in Lima, Peru on 17 December 1996, the Movimiento Revolucionario Túpac Amaru (MRTA or Túpac Amaru) launched a new era in terrorist media operations. By the following morning, the group had a website up and running out of Germany. The site had over 100 pages, which were updated using a laptop computer and satellite telephone uplink. Mainstream media, including the *New York Times*, received their information about the incident from the terrorists' website (Regan 1999). During the initial hours of the conflict, the terrorists effectively owned the information environment relating to their operation.

MRTA's use of the Web represented a strategic innovation in terrorism. For the first time, terrorists could bring their message to a world audience without mediation by the established press or interference by the government. Further, they could offer news reports of world events that were favourable to their cause, thereby enhancing the propaganda value of their websites. In addition, they could use the Web to distribute information directly to their own members and supporters. The advantage the Web offered was immeasurable and recognised by terrorist groups worldwide. By 1998, 12 of the 30 groups on the US State Department's list of terrorist organisations that year were said to have websites (Whitelaw 1998), and by January 2002, researchers at Haifa University in Israel had found 29 sites from 18 organisations on the State Department's 2000 list (Tsfati and Weimann 2002). Today, it would be surprising to find a terrorist group that did not have some presence on the Web. Islamic terrorists have been particularly active on the Web. In October 2003, Internet Haganah, a project devoted to combating terrorism, listed 65 active websites with affiliations to six Islamic terrorist organisations. These included Al Aqsa Martyrs Brigades (10 websites), al-Qaeda (24), Hamas (19), Hizballah (5), Hizb ut-Tahrir (4), and Palestinian Islamic Jihad (2). The project claimed to have got approximately 300 additional terrorist-supporter websites shut down through their volunteer efforts.

Al-Qaeda has been on the Web since the late 1990s, initially through the website alneda.com (Weimann 2006: 67). Representing the Center for Islamic Studies and Research, the site was used to publish propaganda and send messages to al-Qaeda members. According to Bruce Hoffman, the site emphasised three themes:

1 the West is implacably hostile to Islam;
2 the only way to address this threat and the only language the West understands is the logic of violence;
3 jihad is the only option. (Hoffman 2003)

The site contained audio and video clips of bin Laden and justification for the September 11 suicide attacks against Americans. Poetry was used to glorify the martyrs and the importance of the struggle against the enemies of Islam. The English-language version of their site included a 'Message to the American People,' calling on Americans to denounce their Administration and follow Islam, threatening more terror until Americans stop their transgression or 'one of us dies'. By 2002, the site was on the run, moving to different domains and service providers, as it was taken down at the request of federal officials. At one point, the domain name itself was hijacked by a Maryland hacker, who posted copies of the original web pages and operated the site as a decoy. After five days, however, his cover was blown when a message appeared on an Islamic message board saying the site was a trap (Di Justo 2002). After that, al-Qaeda supporters purportedly began using hackers to place their files in obscure directories of other websites (Delio 2003).

Today, the al-Qaeda movement makes extensive use of the Web, with an estimated 5,600 sites as of January 2008 and 900 more appearing each year (Weimann 2008). These sites include static (non-interactive) websites and interactive forums, chat rooms, message boards, and blogs. Not all of these websites play a significant role, however. Internet Haganah identified a list of key sites in 2007, based on the extent to which members of the global movement link to the site and draw content from it. Their top 12 included muslm.net, alfirdaws.org, alhanein.com, tajdeed.or.uk, al-boraq.com, alhesbah. org, alnusra.net, ikhwan.net, ekhlaas.org, al-faloja.com, farouqomar.net, and al-ommh.net (Internet Haganah 2007). Many of these were active in 2006 and have remained active in 2008, although exact domain names change.

Jihadist websites are used to distribute a wide variety of materials to members, supporters, potential recruits, adversaries, and the public at large. These include writings and audio and video recordings of Osama bin Laden, Ayman al-Zawahiri, and other al-Qaeda leaders and operatives; horrific videos of bombings, beheadings, and other terrorist acts; fatwas (religious edicts); electronic magazines; training manuals and videos; news reports; calls to join the jihad; threats to 'infidels'; and software tools. To illustrate, before his death in 2006, Abu Musab al-Zarqawi, leader of the al-Qaeda affiliated Islamic State of Iraq (ISI), posted gruesome videos of ISI's deadly terrorist operations on the Internet along with videos to immortalise ISI's suicide bombers (Glasser and Coll 2005). He started a monthly Internet magazine, offering religious justifications for jihad and advice on how to conduct it, and posted films of his bomb making classes so that his expertise would not be lost. In summer 2005, ISI averaged nine online postings per day (Kimmage 2008). By 2008, however, their postings had dramatically declined, most likely because of the stepped-up efforts against ISI, including the capture or killing of 39 ISI members responsible for producing and disseminating materials on the Internet (Reuters 2008).

Al-Qaeda's media operations are supported by a network of quasi-official production and distribution entities that 'brand' jihadist media and provide an authorised channel for distribution on approved websites (Kimmage 2008). These entities serve the core leaders of al-Qaeda and the armed groups associated with it. Posted materials bear the logos of the originating armed groups and the media centres they used. Focus is on conflict zones, to include Iraq, Afghanistan, and Somalia. Three of the most prominent media entities are the al-Fajr Media Center, the as-Sahab Institute for Media Production, and the Global Islamic Media Front. Most of the products are in the form of text, but videos and audio recordings are also distributed. In 2007, as-Sahab alone released videos at the rate of, about one every three days (IntelCenter 2007).

The high quality products are often posted in multiple languages, including Arabic and English, and in multiple formats such as Windows Media, MPEG4, flash, and a format for mobile devices. In addition, audio and video clips are often broadcast by major media such as CNN and al-Jazeera, so al-Qaeda's audience is not limited to Internet users.

Besides operating their own websites, jihadists have established groups in commercial networks such as Yahoo! and communities of interest on social networking sites. In 2006, Orkut reportedly had at least 10 communities devoted to praising bin Laden, al-Qaeda, or jihad against the United States, with one community drawing over 2,000 members (Hunt 2006). In 2008, a posting on a jihadist forum advised 'all of the brothers' to create Yahoo! email accounts and use email groups to exchange messages. The author noted that authorities were striking jihadist websites, and the use of email was intended to ensure jihadists were able to communicate (Internet Haganah 2008).

Mass emailings have been used to reach broad audiences. The Jihadist Cyber-Attack Brigade, for example, announced in May 2008 they had success-fully sent 26,000 emails to 'citizens of the Gulf and Arab countries explaining the words of our leader Usama Bin Ladin'. The announcement, which was posted to a jihadist website with links to a past bin Laden tape on 'Defending the Prophet', claimed the operation was part of the 'Irhabi 007 Campaign'.

Irhabi (Terrorist) 007 was the codename for Younes Tsouli, a young man born in Morocco and living in West London. Tsouli assisted al-Qaeda by operating websites for the terrorist group. He posted videos, statements, manuals and other materials from Zarqawi and others on websites he set up and on anonymous File Transfer Protocol (FTP) servers he hijacked. For example, in July 2004 he uploaded about 60 files to an FTP server owned by the Arkansas State Highway and Transportation Department. He then posted a link to the files on al-Qaeda's al-Ansar site (Labi 2006).

Jihadists also recognise the value of using non-jihadist websites to reach a larger audience, including the mainstream Arabic media. One outlet they have recommended is Wikinews. According to the Terrorism Research Center (TRC), a statement circulating on jihadist forums extols members to 'go to Wikinews and circulate the news of the Jihad and the Mujahideen.' TRC also noted that for a couple of days, the Arabic page of Wikinews (ar.wikinews. org) featured a statement from Omar al-Baghdadi, an Iraqi terrorist leader. However, the statement was removed and replaced with the message 'This is a terrorist article and has been deleted' (TRC 2007). In addition to distributing news, jihadists see the potential of posting misinformation. For example, in response to a proposal on a jihadist forum to 'bankrupt American banks' by bombing them and causing 'a wave of withdrawals' by panicked customers, one respondent suggested that it might suffice to spread rumours through the Internet (Open Source Center (OSC) 2008b).

Cyber-attacks

The term 'terrorism' generally refers to acts of violence, or threats thereof, against non-combatants. These acts, which are intended to coerce governments or institutions for social or political objectives, typically involve bombings, kidnappings, and other physical acts of murder or destruction. The Internet has transformed terrorism by adding another means of inflicting harm on non-combatants, namely through cyber-attacks. While such attacks have so far resulted in neither death nor damage to physical property, the potential is there for producing these effects. A cyber-attack against the electric power grid, for example, could potentially destroy equipment and shut down power for an extended period of time, leading to loss of life and severe economic damage.

In the 1980s, Barry Collin, a former intelligence officer, coined the term 'cyber-terrorism' to refer to the changing face of terrorism brought on by the convergence of the physical and virtual worlds. Collin later went on to outline scenarios in which terrorists could conduct cyber-attacks with effects commensurate to physical acts of violence. In one, a cyber-terrorist attack against the next generation of air traffic control system causes two large civilian aircraft to collide (Collin 1997).

The term 'cyber-terrorism' has been used to characterise everything from minor hacks to devastating attacks such as outlined by Collin. In 2001, the US National Infrastructure Protection Center defined it as 'a criminal act perpetrated by the use of computers and telecommunications capabilities, resulting in violence, destruction and/or disruption of services to create fear by causing confusion and uncertainty within a given population, with the goal of influencing a government or population to conform to particular political, social or ideological agenda.' Although this definition allows for non-violent attacks, to include denial-of-service (DoS) attacks against Internet servers, government officials and scholars have been reluctant to label any cyber-attack that has occurred so far as an act of cyber-terrorism. This is because cyber-attacks associated with terrorists have yet to produce damages or psychological effects comparable to those caused by bombings and other acts of violence. Indeed, they resemble those of other hackers who have nothing to do with terrorism. As a consequence, cyber-terrorism is often dismissed as fear mongering.

The real issue, however, is not whether cyber-terrorism is taking place today or whether it is a serious threat for the future. It is that the Internet has introduced a venue whereby hackers who align themselves with terrorist groups can inflict damage, particularly economic harm, without engaging in violence. They can do this at little cost and risk, and from anywhere in the world. Individuals and groups who would never detonate a bomb or gun down another human being are thus able to support terrorist objectives. Moreover, not only can they launch attacks through the Internet, they can obtain hacking tools and information from the Net as well. They do not need to worry about acquiring or manufacturing explosives, crossing borders, or funding their operations. The Internet has thus brought about an expansion of damaging acts in support of terrorist objectives, regardless of whether these acts are characterised as cyber-terrorism or not.

The first reported incident of this nature took place in 1997 when a group aligning itself with the Liberation Tigers of Tamil Eelam (LTTE) claimed responsibility for 'suicide email bombings' against Sri Lankan embassies over a two-week period. Calling themselves the Internet Black Tigers, the group swamped Sri Lankan embassies with about 800 emails a day. The messages read, 'We are the Internet Black Tigers and we're doing this to disrupt your communications' (CSI 1998). Two years later, the Kosovo conflict inspired numerous hackers to join the conflict on one side or the other, or to protest the whole thing. Most of the cyber-attacks took the form of web defacements and DoS attacks. Of particular interest here are the activities of the Serb Black Hand (Crna Ruka) group, because of the radical nature of Crna Ruka. According to reports, they crashed a Kosovo Albanian website, planned daily actions against NATO computers, and deleted data on a Navy computer (Denning 2001).

The first appearance of an al-Qaeda-associated hacker group appeared a few weeks after the September 11 2001 terrorist attacks, when GForce Pakistan announced the formation of the 'Al-Qaeda Alliance Online' on a US government website it had just defaced. Declaring that 'Osama bin Laden is a holy fighter, and whatever he says makes sense', the group of Pakistani Muslim hackers posted a list of demands and warned that it planned to hit major US military and British websites (McWilliams 2001). Another GForce defacement contained similar messages along with heart-wrenching images of badly mutilated children said to have been killed by Israeli soldiers. A subsequent message from the group announced that two other Pakistani hacking groups had joined the alliance: the Pakistan Hackerz Club and Anti India Crew. Collectively, the groups had already defaced hundreds of websites, often with political messages, in support of the objectives sought by Muslim terrorists fighting in Kashmir or against Israel. Although the group expressed support for bin Laden, they distanced themselves from terrorism. On 27 October, GForce defaced a US military website with the message that it was 'not a group of cyber terrorists'. Condemning the attacks of September 11 and calling themselves 'cyber crusaders', they wrote, 'ALL we ask for is PEACE for everyone.' This turned out to be one of their last recorded defacements. GForce Pakistan and all mention of the Al-Qaeda Alliance Online disappeared (Denning 2006).

Other hackers, however, have emerged in their place, engaging in what is sometimes called 'electronic jihad'. Jihadist forums are used to distribute manuals and tools for hacking, and to promote and coordinate cyber-attacks, including a DoS attack against the Vatican website, which mainly fizzled, and an 'Electronic Battle of Guantanamo' attack against American stock exchanges and banks, which was cancelled because the banks had been notified. The al-Jinan forum has played a particularly active role, distributing a software tool called Electronic Jihad, which hackers can use to participate in DoS attacks against target websites that are deemed harmful to Islam. The forum even gives awards to participants who are the most effective (Bakier 2007). The objective is to 'inflict maximum human, financial and morale damage on the enemy by using the Internet'.

The al-Farouq forum has also promoted electronic jihad, offering a hacker library with information for disrupting and destroying enemy electronic resources. The library held keylogging software for capturing keystrokes and acquiring passwords on compromised computers, software tools for hiding or misrepresenting the hacker's Internet address, and disk and system utilities for erasing hard disks and incapacitating Windows-based systems. Postings on the forum in 2005 called for heightened electronic attacks against US and allied government websites (Pool 2005a). On another jihadist forum, a posting in October 2008 invited youths to participate in an 'electronic jihadist campaign' against US military systems by joining the 'Tariq Bin-Ziyad Brigades'. The recently formed group was looking to increase its ranks so it could be more effective (OSC 2008a).

In a February 2006 report, the Jamestown Foundation reported that 'most radical jihadi forums devote an entire section to (hacker warfare)'. The al-Ghorabaa site, for example contained information on penetrating computer devices and intranet servers, stealing passwords, and security. It also contained an encyclopaedia on hacking websites and a 344-page book on hacking techniques, including a step-by-step guide for 'terminating pornographic sites and those intended for the Jews and their supporters' (Ulph 2006). The forum Minbar ahl al-Sunna wal-Jama'a (The Pulpit of the People of the Sunna) offered a hacking manual that was said to be written in a pedagogical style and discussed motives and incentives for computer-based attacks, including political, strategic, economic, and individual. The manual discussed three types of attack: direct intrusions into corporate and government networks, infiltration of personal computers to steal personal information, and interception of sensitive information such as credit card numbers in transit (Pool 2005b). Younis Tsoulis (Irhabi 007) also promoted hacking, publishing a 74-page manual 'The Encyclopedia of Hacking the Zionist and Crusader Websites' with hacking instructions and a list of vulnerable websites (Jamestown 2008).

Electronic jihad often coincides with physical forms of terrorism and protest. Publication of the Danish cartoons satirising the Prophet Muhammad, for example, sparked a rash of cyber-attacks as violence erupted on the streets in early 2006. Zone-h, a website that records web defacements, recorded almost 3,000 attacks against Danish websites by late February. In addition, the al-Ghorabaa site coordinated a 24-hour cyber attack against *Jyllands-Posten*, the newspaper that first published the cartoons, and other newspaper sites (Ulph 2006). A video purporting to document a DoS attack against the *Jyllands-Posten* website was later released on the jihadist site 3asfh.com. The video was in the style of jihadist videos coming out of Iraq, showing that the hackers were emulating the tactics of violent jihadists (Internet Haganah 2006b).

Jihadists often target websites that are used to actively oppose them. For example, a message posted to a Yahoo! group attempted to recruit 600 Muslims for jihad cyber attacks against Internet Haganah's website. The motive was retaliation against Internet Haganah's efforts to close down terrorist-related websites. Muslim hackers were asked to register to a Yahoo! group called Jehad-Op (Reynalds 2004). According to the Anti-Terrorism Coalition (ATC), the jihad was organised by a group named Osama Bin Laden (OBL) Crew, which also threatened attacks against the ATC website (ATC 2004).

The use of electronic jihad to support al-Qaeda is explicitly promoted in a book by Mohammad Bin Ahmad As-Sālim titled *39 Ways to Serve and Participate in Jihâd*. Initially published on al-Qaeda's al-Farouq website in 2003

(Leyden 2003), principle 34 in the book discusses two forms of 'electronic *Jihâd:*' discussion boards (for media operations) and hacking methods, about which the book writes: 'this is truly deserving of the term "electronic *Jihâd*", since the term carries the meaning of force; to strike and to attack. So, whoever is given knowledge in this field, then he should not be stingy with it in regards to using it to serve the *Jihâd*. He should concentrate his efforts on destroying any American websites, as well as any sites that are anti-*Jihâd* and *Mujâhidîn*, Jewish websites, modernist and secular websites' (As-Sālim 2003).

Al-Qaeda has long recognised the value of inflicting economic harm on the US, and electronic jihad is seen as a tool for doing so. After the Electronic Battle of Guantanamo was cancelled, a message posted on an Islamist website stated how 'disabling (stock market and bank websites) for a few days or even for a few hours ... will cause millions of dollars worth of damage' (Alshech 2007). A message on al-Jinan noted that hacking methods could 'inflict the greatest (possible) financial damage' on their enemies. According to Fouad Husseing, economically damaging cyber-attacks are part of al-Qaeda's long-term war against the US. In his book, *al-Zarqawi-al-Qaeda's Second Generation*, Husseing describes al-Qaeda's seven-phase war as revealed through interviews of the organisation's top lieutenants. Phase 4, which is scheduled for the period 2010–2013, includes conducting cyber-terrorism against the US economy (Hall 2005).

Although damages from cyber-attacks attributed to al-Qaeda and associated hackers so far have been minor compared to the damages from al-Qaeda's violent acts of terror and even the cyber-attacks of other actors such as the Russians who attacked Estonian websites in 2007, Husseing's book and other writings suggest that al-Qaeda may be thinking bigger. A posting in a jihadist forum advocated attacking all computer networks around the world, including military and telecommunication networks, in order to 'bring about the total collapse of the West' (Alshech 2007). Of course, the idea of shutting down every single network is utter fantasy, so vision by itself does not translate into a threat.

Recruitment

The Internet has transformed terrorist recruitment by providing a venue through which potential terrorists and supporters worldwide can learn about terrorist groups, join or provide assistance through Internet forums and groups, and engage in direct actions that serve terrorist objectives. They can contribute to Internet media operations, engage in cyber-attacks, and donate money, software, and expertise through Internet channels. If desired, they can do all this without travelling or even formally joining. They simply sign up through their deeds. However, for those wishing to be part of the physical action, the Internet has facilitated the processes of joining and getting to a terrorist location as well.

The Internet has been particularly instrumental to the spread of al-Qaeda. Indeed, it is probably fair to say that the jihadist social movement associated with the terrorist organisation would not exist without the Internet. The

Internet has allowed self-selected individuals and groups of friends to formally or informally join the network, while operating independently from the central organisation. And they can live anywhere in the world. The effect is a highly decentralised network of participants who operate in closely knit groups (cells) with little or no direction or even recognition from al-Qaeda's core leadership. This social network is held together largely through the Internet.

Jihadist forums have played a prominent role in al-Qaeda's recruitment strategy. In one forum, a participant nicknamed Wali al-Haq posted the steps a candidate should take to join al-Qaeda:

1 Understand and adhere to the identity, ideology, and objectives of al-Qaeda;
2 Prepare physically, scientifically and spiritually;
3 Either directly join a jihadist faction or pursue a solitary path in taking up the jihadist cause.

According to al-Haq, any Muslim who supports al-Qaeda in any way, be it financially, physically or by simply showing desire or intent to join, is considered to be a jihadist in al-Qaeda (Bakier 2008a). On another forum, would-be jihadists were invited to sign an oath of loyalty to bin Laden, al-Zawahiri, Zarqawi, and Taliban chief Mullah Muhammad Omar. The announcement said, 'This is the Internet that Allah operates in the service of jihad and of the mujahedoun ... such that half the mujahedoun's battle is waged on the pages of the Internet, which is the only outlet for passing announcements to the mujahedoun' (Middle East Media Research Institute (MEMRI) 2005).

As-Sālim's book, *39 Ways to Serve and Participate in Jihad*, calls upon every Muslim to 'obey the Jihad against the infidels'. In addition to engaging in electronic jihad (principle 34), the book suggests participating in martyrdom and other operations, supplying money and equipment to fighters, fund-raising, assisting families of fighters, preaching, prayer, educating children, and so forth (As-Sālim 2003). In effect, there is something for everyone.

Marc Sageman, author of *Leaderless Jihad*, has observed that while websites have been instrumental for distributing documents and other materials, it is through the interactive forums that relationships are built, bonding takes place, and beliefs are hardened. He writes, 'It is the forums, not the images of the passive websites, which are crucial in the process of radicalisation. People change their minds through discussion with friends, not by simply reading impersonal stories' (Sageman 2008: 116). Sageman believes that the forums are to the current generation of jihadists what the mosques were to the previous generation. They play a much larger role in al-Qaeda's efforts to recruit jihadists than the passive websites, where the visitors are already predisposed to the views that are promulgated. Moreover, it is in conversation that commitments are made, plans are hatched, and actions are put into motion. In today's networked world, these conversations can as easily be online as in person. However, William McCants, a fellow at the Combating Terrorism Center at West Point, notes that face-to-face contact with committed militants usually precedes online activity and is essential for continued radicalisation. He also says that the mainstream Muslim forums play a bigger role in Jihadist missionary activity than the jihadist forums (McCants 2008).

Jihadi Web forums have helped bring would-be jihadists to Iraq. Citing Rita Katz, director of the SITE Institute, the *New York Post* reported in September 2003 that a 'maze of secret chat rooms' was used to direct potential recruits into Iraq (Lathem 2003). After expressing interest in one of these rooms, a candidate received a propaganda video from someone calling himself Merciless Terrorist. The video instructed him to download software called Pay Talk, which would allow him to communicate by voice in an 'impossible to monitor "talking chat room"'. There, the would-be-terrorist is given more detailed instructions and directed to a sympathetic Islamic centre or mosque for screening.

According to Evan Kohlmann, Al-Qaeda's al-Ansar forum was 'a virtual matchmaking service for budding Islamic militants searching for a path to jihad, and particularly for the emerging mujahidin frontline in Iraq. In one case, a Moroccan user asked for help contacting Zarqawi's network in Iraq, whereupon his travel arrangements were brokered on his behalf over email (Kohlmann 2008). For jihadists transiting Syria on their way to Iraq, the forum www.nnuu.org offered instructions about what to do (Ulph 2005). Another forum held a live interview with a militant in Iraq, who answered questions about the progress of the conflict in Iraq and how to emigrate and join the fighting (Drennan and Black 2007).

Terrorists use the Internet to recruit children as well as adults, offering slick videos, comic-book style readings, and computer games. For example, a radical Islamic website in the UK posted a rap video designed to inspire young people to take up jihad against the West. The Investigative Project, a counterterrorist research and investigative centre, characterised the video as 'undeniably entertaining, as professionally produced as any video you might see on MTV'. On one of Hizballah's websites, kids can download a computer game called 'Special Force'. The game, which is based on the Israeli invasion of Lebanon in 1978 and 1982 and their forced withdrawal in 2000, involves liberating the military posts occupied by the Israelis. It was designed to introduce young people to the resistance and help win the international media war with Israel (WorldNetDaily 2003).

In addition to recruiting supporters of terrorism, the Internet has been used in at least one case to entrap an unsuspecting victim for a terrorist act. In January 2001, a Palestinian woman in Yassir Arafat's Fatah organisation went to an Internet chat room, where she presented herself as an Israeli woman of Moroccan background to a young Israeli man. After he agreed to meet her in Jerusalem, she drove him into Palestinian territory, where a gunman was waiting to end the man's life (Nacos 2002: 103–104).

Learning

The Internet gives terrorists a fast and easy way to learn ideology, methods, and targets. Terrorists can educate themselves, alone or in small groups, without the need to visit a library, travel to a terrorist training camp, or enroll in a university. Al-Qaeda clearly recognises the value of the Internet for education and training: one prominent leader, Aub Musab al-Suri (now in US custody), contended that by taking advantage of information technology, Muslims can access military and ideological training in any language, at any time, anywhere (CTC 2006: 54). In November 2003, the Saudi-owned London daily *Al-Shrq al-Awsat* reported that al-Qaeda had opened Al-Qaeda University for Jihad Sciences on the Internet. The virtual university was said to comprise several 'colleges', including colleges for the technology of explosive devices, booby-trapped cars and vehicles, electronic jihad, and media jihad.

Al-Qaeda's online 'university' is realised by a collection of web forums with instructional materials in the form of manuals, magazines, and videos, as well as online discussions and coaching. In addition to the hacking manuals described earlier, jihadist sites provide documents and videos on how to build and use various types of physical weapons such as explosives, poisons, AK-47s, and surface-to-air missiles. Information about explosives has included chemical formulas and diagrams for the large-scale production of explosives such as TNT, C4, and PETN; a blueprint for a nitrate-producing machine for making improvised explosives; instructions for evading airport scanning machines (Nathan 2003); a do-it-yourself plan for making dirty bombs (Al-Matrafi 2005); and a video for constructing a suicide bomb vest (Myers 2004). In one forum, a terrorist who had trouble building a bomb received coaching that allowed him to succeed. Besides weapons, Jihadist manuals provide instructions on such topics as intelligence, interrogations, kidnapping, assassinations, operations security, and terrorist cells. There is even a 51-page manual on recruiting, explaining how to select candidates and a three-phase process for winning them over (Bakier 2008b).

At least some of the instructional materials are rather archaic. For example, the 'Al-Qaeda Training Manual', found by British police and released by the Department of Justice in 2001, says nothing about computers, software, the Internet, cellphones, satellite phones, or other modern information technologies known to be used by al-Qaeda. The section on secret writing and ciphers (lesson 13) makes no mention of modern cryptographic systems and is based entirely on manual methods that appear to be at least 50 to 100 years old. More recent training documents, however, cover computers, email, the Internet and Web, encryption, and other modern information technologies.

In January 2004, jihadists launched two educational magazines on the Internet. The first, called the *Al-Battar Training Camp*, was introduced to give Muslim youth jihad training without the need to travel to a terrorist training camp. Published by the Military Committee of the Mujahideen in the Arabian Peninsula, the electronic publication offered instruction and exercises in the use of arms (WorldNetDaily 2004). The sixth issue, published in March 2004, gave a detailed description of the organisation structure of a project cell, described desired skill sets, and emphasised the importance of security, including the use of compartmentalisation within project cells and dead drops (including websites) for communications up and down the chain of command (Mansfield 2004). The magazine appeared to have been discontinued by the end of the year. The second magazine, called the *Base of the Vanguard*, was directed at new recruits who could not break cover to undergo formal training. Spearheaded by Saif al-Adel, the manual contains quotes and articles by al-Qaeda leaders, including bin Laden and al-Zawhiri. It gave technical advice on physical training, operations security, and light weapons; encouraged the use of weapons of mass destruction, and warned operatives to resist counterterrorist psychological operations: 'They will try and wear down your morale by publishing false reports about the arrest of other cells' (Burke 2004). In late 2006, jihadists launched a third educational magazine that focused on technical issues. Called *The Technical Mujahid*, the first two issues covered information security technologies, including software tools for encryption (discussed later in this paper). The magazine was released by the Al-Fajr Media Center (Center for International Issues Research (CIIR) 2007).

Al-Qaeda's online training materials have been instrumental to jihadists planning attacks. According to the *Daily Telegraph*, Nick Reilly, the 22-year-old suicide bomber in the UK who tried unsuccessfully to detonate a series of nail bombs, learned how to make the bombs from videos posted on YouTube. The *Telegraph* also reported that Reilly had been 'groomed by two men on the YouTube website who claimed to be living on the Afghan-Pakistan border and to be in touch with al-Qaeda' (Gardham 2008).

Jihadists have expressed an interest in virtual reality tools, in particular flight simulation software (Internet Haganah 2006a). Virtual reality might also be used for instruction in particular weapons such as surface-to-air missiles or to lead would-be suicide bombers through the process of detonating their bombs and receiving their promised virgins and other heavenly rewards.

Despite the benefits of online training, it comes at a price, as potential terrorists do not have the opportunity to meet established terrorists and develop personal bonds of trust. Further, online training in the use of physical weapons is not likely to be as effective as getting hands-on experience in a camp with experienced instructors. However, these limitations can be overcome if terrorists work in small groups that meet physically, and use online coaching to help them through difficulties. Al-Suri envisioned Muslim homes serving as training camps as well as staging grounds for waging jihad (CTC 2006: 54).

In addition to learning from materials posted on jihadist websites, jihadists use the Internet for research. For example, in January 2002, the National Infrastructure Protection Center (NIPC) reported that al-Qaeda members had 'sought information on Supervisory Control and Data Acquisition (SCADA) systems available on multiple SCADA-related websites. They specifically sought information on water supply and wastewater management practices in the US and abroad' (NIPC 2002). Such information could be useful in planning either physical or cyber-attacks against SCADA-controlled critical infrastructures.

Although most jihadist research may be conducted on public websites, there has been at least one reported incident of jihadists breaking into accounts to collect intelligence. According to Magnus Ranstorp, al-Qaeda hackers used simple password cracking tools, freely available on the Internet, to gain access to the email account of a US diplomat in the Arab world. They had retrieved his bank statements, which revealed information about his location and movement (Ranstorp 2004).

Finance

The Internet has given terrorists new ways of raising, spending, and hiding money. Funds are raised through online solicitations and various cybercrimes such as identity theft and credit card fraud. The Tamil Tigers pioneered both in a single operation. After compromising a computer system at Sheffield University in England in 1997 and capturing the user IDs and passwords of faculty, they used the email accounts to send out messages asking donors to send money to a charity in Sri Lanka (Vatis 2001).

Al-Qaeda has used the Internet to solicit and move funds. In addition, they have funded purchases through online credit card fraud. Younes Tsouli (Irhabi 007), for example, used stolen identities and credit card numbers to pay for web hosting services. To acquire card numbers, he and his two cohorts planted keystroke loggers on their websites and sent out emails with links to fake websites requesting financial information (Krebs 2007; Mansfield 2006). The trio ran up $3.5 million in fraudulent charges, registered more than 180 website domains with 96 different web hosting companies, purchased hundreds of prepaid cellphones and more than 250 airline tickets, and laundered money through online gaming sites (Lormel 2008).

In his autobiography *Me Against the Terrorist!*, Imam Samudra, one of the terrorists convicted in the 12 October 2002 Bali bombings, advocates the use of computer attacks to raise funds for terrorist activities. A chapter titled 'Hacking: why not?' offers rudimentary information on hacking, particularly as it applies to credit card fraud. Evidence found on his seized computer showed he at least had made an attempt at carding (Sipress 2004).

Even if terrorists do not use stolen card numbers to make purchases, online transactions can lower procurement costs and speed transaction times. They also can provide some level of secrecy. On one jihadist forum, a participant suggested establishing phoney online retail stores for receiving contributions to the jihad. Another suggested using the CashU online service, which was said to allow money payments and transfers without risk of theft, fraud, or exposure of personal information (MEMRI 2007).

Security

Operations security has always been a concern for terrorists. Because of their violent acts, they must hide from police and military forces. Traditionally, this has entailed using safe houses, code words, encryption, dead drops, false identities, and other methods of concealment. In using the Internet, terrorists expose themselves to a new set of risks. If they take no security precautions at all, authorities can monitor their online activities, collect evidence, and determine their physical locations. Terrorists are generally aware of these vulnerabilities, and so have learned and adopted new security practices.

Some of the tools they use include the use of cyber cafes, anonymous email accounts, virtual dead drops, coded and encrypted email, encrypted files and disks, hidden files and directories, password-protected websites and forums, and anonymous web browsing via proxies. The September 11 hijackers, for example, accessed anonymous Hotmail and Yahoo! accounts from computers at Kinko's and at a public library (Ross 2001). They also used secret code words and phrases. Three weeks before the attacks, Mohammad Atta reportedly received a coded email message that read: 'The semester begins in three more weeks. We've obtained 19 confirmations for studies in the faculty of law, the faculty of urban planning, the faculty of fine arts and the faculty of engineering' (Ha'aretz 2002). The faculties referred to the four targets (World Trade Center twin towers, Pentagon, and Capitol); the faculty for urban planning may have represented the tower hit by Atta's plane since he had studied urban planning in Hamburg, Germany.

According to reports, the principal architect of the 9/11 attacks, Khalid Shaikh Mohammed, trained high-level al-Qaeda operatives in the use of encryption (AFP 2005). One of his pupils might have been his nephew, Ramzi Yousef, a key operative in the 1993 World Trade Center bombing. Yousef stored information about his Bojinka plot to destroy 11 airliners on his laptop in encrypted files. The encryption was sufficiently robust that it took cryptanalysts more than a year to break the code (Freeh 1997). However, some of the encryption used by al-Qaeda has been much easier to crack. Files on al-Qaeda computers acquired by the *Wall Street Journal* in Afghanistan in November 2001, for example, were encrypted with Microsoft's 40-bit version of the Data Encryption Standard (DES), a weak version of DES that had been approved for export (stronger codes are now exportable) (Hooper 2001).

Jihadists have developed encryption software that at least superficially rivals strong products like Pretty Good Privacy (PGP). Al-Qaeda's Mujahideen Secrets, for example, offers 2048-bit asymmetric (public-key) and 256-bit symmetric (single-key) encryption using the latest US standards, including the Advanced Encryption Standard. The tool, initially released in 2007 by the Global Islamic Media Front, is described in the second issue of *The Technical Mujahid*. According to the magazine, the GIMF developed their own software because they did not trust 'foreign' programs such as PGP. The software can be run from a memory stick, allowing easy portability. While encrypting files with the tool is fairly straightforward, sending encrypted messages is more complicated, as users must first acquire the public keys of their correspondents and then copy-paste encrypted text into message windows (CIIR 2007).

The second issue of *The Technical Mujahid* also discusses steganography, or methods of hiding messages in cover media such as image and audio files (CIIR 2007). A steganographic technique was introduced in the first issue as well, as part of a general discussion about how to conceal files on computer. The method, called Alternate Data Streams (ADS), allows hidden data to be associated with a file (TRC 2006b).

Despite al-Qaeda's interest in steganography, there have been no confirmed reports of jihadists actually using it. There have been indicators of possible use, including jihadist files that tested positive with steganographic detection tools. However, the codes could not be cracked, so the test results may have been false positives. In one case, reported by *ABC News* in October 2001, French investigators believed that suspects arrested in an alleged plot to blow up the US Embassy in Paris planned to transmit the go-ahead for the attack hidden inside a picture posted on the Internet. Investigators found a notebook full of secret codes on one of the men, who was characterised as a 'computer nerd well versed in the messaging technique' (Ross 2001).

In addition to having expertise in encryption, Khalid Shaikh Mohammed is said to have communicated through an email 'virtual dead drop', where messages are composed but never sent. Instead, they are saved as drafts and then read by the intended recipient from the draft message folder of a shared email account (AFP 2005). Other jihadists have also used this technique, including one of the convicted terrorists behind the Madrid train bombings in 2004 (Johnson 2005).

Jihadists make extensive use of password-protected web forums for private meetings and discussions. They are like virtual safe houses, but more vulnerable to monitoring and infiltration than their physical counterparts. Jihadists are aware of these risks and urge caution on the private forums, as well as on public ones. They tell members to access the sites from Internet cafes, but not the same one repeatedly, and to use proxies to conceal their IP addresses; to be suspicious of other participants and wary about what they read and post; to use different usernames and passwords on different forums, and to guard their passwords; to be careful about giving out personal information; and to watch out for spyware and other forms of malicious software. To mitigate the risks, some jihadist forums have implemented 'cloaking' technology, which blocks forum access from IP addresses in the US in order to keep US intelligence services from monitoring the forums. However, if the IP check is only performed for accesses via the website's home page, spies may still be able to gain access by going to an inner page on the site (TRC 2006a).

Implications for counterterrorism

Just as the Internet is transforming terrorism, it is also transforming counterterrorism by providing another channel whereby terrorists can be monitored and potentially subverted. Further, such counterterrorism activities can be performed remotely and from a safe location, avoiding the difficulties and risks associated with infiltrating terrorists' physical space. One effect is that individuals and groups from all over the world can participate in counterterrorism as independent agents. In effect, al-Qaeda's own network of jihadists is matched by a global network of counter-jihadists. The following briefly describes four counterterrorism strategies that explicitly take advantage of al-Qaeda's Internet presence: intelligence collection, denial, subversion, and engagement.

The first strategy, intelligence collection, involves monitoring al-Qaeda's Internet forums and message exchanges in order to develop actionable intelligence regarding their members and social networks; safe houses and other facilities where members gather and weapons are produced; proposals and plans for terrorist acts; financial sources and transactions; and other relevant information. Information gleaned from such surveillance can be used to thwart plots and facilitate arrests and convictions. Law enforcement and intelligence agencies engage in such monitoring, and it has been valuable in the fight against al-Qaeda. Individuals working alone and with groups such as Internet Haganah and SITE also contribute to the effort. Posing as a jihadist from the safety of her home, retired Montana judge Shannen Rossmiller has infiltrated al-Qaeda websites and passed along information to the FBI. Her findings have led to numerous terrorist arrests and convictions (Rossmiller 2007).

The second strategy, denial, involves taking actions that deny al-Qaeda access to the Internet, for example, by shutting down their email accounts, websites, and forums, and by removing jihadist content from other sites. The premise is that by getting al-Qaeda off the Net, they will be unable to post materials and engage with potential recruits. Further, communications among jihadists will be severely hampered, making it more difficult for them to plan and organise actions. Internet Service Providers already practise some denial by shutting down websites that directly advocate violence or provide support to known terrorist organisations in violation of laws. In addition, sites such as YouTube help by removing videos that train terrorists or incite violence. However, the sites and content often reappear elsewhere, so the effects may not last. Another problem with denial is that much of the content posted by jihadists is permissible under principles of free speech. Denial also has adverse effects on intelligence collection, potentially taking away valuable sources of information as sites move and jihadists move further underground on the Internet or off the Net entirely. Further, denial requires international cooperation to be fully successful, as jihadist accounts and websites can be hosted all over the world. Such cooperation can be difficult to achieve.

Still, denial can impair al-Qaeda's efficiency and undermine trust in their online sites. To illustrate, in September 2008, al-Qaeda's media arm was severely hampered when several of its key websites went down. A month later, only one forum, al-Hesbah, was back online. The effect was to curtail the dissemination of videos and other materials from al-Qaeda's leadership and to raise suspicions about infiltrators and the authenticity of lookalike sites (Knickmeyer 2008). On one jihadist forum, a participant posted a message expressing alarm over the attacks and urging the recruitment of computer specialists to address the problem. He asked what would happen if they had no jihadist forums or websites, and then answered that it 'would bring all communication between the mujahidin and the children of the Islamic nation to an end'. He said it would 'delay the carrying out of operations and the transmission of jihadist news' (OSC 2008c).

The third strategy, subversion, involves infiltrating al-Qaeda forums, disrupting their operations, and undermining al-Qaeda objectives, for example, by injecting misinformation into a forum discussion in order to erode trust in a leader or sow seeds of discord. One drawback of subversion strategies is that they are risky – operations can have unintended consequences and backfire. Also, if not coordinated with intelligence operations, they can undermine collection efforts and lead to false conclusions. However, the strategy should not be dismissed outright, as subversive techniques can be effective. Already, participants in some jihadist forums have warned that intelligence services and other opponents may have infiltrated the forums in order to fuel discord and distort the forum, suggesting that the forums were not operating as smoothly and effectively as they would like (OSC 2008d, 2008e).

The fourth strategy, engagement, involves conversing with jihadists and potential recruits in online forums, challenging basic premises and beliefs through dialogue and writings. The goal is to draw people out of the movement and deter potential recruits from joining. If indeed it is through conversations that potential recruits are radicalised and become committed to the jihad, then alternative conversations may be employed to lead them in the opposite direction. Saudi Arabia's online Al-Sakinah ('Tranquillity') campaign illustrates this. Muslim scholars and sheikhs with expertise on Islam, aided by experts in sociology and psychology, enter extremist web forums and engage with participants, encouraging them to renounce their extremist ideas. According to reports, the campaign has been successful. About 700 individuals recanted their beliefs, including high-ranking members of al-Qaeda (Cilluffo *et al.* 2007; Yehoshua 2006).

These four strategies can be used together and in combination with other strategies that are not Internet specific, for example, capturing al-Qaeda terrorists, countering al-Qaeda's ideology, and winning 'hearts and minds'. They have the advantage of directly targeting the media that is holding the global movement together. Without the Internet, al-Qaeda would not likely have its global reach, either as a terrorist network or as an inspiration.

Further reading

Despite the large number of books on terrorism, only one is devoted to terrorist use of the Internet, namely Gabriel Weimann's *Terror on the Internet* (2006, United States Institute of Peace). Fortunately, it is very good. For new developments, Internet Haganah (internet-haganah.com/haganah/) is an excellent resource.

References

AFP (2005) 'Cyber-jihadists Weave a Dangerous Web', *Agence France-Presse*, 27 October.

Al-Matrafi, S. (2005) 'Terrorist Website Drops Dirty Bomb', *Arab News*, 11 March.

Alshech, E. (2007) 'Cyberspace as a Combat Zone: The Phenomenon of Electronic Jihad', *MEMRI Inquiry and Analysis Series*, No. 329 (The Middle East Media Research Institute), 7 February.

As-Sālim, M. (2003) *39 Ways to Serve and Participate in Jihâd* (At-Tibyân Publications), http://tibyan.wordpress.com/2007/08/24/39-ways-to-serve-and-participate-in-jihad/ (accessed June 30, 2008).

ATC (2004) 'ATC's OBL Crew Investigation', Anti-Terrorism Coalition, 1 July.

Bakier, A.H. (2007) 'Forum Users Improve Electronic Jihad Technology', *Terrorism Focus*, 4(20): 26 June.

Bakier, A.H. (2008a) 'Jihadi Website Advises Recruits on How to Join al-Qaeda', *Terrorism Focus*, 5(18): May 6.

Bakier, A.H. (2008b) 'Jihadis Publish Online Recruitment Manual,' *Terrorism Focus*, 5:34, September 24.

Burke, J. (2004) 'Al-Qaeda Launches Online Terrorist Manual,' *Observer*, 19 January.

CIIR (2007) 'Al-Qaida Media Arm Releases the Second Issue of Its Tech Magazine', Global Issues Report, Center for International Issues Research, 19 March.

Cilluffo, F. *et al.* (2007) 'NETworked Radicalization: A Counter Strategy,' The George Washington University Homeland Security Policy Institute and the University of Virginia Critical Incident Analysis Group.

Collin, B. (1997) 'The Future of Cyberterrorism: The Physical and Virtual Worlds Converge', *Crime and Justice International*, March.

CSI (1998) 'Email Attack on Sri Lanka Computers', *Computer Security Alert*, No. 183, Computer Security Institute, June, p. 8.

CTC (2006) 'Harmony and Disharmony: Exploiting al-Qa'ida's Organizational Vulnerabilities', Combating Terrorism Center, United States Military Academy, West Point, 14 February.

Delio, M. (2003) 'Al-Qa'ida Website Refuses to Die', *Wired News*, 7 April.

Denning, D.E. (2001) 'Activism, Hacktivism, and Cyberterrorism,' in J. Arquilla and D. Ronfelt (eds), *Networks and Netwars*. Santa Monica: RAND, 273.

Denning, D.E. (2006) 'A View of Cyberterrorism Five Years Later', in K. Himma (ed.), *Readings in Internet Security: Hacking, Counterhacking, and Society*. Boston: Jones and Bartlett.

Di Justo, P. (2002) 'How Al-Qaida Site Was Hijacked', *Wired News*, 10 August 2002.

Drennan, S. and Black, A. (2007) 'Jihad Online – The Changing Role of the Internet', *Janes*.

Freeh, L.J. (1997) Statement before the Senate Committee on Commerce, Science, and Transportation, regarding the Impact of Encryption on Law Enforcement and Public Safety, 19 March.

Gardham, D. (2008) 'Al-Qaeda Terrorists Who Brainwashed Exeter Suicide Bomber Still on the Run', *Daily Telegraph*, 16 October.

Glasser, S.B. and Coll, S. (2005) 'The Web as Weapon: Zarqawi Intertwines Acts on Ground with Propaganda Campaign on the Internet', *Washington Post*, 9 August.

Ha'aretz (2002) 'Virtual Soldiers in a Holy War', *Ha'aretz Daily*, 16 September.

Hall, A. (2005) 'Al-Qaeda Chiefs Reveal World Domination Design', *The Age*, 24 August.

Hoffman, B. (2003) 'Al Qaeda, Trends in Terrorism, and Future Potentialities: An Assessment', *Studies in Conflict and Terrorism*, 26: 429–42.

Hoffman, B. (2006) 'The Use of the Internet By Islamic Extremists', Testimony presented to the House Permanent Select Committee on Intelligence, 4 May.

Hooper, I. (2001) 'Kabul Computer Reveals Files of Top Al Qaeda Officials', Associated Press, 21 December.

Hunt, K. (2006) 'Osama Bin Laden Fan Clubs Build Online Communities', *USA Today*, 9 March.

IntelCenter (2007) 'al-Qaeda Messaging Statistics (QMS)', 3(3), 9 September.

Internet Haganah (2006a) 'Don't You Just Love It When …', 28 January, http://internet-haganah.com/harchives/005435.html (accessed 21 October 2008).

Internet Haganah (2006b) 'How the Brothers Attacked the Website of Jyllands-Posten', 7 February, http://internet-haganah.com/harchives/005456.html (accessed 21 October 2008).

Internet Haganah (2007) 'Top … Nineteen List of Arabic Salafist/Jihadist Sites', 22 April, http://internet-haganah.com/harchives/006013.html (accessed 24 April 2007).

Internet Haganah (2008) 'Portrait of Rats, Preparing to Drown', 10 October, http://internet-haganah.com/harchives/006420.html (accessed 10 October 2008).

Internet World Stats (2008) 'Internet Usage Statistics', http://www.internetworldstats. com/stats.htm (accessed 8 October 2008).

Jamestown (2008) 'Hacking Manual by Jailed Jihadi Appears on Web', *Terrorism Focus*, 5(9), Jamestown Foundation, 4 March.

Johnson, K. (2005) 'Terrorist Threat Shifts as Groups Mutate and Merge', *The Wall Street Journal*, 14 February.

Kimmage, D. (2008) 'The Al-Qaeda Media Nexus', RFE/RFL (RadioFreeEurope/ RadioLiberty) Special Report, March.

Knickmeyer, E. (2008) 'Al-Qaeda Web Forums Abruptly Taken Offline', *Washington Post*, 18 October.

Kohlmann, E.F. (2008) 'Al-Qa'ida's "MySpace": Terrorist Recruitment on the Internet', *CTC Sentinel*, 1: 2, January.

Krebs, B. (2007) 'Terrorism's Hook Into Your Inbox', *Washington Post*, 5 July.

Labi, N. (2006) 'Jihad 2.0,' *The Atlantic Monthly*, July/August.

Lathem, N. (2003) 'Al-Qa'ida Trolls Net', *New York Post*, 15 September.

Leyden, J. (2003) 'Al-Qaeda: The 39 Principles of Holy War', *Virtual Jerusalem*.

Lormel, D. (2008) 'Credit Cards and Terrorists', Counterterrorism Blog, 16 January.

McCants, W. (2008) 'How Online Recruitment Works', 18 September, http://www. jihadica.com/how-online-recruitment-works/ (accessed 10 October 2008).

McLeod, J. (2007) 'Exposing On-Line Jihadists', *Canada Free Press*, 10 August.

McWilliams, B. (2001) 'Pakistani Hackers Deface U.S. Site With Ultimatum', *Newsbytes*, 17 October.

Mansfield, L. (2004) 'Everything You Always Wanted to Know About Becoming a Terrorist, but Were Afraid to Ask', Northeast Intelligence Network, March.

Mansfield, L. (2006) 'Me and Terrorist 007', 1 March 2006, http://www.lauramansfield. com/j/007.asp (accessed 27 March 2008).

MEMRI (2005) 'Now Online: Swear Loyalty to al-Qa'ida Leaders', *MEMRI Special Dispatch Series*, No. 1027 (The Middle East Media Research Institute), 18 November.

MEMRI (2007) 'Islamists Propose Ways to Transfer Funds to Islamic State of Iraq', Islamic Websites Monitor No. 84, *MEMRI Special Dispatch*, No. 1543 (The Middle East Media Research Institute), 13 April.

Myers, L. (2004) 'Web Video Teaches Terrorists to Make Bomb Vest', *MSNBC News*, 22 December, http://www.msnbc.msn.com/id/6746756/ (accessed 9 October 2008).

Nacos, B.L. (2002) *Mass-Mediated Terrorism*. Oxford: Rowman and Littlefield Publishers, Inc.

Nathan, A. (2003) 'Bomb Designed to Evade Airport Scanning Machines', *Times Online*, 26 October.

NIPC (2002) 'Terrorist Interest in Water Supply and SCADA Systems', Information Bulletin 01-001, National Infrastructure Protection Center, 30 January.

OSC (2008a) 'Jihadist Forum Invites Youths to Join "Electronic Jihadist Campaign"', Open Source Center, 6 October 2008.

OSC (2008b) 'Jihadist Forum Member Proposes Attacking US Banks, Elicits Discussion', Open Source Center, 6 October 2008.

OSC (2008c) 'Forum Member Discusses Importance of Jihadist Websites; Suggests Asking for Help', Open Source Center, 8 October.

OSC (2008d) 'Jihadist Forum Member Warns of "Intellectual Discord" in Forums', Open Source Center, 9 October.

OSC (2008e) 'Website Posts Article Expressing Concern That Members May Belong to Intelligence Services', Open Source Center, 10 November.

Pool, J. (2005a) 'New Web Forum Postings Call for Intensified Electronic Jihad Against Government Websites', Jamestown Foundation, 23 August.

Pool, J. (2005b) 'Technology and Security Discussions on the Jihadist Forums', Jamestown Foundation, October 11.

Ranstorp, M. (2004) 'Al-Qaida in Cyberspace: Future Challenges of Terrorism in an Information Age', in L. Nicander and M. Ranstorp (eds), *Terrorism in the Information Age – New Frontiers?* Stockholm: Swedish National Defence College.

Regan, T. (1999) 'How Terrorists Use the Internet to Spread Their Messages', *Christian Science Monitor*, 1 July.

Reuters (2008) 'US Military Says Hits Al Qaeda Propaganda Units', Reuters, 22 March.

Reynalds, J. (2004) 'Internet "Terrorist" Using Yahoo to Recruit 600 Muslims for Hack Attack', *Mensnewsdaily.com*, 28 February, http://www.mensnewsdaily.com/archive/r/reynalds/04/reynalds022804.htm (accessed October 21, 2008).

Ross, B. (2001) 'A Secret Language', *ABCNEWS.com*, 4 October.

Rossmiller, S. (2007) 'My Cyber Counter-Jihad', *Middle East Quarterly*, Summer.

Sageman, M. (2008) *Leaderless Jihad*. Philadephia: University of Pennsylvania Press.

Salomon, A (2003) 'Terrorists Twin Tower Images, Secret Porn Messages', *ABCNEWS.com*, 8 May.

Sipress, A. (2004) 'An Indonesian's Prison Memoir Takes Holy War Into Cyberspace', *Washington Post*, 14 December, p. A19.

TRC (2006a) 'Al Qaeda Has No Cloak', Terrorism Research Center, 21 July.

TRC (2006b) 'The Technical Mujahid Takes on Covert Communication', Terrorism Research Center, 11 December.

TRC (2007) 'Jihadists See Wiki News Service as Potential Propaganda Tool', Terrorism Research Center, 26 January.

Tsfati, Y. and Weimann, G. (2002) 'www.terrorism.com: Terror on the Internet', *Studies in Conflict and Terrorism*, 25: 317–32.

Ulph, S. (2005) 'Islamist Website Issues Travel Warning for Syrian Mujahideen Crossing Into Iraq', *Terrorism Focus*, 2: 7, Jamestown Foundation, 31 March.

Ulph, S. (2006) 'Internet Mujahideen Refine Electronic Warfare Tactics', *Terrorism Focus*, 3(5), Jamestown Foundation, 7 February.

Vatis, M. (2001) 'Cyber Terrorism and Information Warfare: Government Perspectives', in Y. Alexander and M.S. Swetnam (eds), *Cyber Terrorism and Information Warfare*. Transnational Publishers, Inc.

Weimann, G. (2006) *Terror on the Internet*. Washington, DC: United States Institute of Peace.

Weimann, G. (2008) 'Al-Qa'ida's Extensive Use of the Internet', *CTC Centenial*, 1(2): 607.

Whitelaw, K. (1998) 'Terrorists on the Web: Electronic "Safe Haven"', *U.S. News and World Report*, 22 June, p. 46.

WorldNetDaily (2003) 'Trouble in Holy Land: Hezbollah's New Computer Game', 3 March.

WorldNetDaily (2004) 'Al-Qaida Offers Do-It-Yourself Terror Training', 5 January.

Yehoshua, Y. (2006) 'Reeducation of Extremists in Saudi Arabia,' *MEMRI Inquiry and Analysis Series*, No. 260 (The Middle East Media Research Institute), 18 January.

Chapter 11

Cyber-terror: construction, criminalisation and control

Maggie Wykes with Daniel Harcus

Introduction

There are several problems with much that has been said and done, both within and about, mediated accounts of crime that this chapter tries to find ways of addressing in approaching cyber-terror. The first is that most research that focuses on mediated accounts of both crime and public responses to it is actually based on assumptions about 'effects' (not least by academics, certainly by journalists and politicians). Public perceptions are assumed at best, but perhaps even invoked, by the media and in either case a consensus is assumed particularly in relation to violence. In other words whether people are *actually* concerned about terror, the Internet or cyber-terror is simply unknown.

The second problem follows from this in that very little research actually deals with perceptions of insecurity by means of interviewing the public in any representative or rigorous way. Moreover, when, rarely, the public is asked about their perceptions and insecurities these are often very different from those that dominate mediated and political discourses, which raises questions about how and why some 'events' are represented to the public as if the public are concerned.

Third, those crime and fear discourses that dominate mass-mediated accounts do not necessarily (or even normally) address the realities of crime, threat and risk for citizens as individuals. The chances, for example, of any of our children being lured to their death by a dangerous paedophile prowling the Internet are nothing compared to the risks to children in their own homes and communities from someone they know, as in the cases of Fred and Rose West, Ian Huntley, 'Baby P' and Hans Fritzl (Wykes 1998; Wykes and Welsh 2009).

In truth we know very little about what people actually know or think about either terrorism or the Internet, nor whether what the media says about either has any impact. There is little relation between accounts of violence in the media (which very often prefer the 'dangerous stranger') and the real experience of violence in everyday lives (within families and intimate relationships; see Wykes and Welsh 2009). Where a correlation exists it is between press accounts, political discourse and policy, and this chapter argues that this is at least partly enabled because of these three 'problems' with both the media and much criticism of its role.

There are several twenty-first century instances of the represented invocation to audiences of fear and insecurity about violence and danger in the UK. These representations often are discontinuous with 'real' data, but they nearly always result in changes in policy and legislation. These have included in no particular order: the media itself as causal of crime; dangerous dogs; beggars; mental health patients in the community; AIDS; immigrants; youths; 'pretend' families/single parents; binge-drinkers; paedophiles; drugs; absconding offenders; gun crime; terrorists and Internet crime. All offer little hard evidence of genuinely impacting on the vast majority of ordinary people's lives despite media furore and acres of 'papers' calling for and realising policy and legislative change. The most pervasive, persistent and perhaps significant in broader moral and political terms, of these panics, are allied to the Internet; paedophiles (see Bryce, Chapter 16) and, the subject of this chapter, terrorists.

Terror

> It has been said that the first casualty of war is truth. In the digital war on terrorism the first victim may be our civil liberties. (Weimann 2006: 12)

This is a particularly salient observation not only because it encapsulates the impetus for this chapter but also because terrorism's meaning was never less clear than today. Although most people know terrorism when they see it, there is much debate as to what actually constitutes terrorism in a postmodern society. Yet, an international definition is crucial as a basis for counterterrorist activities (Herren n.d.), now placed in global context since the twin towers at the gates of the West were blown apart by suicide hijackers from the Middle East. In general terms, a terrorist act is a pre-planned violent attack or threat, which aims to cause psychological effect and fear amongst the target citizens, with the underlying premise of promoting a political stance (see Schmidt and Jongman 1988). This concept of terrorism has developed significantly though. 'Old' terrorism was generally local, structured, secular, nationalist, ideologically socialist and political, and it predated globalisation so its messages were low key. In comparison, 'new' terrorism is global, based within loosely knit networks, fundamentalist, imperialistic, ideologically theological, and operates in a world of cheap and fast global communication rendering such messages immeasurably more intense. The potential for mass-scale destruction has also increased significantly (Shavit 2004: 65–6) and has led to a more 'pre-emptive' definition being mediated. The UK has been pre-emptive before, by preventing IRA activity in Britain under the Prevention of Terrorism Act 1974, but has never been so 'broad brush' in its encapsulation. Although argued as essential in the interests of national security, the pre-emptive definition has arguably actually developed to accommodate the global interests of the West, such as oil (Livergood 2007) and therefore the interests of global capital, shifting the legitimation of a defensive strategy covertly toward economic rather than political interests (maybe it was ever thus).

Terrorism has apparently significantly broadened in its scope since its use as an instrument of state control under the French revolutionaries in the eighteenth century. Indeed it has arguably been inverted in popular and policy accounts. Then, the weapon of terror was the guillotine, and the threat of it was invoked by the public spectacle of beheadings to massive crowds. Now, the advent and exponential growth of the Internet plays a pivotal role in the world we live in. It is the public space of the twenty-first century. Its global reach, chaotic structure, ease of access, anonymity and our increasing dependence on it for the information, education, entertainment and communication it offers makes it appear to be both a perfect tool for terrorists and site of terror activity, worldwide.

Authorities and the media alike have been quick, and often wrong, to sensationalise the benefits the Internet offers to terrorists. This public alarm has been used as a shield by social control agencies in the 'War on Terror' to impose laws and practices which have wider implications on matters of privacy and liberty. The 'threat' of terror attacks is indeed a realistic one, and Internet technology is an ideal medium to facilitate such 'threats'. However, mass mediatisation enables a significant overstatement of risk while the technology also provides a platform for authorities to exert controls over crime and public use of the Internet on a wider basis; controls based not on terror but on *perceived threat* of terror. This reworking has happened with subtlety but remarkable speed. It began before, but accelerated post 9/11, when terrorism was shifted from meaning 'motivated violence for political ends' (Crozier 1974) towards a reconstruction in the interests of the 'state to represent threats against its sovereignty' (Oliverio 1998). Those threats in many guises have rapidly been repositioned as terror, aided and abetted by the Internet, and the media has been complicit.

Myth, meaning and 9/11

Since September 11 2001 terror has absorbed politicians, police and journalists alike. There is of course a natural affinity of interests between these groups not only ideologically in terms of class, race and gender in the UK (Tunstall 1996) but in terms of journalistic practices whereby most 'stories' come from government, police, courts, local government and press officers of one kind or another (Franklin 1997). Crime satisfies many news value criteria[1] and the more extreme the crime the better 'fit' to journalists' professional imperatives. Chibnall (1977) focused on the reporting of violent crime and added to these criteria five further aspects of a crime story that make it essential news: high visibility; political or sexual connotation; graphic presentation; individual pathology and a deterrent potential. News about extreme violence also allows for the narrative playing out of familiar cultural myths of good versus evil: such news thrills because it threatens – but only symbolically. It 'evokes threats to but also re-affirms the consensual morality of the society' (Hall *et al.* 1978: 66) and how violent crime is reported matters because, for most people, most of the time, news is our only experience of (and means of constructing an opinion about) violence. Yet that news is necessarily selected and represented within very particular sets of value criteria allied to external and internal ideological and practical controls on the practice of news-making.

News about 9/11[2] was generated by a British media industry deeply entrenched in delineating economic, cultural and professional conditions. It was news about suicidal and murderous assaults using jetliners as weapons, against a symbol of the most powerful nation's global dominance, the World Trade Center, and on 'the heart of America's military machine' (*Daily Telegraph*, 12 September 2001). The attacks destroyed not only two huge buildings, damaged the Pentagon and killed over two thousand people but also assaulted the USA's sense of itself and of its security; and, indeed, the rest of the world's sense of American power and autonomy. It was an 'act of callous ferocity … crimes against humanity … mutant, predatory "final solution" politics' (Scraton 2002b: 2). Nine-eleven demanded journalism because it epitomised everything that constitutes news. It threatened Western/ white power, so fitted the theorised meta-political agenda of the UK press. Its visual drama required little more than mere description to tell the story in clear, simple, populist, saleable terms – hence the heavy use of images, and it complied to many news values, not least rarity and negativity (Galtung and Ruge 1965; Chibnall 1977; Wykes 2001; Jewkes 2004). However, the meagre explanations that were offered left powerful resonances and legacies.

Clearly evident in the accounts were the beginnings of an Occidentalism and Islamophobia that continue to imbue accounts of terror. All the British press used the analogy with Pearl Harbor to try and explain the events of 9/11, conjuring up memories, myths and stereotypes, reinforcing the 'special relationship' between the UK and USA, and presenting danger to both from the East. This was compounded by each of the newspapers referring to Arabs in Jerusalem as celebrating the attack. For example, the *Sun* (12 September 2001) offered: 'Children dance as Palestinians cheer revenge on enemy'. Also present was an assumed consensus of experience and perspective: a representational binding together of the West, or at least the old transatlantic allies, as vulnerable victims. It was the start of the creation of all of 'us' as potential victims. That vulnerability was emphasised by the publishing of images of people jumping from the flaming Trade Center, one pair hand-in-hand. These were so terrible that they were rarely shown again – yet when 9/11 is mentioned in the UK it is those images that most affected people and those they remember. The images made us all potential 'jumpers' as we were offered modes of identifying and empathising with the victims through vignettes of lives and loved ones.

Family was a predominant mode of identification and also a deeply ideological framing. Prominence was given to the 'ordinariness' of those who were already dead or dying; these were workers, fathers, wives, sweethearts, sons and friends. Almost immediately relatives of some were named and interviewed and last messages of love on mobile phones were broadcast for all. Community was a further mode of identification: aircraft were grounded;

public transport halted; the stock market crashed; the 'city's subway system was closed' and 'cell phones were no longer functioning' (*Guardian*, 12 September 2001), affecting many more than those in the buildings and rescue teams. With unprecedented immediacy the broader public was implicated and threatened. A third mode of identification was Nation: the (re) building of the special relationship between the UK and USA in an invocation to all who believed in peace and democracy. Blair declared that he stood 'shoulder to shoulder' with the American people in a battle between the 'free and democratic world and terrorism' (www.guardian.co.uk). On 12 September 2001, the British press was relatively uniform and news accounts were measured. Populism, political partisanship and jingoism were suspended to promote a Westerncentric unity, obfuscating the integral differences over class, race, creed and gender, and reiterating shared values of family, community and nation. This was portrayed as a collaboration of all right-thinking peoples against the threat of the 'other'.

Interestingly, there has been an almost complete lack of any criminological critique of 9/11 or subsequent terror in the UK. Hundreds of surviving Taliban and al-Qaeda fighters were shipped, manacled and blindfolded, to a US naval base at Guantanamo Bay, Cuba. Many remain held as the 'tangible manifestation of the terrorism responsible for the deaths at the World Trade Center and the Pentagon' (Scraton 2002a: 228). Yet they can only be held because they are not defined as 'prisoners of war' because the war on terrorism that justified invading Afghanistan was redefined in order to imprison without trial. There has been little fury about such contempt for the law itself. Also invisible was any account of America's interest in the oil reserves of the Middle East and Bush's personal and political dependence on oil money. Increasingly, 9/11 became an excuse for US imperialism and a deflection from US internal economic corruption and collapse. One further lasting effect has been the silencing of liberals, pacifists and anti-racists because to be against American actions since 9/11 was for a long time seen as an abuse of the dead: much as to query the aggression of Israel provokes cries of anti-Semitism. The legacy has been a closing down of alternative perceptions on offer to the public by politicians and journalists and an increasing link in mediated discourses of other violences/crimes to the *terror* threat as if we all agree it is there, we know what it is and are united in war against it. The terror threat has, then, been irrevocably linked to Islam, placing the race card high on the criminalising agenda once again (see Hall *et al.* 1978). This, of course, has in turn supported increasing controls over and invasions of new communications spaces with the excuse of searching for threats of terror and also increasingly a criminalisation of those new electronic spaces.

New myth, old stereotypes

The coverage of 9/11 set the agenda for later accounts of terror and war and the context was thoroughly criminalised and linked to Islam; that is, to religious rather than political radicalism. This was reflected in anxiety about the wearing of the burka and nijab by women, with cases of the barring of classroom assistants who chose the veil (BBC, 10 November 2006) and worries about their use in court. In the UK the bombers of the London Underground on 21/7 were tried in February 2007 and 'CCTV images of one of the alleged July 21 terror plotters escaping disguised as a Muslim woman in a burka' (*The Guardian*, 20 February 2007) only appeared to confirm the 'problem'. In Britain, there were also wider repercussions as old racial stereotypes began to be reworked linking race to this new violence and often pivoted around the modes of family, community and nation evoked in accounts of 9/11.

The ideal 'functional' family is still the mythical Victorian Western Judaeo-Christian model and the sentimentalisation of the family post 9/11 seems to have enabled a racialised criminalising critique of 'other' families. Black families are increasingly blamed for street violence while Asian families are more and more associated with forced marriage, honour killings and terror. 'Honour' killings in Britain have been linked with extremist groups abroad by the Crown Prosecution Service (CPS). The CPS told a BBC investigation that Islamist terror groups were behind the murder five years ago of Heshu Yones, 16, who was stabbed to death by her father, Abdalla Yones: 'they feel very strongly that how you treat your women is a demonstration of your commitment to radicalism and extremist thought' (Lowe 2007). In each case family is used as a trope to 'criminalise' and distance 'them' from us.

The blurring of boundaries in news accounts of race and crime since 9/11 has had a long reach. Explanations for crime have been threefold: dysfunctional families; 'other' communities, particularly immigrant, and threats to the nation, and in each case 'terror' features prominently. At the level of threat to the nation, family and community are mobilised as potential victims with the state as 'protector', given the right to pass legislation and exert authority despite the lack of any publicly known threat to, or realised attack on, the UK from outside its borders since the last attacks by the IRA. The redefining and extending of terror has evolved as a whole new discourse of racial organisation, demarcation and degradation. This is othering of an extreme kind. Race, community, violence and terror accounts blur black and Asian identity boundaries with criminal motives, with not a hint of even a 'quasi' political account. The effectiveness of the mediated terror discourse in criminalising has partly been due to its association with the Internet and cyberspace.

Already mysterious and infinite the Net has been readily labelled a dangerous place full of identity thieves (Finch 2007) and cyber-stalkers (Wykes 2007). The unknowableness of terror, its immeasurable presence, secrecy and ability to cross boundaries and borders makes associations with cyber activity particularly evocative and there has been since 9/11 much evidence of this association being made by journalists and politicians, if rather less actual evidence of any fit between terror and cyber.

Cyber-terror

Much in this shift of meanings around terror, race and threat depends on the mysterious pervasive unknowable presence of the Internet with its potential to hide, disguise, accelerate and infiltrate our lives. Indeed there has been a doubling of discursive criminalisation that has linked terror both back to old myths of race and crime and forward to new technology. The Internet offers the cyber-mac of paedophiles and the cyber-cell of terror: allowing all manner of attributions, deflections and restrictions in the blurring of its real and represented boundaries. It has become a bête noir, scapegoat and black hole. Yet the Internet is poorly researched, massively complex in use and content, still in global terms often inaccessible and too expensive. Like the rest of the media it is over-hyped in relation to any genuinely known effects and offers huge potential to those who oppose terror: perhaps more than it does to those who may wish to commit terror.

What modern terrorism actually does do effectively online is to exploit the very nature of cyberspace in support of conventional activities rather than as a source or site of new ones such as cyber-terror (Yar 2006). The anonymity of the Internet is ideal for hiding extremist ideologies which would be negatively perceived in the real world. Its global character allows terrorists to discuss views and beliefs without having to be in the country. This international element exacerbates difficulties for crime control because the technology provides an arena where terrorists can operate without regulation, censorship, or government control (Rosenblatt 2006). Cyberspace therefore hinders crime control by providing terrorists a network to operate within which is outside the physical domain of conventional investigative techniques.

One of the main benefits the Internet offers terrorists is for information gathering. It can, for example, be used as a tool to gather data and study vulnerabilities such as weaknesses in bridges, dams and buildings (Verton 2003: 86). Although data mining is available by traditional means, online searching capabilities add a new dimension in regards to quantity, ease of access and anonymity. Secondly, terrorists can use the Internet for publicity, propaganda and psychological warfare. Internet technology allows terrorists to reach an audience in a direct, interactive and uncensored way, which was previously unavailable in the mass media (Pries-Shimshi 2005). On websites terrorists can publicise their campaigns in any manner they wish, through mission statements, broadcasts and by posting videos of attacks on the enemy. Every martyr prays for immortality and for the first time the Internet has created a medium where this can be achieved (Custer 2007, cited in Fager 2007). Shutting down a site in one location will simply lead to the material reappearing elsewhere, allowing testimonies and information to be accessed infinitely. Third, Internet technologies are used to great effect to target and recruit individuals. Such recruitment tends to be a self-selecting, bottom up, process and terrorists use the Internet to appeal to people looking to join in secrecy (Sageman 2004: 122). Fourth, the Internet provides a new training medium. Crime control is particularly hindered here because new recruits are able to train anywhere, making surveillance difficult and more expensive to track. Regular issues of online training manuals like al-Qaeda's *Al Battar* provide detailed instructions of terrorism skills. Another instrumental use is for planning and networking (Weimann 2006: 126). The fast flows of information and encryption technologies help to conceal such communications, making it impossible for law enforcement agencies to obtain information (Denning and Baugh 2000). For example, Hamas reportedly use encrypted Internet communication to transmit maps and other information pertaining to terrorist attacks (Denning 2000). Other uses of the Internet include fund-raising and attacking other terrorists (Weimann 2006). There is competition in cyberspace for hearts, minds and funds.

Much of this evidence of terrorist Net use in relation to terrestrial operations, however, is gathered from American and Israeli authorities, which raises questions anyway about what to believe about the extent terrorists are using the Internet. Cere (2007) argues that, while terrorism has a presence in cyberspace in regards to everyday activities, the use of instruction manuals and encrypting files is clearly not widespread because of the technical difficulty. There are possibly around 5,000 websites dedicated to terrorism hidden amongst billions of web pages (Pelley 2007) but no indication of joined-up ideologies or interchanges. If anything, searches suggest there are isolated cyber-cells and educational and publicity clusters from more established groups but certainly no sense of cohesion or strategy. In fact, there are many conflicting messages and examples of downright incoherence. In any case, size and scope of the technology arguably doesn't matter when it took 19 suicide bombers with penknives to attack the United States in 2001, killing thousands and causing billions of dollars of damage (*Guardian*, 15 September 2001).

Perhaps of more significant a concern for criminologists and lawyers is that, despite the advantages it offers terrorists, Internet technology has also proved highly beneficial for counterterrorism efforts. Internet users leave an electronic trail for investigators to track movements such as web pages visited, credit card transactions or emails sent. Internet technologies such as the FBI's DCS1000, formally 'Carnivore', are able to track trigger words when filtering through vast quantities of information including email, chat rooms and websites. Such a tool is only effective in cyberspace because it is impossible to filter suspect activity in the real world so accurately. Surveillance of terrorist activity online contributed to the evidence which led to the detection and conviction of the 'fertiliser bombers' in April 2007 (Gardener 2007). The Internet also facilitates other unconventional methods of crime control. MI5 has launched anti-terrorism campaigns on its website, providing risk assessments, practical advice on how to protect oneself and a tool whereby people can anonymously report suspect activity (Weimann 2006: 240). It also plans to send out email terror alerts, in an effort to use the Internet to warn of heightened risk to the public (Ward 2007). The effectiveness of both of these procedures is questionable, but highlights an attempt to counterclaim the flow of anti-Western rhetoric online, as well as utilising interactive facilities.

Also, although not widespread, Internet technology is facilitating indirect crime control from vigilante groups responding to the changed meanings and hyped threat. From his home in Illinois, US computer programmer Aaron Weisburd identifies terrorist sites then informs ISPs to remove them, as well as occasionally defacing them. In some instances such activity is more structured, such as the SITE Institute which is a private firm hired by businesses and the US government to obtain information online crucial in the fight against terror. In addition there are also hackers, such as Israeli hackers 'm0sad', who infiltrate terrorist sites and deface them (Weimann 2006). In this sense, then, crime control has been broadened since the advent of the Internet (see Chapter 27).

Vigilantism is just one aspect of the threat of Net-related terror activity that has had a direct impact on civil liberties. The UK Terrorism Act 2000[3] encompasses a wide definition for terror activities, and allows for surveillance and detention laws outside any boundary seen in UK law before. Similarly, the USA PATRIOT Act significantly increased the surveillance and investigative powers of law enforcement agencies including the ability to track terror suspects online (Verton 2003). Western authorities are arguably justifiably monitoring terrorist behaviour online (Klang 2005) but allowing authorities the ability to spy on all our activity online in order to identify terror potential would threaten privacy rights.

In reality, little is known about the use of the Internet to promote terrestrial terror but it seems unlikely to be generating any more actual attack than we witnessed in the days of the IRA, Red Brigade and Baader Meinhof. Indeed we arguably live in a less terrorised real world post-Internet. However, discourses about that potential are not limited to terrestrial threat but to the insidious, invisible, invasive area of 'cyber-terror', attacks by invisible ghosts on the Internet and its component interconnected electronic technologies.

The 'ghost in the machine'

Modern terrorists must be well aware of the importance of the Internet but, significantly, continue to focus on conventional tactics to physically bring infrastructures down as opposed to electronically disrupting them (Leppard 2007). At present, cyber-terrorism remains 'a ghost in the machine rather than a serious threat' (Klang 2005: 136). The column inches are related to distorted media sensationalism rather than a considered account of the actual threat. The closest thing to a cyber-terrorism attack so far was the email bombing by the Internet Black Tigers in Sri Lanka in 1998. However, this flood of emails directed at authorities must be considered no more than a nuisance compared to the deaths of 240 people from the physical bombings of US embassies in Africa that same year (Taylor 2001: 70).

State systems are well protected; indeed the Internet was only released to the public at the end of the 1980s once the US had established MILNET to support its defence systems. Military and intelligence computer systems are 'air gapped', meaning they are on separate networks so the threat is indeed one to investigate but the apocalyptic nightmares are simply unfounded at present. The UK government reacted to the fears by including actions which 'interfere with or seriously disrupt an electronic system' as a terrorist offence under section 2(e) of the Terrorism Act 2000. Such a wide definition includes denial-of-service hackers and is too far removed from traditional perceptions of terrorism to justify that label. Cyber-terrorism which could cause injury, loss of life or damage to property is clearly covered within s.2 (a–d), and rightly so. However, the inclusion of s.2(e) is unjustifiable, and wrongly warrants a broad range of surveillance techniques for crime controllers to use in order to regulate Internet activity more widely.

Alternatively, authorities and companies alike who use electronic systems should encrypt systems and remove information which could be used to plan such an attack. Such a requirement would not hinder individual privacy rights but would of course cost money and impact on profit margins and not be politically popular with business. Rather the government promotes anxiety and seeks state powers to address the purported threat of cyber-terror: 'It is easy to appreciate the devastation of a physical attack and what it can bring but we must not underestimate the potentially devastating consequences of an electronic attack' (BBC 2007), so justifying instead invasive policy and practice.

Certainly, the Internet is playing an increasingly central role in the economic life of Western nations, and a serious attack on these critical infrastructures could have a debilitating impact on the economy (Yar 2006). Theoretically, there is potential for terrorists to hack, from anywhere in the world, into the ever-integrated networks of defence, power, or water systems, causing large-scale devastation. Cyber-terrorism has been defined as attacks and threats of attack against computers, networks and the information stored therein that are carried out to intimidate citizens and governments in furtherance of political or social objectives (Denning 2000) but it has far-reaching boundaries. Airlines use online wireless technology for self check-in, but often these systems lack encryption protection. Investigations have shown the ease with which core operational systems can be hacked in order to access flight operations, bag matching, and passenger reservations (Verton 2003). Similarly, train signalling is often controlled by remote communication technology which could be interfered with to cause derailment or collision. Without deploying proper security protections, companies are putting themselves and the public at risk of terrorist activity (Verton 2003: 70).

Another problem in anticipating potential cyber-terrorism is that in many states the majority of the nation's critical networks are now in the hands of private companies; 85 per cent in the case of the USA (Verton 2003). Protection systems are outside public control and have proved weak due to a perceived low return on investment, again indicating a preference for profit over protection of the public. All that said, very little cyber-terror has yet happened. Instead we have witnessed 'cyber-error', causing all manner of problems for public institutions such as the National Health Service for example in the UK (*Guardian*, 1 October 2006), as well as causing nuisance, loss and delay for ordinary netizens.

Concluding comments

Anxiety over terrorists utilising the Internet will always support someone's agenda. The government have used such fears to widen the scope of terror activity to include hackers and denial-of-service attacks, and to legitimate detection and control cybercrime on a wider basis. Online surveillance technologies are now available to significantly improve crime control but of course this comes at the expense of civil rights and privacy. It is postulated that authorities use the law, and especially s.2 (e), to warrant increased surveillance online. However, this can lead to vigilantism, which purports to aid control and disrupt terrorist electronic systems, but can actually fall within the ambit of terrorist activity itself. If we continue to support vigilantism we risk becoming terrorist states ourselves (Ganor 2002). Clearly such a scenario would be unacceptable but there is no call to stop it even though at present the very virtuality of the Internet makes it an unsuitable target to generate the desired effect of terror (Yar 2006). Of course, it is inevitable that terrorists will continue to utilise Internet technologies to hinder surveillance and promote their activities. However, Internet technologies are successfully being used by authorities and vigilantes alike to foil attacks, gather intelligence, and control terrorism. Moreover, other mediations, electronic and terrestrial, continue to promulgate the threat of cyber-terror alongside that of real terror, conflating the two and yet doubling the discursive effect and potential for damage.

The Internet is, in many ways, key to all sensibilities in this process and is the latest incantation of the media as 'dangerous'. It is the space where, purportedly, cyber-paeds prey in chat rooms; al-Qaeda encrypt missions, recruit martyrs and hide funds; drugs are traded and funds for terror are raised: youth is corrupted and the country's moral backbone eroded while the very basis of national security is under threat 24/7. Much millennial crime news has made connections between the differing foci of discourses of fear and insecurity, with even an attempt to link terror, race, Internet and paedophilia, as in the case of: 'The man shot during an anti-terrorism raid by police in east London in June was arrested yesterday on suspicion of possessing and making images of child sexual abuse' (*Guardian*, 4 August 2006; see also Greer and Jewkes 2005). Yet:

> The Crown Prosecution Service announced last night that it had advised the Metropolitan Police not to charge the 23-year-old supermarket employee. After the development, he has no blemish on his character and the two brothers are expected to file compensation claims totalling more than £1m against the Metropolitan Police. (*Independent*, 20 October 2006)

Does such journalism matter? To return to the problem posited at the outset of this chapter: when, rarely, the public is asked about their perceptions and insecurities these are often very different from those that dominate mediated and political discourses. Simply, a local government survey of perceptions of crime found concerns not about terror but about: 'Young people causing a nuisance. Having your car broken into or vandalised. Vandalism or damage to property. Abandoned vehicles' (Wealden District Council 2004). This was confirmed by work by the Department of Transport on issues of concern: 'Graffiti and vandalism strongly affect people's perceptions of crime and personal security. They give the impression that the area is unmanaged and out of control' (Dept of Transport n.d.). Both these offer some confirmation of Marie Gillespie's findings that when people are actually asked about terror:

Interviewees showed high levels of political cynicism; they believe that government and media create a climate of multiple uncertainties and insecurities; chief among these insecurities is terrorism, as interviewees believe the government exploits public insecurity to deliver security solutions and hold on to their power base; perceived threats to personal and local security – jobs, health, schools, money and crime – are much more important to interviewees than the threat of terrorism. (Gillespie *et al.* 16 June 2006)

So those crime and fear discourses that dominate mass-mediated accounts do not necessarily or even normally address the actual perceptions of crime, let alone the realities of crime, threat and risk for citizens as individuals, either by accurately portraying terror and cyber issues or by addressing the real experiences of the public. Yet they do inform significant changes in policy, law and the empowerment of control agencies. All this shows that what they do address is the fear not of the public but of the nation state, the government and all those with allied vested interests.

Obfuscations and diversions continue as the Internet is increasingly portrayed as responsible for crime and fear because it is so secret, so fast, so vast and so invasive. It is supposedly the site of identity theft; fraud; terrorism; hate crime; stalking; hackers; child pornography; paedophile activity and piracy. Actually, as David Wall argued in 1999, these are not new crimes but 'old crime, no bottles'. In effect there is little known about levels or types of cybercrime or even if they count as offences in cyber-contexts; it is unclear who is harmed, whose laws/morals apply and how they might be applied if so desired. Similarly no one knows much about cyber-terror (or arguably much about real terrorists) but many inferences have filled that space of not knowing; inferences that have changed meanings about our world and on the basis of those, also changed practices and policies.

Furedi (in Hale *et al.* 2005) identified a shift from political terrorism by identifiable groups against identifiable states to a much looser ideological terrorism, bound together by the Internet but largely anonymous and characterised by a moral or religious agenda. The difficulty in labelling or explaining these twenty-first-century terrorists is exacerbated by their lack of coherent identity or nation state goals. This has led to the use of terms like 'evil', 'extremist', 'zealot' in the media, placing terror in the realms of psychosis.

Alternatively, terror has been simply criminalised and associated with old stereotypes of criminality. By identifying terror firmly with Islam it has been easy to ally it to both race and religion, offering explanations that foster racism and fear of the other and shore up nation state sovereignties united by western Judaeo-Christianity. Further, 'the elevation of terrorism to the status of a national security threat ... has deflected careful scrutiny of the government's domestic and foreign policies' (Said 1986/2006); again acting ideologically to secure state power by diversion. Finally, the furore over the alliance of the Internet with terror has justified the increasing use of overt legislation like RIPA 2000, way beyond the remit of the War on Terror: 'Some local authorities have used the Regulation of Investigatory Powers Act (RIPA) more than 100 times in the last 12 months to conduct surveillance' (BBC, 27 April 2008); in some cases to catch benefit frauds and in others 'to spy on a family for three weeks to find out if they were really living in a school catchment area' (*ibid.*). Meanwhile, levels of covert practices like electronic surveillance, data-exchange and entrapment are impossible to estimate.

In practice, massive resources have been diverted to monitoring the Internet, and using new technologies to monitor 'crime' on the basis of a threat achieved by conjoining cyber, terror and race, with race being used as an aide-memoire for the public that the 'other' is a threat. Yet there is little evidence that crime or deviance of any kind can be recognised, tracked, prosecuted or prevented with any degree of efficiency in cyberspace. Nonetheless, RIPA 2000, the Regulation of Investigatory Powers Act geared towards monitoring communications, is now being deployed in ways that raise serious concerns about civil rights, surveillance, data-protection, freedom of expression and privacy; implications that are perhaps now so real they are beyond exorcising. Moreover RIPA is increasingly interacted with terrorism. The Terrorism Act (2006) refers not just to an act but the perceived 'threat' of action and acknowledges the use of RIPA. It is:

> an Act to make provision for and about offences relating to conduct carried out, or capable of being carried out, for purposes connected with terrorism; to amend enactments relating to terrorism; to amend the Intelligence Services Act 1994 and the Regulation of Investigatory Powers Act 2000; and for connected purposes. (Terrorism Act 2006)

It appears that terrorism has not broadened too significantly from its use by the French State as an instrument to exert control. Nowadays, the threat of terror, aligned to old racial stereotypes and new cyber-secrecies, is being used by governments as justification to control the public's civil rights, movements and communications freedoms; maybe not so different from the guillotine after all.

Notes

1 News values have been thoroughly rehearsed, researched and written about for four decades (Galtung and Ruge 1965; Chibnall 1977; Fowler 1991; Wykes 2001; Jewkes 2004) but remain vital to any proper investigation of the mass mediation of ideas or theorising of the role of the media. Briefly:

> The gathering of news immediately excludes all but a very few events that can be considered newsworthy. News is a selection of history made by journalists. The selection of stories is not arbitrary but highly systemised and conventionalised by conditions external to the story, as well as integral. External controls may include time, cost, access, expertise, publication space and news agenda. Potential news events have to be, practically, reportable but they also have to have particular internal features. Galtung and Ruge (1965) offered a model of news attributes and pointed out that these are mainly cultural not natural (Wykes 2001: 22–3).

2 Wykes 2003 offers a full account of the UK press coverage of 9/11 from which this
   section is abridged.
3 Terrorism Act 2000 is worryingly broad, especially (1)(c):
   1. (1) In this Act 'terrorism' means the use or threat of action where –

       (a) the action falls within subsection (2),
       (b) the use or threat is designed to influence the government or to
            intimidate the public or a section of the public, and
       (c) the use or threat is made for the purpose of advancing a political,
            religious or ideological cause.

       (2) Action falls within this subsection if it –

       (a) involves serious violence against a person,
       (b) involves serious damage to property,
       (c) endangers a person's life, other than that of the person committing
            the action,
       (d) creates a serious risk to the health or safety of the public or a section
            of the public, or
       (e) is designed seriously to interfere with or seriously to disrupt an
            electronic system.

       (3) The use or threat of action falling within subsection (2) which involves
            the use of firearms or explosives is terrorism whether or not subsection
            (1)(b) is satisfied.

       http: //www.opsi.gov.uk/ACTS/acts2000/20000011.htm

Further reading

The References contain many readings that an interested reader might delve into.
In particular, to better understand the way in which the mainstream media report
terrorism, try Chermak, S., Bailey, F. and Brown, M. (eds) (2003) *Media Representations
of September 11* (Westport: Praeger). It is very diffuclt to find objective accounts of
the relationship between terrorism and the Internet so further reading in this area
needs to be done critically. Try Weimann, G. (2006) *Terror on the Internet: The new
arena, the new challenges* (United States Institute of Peace); Shavit, S. (2004) 'Contending
with International Terrorism', in *The Journal of International Security Affairs*, 6 (Winter)
www.securityaffairs.org/issues/2004/06No_6_Winter_2004_Full_Issue.pdf; or Verton,
D. (2003) *Black Ice: The Invisible Threat of Cyber-Terrorism* (New York: McGraw-Hill/
Osborne). For broader discussions of terrorism, Said, E. (1986) 'The Essential Terrorist',
available at *The Nation* 14 July 2006, http://www.thenation.com/doc/19860614/said,
is a stimulating account. Hall, S., Critcher, C., Jefferson, T. and Clarke, J. (eds) (1978)
Policing the Crisis: Mugging, the State, Law and Order (London: Macmillan) is a seminal
account of the way in which power uses crime/threat to legitimate increased legislation
and control.

References

BBC (2007) 'No guarantee in terrorism fight', 25 April. http://news.bbc.co.uk/1/hi/
   uk_politics/6590111.stm

Bromley, M. and Cushion, S. (2002) 'Media Fundamentalism: the immediate response of the UK national press to September 11', in B. Zelizer and S. Allan, *Journalism after September 11*. London: Routledge.

Cere, R. (2007) 'Digital Undergrounds: alternative politics and civil society', in Y. Jewkes (ed.), *Crime Online*. Cullompton: Willan Publishing.

Chermak, S., Bailey, F. and Brown, M. (eds) (2003) *Media Representations of September 11*. Westport: Praeger.

Chibnall, S. (1977) *Law and Order News*. London: Tavistock.

Crozier B. (1974) *A Theory of Conflict*. London: Macmillan.

Denning, D. (2000) 'Cyberterrorism: The Logic Bomb Versus the Truck Bomb', *Global Dialogue*, Autumn.

Denning, D. and Baugh, W. (2000) 'Hiding Crimes in Cyberspace', in D. Thomas and B.D. Loader, *Cybercrime*. London: Routledge.

Dept of Transport (n.d.) (http://www.dft.gov.uk/pgr/crime/reducinggraffiti/graffitiva ndalismbriefpaper?page=1#a1000).

Ericson, R., Baranek, P. and Chan, J. (1991) *Representing Order*. Milton Keynes: Open University Press.

Fager, J. (2007) *60 Minutes* [video], March 05. NY: CBS.

Finch E. (2007) 'The Problem of stolen identity and the Internet', in Y. Jewkes (ed.), *Crime on-line*. Cullompton: Willan Publishing.

Fowler, R. (1991) *Language in the News: Discourse and Ideology in the Press*. London/ New York: Routledge.

Franklin, B. (1997) *Newzak and Newspapers*. London: Routledge.

Galtung, J. and Ruge, M. (1965) 'Structuring and selecting news', in S. Cohen and J. Young (1982 edn) *The Manufacture of News: Deviance, Social Problems and the Mass Media*. London: Constable.

Ganor, B. (2002) *Defining Terrorism: Is One Man's Terrorist Another Man's Freedom Fighter?* http://www.ict.org.il/index.php?sid=119&lang=en&act=page&id=5547&str=definiti on%20of%20terrorism (accessed on 10 May 2007).

Gardener, F. (2007) 'MI5 watch 2,000 terror suspects'. *BBC News* http://news.bbc. co.uk/1/hi/uk/6613963.stm (accessed 2 May 2007).

Gillespie, M. *et al.* (2006) 'Beyond the Iraq War 2003: the gap between security policy-makers' perceptions and those of the public', 16 June 2006, at http://www3.open. ac.uk/media/fullstory.aspx?id=9114

Greer, C. and Jewkes, Y. (2005) 'Images and processes of social exclusion', *Social Justice*, 32(1): 20–31.

Gunter, B., Harrison J. and Wykes M. (2003) *Violence on Television: Distribution, Form, Context and Themes*. USA: Lawrence Erlbaum.

Hale, C., Hayward, K., Wahidin, A. and Wincup, E. (2005) *Criminology*. Oxford: Oxford University Press.

Hall, S., Critcher, C., Jefferson, T. and Clarke, J. (eds) (1978) *Policing the Crisis: Mugging, the State, Law and Order*. London: Macmillan.

Herren, E. (n.d.) *Tools for Countering Future Terrorism* www.ict.org.il/index.php?sid=119 &lang=en&act=page&id=5521&str=Internet (accessed 1 May 2007).

Home Office Research Development and Statistical Directorate (1999) *Information on the Criminal Justice System in England and Wales: Digest 4*.

Jewkes, Y. (2004) *Media and Crime*. London: Sage.

Klang, M. (2005) 'Virtual Sit-Ins, civil disobedience and cyberterrorism', in M. Klang and A. Murray, *Human Rights in the Digital Age*. London: Glasshouse Press.

Laquer, W. (1999) *Postmodern Terrorism*. NY: OUP.

Leppard, D. (2007) 'Al-Qa'ida plot to bring down UK Internet', *The Sunday Times*, www.timesonline.co.uk/tol/news/uk/crime/article1496831.ece

Livergood, N.D. (2007) *The New U.S.-British Oil Imperialism*, www.hermes-press.com/impintro1.htm

Lowe, F. (2007) the *The Daily Telegraph*, 27 June, http://www.telegraph.co.uk/news/uknews/1555670/'Honour'-killings-linked-to-terror-groups.html

Oliverio, A. (1998) *The State of Terror*. Albany, New York: SUNY Press.

Pelley, S. (2007) 'Terrorists Take Recruitment Efforts Online', www.cbsnews.com/stories/2007/03/02/60minutes/main2531546_page3.shtml

Pries-Shimshi, Y. (2005) *Creating a Citizenry Prepared for Terrorism: Education, Media, and Public* (http://www.ict.org.il/Articles/tabid/66/Artic/sid/184/currentpage/13/Default.aspx

Rosenblatt, D. (2006) 'Cyber-spies tracking terror on Web', CNN, http://ucg.net/2006/WORLD/europe/09/28/Internet.spying/index.html

Sageman, M. (2004) *Understanding Terror Networks*. Pennsylvania: University of Pennsylvania Press.

Said, E. (1986/2006) 'The Essential Terrorist', available online at *The Nation*, 14 August 2006, http://www.thenation.com/doc/19860614/said

Schmidt, A. and Jongman, A. (1998) *Political Terrorism*. Amsterdam: North Holland Publishing.

Scraton, P. (2002a) 'In the name of a just war', in P. Scraton (ed.), *Beyond September 11: An anthology of dissent*. London: Pluto Press, 216–33.

Scraton, P. (2002b) 'Introduction: Witnessing "terror", anticipating war', in P. Scraton (ed.), *Beyond September 11: An anthology of dissent*. London: Pluto Press, 1–10.

Shavit, S. (2004) 'Contending with International Terrorism', in *The Journal of International Security Affairs*, 6: Winter, www.securityaffairs.org/issues/2004/06/No_6_Winter_2004_Full_Issue.pdf

Taylor, P. (2001) 'Hacktivism: In search of lost ethics?', in D. Wall, *Crime and the Internet*. London: Routledge.

Terrorism Act 2006 http://www.opsi.gov.uk/acts/acts2006/ukpga_20060011_en_5#pt2-pb5-l1g34

Tunstall, J. (1996) *Newspaper Power*. Oxford: Clarendon Press.

Van Dijk, T. (1991) *Racism and the Press*. London: Routledge.

Verton, D. (2003) *Black Ice: The Invisible Threat of Cyber-Terrorism*. New York: McGraw-Hill/Osborne.

Wall, D.S. (1999) 'Cybercrimes: New wine, no bottles?', in P. Davies, P. Francis and V. Jupp (eds), *Invisible Crimes: Their Victims and their Regulation*. London: Macmillan, 105–39.

Ward, M. (2007) 'Alert system dubbed a "shambles"', BBC, http://news.bbc.co.uk/1/hi/technology/6262719.stm

Wealden District Council (2004) http://www.wealden.gov.uk/Health_and_Public_Safety/Crime_and_Disorder/PublicPerceptionsurveyresults.aspx

Weimann, G. (2006) *Terror on the Internet: The new arena, the new challenges*. United States Institute of Peace.

Wykes, M. (1998) 'A family affair: sex, the press and the Wests', in C. Carter *et al.* (eds), *News, Gender and Power*. London: Routledge, 233–47.

Wykes, M. (2001) *News, Crime and Culture*. London: Pluto Press.

Wykes, M. (2003) 'September 11th 2002: Reporting, Remembering, Reconstructing 9/11/2001', in S. Chermak, F. Bailey and M. Brown, *Media Representations of 9/11*. USA: Praeger Publishing, 117–34.

Wykes, M. (2007) 'Constructing crime: culture, stalking, celebrity and cyber', *Journal of Crime, Media, Culture*, 3(2): 158–74.

Wykes, M. and Welsh, K. (2009) *Violence, Gender and Justice*. London: Sage.

Yar, M. (2006) *Cybercrime and Society*. London: Sage.

Chapter 12

Cyber-protest and civil society: the Internet and action repertoires in social movements

Jeroen Van Laer and Peter Van Aelst

Introduction

A notable feature of recent public engagement with the Internet is its use by a wide range of activists and groups in social and political protest. The Internet is not only said to greatly facilitate mobilisation and participation in traditional forms of protest, such as national street demonstrations, but also to give these protests a more transnational character by effectively and rapidly diffusing communication and mobilisation efforts. The uprising of the Zapatista movement in 1994 is a case in point (see among many others: Cleaver 1998; Schulz 1998; Ronfeldt and Arquilla 1998; Martinez-Torres 2001; Cere 2003; Olesen 2004). Started as a local rebellion – a struggle for more rights and greater autonomy for the indigenous people of Chiapas in the rainforest of southern Mexico – their cause rapidly gained momentum thanks to a vast growing, global network of support that successfully linked the Zapatista rebellion with many other local and international struggles against neoliberal globalisation. The Internet was decisive to the global diffusion of protest and solidarity.

Another frequently used example of how the Internet shapes social movement tactics and actions is the anti-WTO (World Trade Organisation) mobilisations in Seattle in late 1999 (e.g. Eagleton-Pierce 2001; Smith 2001; Van Aelst and Walgrave 2004; Juris 2005). By means of the open network of the Internet, a diverse range of activists, groups and social movement organisations could loosely knit together and coalesce in coordinated actions against the WTO summit both offline, in the streets, as well as online, in cyberspace. The Internet contributed to the organisation of activists' street blockades, disturbing the normal WTO summit, and attracting the attention of news media around the world. During the blockades, activists with portable computers connected to the Internet were constantly updated with reports from the streets and details of changing police tactics (de Armond 2001). At the same time the Internet was the site of anti-WTO action itself, with groups like ®™ark (Artmark) creating a sophisticated parody, a 'spoof site', of the

WTO's homepage (Meikle 2002). Also, in the advent of the Seattle protests, the first independent online media centre, Indymedia, was set up, allowing for real-time distribution of video, audio, text and photos, enabling activists to provide coverage, and especially the necessary analyses and context to counterbalance the poor US corporate media coverage of the WTO meetings and the claims of the Global Justice Movement (Smith 2001; Kidd 2003).

Although the precise contribution of the Internet is hard to establish, these examples show that the Internet has given civil society new tools to support their claims. In this chapter we will document how the Internet has shaped and is shaping the collective action repertoire of social movements pursuing social and political change. Two main suggestions can be identified in the literature. On the one hand, the Internet facilitates and supports (traditional) offline collective action in terms of organisation, mobilisation and transnationalisation and, on the other hand, it creates new modes of collective action. The Internet has indeed not only supported traditional offline social movement actions such as the classical street demonstrations and made them more transnational, but is also used to set up new forms of online protest activities and to create online modes of existing offline protest actions. By doing so the Internet has expanded and complemented today's social movement 'repertoire of collective action' (Tilly 1984; McAdam *et al.* 2001). Virtual activities may range from online petitions, email bombings and virtual sit-ins to hacking the websites of large companies and governments.

Before we elaborate on the role of the Internet we will define what we mean by social movements and their action repertoire. Social movements, following Diani (1992), can be defined as 'networks of informal interaction between a plurality of individuals, groups and/or organisations, engaged in a political or cultural conflict on the basis of a shared collective identity' (Diani 1992: 13). Their 'repertoire of collective action' is, as Charles Tilly originally pointed out, the 'distinctive constellations of tactics and strategies developed over time and used by protest groups to act collectively in order to make claims on individuals and groups' (Tilly 1984; Taylor and Van Dyke 2004: 265). The repertoire of actions supported and/or created online that we scrutinise in this chapter thus are *collective* undertakings, either in terms of participants or in terms of outcome. The action repertoire of social movements is as broad as there are social movements and activists, goals and causes, claims and grievances. Here we explicitly focus on what has been termed 'unorthodox' or 'unconventional' political behaviour (Marsh 1977; Barnes and Kaase 1979): those actions and tactics that, on the one hand, are 'performed' on the non-institutional side of politics, outside the realm of conventional or orthodox political participation (i.e. voting, being a member of a political party, lobbying), and on the other hand, do not equal severe political crime: hijacking, terrorism, guerrilla warfare etc. (Marsh 1977: 42).

However, the boundaries between unconventional tactics and crime or illegal action remain diffuse and are often the object of discussion both between activists and official institutions as well as among scholars investigating them. Whether a particular tactic is defined as a legal or illegal action heavily depends on time and place. Organising a protest demonstration used to be an illegal practice in many Western countries and still is in many non-democratic countries today. Since the 1960s mass street demonstrations have, at least in Western democracies, undergone a 'normalisation' (Van Aelst and Walgrave 2001) leading to what Meyer and Tarrow (1998) call 'the social movement society'. Also, the use of a particular tactic is often subject to a struggle of 'meaning' between activists, media and authorities. Take, for instance, the example of the notion 'hacktivism': some activist groups like the Critical Art Ensemble (CAE) tried to introduce the less pejorative term of 'electronic civil disobedience' to describe the protest actions they perform on the Internet (Meikle 2002). Finally, also *within* social movements disagreement about the use of 'legal' or 'illegal' tactics can result in major disputes. In the early 1980s some peace groups in Western Europe rejected the use of 'illegal' actions such as train rail blockades ('trainstoppings') because they would likely marginalise the general peace movement's objectives (Van Laer 2009). At present these techniques are much more accepted, also by 'established' peace movements, which became clear during the mobilisations against (the build-up of) the military interventions in Afghanistan and Iraq in 2002 and 2003.

In this chapter we include forms of direct action and civil disobedience that cross the legal boundaries of society, because they are and always have been an inherent part of the social movement action repertoire. The constant innovation of action repertoires, touching the edge of legality, is an important aspect of mobilising a social movement's constituency and forcing its causes onto the mainstream media agenda (Klandermans 1997; Tarrow 1998). 'If there is one thing that distinguishes social movements from other political actors, then it is their strategic use of novel, dramatic, unorthodox, and non-institutionalised forms of political expression to try to shape public opinion and put pressure on those in positions of authority' (Taylor and Van Dyke 2004: 263).

The remainder of this chapter is structured as follows: in the next section we will elaborate on a typology of the 'new' repertoire of collective action. This section is the largest part of this chapter, since we will extensively illustrate our typology with a near endless list of examples that can be found in the literature. This section thus provides evidence of all the (new) *possibilities* thanks to the Internet. In a subsequent section we will then present important *limitations* about the use of the Internet and the impact of this new medium on social movement's action repertoire as well as on its democratising potential at large. We wrap up with a discussion and conclusion section.

1. A typology of a new digitalised action repertoire

The typology we present in this chapter is pretty straightforward and centres around two related dimensions: first of all, there is the distinction between 'real' actions that are supported and facilitated by the Internet, and 'virtual' actions that are Internet-based (Gurak and Logie 2003; Vegh 2003). Both the 'old' repertoire, supported by the Internet, and the 'new' or modified online tactics concatenate in a new 'digitalised' social movement repertoire of collective action. Secondly, we introduce a classic dimension that makes a distinction between tactics with low and high thresholds and show how the Internet may have lowered action-related barriers. Figure 12.1 presents a broad overview of both dimensions and a selection of different types of action used or supported by social movements. Before supporting this typology with examples, both dimensions will be discussed within the broader social movement literature.

1.1. Dimension 1: Internet-supported versus Internet-based

Our first dimension distinguishes between 'old' and 'new' forms of collective action. We call these new forms 'Internet-based' because they exist only because of the Internet. Internet-supported actions refer to the traditional tools of social movement that have become easier to organise and coordinate thanks to the Internet. This *facilitating function,* lowering tactic-related thresholds and making traditional protest action more transnational, will be further discussed as part of the second dimension. This first dimension highlights more the Internet's *creating function* of new and modified tactics expanding the action toolkit of social movements. This increase of available tactics online has opted some scholars to speak of an additional 'repertoire of electronic contention' (Constanza-Chock 2003; Rolfe 2005). These can be tactics, for instance, directed towards the online presence or activities of particular groups, governments or companies, pinning down their servers. Some of these tools such as the email petition can be seen as an extension of an existing protest technique, and

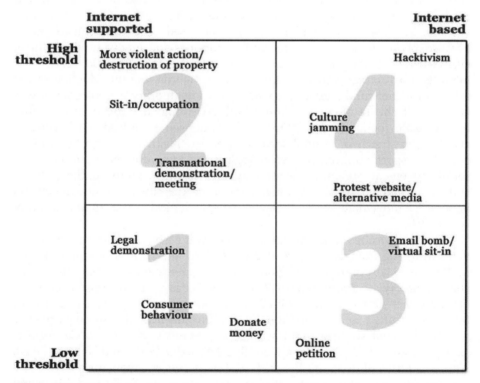

Figure 12.1 Overview of both Internet-supported and Internet-based types of action used by social movements

are therefore placed closer to the 'Internet-supported' side of the continuum. The same holds true for other action forms such as culture jamming, which illustrates that the distinction between Internet-based and Internet-supported actions is subtle and permeable. Moreover, the distinction is further blurred since action groups almost never use just one single tactic, but instead draw on a myriad of tactics both offline and online. 'Net activism has never been *exclusively* Net-centered,' Meikle (2002: 41) notes. And likewise offline actions today are almost always accompanied with tactics online. Some scholars even make a strong case to completely abandon the sharp distinction between the on- and offline worlds, since both spheres are heavily interdependent (Bimber 2000).

The development and expansion of the action repertoire can be seen as a mere result of the technological evolution that has given the civil society more sophisticated opportunities for their actions. As the history of social movements shows, the action repertoire only changes slowly (Tilly 1977, 1984). If the prevailing repertoire changes significantly at some point, the change is prima facie evidence of a substantial alteration in the structure of power, due to social, economic or political transformations. In the eighteenth century people targeted the power holders in their community with local rebellions likely claiming food and other stock supplies (Tilly 1984). In the nineteenth century this kind of 'mutiny' almost completely disappeared and the action repertoire changed to mass strikes and demonstrations, which was, according to Tilly, the immediate result of the rise of capitalism and the nation state. But since then, most of the tactics that were used 100 years ago are, at present, still widely known and used. The reason therefore is because 'people generally turn to familiar routines and innovate within them, even when in principle some unfamiliar form of action would serve their interests much better' (Tilly 1984: 4). In other words, the introduction of the Internet did not fundamentally change the contemporary action repertoire at large, yet it chiefly offers new opportunities to innovate and expand within the available toolkit of action forms. Tilly himself is indeed very sceptical about a far-stretched technological emphasis: 'Neither in communications nor in transportation, did the technological timetable dominate alterations in social movement organisation, strategy, and practice. Shifts in the political and organisational context impinged far more directly and immediately on how social movement worked than did technological transformations' (Tilly 2004a: 104).

The last decades and important 'repertoire shift' occurred from the national to the transnational level provoked by the increased influence that multinational corporations and global trade regimes have over national policy and regulatory decisions (Ayres 2005; Tilly 2004a). An impressive body of literature has started to deal with how the locus of (economic and political) power has shifted to a transnational and even global level, and consequently social movement strategies and actions (e.g. Smith *et al.* 1997; della Porta *et al.* 1999; Clark 2003; Bandy and Smith 2005; della Porta and Tarrow 2005). And a prominent tool in this tactical but necessary reorganisation is the Internet (Bennett 2003; Ayres 2005). Carty (2002) and Stolle and Micheletti (2005) made a similar point when investigating culture jamming as a new kind of protest tactic addressing corporate multinationals like Nike. However, the shift towards new Internet-based actions and tactics heavily related to the Internet has not resulted in the replacement of the old action forms, but rather complemented them. The existing tools are still used, and probably more than ever, as the Internet contributes to lowering participation thresholds. This will be explained in our second dimension.

1.2. Dimension 2: low versus high thresholds

Since scholars have started to investigate different forms of actions they have noticed a 'hierarchy of political participation' (Marsh 1977; Barnes and Kaase 1979; Dalton 1996). Some action forms entail more risk and higher commitment than other tactics, thus providing lower and higher thresholds for people to (consider to) participate (McAdam 1986; Tarrow 1998). Tarrow (1998), for instance, makes a distinction between conventional protest tactics, disruptive tactics and violent tactics. Earlier, Barnes and Kaase (1979) have ranked political actions according to their 'intensity' (moderate versus militant), while Klandermans (1997) made a typology based on 'low effort' and 'high effort'. Asking people how much they approved or disapproved of a certain tactic, Marsh (1977) ranked different social movement tactics with low thresholds (signing petitions, legal demonstrations) to high thresholds (illegal demonstrations, violent action). Collom (2003) has put this logic of an 'activism hierarchy' to the test and found empirical evidence that people engaging in unconventional political activity with higher intensity (e.g. demonstrations) were most likely to have already participated in low intensity forms of actions, like signing petitions, leading to some kind of 'stepping-stone theory' of political participation (Verhulst and Van Laer 2008). This 'hierarchy of (offline) political participation' can of course be easily attributed to online tactics as well, with no or marginal thresholds towards signing an online petition and much higher thresholds when dealing with particular forms of 'hacktivism', like denial-of-service (DoS) tactics. Postmes and Brunsting (2002), for instance, made a comparable distinction between 'persuasive' (like email petitions) and 'confrontational' (like virtual sit-ins) online tactics, the latter entailing higher risks and thus higher thresholds.

The reasons why social movements may or may not use a particular action form, or why individual people decide to participate in a particular action form, are manifold. They might feel, for instance, unfamiliar with a specific tactic, or think some kind of action is inefficient to obtain the goals put forward and other means should be used instead. The 'tactical question' is persistent for social movements, and entails instrumental calculations as much as identity or ideological considerations (Ennis 1987; Jasper 1997). A pacifist group of activists, for instance, will probably refuse to take up more violent forms of action, even though this would perhaps be more effective to gain media attention or alter significant policy change. One crucial variable we will focus on here, however, is the practical participation costs inherent to a particular action form, thus, the amount of *resources* needed to engage in a particular tactic (e.g. time, money and skills). These costs also refer to *potential* costs, like the costs related to getting arrested. For instance, signing petitions can be considered a tactic entailing minimal costs, because of minimal commitment and risk, thus consisting of a low participation threshold. But in order to participate in a street demonstration you need some spare time on a Saturday afternoon, and maybe money to pay your travelling expenses, which is especially the case with a transnational demonstration located outside your national boundaries. Moreover, you might risk a violent confrontation with police forces. Here, thresholds to participate are obviously much higher.

The reason why we focus on these practical participation *costs* is because of the Internet's principal potential to reduce the 'transaction costs' for groups and activists organising, mobilising, and participating in collective action (Bonchek 1995; Naughton 2001). Technically, with its global architecture, the Internet allows for collaboration and participation beyond time and space constraints. As a many-to-many medium it stimulates diffusion of ideas and issues on an unprecedented scale, significantly reducing mobilisation costs of social movement actors. Moreover, defining social movements as 'sustained interactions' communication is key, which in turn explains the Internet's attractiveness as a tool for social movements to overcome often limited available resources (van de Donk *et al.* 2004a).

Although the Internet can resolve participation thresholds common to particular action forms, it certainly creates new ones too. Especially regarding hacktivist tactics special skills might be acquired to be even able to engage. We will come back to this as we discuss the limitations of Internet use on action repertoires. First we illustrate the various possibilities of the Internet as a new space for social movement tactics, and lowering participation thresholds of existing tactics.

2. The 'digitalised' action repertoire: a snapshot of possibilities

In the next section we will support our typology by giving multiple examples of how the Internet created new or facilitated old action forms. The four quadrants depicted in Figure 12.1 will structure the discussion of these cases.

2.1. Quadrant 1: Internet-supported action with low thresholds

Traditional forms to support or engage in collective action are, among others, donating money, being active as a conscious consumer, or participating in a legal demonstration. In almost all Western democracies these kinds of actions have become quite 'normal' as ever more people participated or used them (Norris *et al.* 2005). This success can be related to their limited thresholds, but as we will show the Internet has made them even easier and more accessible.

Donation of money
Donating money is a way of active participation that involves no risk or commitment, only money (and sometimes even no money at all). Garrett (2006) sees great opportunities with the Internet for this particular kind of action.

Before the Internet, Garrett contends, coordination costs largely outweighed the benefits of small contributions. With the Internet, organisations can now 'more effectively pool small-scale acts of support' by using click-and-give websites (Garrett 2006: 206). A well-known example is The Hunger Site that initially promoted food programmes by asking people to click on a button and watch a new page with different ads from the site's sponsors. The Hunger Site warrant that 100 per cent of the money of these sponsors directly goes to their charity partners. So there is not a penny of donation money involved from participants themsleves. After two years of operation the site reached a stunning 198 million donations (Meikle 2002: 11). The Hunger Site now has several other projects like The Breast Cancer Site, where you can click and give free mammograms, or The Rainforest Site where you can click and protect endangered habitats. Entering the term 'click-and-give' in any online search engine will give you an infinite list of websites promoting an infinite list of causes.

Consumer behaviour

Consumer behaviour as an action form has always been heavily related to the Fair Trade Movement, which is, at present, in terms of popularity and supporters, fast growing. For this movement the Internet provides important new assets to be exploited. If you intend to boycott certain products or to buy specific food or clothes for ethical or political reasons, you need to be knowledgeable about different alternatives. The Internet offers clear advantages in terms of information dissemination. A very young but successful example is the US-based fair trade organisation World of Good, Inc. (Krier 2008). Together with its sister organisation World of Good Development it has initiated a web-based tool which allows producers and buyers to calculate a 'fair' minimum wage for their product. Also this company is involved in a large-scale project with eBay, a popular online reseller, aimed at setting up a new online marketplace which should link Fair Trade producers and resellers to conscious consumers (Krier 2008). As such, the Internet lowers the thresholds for many potential conscious consumers to effectively buy specific fair trade products.

Legal demonstrations

Social movement organisations wanting to mobilise for a mass street demonstration make extensive use of the Internet to enhance coordination and mobilisation efforts (Van Laer 2007a). This concerns mainly the distribution of information, both about the reasons for and goals of the action, as well as more strategic information concerning the action itself. Via the Internet organisations provide detailed information on time, place, and perhaps even a practical field guide for activists to 'inform people on how to organise, on their rights and how to protect themselves from harm' as was the case during the FTAA (Free Trade Area of the Americas) protests in Quebec city, 2001. This lengthy document took activists by the hand and guided them through all the obstacles to effective participation (Van Aelst and Walgrave 2004). During the Seattle WTO (World Trade Organisation) protests, a main rallying point was the StopWTORound distribution list, which enabled subscribers to receive detailed information on different aspects of the WTO (George 2000). A recent study among diverse types of demonstration (like trade unions, antiwar, immigrant rights, but also right-wing mobilisations), showed how activists use the Internet to cross movement and protest issue boundaries, thereby significantly increasing their mobilisation potential (Walgrave *et al*. 2008). The processes of 'brokerage' and 'diffusion' these authors describe are important mechanisms that in cyberspace do not stop at national boundaries either, making every mobilisation call in theory inherently transnational. Carty's (2002) account of various anti-sweatshop movements offers a first example. She describes how groups like the NGO Global Exchange provide complete campaign starter kits via their website to organise rallies and demonstrations. In October 1997 this strategy resulted in more than 84 communities in 12 different countries demonstrating simultaneously outside of Nike retailers (Carty 2002: 135). These several 'national' demonstrations are thus transnationally linked via their similar cause and tactical choice. In another study, Fisher and colleagues (2005) show how, in the case of five Global Justice demonstrations (mostly directed against the powerful economic institutions such as the World Bank and the G8), the Internet was successfully used by social movement organisations to connect domestically grounded activists to transnational struggles, thereby spurring local, large-scale protest events. We provide a more extensive discussion about the Internet's transnationalisation function in the following section on transnational social movement demonstrations and meetings.

2.2. Quadrant 2: Internet-supported action with high thresholds

In this second quadrant we discuss action forms that have been used before but have far higher thresholds, both legally and practically. It concerns transnational demonstrations and meetings, and more obstructive action forms such as sit-ins and (street) blockades. Again we believe the Internet can lower especially the practical barriers by facilitating the organisation and coordination of these events.

Transnational demonstration
We started this chapter with reference to the Zapatista movement and the so-called 'Battle of Seattle', two well-known moments of transnational mobilisation. A more recent example is the worldwide protest against the imminent war in Iraq on 15 February 2003. On that day several million people took to the streets in more than 60 different countries around the world. Several authors have shown that this protest event would not likely have been as massive and diverse without the coordinating and mobilising capacity of the Internet (Vasi 2006; Bennett *et al*. 2008; Verhulst 2009). Van Laer (2009) contends that the Internet was especially conducive in terms of 'mesomobilisation', that is the efforts of groups and organisations to coordinate and integrate other groups, organisations, and networks for protest activities (Gerhards and Rucht 1992: 558). In a historical comparison of three eras of peace and anti-war mobilisation, Van Laer (2009) showed how several face-to-face international meetings each time served as the principal basis for

coordination and collaboration, but that in the advent of the second war in Iraq in 2003 the Internet was fundamental in 'spreading the fire', bringing the call for a global day of action on an unprecedented worldwide scale, among hundreds of other national anti-war networks and social movement organisations, with a speed and efficiency that was not possible before.

However, we should notice that this event was transnational because all around the world people took to the streets for the same reasons, but that the event was hardly transnational on the individual level. A survey among the participants revealed that only a handful of demonstrators travelled more than 200 kilometres to participate in an anti-war march, even in large countries like the UK, Germany and the US (Walgrave and Verhulst 2003). The barriers for people to participate in an event abroad remain high and difficult the overcome. In their efforts to get people from around the world to an international summit social movements have used the Internet to distribute useful information on how to travel or where to sleep (Ayres 2005), but often that has proven not to be enough to significantly lower the practical thresholds (Bédoyan et al. 2004; Lichbach and de Vries 2004; Fisher et al. 2005; Walgrave and Van Laer 2008). Perhaps this might be one reason that 'global days of action' appear to be on the rise as a tactic of transnational activists (Tilly 2004a). Thanks to Internet technology activists do not need to be in the same geographical location to protest against, for instance, climate change, but can link their dispersed protest actions effectively online. This may well lead to Wellman's (2002) so-called 'glocalisation' of communities, meaning the combination of intense local and extensive global interaction.

Transnational meetings
Instrumental advantages of the Internet have also been well documented in the case of transnational social movement meetings and summits, especially those of the Global Justice Movement. A recurrent key event of the Global Justice Movement, for instance, is the various social forums they organise both on a global level (the World Social Forum (WSF)), the regional level (e.g. European Social Forum) and even the national and local level. In his study on the second World Social Forum in Porto Alegre (Brazil), Schönleitner (2003) found that the Internet was a major tool for mobilisation and organisation for this kind of event: the registration of the delegates and the planning of workshops are achieved through the Web; email bulletins keep delegates and others updated; and almost all internal communication and external liaison has been done via Internet and mobile phones. Without the Internet the WSF would hardly be possible in its current form (Schönleitner 2003: 130). Kavada (2006) showed how the use of mailing lists contributed to an effective division of labour, spurring deliberative coordination and discussion in the advent of the third European Social Forum in London. Finally, a study of Van Laer (2007b) empirically addressed the importance of the Internet as a tool that allowed activists participating in the fourth European Social Forum in Athens to contact fellow participants from other organisations and countries before the summit in order to meet each other and exchange experiences and information at the Forum itself.

Sit-in/occupation and more violent forms of protest

McPhail and McCarthy (2005) contend that the Internet is also changing the way in which anarchistic groups like the 'Black Bloc' are engaged in more confrontational protest actions by providing access to email alert lists, schedules of planning meetings and marshal training sessions, information about protection against tear gas and pepper spray as well as legal information about rights of assembly, speech, etc. Especially, the Internet allows for the secure dissemination of messages about time and place of extra-legal and illegal activities, thereby significantly reducing the possibility of surveillance by the police and other opponents, and – during a protest event – Internet and other communication technology makes it possible to continuously document activists 'on the spot' about actions and interaction with the police. During the Seattle protests protesters made extensive use of Internet technology to tactically relocate groups of activists according to police locations. In the advent of the G8 protests in Genoa, July 2001, there were detailed city maps that circulated on the Internet with various 'battle grounds' coloured differently.

Another, less confrontational example, is that of the Harvard Progressive Student Labor Movement (PSLM) at Harvard College, in the United States, demanding higher living wages for the institution's security guards, janitors, and dining-room workers. In 2001 this movement started with the occupation of several university administrative offices, relying heavily on the Internet to coordinate the action and to fuel support among academic personnel, student parents, and other student communities on other university campuses in the US (Biddix and Park 2008). Via websites experiences about the sit-in were shared so that other student communities could learn and start a sit-in themselves. An interesting aspect of this case is that the 'real-life' sit-in at Harvard College eventually was accompanied with a 'virtual sit-in' in order to 'escalate' the campaign as media attention seemed to wither and administration officials continued to refuse to negotiate with the activists (Constanza-Chock 2003).

2.3. Quadrant 3: Internet-based action with low thresholds

In this section we discuss actions that are solely performed online: online petitions, email bombs and virtual sit-ins. The examples here clearly illustrate the advantages of the Internet in terms of mobilisation and reduction of participation thresholds.

Online petition

In a study among global justice activists della Porta and Mosca (2005) found that online email petitions were the most widespread form of action that was used online. Earl (2006) makes a distinction between online petitions that are performed by social movements themselves, and petitions that are centralised on a specialised 'warehouse site', like *ipetition.com, thepetitionsite. com* or *MoveOn.org. MoveOn.org* became widely known as the petition site opposing the impeachment of Bill Clinton in 1998 and the war in Iraq in 2003 (Earl 2006) and eventually become much more than a simple petition site, but incarnated as a distinct movement appealing to a new generation of American politically engaged citizens (Pickard 2008). Especially these warehouse sites illustrate how the Internet can reduce costs of setting up or participating in an online petition: a social movement or random activist can easily make a new account on a warehouse site, choosing a cause and statement and then start to invite people to sign a petition. But with a little knowledge of html, you can easily start your own online petition as well. In May 2006, for instance, a union of French wine farmers in the region of Margaux quickly started with a blog and an online petition against a possible new highway across their precious vineyards. Also the Internet, as a medium that neatly integrates different kinds of media forms, offers new possibilities for setting up petitions, like, for example, the visual petition a 'Million Faces' initiated by the international campaign *Control Arms*. People sign this petition against the spread of arms around the world by uploading a picture of themselves optionally displaying a personal message. In July 2007 Friends of the Earth in the UK launched its 'Big Ask online march', a video wall of 'filmed signatures' to lobby for a climate change bill.

Today, popular social network sites like Facebook are extensively used to do similar things. Anyone with a Facebook profile can form a group against or in favour of a particular cause and invite other Facebook members to 'sign' this cause by becoming a member of this group. One such group, 'Hey, Facebook, breastfeeding is not obscene', was set up to protest against Facebook itself, asking to allow breastfeeding pictures that are now classified by Facebook as 'obscene' and removed from the network site.[1] Dubbed as the Mothers International Lactation Campaign (MILC), they also organised a virtual 'nurse-in', asking Facebook members to change their profile picture into a breastfeeding one. In January 2008 Colombian engineer Oscar Morales Guevara created a Facebook group, 'Un Million De Voces Contra La FARC' (One Million Voices Against the FARC), opposing president Chavez's request to the European Union to remove the FARC from the list of terrorist organisations, as well as protesting against the FARC in general. Within hours several thousand people had subscribed to this new group. This Facebook petition eventually resulted in a global day of action on 4 February 2008 against the FARC with over four million people protesting in dozens of Colombian cities and other cities worldwide.[2]

Email bomb and virtual sit-in

A more disruptive form of the online petition is the email bomb, which comprises large amounts of emails sent to email accounts of, for instance, a minister or corporate CEO, or to a target system in order to pin down the targeted mailing server, demonstrating the extent of support for a specific cause (Meikle 2002). A very similar tactic is that of the virtual sit-in. Here people do not send an email, but instead ask for information from a website but in such numbers that the server cannot deal with the amount of requests and eventually crashes. In fact, these tactics are often treated as hacktivist action forms. However, to the extent that it involves hundreds or thousands of people sending an email or requesting information from a website at the same time, we believe this tactic is a collective action form still entailing lower thresholds than other kind of hacktivist tactics, like more specialised actions altering website source codes (see below) or using special software to disrupt Internet traffic, although the outcome (denial of service) indeed might be the same. On 30 November 1999, the day the WTO summit started in Seattle, several thousands activists requested information from the WTO website at the same time, which caused a crash of the WTO server. An early example of the use of email bombing is, for instance, *Workers Online*, the webzine of an Australian labour organisation, which organised in July 2001 a massive email jam session in response to legislation on workers' compensation. Within hours, a reported 13,000 emails were sent to the government (Meikle 2002: 163).

2.4. Quadrant 4: Internet-based action with high thresholds

In the last section we discussed actions that are made possible largely or totally thanks to the Internet, but demand more resources than signing a petition or sending an email. We will discuss examples of protest websites, culture jamming and hacktivism. It is important to note that culture jamming is not a totally new technique, as its origins can be traced to the 1960s, nor is it totally Internet-based, as it has offline versions. However, as it has grown together with the Internet and has its main features online we discuss it in this section.

Protest websites
The examples we present in this section are heavily related to what Clark and Themudo (2003: 110) have termed 'Internet-based dot causes', which can apply to any social movement or citizen group that 'promotes social causes and chiefly mobilises support through its website'. One of the earliest examples of a 'dot cause' is perhaps the Free Burma Campaign (FBC). Its website, initially created by exiled Burmese graduate student Zar Ni, generated unprecedented global attention to the Burmese military junta, worldwide support from scholars and activists, and even the withdrawal of global firms such as Levi Strauss and Texaco out of Burma (O'Neill 1999; Danitz and Strobel 2001). Another example is the McSpotlight campaign (O'Neill 1999; Meikle 2002), also claiming to be among the first to exploit the potential of the Internet into a successful grass-roots advocacy campaign against fast food giant McDonalds (Meikle 2002: 85). The heart of McSpotlight was its website which was launched in 1996 following the longest-running trial in English history: the McLibel case, where McDonald's took legal action against two individuals who distributed a leaflet accusing McDonald's of socially and environmentally harmful practices. The McSpotlight campaign offers a great example of how cyberspace acts as a new area of contention: in order to avoid censorship mirrors of the McSpotlight site were created in Chicago, London, Auckland and Helsinki, making it very difficult if not impossible for McDonalds to start legal action coordinated across a number of different legal systems and jurisdictions against the McSpotlight website (O'Neill 1999; Meikle 2002). Rosenkrands (2004) provides an extensive list of different Web-

based movements encompassing a wide range of different causes, like for instance *No Logo.com*, a website to support the movement against big brands and corporate globalisation launched by *No Logo* author Naomi Klein and a few other activists. Other examples include *CorpWatch.org*, *Nike Watch*, or *CokeSpotlight*, just to name a few.

Alternative media sites

A little bit different from the sites we described in the previous section, but taking advantage of the same possibilities of the new Internet space to publish and disseminate alternative points of view about political and cultural struggles, are those sites from alternative media (activist)groups, such as Indymedia. The Internet provides activists and social movements with alternative channels for the production of media, thereby circumventing mainstream media channels. The first independent media centre (IMC), Indymedia, was set up in the wake of the Seattle WTO protests in 1999, and soon after dozens of other IMCs were set up creating a worldwide network of radical social movement publics for the circulation of alternative news and information (Kidd 2003; Juris 2005). The ideas behind these alternative media sites are closely related to the open source movement that in turn very much intermingles with the global justice movement and its process of archiving and systematising their work and actions in 'memory-projects' like *Euromovements.info*. From another point of view, these alternative media sites are also struggling with information monopolisation and the production of meaning. And the latter is where we enter the field of culture jamming.

Culture jamming

Culture jamming 'changes the meaning of corporate advertising through artistic techniques that alter corporate logos visually and by giving marketing slogans new meaning' (Stolle and Micheletti 2005: 10). Culture jammers make use of techniques such as appropriation, collage, ironic inversion and juxtaposition through diverse tactics like billboard pirating, physical and virtual graffiti, and website alteration (Meikle 2002: 131; Juris 2008: 275). This action form is perhaps most vividly exemplified by the *Nike Email Exchange Campaign*, which started with one MIT graduate student emailing the Nike Company about printing the word 'sweatshop' on his personalised Nike shoes, but eventually generating unexpected media attention and thousands of other reactions worldwide (Peretti 2006).[3] Humour, satire and irony are very important and powerful features of culture jam-like tactics.

Pinning down the roots of culture jamming is near impossible, foremost because many of the groups involved in this kind of cultural production predate the Internet era as well as the techniques they use (Klein 2002). Well-known groups like Adbusters (notorious for their 'uncommercials' or 'subvertisement'), the Yes Man, or ®™ark, however, all credit the Internet for making the creation of ad parodies immeasurably easier and providing a platform to take their campaigns and artistic productions to a much wider and international audience (Meikle 2002; Klein 2002). By their online presence they are able to spur local offline action too, as for instance in the following example. Although initially the idea to alter the voices of typical girls and boys' toys was posted by ®ᵗᵐark on its website, it was a handful of war veterans that made the culture jamming more concrete: only days from Christmas Eve, the Barbie Liberation Organisation bought several hundred Barbie and GI Joe dolls, changed the voice boxes, and put them back on the shelves. You can imagine the surprised faces of parents and kids finding their Barbie saying, 'Dead men tell no lies' or GI Joe suggesting, 'Wanna go shopping?' (Rosenkrands 2004: 57–8).

Next to the alteration of specific ads online and offline, there is another often-used online technique of creating 'spoof sites'. These are clones of existing sites of, for instance, multinational corporations, governments, politicians and the like. During the WTO protests in Seattle, 1999, the group ®ᵗᵐark set up a spoof site www.gatt.org, cloning the WTO/GATT home page with mock stories and quotes from WTO officials provided with 'helpful commentary' in an often ironic or cynical sense (Meikle 2002: 118).

Hacktivism

Finally, the Internet has also created a new space for confrontational activities like denial-of-service (DoS) attacks via automated email floods, website defacements altering the source code of targeted websites, or the use of malicious software like viruses and worms. These are all actions that touch the boundary of what is seen or held as legal and what as illegal. Depending on the point of view these tactics are than labelled as 'electronic civil disobedience', 'hacktivism' or as 'cyber-terrorism' (Denning 2001; Vegh 2003). Meikle (2002) provides a detailed account of one of the first social movement hacktivist groups: the Electronic Disturbance Theatre, which became active in response to the solidarity call of the Zapatista movement in Mexico. Via a Java applet called *Floodnet* they initiated several automated 'virtual sit-ins' against, among others, President Zedillo of Mexico's home page, and the Pentagon site. The Floodnet software makes use of the server and bandwidth of individual participants that downloaded and activated the software on their computers. This kind of software is used to perform a DoS attack forcing a website to shut down or rendering a server system inoperative, or to leave politically tinted messages on the server logs. Another tactic is to alter the source code of a particular website in order to reroute visitors to another website. In July 1998 a group of international hackers succeeded in probably the largest homepage takeover ever (Denning 2001: 273). They changed over 300 websites, redirecting possible visitors to their own site, greeting them with a message protesting the nuclear arms race. This tactic was also used extensively during the WTO protests in Seattle. Another often-used tactic is more like 'cybergraffiti' (Vegh 2003). By hacking into a website's source code a hacker changes the homepage or leaves a 'statement' (a slogan or picture) on the original homepage. F-Secure Corp, a Finnish Internet security firm, reported in 2003 that over 10,000 websites had been marred with digital graffiti by protesters and supporters of the US-led war in Iraq.[4]

That some of these tactics make it very complicated to delineate what is 'acceptable' and what should be labelled as 'crime' is illustrated by the group *Condemned.org* who broke into the servers of a number of child porn sites and erased their hard drives (Meikle 2002: 164). We do not engage in a full outline of this discussion but refer readers to Chapter 17 in this book, which deals with this subject.

3. Limitations of the Internet and the action repertoire of social movements

The numerous examples discussed in the previous section are somehow anecdotal, yet they show that the Internet has improved and broadened the toolkit of social activists. However, we should not be blind to the limitations that accompany these new technological opportunities. There is the 'classical' problem related to unequal Internet access, also referred to as the digital divide. Other shortcomings are more directed to social movements and their particular use of actions. In some cases the Internet has made collective action still not easy enough, while in others it has made it perhaps too easy. Finally we will argue that the new media seem to lose their newness quickly and more fundamentally are unable to create stable ties between activists that are necessary for sustained collective action.

3.1. Still a digital divide

The term *digital divide* refers in the first place to the inequality in Internet access between the rich industrialised countries and the developing countries in the South (Norris 2001). According to recent estimates around 75 per cent of the people living in North America can be considered as Internet users, while this percentage drops to hardly five in Africa.[5] Besides the clear geographical variation also within (Western) societies certain people remain behind in the digital evolution; not only because of the absence of a computer or Internet access, but also because they lack the skills to use the new media technology. In that respect social movement actions may fail to reach the socially weaker groups in society if they rely too much on the new media to organise their protest events, which is even more the case for pure Internet-based action forms. The digital divide argument goes to the core of many social movements as it weakens their democratic potential (Tilly 2004b). And this is even more apparent in the light of the global digital divide, which seriously endangers the representation of a 'global civil society' in the repertoire shift from the national to the transnational level.

There is also a digital divide within cyberspace, what Norris (2001) has termed the 'democratic divide' between those who use the Internet for political aims and those who do not. In this sense, the Internet will chiefly serve those activists and groups that are already active, thus reinforcing existing patterns of political participation in society. In this sense the early 'cyber-enthusiasm' of the Internet's potential to reinvigorate democracy (see for example Rheingold 1993; Davis and Owen 1998; Coleman 1999) has gradually been replaced by more sceptical and even pessimistic accounts of the Internet's democratising potential (see for example Hill and Hughes 1998; Margolis and Resnick 2000; Scheufele and Nisbet 2002).

3.2. The Internet makes it not easy enough

As mentioned before 'real' transnational demonstrations, getting people from different parts of the world to protest against international institutions and world leaders has remained difficult. Most international protests are in fact overwhelmingly local, or at best national demonstrations (Fisher *et al.* 2005). And in the rare cases that protests were able to get an internationally diverse public to the streets, it was not so much because of the Internet but rather because of 'stronger' mobilising factors. These can be resources such as time (to travel) or free transportation (provided by an organisation involved) (Bédoyan *et al.* 2004). The fact that information on these events is distributed easily and rapidly is certainly helpful, but often not enough to lower the practical barriers significantly.

As indicated, the Internet certainly creates new thresholds too. Meikle (2002) noticed how the Electronic Disturbance Theater (EDT) explicitly warned potential participants of possible risks in a virtual sit-in , which they organised to raise awareness about the Zapatista struggle in Mexico:

> We're met with a set of instructions ... and warnings: 'This is a protest, not a game, it may have personal consequences as in any off-line political manifestation on the street.' We're warned that our computer's IP addresses will be collected by 'the government', in the same way that our pictures might be taken during a street action. We're warned of possible damage to our computers, in the same way that 'in a street action the police may come and hurt you'. (Meikle 2002: 144)

Finally, although the bits and bytes are hard to repress in cyberspace, in some cases the use of the Internet seems futile in light of enduring barriers related to political constraints. Earlier we gave the example of the exiled Burmese people protesting against the military junta in their home country. However, despite raising global awareness it became very clear that in late 2007 still nothing fundamentally had changed. Thousands of people, among them many Buddhist monks, took to the streets again in the Saffron Revolution (referring to the colour of the monks' habits). The junta's first reaction was to block any possible Internet traffic in the country, making it impossible to blog about the demonstrations and the way the junta repressed them. In 2003 millions of people demonstrated against the imminent war in Iraq, in many ways thanks to the Internet, commentators and scholars said, but voices were deadly silent in mainland China.

3.3. The Internet makes it too easy

As some action forms still demand high efforts of participants, the opposite argument can be made for some new online tactics. At first glance, the email petition seems a brilliant continuation of its offline predecessor since it is a familiar tactic, can be easily used, set up, and immediately forwarded to an infinite number of people across time and geographical boundaries. Yet, decision-makers may likely be 'unimpressed by a haphazard list of names that arrives piecemeal, with repeated signatures or pseudonyms from people well outside their jurisdiction' (Meikle 2002: 25). Does a hardly personalised email show the same commitment as a handwritten letter? Many power holders believe it does not and so potential subscribers may also feel that this kind of tactic is not appropriate. Again, what are we to think of the idea of pursuing social and political change by clicking on a button and watching some ads?

3.4. The new media lost their newness

When social movements as 'early adopters' started to use the Internet more than a decade ago their opponents were taken off guard. Some people indicate the failure of the MAI[6] agreements on free trade as the first example of a new style of Internet-based contentious politics (Ayres 1999: 133). Yet, we are not sure whether this first obvious success indeed heralded a new era of activist repertoire. The example of the MAI may well illustrate how politicians and negotiators were somehow overwhelmed and surprised by the enormous attention to the MAI and the rapid diffusion of critical and substantial information about the exact content of the agreements. Today, more than 10 years after the MAI, the Internet is widely introduced and used in all kinds of different life spheres, and new opponents are probably not so easily taken by surprise any more. Furthermore, targeted companies or authorities do not passively wait for future online hacktivist actions, but proactively invest in software to hinder new attacks. This means social activists are forced to renew their action repertoire ever faster, only to spark the same amount of public attention or political pressure.

3.5. The Internet only creates weak ties

The Internet is a 'weak-tie instrument' par excellence (Kavanaugh *et al.* 2005); as such it is able to attract easily and rapidly a large number of people to join an action ore event. Walgrave and colleagues (2008) have pointed to weak ties crossing movement and issue boundaries as an important asset for social movement actors expanding their mobilisation potential. However, critics have noticed that this growth in support is often followed by an even faster decline in support. Earl and Schussman (2003) noticed that in the rising era of e-activism 'members' have become 'users', who after the action they supported is over often choose to move on and don't feel a need to get permanently engaged. According to several scholars the Internet is unable to create the necessary trust and strong ties that are necessary to build a sustainable network of activists (Diani 2000; Clark and Themudo 2003; Tilly 2004b).

4. Discussion and Conclusion

In this chapter we have focused on how the Internet has changed the action repertoire of social movements in two fundamental ways. First, by facilitating existing actions forms making it possible to reach more people, more easily, in a time span that was unthinkable before. Second, by creating new (or adapted) tools for activism. We have tried to capture this 'double impact' in a typology of collective action with two dimensions. The creation of new e-tools for activism was represented in the first dimension ranging from Internet-supported to Internet-based actions. The second dimension referred to the (practical) thresholds that have been lowered, but not broken down, by the Internet. On the basis of these two dimensions four quadrants of activism were discussed and illustrated with numerous examples. However, the dimensions should not be seen as clear and stable divisions between the different forms of activism, but rather as fluid lines that are permanently redefined by technological innovations and the creativity of activists.

In our discussion of the typology we have tried to build a strong case in favour of the Internet as it has given social movements new and improved opportunities to engage in social and political action. At the same time we have avoided a naive Internet-optimism, by pointing out several limitations. However, those limitations do not outweigh the advantages, as we believe the overall balance is positive. This does not mean that social movements have suddenly become a more powerful force in society or that the power balance has shifted in their favour. As mentioned before political and economic power has gradually moved to the international level. The Internet enabled social movements to follow that transition and operate more globally. One could state that the Internet has made it possible to maintain the status quo, but has not changed it. What has changed is that powerful actors such as multinationals, governments or supranational institutions can be held accountable at any time. Civic groups with little resources can mobilise support and public attention against a far more powerful competitor more easily and independently than in the past. Although Goliath can use the Internet as well, the relative advantage of this new technology is bigger for David. Several authors have indeed shown that social movements, being networks of diverse groups and activists, are especially keen on using the Internet because of its fluid, non-hierarchical structure, which 'matches' their ideological and organisational needs (Klein 2001; Bennett 2003; van de Donk *et al.* 2004b). This is far less the case for organisations or actors that have a more hierarchical and formal structure, where the Internet is often seen more as a threat and less an opportunity.

In this chapter we have tried to explain and illustrate how the Internet has changed the action repertoire of social movements. By focusing on the action repertoire we have not been able to discuss the much broader consequences of the use of electronic media for civil society. As stated by McCaughey and Ayers: 'Activists have not only incorporated the Internet into their repertoire, but also ... have changed substantially what counts as activism, what counts as community, collective identity, democratic space, and political strategy' (McCaughey and Ayers 2003: 1–2). As such activists and social movements have now often found straightforward ways to reconnect with ordinary citizens, and especially with youngsters, in the face of apparently ever-increasing public disengagement from formal political institutions and processes (cf. Dalton 2008). The interested reader still has a lot to explore, and so have social movement scholars that try to keep up with the new developments in the Internet age.

Notes

1 Link to Facebook group: http://www.facebook.com/group.php?gid=2517126532
2 Mario Vargas Llosa. 'No más FARC.' El Pais, 10 February 2008, available online: http://www.elpais.com/articulo/opinion/FARC/elpepiopi/20080210elpepiopi_12/Tes. Link to Facebook group: http://www.facebook.com/group.php?gid=6684734468
3 By adding the word 'sweatshop' to his shoes Jonah Peretti wanted to address the issue of child labour. The complete correspondence between Peretti and Nike can be read at http://www.shey.net/niked.html (see also McCaughey and Ayres 2003).
4 Brian Krebs, 'Hackers Plan Attacks To Protest Iraq War', *Washington Post*, 1 April 2003.
5 http://www.internetworldstats.com/stats.htm
6 Multilateral Agreement on Investment, negotiated between members of the OECD (Organisation for Economic Co-operation and Development).

Further reading

In addition to the References for this chapter we would like to highlight a few useful articles and books for the interested reader.

Recommended introductions to social movement activism and the impact of new communication technology are van de Donk, Loader, Nixon and Rucht's (2004) reader, *Cyberprotest. New Media, Citizens and Social Movements* and McCaughey and Ayers' (2003) reader, *Cyberactivism: Online Activism in Theory and Practice*. For more on electronic civil disobedience, with lots of interesting examples, certainly read Graham Meikle's (2002) *Future Active: Media Activism and the Internet*. On culture jamming and new sites of activism the work of activist-researcher Naomi Klein is suitable, but recent interesting accounts can be found in Christine Harolds' (2007) *Our Space: Resisting the Corporate Control of Culture*, or the ethnographic work of Jeffrey Juris (2008), *Networking Futures: The Movements against Corporate Globalization*.

For general reading, empirical as well as theoretical, on social movements and contentious action, the following two readers are very helpful: Goodwin and Jasper's (2003) *The Social Movement Reader: Cases and Concepts* (Blackwell Readers in Sociology) and Snow, Soule and Kriesi's (2004) *Blackwell Companion to Social Movements*.

References

Ayres, Jeffrey M. (1999) 'From the Streets to the Internet: The Cyber-Diffusion of Contention', *The ANNALS of the American Academy of Political and Social Science*, 566: 132–43.

Ayres, Jeffrey M. (2005) 'Transnational Activism in the Americas: The Internet and Innovations in the Repertoire of Contention', in Patrick G. Coy and I. Wallimann (eds), *Research in Social Movements, Conflicts and Change*. London: JAI Press, 35–61.

Bandy, Joe and Smith, Jackie (eds) (2005) *Coalitions across Borders: Transnational Protest and the Neoliberal Order*. Lanham: Rowman and Littlefield Publishers.

Barnes, Samuel and Kaase, Max (1979) *Political Action: Mass Participation in Five Western Democracies*. Beverly Hills, CA: Sage.

Bédoyan, Isabelle, Van Aelst, Peter and Walgrave, Stefaan (2004) 'Limitations and Possibilities of Transnational Mobilization: The Case of EU Summit Protesters in Brussels, 2001', *Mobilization: An International Journal*, 9(1): 39–54.

Bennett, W. Lance (2003) 'Communicating Global Activism. Strenghts and Vulnerabilities of Networked Politics', *Information, Communication & Society*, 6(2): 143–68.

Bennett, W. Lance, Breunig, Christian and Givens, Terri E. (2008) 'Communication and Political Mobilization: Digital Media and the Organization of Anti-Iraq War Demonstrations in the U.S.', *Political Communication*, 25: 269–89.

Biddix, J. Patrick and Park, Han Woo (2008) 'Online Networks of Student Protest: The Case of the Living Wage Campaign', *New Media and Society*, 10(6): 871–91.

Bimber, Bruce (2000) 'The Study of Information Technology and Civic Engagement', *Political Communication*, 17(4): 329–33.

Bonchek, Mark S. (1995) *Grassroots in Cyberspace: Recruiting Members on the Internet or do Computer Networks Facilitate Collective Action? A Transaction Cost Approach*. Paper presented at the 53rd Annual Meeting of the Midwest Political Science Association, Chicago, IL.

Carty, Victoria (2002) 'Technology and Counter-hegemonic Movements: the Case of Nike Corporation', *Social Movement Studies*, 1(2): 129–46.

Cere, R. (2003) 'Digital Counter-Cultures and the Nature of Electronic Social and Political Movements', in Y. Jewkes (ed.), *Dot.cons: Crime, Deviance and Identity on the Internet*. Cullompton: Willan Publishing.

Clark, John D. (ed.) (2003) *Globalizing Civic Engagement. Civil Society and Transnational Action*. London: Earthscan Publications Ltd.

Clark, John D. and Themudo, Nuno S. (2003) 'The Age of Protest: Internet-Based "Dot Causes" and the "Anti-Globalization" Movement', in John D. Clark (ed.), *Globalizing Civic Engagement. Civil Society and Transnational Action*. London: Earthscan Publications Ltd, 109–26.

Cleaver, Harry (1998) 'The Zapatista effect: The Internet and the Rise of an Alternative Political Fabric', *Journal of International Affairs*, 51(2): 621–40.

Coleman, Stephen (1999) 'Can the New Media Invigorate Democracy', *Political Quarterly*, 70(1): 16–22.

Collom, Ed (2003) *Protest Engagement in America: The Influence of Perceptions, Networks, Availability, and Politics*. Paper presented at the American Sociological Association, Chicago.

Constanza-Chock, Sasha (2003) 'Mapping the Repertoire of Electronic Contention', in Andrew Opel and Donnalyn Pompper (eds), *Representing Resistance: Media, Civil Disobedience and the Global Justice Movement*. London: Praeger.

Dalton, Russell J. (1996) *Citizen Politics: Public Opinion and Political Parties in Advanced Industrial Democracies*. Chatham, N.J.: Chatham House Publishers.

Dalton, Russell J. (2008) 'Citizenship Norms and the Expansion of Political Participation', *Political Studies*, 56(1): 76–98.

Danitz, Tiffany and Strobel, Warren P. (2001) 'Networking Dissent: Cyber Activists Use the Internet to Promote Democracy in Burma', in John Arquilla and David Ronfeldt (eds), *Networks and Netwars: The Future of Terror, Crime, and Militancy*. Santa Monica: RAND Corporation, 129–69.

Davis, Richard and Owen, Diana (1998) *New Media and American Politics*. New York: Oxford University Press.

de Armond, Paul (2001) 'Netwar in the Emerald City: WTO Protest Strategy and Tactics', in John Arquilla and David Ronfeldt (eds), *Networks and Netwars: The Future of Terror, Crime, and Militancy*. Santa Monica: RAND Corporation, 201–35.

della Porta, Donatella, Kriesi, Hanspeter and Rucht, Dieter (eds) (1999) *Sociale Movements in a Globalizing World*. London: Macmillan.

della Porta, Donatella and Mosca, Lorenzo (2005) 'Global-net for Global Movements? A Network of Networks for a Movement of Movements', *Journal of Public Policy*, 25(1): 165–90.

della Porta, Donatella and Tarrow, Sidney (eds) (2005) *Transnational Protest and Global Activism*. Boulder: Rowman and Littlefield.

Denning, Dorothy E. (2001) 'Activism, Hacktivism, and Cyberterrorism: The Internet as a Tool for Influencing Foreign Policy', in John Arquilla and David Ronfeldt (eds), *Networks and Netwars: The Future of Terror, Crime, and Militancy*. Santa Monica: RAND Corporation, 239–88.

Diani, Mario (1992) 'The Concept of Social Movement', *Sociological Review,* 40(1): 1–25.

Diani, Mario (2000) 'Social Movement Networks. Virtual and Real', *Information, Communication & Society*, 3(3): 386–401.

Eagleton-Pierce, Matthew (2001) 'The Internet and the Seattle WTO Protests', *Peace Review*, 13(3): 331–37.

Earl, Jennifer (2006) 'Pursuing Social Change Online: The Use of Four Protest Tactics on the Internet', *Social Science Computer Review*, 24(3): 362–77.

Earl, Jennifer and Schussman, Alan (2003) 'The New Site of Activism: On-line Organizations, Movement Entrepreneurs, and the Changing Location of Social Movement Decision-Making', in Patrick G. Coy (ed.), *Consensus Decision Making, Northern Ireland and Indigenous Movements*. London: JAI Press, 155–87.

Ennis, James G. (1987) 'Fields of Action: Structure in Movements' Tactical Repertoires', *Sociological Forum*, 2(3): 520–33.

Fisher, Dana R., Stanley, Kevin, Berman, David and Neff, Gina (2005) 'How Do Organizations Matter? Mobilization and Support for Participants at Five Globalization Protests', *Social Problems*, 52(1): 102–21.

Garrett, R. Kelly (2006) 'Protest in an Information Society. A Review of the Literature on Social Movements and New ICTs', *Information, Communication and Society*, 9(2): 202–24.

George, Susan (2000) 'Seattle Turning Point: Fixing or Nixing the WTO', *Le Monde Diplomatique*, January.

Gerhards, Jürgen and Rucht, Dieter (1992) 'Mesomobilization: Organizing and Framing in Two Protest Campaigns in West Germany', *American Journal of Sociology*, 98(3): 555–96.

Gurak, Laura J. and Logie, John (2003) 'Internet Protest, from Text to Web', in Martha McCaughey and Michael D. Ayers (eds), *Cyberactivism. Online Activism in Theory and Practice*. New York, London: Routledge, 25–46.

Hill, Kevin A. and Hughes, John E. (1998) *Cyberpolitics: Citizen Activism in the Age of the Internet*. Maryland: Rowman and Littlefield Publishers.

Jasper, James M. (1997) *The Art of Moral Protest: Culture, Biography, and Creativity in Social Movements*. Chicago: University of Chicago Press.

Juris, Jeffrey S. (2005) 'The New Digital Media and Activist Networking within Anti-Corporate Globalization Movements', *Annals of the American Academy of Political and Social Science*, 597: 189–208.

Juris, Jeffrey S. (2008) *Networking Futures: The Movements against Corporate Globalization*. Durham, NC: Duke University Press.

Kavada, Anastasia (2006) *The 'alter-globalization movement' and the Internet: A case study of communication networks and collective action*. Paper presented at the Cortona Colloquium 2006 – Cultural Conflicts, Social Movements and New Rights: A European Challenge, 20–22 October 2006, Cortona, Italy.

Kavanaugh, Andrea, Reese, Debbie Denise, Carroll, John M. and Rosson, Mary Beth (2005) 'Weak Ties in Networked Communities', *Information Society*, 21(2): 119–31.

Kidd, Dorothy (2003) 'Indymedia.org: A New Communication Commons', in Martha McCaughey and Michael D. Ayers (eds), *Cyberactivism:Online Activism in Theory and Practice*. New York and London: Routledge, 47–70.

Klandermans, Bert (1997) *The Social Psychology of Protest.* Oxford: Blackwell Publishers.

Klein, Naomi (2001) 'Reclaiming the Commons', *New Left Review*, 9: 81–90.

Klein, Naomi (2002) *No Logo: No Space, No Choice, No Jobs.* New York: Picador.

Krier, Jean-Marie (2008) *Fair Trade 2007: New Facts and Figures from an Ongoing Success Story.* Culemborg, Netherlands: DAWS – Dutch Association of Worldshops.

Lichbach, Mark Irving and de Vries, Helma G.E. (2004) 'Global Justice and Antiwar Movements: From Local Resistance to Globalized Protests', unpublished manuscript. Department of Government and Politics, University of Maryland.

McAdam, Doug (1986) 'Recruitment to High-Risk Activism: The Case of Freedom Summer', *American Journal of Sociology*, 92(1): 64–90.

McAdam, Doug, Tarrow, Charles and Tilly, Charles (eds) (2001) *Dynamics of Contention.* Cambridge: Cambridge University Press.

McCaughey, Martha and Ayers, Michael D. (eds) (2003) *Cyberactivism. Online Activism in Theory and Practice.* New York and London: Routledge.

McPhail, Clark and McCarthy, John D. (2005) 'Protest Mobilization, Protest Repression and Their Interaction', in Christian Davenport, Hank Johnston and Carol Mueller (eds), *Repression and Mobilization.* Minneapolis, MN: University of Minnesota Press, 3–32.

Margolis, Michael and Resnick, David (2000) *Politics as Usual: The Cyberspace 'Revolution'.* Thousand Oaks, CA: Sage Publications.

Marsh, Alan (1977) *Protest and Political Conciousness.* Beverly Hills and London: Sage Publications.

Martinez-Torres, Maria Elena (2001) 'Civil Society, the Internet, and the Zapatistas', *Peace Review*, 13(3): 347–55.

Meikle, Graham (2002) *Future Active: Media Activism and the Internet.* New York and London: Routledge.

Meyer, David S. and Tarrow, Sidney (eds) (1998) *The Social Movement Society: Contentious Politics for a New Century.* Lanham, MD: Rowman and Littlefield.

Naughton, John (2001) 'Contested Space: The Internet and Global Civil Society' in Helmut Anheier, Marlies Glasius and Mary Kaldor (eds), *Global Civil Society 2001.* Oxford: Oxford University Press, 147–68.

Norris, Pippa (2001) *Digital Divide. Civic Engagement, Information Poverty, and the Internet Worldwide.* Cambridge: Cambridge University Press.

Norris, Pippa, Walgrave, Stefaan and Van Aelst, Peter (2005) 'Who Demonstrates? Antistate Rebels, Conventional Participants, or Everyone?', *Comparative Politics*, 37(2): 189–205.

Olesen, T. (2004) 'The Transnational Zapatista Solidarity Network: an Infrastructure Analysis', *Global Networks – a Journal of Transnational Affairs*, 4(1): 89–107.

O'Neill, Kelly (1999) *Internetworking for Social Change: Keeping the Spotlight on Corporate Responsibility.* Discussion Paper No 111. Geneva: United Nations Research Institute for Social Development.

Peretti, Jonah (2006) *Culture Jamming, Memes, Social Networks, and the Emerging Media Ecology*, retrieved online 18 December 2006, http://depts.washington.edu/ccce/polcommcampaigns/peretti.html.

Pickard, Victor W. (2008) 'Cooptation and Cooperation: Institutional Exemplars of Democratic Internet Technology', *New Media and Society*, 10(4): 625–45.

Postmes, Tom and Brunsting, Suzanne (2002) 'Collective Action in the Age of the Internet. Mass Communication and Online Mobilization', *Social Science Computer Review*, 20(3): 290–301.

Rheingold, Howard (1993) *The Virtual Community: Homesteading on the Electronic Frontier.* Reading, MA: Addison-Wesley.

Rolfe, Brett (2005) 'Building an Electronic Repertoire of Contention', *Social Movement Studies*, 4(1): 65–74.

Ronfeldt, David and Arquilla, John (1998) 'Emergence and Influence of the Zapatista Social Netwar', in John Arquilla and David Ronfeldt (eds), *Networks and Netwars: The Future of Terror, Crime, and Militancy*. Santa Monica, CA: RAND Corporation, 171–99.

Rosenkrands, Jacob (2004) 'Politicizing *Homo Economicus*: Analysis of Anti-Corporate Websites', in Wim van de Donk, Brian D. Loader, Paul G. Nixon and Dieter Rucht (eds), *Cyberprotest. New Media, Citizens and Social Movements*. London: Routledge, 57–76.

Scheufele, Dietram A. and Nisbet, Matthew C. (2002) 'Being a Citizen Online: New Opportunities and Dead Ends', *Harvard International Journal of Press/Politics*, 7(3): 55–75.

Schönleitner, Günther (2003) 'World Social Forum: Making Another World Possible?', in John D. Clark (ed.), *Globalizing Civic Engagement. Civil Society and Transnational Action*. London: Earthscan Publications Ltd, 127–49.

Schulz, M.S. (1998) 'Collective Action across Borders: Opportunity Structures, Network Capacities, and Communicative Praxis in the Age of Advanced Globalization', *Sociological Perspectives*, 41(3): 587–616.

Smith, Jackie (2001) 'Globalizing Resistance: The Battle of Seattle and the Future of Social Movements', *Mobilization: An International Journal*, 6(1): 1–19.

Smith, Jackie, Chatfield, Charles and Pagnucco, Ron (eds) (1997) *Transnational Social Movements and Global Politics: Solidarity Beyond the State*. New York: Syracuse University Press.

Stolle, Dietlind and Micheletti, Michele (2005) *The Expansion of Political Action Repertoires: Theoretical Reflections on Results from the Nike Email Exchange Internet Campaign*. Paper presented at the 101st Annual Meeting of the American Political Science Association, September 1–4, Washington, DC.

Tarrow, Sidney (1998) *Power in Movement: Social Movements and Contentious Politics*. Cambridge: Cambridge University Press.

Taylor, Verta and Van Dyke, Nella (2004) '"Get up, Stand up": Tactical Repertoires of Social Movements', in David A. Snow, Sarah A. Soule and Hanspeter Kriesi (eds), *The Blackwell Companion to Social Movements*. Malden, Mass.: Blackwell Publishing, 262–92.

Tilly, Charles (1977) 'Getting it Together in Burgundy, 1675–1975', *Theory and Society*, 4(4): 479–504.

Tilly, Charles (1984) 'Social Movements and National Politics', in Charles Bright and Susan Harding (eds), *Statemaking and Social Movements: Essays in History and Theory*. Ann Arbor, MI: University of Michigan Press, 297–317.

Tilly, Charles (2004a) *Social Movements, 1768–2004*. Boulder, CO: Paradigm Publishers.

Tilly, Charles (2004b) 'Trust and Rule', *Theory and Society*, 33(1): 1–30.

Van Aelst, Peter and Walgrave, Stefaan (2001) 'Who Is that (Wo)man in the Street? From the Normalisation of Protest to the Normalisation of the Protester', *European Journal of Political Research*, 39(4): 461–86.

Van Aelst, Peter and Walgrave, Stefaan (2004) 'New Media, New Movements? The Role of the Internet in Shaping the "Anti-globalization" Movement', in Wim van de Donk, Brian D. Loader, Paul G. Nixon and Dieter Rucht (eds), *Cyberprotest. New Media, Citizens and Social Movements*. London: Routledge, 97–122.

van de Donk, Wim, Loader, Brian D., Nixon, Paul G. and Rucht, Dieter (2004a) 'Introduction: Social Movements and ICTs', in Wim van de Donk, Brian D. Loader, Paul G. Nixon and Dieter Rucht (eds), *Cyberprotest. New Media, Citizens and Social Movements*. London: Routledge, 1–26.

van de Donk, Wim, Loader, Brian D., Nixon, Paul G. and Rucht, Dieter (eds) (2004b) *Cyberprotest. New Media, Citizens and Social Movements*. London: Routledge.

Van Laer, Jeroen (2007a) 'Internet Use and Protest Participation: How do ICTs affect mobilization?', *PSW Papers*, 1: 1–24.

Van Laer, Jeroen (2007b) 'Van muisklik tot handdruk: netwerking online en offline tussen andersglobalisten voor, tijdens en na het Europees en Belgisch Sociaal Forum in 2006', unpublished manuscript, University of Antwerp, Media, Movements and Politics research group (M²P).

Van Laer, Jeroen (2009) 'Internationale Coördinatie van Wereldwijd Protest en de Impact van Veranderende Communicatietechnologieën', *Brood & Rozen*, 2.

Vasi, Ion Bogdan (2006) 'The New Anti-war Protests and Miscible Mobilizations', *Social Movement Studies*, 5(2): 137–53.

Vegh, Sandor (2003) 'Classifying Forms of Online Activism: The Case of Cyberprotests against the World Bank', in Martha McCaughey and Michael D. Ayers (eds), *Cyberactivism. Online Activism in Theory and Practice*. New York and London: Routledge, 71–95.

Verhulst, Joris (2009) 'February 15, 2003: The World Says No to War', in Stefaan Walgrave and Dieter Rucht (eds), *Protest Politics. Demonstrations against the War on Iraq in the US and Western Europe*. Minneapolis: University of Minnesota Press.

Verhulst, Joris and Van Laer, Jeroen (2008) *Determinants of Sustained Activism Across Movement Issues*. Paper presented at the 2nd ECPR Graduate Conference, 25–27 August 2008, Barcelona.

Walgrave, Stefaan, Bennett, W. Lance, Van Laer, Jeroen and Breunig, Christian (2008) 'Network Bridging and Multiple Engagements: Digital Media Use of Protest Participants', unpublished manuscript, University of Antwerp, Media, Movements and Politics research group (M²P).

Walgrave, Stefaan and Van Laer, Jeroen (2008) 'Transnational versus National Activism. A Systematic Comparison of "Transnationalists" and "Nationalists" Participating in the 2006 European and Belgian Social Fora', unpublished manuscript, University of Antwerp, Media, Movements and Politics research group (M²P).

Walgrave, Stefaan and Verhulst, Joris (2003) *The February 15 Worldwide Protests against a War in Iraq: An Empirical Test of Transnational Opportunities. Outline of a Research Programme*. Paper presented at the International Workshop on Contemporary Anti-War Mobilizations, 6–7 November 2003, Corfu, Greece.

Wellman, Barry (2002) 'Little Boxes, Glocalization, and Networked Individualism', in Makoto Tanabe, Peter van den Besselaar and Toru Ishida (eds), *Digital Cities II: Computational and Sociological Approaches*. Berlin: Springer, 10–25.

Chapter 13

Intellectual property crime and the Internet: cyber-piracy and 'stealing' information intangibles

David S. Wall and Majid Yar

Introduction

Perhaps the most prominent characteristic of the Internet and the cyberspace it creates is that it is entirely constructed by informational flows. In one way or another each of these flows represents expressions of ideas that are the product of creative (intellectual) labour: ideas over which some form of moral or financial claim can be made to ownership. They range from the very TCP/IP protocol (Transmission Control Protocol/Internet Protocol) that the Internet is based upon, to the intangible artefacts that have become the new real estate of digital or virtual worlds. While some of these ideas, such as the TCP/IP protocol itself, have been expressly 'released' into the public domain others are fiercely contested. The fight that is, and has been, taking place for control over intellectual real estate is a prominent feature of the contemporary landscape of debates over the Internet because they tend to focus upon issues relating to the ownership and control of an environment that was initially designed to facilitate the free flow of information.

The ability of networked technologies to disseminate, share or trade informational or intellectual properties in the form of text, images, music, film and TV through information services is what has made the Internet and World Wide Web what it is today, and the same ability is arguably driving the further development of the information age. Networked information technologies are, however, not simply characterised by informational flows. It is significant that these flows are also networked and globalised (see Wall 2007: 50). These three qualities on the one hand give the authors, creators or their licensees – who have a right of ownership or control over the creations – a highly efficient means by which to disseminate their 'properties'. On the other hand, however, the very fact that they are informational, networked and globalised means that traditional physical and/or 'centralised' means of controlling intellectual properties can be circumvented. The increased market values of informational property in an information age combined with relatively low levels of control that can be exerted over them simultaneously creates new opportunities and motivations for unauthorised appropriation or use – what has become known as cyber-piracy. Yet, these debates are also taking place within the context of changing cultural, social and legal meanings of intellectual property. It is a process of change that is beginning to challenge conventional orthodoxies and legal attitudes towards intellectual properties.

This chapter will look at the above-mentioned tensions (and others) to critically explore what is being understood as intellectual property crime online. The first part will look at what intellectual property is, at how it is being transformed by 'the digital', and why it has become significant to the information economy. The second part will look at 'virtual theft' and specifically at how different forms of informational intangibles (virtual intellectual property online) are being appropriated and causing concern for creators and owners: intellectual property piracy of music, video and software and the theft of virtual artefacts. Part three will discuss critically some of the broader issues that are emerging in the debate over intellectual property online.

Part one: What is intellectual property and how it is being transformed by 'the digital'

We begin here by briefly mapping out just what is meant by the term 'intellectual property' and intellectual property law. Intellectual property is the creative product of intellectual labour and is manifested in the form of so-called 'intangibles', such as ideas, inventions, signs, information and expression. Whereas laws covering 'real' property establish rights over 'tangibles', intellectual property laws establish proprietary rights over 'original' forms of intellectual production (Bently and Sherman 2001: 1–2; WIPO 2001: 3). Intellectual property can take a number of recognised forms – patents, trademarks, trade secrets, industrial designs and copyright.[1] Copyright establishes the holder's (e.g. an author's) rights over a particular form of original expression (WIPO 2001: 40–41). Typical objects of copyright include literary, journalistic and other writing, music, paintings, drawings, audio-visual recordings, and (most recently) computer software. As the term suggests, copyright law grants the holder rights over the copying, reproduction, distribution, broadcast and performance of the designated 'work' or content. In essence, the holder retains ownership of the expression and the right to exploit personally or by licensing its copying, distribution, or performance in return for the payment of a royalty or fee. Thus, for example, if you purchase a CD recording of songs, you have ownership over the tangible object (the CD), *but not of the musical content* of the CD, whose ownership remains with the copyright holder. Therefore, you are legally prohibited from multiply copying, distributing, broadcasting or performing the content without authorisation from the holder and the payment of some agreed compensation. A trademark, in contrast, is 'any sign that individualises the goods of a given enterprise and distinguishes them from the goods of its competitors' (WIPO 2001: 68). Trademarks indicate the source of the product, such that the consumer can distinguish it from the products of other manufacturers.

Words, such as slogans and company names, drawings and symbols like logos and audible signs such as music can all function as trademarks (WIPO 2001: 70). The recognised holder of a trademark enjoys proprietary rights over its use, and other parties are prohibited from using the holder's mark to (mis)identify their own products (Bently and Sherman 2001: 900–901). Patents have as their object inventions (products or process) over which the state grants the inventor rights in relation to the exploitation (e.g. manufacture and sale) of the invention. Once an invention is patented, it cannot be exploited by any party without the prior permission of the patent holder (WIPO 2001: 17). Historically, patents have been associated with tangible properties such as the chemical formulae for pharmaceutical drugs, or the design specifications of engineered objects such as electronic circuitry or mechanical components. However, in recent years patent protection has come also to cover intangible properties, especially computer software (which is also additionally afforded protection via copyright) (Stobbs 2000). Therefore, taken together, intangible or intellectual properties are created and defended through copyright, trademark and patent laws.

The 'digital revolution' brought about by networked information technologies has had profound consequences for the various different forms of intellectual expression. The ability to digitally copy, transfer or transmit the expression of ideas in the form of code has enabled the perfect reproduction of such content, without deterioration or degradation. Thus a digital copy of, say, a film, image, or sound recording is indistinguishable from the 'original' and can subsequently be copied endlessly without any loss of visual or auditory detail (Yar 2007: 97). Since the Internet is essentially a network designed to enable the effective, fast and worldwide transmission of digitised code, it has become the perfect medium through which such content can be freely circulated, copied and exchanged. Moreover, the rapidly falling costs of the equipment and services necessary to make and share such copies, such as personal computers, CD- and DVD-burners, hard disk storage, and broadband Internet access, have enabled users to share digital content at very little marginal cost (Yar 2005).

A distinctly visible expression of the new informational order that is emerging in the information age has been the dramatic rise in the overall numbers of registrations for trademarks and patents, combined with a new aggression in the application of intellectual property laws to protect both properties and also the expression of the ideas they implement. Whilst not quite yet at the level depicted in the animation series *Futurama*, where the main character Fry calls his new space snack 'Popplers' because it is one of only two names left on Earth that have not yet been trademarked,[2] the granularity of this 'intellectual land grab' (Wall 2007: 23) has become so fine that a Russian entrepreneur has sought to trademark the emoticon ;-) (BBC 2008). These and other examples illustrate how information is now routinely becoming commoditised as intellectual property, including some previously in the public domain. Not only is this practice encouraging the growth of a new political economy of information capital and new power relationships (see Boyle 1996), but the value inherent in it is also encouraging new forms of deviant behaviour to appropriate the value of informational content.

In this way, cyberspace today not only challenges our conventional understanding of ownership and control, but it is also blurring the traditional boundaries between criminal and civil activities along with some of the principles upon which our conventional understandings of criminal harm and justice are based. A good example here is a reduction in the ability of prosecutors to prove the offender's intention to permanently deprive another person of their digital informational property as would be required under s.1 of the Theft Act 1968 in the UK. Consequently, important questions remain unanswered as to what online intellectual property crimes actually are and to what extent they differ from other activities that we currently recognise as intellectual property crime. Wall (2007) argues that cybercrimes are behaviours that are mediated by networked technologies with the premise that were those technologies to be removed then the cybercrime activity would cease. Using this criteria intellectual property crime online is no different and satisfies the criteria as a cybercrime. It is, however, important to distinguish between intellectual property crimes that use the Internet and intellectual property crimes that take place in cyberspace.

Part two: 'virtual theft' – the 'stealing' of informational intangibles[3]

We can break down the types of losses that are incurred by victimisation through virtual theft. Indeed, here we encounter a primary conceptual inconsistency because as stated earlier, digital media can be reproduced exactly. In fact digital media are simulacra (Baudrillard 1994), copies without originals, rather than copies. Because the point in question here is the 'owner's' lack of exclusive control over the property, then the metaphor of piracy is probably more generally appropriate than that of theft – although the latter is commonly featured in many of the online crime narratives.

At the heart of the cyber-piracy debate is the ability of those with legitimate rights to digital intellectual properties to maintain their control over them. The problem of regulating cyber-piracy is largely one of policing its usage, because digital property, whether in written, musical, or video form, has the unique characteristic of being stored as code and, as stated earlier, being produced in its original form each time the file is run. Digital copies are identical, which creates new problems for controlling their dissemination in ways that preserve income streams. They are very different in nature to intellectual properties reproduced by analogue technology, such as vinyl records or film, which degrade in quality with each generation of copy. This characteristic emphasises the value of the original artefact, but also instils an informal policing mechanism into the process. Without adequate controls in place the value of digital property can (arguably) be lost very quickly. Consequently, running in parallel to the growth of the Internet has been an increase in the number and complexity of intellectual property laws and regulations relating to trademarks, copyright, and patents; see for example the debates over the changes in privacy and publicity laws in the USA (Boyle 1996; Madow 1993). These laws have intensified the debates over piracy. Thus, the intersection of the medium of cyberspace and more restrictive intellectual property laws became quite a potent combination, especially at a time when, as Baudrillard observes, economic activity has become the outcome rather than the cause of cultural values and norms (Baudrillard 1994, 1998). Importantly, the fact that productive ideas can now be put into place without the need for expensive mechanical manufacturing processes means that the monetary value of those ideas is further enhanced. These forms of intellectual property, trademarks, domain names and character merchandising are becoming the real estate of cyberspace – especially where the IP is linked to the architecture of the Internet (e.g. domain names). Thus the virtual terrain of cyberspace is marked by the struggle for control over this 'intellectual' real estate and its value increases in proportion to the strength of the legal and technological control that exists over its dissemination. The downside is that this control makes it all the more desirable as something to be acquired for use or to be sold on.

Intellectual property piracy follows the centuries-old practice of hijacking value by counterfeiting products (through design piracy) and making copies of the original and then passing them off as originals. The trademark originally emerged as a trusted sign to counter piracy by indicating to the purchaser that the product is genuine and produced by quality manufacturers (see Sherman and Bently 1999). However, in the age of mass consumption the trademark itself has acquired its own status and value, independent of the quality of work – especially when linked to brands. For goods carrying trademarks, the Internet has become a natural marketplace,[4] especially following the popularity of e-commerce and Internet auctions such as eBay. These sites became a natural forum for selling counterfeit branded hard goods, such as watches and designer clothes and accessories, and also counterfeit branded *soft* goods that have been copied and packaged, or made available to download, and they still are, despite judicious policing efforts. Thus it is unsurprising that one of the most commonly reported forms of misrepresentation on Internet auction sites takes the form of selling counterfeit goods which are advertised as authentic items. There is a growing body of evidence that auction sites are extensively used for trading counterfeit DVDs, CDs, and computer software packages, as well as counterfeit clothing, perfumes and other items (Enos 2000; MPAA 2003: 3).

In many ways, these examples follow the *mens rea* (guilty mind – intent) and *actus reus* (guilty act) of traditional piracy and the primary concern of victims, the intellectual property right holders, is to restore any income lost by piracy that would otherwise have been enjoyed had the goods or services been purchased legitimately. However, other new forms of counterfeiting are emerging solely within the confines of cyberspace that require a further examination. Take, for example, a situation where pictures of a famous pop star are appropriated from (usually official) Internet sites, or scanned from physical sources, or digitally created by 'morphing' different images together. The pictures are then packaged in a glossy, professional format with some additional explanatory text, and then sold through some form of cyber-shopping mall or topic-specific social networking sites typically to young customers who purchase them in good faith. To frustrate detection, the site may be on a server in the USA and the proceeds paid into a bank account halfway round the planet. The whole operation might take as little as a few days, and by the time the deception has been detected, the proceeds of the scam have been removed from the bank account and the perpetrators gone. Alternatively the images may be traded online for other similar pirated informational products. Such piracy does not stop with images, it could just as easily be software, music or video as the later discussion outlines.

The appropriation of informational property may be motivated by libertarian (see Akdeniz 1997)[5] artistic, moral, even educational reasons and not simply by the prospect of financial gain. See, for example, the three culturally different, yet significant, examples of the protection of popular iconography through the WWW with regard to Elvis Presley (imagery), the Tellytubbies (trademark) and the pop group Oasis (copyright) in Wall (2004, 2007: 98) and more latterly the ferocity of the anti-MP3 and MP4 (copyright) anti-piracy campaigns. Although not explored in detail here, these and many more examples nevertheless demonstrate the gravity that owners of intellectual property rights attach to threats to their interests. They also illustrate the new dilemmas that intellectual property right holders face with regard to the paradox of circulation and restriction in an environment of participatory consumption, which requires them to carefully balance their need to restrict the unauthorised circulation of their informational property to maintain income streams, while also allowing enough circulation of the properties to allow the market to consume it as culture in the broadest sense and enabling it to reach new markets (Wall 2004: 35).

Informational piracy differs from traditional intellectual infringement because it blurs the boundaries between criminal and civil actions. It is where owners' intellectual property rights in images, trademarks, copyrighted texts or general character merchandising are threatened by theft or release into the public domain of the Internet. The threat is not just the loss of income streams, but also of the 'dilution' of a 'property's' value. Dilution is a term used in intellectual property law to describe the reduction in value through unrestricted use, but is also a key part of the argument used to justify legal sanctions against infringers. The additional problem for intellectual property rights holders and for law is that the Internet also facilitates new types of participatory consumption and development of informational properties. Indeed the 'wikinomics' of the digital economy, as it has been named (Tapscott and Williams 2007) actively requires the release of some aspects of intellectual property into the public domain so that participants can contribute to it. We return to this discussion later, but the remainder of this section will focus upon specific areas of intellectual property piracy: music, video and software and the theft of virtual artefacts.

Intellectual property piracy (music and video)

Music: If P2P software transformed information sharing, then the invention of MP3 and MP4 file formats have respectively transformed the distribution of music and video. In the case of the former, as long as the appropriate P2P software is available, then the music files can be downloaded to a computer's sound system, a portable MP3 player, or directly onto a CD-Rom or Mini-disc. The recording of music in a computer-readable format was previously possible; however MP3 compression techniques reduced the files to manageable or transferable sizes. Consequently, devices from the early Rio Diamond MP3 player through to the more recent generation of iPods have been specifically designed to play MP3 files. Opinions on the morality and legality of MP3 are divided. On the one hand the record companies and a few rock bands argue that the distribution of unauthorised MP3s is causing the death of popular music by giving away hard-earned and expensive properties and denying the authors the rewards that they deserve. On the other hand, a strong counter argument is emerging that questions the claims of the music industry. A report by the Australian Institute of Criminology argued that the music industry cannot 'explain how it arrives at its statistics for staggering losses through piracy' (Greene 2006). Evidence is also beginning to suggest that illicit MP3 downloads are in fact helping to promote music culture and also expand the capacity of the market. Not only can individual musicians now obtain immediate exposure to a much broader section of the public without having to become contracted to record companies, but MP3 has arguably broadly stimulated the market for old as well as new popular music. Even CD sales, it is alleged, are going up and not down. Oberholzer-Gee and Strumpf disproved the industry claims in their 2004 research into the impact of downloads on physical CD sales with the observation that 'downloads have an effect on sales which is statistically indistinguishable from zero' (Gibson 2005; Potier 2004; Schwartz 2004). Furthermore, this claim is strengthened by the commercial success of recently introduced, and authorised, pay-to-use MP3 sites, such as iTunes, e-music and others, and, of course, the popularity of new MP3 playing hardware devices, such as the iPod. Further evidence of this trend is found in empirical research conducted in 2005 by Leading Question, which found that online file sharers actually buy more music, up to four and a half times more in legal downloads (Gibson 2005; Leading Question 2005).

The counterclaims described earlier illustrate the dynamics of a power play in which the recording industry's highly publicised private legal actions have been framed within a crime discourse to tame the MP3 download market. As soon as the technology of MP3 began to gain popularity, legal actions were launched by the Recording Industry Association of America (RIAA) and British Phonographic Industry (BPI) on behalf of the music industry. They invoked copyright laws and brought lawsuits against MP3 bulk uploaders. Perhaps uniquely, the 16,000 or more cases were mostly brought against individuals, but few have actually gone to court, with the greater majority being settled privately (Vance 2005). Accompanying these cases was a publicity campaign that simultaneously warned the public of the damage to the industry and also to society by suggesting that the proceeds of piracy supported organised crime. The impact of the actions and publicity has been to create the illusion of certainty of prosecution and to exercise a broad chilling effect upon illegal downloading behaviour.

Video (Film and Television): MP4, or MPEG-4, is a computer file compression format that, like MP3 with music, allows video, audio and other information to be stored efficiently on one file. Within a P2P network MP4 files have transformed the dissemination of video, film and televisual materials. Newly released films can, for example, be illicitly videoed in cinemas and then converted into MP4 files; as can television programmes. Similarly, DVDs can be ripped into MP4 files. All can be sold, or traded through illegal 'film portals' or across P2P networks. DVD manufacturers initially protected their products with a security device, however this was broken by a descrambling program, DeCSS, written by Jon Lech Johansen (also known as 'DVD Jon') so that he could watch his own DVDs on his Linux-powered PC. He also posted details of his descrambler on the Internet that led to him being prosecuted 'largely on the behest of the Motion Picture Association of America (MPAA)' (Leyden 2003). The case for the prosecution argued that by sharing his DeCSS descrambler with others over the Internet, Johansen made it easier to pirate DVDs and therefore acted illegally. The case was thrown out by the Norwegian court on the grounds that the DVD scrambling codes had prevented Johansen from using his Linux PC to play back the DVDs he'd bought (Cullen 2004: *Public prosecutor v Jon Lech Johansen* 2003).

The failure to convict Johansen did not prevent the MPAA from continuing to protect its interests. From 2004 onwards, legal actions have been brought against file sharers, particularly the film indexing sites and television download sites (BBC 2005c). The latter action was significant because of the increased use of the Internet as the broadcasting medium for television and the blurring of the boundaries between the two: 'as TV-quality video online becomes a norm' (BBC 2005a). Like the MP3 cases, the MPAA's actions were framed within an even stronger crime discourse that was driven by anti-piracy advertisements showing at the cinema and also on DVDs and containing very vivid crime imagery alleging that piracy supported organised crime and terrorism. Also, as with the cases against individual music file sharers, most of the MP4 cases appear to have been settled privately. The actions and crime discourse have, as with MP3, created a chilling effect on downloading behaviour and evidence of a decreasing volume of downloads is an indication of this trend, although it is an area that requires further research. Initially, these P2P related actions against individual infringers took place alongside legal actions brought against film websites that pose as legitimate film and music download services (BBC 2005g). The current practice is to focus prosecutions upon the latter.

Intellectual property piracy (software)

The final aspect of IP piracy that currently excites major concerns within cybercrime debates is the illegal distribution of software over the Internet. Illicit software was initially distributed though BBS bulletin boards and later across P2P file sharing networks such as 'Drink or Die' (BBC 2005b; USDOJ 2002). The distribution operations were either for profit or for trading (though not necessarily for profit), or to fulfil a broader ethic of helping the Internet community. The latter function is often referred to as Warez, which is a leetspeak (eg. uses non-alphabetical numbers that resemble syllables or sounds in words) derivative of (soft)wares, but also tends to signify copyrighted software that has been illegally offered for trade, but usually not for profit.[6] The computer software industry claims large financial losses to such violations. Global losses were pinned at $13.08 billion for 2002 (BSA 2003: 3). Eastern-Central Europe is deemed to have the highest 'piracy' rate, where 71 per cent of all software is claimed to be an illegal copy; however, rates are also high for North America (24 per cent) and Western Europe (35 per cent) (BSA 2003: 2). Whilst the figures are high, the methodologies used to calculate the losses typically tend to rely upon estimations based upon the generalisation of limited statistics produced by a business victimisation survey.

The theft of virtual artefacts

An emerging problem is the unauthorised appropriation of virtual artefacts that are the product of intellectual labours and which have been created in virtual environments. For many years, for example, the trade in 'game cheats' has been a long-standing practice. Cheats are virtual artefacts that enable players to map their way through computer games more quickly or gain access to hidden spaces within them. Some cheats exploit flaws in gaming programs, while others are strategically placed there by the games-makers in order to sustain players' interest in the game. The problem with 'cheats' is to be able to identify those that are illicit and those that are the legitimate product of game designers. Perhaps the most infamous 'cheat' in recent years has been the software called 'Hot Coffee' which unlocked secret sex scenes in *Grand Theft Auto: San Andreas* (BBC 2005c). Because of these additional scenes, the rating of the game was subsequently changed to 'Adult', which along with the additional publicity attracted by litigation helped to ensure that the game became one of the most popular of all time. Interestingly, there is also a growing online market in the sale or trade of other 'cheat' type activities outside the gaming world, such as assignments by students (plagiarism) on auction sites and P2P networks.

An interesting development in computer gaming has been the increased criminal exploitation of gaming artefacts that have strategic importance in online role play gaming, for example in Project Entropia.[7] Players need to obtain artefacts that sustain their place in their games and help them progress through it. The artefacts are therefore highly desired because they represent not only high levels of ability and power, but also the hours of labour put into their construction. Because of this, players are willing to pay large amounts of real money for them. In 2004, a virtual island was sold on eBay for $26,500 (£13,700) and in 2005 a virtual space station went for $100,000 (£56,200) (BBC 2005f). The space station was to be used as a virtual nightclub to which users paid entry for access and while inside were exposed to real-time advertising as in a real nightclub.

Consequently, the high values of these artefacts have generated a string of new criminal opportunities. Already there have been examples of buyers being defrauded through e-auction sales, artefacts being stolen, by hacking, from players' accounts, and even an 'online mugging' where a Japanese student was subsequently arrested for using automated bots in a 'first person shooter' game to make his avatar move faster than other players and shoot with pinpoint accuracy, thus attacking fellow players and stealing items (BBC 2005e). Police in Korea, Taiwan and also Japan, countries where computer gaming is massively popular, have in recent years had to respond to requests from gamers to investigate the theft of their 'magic swords' – items obtained in computer gaming environments through intense labour.[8]

The challenges that these forms of offending pose for criminal justice systems are considerable, not least because the victims can point to real economic harms done to them through the illegal usage, or sale, of their 'virtual currency'. At the forefront is the question over how best to legally represent the loss in the victims' interests. In their discussion of virtual property crimes, Lastowka and Hunter (2005: 300) argue that the analogy of theft is inappropriate because it implies the destruction of existing value. They favour instead, the language of offences such as 'counterfeiting', which takes into consideration the fact that the 'criminals' are actually creating illegitimate value (Lastowka and Hunter 2005: 315).

Part three: broader issues that are emerging in the debate over intellectual property online

The emergence of intellectual property violations as forms of criminal behaviour must be placed in the context of wider legal, political, economic and social processes, since it is in these spheres of action that the definition of what counts as or constitutes crime ultimately emerges. Below we shall discuss relevant developments in the areas of (1) intellectual property law; (2) policing; and (3) the cultural rhetoric of anti-piracy discourse.

One of the most significant legal developments in recent years has been the incremental criminalisation of intellectual property offences. In the past, violations (such as those related to copyright) have been largely tackled through a range of *civil* remedies available to copyright holders – such as injunctions, 'delivery up' or destruction of infringing articles, and the payment of damages (Bently and Sherman 2001: 1008–23). Even where the law made provision for criminal prosecution of IP violations, there tended to be few such actions – for example, between 1970 and 1980 there were less than 20 prosecutions for copyright offences in the UK (Sodipo 1997: 228). This may be attributed to a number of factors, including the relatively low priority accorded to intellectual property crimes by overstretched and under-resourced criminal justice agencies; the public concern and political emphasis on more visibly 'harmful' offences, such as 'street crimes' and violent crime; difficulties in policing and intelligence gathering; and the reluctance of public prosecutors to involve themselves in a notoriously complex and specialised domain of law. However, recent years have seen moves to redress such copyright violations, bringing them increasingly under the sway of criminal sanctions. This has taken three main forms.

Increased willingness to use existing criminal sanctions against 'pirates'

There has been increased willingness to use existing criminal sanctions against 'pirates', encouraged both by greater political sensitivity to IP rights and their economic importance, and by concerted application of pressure through lobbying by the copyright industry. One key means in achieving this has been the formation of industry organisations (such as the Alliance Against Counterfeiting and Piracy (AACP) and the Federation Against Copyright Theft (FACT) in the UK) that conduct investigations and gather information on 'piracy' activities, and lay complaints before public prosecuting authorities (Bently and Sherman 2001: 1030–31; Sodipo 1997: 229). Recent years have seen a number of high-profile piracy cases in which such procedures have led to criminal convictions carrying substantial custodial sentences – for example, in 2002 a FACT investigation led to a four-year prison sentence for the convicted 'pirate' (Carugati 2003). The overall number of criminal prosecutions for copyright violations has also increased massively – in 2000 alone, there were over 500 such cases in the area of music (CD) counterfeiting alone (Home Office 2002: 2)

Incorporating additional provisions for criminal sanctions into national laws and international treaties

In recent years there has taken place the incorporation of additional provisions for criminal sanctions into both international treaties and national laws. At the national level, we can note for example Section 107 of the Copyright, Designs and Patents Act (1988) in the UK, which places local administrative authorities (such as Trading Standards departments) under a duty to enforce criminal copyright provisions, and significantly strengthens the penalties available in comparison to the previously existing Copyright Act of 1956 (Bently and Sherman 2001: 1031; Dworkin and Taylor 1989: 121–122). In the US, the No Electronic Theft Act (1988) makes provision for up to three years imprisonment for convicted 'pirates'; it also extends the applicability of sanctions beyond those engaging in piracy for commercial gain, to include for example the not-for-profit digital trading engaged in by file-sharers (Drahos and Braithwaite 2002: 185). At an international level, Article 61 of the 1994 TRIPS (Trade-Related Aspects of Intellectual Property Rights) agreement establishes a *mandatory* requirement for signatories to make criminal provisions against commercial copyright violations. Hence the extensions of available criminal sanctions and the greater willingness to pursue them have, taken together, significantly reconfigured piracy, rendering it more grave in an attempt to stem its growth.

Already noted has been the recent increase in policing and enforcement activity, in which industry organisations are playing a leading role. It is also worth noting here the proliferation of industry-financed 'anti-piracy' organisations whose *raison d'être* combines research, intelligence gathering, policing, education and lobbying activities. The past two decades has seen the creation of the Counterfeiting Intelligence Bureau, the International Intellectual Property Alliance, the International Anti-Counterfeiting Coalition, the Alliance Against Counterfeiting and Piracy, the Coalition for Intellectual

Property Rights, the Artists Coalition Against Piracy, the aforementioned AACP and FACT, as well as numerous existing trade organisations that have established specialist groups and initiatives to combat film piracy (such as the Motion Picture Association of America (MPAA) and the Recording Industry Association of America (RIAA)). Such organisations purport to 'lift the burden of investigation from law enforcement agencies' (AACP 2002: 2) by engaging in a range of increasingly intensive policing activities. Where public agencies have been reluctant to invest time and resources in tackling IP violations, industrial and commercial interests have 'filled the void'. In addition to intelligence gathering and undercover operations, they have attempted to bring intellectual property crime into the criminal justice mainstream through, for example, the appointment of specialist liaison personnel to 'assist' and 'advise' responsible agencies in the detection and prosecution of 'copyright theft'. Governments have themselves responded to concerted pressure from these groups by establishing intellectual property strategies and specialist units within criminal justice agencies to address intellectual property violations. The UK, for example, has the local trading standards organisations which operate at a local level and the e-crime unit of SOCA, the Serious and Organised Crimes Agency (formerly the National High-Tech Crime Unit), investigates serious national infringements. In the USA there is the FBI's Internet Fraud Complaint Centre (IFCC), which also takes on a responsibility for policing some intellectual property crimes. At an international level, Interpol has established an Intellectual Property Crimes Unit (2002) and there are concerted efforts at the EU level to strengthen EUROPOL's powers of enforcement in the area of intellectual property.

The development and implementation of 'anti-piracy education' campaigns

Recent 'anti-piracy education' campaigns involving both copyright industries and public agencies have given particular focus to young people because of their apparently disproportionate involvement in illegal Internet downloading, copying and distribution of copyrighted materials. Recent years have seen numerous 'educational' programmes produced by umbrella organisations that represent various sectors of the copyright industries – software, music and/ or motion pictures. Such programmes typically provide a range of materials, exercises and gaming activities that are intended for use in the classroom, thereby incorporating anti-piracy into the school curriculum. Programmes typically target younger children between the ages of eight and 13. For example, there is the FA©E (Friends of Active Copyright Education) initiative of the Copyright Society of America – their child-oriented program is called 'Copyright Kids'. Also notable is the SIAA's (Software & Information Industry Association) 'Cybersmart! School Program'. A third is the BSA's (Business Software Alliance) 'Play It Cybersafe' program featuring the cartoon character Garret the Ferret, aka 'The Copyright Crusader'. A fourth campaign is produced by the Government of Western Australia's Department of Education and Training, and is called 'Ippy's Big Idea'. A fifth campaign is the MPAA's 'Starving Artist' schools' roadshow. This is a role-playing game designed for schoolchildren, which was taken 'on tour' in 2003 in 36,000 classrooms across the US. The game invites students 'to come up with an idea for a record album, cover art, and lyrics' (Menta 2003). Having completed the exercise, the students are told that their album is already available for download from the Internet, and are asked 'how they felt when they realised that their work was stolen and that they would not get anything for their efforts' (Menta 2003). All such campaigns attempt to create a moral consensus that unauthorised copying is a form of theft and, as such, is as immoral as stealing someone else's material possessions; moreover, they also target the children's parents in an attempt to warn them of the possible legal repercussions if their children are caught engaging in piracy.

All of the foregoing developments have served to progressively shift intellectual property offences into the space of criminal conduct. However, as Becker (1963) notes, it is by no means given that those targeted with stigmatising labels of criminality and deviance will automatically accept such labels. Rather, they may resist such efforts, seeking to deflect the label by defending their activities against those who seek to position them as 'outsiders'. Such reactions may be considered as instances of what Sykes and Matza (1957) call 'techniques of neutralisation'. These techniques serve as vocabularies of justification by which the potential 'deviants' deflect negative labels, turning accusations of moral delinquency back upon their accusers. Prime among these techniques are those of the 'denial of harm' (the assertion that no real social damage is caused by the behaviour in question) and 'denial of the deniers' (the assertion that those who mount accusations are themselves corrupt, immoral or otherwise hypocritical). Moments of reaction-resistance have clearly emerged in response to moral entrepreneurs' constructions of Internet piracy as a form of criminality. Music fans, committed to the free circulation and appreciation of popular culture, have established websites where such rhetorical defences are mounted. For example, the activists of BOYCOTTRIAA.com stated in 2005 that:

> Boycott-RIAA was founded because we love music. We cannot stand by silently while the recording industry continues its decades-long effort to lock up our culture and heritage by misrepresenting the facts to the public, to artists, the fans and to our government.

Through such responses, acts of copying and culture sharing are defended as principled stands against corporate interests who are charged with being the true 'villains' in the unfolding confrontation between producers and fans. However, the lines of division within this battle to define criminality are further complicated by the indeterminate role played by recording artists themselves. On the one hand, artists have played a pivotal role in the entrepreneurship that has sought to define Internet copying as harmful and socially unacceptable. For example, the famous controversy over Napster's online music file-sharing service first hit the headlines as a result of legal action taken by the band Metallica (Marshall 2002: 9). Other prominent anti-Napster performers included Madonna and Mick Jagger. In contrast, other artists have made common cause with file-sharers, choosing instead to direct their criticisms against the recording companies rather that the fans. In 2000, rock musician Courtney Love (singer with Hole and widow of rock icon Kurt Cobain) launched what has been dubbed the 'Love Manifesto', a critical reflection on intellectual property theft, artists and the recording industry. Love began her 'Manifesto' thus:

> Today I want to talk about piracy and music. What is piracy? Piracy is the act of stealing an artist's work without any intention of paying for it. I'm not talking about Napster-type software ... I'm talking about major label recording contracts. (Love 2000)

She went on to claim that standard practice within the recording industry deprives musicians of copyrights, and the monies advanced to artists are largely recouped from them by the industry under 'expenses' for recording and promotion. As a consequence, the musicians see little return from their efforts and, she opined, 'the band may as well be working at a 7-Eleven' (Love 2000). In fact, it has been argued that piracy is in the financial interests of most recording artists; most performers make their living from concert performance, and this is best supported and promoted by having their music circulated as widely as possible, including via copying. As musician Ignacio Escolar has put it: 'Like all musicians, I know that 100,000 pirate fans coming to my shows are more profitable than 10,000 original ones' (Escolar 2003: 15).

The need to revise intellectual property regimes and reverse the decriminalisation of IP piracy

What the previous discussion indicates is a process by which intellectual property piracy is increasingly becoming framed by crime debates without any clear evidence that this process will solve the problem. This suggests that the perceived problem – the nature of the piracy – may actually require some critical revision. An emerging and very real problem for intellectual property rights holders and also for law and its related regulations is the very real shift that is now taking place in the ways that intellectual properties are being consumed in the information age. At the level of computer programming, we have already seen the 'open source' movement make major contributions to the development of powerful operating systems such as Linux. The main principle behind the open source movement is that core computer code is freely circulated so that individuals can perfect or develop it themselves and then recirculate for the benefit of others. In this way, the group effort makes the object of everyone's labours stronger and also much more powerful than one individual could possibly manage. At the broader level of the general consumer we are also witnessing significant new types of participatory consumption (prosumption). Sophisticated new software ranging from blogging technology, through to image manipulators, through to recording and publishing software have enabled consumers of information, music, text, images (moving and still) to create their own 'mash ups'. In other words, software is enabling consumers to combine together the different parts of different intellectual properties that they particularly enjoy to create something entirely new that they consume themselves and also share with others.

In both of the examples illustrated above, the consumers also become producers or 'prosumers'. Not only does this cause them to fall foul of conventional IP laws, especially in the second example, but they are also increasingly demanding recognition of, and rights to, their contributions to the intellectual properties that they have enhanced. This 'wikinomics' of the digital economy (Tapscott and Williams 2007) actively requires entirely new ways of thinking with regard to intellectual properties. Not least, the release of some aspects of intellectual property into the public domain so that participants can contribute to it. This process is counter-intuitive to conventional practices; however, Tapscott and Williams argue that allowing participatory consumption has considerable value to IP rights owners and, furthermore, it does not necessarily require core intellectual property to be released, only that which enables participatory consumption. Plus mechanisms could be created – depending upon the characteristics of the intellectual property in question – that would allow prosumers to gain recognition and even income from their contributions. Importantly, such a revision of conventional approaches to IP would also halt the increasing criminalisation process to the benefit of all.

Conclusions

This chapter has illustrated how inventive, reflexive and responsive computer-assisted or mediated crime can be and also how close it sits to legitimate business opportunities. It also shows how the virtual bank robbery, the virtual sting and virtual theft are areas of harmful/criminal activity that are rapidly evolving along with technological developments. As they evolve they create new challenges for law enforcement. For example, in the UK, machines cannot be deceived, only the people who use them; data cannot be stolen; fraud and deception are yet to be fully established as specific crimes and trade secret theft is still not an offence in the UK – only the way that the information was obtained. But is law the most effective local solution to what has become a global problem? The example of MP3 and MP4 file-sharing is a graphic illustration of where private corporate interests compete with the public interest and capture the crime agenda.

The bulk of the chapter has focused upon fraudulent behaviour driven by the desire for economic or informational gain. This profile will gradually broaden as new opportunities for offending are created by the convergence of networked technologies of the home, work, leisure, with those managing identity and location. Importantly, this new world of convergence will be characterised more and more by information brokering, thus 'information capital' will become increasingly more valuable. As a consequence, we shall probably see a further rise in the extent and breadth of information theft. Future computer-assisted crime debates will therefore focus increasingly upon the rights relating to the protection of information and also the restoration of information and reputation once compromised.

Notes

1 This chapter deals with concepts of, and different types of, intellectual property and issues relating to the Internet, rather than specifically focusing upon intellectual property law. Each jurisdiction has its own intellectual property laws.
2 'The Problem with Popplers', episode 15, season 2 *Futurama* (originally aired 7 May 2000).
3 This section is drawn from Wall (2007): 94–101.
4 Quick Reference Sheet of Felony Charges to Consider and Relevant Issues to Consider in Typical Intellectual Property Cases <http://www.usdoj.gov/criminal/cybercrime/ipmanual/chart.htm>
5 Akdeniz describes the case of the Jet Report which was released into the public domain on ethical grounds.
6 'Among warez users, there is often a distinction made between "gamez" (games), "appz" (applications), "crackz" (cracked applications), and "vidz" (movies).' Wilkipedia <http://en.wikipedia.org/wiki/Warez>
7 Project-entropia.com
8 Interview with Korean Police Chiefs by David Wall, October 2008.

Further reading

For further discussion of intellectual property crimes online, see Majid Yar, *Cybercrime and Society* (2006) and David S. Wall, *Cybercrime* (2007). On movie piracy, see Majid Yar, 'The Global "Epidemic" of Movie "Piracy": Crime-Wave or Social Construction?', *Media, Culture and Society* (2005) 27(5); on the criminalisation of music piracy see Majid Yar, 'Teenage Kicks or Virtual Villainy? Internet Piracy, Moral Entrepreneurship, and the Social Construction of a Crime Problem', (in Y. Jewkes (ed.), *Crime Online* (Willan Publishing, 2007); and 'The Rhetorics and Myths of "Anti-Piracy" Campaigns: Criminalisation, Moral Pedagogy and Capitalist Property Relations in the Classroom', *New Media and Society* (2008), 10(4).

References

AACP (2002) *Proving the Connection: links between intellectual property theft and organised crime*. London: Alliance Against Counterfeiting and Piracy.
Akdeniz, Y. (1997) 'The regulation of pornography and child pornography on the internet', *Journal of Information Law and Technology*, 1, at www2.warwick.ac.uk/fac/soc/law/elj/jilt/1997_1/akdeniz1/
Baudrillard, J. (1994) *Simulacra and Simulation*. Ann Arbor: University of Michigan Press.
Baudrillard, J. (1998) *The Consumer Society: Myths and Structures*. London: Sage.
BBC (2005a) 'Net regulation "still possible"', *BBC News Online*, 27 January, at http://news.bbc.co.uk/1/hi/technology/4211415.stm
BBC (2005b) 'Internet piracy pair facing jail', *BBC News Online*, 6 May, at http://news.bbc.co.uk/1/hi/technology/4518771.stm
BBC (2005c) 'TV download sites hit by lawsuits', *BBC News Online*, 13 May, at http://news.bbc.co.uk/1/hi/technology/4545519.stm
BBC (2005d) 'No more "Hot Coffee" sex for GTA', *BBC News Online*, 11 August, at http://news.bbc.co.uk/1/hi/technology/4142184.stm

BBC (2005e) 'Student held over online mugging', *BBC News Online*, 20 August, at http://news.bbc.co.uk/1/hi/technology/4165880.stm

BBC (2005f) 'Virtual club to rock pop culture', *BBC News Online*, 2 November, at http://news.bbc.co.uk/1/hi/technology/4385048.stm

BBC (2005g) 'Hollywood pursues fake film sites', *BBC News Online*, 14 October, at http://news.bbc.co.uk/1/hi/technology/4342910.stm

BBC (2008) 'Russian hopes to cash in on ;-)', *BBC News Online*, 11 December, http://news.bbc.co.uk/2/hi/europe/7778767.stm

Becker, H. (1963) *Outsiders: Studies in the Sociology of Deviance*. New York: Free Press.

Bently, L. and Sherman, B. (2001) *Intellectual Property Law*. Oxford: Oxford University Press.

Boyle, J. (1996) *Shamans, Software and Spleens:Law and the Construction of the Information Society*. Cambridge, MA: Harvard University Press.

BSA (2003) 'Eighth Annual BSA Global Software Piracy Study', *Business Software Alliance* at http://www.bsaa.com.au/downloads/BSA_Piracy_Booklet.pdf

Carugati, A. (2003) Interview with MPAA President Jack Valenti, *Worldscreen*, at http://worldscreen.com/interviewscurrent.php?filename =203valenti.txt

Cullen, D. (2004) 'Norway throws in the towel in DVD Jon case', *The Register*, 5 January, at www.theregister.co.uk/content/6/34706.html

Drahos, P. and Braithwaite, J. (2002) *Information Feudalism: Who Owns the Knowledge Economy?* London: Earthscan

Dworkin, G. and Taylor, R.D. (1989) *Blackstone's Guide to the Copyright, Designs and Patents Act 1988*. London: Blackstone Press.

Enos, L. (2000) 'Yahoo! Sued for Auctioning Counterfeit Goods', *Ecommerce Times*, 29 March, at http://www.ecommercetimes.com/story/2849.html

Escolar, I. (2003) 'Please pirate my songs!', in WSIS, *World Information: Knowledge of Future Culture*. Vienna: Institut für Neue Kulturtechnologien.

Gibson, O. (2005) 'Online file sharers "buy more music" ', *Guardian Online*, 27 July, at www.guardian.co.uk/arts/news/story/0,11711,1536886,00.html

Greene, T. (2006) 'Piracy losses fabricated – Aussie study', *The Register*, 9 November, at www.theregister.co.uk/2006/11/09/my_study_beats_your_study/

Home Office (2002) 'Chipping of Goods Initiative', press release 24 May 2002, *Home Office*, at http://www.homeoffice.gov.uk/docs/pressnotice3.doc

Lastowka, G. and Hunter, D. (2005) 'Virtual crime', *New York Law School Law Review*, 49(1): 293–316.

Leading Question (2005) 'Music pirates spend four-and-a-half times more on legitimate music downloads than average fans', *The Leading Question*, 27 July, at www.musically.com/theleadingquestion/files/theleadingquestion_piracy.doc.

Leyden, J. (2003) 'DVD Jon is free – official', *The Register*, 7 January, at www.theregister.co.uk/2003/01/07/dvd_jon_is_free_official/.

Love, C. (2000) 'Love Manifesto', online at http://www.reznor.com/commentary/loves–manifesto1.html

Madow, M. (1993) 'Private ownership of public image: popular culture and publicity rights', *California Law Review*, 81: 125–240.

Marshall, L. (2002) 'Metallica and morality: the rhetorical battleground of the Napster wars', *Entertainment Law*, 1(1): 1–19.

Menta, R. (2003) 'Let's play starving artist', at http://www.mp3newswire.net/stories/2003/starvingartist.html

MPAA (2003b) '2003 Piracy Fact Sheets: US Overview', *Motion Picture Association of America*, at http://www.mpaa.org

Potier, B. (2004) 'File sharing may boost CD sales: study defies traditional beliefs about Internet use', *Harvard University Gazette*, 15 April, at www.news.harvard.edu/gazette/2004/04.15/09-filesharing.html.

Public Prosecutor v. Jon Lech Johansen (2003) Case No. 02-507 M/94, Oslo Court House, 7 January, at www.eff.org/IP/Video/Johansen_DeCSS_case/20030109_johansen_english_decision.rtf

Schwartz, J. (2004) 'A heretical view of file sharing', *New York Times*, 5 April, at www.umsl.edu/~sauter/DSS/05music.html

Sherman, B. and Bently, L. (1999) *The Making of Modern Intellectual Property Law*. Cambridge: Cambridge University Press.

Sodipo, B. (1997) *Piracy and Counterfeiting: GATT TRIPS and Developing Countries*. London: Kluwer.

Stobbs, G.A. (2000) *Software Patents* (2nd edn). New York: Aspen.

Sykes, G. and Matza, D. (1957) 'Techniques of neutralization: a theory of delinquency', *American Sociological Review*, 22: 664–70.

Tapscott, D. and Williams, A. (2007) *Wikinomics: How mass collaboration changes everything*. London: Atlantic Books.

USDOJ (2002) 'Warez leader sentenced to 46 months', *US Department of Justice press release*, 17 May, at www.cybercrime.gov/sankusSent.htm

Vance, A. (2005) 'Music sales slide despite RIAA's crushing blows against piracy', *The Register*, 31 December, at www.theregister.co.uk/2005/12/31/riaa_2005_piracy/

Wall, D. S. (2004) 'Policing Elvis: legal action and the shaping of post-mortem celebrity culture as contested space', *Entertainment Law*, 2(3): 35–69.

Wall, D.S. (2007) *Cybercrime: The transformation of crime in the information age*. Cambridge: Polity.

WIPO (2001) *WIPO Intellectual Property Handbook: Policy, Law and Use*, WIPO (World Intellectual Property Organization) publication no. 489(E). Geneva: WIPO.

Yar, M. (2005) 'The Global "Epidemic" of Movie "Piracy": Crime-Wave or Social Construction?', *Media, Culture and Society*, 27(5): 677–96.

Yar, M. (2006) *Cybercrime and Society*. London: Sage.

Yar, M. (2007) 'Teenage kicks or virtual villainy? Internet piracy, moral entrepreneurship, and the social construction of a crime problem', in in Y. Jewkes (ed.), *Crime Online*. Cullompton: Willan Publishing.

Chapter 14

Identity theft and fraud

Russell G. Smith

Introduction

This chapter[1] addresses what is, arguably, one of the most pressing financial crime problems that has faced developed societies in recent years – namely the commission of crime through the creation and use of misleading and deceptive identities. Although by no means a new phenomenon, identity-related crime has been greatly facilitated with the advent of information and communications technologies that have provided a rich source of personal information to steal, and technologies with which to fabricate documentary evidence of identity. The genie is certainly 'out of the bottle' and remedying the problem has proved a challenge for businesses, governments and individuals alike.

At the outset, the confusing taxonomy associated with identity-related crime needs to be understood and rationalised. Arguably, the concept of identity-related crime is as diffuse and unhelpful as that of 'white-collar crime'. Hopefully the criminological community will be able to avoid decades of debate similar to that which accompanied attempts to define the concept of white-collar crime (see Geis 1991). Identity-related crime, like white-collar crime, is, to use the words of Weisburd, Wheeler and Waring (1991: 3), 'a social rather than a legal concept, one invented not by lawyers but by social scientists'. Identity-related crime is a compound concept used to refer to a range of methods used to commit specific forms of deception and fraud. The creation and misuse of identification evidence lies at the heart of the concept, but the crimes involved invariably entail fraud or obtaining a financial advantage by deception – rather than crimes that proscribe the misuse of personal information itself. Traditionally, identity thieves were usually charged with counterfeiting, obtaining unauthorised access to a computer, or opening a bank account in a false name, rather than making use of another person's name or other personal information without their permission. This is beginning to change in recent years as new and specific offences of identity-related crime are being enacted in a range of countries. These tend to proscribe

273

the creation, use, supply or possession of so-called identification information with intent that it be used in the commission of a serious criminal offence (see Standing Committee of Attorneys-General 2008).

A variety of terms have been used in connection with the misappropriation of personal information. These include: identity crime, identity theft, identity fraud, identity fabrication, identity manipulation, lent identities, and various other identity-related concepts. In 2006, in Australia, this proliferation of terms led the Australasian Centre for Policing Research and the Australian Transaction Reports and Analysis Centre's Proof of Identity Steering Committee to develop a set of standard definitions for use by law enforcement throughout Australia. It was recommended that the following definitions be adopted:

> The term *Identity* encompass the identity of natural persons (living or deceased) and the identity of bodies corporate;
> *Identity Fabrication* be used to describe the creation of a fictitious identity;
> *Identity Manipulation* be used to describe the alteration of one's own identity;
> *Identity Theft* be used to describe the theft or assumption of a pre-existing identity (or significant part thereof), with or without consent, and, whether, in the case of an individual, the person is living or deceased;
> *Identity Fraud* be used to describe the gaining of money, goods, services, other benefits or the avoidance of obligations through the use of a fabricated identity; a manipulated identity; or a stolen/assumed identity; and
> *Identity crime* be used as a generic term to describe activities/offences in which a perpetrator uses a fabricated identity; a manipulated identity; or a stolen/assumed identity to facilitate the commission of a crime(s). (Australasian Centre for Policing Research and Australian Transaction Reports and Analysis Centre 2006: 15)

To these may be added the concept of *Lent Identities* in which individuals are complicit in the misuse of their personal identification information, usually for some financial reward. In addition, there are a number of other terms and concepts relevant to the ways in which identity crimes may be committed including *Skimming*, in which data are extracted from the magnetic stripe on credit cards, *Cloning* in which the data on plastic cards are copied, and *Phishing* in which Internet sites are copied in order to trick unsuspecting users into disclosing personal information. These and other terms used to describe the methods of identity crime will be discussed in more detail below.

It is suggested that 'Identity Crime' be used as the generic crime category, with the other terms used as specific descriptors of the ways in which such crimes can be committed. From a legislative perspective, the resolution of the taxonomy has been more difficult with most statutes proscribing various specific acts that give rise to identity crimes, such as gaining access to computers without authorisation, counterfeiting documents, opening accounts in false names and altering certificates or other documents used to establish identity. In some countries the list of offences that can be used to prosecute identity crime is extensive with hundreds of relevant offences being available to prosecute these cases – extending from theft through fraud to computer crimes and an extensive range of regulatory offences. As we shall see, this has led some countries to enact specific identity crime statutes that seek to gather together all of the possible criminal acts in one piece of legislation with appropriate sanctions provided that reflect the seriousness of the conduct.

The interrelationship between identity-related crime, Internet crime and fraud raises difficult questions of categorisation and definition. This is, in part, because most economic crimes involving fraud or dishonesty that have been perpetrated in recent years have involved the use of computers and the Internet, simply because modern businesses rely so heavily on digital technologies for accounting purposes and for transfer of funds. Many identity-related crimes are facilitated through the use of the Internet, which provides a rich source of personal information that can be stolen and misused. The vast majority of such crimes seek to extract money from victims through acts of dishonesty, making them fall within the definition of fraud. Figure 14.1 provides an illustration of the interrelationship between the concepts of identity-related crime, Internet crime, and fraud.

We can see that identity-related crime has connections with both Internet crime and fraud. Only a subset of identity-related crime has no fraudulent component in terms of the absence of a financial benefit sought to be derived dishonestly from the activity. Included are cases of violent crime in which the offender makes use of another person's identity in order not to be caught. Another example concerns the terrorists who destroyed the World Trade

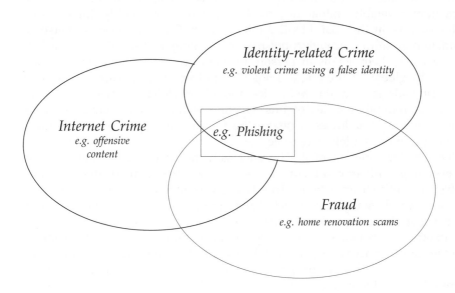

Figure 14.1 The interrelationship between identity-related crime, Internet crime and fraud

Centre who were found to have used other people's names when undertaking their pilot training and when boarding the aircraft prior to 11 September 2001 (National Commission on Terrorist Attacks upon the United States 2004). Similarly, a subset of fraud offences has no misuse of identity involved and no involvement of the Internet. An example would be the traditional scams relating to home improvement such as roofing repairs in which the work is either not carried out satisfactorily, or not at all. Although these may be advertised online, many simply arise from word-of-mouth or traditional advertising media. Finally, a subset of Internet crimes has no misuse of identity and no financial motivation. An example would be the creation and dissemination of offensive content such as racist propaganda. On the other hand, crimes such as phishing lie at the intersection of all three concepts and involve deception as to identity (usually of a business's Internet site), designed for purposes of financial gain, and perpetrated using the Internet.

In view of the focus of the present book on Internet crime, it is appropriate to consider the specific types of identity crime that make use of the Internet as a tool or target of illegality.

The Internet as a source of personal information

As a tool for discovering information, the Internet provides a comprehensive, quick and cheap tool that is accessible to everyone who has a telephone connection, personal computer and service provider. Extensive amounts of personal information are now held on computer networks and shared, intentionally and unintentionally, with others. Having autobiographical information available online has made the work of identity thieves that much easier as, in the past, identity thieves were required to obtain personal information by sifting through rubbish, or by tricking unsuspecting individuals into disclosing their details in person, by mail or by telephone. Information provided by global positioning technologies and street-view maps has assisted many criminals in planning robberies and other violent crimes, as well as in creating in-depth profiles of unsuspecting victims' daily activities. None of these criminal typologies is new – the Internet simply makes them more efficient and more widely accessible.

With the development of the Internet as a means of transacting business and engaging with government, it has become important to identify those involved in online transactions. This has led to an unfortunate consequence of crime control owing to the fact that techniques of identification, such as online registration requirements, have meant that individuals now supply vast amounts of personal information online – simply in order to obtain a password or other access key that can be used to facilitate 'secure transactions' with financial institutions or government agencies. As such, it has been suggested that '[i]dentity is "the new money"' (Crosby 2008), and based on the argument that crime follows opportunity, criminals in the twenty-first century look to identity as a new source of wealth. Owing to the often lax security measures present in organisations to protect electronic data, the theft of personal information by criminals is relatively easy.

The amount of data being generated in society is increasing exponentially and it is predicted that data created will eventually exceed storage capacity. In 2006, for example, the world produced 161 exabytes (billion gigabytes) of data and had 185 exabytes of storage capacity available. By 2010, this is expected to reach 988 exabytes (nearly 1 zettabyte) with only 601 exabytes of storage capacity expected to be available at that time (Glenn and Gordon 2007). The capacity of organisations to ensure the security of these amounts of data is conjectural with, for example, two-fifths of businesses in the United Kingdom spending less than one per cent of their information technology budget on information security, and with only one per cent of companies having a comprehensive approach to identity management. Furthermore, the Department of Trade and Industry (2006) found that only one in ten business people in the United Kingdom with responsibility for information security were aware of the two British Standards on information security (BS 7799, parts 1 and 2 – now ISO 17799 and ISO 27001).

The types of personal information at risk of misuse by identity criminals fall into two categories: life history information, and financial information. Examples of the former include details of a person's name, sex, age, address, and a variety of numbers used as identifiers when dealing with government agencies and businesses. Examples of the latter include bank account information such as account names, numbers, commencement and expiry dates, and secure numbers and passwords used to conduct secure electronic transactions. In addition, biometric data such as that obtained from fingerprint or facial scans, is a form of personal information that can be misused for the commission of identity crime.

Personal identification information can be obtained from a variety of sources including accidental data leakage from government or business networks, deliberate harvesting of data through the use of computer hacking or by gathering documents that contain personal information, or by social engineering in which individuals are persuaded or tricked into disclosing personal information to individuals for use in criminal activities.

Recently, cases of accidental or negligent data leakage continue to be disclosed providing a rich source of personal information available for potential misuse by criminals. The precise extent to which data leakage is correlated positively with the commission of identity crime is unknown – although the risk of abuse is clearly apparent. Levi (2009) argues that in none of these cases was a large proportion of the 'stolen' data *actually* used to commit fraud subsequently. Bearing this limitation in mind, some of the more prominent examples of data leakage include the following.

Over a two-year period and in March 2008, a company TK Maxx lost details of approximately 90 million customers, while in 2008, the HSBC banking group lost a computer disk containing the details (including names and dates of birth) of 370,000 customers (BBC 2008). In the United States in May 2005, the processor of payment card data, CardSystems Solutions Inc, had its database breached and credit card account information including magnetic stripe data and cardholder names relating to over 40 million accounts was stolen (Krim and Barbaro 2005). More recently, in late 2007, HM Revenue and Customs lost, in the ordinary mail, unencrypted CDs containing the financial details of

25 million people (more than one-third of the United Kingdom population) drawing family benefit (Levi 2009: 55; Information Commissioner's Office 2007).

In response to instances of such data loss, the British Payment Card Industry's Security Standards Council established 12 requirements with which organisations that deal with credit and debit card transactions should comply (Payment Card Industry 2006). At present, however, only one-third of retailers in the United Kingdom are deemed to be compliant (Reuters 2008).

In the first half of 2007, Symantec (2007) reported that the primary cause of data breaches that could facilitate identity theft was the theft or loss of a computer or other medium on which data were stored or transmitted such as a USB key or a back-up device. It was found that the loss of such devices comprised 46 per cent of all data breaches reported. A range of high-risk activities are engaged in by users of social networking sites with one study finding that 44 per cent of adults who had a profile allowed their profile to be seen by anyone and that 25 per cent of registered social networking users had posted personal data about themselves on their profiles including their telephone number, home address or email address (Ofcom 2008). The European Network and Information Security Agency (2007) has also identified the danger of phishing offenders making use of information obtained from social networking sites.

A relatively new source of online personal information is the many social networking sites popular with young people such as Facebook, Bebo, Orkut and MySpace. In the United Kingdom, over 10.8 million people are registered with a social networking site (Get Safe Online 2007). This is of concern in view of the fact that one in seven users on Facebook logged into their profile virtually all the time during office hours (Sophos 2008) rendering both themselves and their organisations open to identity theft and/or manipulation. In order to test the ready availability of personal information from these sites, one organisation, Sophos, managed to discover the dates of birth, current email addresses or telephone numbers of other users of sites using a fictitious profile. In addition, the organisation managed to gain access to employer details, résumés and in one case a user's mother's maiden name. It has been suggested (Trend Micro 2007) that such sites, in addition to those that '... run the gamut of social networking, banking/financial, online gaming, search engine, travel, commercial ticketing, local government sectors, news, job, blogging, and e-commerce sites for auction and shopping', will continue to be the attack vectors most sought after by criminals.

Those seeking personal information online are also beginning to make use of an ever-expanding digital underground economy. In North America, Operation Firewall, for example, in 2004 culminated in the arrest of 28 people from six countries for offences including the buying and selling of 1.7 million credit card numbers (McAfee 2005). The digital underground economy is expanding and becoming a lucrative source of income for organised criminals. Trend Micro (2007), for example, summarised the 'going rate' for various programs that could be used in connection with identity crimes and other acts of computer crime (Table 14.1), while Symantec (2007), provided a ranking of the cost of various items for sale in the digital underground market (Table

14.2). Of concern is not only the fact that such information is readily available in the underground online world, but also that the cost of acquiring it is so low, making the commission of identity crime extremely cost-effective.

Arguably the most successful means of dishonestly obtaining personal information online is through the range of activities known as phishing. Phishing involves the use of technological means coupled with social engineering designed to trick unsuspecting users of the Internet into disclosing personal information in response to an unsolicited request, usually received

Table 14.1 Nature of the digital underground market

Asset	Going rate (US$)
Pay-out for each unique adware installation	30 cents in the United States
	20 cents in Canada
	10 cents in the UK
	2 cents elsewhere
Malware package, basic version	$1,000–$2,000
Malware package with add-on services	Varying prices starting at $420
Exploit kit rental – 1 hour	$0.99–$1
Exploit kit rental – 2.5 hours	$1.60–$2
Exploit kit rental – 5 hours	$4, may vary
Undetected copy of an information-stealing certain Trojan	$80, may vary
Distributed Denial of Service attack	$100 per day
10,000 compromised PCs	$1,000
Stolen bank account credentials	Varying prices starting at $50
1 million freshly harvested emails (unverified)	$8 up, depending on quality

Source: Trend Micro (2007)

Table 14.2 Rank order of the cost of items for sale in the digital underground market

Item	Percentage	Price range (US$)
Credit cards	22	0.50–5
Bank accounts	21	30–400
Email passwords	8	1–350
Mailers	8	8–10
Email addresses	6	2/MB–4/MB
Proxies	6	0.50–3
Full identity	6	10–150
Scams	6	10/week
Social security numbers	3	5–7
Compromised UNIX® shells	2	2–10

Source: Symantec (2007)

by email. Once this information has been obtained, criminals may sell it to another person or use it to commit identity fraud. Phishing can target potential victims in three types of ways: syntactic, semantic and blended methods (Smith 2008a). Syntactic attacks involve exploitation of technical vulnerabilities such as the use of malicious computer code transmitted via email. Semantic attacks involve the use of social engineering or the exploitation of human vulnerabilities to obtain personal information by deception. Blended attacks entail the use of technical means to facilitate acts of social engineering. Phishing represents a clear example of a blended attack as a spam email is disseminated requiring the recipient to 'validate' their credit card or Internet banking account log-in details by replying to the email. Syntactic strategies used to obtain the user's email address include the use of password sniffers that can be used to intercept encrypted passwords travelling over a network, or Internet Protocol spoofing, 'Trojan horse' software and keylogging, all of which seek to obtain logon, password, or other personal information from the unsuspecting user's computer. Technological ploys and social engineering come together in techniques known as 'man in the middle' attacks in which a hacker routes messages between a vendor and client through a bogus website that mimics the vendor's site. Blended attacks that combine human nature and technical disguise include false websites that rely on domain name service (DNS) poisoning, 'DNS hijacking', and cross-site scripting to hijack web users. Such attacks that do not require a user to respond to a lure are sometimes referred to as 'pharming'.

The success of phishing was demonstrated in a study by Dhamija *et al.* (2006) in which 20 websites, seven of which were legitimate and 13 of which were fabricated, were presented to participants for examination. The study involved 22 university-based participants who examined the 20 sites to determine their authenticity. It was found that 90 per cent of participants were deceived by good-quality phishing sites, 23 per cent relied only on content to determine authenticity (without examining browser address bars, status bars, or security indictors), and 68 per cent ignored pop-up warnings as to content risk. Neither education, age, sex, previous experience, nor hours of computer use showed any significant correlation with phishing risks.

The growth in the number of phishing attacks has been exponential until recently, although now seems to be declining slightly. The actual number of phishing sites is, however, still substantial. The Anti-Phishing Working Group (APWG), which is an industry association formed in 2003 to eliminate identity theft and fraud that results from phishing and email spoofing, received 23,187 unique email phishing reports in the month of December 2008. This however, represents a 140 per cent decline from the 55,643 reports received in April 2007. In addition to these phishing emails reported, the APWG itself detected a further 15,709 sites in December 2008. Despite this decrease in phishing reports, the number of website addresses (URLs) that infected personal computers with password-stealing crimeware increased substantially to a record high of 31,173 at the end of December 2008, an increase of 827 per cent from the 3,362 URLs with crimeware at the end of January 2008. However, the number of unique keyloggers and malicious code applications detected declined from a high of 1,518 in July 2008 to 559 in December 2008.

In terms of hijacked brands, the number increased slightly from 237 to 252 between July and December 2008 while for targeted industry sectors, financial services continued to be the most targeted sector accounting for 46 per cent of attacks in the last quarter of 2008. Between the third and fourth quarters of 2008, there was a large increase in payment services brands attacked (24 to 38 per cent). There was also a continued increase in attacks directed towards social networking sites such as MySpace and Facebook. The United States remained the top country hosting phishing sites, although in the month of September 2008, Sweden became the leading country hosting 63 per cent of phishing sites. Another important trend has been an increase in rogue anti-malware programs that can be used for phishing, extortion or the sale of worthless anti-virus products. Such detected programs increased 225 per cent from 2,850 in July 2008 to 9,287 in December 2008 (APWG 2009).

In addition to these online sources of personal information, identity thieves can obtain data from conventional social engineering techniques and other technological means (see Pontell *et al.* 2008).

Types of Internet-based identity crime

Armed with personal information obtained from data leaked publicly, or extracted from online databases or from users by sophisticated social engineering and other technological means, criminals have been able to commit a wide range of criminal activities. The following examples represent some of the most recent and productive ways in which personal information has been misused for financial gain.

Electronic financial transactions

Advances in information and communications technologies and the market demand for efficient consumer transactions have resulted in an increase in the use of electronic payment systems over conventional paper-based or face-to-face transactions. In the past, identity thieves were required to counterfeit or alter cheques in order to commit transaction-based identity fraud. Now, all that is required is the ability to gain access to a network using a stolen logon and password and funds can be transferred seamlessly and instantaneously. In recent years, the use of electronic transactions has increased considerably and electronic payment systems are an increasingly important part of the retail and commercial sectors. In Australia, for example, the volume and value of cheque transactions in paper-based clearing systems fell from an average of 2.7 million per day in 2001, to 1.07 million in 2008, representing an average of A$8.3 billion per day in 2001 to A$4.8 billion in 2008 (APCA (Australian Payments Clearing Association 2009). There has been a corresponding decline in cheque-based fraud and an increase in debit card and credit/charge card fraud over the 24 months from 2005–06 to 2007–08, as shown in Table 14.3.

Arguably of greater relevance to the question of Internet-based identity fraud are so-called 'card-not-present' transactions. These use account information including pseudo-account information without the physical card being involved, via the telephone, mail, Internet etc, without the authority of

Table 14.3 Fraud perpetrated on Australian issued payment instruments, 2005–06 to 2007–08

Instrument	No. of fraudulent transactions		Value of fraudulent transactions (A$ million)	
	2005–06	2007–08	2005–06	2007–08
Cheque	2,942	1,742	40,706,011	14,553,976
Debit card	29,357	44,542	14,471,065	15,494,628
Credit/charge card	236,271	361,124	87,432,913	131,729,930
Total	268,570	407,408	142,609,989	161,778,534

Source: APCA (2009)

the cardholder. Also included are instances in which a card should normally be present, such as in a retail transaction, but the merchant has chosen to accept the transaction based on a card number only, and this then turns out to be a fraudulent transaction (APCA 2009). Table 14.4 shows the increase in card-not-present transactions in Australia between 2005–06 and 2007–08, both with respect to transactions on cards issued in Australia and on overseas-issued cards. Overall, there was an increase of 110 per cent between 2005–06 and 2007–08 in relation to card-not-present fraudulent transactions, a large proportion of which was Internet-based. An even higher percentage increase of 132 per cent related to the change in the total value of fraudulent transactions over this period.

A recent example of a large-scale card-not-present fraud in Australia that resulted in arrests in March 2009, concerned a syndicate of individuals based in New South Wales who were alleged to have purchased more than A$4.5m in goods using credit cards bearing bank account details 'skimmed' or stolen from legitimate cardholders. The goods, including brand new LCD televisions, laptop computers, cameras, power tools, GPS systems and iPods, were then allegedly sold on various online auction sites at reduced prices, allowing the syndicate to launder the profits. The syndicate had been in operation for some time and had allegedly sold 6,000 items for A$1.3 million (New South Wales Police Force 2009).

In the United Kingdom, in the first quarter of 2008, 1.8 billion plastic card purchases were reportedly made totalling £91.1 billion (APACS (Association of Payment Clearing Services) 2008) and in the calendar year 2007, more than 18 billion automated clearing-house payments were reportedly made in the United States (NACHA (the Electronic Payments Association) 2008). In March 2008, the Association of Payment Clearing Services, now the UK Payments Administration Ltd (APACS 2008) reported that there had been a 25 per cent rise in the fraudulent use of United Kingdom credit and debit cards in 2007, with losses amounting to £535m. Some £290.5m of this took place on the Internet, via phone or mail order, where the credit or debit cardholder was not present, a year-on-year rise of 37 per cent. APACS indicated that the first rise in three years of overall card fraud was mainly due to stolen and counterfeit

Table 14.4 Card-not-present fraudulent transactions in Australia 2005–08

Category	2005–06		2006–07		2007–08		% change 2005–08	
	No.	A$	No.	A$	No.	A$	No.	A$
CNP Aust cards	97,279	27,223,045	150,646	39,959,984	211,444	63,491,661	117	133
CNP o/s cards	39,998	10,774,335	47,795	16,552,405	76,452	24,583,640	91	128
Total	137,277	37,997,380	198,441	56,512,389	287,896	88,075,301	110	132

Source: APCA (2009)
CNP Aust cards – credit card and charge card fraud perpetrated in Australia or overseas on Australian-issued cards
CNP o/s cards – fraud perpetrated in Australia on cards issued overseas

cards used abroad. Card fraud overseas rose by 77 per cent in 2008 to £208m and accounted for 39 per cent of the total (APACS 2008).

The British Crime Survey 2005–06 found that four per cent of card users had been victims of card fraud in the last year, equating to one per cent of all adults. The recent introduction of Chip and PIN cards has made it more difficult to commit fraud in the United Kingdom, although evidence has emerged of the ability to compromise even the more secure Chip and PIN reader technologies (Drimer *et al.* 2008). Concerns of displacement are also evident, for although incidents of payment card fraud may be decreasing in the United Kingdom, there has been an increase in overseas fraud involving British victims as data from stolen Chip and PIN cards is transferred to magnetic stripe cards and used in jurisdictions that have not yet integrated Chip and PIN technologies (APACS 2008).

Mobile and wireless transactions

Identity crime facilitated through the Internet is also beginning to be perpetrated through wireless communication systems, some of which have less robust security measures in place. Mobile and wireless devices, such as third-generation (3G) and fourth-generation (4G) mobile phones and PDAs equipped with global system for mobile communications/general packet radio service (GSM/GPRS), will become increasingly important tools for accessing information when personal (desktop) computers are no longer the main means of computing. Mobile devices and networks will continue to become more capable and better able to support a wide range of communication and collaboration functions (Jones 2006).

Recent reports on mobile device penetration rates consistently reflect the rising uptake of mobile phones internationally. In Australia, for example, it is estimated that 'there is more than one mobile service for every Australian, with 21.26 million mobile phone services in operation at 30 June 2007' (ACMA

(Australian Communications and Media Authority) 2008). At the end of 2007, the four major mobile network operators in the United Kingdom (Vodafone, O2, T-Mobile and Orange) reported a combined mobile phone subscription of 7,588,000 (Ofcom 2008). The recent study by Datamonitor further suggested that global enterprise expenditures on mobile devices will increase to an estimated US$17 billion by 2012 from the current US$6 billion (Anjum 2008).

Wireless networks create a number of risks of relevance to identity crime. Of particular concern is the potential for users who have created an insecure, and unencrypted network to have their network used by nearby users within wireless range of the available computer. This, itself, is a form of identity theft as the individual who makes use of an unsecured network is pretending to be the person who created that network and the person who is paying the ISP for the service provided. Acts of so-called 'war driving' are becoming more common with individuals scanning for unsecured wireless networks to use, not only to avoid having to pay ISPs, but also for the transmission of illegal content which would be transmitted using another person's broadband connection. In one survey conducted by AusCERT of the security measures used by a sample of 1,001 adult home computer users with Internet access in Australia, it was found that 16 per cent of those surveyed used insecure wireless networks, and 5 per cent of those surveyed admitted to using a neighbour's wireless connection (AusCERT 2008).

Consumer scams

The development of the Internet has been identified as a key factor in the expansion of consumer fraud (Choo et al. 2007) as large numbers of potential victims can be located easily and unsolicited invitations can be sent without disclosing the true identity of the fraudsters. The principal technology used involves 'spamming' in which scam invitations can be sent in bulk by email to countless recipients at once, in any location in the world. The use of networks of millions of compromised computers known as botnets has created the opportunity to target an ever-increasing pool of potential victims and greater opportunities for organisation and networking between groups and perpetrators of fraud.

Criminal misuse of identity lies at the heart of most consumer scams, with offenders pretending to be other people or businesses in order to trick the victim into participating in the scam, while at the same time making their own identity hard for police to discover. A good example of this concerns the various advance fee frauds perpetrated by a group of West Africans and others since the 1980s globally. Various offenders began working from Nigeria targeting victims across the globe. Confederates and other fraudsters in other African countries, the United States, Britain, Canada, Hong Kong, and Japan then began using the same techniques. The scale of these frauds increased considerably and created a global problem for law enforcement. Email has proved to be an effective way of disseminating advance fee letters as the true identity of the sender is easy to disguise and original supporting documentation unable to be checked for authenticity.

Levels of concern about scam victimisation are high with consumers across the globe expressing fear that their personal information may be compromised when transacting business online. In a global survey conducted for Visa International (2006) in November and December 2005 across 12 countries, attitudes towards data security and consumer behaviour were examined. Of the more than 6,000 respondents, 64 per cent said that loss or theft of personal information was their biggest concern, even above terrorism (58 per cent), job loss (57 per cent), disease epidemics (55 per cent) and natural disasters (48 per cent). Interestingly, the higher the awareness among consumers, the higher their level of apparent concern.

In May 2006, the *Unisys Security Survey and Index 2006* was conducted by Newspoll. A large, representative national sample of 1,200 respondents aged 18 years and over was surveyed for the quarterly report on national security concerns. It was found that 56 per cent of the respondents had high levels of concern (very/extremely) about unauthorised access to personal information or its misuse, while 53 per cent had high concern about other people obtaining their credit card or debit card details. Women were much more likely to be extremely or very concerned about people obtaining their credit or debit card details than men. These levels of concern were higher than the perceived threat of war/terrorism (41 per cent) and much higher than concerns about their personal safety over the forthcoming six months (14 per cent) (Unisys 2006).

As we shall see below, evidence now exists that large numbers of consumers are exposed to scams, and quite high proportions of the population actually respond to them and lose money as a result. Despite this, as Levi (2009) so eloquently argues, the level of concern about identity crime has yet to reach the status of 'moral panic' as conventionally understood in criminology.

Online gaming

The Internet has also enabled the development of a variety of online gaming activities ranging from simple games such as puzzles or word games, to Massively Multiplayer Online Role-Playing Games (MMORPGs) like World of Warcraft. These can be played online through consoles, across mobile phones or via peer-to-peer networks (Byron 2008: 191). Online gaming is a growing industry with the market worldwide expected to exceed US$13 billion by 2012 (Ong 2008). Research by Gartner predicted that end-user revenue will increase to US$9.6 billion in 2011 (Nguyen *et al.* 2007). This level of financial activity provides a clear goal for identity criminals.

The virtual worlds in MMOG (Massively Multiplayer Online Games) and MMORPG provide an environment in which people communicate with each other using a virtual persona, known as an avatar. This allows strangers who may not even speak the same language to establish a relationship in the virtual world. To participate in the games, players have to exchange real cash for virtual currency from the gaming site (e.g. LindeX, the official Second Life currency exchange) or from third-party trading websites (e.g. http://www.ige.com/). Using these virtual currencies, players can purchase virtual property, virtual accommodation and virtual merchandise such as weapons to use in the 'World of Warcraft' games, and to inflate their virtual status in their virtual worlds. A study by Chen *et al.* (2004) suggested that as of March 2003, a virtual exchange rate was estimated to be 10,000 in virtual cash unit to US$1. It was also reported on LindeX™ that a virtual exchange rate was estimated to be L$264 (Linden Dollars) to US$1 as at 1 June 2008.

> Various risks of identity-related crime arise in connection with online gaming. [I]t is possible for one virtual world Avatar to arrange a meeting with another one, who may or may not be in another country or continent, and drop off goods or monies worth significant sums of hard currency for the other party to take up. Thereby, the digital transfer of a potentially significant sum may take place without being reported to any regulatory or investigative agency. The individual controlling the second Avatar could potentially then immediately access the monies through the use of the Entropia Universe ATM card. All of this has been done quickly and easily, resulting with one party now having 'virtually clean' money, pun intended, without leaving a trail for investigators to follow. Therefore, if Entropia Universe accounts, or those provided by other gaming companies that will likely follow suit, are able to continue to operate outside the reach of current federal regulations, laundering funds through an MMO may become the easiest method ever. (Kane 2008: 20)

Because life in virtual gaming worlds mirrors many aspects of life in the real world, risks of identity crime are ever present. The use of compromised passwords and access codes could result in theft of property, and impersonation of other Atavars who could commit a range of virtual crimes and then be unable to be located by virtual or real world police. Already examples have begun to emerge of ATM fraud, theft of furniture, and money laundering in virtual worlds (Warren 2008). In one case a 17-year-old in the Netherlands allegedly stole about €4,000 worth of virtual objects including furniture from the Habbo Hotel social networking site. The accused lured victims into disclosing their Habbo login and password details by creating fictitious Habbo websites and then stealing their virtual 'furniture' from their online 'hotel rooms'. Police in China have also investigated cases of virtual theft, including instances of organised gangs engaging in online robbery. In 2006, officers from Shenzhen arrested more than 40 suspects who were accused of stealing up to 700,000 yuan worth of virtual items from users of the social networking site 'QQ' (Johnson 2007).

The extent of the problem

Determining the size of the problem of identity crime can be approached from a number of perspectives, each of which has its own problems and limitations. The following discussion focuses on the quantification of identity crime that has been facilitated through the use of the Internet. Some of the main impediments to the effective quantification of the extent of the problem of identity crime are as follows. First, as already noted, the concept of identity crime is far from settled, making categorisation for the purpose of counting crimes and offenders in official statistics problematic. Secondly, the units of measurement are often not clearly delineated, varying from exposure to risks, through participation in criminal conduct, to actual victimisation and financial loss. Survey research also presents problems in this area, although the difficulties of conducting large-scale, costly surveys, achieving meaningful response rates, and representative results are by no means unique to the field of identity crime. Further, because many identity criminals implicate victims in the criminal enterprise, official reporting rates tend to be low as victims may be fearful of official action being taken against them for participating in a criminal activity. Victims are also often unwilling to publicly describe the details of their sometimes less than cautious conduct in sharing passwords or failing to secure personal information. Bearing these limitations in mind, the following data have been collected concerning identity crime incidence and cost.

Consumer victimisation surveys

Research into consumer fraud is often specific to a location or a victim group, rather than the general population. To address this perceived lack of generalisable data, the Australian Bureau of Statistics (ABS) undertook a study on personal fraud in 2007 after a recommendation from the Australasian Consumer Fraud Taskforce, a group of government agencies and private sector partners in Australia and New Zealand dedicated to eradicating consumer fraud. The ABS Personal Fraud Survey is currently the largest survey of personal fraud ever undertaken in Australia (ABS 2008). The survey measured respondents' experience of personal frauds, which included both identity fraud and consumer scams. Under these umbrella terms, there were a number of categories of each type of fraud including various scam types, and bank and credit card fraud.

The personal fraud survey was conducted as part of the ABS's regular household survey, and involved over 14,000 participants in Australia aged 15 years and over. The inclusion of the survey within the household survey allowed the results to then be generalised to the Australian population, giving estimates of fraud victimisation across all risk categories, rather than specific groups of people. The survey participants were asked about all fraud incidents that they had experienced in the previous 12 months, and detailed responses were sought about the most recent of these incidents. A person was considered a victim if they had responded positively to a scam invitation including requesting additional information up to and including supplying personal information or money. The results of the survey indicated that a total of 806,000 Australians aged 15 and over had been victims of personal fraud in the preceding 12 months. This equated to approximately 5 per cent of the Australian population. Of these, over 450,000 victims lost money as a result of the fraud. Of this 5 per cent, identity fraud accounted for 499,500 victims in Australia or 3 per cent of the population. Of the 499,500 victims of identity fraud, the majority (383,300 or 77 per cent) were victims of credit or bank card fraud. This equated to a victimisation rate of 2.4 per cent. These victims experienced at least one unauthorised, fraudulent transaction using their cards or account details. Identity theft accounted for 124,000 victims of identity fraud. These victims included those who experienced unauthorised use of their personal details, such as a driver's licence, tax file number, or passport through fraudulent or forged identification documents, or unauthorised appropriation of their identity through any other means to conduct business, open accounts or take out loans illegally in their name. Interestingly, when asked about how the most recent incident of identity theft had been committed, the highest percentage of respondents (27.3 per cent) indicated that it occurred in person. Some 21.2 per cent of respondents said that it was perpetrated by email or via the Internet and a further 7.7 per cent by landline or mobile phone.

It was estimated that over 5.8 million people were exposed to a scam in the preceding 12 months, which equated to 35.8 per cent of the population. The most prevalent scams were lotteries (2,437,400 people), phishing and related scams (2,374,700 people) and chain letters (2,054,000 people). Of those who received a scam invitation, 5.7 per cent responded positively which equated to 2 percent of the Australian population. Lotteries were the most successful scam with 0.5 per cent of respondents falling victim to one; this was followed by pyramid schemes (0.4 per cent) and phishing and related scams (0.4 per cent). A further breakdown of personal fraud victimisation is shown in Table 14.5.

The survey also asked respondents to indicate the manner in which the most recent scam invitation had been delivered. Interestingly, although the Internet (online/email delivery) was reported by 21 per cent of respondents, physical delivery continued to be a problem with more than one quarter of respondents indicating that identity theft scams had been received 'in person' (see Table 14.6).

In terms of the impact of victimisation, the Australian Bureau of Statistics (2008) survey found that victims of scams often changed their behaviour as a direct result of victimisation. Table 14.7 shows how behaviour changed as a result of victimisation for the respondents to the survey.

Table 14.5 Personal fraud victimisation rates in Australia, 2007

Fraud type	Victimisation rate
Identity fraud	3.1%
Credit or bank card fraud	2.4%
Identity theft	0.8%
Scams	2.0%
Lottery scams	0.5%
Pyramid schemes	0.4%
Phishing and related scams	0.4%
Financial advice	0.2%
Chain letters	0.2%
Advance fee fraud	0.1%*
Other scams	0.4%

Source: Australian Bureau of Statistics (2008)
*Relative standard error 25–50%

Table 14.6 Mode of delivery of fraud for most recent incident (percentage of respondents)

Type	Mode of delivery					
	Phone	In person	Post	Email	Other	Unknown
Pyramid	19.4*	59.2	10.8*	10.7*		
Lotteries	20.2*		39.2	40.6		
Phishing	27.1	20.2*		52.7		
Financial		67.6		32.4*		
Chain letters			51.7	48.3*		
Other scams	28.1	6.5*	13.0*	45.9	6.5*	
Card fraud	3.3*	29.2	2.5*	19.8	8.9	36.3
ID theft	7.7*	27.3	4.8**	21.2	12.2*	26.8

Source: Australian Bureau of Statistics (2008)
*Relative standard error 25–50% **Relative standard error > 50%

Table 14.7 Behaviour changes as a result of personal fraud victimisation (percentage of respondents)

Type	More aware/ careful	Reduced well-being	Change ISP, email etc.	Stopped dealing	Other
Pyramid	16.5*	8.7**		9.5**	
Lotteries	20.3*	7.7**		21.3*	5.0**
Phishing	19.5*			19.7*	
Other scams	43.0			21.0*	6.1*
Card fraud	28.1	4.7*	11.8	3.5*	3.4*
ID theft	24.5	8.8*	3.9**	6.7*	6.6*

Source: Australian Bureau of Statistics (2008)
*Relative standard error 25–50% **Relative standard error > 50%

Almost one quarter of the victims of identity theft reported being more aware or more careful following their scam experience, while smaller proportions of respondents reported levels of reduced well-being, or needing to change their ISP or email address following victimisation.

Also in Australia, in 2007, a study commissioned by the Office of the Privacy Commissioner, *Community Attitudes to Privacy 2007*, was undertaken in which respondents were asked, *inter alia*, whether they or someone they knew had been the victim of identity fraud or theft. Despite the generality of the question, overall, 9 per cent of Australians claimed they had been victims themselves and 17 per cent knew someone who had been the victim (Office of the Privacy Commissioner 2007).

In the United States, Javelin Strategy and Research conducted a survey of 5,075 consumers, representative of the United States population, to determine the manner in which identity theft occurred. Some 445 (8.8 per cent) of those interviewed were victims of identity fraud. Contrary to popular belief, in cases where victims knew how their data had been stolen, online identity theft methods (phishing, hacking and spyware) only constituted 12 per cent of fraud cases. The vast majority of known cases occurred through traditional methods (79 per cent), when a criminal made direct contact with the consumer's personal identification. These instances include stolen and lost wallets, chequebooks, or credit cards, 'shoulder surfing' (when someone looks over your shoulder at an ATM or cash register), and stolen mail from unlocked letterboxes. So-called 'friendly theft' was reported by 17 per cent of victims, such as when friends, family or in-home employees took private data for their personal gain (Javelin Strategy and Research 2008: 5–6).

Business victimisation surveys

The incidence of identity crime can also be examined from the point of view of businesses which have been victimised, either as the specific victims of dishonesty themselves, or because they have been required to compensate consumers and other individuals who have suffered loss at the hands of identity thieves – namely, financial institutions and card issuers. In August 2008, KPMG Forensic, in collaboration with the University of Melbourne and the University of Queensland, sent a fraud survey questionnaire to 2,018 of Australia and New Zealand's largest public and private sector organisations. The questionnaire sought information about fraud incidents within the respondents' business operations during the period February 2006 to January 2008. Usable replies were received from 420 organisations – 20 per cent of those surveyed (KPMG 2009). Survey respondents reported 222,577 incidents of fraud during the survey period. The total value of fraud reported (before taking into account associated costs and recoveries) was A$301.1 million with 45 per cent of all respondents experiencing at least one fraud during the survey period. In the survey respondents were asked if their largest reported fraud incident involved identity fraud. Fifteen per cent of the largest fraud incidents involved some form of identity fraud. The most common form of identity fraud reported by respondents in 2008 was the unauthorised use of a credit card or credit card number stolen from the cardholder. Respondents reported 154,602 cases of this kind of fraud with a total value of over A$90 million.

Within the financial services sector, credit card fraud accounted for 39 per cent of the value of fraud attributable to external parties, while within the non-financial services sector, credit card fraud accounted for 29 per cent of the value of fraud attributable to external parties. In terms of the largest single cases of fraud reported by respondents, identity fraud accounted for only 2 per cent of cases, but involved A$1,231,207 in total losses, with a mean value per case of A$410,402 (KPMG 2009). Although not all of the identity fraud detected by the respondents would have been enabled through the use of the Internet, it is clear that a high proportion of identity fraud involving misuse of plastic cards would have been facilitated through the use of the Internet. A number of other cases would also have involved card-not-present fraud in which account information had been obtained from the Internet.

In a much smaller-scale survey, 150 United Kingdom-based online merchants and 1,000 online shoppers were surveyed in 2008 (CyberSource 2009). It was found that online fraud had increased since the 2007 survey, and that fraud losses in 2008 consumed more than 1 per cent of revenue for 37 per cent of United Kingdom online merchants. Some 13 per cent lost more than 5 per cent of their revenue and 54 per cent of merchants indicated that theft of customer data was their greatest business threat, followed by 52 per cent who identified online fraud as the greatest threat. Merchants also identified as the two most common methods used by fraudsters, making multiple orders with similar identity data but different card numbers (38 per cent) and using multiple identities using the same card number (34 per cent) – both examples of online identity crime (CyberSource 2009: 9). CyberSource also interviewed 1,000 adults in the United Kingdom, aged 16 years or more, during the weekend of the 17 to 19 October 2008. The survey group was designed to be nationally representative of adults throughout the United Kingdom, and weighting was applied to the results to bring the data in line with national profiles. It was found that 66 per cent of those who responded indicated that they were concerned about the level of risk when shopping online. Over one in three claimed to have been a victim of online credit card fraud, or to have known someone who was (CyberSource 2009: 16).

The cost of identity crime

Attempts to quantify the overall cost of identity crime have faced a range of challenges as official crime statistics rarely include a discrete category of identity crime, or identity fraud, while surveys have often been small in scale and insufficiently specific to permit accurate costing of the cost of identity crime categories. The most recent available evidence is as follows.

United Kingdom

Fraud in the United Kingdom was conservatively estimated by Levi *et. al* (2007) to cost at least £12.98 billion in 2005, while fraud committed against private individuals was estimated at £2.75 billion. Identity fraud was estimated to cost £1.3 billion involving 80,000 victims in 2005. Another survey by CIFAS (2006), the United Kingdom's Fraud Prevention Service, found the number of victims of impersonation to be more than 67,000, with total cases of identity fraud reported at over 80,000. Other research by CIFAS (2004) indicated that deceased fraud (or impersonation of deceased persons) was the United Kingdom's fastest growing identity theft crime, estimated to cost £250 million a year.

Australia

In Australia, the Australian Institute of Criminology estimated the cost of all types of fraud to be at least A$8.5 billion in 2005 (Rollings 2008). A breakdown of individual fraud types was not provided in this study although an earlier investigation by the Securities Industry Research Centre of Asia–Pacific (SIRCA) in 2003 for the Australian Transaction Reports and Analysis Centre (AUSTRAC), claimed that identity fraud cost Australian large business

$1.1 billion in the year 2001–02 (Cuganesan and Lacey 2003). Again, it was not possible to say how much of this was related to misuse of the Internet. As we have seen, victims of personal fraud in Australia reported losses of A$977 million in 2007. Some 16.3 per cent of respondents said that in respect of the most recent incident of identity theft, they had incurred a financial loss, with 8.0 per cent losing A$500 or less and a further 8.2 per cent losing more than A$501 (ABS 2008: 15).

In a pilot study conducted by the Australian Bureau of Criminal Intelligence (2002)(now part of the Australian Crime Commission), 23 law enforcement and other public sector agencies, and one private sector organisation provided information relating to identity fraud offenders, fraudulent identities and victims of identity takeovers known to them. The study found that between 25 February 2002 and 23 August 2002, 1,195 fraudulent identities were identified relating to 597 suspects and involving 1,404 documents; 1,183 cases involved fraudulent identities, 12 cases involved identity takeovers, and 12 involved known identity fraud offenders. In all, 1,404 offences were identified in which A$2,639,797 had been obtained and a further A$239,532 attempted to be stolen. The study found that fraudulent identities were used to support or to commit a variety of criminal activities such as obtaining finance, opening bank accounts, money laundering, car rebirthing, credit card skimming, obtaining family allowance benefits, obtaining security guard licences, boat licences and shooters' licences, avoiding driving demerit points and producing English language certificates for migrants. Interestingly, no suspects or offenders identified by the participating agencies used online service delivery to establish contact with the agencies in question.

United States

In the United States in 2008, Javelin Strategy and Research conducted a survey of 5,075 consumers, representative of the United States population, to determine the nature and extent of identity theft. Some 445 (8.8 per cent) of those interviewed reported being victims of identity theft. Between 2007 and 2008, 8.1 million Americans (4 per cent of the adult population) reported being victimised by identity fraud, losing an estimated US$45 billion. Over the four years since 2003, both the total number of victims and the overall monetary losses have steadily decreased. However, the time spent by victims in resolving identity fraud cases increased. The study also found that only a small percentage of identity fraud occurred over the Internet, with most cases involving traditional offline channels (Javelin Strategy and Research 2008: 5–6).

In the United States between January and December 2005, Consumer Sentinel, the complaint database developed and maintained by the Federal Trade Commission, received over 685,000 consumer fraud and identity theft complaints, 37 per cent of which concerned identity theft. Consumers reported losses from fraud of more than US$680 million in 2005 (Federal Trade Commission 2006).

Canada

In Canada, a national survey of 1,000 Canadians, aged 18 years and older, conducted in mid-March 2005, found that 20 per cent had been victims of identity theft, an increase of five per cent on the corresponding figure in the 2003 survey (Canadian Competition Bureau 2005). In 2002, Public Safety and Emergency Preparedness Canada (2004) estimated that total losses due to identity theft were approximately Can$2.5 billion.

Summary

Although it is difficult to reconcile these differing estimates of the incidence and cost of identity crime, it is clear than substantial numbers of individuals are victimised each year in developed countries alone, with losses for major countries in excess of the equivalent of £1 billion annually per country. A good deal of identity crime continues to be committed offline, and the number of offences and cost are beginning to decline in some countries, presumably owing to increased computer security measures being used and the ever-increasing awareness-raising activities of consumer protection agencies and the plastic card industry sector. Nonetheless, the Internet continues to provide an extensive source of personal information that is capable of misuse by criminals intent on committing financially motivated crimes.

Addressing identity theft and fraud

A wide range of measures have been developed to deal with identity crime, many of which are described in the extensive compendia produced by the United States President's Taskforce on Identity Theft (2008) and in reports on identity crime to the United Nations Commission on Crime Prevention and Criminal Justice (2007). White and Fisher (2008), in the United States, and Smith (2003), in Australia, have also provided full reviews of the specific measures designed to reduce identity crime committed in the transnational online environment. Many of these initiatives remain in their infancy, and few have been subjected to rigorous evaluation (see Smith 2008b), although some of the biometric solutions and some electronic payment system fraud prevention measures have received extensive critical appraisal – and, unfortunately, have been found wanting in terms of crime reduction on occasions (see Smith 2007). Others such as the use of Chip and PIN to secure plastic card transactions have largely been found to be successful in reducing fraud, although these solutions have not universally been implemented globally to date. As a result, spatial displacement has taken place with identity criminals targeting countries in which these novel payment system solutions have yet to be implemented – such as the United States and Australia where Chip and PIN are not generally available for use with plastic card payment systems.

The most frequently adopted responses to identity crime risks relate to legislative reform, improvement of identification procedures, user education and victim support.

Legislative reform

The legislative responses to identity crime generally fall within four areas: amendments to laws that proscribe financial crime and fraud; laws which proscribe the criminal misuse of computers and computer networks; laws which provide for the introduction and use of identity cards and other types of identifiers; and laws which proscribe identity crime specifically. Legislative reform to deal with identity-related crime is one of the specific measures identified at the Eighteenth Session of the United Nations Commission on Crime Prevention and Criminal Justice that will contribute to the delineation of a guidance framework on the most appropriate initiatives to be prioritised and pursued in the future (United Nations 2009). Some of the specific legislative reforms pursued by individual countries are as follows.

In the United Kingdom an example of the first type of legislation is the Fraud Act 2006, which creates a single and flexible offence of fraud that has made the prosecution of offenders easier and more likely to be successful. The Act created a general definition of fraud as well as specific offences in connection with acting dishonestly.

In Australia, model laws on theft, fraud, bribery and related offences were created with the *Criminal Code Amendment (Theft, Fraud, Bribery and Related Offences) Act 2000* (Cth) which commenced operation on 24 May 2001. Relevant offences introduced into the Commonwealth Criminal Code include obtaining property or a financial advantage by deception (Division 134), offences involving fraudulent conduct (Division 135), forgery (Division 144) and falsification (Division 145). In addition to the obtaining offences (ss. 134.1 and 134.2), the 'general dishonesty' offence in section 135.1 provides a maximum penalty of five years' imprisonment 'where a person does anything with the intention of dishonestly obtaining a gain from, or causing a loss to, the Commonwealth'. This legislation also amends the law governing geographical jurisdiction to facilitate the prosecution of cross-border fraudulent criminal activity.

In addition, efforts have been made to amend computer crime laws to ensure that identity-related crimes carried out electronically can be prosecuted. The Australian parliament has, for example, enacted the *Cybercrime Act 2001*, which commenced operation on 21 December 2001. This Act inserts a new Part into the Commonwealth *Criminal Code Act 1995* and largely follows the provisions of the Council of Europe's *Convention on Cybercrime*, which was adopted by the Committee of Ministers of the Council of Europe on 8 November 2001 and opened for signature on 23 November 2001 in Budapest (Council of Europe 2001). Some of the *Cybercrime Act* provisions could be used to prosecute identity-related frauds carried out through the misuse of computers, such as where a person gains access to a computer by using another person's password without authorisation.

In the United States, specific legislation was introduced to deal with identity-related crime some time ago. The Federal *Identity Theft and Assumption Deterrence Act 1998* (18 USC 1028) which became effective on 30 October 1998, made identity theft a crime with maximum penalties of up to 15 years' imprisonment and a maximum fine of US$250,000. It established that the person whose identity has been stolen is a victim who is able to seek restitution following a conviction. It also gives the Federal Trade Commission power to act as a clearing house for complaints, referrals, and resources for assistance for victims of identity theft.

On 16 October 2007, the Canadian government introduced legislation amending the Criminal Code, RSC 1985, c. C-46. The Bill created offences of obtaining personal information from a third party by false pretence or by fraud, and selling or otherwise disclosing personal information obtained from a third party by a false pretence or by fraud. The amendments permit police to intervene at an earlier stage of criminal operations, before identity fraud or other crimes that cause financial or other harm are attempted or committed (Standing Committee of Attorneys-General 2008).

In Australia, three states, South Australia, Queensland and Victoria, currently have specific identity fraud legislation. The Victorian Crimes Amendment (Identity Crime) Act 2009 created new offences of assuming a false identity with intent to commit a serious offence, making, using or supplying identification information with intent to commit an indictable offence (which carries a maximum penalty of five years' imprisonment), possessing identification information with intent to commit an indictable offence (which carries a maximum penalty of three years' imprisonment), possessing equipment capable of making identification information with intention to use in the commission of an indictable offence (which also carries a maximum penalty of five years' imprisonment). The legislation does not apply to using one's own identification information and it is not a defence to a charge that the victim consented to the use of the victim's personal information. Attempting to commit these offences is also not a separate criminal offence and the law applies even if the commission of the indictable offence is impossible. The Victorian law also applies to deceased persons' identities that have been misused and to entirely fictitious identities. Finally, the legislation gives power to courts to issue an identity crime certificate to victims to verify the fact of their victimisation. This can be used to assist victims in re-establishing their stolen identities and in ensuring that they are not liable for crimes committed in their name. The certificate is, however, not a remedy in that it does not compel others to take restorative action – for example, it does not compel financial institutions to reinstate a person's credit rating. Rather, the certificate provides a means to present the outcome of a court's decision in a way that may be readily used by the victim to ensure the outcome of the legal proceeding (Standing Committee of Attorneys-General 2008).

Australia has not, however, moved down the path of authorising the creation and use of identity cards on a national basis, although some states and territories have cards to verify the fact and date of a person's birth. In the United Kingdom, the Identity Cards Act 2006 (Eng.) prohibits the use of all false identity documents. This is supported by new measures to help businesses verify whether passports are genuine. From 25 November 2008, Britain began issuing identity cards to foreign nationals from outside the European Economic Area and Switzerland who were given permission to extend their stay in the United Kingdom as students and their dependants, and husbands, wives, civil partners, or unmarried or same-sex partners of permanent residents, and the applicant's dependants. By 2015, it is expected that 90 per cent of nationals from outside the European Economic Area or

Switzerland will have an identity card. The identity card for foreign nationals is the first part of the national identity scheme to be phased in over the period 2009–2012 for all those coming to the United Kingdom for more than six months or extending their stay in the United Kingdom (National Fraud Strategic Authority 2009).

Also, since October 2008, the General Register Office in the United Kingdom has provided updated death records on a weekly basis to vetted organisations to combat the theft of identity from the deceased. In the first half of 2009, a strategic review was undertaken to examine the overall national response to identity crime and related fraud. This review examined the evolving nature of identity crime and related fraud, assessed the national response to identity crime in Britain, identified strengths and weaknesses in the government's capabilities and developed appropriate and achievable plans to close the gaps identified (National Fraud Strategic Authority 2009: 45).

The problems associated with national identity card systems lie in the risk that the security of a networked identity database could be compromised and that data could be used for unauthorised purposes in breach of privacy principles (see Smith 2008b). There is also the reluctance of the public to find such a solution acceptable, especially in non-European and non-Asian countries such as Australia where the introduction of a national identity card has been generally opposed.

Identification procedures

A range of policy reforms have also been devised to improve identification procedures used by government and business and, importantly, to enable agencies to verify documents and information tendered as evidence of identity with issuing agencies. In many countries, documents used to establish identity are issued by a number of government agencies including passport offices, birth registries and drivers' licence issuing agencies. Cross-validation enables inconsistencies to be ascertained and identity-related fraud minimised. The solutions to the problem lie not so much in increasing the number of proof of identity documents required, but in improving the security features of documents, enabling staff who inspect documents for authenticity to be able to detect counterfeits and to verify the information contained on documents with the issuing source, and for alternative means of identification to be used, such as interviews, or biometrics.

In London, in 2008, the Metropolitan Police Service engaged with the printing industry and met with United Kingdom and international sales managers alongside commercial directors to establish a voluntary code of conduct to raise industry standards around the sale of equipment to minimise risks of false identity documents being created and used (National Fraud Strategic Authority 2009: 45).

Biometric identification systems are also attracting great interest for the apparently higher level of integrity that they offer in comparison to the standard knowledge-based and token-based systems of identification (see Smith 2003). There is a wide variety of such systems being used that make use of an individual's unique physical properties. Common biometric identifiers today include fingerprints, voice patterns, typing patterns, retinal images, facial or hand geometry, and even the identification of a person's subcutaneous vein structures or body odours. Although such systems achieve much higher levels of security than those which rely upon passwords, they are expensive to introduce and raise potential problems in terms of privacy and confidentiality of the personal data stored on computer networks (see Smith 2003).

User education and victim support

Considerable effort is made each year by government and private sector organisations in seeking to educate consumers as to the risks of identity crime, especially those forms that occur online. Targeted education campaigns are conducted each year by members of the International Consumer Protection and Enforcement Network (ICPEN). Each year, for example, members of the Australasian Consumer Fraud Taskforce (ACFT) participate in a period of fraud prevention awareness-raising activities based around an agreed theme designed to achieve the greatest impact on consumers living in their respective countries. For the 2007 campaign, the ACFT developed the theme for Australia and New Zealand: 'Scams target you – protect yourself' with four targeted risk areas examined in each of the four weeks of the campaign respectively: protect your money, protect your phone, protect your computer and protect your identity (Smith and Akman 2008).

In the United States, the Identity Theft and Assumption Deterrence Act 1998 created a centralised victim assistance, complaint and consumer education service for victims of identity theft. This means that victims need not contact each of the relevant agencies separately. Instead, there is a 'joint fraud alert' that the three major credit reporting agencies administer. Victims can access assistance in the absence of a conviction for identity theft. The Fair and Accurate Credit Transactions Act 2003 also introduced a series of protections for consumers. Consumers are able to obtain a free credit report on request, to help them monitor their financial information and provide an early alert of unlawful activity. Consumers can also place a fraud alert on their account. Once the alert has been placed on the account, credit-reporting agencies must block potentially fraudulent information on consumer credit reports from being released. In Britain, similar support services for victims are being introduced as part of the National Fraud Strategy (National Fraud Strategic Authority 2009).

Conclusions

This chapter has outlined various identity crime risks that arise in connection with the Internet and identified some of the key issues to be addressed in responding to the problem. It is clear that there is not a single solution to the problem of online identity crime and that a range of measures will need to be adopted that will involve both government agencies as well as organisations in the private sector all working cooperatively. Technology will provide some solutions, such as the development of biometric identification systems. However, these will not solve all of the problems because technological solutions, no matter how sophisticated, can be circumvented by those with the necessary skills and resources. Adopting a range of identification strategies is likely to be the most effective response coupled with appropriate and secure sharing of information across agencies. At the same time, privacy considerations need to be taken into account and legislation reviewed to keep pace with technological developments.

Note

1 I am grateful to Dr Kim-Kwang Raymond Choo, Research Analyst at the Australian Institute of Criminology, for alerting me to a number of the sources used in this chapter.

Further reading

Regular updates on the nature and extent of identity crime can be found in the regular reports of the Anti-Phishing Working Group (www.antiphishing.org), CyberSource (www.cybersource.com), Javelin Survey and Research (www.javelinstrategy.com), KPMG (www.kpmg.com.au), Sophos (www.sophos.com), Symantec (www.symantec.com) and Unisys (www.unisys.com). Statistics on payment card fraud are published by the Australian Payments Clearing Association (www.apca.com.au), NACHA – The Electronic Payments Association (www.nacha.org) and CIFAS (www.cifas.org.uk). Material on prevention is available from Get Safe Online (www.getsafeonline.org), the Office of Fair Trading (http://www.consumerdirect.gov.uk) and the Australasian Consumer Fraud Taskforce (www.scamwatch.gov.au). Finally, international normative developments can be tracked by following the meetings of the United Nations Commission on Crime Prevention and Criminal Justice (http://www.unodc.org/unodc/en/commissions/CCPCJ/index.html).

References

Anjum, Z. (2008) 'IT managers daunted by mobile device security', *Computerworld Singapore*, 27 May. http://www.computerworld.com/action/article.do?command=viewArticleBasic&taxonomyName=mobile_devices&articleId=90895398taxonomyId=758intsrc=kc_top

Anti-Phishing Working Group (2009) *Phishing Activity Trends Report* – July to December 2008, at www.antiphishing.org

Association of Payment Clearing Services (APACS) (2008) *Fraud: The Facts 2008*. London: APACS.

AusCERT (2008) *Home Users Computer Security Survey*, at www.auscert.org.au

Australasian Centre for Policing Research and Australian Transaction Reports and Analysis Centre (2006) *Standardisation of Definitions of Identity Crime Terms: A Step Towards Consistency*. Adelaide: Australasian Centre for Policing Research.

Australian Bureau of Criminal Intelligence (2002) *Identity Fraud Register Pilot: Final Report*. Canberra: Australian Bureau of Criminal Intelligence.

Australian Bureau of Statistics (2008) *Personal Fraud 2007* cat. no. 4528.0. Melbourne: Australian Bureau of Statistics.

Australian Communications and Media Authority (ACMA) (2008) 'Number of Mobile Phones Now Exceeds Australia's Population', *Media Release* 28 April. http://www.acma.gov.au/WEB/STANDARD/1001/pc=PC_311135

Australian Payments Clearing Association (APCA) (2009) *Fraud Perpetrated on Cheques and Plastic Cards*, at www.apca.com.au

British Broadcasting Corporation (BBC) (2008) 'HSBC Loses Customers' Data Disc', 7 April, http://news.bbc.co.uk/1/hi/business/7334249.stm

Byron, T. (2008) *Safer Children in a Digital World: The Report of the Byron Review.* Nottingham: DCSF Publications.

Canadian Competition Bureau (2005) *Findings from the 2005 Fraud Awareness Tracking Study.* Ottawa: Canadian Competition Bureau

Chen, Y.C., Chen, P.S, Song, R. and Korba, L. (2004) *Online Gaming, Crime and Security Issue: Cases and Countermeasures from Taiwan.* Paper presented to the Second Annual Conference on Privacy, Security and Trust, University of New Brunswick, at http://dev.hil.unb.ca/Texts/PST/pdf/chen.pdf

Choo, K-K.R., Smith, R.G. and McCusker, R. (2007) *Future Directions in Technology-enabled Crime.* Research and Public Policy Series no 78. Canberra: Australian Institute of Criminology.

CIFAS (2004) *Deceased Frauds – Research Results*, at http://www.cifas.org.uk/reports_deceased_fraud.asp

CIFAS (2006) *Online Fraud Trends*, at http://www.cifas.org.uk/press_20070130.asp

Council of Europe (2001) *Convention on Cybercrime*, European Treaty Series no. 185, Budapest, 23 November, at http://conventions.coe.int/treaty/EN/projets/projets.htm

Crosby, J. (2008) *Challenges and Opportunities in Identity Assurance.* London: HM Treasury.

Cuganesan, S. and Lacey, D. (2003) *Identity Fraud in Australia: An Evaluation of its Nature, Cost and Extent.* Sydney: SIRCA.

CyberSource (2009) *Fifth Annual UK Online Fraud Report.* Reading: CyberSource.

Department of Trade and Industry (2006) *Information Security Breaches Survey 2006.* London: Department of Trade and Industry.

Dhamija, R., Tygar, J.D. and Hearst, M. (2006) 'Why Phishing Works', *CHI 2006*, April 22–27. Montreal: CHI.

Drimer, S., Murdoch, S.J and Anderson, R. (2008) 'Thinking Inside the Box: System-level Failures of Tamper Proofing'. Paper presented at the *IEEE Symposium on Security and Privacy*, May, Oakland, California.

European Network and Information Security Agency (2007) *Security Issues and Recommendations for Online Social Networks*, ENISA Position Paper no. 1. Heraklion: European Network and Information Security Agency.

Federal Trade Commission (2006) *Consumer Fraud in the United States: An FTC Survey.* Washington: Federal Trade Commission.

Geis, G. (1991) 'White-Collar Crime: What Is It?', *Current Issues in Criminal Justice*, 3(1): 9–24.

Get Safe Online (2007) 'Social Networks and Wireless Networks Provide "Rich Pickings" for Criminals', Press Release no. 8, at www.getsafeonline.org/nqcontent.dfm?1_id=1469

Glenn, J.C. and Gordon, T.J. (2007) *State of the Future: Executive Summary*, at http://www.millennium-project.org/millennium/sof2007-exec-summ.pdf

Information Commissioner's Office (2007) *Confidential Details Lost by Revenue and Customs*, 20 November, at http://www.ico.gov.uk/upload/documents/pressreleases/2007/personal_details_lost_by_hmrc_201107003.pdf

Javelin Strategy and Research (2008) *2008 Identity Fraud Survey Report: Consumer Version*. Pleasanton, CA: Javelin Strategy and Research.

Johnson, B. (2007) 'Virtual Robber Nabbed for Real', *Age (Melbourne)*, 16 November, at http://www.theage.com.au/news/world/virtual-robber-nabbed-for-real/2007/11/15/1194766867217.html

Jones, N. (2006) *Europeans Expect Mobile Technology to Facilitate Collaboration in 2009*. Stamford, CT: Gartner.

Kane, S.F. (2008) Virtually Lawless: Legal and Economic Issues in Virtual Worlds, *The Computer and Internet Lawyer*, 25(6): 13–24.

KPMG (2009) *Fraud Survey 2008*. Sydney: KPMG Australia.

Krim, J. and Barbaro, M. (2005) '40 Million Credit Card Numbers Hacked', *Washington Post*, 18 June: A01, http://www.washingtonpost.com/wp-dyn/content/article/2005/06/17/AR2005061701031_2.html

Levi, M. (2009) 'Suite Revenge?: The Shaping of Folk Devils and Moral Panics about White-Collar Crimes', *The British Journal of Criminology*, 49(1): 48–67.

Levi, M., Burrows, J., Fleming, M.H., Hopkins, M. and Matthews, K. (2007) *The Nature, Extent and Economic Impact of Fraud in the UK: Report for the Association of Chief Police Officers Economic Crime Portfolio*. London: Association of Chief Police Officers.

McAfee (2005) *McAfee Virtual Criminology Report*. Santa Clara: McAfee.

NACHA – The Electronic Payments Association (2008) 'Electronic Payments Make Sense as Postage and Fuel Costs Continue to Rise', *Press Release*. Herndon, VA: NACHA.

National Commission on Terrorist Attacks upon the United States (2004) *The 9/11 Commission Report*. Washington: National Commission on Terrorist Attacks upon the United States.

National Fraud Strategic Authority (2009) *The National Fraud Strategy: A New Approach to Combating Fraud*, at http://www.attorneygeneral.gov.uk/attachments/NFSA_STRATEGY_AW_Web.pdf

New South Wales Police Force (2009) 'Police and eBay Smash Multi-million Dollar Fraud Syndicate' *Media Release*, 10 March. Sydney: New South Wales Police Force.

Nguyen, T.H., Ekholm, J. and Ingelbrecht, N. (2007) *Dataquest Insight: More Growth Ahead for Mobile Gaming*. Stamford, CT: Gartner.

Ofcom (2008) *Social Networking: A Quantitative and Qualitative Research Report into Attitudes, Behaviours and Use*, at www.ofcom.org.uk/advice/media_literacy/medlitpub/medlitpubrss/socialnetworking/report.pdf

Office of the Privacy Commissioner (2007) *Community Attitudes Towards Privacy*. Melbourne: Wallis Consulting Group.

Ong, B.H. (2008) 'In the Real World, Virtual Gaming Spells Big Business', *Straitstimes. com* 28 April, at http://www.straitstimes.com/Free/Story/STIStory_231774.html

Payment Card Industry (2006) *Payment Card Industry Data Security Standard*, at https://www.pcisecuritystandards.org/pdfs/pci_dss_v1-1.pdf

Pontell, H.N., Brown, G.C., and Tosouni, A. (2008) 'Stolen Identities: A Victim Survey', in M.M. McNally and G.R. Newman (eds), *Perspectives on Identity Theft: Crime Prevention Studies*, vol 23. Monsey, New York: Criminal Justice Press.

Public Safety and Emergency Preparedness Canada (2004) *Report on Identity Theft*. Ottawa: Public Safety and Emergency Preparedness Canada.

Reuters (2008) 'MegaPath Survey Finds Only One Third of Retailers Have Strong PCI Compliance', 1 April, at http://www.reuters.com/article/pressRelease/idUS135077+01-Apr-2008+BW20080401

Rollings, K. (2008) *Counting the Costs of Crime in Australia: A 2005 Update*, Research and Public Policy Series no. 91. Canberra: Australian Institute of Criminology.

Smith, R.G. (2003) 'Travelling in Cyberspace on a False Passport: Controlling Transnational Identity-related Crime', in R. Tarling (ed.), *The British Criminology Conference: Selected Proceedings*, vol 5, Papers from the British Society of Criminology Conference, Keele, British Society of Criminology, at http://www.britsoccrim.org/bccsp/vol05/smith.htm

Smith, R.G. (2007) 'Biometric Solutions to Identity-related Cybercrime', in Y. Jewkes (ed.) *Crime Online*. Cullompton: Willan Publishing.

Smith, R.G. (2008a) 'Online Personal Fraud: Quantifying the Extent of Semantic and Syntactic Attacks in Australia.' Paper presented at the *Twenty-Sixth International Symposium on Economic Crime*, 3 September, Jesus College, Cambridge.

Smith, R.G. (2008b) 'Preventing Identity-related Crime: The Challenges of Identification', in M.M. McNally and G.R. Newman (eds), *Perspectives on Identity Theft: Crime Prevention Studies*, vol 23. Monsey NY: Criminal Justice Press.

Smith, R.G. and Akman, T. (2008). 'Raising Public Awareness of Consumer Fraud in Australia', in *Trends and Issues in Crime and Criminal Justice*, no. 349. Canberra: Australian Institute of Criminology.

Sophos (2008) *Security Threat Report 2008*. London: Sophos.

Standing Committee of Attorneys-General (2008) *Final Report: Identity Crime*. Canberra: Model Criminal Law Officers' Committee of the Standing Committee of Attorneys-General.

Symantec (2007) *Internet Security Threat Report*. Cupertino: Symantec.

Trend Micro (2007) *Threat Report 2008: Threat and Technology Forecast*. Cupertino: Trend Micro.

Unisys (2006) *Security Survey and Index 2006: A Newspoll Survey*, June Quarter. Sydney: Newspoll.

United Nations (2007) *Results of the Second Meeting of the Intergovernmental Expert Group to Prepare a Study on Fraud and the Criminal Misuse and Falsification of Identity*, Report of the Secretary-General, E/CN.15/2007/1. Vienna: Commission on Crime Prevention and Criminal Justice Sixteenth Session.

United Nations (2009) *International Cooperation in the Prevention, Investigation, Prosecution and Punishment of Economic Fraud and Identity-related Crime*, Report of the Secretary-General, E/CN.15/2009/1. Vienna: Commission on Crime Prevention and Criminal Justice Eighteenth Session.

United States President's Taskforce on Identity Theft (2008) *President's Identity Theft Taskforce Report*. Washington: United States President's Taskforce on Identity Theft.

Visa International (2006) *Consumer Attitudes and Behaviours Toward Data Security in Asia Pacific*. Hong Kong: Harris Interactive.

Warren, I. (2008) 'Regulation, Governance and Second Life', Paper presented at the *Australian and New Zealand Society of Criminology 21st Annual Conference, Criminology: Linking Theory, Policy and Practice*, 26 November, Canberra.

Weisburd, D., Wheeler, S. and Waring, E. (1991) *Crimes of the Middle Class: White Collar Offenders in the Federal Courts*. New Haven: Yale University Press.

White, M.D and Fisher, C. (2008) 'Assessing Our Knowledge of Identity Theft: The Challenges to Effective Prevention and Control Efforts', *Criminal Justice Policy Review*, 19(1): 3–24.

Chapter 15

The sex industry, regulation and the Internet

Teela Sanders

Introduction

This chapter explores the relationship between the sex industries and the Internet. It will be argued throughout this chapter, that the diversification of the sex markets, and the purchase of sex, has been greatly assisted by new technologies, specifically the Internet. First, the overall impact of the Internet on the shape and nature of the sex markets is explored. Second, I explain how those who sell sex (not only women) use the Internet to advertise and manage their services and business using empirical data collected from an ethnographic project. Third, the role of the buyer is explored, highlighting that the sex markets have been increasingly accessible and available through the privacy and anonymity afforded computer usage. Fourth, this section will explain how men who sell sex use the Internet as a forum for advertising to a range of customers, including the gay community. Fifth, looking at both the sellers and the buyers of commercial sex, I use empirical research findings from two projects (explained below), to look at what can be described as an online 'sex work community'. How this group communicates, the purposes of their online interactions and their role in self-regulation are explored. Finally, I return to a global perspective that examines the wider diversification of the sex markets and the expansion of markets given the impact of the sex industry. The conclusion looks forward to further implications of the Internet as it becomes an intricate part of the infrastructure of commercial sex.

Empirical research

The sex industries are made up of many different sex markets that offer an array of sexual services, from the very mundane and basic, to fantasies and fetishes to match a myriad of tastes. Harcourt and Donovan (2005) document 25 different types of sex market which occur in everyday settings as well as specific sex work venues. Increasingly the Internet has been identified as a space through which more can be learnt about sexual behaviour and commercial sex. Durkin and Bryant (1995: 197) note that the prognosis for computer sex research brings an opportunity for systematic data gathering using computer-mediated communication to understand electronic erotica and sexual behaviour. Monto (2004) refers to bulletin boards online as a medium to access men who buy sex and explore the purchaser's side of the sexual exchange. Sharp and Earle (2003) describe how the Internet reveals the secret and 'deviant' world of what they crudely term 'cyberpunting' and 'cyberwhoring', yet these suggestions are made with little acknowledgement of the ethical, methodological and epistemological complications of this form of research.

The place of the researcher in commercial sex research is potentially even more central to the relationship between the subject and object, the quality of information shared and the ethical responsibility of the researcher. Establishing research relationships online or observing interactions in the virtual arena take on a range of issues regarding the identity of the researcher and how they manage the disclosure of their status and purpose. The ambiguity of the public virtual domain of bulletin boards and chat rooms poses a set of ethical dilemmas for the researcher who 'lurks' in virtual spaces to find out about behaviour, and possibly use the verbatim text that is exchanged through this platform. I found that the sex work community are incredibly suspicious of engaging in online relationships with others who do not appear to be legitimate members of their self-defined community. Contributors to specific British-based websites that I observed were vocal in expressing their realisation that their interactions were monitored by 'outsiders' such as law enforcers, journalists and researchers. As I argue elsewhere (Sanders 2005b), this level of suspicion and the public nature of the forum through which a private, intimate sexual behaviour is discussed meant that as an ethnographer in the 'virtual' field, establishing bona fide status was carried out in a more rigorous manner than in face-to-face fieldwork situations.

Throughout this chapter, I draw on two empirical research projects which have both used the Internet in various ways as access points for individuals and as fieldwork sites. The first project, written up in the book *Sex Work: A Risky Business* (Sanders 2005b), is primarily about the indoor sex markets from sex workers' perspectives. Here, I explore the concept of risk and examine the risk management strategies that sex workers use to manage the risks they encounter in their working and private lives. As I was looking across the sex markets, I included in the sample, women who worked as entrepreneurial escorts and independent sex workers, managing their business online. I also interviewed managers and owners from an online escort agency as well as women who worked for them. As part of this project, I conducted a content analysis of 30 sex workers websites, to investigate the content of their websites, and the mechanisms that are used to manage the business. Both the interviews with sex workers and observations of the websites will be drawn on to evidence points made throughout the chapter.

The second project concentrated on men who buy sex and is recorded in the monograph *Paying for Pleasure: Men who Buy Sex* (Sanders 2008a). It involved 50 in-depth interviews to explore the role of commercial sex in the men's lives. The main access point was two key Internet sites which are UK-based and acted as virtual spaces where men who buy sex (and those who sell sex) congregate. Male clients were recruited through Internet message boards and snowball sampling. In total, 50 male clients were interviewed: 37 interviews were conducted face to face and 13 over the telephone. The sample was generally made up of middle-class, white, middle to older aged men due to Internet-based recruitment methods. The mean age was 45 years with a range of 22–70 years. Forty-two members of the sample described themselves as White British, while four stated they were British Asian. Four participants were respectively White Irish, British-born Canadian, Australian and Italian. Eighteen of the 50 were married and a further eight were in long-term relationships. Twelve men said they were single, four were widowers, and eight stated they were either divorced or separated. Only seven men did not have any formal qualifications: 34 had a higher education degree. Occupations were predominantly middle-class including a lawyer, pilot, several men involved in teaching or academia, engineering, banking, media, sales and IT.

The sample was varied in terms of the length of time men had experience of the sex industry: the average numbers of years was nine, with a range of between one and 33 years. The average expenditure on sexual services per month was £170 with a range of £45–£500. Only two of the 50 said they currently purchased sex from the street market, although a further eight men said they had done this in the past but had stopped for a range of reasons such as (perceived) concern about disease and drugs, concerns about the police and scams such as robbery they could fall victim to. The greater part of the sample (32/50) visited both massage parlours and independent escorts who operated their own businesses online; seven others only went to parlours and nine only saw escorts (six in their own home and three in either a hotel or the sex worker's apartment). Twenty-eight of the 50 participants described themselves as 'regulars' who visit the same sex worker (sometimes more than one sex worker). In addition to these in-depth interviews, observations were carried out on message boards and chat rooms over a period of 18 months. These data sources will be drawn upon to explain the relationship between buyers and sellers and the self-regulating nature of the online sex industry.

The UK law on commercial sex

In the UK, it is legal to be a sex worker and engage in adult consensual commercial sex, whereby an exchange of money or other commodities is agreed for sexual services. However, increasingly, many of the relationships around selling, organising and buying sex have become illegal. Dating back to the Street Offences Act (1957), it is illegal to solicit or loiter, and laws introduced under the 1985 Sexual Offences Act make it a crime to kerb-crawl for sex in public. The indoor sex markets have been targeted under the 2003 Sexual Offences Act, where brothel-keeping and procuring (encouraging) prostitution can be met with a seven-year prison sentence (for a review of the laws see Brooks-Gordon 2006: ch. 2). More recently, in 2008, the Home Office

(2008) have pushed for a new crime to be made of buying sex from anyone 'controlled for gain'. This would mean that anyone who purchased sex, even consensually, from someone who was managed, had a receptionist, or paid money to work in a brothel, would be made a criminal. This prohibitionist approach to managing the sex industry stems from a desire to eradicate the sex industry and make moral, symbolic legislation, sending the message that buying and selling sex is wrong.

The laws relating to advertising sexual services have also undergone recent changes. In the 2001 Criminal Justice and Police Act, legislation was introduced to make it a crime to advertise in public places, particularly phone boxes. In an attempt to reduce what is known as 'carding' escort and brothel advertisements in the telephone boxes of London, a prosecution for advertising violations could lead to a summary conviction of six months imprisonment or a fine. There has also been a move to ban the advertisements of personal services in newspapers. The Minister for Women and Equality, Harriet Harman MP, commissioned the report 'Women Not for Sale. A Report on Advertising Women in Small Ads in Local Newspapers', published in January 2008. The report found from 79 newspapers across the UK that advertisements of personal services represented £44 million of advertising revenue. The findings that were highlighted, although it was noted that the reality of these adverts was not proven, was that half of the ads indicated nationality or race as a 'selling point'. These findings were used to fuel the idea that sex workers who are not 'British' are trafficked to the UK for purposes of prostitution. Harriet Harman made the following evaluation: 'Next to the ads where it says skip hire and lost pets you'll find "fresh girls in every week", "girls age eighteen to twenty four from Africa, from South East Asia". Within these ads are girls who've been trafficked into modern day slavery.'[1] The concern over the trafficking of women, and the confusion between trafficking and economic migrant women who move to work in the sex industry, is increasing the pressure to create punitive legislation in efforts to stop the sex industry.

There is no direct legislation that attempts to regulate advertising on the Internet because being a sex worker is not a crime. Often sex workers have statements (usually for the benefit of their customers) which state that they are not coerced, do not give their earnings to anyone they do not choose to, and are not working against their own wishes. Whilst individual escorts who work alone within the law are at this point safe from police attention, escort agencies and brothels who advertise online are exposed to police attention as they are culpable under brothel-keeping, money-laundering and procuring laws.

The impact of the Internet on the sex industry

Castells (1996) has identified that the Internet is one of the most significant drivers in social change in late modernity. Nowhere is this more evident than in the changing nature and social organisation of the global commercial sex industries. Any growth in both women setting up as entrepreneurial sex workers and the methods through which men come to know and negotiate sexual services is almost certainly attributable to the prevalence of computer-mediated communication that has occurred in late modernity (see Sharp and Earle 2003; Soothill and Sanders 2005). As Kilvington, Day and Ward (2001) note, the Internet provides the opportunity to work in the sex industry without the costs associated with physical visibility on the streets. O'Neill (2001: 150) recognises the shift to the Internet is driven by the high costs of advertising space in contact magazines and telephone booths; these are also more open to surveillance and policing than the Internet which remains outside the capabilities of everyday law enforcement. Reflecting on the changes in the UK, Sharpe and Earle (2003: 36) claim 'In recent years, demand for commercially available sexual services has soared, and the nature of the relationships involved in the selling of sexual services is undergoing a significant transformation in a number of ways, owing to the emergence and near exponential spread of the Internet.' Although it is very hard to measure and quantify growth in an unaccountable and largely hidden industry, what is indisputable is that new information technology has created new conditions of sexual commerce and consumerism in the digital age.

These new conditions have been created largely because the global reach of the Internet has meant that the sex markets, and individual sellers, are accessible without boundaries or limits. Websites can be perused 24 hours a day, without geographical, spatial or time restrictions. Moreover, looking for commercial sex, which is generally considered a 'deviant' if not at least a private activity, can be done in the privacy of one's own home or office space, entirely when it suits. The level of control that a buyer has over the knowledge process has massively increased because all the information required to find, negotiate and arrange commercial sex is all available at the touch of a button. The significance of the Internet on the shape, nature and organisation of the sex markets throughout the world has led Weitzer (2005) to state that the new directions of research into the sex industry need to prioritise the relationship between the Internet and commercial sex.

Promoting commercial sex

The relationship between the Internet and commercial sex is relatively recent, but was also one of the early uses applied to the Internet. The Internet became a promoter of the sex industry when the first online escort agency, based in Seattle, USA, was advertised in 1994 (Hughes 2001: 2). This has been considered by some radical feminists as a markedly negative aspect of the exploitation of women, and some have stated that commercial sex advertised online is nothing short of 'cybersexploitation' (O'Connell 2003; Hughes 2004).

Largely, the main function of the Internet is for advertising. Websites range from the very simple (with a few semi-naked pictures, list of services and contact details), to the more elaborate (with extensive information, narrative about the individual or place, gallery of photos, feedback from customers), promote brothels, massage parlours, sex clubs, domination dungeons, and individual sex workers. The explicit advertisement of sex is generally not evident because of the laws against advertising (see below). Instead, suggestions of prices are based on time (e.g. 30 minutes = £150; 60 minutes = £300). Some sites have a disclaimer of 'adult content', asking viewers to click if they are over 18.

I have identified how the sex markets create ancillary industries which exist to support the sex industry, and in part are essential to the operation and running of different markets (Sanders 2008b). There is an identifiable ancillary industry which supports websites in the sex industry and has three main forms:

- Clients who are in the IT job market offer individual sex workers, either as a favour, for a fee, or in exchange for free or favourable sexual services, to create and manage a website.

- Sex workers who have IT skills (or train) manage their own websites, and offer their skills to other sex workers for a fee. This model of 'women supporting women' is often preferred in order to cut out any financial exploitation from clients.

- Individual IT companies specialise in selling web skills to sex businesses.

This ancillary industry is not necessarily like other IT business relationships, because of the illegal element to some of the work. For instance, managers could be charged with brothel-keeping, and those who work together could be charged with procuring (encouraging prostitution) offences. Hence, high levels of discretion and confidentiality are key when work is carried out for sex workers or managers of sex businesses.

New markets

The changing nature of the sex markets due to technological advancement has reshaped, expanded and repackaged the availability of all types of sexual services over the past decade. For instance, using a combination of the Internet as the main advertising mechanism, and other new technologies such as webcams and mobile telephones, hybrid sex markets have been developed, often by entrepreneurial female sex workers. Harcourt and Donovan (2005) make distinctions between 'direct' and 'indirect' sexual services. Direct sexual services refer more specifically to types of commercial sex where physical contact of a sexual nature is exchanged for money. Direct sex work involves some aspect of genital contact, although does not always mean penetrative intercourse. Direct sexual services usually take place in a known and recognised sex market such as in a brothel or on the street. Indirect sexual services refer to a whole range of other types of sexual services which do not necessarily involve physical genital contact but the exchange is sexual in nature and is characterised by money or gifts. Lap dancing, stripping, erotic telephone sex work, massage and bondage are some examples of indirect sex work. Lucas (2005) notes that there is a hierarchy of prostitution markets where elite prostitution has adapted to benefit from using technologies.

The Internet and other new communication technologies have played a role in developing and diversifying both direct and indirect sexual services.

In terms of indirect sexual services, watching 'private' sexual activities (sexual voyeurism) or watching live pornographic shows online have become popular as cash transactions can be made instantly direct into a bank account. In these new markets, sex workers have only virtual contact with those who buy the service, and for some this is a more palatable means of earning money. Live sex chat lines have taken on a more visual element through websites offering speedy connections and down the line visuals via webcams to paying customers all over the world.

Agustin (2005) reminds researchers that the cultural context of commercial sex is needed to understand the nature and organisation of the sex industries in late capitalism. This is a relevant point when understanding recent changes in how the sex markets are formed, managed and organised. The Internet, as demonstrated above, is creating opportunities for commercial sex which move beyond the traditional, face-to-face contact. As a result of the trend towards independent sex workers and establishments moving to the Internet, directories, website hosts and other online guides and manuals have become another part of the ancillary Internet industry that makes money from the sex industry. Recently a sex worker wrote a guide, 'The Internet Escort's Handbook', which has turned into a series of manuals to discuss issues such as mental, emotional and physical conditions of working as an escort; health and personal boundaries; marketing your image; and myths and deceptions.

Sellers advertising online

There has been a noted transition from advertising in print format (specialist magazines, newspaper small adverts in the 'personal' column, even simple handwritten adverts in shop windows), to online advertising. This has been facilitated in two ways:

- Individual entrepreneurs, who either have web design skills, or hire someone with the skills, create their own websites and take control over their own advertising and service management. This quote from Lucy, who worked from a rented house alone, explained how she changed her advertising methods in 2000: 'Previously I was advertising in a local paper. Previous to this I was doing domination and I worked as a dominatrix for 18 months which wasn't on the Internet but did not involve any personal services. So I decided to branch out and I tried advertising in the paper for about three months and it did not suit me at all. They [potential customers] would phone you from 10 in the morning till nine at night. So I was just about to give it up and then I went on the Internet and found XXX [a large marketing website for the sex industry] and I thought a website was in order and I started from there.'

- Online advertisers approach sex workers to encourage them to buy online advertising.

These transitions involve hiring a photographer to take pictures and commissioning a 'webmaster' to create a domain name, set up a webpage and manage the site. As newspaper and print advertising has become increasingly expensive and needs maintaining weekly, as well as a surge of newspapers withdrawing these adverts, the Internet offers a more streamlined and efficient method of reaching the desired audience. Not only is the Internet more efficient for sex workers, there are some fundamental benefits from advertising and managing sexual services online.

Advantages of the Internet: safety and security

New technologies are offering opportunities for sex workers across the globe. Veena (2007) reports on a small qualitative study with 10 freelance sex workers who all work from the Internet in Bangkok, Thailand. The opportunities that the Internet provides these sex workers can be generalised to the basic benefits of using technology as a tool to organise business for independent women. Sex workers in Veena's study reported that through the Internet women could maximise their earnings by reducing costs such as those incurred when arranging to meet clients and a third party who would be part of the organisational triangle. Alongside financial independence, women could charge higher prices. Beyond the financial benefits, the sex workers in Veena's (2007: 105) study identified 'the privacy factor' as a key benefit of using the Internet. Many of the sex workers were students and wanted to keep their sex work employment hidden from the university community.

What was also evident in Veena's study and concurs with work from Sanders (2005a: 68) on independent Internet-based escorts, is that the Internet sex work community becomes a prime place where safety is discussed between women and strategies and advice are shared for choosing safe customers and how to work in a way that minimises risks. Several websites have spaces where sex workers can write about individuals with whom they have had negative experiences and even exchange identifying features such as car registration and mobile phone number as a means of warning other sex workers to beware. These established activities identify a real sex work community. On these websites, there is a sense of collective concern and effort to supply information that can help each other stay safe. This is particularly the case between escorts who often work alone in their own apartment, or visit customers alone. These websites that are hosted by sex workers for sex workers usually have guides on how to be safe in different working environments, how to ensure that other people know their whereabouts, and how to act if the customer becomes agitated or violent.

In addition to the sense of community that is evident among sex workers who contribute to and use websites, using the Web to organise business, and select clients is the first step in ensuring that only genuine customers are chosen. For instance, on the website, sex workers will advertise which types of service are on offer, and therefore those that are not. Kinnell (2006) notes that often a trigger point for violence from a client is when the service he is expecting is not provided, or when there is a dispute over money. By stating upfront the services, and then in conversation before the meeting, the price, the terms of the contract are clearly negotiated by the two parties. This means that the customer is very clear when he meets the sex worker about the exact parameters of the commercial sex liaison.

Sex workers described how they would use the very first contact with clients as a means of screening 'good' from 'bad' clients. If clients would speak in depth and at length about a sexual fantasy, this was not seen as appropriate and it was easy to spot those who were time wasters. Jeanie, who had worked online for two years, explained:

> Of the emails that I get there are fifty per cent that I automatically bin them because you can tell a lot by the way someone phrases an email. If someone goes into too much detail in the first email, or some of them you can tell it is kids messing about on their dad's computer. You get a good judge from the way they phrase their emails as to whether it is the type of customer that you want. Some are too young or will go into really graphic detail. It allows you to be a lot more picky and you have got to have the confidence to be able to sit there on the Internet and think, well, I would rather lose the money than see this person.

The very first email contact, how the prospective customer explained themselves and their requirements, was the point where sex workers decided whether to pursue the inquiry or not. Arranging appointments via email and then the telephone was considered to provide more security in terms of reducing the number of time wasters who would book appointments and not turn up:

> ... with the email, as you know I don't give out a phone number on my site so with the email all it takes is when it suits me I go check my email and email them back. With the phone you have basically got to be sat there working from 10 until six plus over the phone, because they don't know you, and through the Internet they have found your reviews or whatever, so there is trust worked up and they are quite happy to book definite appointments and give mobile numbers for your own security and they are happy to make their way into an area and phone at a set time. (Jeanie, 34, escort)

In my research it was a common theme that sex workers who had moved their advertising onto the Internet believed that customers who surfed the net were higher paying and from a professional background. Twenty-eight-year-old Verity (who visited customers in hotels) saw only men in the higher income bracket:

> I usually get thirty to sixty professionals, lawyer, doctor, computing, finance or own their own company. I think the Internet has changed the clients at the moment but I think it will broaden out as people get more used to looking online. At the moment a lot of people surf at work and it is not everyone who has a computer at home. I do get more inquiries now as more people are getting PCs in their home. I suppose the price is higher than average, that is going to reflect on the client group.

Verity identified a common theme among female sex workers, who felt that those people who had access to computers in order to arrange sexual services were those in professional jobs who could afford to pay higher prices compared to those in a sauna, for instance.

There were other advantages that several female sex workers explained were a by-product of the Internet. These were related to educating men about the types of women (e.g. not stereotypes) who worked in the Internet, as well as establishing business links between women:

> I think the websites opens up the men's eyes that you have a personality and a sense of humour rather than just being on your back. I don't use the chat but the message boards I do. A lot of the people will decide to see you on the basis of what they have seen of your personality on the message boards. It is getting a lot more that the clients want to spend quality time with not only someone who is attractive but someone whom they are going to get on with. That is what they are looking for on the Internet. They must just read the post and pick up on it. I have done work with three other girls and it is from reading their messages on the board that I have decided that we could probably get on. (Flo, 36, escort)

Disadvantages: being found out

New technologies have allowed many sex workers to transform their businesses, appeal to wider audiences, have greater control over their work, and make a profit from providing sexual services safely. However, there are always disadvantages and these relate to the constant updating of technologies, the increasing competition from other sex workers, and the threat of being 'found out' by family and friends, and of course officials.

Advertising online creates problems in terms of being identified as a sex worker. The norm is to have some images on the website to attract customers. Often these images hide or blur out the face to avoid direct recognition. However, this disguise is not always successful and several sex workers gave me accounts of how they had been discovered working through the Internet by close family and friends. Jeanie, a 34-year-old escort, revealed how a picture on the Internet caused problems with her boyfriend:

> When I met the partner I am with now, he doesn't actually know that I do this and a friend had actually fallen out with her partner. He knew that I used to do domination and I used to show my face in the photos then. And when I had been with my current partner for about a month this chap just walked up to him in a nightclub and handed him the picture. So I had to tell him about that and from the reaction I got from that I made the decision that I was not going to tell him about anything else. It didn't go down very well, so I told him about the web design instead. It is a bit of a double life but I just don't think about it too much. Work is so separate. I find it easy to switch on and off.

In addition to the fear of being found out by someone you know, sex workers were constantly fearful of the media finding out about their websites and making salacious headlines that could cause devastation in their personal and public lives. Sex workers were particularly concerned about the impact of exposure on their children.

Buying sex online

In *Paying for Pleasure: Men who buy Sex* (Sanders 2008a) I describe how the sex industry has expanded due to 'push factors' that act as drivers from the lives of individual men and 'pull factors', which attract men to commercial sex. One of the most powerful pull factors is the Internet and the prolific amount of information about the sex industry that is freely available at the click of a mouse. This material is not illicit, and is not particularly sexual in nature, but does provide all the information a novice needs to enter into the negotiations as a customer of sex workers. For men seeking to buy sex, the Internet provides a space to explore this activity, with minimum risk of being found out or apprehended by the police. Given that many men who buy sex are in long-term relationships or married, the secrecy of the Internet provides additional security that their 'deviant' activities will not be identified. The information sharing facilities enable men to engage in online discussion about offline sex markets which range from those indoors, including stripping and lap dancing, to the street markets.

What do the websites offer?

In the UK, the first website, Punternet, which facilitates adult consensual sexual services, appeared in 1999 with the purpose 'to facilitate the exchange of information on prostitution in the UK'. Designed initially as a site for men looking for sexual services, the website sets out its primary functions: 'Here you will find information on where to find services, what to expect, legalities etc. ... and read reviews of encounters with working girls.' Another regional-based website states that its aims are 'to play parlours off against one another. It increases the stakes and competition between rival parlours such that the best survive and prosper and the worst places vanish.' These types of website receive, at times, several hundred contributions each day and an unknown amount of observers, known as 'lurkers', who simply read and use the information without contributing. Soothill (2004a) recorded that one website for the north-west of England hosted 900 topics in 2003 and received 3,900 replies. Since the Punternet website pioneered these forums in the UK, several others have sprouted with a geographical specificity. Clearly, this is just one example of the many different Internet sites that are geographically specific that speak to the sex work community of both men and women involved.

Although less popular, some websites have been created where men discuss the street sex market. Holt and Blevins (2007) conducted virtual research on active web forums of 'johns' in 10 US cities and examined 6,899 posts in 2005. These researchers found that in the posts, 45 per cent referred to street markets, although there was some geographical variability and in some cities, escort services were talked about the most (for instance, in Atlanta, 75 per cent of posts referred to escorts). The forums were all used to exchange knowledge of where to buy sex, and often in response to inquiries from men visiting the region: 'users ... even assembled maps detailing specific hotspots for prostitutes around the city' (Holt and Blevins 2007: 342).

The website hosted in the UK that I researched provided a range of facilities for both men and sex workers. Chat rooms, message boards, advertisements from sex workers, a 'beginners guide to saunas and massage parlours' and 'field reports' were the main facilities. The field reports are sexual accounts that men write about their commercial liaisons with sex workers. These field reports are categorised under the sex worker's name, and act as free advertising for sex workers. On 13 December 2008, there had been 43,539 field reports posted since 1999, which accounts for a total expenditure of £5,414,708, with an average cost of £125 for each visit. The prevalence of the field reports demonstrates the importance of this mechanism on the website, both for men who buy services and women who sell services. Men I have interviewed who have both contributed and read field reports, note the value of these and other aspects of the website:

> It's got a lot of information on there and if you are not sure about something or what have you then sometimes a thread comes up that can answer your question but obviously the main sort of source for it is the field reports that are on there and that is quite important really if you want to choose the right person if you like. (Jonny, 51, married, IT)

Sex workers have noted the value of the reports. Natasha, an entrepreneurial sex worker who charges £250 for each service, described how her business depended on field reports:

> A lot of the people who see me only do after reading a good report. They always say I have written a report or I have been recommended because obviously they are paying a lot of money and they want to know that what they are getting is good. I quite like that because they know what they are coming for and who they are seeing.

The reports are moderated and sex workers can request for a report to be removed if it is unfavourable or salacious. Not recommending a sex worker is the outcome in only 9 per cent of the reports, suggesting that the majority of reports are favourable and therefore provides positive marketing in a competitive arena.

Applying a sociological analysis of these field reports has led me to argue that these public accounts of intimate private sexual stories reveal the sexual self in the virtual safety of cyberspace (Sanders 2008a: ch. 4). Men talk about their own masculinity, their sexual performance, and often self-analyse their encounters for others (men) to read. Hiding behind pseudonyms both in the reports and the message boards, these anonymous accounts create the feeling of being part of a community. Part of the role of this community is maintaining expected norms of behaviour in the sex industry. One of the older male interviewees described how benchmarking happened by men responding to issues about unsafe sexual practices:

> I mean there's something on the message board at the moment about that, you know, bareback [sex without a condom]. The other day there was a hell of a commotion and one of the girls was throwing somebody out because I think he'd asked for bareback sex. And I thought perhaps he'd tried to take the condom off which was obviously the justification for throwing him out. But no, she'd thrown him out very forcibly, shouting at him and you know, door slamming, just because he'd asked for it! (Benny, 70, widower, retired trucker)

The research on websites where men discuss their commercial sex habits has a strong emphasis on sharing information about specific sex workers in the spirit of recommending services that they were satisfied with. Holt and Blevins (2007: 342) note that posters recommend individuals by posting weblinks and where names and phone numbers were posted it was usually with permission from the sex worker. However, these researchers noted that there were also derogatory comments about the appearance and characteristics of some women who worked on the street, often in relation to their drug use.

Another interviewee in my research summarised the impact of the Internet on real-life commercial sex:

> The Internet has transformed part of the paid sex industry. There are websites with message boards where punters can exchange information. These message boards have an educative function, and amongst other things do set benchmarks. To give examples: Any mention of unprotected sex (bareback) will be met with a barrage of both criticism and informed argument. Just before the law was changed regarding sex with under 18-year-olds someone attempted to advertise the availability of a 16-year-old; despite this being technically legal at that time strong negative responses were expressed, leaving any possible user in no doubt as to what others would think of him. Message boards often contain links to Crime Stoppers or similar resources, encouraging users to report illegal activity such as the use of those under age. Boards often contain sections where both punters and service providers can warn others about dangerous people or practices. (Henry, 56, teaching)

There were other clear benefits to men sharing information about themselves and their identities, lives and routines as 'clients'. Sharing knowledge of what society generally views as a 'deviant' sexual behaviour, means that the men are constantly involved in strategies to manage their stigma and identity. Holt and Blevins (2007: 347) note that 'johns discussed the risks and threats they faced while seeking out paid sexual encounters'. This often centred on alerting other posters to police activity and areas which were heavily policed in the city and were known for 'active stings and busts'. In addition, men would post about their negative experiences of violence and robbery when trying to buy sex, or when a sex worker had taken advantage by robbing their wallet.

Communication between sex workers and clients who buy sexual services acts as a means of establishing group rules and codes of behaviour. Although this is an area where little empirical data has been gathered, Soothill (2004b: 51) documents the moral integrity of clients in relation to sex with young women under the age of 18 years, suggesting that a sex code and a moral code exist among the patrons of prostitution. The online forums provide this space for dialogue outside real-time physical contact, as many sex workers operate in isolation and the majority of clients go about their commercial sex in secret.

Men selling sex via the Internet

The discussion so far has centred on men buying sex from female sex workers. However, the Internet has been the central driver in expanding the male sex industry. Men selling sex to men, across a spectrum of sexual orientations, have used the Internet as a place where the taboos of same sex and commercial sex can be overcome.

Although the main types of male sex worker have been identified as escorts, independent workers and street workers (Connell and Hart 2003), there is evidence to suggest that the online escort worker forms the largest group. Although much early research focused on street-based sex work, the evidence shows that selling sex on the street is less prevalent for men than indoor work, except in certain urban centres and known outdoor spaces for public sex.

The majority of men selling sex do so indoors, in brothels, or bars in some countries, independently in flats, or as agency or independent escorts, often advertising through the gay press, over the Internet and on websites such as 'Gaydar' (Gaffney 2007). Men who sell sex to men use online advertising in a similar way to female entrepreneurial sex workers.

Regulating sexual services

The description of the sex work community above, and those that manage websites for the sex industry, demonstrates that there is a certain degree of informal self-regulation about the communication. The message boards have moderators who manage the information flow, reply to requests, and protect individuals from comments that are not appropriate. There is a degree of integrity about the sites, in that they are seen as communal for all and a place to share information in a non-stigmatised environment. Formally policing the websites and forums would be an impossible task. There is evidence that the self-regulating nature of the online communication has a direct effect on what happens in real-life encounters. As Soothill (2004b: 52) concludes, 'An Internet site that is developed responsibly can help to ensure that the parlour game can continue without unnecessary conflict.'

Activities on the Internet can also be seen to be in direct conflict with efforts to police the sex industry. Holt and Blevins (2007: 350) note that the web forums where 'johns' post have an impact on how efficient law enforcement can be: 'computer mediated communication may enable johns to negate law enforcement efforts no matter how surreptitious or dynamic they may be.' This is equally the case for sex workers who may be breaking the law by working together, or employing a receptionist. They can remain as invisible as possible by not including addresses and screening clients via email and telephone. However, this does not make them immune from decoys who pose as clients only to carry out raids. The mismatch between the sheer expanse of the sex industry on the Internet and limited policing resources for 'vice' is at the heart of the modern-day irony of the nature of the sex industry.

An expanding industry in a criminalised climate?

This chapter has outlined the landscape of the sex industry in relation to new technologies. Just as the Internet and the virtual arena expand and create new opportunities for sellers, organisers and buyers, the sex industry will adapt and remodel itself driven by the desire to make profit. The rise of the interconnections between the Internet and the sex industries has had three significant impacts. First, there has been an opening up of the market from both the supply and demand side of the relationship. Bernstein (2007a) writes that the sex industries are increasingly for the middle classes in that working in the sex industry is becoming a mainstream option for women (and men) who have educated backgrounds, dispelling the idea that prostitution is only about 'survival' by those that are destitute. In addition, middle-class men have increased opportunities to come to know about the sex industry in a way that was too removed from their everyday lives before the widespread nature of the Internet.

Second, there has been a professionalisation of the sex industry through the Internet. Bernstein (2007a) identifies the Internet and entrepreneurial activities as clear signs of how parts of the sex industry are becoming professionalised. An example of such professionalisation, where the sex industry mirrors features of mainstream employment, is that of the website 'EscortSupport. com'. Bernstein (2007a: 482) explains how this is an example of 'a website for sex workers which extends tips and networking to a broad online community'. The benchmarking of rules and etiquette that I demonstrate above, and the sharing and camaraderie displayed by sex workers to help each other work safely, are examples of how the business is developing and becoming more formalised.

Thirdly, the overall impact of the Internet, given the evidence of entrepreneurialism and 'mainstreaming', shows how the sex industries are embedded in consumption and work patterns in contemporary society.

Brents and Sanders (forthcoming) note that the economic mainstreaming of sex industries as acceptable businesses on the high streets (in particular lap dancing venues) in many parts of the Western world, has been equalled, to some extent, with a social acceptability of the sex industry. Economically, there has been support from multinationals to create mass business out of sex, which in turn has created an expanding employment sector in the informal economy.

This has had the impact that women are considering the sex industry as a viable alternative to long hours in low-paid, unskilled employment; and for certain sectors of female labour, such as migrant workers and students, the sex industry is a mainstream, rather than alternative, option.

The economic strength of the sex industry has gathered momentum from more fundamental changes in sexual relationships and relationship patterns in modernity. Bernstein (2007b: 6) claims that there has been a rise in 'recreational sexuality' which is free and outside the bonds of traditional notions of sexuality that is bound by marital relations: '... the proliferation of forms of service work, the new global information economy, and "postmodern" families peopled by isolable individuals have produced another profound transformation of the erotic sphere'. Bernstein (2007b: 7) evaluates that there has been some social acceptance of the modern sex industry because 'recreational sexuality' becomes 'available for sale and purchase as readily as any other form of commodity packaged leisure activity'. The Internet has assisted the economic, social and cultural change to move the sex industry from the margins of leisure and employment, to a more central position in late capitalist society.

Juxtaposed with the process of mainstreaming the sex industry, there is a move by many states to criminalise the sex industry, both the sex workers and those who sell sex (see the edited collection by Phoenix 2009). European models of making it a crime to pay for sex have been encouraged by Sweden, which criminalised the purchase of sex in 1999 (Scoular 2004). The UK model is one of prohibition which seeks to eradicate the street markets, disrupt the rest of the sex markets and make it a crime to buy sex from those 'controlled for gain'. This move towards abolitionism, driven by a model that provides welfare assistance through the criminal justice system for sex workers to 'exit' prostitution, is at odds with the larger markets that have moved online. This has, in effect, created a chasm between the markets where women are more vulnerable and disenfranchised on the street compared to the indoor markets where women potentially have more control over their working conditions. A model of regulation that makes no distinction between voluntary and forced prostitution will only fail to provide adequate support, provision and safety to either group of sex workers, while pursuing the eradication of commercial sex.

Note

1 http://www.equalities.gov.uk/news/prpage9.htm (accessed 15 December 2008).

Further reading

The relationship between the Internet and the sex industry is in its infancy in terms of research and writings about this. For an overview of the changes, read Sharp, K. and Earle, S. (2003) 'Cyberpunters and Cyberwhores: Prostitution on the Internet', in Y. Jewkes (ed.), *Dot Cons. Crime, Deviance and Identity on the Internet*, pp. 36–52 (Cullompton: Willan Publishing). On women who use the Internet to sell sex, see: Veena, N. (2007) 'Revisiting the Prostitution Debate in the Technology Age: Women Who Use the Internet for Sex Work in Bangkok', *Gender, Technology and Development*, 11(1): 97–107. A wider overview of this subject can be found in Bernstein, E. (2007) *Temporarily Yours: Intimacy, Authenticity and the Commerce of Sex* (Chicago: University of Chicago Press). Men who use the Internet to buy sex is the subject of Holt, T. and Blevins, K. (2007) 'Examining sex work from the client's perspective: assessing Johns using on-line data', in *Deviant Behaviour*, 28(3): 333–54. In addition, Chapter 4 in Sanders, T (2008) *Paying for Pleasure: Men who Buy Sex* (Cullompton: Willan Publishing) looks at the male sex work community. Finally, for detail on methodology, perhaps look at Sanders, T. (2005) 'Researching the online sex work community', in C. Hine (ed.), *Virtual Methods in Social Research on the Internet* (Oxford: Berg).

References

Agustin, L.M. (2005) 'New Research Directions: The Cultural Studies of Commercial Sex', *Sexualities*, 8(5): 618–31.

Bernstein, E. (2007a) 'Sex work for the Middle Classes', *Sexualities*, 10(4): 473–88.

Bernstein, E. (2007b) *Temporarily Yours: Intimacy, Authenticity and the Commerce of Sex*. Chicago: University of Chicago Press.

Brents, B. and Sanders, T. (forthcoming) 'The Mainstreaming of the Sex industry: Economic Inclusion and Social Ambivalence', *Journal of Law and Society*.

Brooks-Gordon, B. (2006) *The Price of Sex: Prostitution, Policy and Society*. Cullompton: Willan Publishing.

Castells, M. (1996) *The Rise of the Network Society*. Oxford: Blackwell.

Connell, J. and Hart, G. (2003) *An Overview of Male Sex Work in Edinburgh and Glasgow: The Male Sex Work Perspective*. MRC Social and Public Health Sciences Unit, Occasional Paper, June.

Durkin, K. and Bryant, C. (1995) '"Log on to sex": some notes on the carnal computer and erotic cyberspace as an emerging research frontier', *Deviant Behaviour*, 16(2): 179–200.

Gaffney, J. (2007) 'A Co-ordinated Prostitution Strategy and Response to Paying the Price – but what about the men?', *Community Safety Journal*, 6(1): 27–33.

Harcourt, C. and Donovan, B. (2005) 'The Many Faces of Sex Work', *Sexually Transmitted Infections*, 81(3): 201–06.

Holt, T. and Blevins, K. (2007) 'Examining sex work from the client's perspective: assessing Johns using on-line data', *Deviant Behaviour*, 28(3): 333–54.

Home Office (2008) *Tackling The Demand for Prostitution: Review*. Home Office: HMSO.

Hughes, D. (2001) Prostitution Online. www.uri.edu/artsci/wms/Hughes/demads.htm

Hughes, D. (2004) 'The use of new communication technologies for sexual exploitation of women and children', in R. Whisnant and C. Stark (eds), *Not for Sale: Feminists Resisting Prostitution and Pornography*. Toronto: Spinifex Press, 38–55.

Kilvington, J., Day, S. and Ward, H. (2001) 'Prostitution Policy in Europe: A Time for Change?', *Feminist Review*, 67(Spring): 78–93.

Kinnell, H. (2006) 'Clients of Female Sex Workers: Men or Monsters?', in R. Campbell and M. O'Neill (eds), *Sex Work Now*. Cullompton: Willan Publishing, 212–62.

Lucas, A. (2005) 'The Work of Sex Work: Elite Prostitutes' Vocational Orientations and Experiences', *Deviant Behavior*, 26(5): 513–46.

Monto, M. (2004) 'Female Prostitution, Customers and Violence', *Violence Against Women*, 10(2): 160–88.

O'Connell, R. (2003) *A Typology of Child Cybersexploitation and Online Grooming Practices*. Preston: Cyberspace Research Unit, University of Central Lancaster.

O'Neill, M. (2001) *Prostitution and Feminism*. London: Polity Press.

Phoenix, J. (ed.) (2009) *Regulating Sex for Sale: Prostitution Policy Reform in the UK*. Bristol: Policy Press.

Sanders, T. (2005a) 'Researching the online sex work community', in C. Hine (ed.), *Virtual Methods in Social Research on the Internet*. Oxford: Berg.

Sanders, T. (2005b) *Sex Work: A Risky Business*. Cullompton: Willan Publishing.

Sanders, T. (2008a) *Paying for Pleasure: Men who Buy Sex*. Cullompton: Willan Publishing.

Sanders, T. (2008b) 'Selling Sex in the Shadow Economy', *International Journal of Social Economics*, 35(10): 704–28.

Scoular, J. (2004) 'Criminalising "Punters": Evaluating the Swedish Position on Prostitution', *Journal of Social Welfare and Family Law*, 26(2): 195–210.

Sharp, K. and Earle, S. (2003) 'Cyberpunters and cyberwhores: prostitution on the Internet', in Y. Jewkes (ed.), *Dot Cons. Crime, Deviance and Identity on the Internet*. Cullompton: Willan Publishing, 36–52.

Soothill, K. (2004a) 'Sex Talk', *Police Review*, 20–21.

Soothill, K. (2004b) 'Parlour Games: The Value of An Internet Site Providing Punters' Views of Massage Parlours', *The Police Journal*, 77(1): 43–53.

Soothill, K. and Sanders, T. (2005) 'The Geographical Mobility, Preferences and Pleasures of Prolific Punters: A demonstration study of the activities of prostitutes' clients', *Sociological Research Online*, 10(1).

Veena, N. (2007) 'Revisiting the Prostitution Debate in the Technology Age: Women Who Use the Internet for Sex Work in Bangkok', *Gender, Technology and Development*, 11(1): 97–107.

Weitzer, R. (2005) 'New Directions in Research on Prostitution', *Crime, Law and Social Change*, 43: 211–35.

Chapter 16

Online sexual exploitation of children and young people

Jo Bryce

Introduction

Internet safety is a significant concern for parents, education and child protection services, service providers, enforcement and the government. The Internet, social networking sites[1] and use of mobile phones are now an integral part of the everyday social lives, identities and relationships of young people. Their active engagement with these technologies focuses on creating and sharing content, communicating with friends, and meeting new people. Whilst this has potential benefits for creativity, education and the development of media literacy, it also creates opportunities for exposure to a number of online risks that can have a potentially negative impact on their psychological and physical well-being (e.g. cyberbullying, access to sexual and violent content, and so on). One of the greatest concerns over risks associated with young people's online behaviour is the potential for sexual exploitation. This can include behaviours such as experiencing inappropriate sexual contact and communication with adults or other young people online; involvement in the production and distribution of illegal or age-inappropriate sexually explicit content; and initiating inappropriate and abusive sexual contact with others.

This chapter provides a critical review of the existing research on the online sexual exploitation of young people. It examines definitions of the associated behaviours and offences, and highlights difficulties with establishing the prevalence of the problem. It also critically reviews the available literature on offender motivations and characteristics, and considers the applicability of offender profiling techniques to this category of criminal behaviour. The processes that characterise online sexual exploitation are then examined, focusing on victim identification and approach, and the stages of the grooming process identified in previous empirical research (e.g. O'Connell 2003). Online behaviours, victim characteristics and factors that are known to increase the vulnerability of young people to online sexual exploitation are then discussed. The chapter also considers the need to develop further understanding of the dynamics of victim–offender interactions during the offending process, and critically examines the way in which research and educational strategies conceptualise this relationship. The final section of the chapter examines legal, regulatory and educational approaches to preventing and responding to the online sexual exploitation of young people, and considers current challenges in protecting them from this form of online behaviour.

Prevalence

The online sexual exploitation of young people involves a variety of different offender behaviours and interactions with young people using a variety of different technologies, and may lead to offline meetings that result in contact sexual abuse. The term Internet sex offender used in the research literature generally relates to those convicted of downloading, accessing or disseminating Child Sex Abuse Images (CSAIs), though this term is also used in the media and by researchers to refer to offenders who use the Internet to contact and groom young people with the intention of meeting them offline to commit contact sex offences. This category of offending may also include adults attempting to engage young people in abusive activities such as cybersex or masturbation, causing them to watch sexual activity or send sexually explicit images of themselves (non-contact abuse). The terms 'child molester' or 'paedophile' are also widely applied to both categories of offender, and these categorisations predate the use of the Internet and related technologies by offenders to sexually abuse young people. There is also often an overlap between these two types of offending behaviour which creates difficulties in classification and research, as there is evidence that many offenders involved in grooming and contact offending also access, produce and disseminate CSAIs.

Media reporting of convictions of offenders who have used the Internet as part of the sexual exploitation of young people is frequent, creating societal perceptions that this type of online behaviour is common and amplifying concerns over the associated risks for young people (Sheldon and Howitt 2007; Wolak *et al.* 2008). Estimating the prevalence of the online sexual exploitation of young people depends on their awareness, recognition and reporting of problems experienced. They need to be aware of mechanisms for reporting inappropriate behaviours and have the confidence to talk to adults about problems. The similarities between many of the stages of the online grooming process, and general processes of online relationship formation and sexual experimentation can make it difficult for young people to identify sexual exploitation. They may not realise that the people they are interacting with online are adults or have the intention to sexually exploit them. Initial relationships may end before sexual themes are introduced or an offline meeting occurs, so the potential victim is never aware of the true intentions of their online 'friend'. If young people become concerned and attempt to end what they perceive to be an inappropriate online relationship, the offender may use coercion or threats to scare the victim and prevent them reporting the problem. Young people may also not necessarily report sexually abusive interactions or meetings because they perceive what has happened to be part of a romantic relationship rather than abuse (Wolak *et al.* 2004).

These difficulties in recognising and reporting online sexual exploitation suggest that its prevalence is likely to be under-reported, and the fragmentation of available figures between different sources makes it difficult to determine the scale of the problem. Carr (2004) estimated that the media had reported 27 UK cases of Internet grooming and contact offences up to 2004, while Childline (2005) reported that 34 per cent of the 389 calls received about Internet risks related to actual or risk of sexual abuse. The Child Exploitation and Online Protection Centre (CEOP) received 5,812 reports of suspected suspicious online behaviours for 2007–8 and were responsible for 297 arrests during the same period (CEOP 2008). British Crime Survey and Home Office figures indicate that charges and convictions for these categories of offence are relatively infrequent in comparison to general figures for sexual crimes against young people, though it has been argued that conviction rates are poor indictors of the prevalence of offending (Howitt 1995; Sheldon and Howitt 2007). British Crime Survey figures for 2006 reported that 36 adults were charged with meeting a female child following grooming, with two convictions. In the same period, seven adults were charged and convicted of meeting a male child following grooming. These figures only reflect the number of charges and convictions per offence category, and do not account for the number of ongoing investigations or reports made to enforcement or other agencies.

Although these figures come from diverse sources and have their limitations, they suggest that the prevalence of online sexual exploitation is relatively small given the wider context of sexual offending against young people in society (Wolak *et al.* 2008). However, given the potential difficulties associated with recognition and reporting of associated behaviours, it seems likely that recorded figures represent only a small proportion of sexual offending against young people which involves the Internet and related technologies (see Sheldon and Howitt 2007 for a more detailed discussion). Regardless of the exact prevalence, online sexual exploitation is a significant societal problem because of the potentially negative physical and psychological impacts of victimisation. The potential for this to occur to young people as a result of their online interactions has important implications for child protection, the involved industries, enforcement and education, and has been the focus of sustained multi-stakeholder collaboration in developing prevention and response strategies.

Offender characteristics

Research examining the demographic and psychological characteristics of Internet offenders has tended to focus on those convicted of downloading, producing and disseminating child sex abuse images (CSAIs), rather than those convicted of contact sex offences involving use of the Internet. Although published research evidence is limited, there appears to be no clear demographic profile of offenders involved in the online sexual exploitation of young people other than being male. Offenders come from a range of age, socio-economic and educational backgrounds as demonstrated by offenders prosecuted as a result of Operation Ore, and this appears to be the same for Internet-related contact offenders. Research examining the demographic characteristics of offenders convicted of accessing CSAIs found them to be aged 25–50 years, lacking prior criminal convictions, of higher intelligence and educational achievement, and more likely to be in a relationship compared with contact offenders (Burke *et al.* 2001). Other research found that both internet and contact offenders are likely to be in a relationship and have children or stepchildren (Sheldon and Howitt 2007). Webb *et al.* (2007) studied the demographic characteristics of 210 offenders (43 per cent convicted of a CSAI offence and 57 per cent of a contact offence) and found similarity in the demographic characteristics consistent with previous research on community contact offenders.

Psychological characteristics and motivations

There is extensive research on the psychological and motivational characteristics of contact sex offenders that predates the involvement of the Internet in sexual offending, but there is little empirical research on offenders involved in the online sexual exploitation of young people (Middleton *et al.* 2006; Quayle and Taylor 2003; Sheldon and Howitt 2007). Developing a deeper understanding of the motivations and characteristics of this category of offender, and the efficacy of associated therapeutic interventions for attitudinal and behavioural change, is an important area requiring further research.

Recent research on Internet sex offenders has used psychometric testing to investigate the applicability of the 'pathways model' (Ward and Siegert 2002) to understanding the psychological and motivational factors associated with accessing and distributing child sex abuse images and potential implications for risk assessment and treatment (Middleton *et al.* 2006). As the pathways model was developed from research on community contact sex offenders that predates the use of the Internet in offending, it is likely that the pathways and associated psychological deficits would be expected to be similar for offenders using the Internet to target and groom children. The model suggests that there are multiple pathways leading to sexual offending against children, with each pathway containing a core set of multiple dysfunctional mechanisms (e.g. intimacy deficits, distorted sexual scripts, emotional dysregulation, antisocial cognitions, and multiple dysfunctional mechanisms) leading to contact and non-contact offences (Middleton *et al.* 2006). Seventy-two convicted sex offenders who had completed treatment were recruited from National Probation Service records and were tested using standardised psychometric assessment tests (Beech *et al.* 1999). Each of the pathways specified in the model is outlined below, before considering how these pathways are hypothesised to operate in Internet (CSAI) and Internet-related contact offenders.

The *intimacy deficits pathway* is characterised by difficulties in forming close personal relationships with adults due to fear of rejection resulting from insecure childhood attachments (Middleton *et al.* 2006). High levels of associated emotional loneliness motivates offending during periods of loneliness and difficulties in forming adult relationships. This leads some offenders to access CSAIs and others to seek out children as sexual partners. Offenders in this pathway show no emotional dysregulation or cognitive distortions about sexual contact with children, though they are perceived to be more accepting partners or 'adult substitutes' despite offenders having a sexual preference for adults.

The *distorted sexual scripts pathway* is characterised by high levels of emotional congruence with children, but no emotional dysregulation, loneliness or cognitive distortions (Middleton *et al.* 2006). Early sexual experiences lead to distorted sexual scripts and dysfunctional attachment styles, leading offenders to equate sex with intimacy and relationships. Offending occurs as children are perceived to be more trustworthy and accepting in meeting sexual needs during periods of rejection or relationship difficulties.

The *emotional dysregulation pathway* is characterised by high levels of difficulties controlling negative emotions, but no emotional loneliness, cognitive distortions or emotional congruence with children (Middleton *et al.* 2006). Offenders experience strong negative emotions that they are unable to control and manage effectively, leading to disinhibition and use of sex as a coping strategy. Depending on availability, offenders access child images or commit contact offences to alleviate negative emotions without specific sexual interest in children, justifying their behaviour as a loss of control.

The *antisocial cognitions pathway* is characterised by high levels of impulsivity and self-esteem (Middleton *et al.* 2006). These offenders do not have distorted sexual scripts, problems with intimacy or emotional regulation. They may have feelings of superiority over children but are not sexually interested in them. Use of CSAIs or contact offending against children is an extension of pro-criminal attitudes and behaviours, high levels of impulsivity and opportunism.

The *multiple dysfunction pathway* is characterised by high levels of emotional dysregulation, distorted sexual scripts, and cognitive distortions and these offenders are described as 'pure paedophiles' (Middleton *et al.* 2006). Children are preferred or ideal sexual partners, and accessing CSAIs and contact offending are extensive. Middleton *et al.* (2006) claim that the small number of offenders classified by this pathway in their sample suggests such individuals may have preference for contact offences and are, therefore, more likely to be convicted for them. It would be expected that the relative frequency of this pathway would be higher in samples of Internet-related contact offenders than in the sample in this study.

Middleton *et al.* (2006) were able to classify a substantial proportion of their sample of Internet offenders (convicted of CSAI offences) into one of the pathway categories, suggesting that a large number of offenders are characterised by psychological deficits similar to those of non-Internet contact offenders. However, the inability to assign approximately half of the sample to a specific pathway also suggests the existence of a group of offenders who access CSAIs but do not display these psychological deficits and may experience different pathways to offending not specified by the model (Middleton *et al.* 2006). The characteristics of the Internet, online communication and the ways in which this facilitates victim identification, approach and grooming may also have specific influences on the identified pathways or suggest the existence of alternative offending pathways for Internet-related contact offenders. This is consistent with the claim by Middleton *et al.* (2006) that an assessment of levels of problematic Internet use might be a useful addition to the model, given evidence that this may be an additional factor causing offenders to access CSAIs (Quayle and Taylor 2003). This may also be the case for Internet-related grooming and contact offending as the relative accessibility of young people online, and potential ease of approach and interaction without parental monitoring, could be related to this factor, have a reinforcing effect or play a role in this category of offending behaviour. As the pathways model was developed on samples of community contact offenders, it would be expected that a similar pattern of results for pathways to Internet-related contact offending would be found. There are no published studies solely on this category of offender, but the results of the Middleton *et al.* study also has implications for considering the applicability of this theoretical framework to the online sexual exploitation of young people. It is possible that some Internet-related contact offenders might not exhibit the included psychological deficits or be classifiable to the identified pathways in the Ward and Siegert model, suggesting the need for further research which focuses specifically on this group of offenders in order to inform understanding, risk assessment and treatment.

It is also important to recognise the potential bias associated with self-presentation or underestimation of psychological deficits in offender respond-ing to psychometric tests, although Middleton *et al.* (2006) found no evidence of self-deceptive enhancement or image management in their sample. This potential bias in models of offender motivations and psychological character-istics assumes that offenders respond truthfully when completing psychometric tests. Where offenders participate in research during or after a prison sentence and treatment, their responding may reflect clinical explanations for offender behaviour learned through treatment and obscure experienced motivational and emotional states at the time of offending (Howitt and Sheldon 2007). This could explain the high incidence of offending as a response to inappropriate reactions to problematic situations and relationship difficulties, rather than a sexual interest in children, in the sample used in the study by Middleton *et al.* (2006).

However, if responding is not influenced by social desirability, there is a need to further understand why CSAIs are used as a coping mechanism during periods of interpersonal difficulties given the low levels of sexual interest in children and cognitive distortions found in the study (Middleton *et al.* 2006). This behaviour seems difficult to understand unless the choice of material reflects an underlying sexual interest in children, or it would seem more likely that offenders would instead access adult sexually explicit content which does not carry the strong moral and legal sanctions associated with CSAIs. This issue is often overlooked in the literature on Internet offenders convicted of accessing CSAIs, and is also relevant to understanding the motivations and pathways to Internet-related contact offending (Sheldon and Howitt 2007).

Cognitive distortions (CDs)

The pathways model described above places particular importance on the role of cognitive distortions (CDs) in the offending process, and they are hypothesised to be an important psychological deficit in offenders and the specified pathways. Howitt and Sheldon (2007) emphasise the central role of cognitive distortions in Internet and Internet-related contact and non-contact offending against children, and they claim that this highlights the importance of research on their development, function, and influence on offending behaviour. Cognitive distortions were originally conceptualised as pre-offence beliefs generated by offenders to enable them to overcome the guilt associated with breaking the social taboo against sexual contact with children (Abel *et al.* 1984; Howitt and Sheldon 2007). Other researchers view cognitive distortions as post-offence rationalisations generated by offenders to explain and justify their behaviour after the offence has been committed (Gannon and Polaschek 2005; Howitt and Sheldon 2007). An alternative perspective views them as reflecting the distorted early experiences of offenders, particularly early childhood experiences of sexual abuse by adults or sexual activity with other children (Howitt 1995; Howitt and Sheldon 2007). Regardless of these differing perspectives, it is likely that cognitive distortions are important in overcoming moral sanctions against viewing images and engaging in sexual contact with children (Howitt and Sheldon 2007).

Ward and Keenan (1999) developed a taxonomy of five categories of contact offender cognitive distortions: children as sexual objects who are able to enjoy sexual relationships with adults; beliefs in entitlement to have sexual needs met due to perceived self-importance; belief in a dangerous world in which children are perceived to be more trustworthy and reliable than adults; uncontrollability of behaviour due to external factors such as stress, alcohol or drugs; and the belief that not all sexual activity with children is harmful and can be positive. Sheldon (2004) identified these factors in a mixed sample of Internet and contact sex offenders, as did Beech and Ward (2004) in a sample of contact offenders. It is, therefore, likely that these distortions will be found in accounts of the offending behaviour of those who commit contact offences which involve the Internet. Ward and Siegert (2002) claim that the pathways identified in their model are influenced by these five underlying cognitive schemas, though this has been criticised for being based on subjective analysis of cognitive distortions without supporting quantitative or psychometric data demonstrating the distinctiveness of the categories or how these might vary in different groups of child sex offenders (Howitt and Sheldon 2007).

Evidence that child molesters differ significantly from controls on the acceptability of cognitive distortions is contradictory (Howitt and Sheldon 2007). Bumby (1996) provides evidence that this is the case, but other researchers claim offenders are reluctant to overtly accept them, and suggest that instead offenders accept cognitive distortions less strongly than controls (e.g. Arkowitz and Vess 2003; Marshall *et al.* 2003). Howitt and Sheldon (2007) conducted a psychometric and qualitative study of 51 offenders recruited from a privately run UK prison and the National Probation Service that included measures of cognitive distortions reflecting the categories identified by Ward and Keenan (1999). There were three categories of offender in the study: those who had committed contact offences only (N=25); those who had committed Internet or non-contact offences only (N=16); and those who had committed both contact and non-contact offences (N=10). The results of the study suggested that a large number of cognitive distortions were accepted by the majority or a substantial minority of the sample, contrasting with claims that offenders are reluctant to acknowledge cognitive distortions (Arkowitz and Vess 2003; Marshall *et al.* 2003; Howitt and Sheldon 2007).

The concept and measurement of cognitive distortions has been criticised for its reliance on the truthful responding of offenders which may be influenced by social desirability (Blumenthal *et al.* 1999; Horley 2000; Kolton *et al.* 2001). However, later studies have also measured social desirability and impression management and found them to have no influence on responding (Gannon and Polaschek 2005). There was no evidence of the influence of social desirability in this study, and Howitt and Sheldon (2007) suggest that offenders are unlikely to recognise the social undesirability of a cognitive distortion and agree with the associated statement or use it as post-offence justification. They conclude that this suggests that cognitive distortions are believed by offenders and result from personal experience (Howitt and Sheldon 2007). Contact offenders scored lower on cognitive distortions associated with 'children as sexual beings' compared with Internet offenders, contradicting the claim that cognitive distortions justify offending against children. Quayle and Taylor (2003) suggest that Internet offenders' sexual interest in children is primarily fantasy driven, which may lead them to endorse such cognitions more than contact offenders whose direct experience of sexual activity with children may contradict the belief that they are sexual beings (Howitt and Sheldon 2007). The pattern of identified results and lack of social desirability in responding suggests that cognitive distortions are important aspects of offence-conducive thinking that reflect the early distorted experiences of the offender (Howitt and Sheldon 2007).

Howitt and Sheldon (2007) identify a number of limitations with the psychometric approach to examining cognitive distortions in sex offenders, particularly the use of an overall score which fails to recognise the complex interaction of different social and psychological factors over time leading to their development. They claim that there is a need for further research comparing the cognitive distortions of Internet and Internet-related contact offenders, particularly as the distancing potentially facilitated by the Internet may reinforce beliefs which themselves influence the offending process.

Howitt and Sheldon (2007) conclude that there are some similarities in the agreement with cognitive distortions between contact and Internet offenders, but also important differences which may explain why some Internet offenders progress to contact offending and others do not. There is a need to further explore factors that account for these differences and subsequent outcomes for offending (Howitt and Sheldon 2007). This is particularly important as these different offender groups were not available to study when models of offending were developed, and provide a new source of information about the motivations, behaviours and psychological characteristics of offenders. Research on the role of cognitive distortions in the offending process of both Internet and Internet-related contact offenders is another key area for further development.

Critical perspectives

Empirical research examining Internet sex offenders has drawn on a number of forensic or offender profiling techniques, particularly those associated with the development of typologies for classifying offenders as part of risk assessment and treatment. The assumption underlying offender profiling is that personality is reflected in offender crime scene behaviour leads, and that offender behaviour is consistent when committing specific offences and between offences in that same category (behavioural consistency) (Alison *et al.* 2008; Mokros and Alison 2002). The 'homology assumption' suggests that offenders with similar psychological/demographic characteristics display similar crime scene behaviours enabling crime scene analysis to generate predictive inferences about the psychological and demographic characteristics of offenders (Alison *et al.* 2008; Mokros and Alison 2002). These assumptions are particularly important in the development of typologies for classifying offender behaviour, and their associated social and psychological characteristics (Alison *et al.* 2008; Mokros and Alison 2002). However, researchers have critiqued the assumptions of behavioural consistency and homology as reflecting a naive trait approach to personality which is undermined by recent research suggesting the unstable nature of personality and behaviour over time, across different situations and in interactions with others (Alison *et al.* 2008; Mokros and Alison 2002). The implications of such critiques for research on Internet and Internet-related contact offending have not yet been fully considered in the literature. Such critiques do not suggest that typologies and related offender profiling techniques do not have scientific or practical value for risk assessment, treatment or enforcement, but that their potential limitations should be more fully recognised and addressed.

Such critiques also emphasise the importance of the context of the offence, and dynamic interaction between victim and offender shaped by their characteristics as influencing crime scene behaviour (Mokros and Alison 2002). This suggests that focusing on offender characteristics alone cannot provide a full understanding of the dynamic nature of the offending process, and has important implications for research examining the online sexual exploitation of young people. The greater part of existing research focuses on offender psychological functioning and pathways to offending in order to develop typologies that are useful for understanding offending motivations, treatment and risk assessment. However, fuller understanding of the offending process requires further recognition of its dynamic nature and the complex interaction of victim and offender, shaped by technological and individual characteristics.

There is also the issue of obtaining access to data that would enable analysis of the grooming process and the interaction between victim and offender. Whilst information of this nature is collected by enforcement agencies during the investigation and prosecution of offenders, obtaining access to this information for academic research is complicated by a number of ethical and legal constraints. However, this data (e.g. copies of chat logs, emails etc.) represents naturalistically occurring data about the offence in process. This could be used to analyse the dynamic nature of the interaction between victim and offender, and develop further understanding of the key stages in the grooming processes outlined by O'Connell (2003). It could also be used to identify specific linguistic techniques used by the offender to develop the relationship, particularly during the shift into its sexual stages, and how the victim responds. Such information would make a valuable contribution to informing educational strategies for young people, as well as informing the grooming libraries used by commercial educational and domestic monitoring software. It could also lead to the development of typologies for classifying victim and offender characteristics, interactions and locations for use in enforcement and educational strategies, while recognising the potential limitations outlined above.

Processes of sexual exploitation

Online sexual exploitation is a dynamic interaction between the victim and offender influenced by their psychological and social characteristics, as well as the technologies through which interaction occurs. Understanding the complexities of this process is complicated by the similarities between the characteristics of grooming, at least in the earlier stages of the process, and routine online friendship formation between young people. Even the specifically sexual stages may be difficult to distinguish from the sexual interactions that are increasingly characteristic of young people's online exploration of sexual identity and relationships.

Victim identification

The increasing popularity of social networking among young people in recent years has led to concerns that the personal information included on profile pages and disclosed online could be used by adults with a sexual interest in young people to identify, contact and groom potential victims (Wolak *et al.* 2008). Online grooming is a process by which adults with a sexual interest in young people engage them in online interactions and relationships for the purposes of committing contact or non-contact offences. It is defined in UK law as 'A course of conduct enacted by a suspected paedophile, which would give a reasonable person cause for concern that any meeting with a child arising from the conduct would be for unlawful purposes' (Home Office 2002: 25). Offering incentives such as money, gifts, concert tickets, modelling contracts, day trips, phones, and games may also be used as part of the grooming process or to encourage young people to produce and send images of themselves to offenders (CEOP 2008). Meeting a child following grooming is illegal under the Sexual Offences Act (2003).

Process of grooming

O'Connell (2003) developed a general framework specifying the different stages of the grooming process. The length of time taken to progress between stages differs depending on the motivations and intentions of the offender, and some stages may also be absent from the process. For example, the risk assessment stage may be less important where the offender intends to engage in non-contact sexual offences (e.g. obtaining images, cybersexual and masturbatory activities) (O'Connell 2003).

After a potential victim has been identified, the offender will attempt to initiate a conversation or relationship through email, chat, Instant Messaging (IM) or friend requests on social networking sites (Wolak *et al.* 2008). The friendship and relationship forming stages are similar to those of the development of other online friendships, and involve the offender approaching and befriending the young person, and encouraging them to discuss their life in order to initiate friendship (O'Connell 2003). During the relationship forming stage, the offender may also give hints about the sort of future relationship they would like by making comments about love and romance, future meetings, or exchanging images (O'Connell 2003). This is followed by the risk assessment stage where the offender attempts to assess the likelihood of their activities being detected by other people in the victim's family or home by asking about the location of their computer and other users (O'Connell 2003).

Following the risk assessment stage, the offender develops the emotional and romantic aspects of the relationship in order to ensure they have the trust of the victim (O'Connell 2003) and moves the relationship to a more explicitly sexual stage in which the offender tries to engage the victim in sexual conversations which may be confusing or uncomfortable, or are more explicit than they would expect to have with someone of their own age (O'Connell 2003). They may also try to persuade them to engage in sexual activity and describe it to the offender, or use a webcam so they can watch. They may also send the victim sexually explicit images or CSAIs to normalise sexual contact between adults and young people, and make requests for them to send images in return (O'Connell 2003). Offenders may become abusive, threatening, and/or harassing to ensure compliance with their requests if the victim is reluctant. CEOP (2008) report an increase in the number of cases that involve the use of blackmail and coercion in attempting to ensure victim compliance.

Some offenders may terminate the relationship at the point at which they have obtained sexual gratification without ever meeting the victim offline, though non-contact offences may have occurred (e.g. encouraging the victim to engage in sexual activity or send sexually explicit images) (O'Connell 2003). This abrupt end to the online relationship may leave the victim feeling hurt and humiliated by the deception of the other person, and afraid to tell an adult because they feel embarrassed and are concerned about the potential repercussions (O'Connell 2003). However, many offenders request private offline meetings with the victim in order to commit contact sexual offences. It is difficult to estimate the frequency of these different types of offender behaviour given the problems associated with obtaining general prevalence figures described earlier. However, figures from CEOP (2008) indicate that 40 per cent of reports made to them in 2007–8 related to grooming, while only 7 per cent related to contact abuse. This suggests that grooming is more frequent than contact abuse though these figures may be explained by under-reporting of contact offences, and increased awareness of grooming and reporting of suspected suspicious behaviour which may be reducing the number of contact offences committed.

Victim characteristics

There is less published research examining the characteristics of the victims of online sexual exploitation, but this is also an important aspect of developing an understanding of the dynamic nature of the interaction between victim and offender during the offending process. It is also important to identify demographic, social and psychological factors which place specific groups of young people at risk of online sexual exploitation, as well as the frequency of engagement in online behaviours which are potentially risky. One of the key concerns associated with the increasing popularity of social networking among young people is the amount of personal information posted and shared online, and the potential for this to be used by offenders to identify and contact victims (Wolak *et al.* 2008). Internet safety messages generally advise young people against disclosing personal information online, but communicating with friends and meeting new people is an essential part of social networking. This highlights the contradiction between educational messages and the everyday online motivations, behaviours and experiences of young people. A number of studies have examined the frequency of young people's engagement in online behaviours which potentially place them at risk of sexual exploitation (e.g. Bryce 2008; Livingstone and Bober 2005; OFCOM 2008). Behaviours include posting or disclosing personal information and images online, interacting with 'strangers', talking about sex with 'strangers' and meeting 'strangers' offline. A multi-method research project conducted by the Cyperspace Research Unit (CRU) in 2008[2] examined the frequency of engagement in these behaviours and associated risk perceptions in a sample of young people aged eight to 18 years in the north-west of England.[3] Some of the key findings of the study which relate to engagement in potentially risky online behaviours are presented below and related to other relevant research.

Disclosure of personal information online

Despite educational messages which advise against disclosure of personal information online, a significant number of young people frequently engage in this behaviour. Twenty-six per cent of the sample of young people in the CRU Orange Project (Bryce 2008) disclosed personal information about themselves online. The qualitative data suggested that young people recognise the risks associated with this behaviour, but perceive themselves to have the skills and confidence to manage any problems encountered. Given that the main motivation for using social networking sites is to communicate and meet people, young people felt that disclosing personal information was essential. Similar views were found in the OFCOM social networking research (OFCOM 2008). The UK Kids Go Online Study (Livingstone and Bober 2005) found that 46 per cent of 9–19-year-olds who used the Internet had disclosed personal information to people they met online. The difference in figures between the two studies can be explained in the ways in which disclosure and personal information was conceptualised. |

Uploading and sending images

Image sharing is another central aspect of social networking which raises safety concerns. Fifty-four per cent of the sample in the CRU Orange Project (Bryce 2008) had uploaded an image of themselves online, and 26 per cent had sent an image of themselves to someone they met online. Images were viewed as an important way of establishing and developing identity online by the focus group participants, as well as a strategy for verifying the online identity of others and building trust in online interactions (Bryce 2008). This is consistent with other research suggesting similar use of images by young people (OFCOM 2008; Withers and Sheldon 2008).

Talking to strangers and making friends

Sixty-two per cent of the sample in the CRU Orange Project (Bryce 2008) had talked to people that they had never met before online and 52 per cent had made friends this way. This figure is higher than Livingstone and Bober (2005) who found that 30 per cent of their sample of Internet users formed a friendship with someone they had met online, but this study was conducted before social networking became a popular adolescent activity. The relatively high proportion of young people talking to strangers and making friends online is not surprising given the centrality of maintaining and making friends online, despite educational messages to the contrary. Focus group participants in the CRU Orange Project (Bryce 2008) were aware of the potential risks of talking to strangers online and were concerned about unwanted contact, but accepted this as a routine aspect of online interactions and experiences.

Sexual approaches to young people

There have been a number of studies examining the frequency of sexual approaches to young people online in recent years. Mitchell et al. (2003) found that 13 per cent of their sample had received unwanted sexual approaches in the previous year, though only 4 per cent of the sample felt scared or upset by these contacts. Forty-three per cent of solicitations were believed to have been made by someone aged 18 or younger. Seventy-five per cent of those making solicitations asked to meet the young person offline. Mitchell *et al.* (2007a) reported that 4 per cent of 10–17-year-olds in the YISS-2 (Youth Internet Safety Survey – 2) had received a request to send sexual images to someone they met online. The prevalence of sexual approaches to young people appears to be decreasing, suggesting the success of associated awareness raising and educational strategies (Wolak *et al.* 2008). Young people may be less likely to respond to such approaches and decrease the likelihood of the grooming process being initiated (Wolak *et al.* 2008). However, enforcement agencies have reported the displacement of these activities onto activities such as hacking, blackmail, threats and coercion (CEOP 2008).

Meeting offline

The potential for young people to attend offline meetings with people they meet online is a key child protection concern relating to sexual exploitation. Twenty-four per cent of the sample in the CRU Orange Project (Bryce 2008) had met someone offline that they met online. This percentage is higher than in earlier research studies which suggested that 8 per cent of 9–19-year-olds (Livingstone and Bober 2005) had attended offline meetings with friends they made online. The CRU Orange Project (Bryce 2008) and Livingstone and Bober (2005) found that the majority of these meetings were positive, with young people taking necessary precautions to ensure their safety (for example, taking friends, ensuring someone was aware of where and when the meeting was arranged). Many participants felt that meeting people offline was another important part of the social networking experience, consistent with other recent research (OFCOM 2008; Withers and Sheldon 2008). The higher figures for meeting offline in the CRU Orange Study (Bryce 2008) can be accounted for by the increasing popularity of social networking since the earlier studies were conducted, and the importance placed on making friends online and meeting them offline.

Risk awareness

The qualitative research conducted as part of the CRU Orange Project (Bryce 2008) suggests that educational messages are successful in raising the awareness of young people about the risks and consequences associated with communicating with previously unknown people or 'strangers' online. Young people felt that they were adequately protected from such risks, and were confident that they could identify and deal with potentially inappropriate contact, consistent with other recent research (OFCOM 2008; Withers and Sheldon 2008). However, these results suggest that a significant number of young people frequently engage in online behaviours which potentially place them at risk of sexual exploitation, despite awareness of the risks and being exposed to educational messages to the contrary (Livingstone 2008). The perceived centrality of these behaviours to social networking and online interaction among young people highlights the need for educational strategies to encourage greater consideration of their potential consequences and associated risk reduction strategies. Research examining young people's engagement in behaviours that potentially place them at risk of online sexual exploitation is an important aspect of understanding factors which increase their vulnerability to victimisation.

It is also important to understand the ways in which young people talk about these issues to enable the development of awareness campaigns and educational materials which have relevance to their everyday lives through the framing of safety messages in familiar language. This will increase the ecological validity and impact of awareness materials and educational campaigns. Particular attention should be paid to the everyday lives and social worlds of young people as the context in which communicated educational and awareness messages are received, interpreted and their relevance evaluated, and behavioural and attitudinal impact achieved. The use of both quantitative and qualitative methodologies is essential to enable a broad and dynamic understanding of young people's online behaviour and experiences within the contexts of their everyday lives to inform the content of educational and risk reduction strategies to accurately reflect the online behaviours and experiences of young people (Bryce 2008).

Self-victimising behaviours

An emerging area of concern is the use of the Internet and related technologies by young people for 'sexting' (*Daily Mail* 2009) or self-victimising activities (Quayle 2007 and this volume). The creation and dissemination of user-generated content (e.g. images, video clips) by young people online is increasingly popular, and this commonly includes provocative or sexually explicit content that may be posted online or sent to peers and romantic partners (see cases reported in the *TES* Cymru 2005 for example). Young people often lack understanding of how their content and communications could be disseminated until they are exposed to ridicule, bullying, humiliation and other negative consequences (Boyd 2007; *TES* Cymru 2005). Given that the Internet is an increasingly important part of the everyday lives of young people, it is unsurprising that it is being used as a means of communicating and exploring sexual identity and relationships. This highlights the need for educational strategies which address online sexual exploitation to encourage young people to think about the potential outcomes of posting private or provocative content online or sharing it with peers.

Vulnerability to online sexual exploitation

Research can also enable identification of factors that place specific groups of young people at risk of online sexual exploitation (Wolak *et al.* 2004, 2008). These factors have been linked to the likelihood of young people forming close personal relationships online and include: girls who have a high degree of conflict with their parents; boys who experience low levels of monitoring by their parents; young people with questions about their sexuality and who lack other appropriate sources of help, information and support; and young people experiencing depression, loneliness or social isolation (Wolak *et al.* 2004). Mitchell *et al.* (2007b) found that children aged over 14 who had experienced negative life events, maltreatment or depression were also more likely to be approached.

Effects of online sexual exploitation on the victim *ethic*

The effects of sexual abuse on young people are severe and can have a number of associated negative outcomes including delinquency, depression, substance abuse, guilt, post-traumatic stress disorder (Finkelhor 1984; Molnar *et al.* 2001). It has also been identified as a significant risk factor for psychiatric disorders in later life (Beitchman *et al.* 1991; Kendall-Tackett *et al.* 1993). However, less is known about the effects of online sexual exploitation on the victim. Although it is likely that the psychological and social impacts will be similar to those for victims of contact sexual abuse, the extent to which the involvement of the Internet and related technologies intensifies victimisation and its potential outcomes has yet to be fully determined.

Conceptualising the victim–offender relationship

Society and the media construct the perpetrators of online sexual exploitation as 'strangers' using the personal information disclosed online by young people to initiate contact and develop deceitful relationships with the intention of meeting them offline to facilitate sexual abuse (Medina 2007; Rawe 2006; Wolak *et al.* 2008). To some extent, this is an extension of concerns about offline 'stranger danger' (Sheldon and Howitt 2007), and this is reflected in many of the educational strategies targeted at young people. However, the concept of the offender as a stranger has been criticised as not fully reflecting the ways in which young people meet and interact with the people they meet online, or the complexity of the grooming process and related victim–offender relationships (Sheldon and Howitt 2007; Wolak *et al.* 2008). Whilst the offender may initially be a stranger when contact is made, by the time non-contact or contact offences occur, the victims often perceive themselves to be in a friendship or romantic relationship with the offender (Wolak *et al.* 2004, 2008).

Wolak *et al.* (2004) studied 129 cases of Internet-initiated sexual contact between adults and young people, and found that the stereotype of the online sexual predator as a stranger and paedophile deceiving young people into sexually abusive relationships is potentially misleading. The majority of the victims in their sample were females aged 13–15 years old, and they were generally aware of the age and sexual motivations of the offender (80 per cent of offenders mentioned sex in their conversations before meeting). Seventy-four per cent of the victims agreed to meet the offender, despite being aware that there was a sexual aspect to the meeting and 50 per cent described themselves as being in love with the offender. In the majority of cases, there was also a lack of violence or coercion. This suggests that victim experience of online sexual exploitation and related contact offences may not be consistent with the way it is conceptualised in educational and risk reduction strategies. It is important that such approaches address this issue in greater detail to encourage young people to give greater consideration to the nature of their online relationships and potential offline consequences.

It is also important to recognise that the online sexual exploitation of young people is not solely perpetrated by individuals who are initially strangers to them. The vast majority of the sexual abuse of young people occurs within the family or local community, and is generally committed by an offender already known to the victim. For example, the NSPCC (2009) reported that of the 13,237 children counselled for sexual abuse by ChildLine in 2007/08, only 4 per cent said that the offender had been a stranger. Many of the cases reported in the media involve the use of the Internet and related technologies to facilitate contact and non-contact sexual offences within the context of pre-existing victim–offender relationships. Mitchell *et al.* (2005) analysed 126 US cases of family and acquaintance Internet-related offences, and found that 70 per cent of the victims were female, with 45 per cent being aged 6–12, and 48 per cent aged 13–17. In 44 per cent of the cases, the victim and offender were family members, and in 56 per cent they were acquaintances. The authors suggest that these findings also challenge the perception that online sexual exploitation is perpetrated only by 'strangers'. Offenders are using the Internet within the context of intra-familial and acquaintance sexual abuse to groom and communicate with victims, and this needs to be more clearly recognised within educational strategies that address the online sexual exploitation of young people. This highlights the need to recognise the problems associated with conceptualising online sexual exploitation as only an issue of 'stranger danger' and to recognise how the dynamics of the offending process may be influenced by these different forms of the victim–offender relationship, in addition to the individual characteristics of the victim and offender.

Risk reduction strategies

A variety of risk reduction strategies for preventing and responding to the online sexual exploitation of young people have been developed and implemented as a result of multi-stakeholder collaboration between government, enforcement agencies, industry, educational agencies and NGOs. Strategies include the development and implementation of self-regulatory codes of conduct for the involved industries which address the provision of safety information, mechanisms for dealing with reports of suspicious behaviour and liaising with the police. The creation of CEOP as a specialist police agency, and the expanded range of new offences created by the Sexual Offences Act[4] (2003) to address online sexual exploitation are important enforcement and legal developments. Technical solutions including monitoring software for use in domestic and educational contexts, as well as filtering and monitoring solutions for service providers, have also been developed to protect young people online.

These strategies are supplemented by a wide range of educational strategies that emphasise minimising risk of sexual exploitation, and empowering young people to be safe and responsible users of the Internet. Parents and carers, education and child welfare professionals are also key educational audiences, and attempting to close the recognised skills and knowledge gap between adults and young people is an ongoing challenge. A variety of educational strategies and materials have been developed for parents, teachers and other relevant adults. These focus on the function of the Internet and related technologies, how they are used by young people, the risks associated with their online behaviour, strategies for preventing and responding to online problems, as well as strategies for effective communication about online safety. All involved stakeholders (e.g., government, industry, enforcement, educators) have developed a wide variety of online and offline resources for all key educational audiences. This includes the development of resources and lesson plans for young people that can be embedded within the school curriculum (e.g. in PSHE (Personal, Social and Health Education) or ICT lessons), and many of these have a specific focus on online sexual exploitation (e.g. the Thinkuknow series of resources developed by CEOP).

Conclusions

The online sexual exploitation of young people is a significant problem in contemporary society that has a range of negative psychological and social consequences for victims. The recognised need to ensure that young people are safe in their online behaviour and interactions has led to the development of a variety of multi-stakeholder collaborative prevention and response strategies. Despite this, understanding the dynamic nature of the offending process, offender and victim characteristics is still in the early stages. It is clear that offenders use a number of different strategies to initiate and develop relationships with victims, and that these vary according to their motivations and underlying psychological and social characteristics. There is evidence that many Internet-related contact sexual abuse cases do not involve deception, coercion or threats, but are characterised by building trusting and romantic relationships in which the victim is fully aware of the true identity and intentions of the offender (Wolak et al. 2004); although recent UK enforcement reports suggest the increasing use of blackmail, hacking and coercion by offenders to ensure victim compliance (CEOP 2008).

Further development of research examining the motivations, behaviours and psychological characteristics of offenders is essential. The relatively new nature of this set of offending behaviours and processes, and difficulties associated with access to relevant empirical data raise a number of methodological and theoretical challenges. This suggests the need to explore collaborative relationships with enforcement to access relevant data about the offending process to enable further development of theoretical understanding and inform risk assessment, management and treatment of offenders. The existing research suggests that there are important similarities between offenders convicted of accessing CSAIs and those who use the Internet to communicate with and groom young people, but also a variety of psychosocial and behavioural characteristics that differentiate between them. The extent to which pathways to offending behaviour and characteristics differ between these categories of offender requires further research, as does the role of fantasy in accessing CSAIs, grooming and contact offending (Howitt and Sheldon 2007).

It is particularly important to map the variety of victim–offender relationships and interactions within the grooming and offending process, and consider the associated implications for risk assessment, management and treatment of offenders. It is also clear that perceptions of offenders as 'strangers' often conflict with the way in which young people conceptualise the people they interact with online, and that the use of the Internet and related technologies by intra-familial and acquaintance offenders is an important area which should be more fully addressed in educational strategies.

Research on victims, offenders and the offending process is also important for informing educational and risk reduction strategies for young people, as well as training and operational procedures for law enforcement, treatment programmes and risk assessment. This highlights the need for continuing research on the motivations, experiences, and risk perceptions associated with young people's online behaviour, and its potential psychological, social and educational outcomes. A comprehensive investigation of these factors will enable the identification of profiles of risk and vulnerability for different groups of young people, and assist in the development of targeted educational strategies. Young people are not a socially, psychologically or developmentally homogeneous group who can be uniformly targeted by safety messages. Whilst general safety initiatives and educational strategies have an important role in preventing online sexual exploitation, greater recognition of the existence of different groups of young people distinguished by different profiles of risk and vulnerability is required in order to develop targeted educational strategies (Byron 2008; Wolak *et al.* 2008).

It is also necessary to consider the prevalence of this problem within the context of continuing technological change and its influence on young people's online behaviours, interactions and experiences. In particular, the ability to access the Internet and social networking sites via mobile phones is of concern because of the potential problems of ensuring effective monitoring of online behaviour. It is also important to consider the online sexual exploitation of young people within the wider societal context of the high incidence of child sex abuse. It is well documented that the majority of instances of child sexual abuse occur within the home or local community where the offender is already known to the victim, while only approximately 5 per cent of child abuse cases are estimated to involve strangers (NSPCC 2009). The construction of online sexual exploitation as a new form of 'stranger danger' has a number of limitations which have been discussed in this chapter, and suggests that strategies for dealing with this problem should also be addressed within the wider societal issue of the sexual abuse of young people.

Notes

1 Social networking sites are online communities in which members can view information about other users, and develop a network of friends and contacts through invitations. Members can contact each other using the comments facility to leave a message on a person's profile page, messaging or using chat rooms and forums. Popular social networking sites include MySpace, Bebo, Facebook. Users, including young people, are asked to provide personal information at registration and also include this in their profile pages. Information disclosed may include age, name/nickname, gender, date of birth, location, email address, images of the user and their friends, information about personal appearance, personal likes and dislikes (e.g. music, films, hobbies, celebrities).
2 This project was funded by Orange.
3 The quantitative phase of the project involved a questionnaire study with a sample size of 650. The qualitative phase consisted of 20 focus groups.
4 See Gillespie (2008) for a detailed discussion of the Sexual Offences Act (2003) and related offence categories.

Further reading

Sheldon, K. and Howitt, D. (2007) *Sex Offenders and the Internet*. London: John Wiley and Sons.
Taylor, M. and Quayle, E. (2003) *Child Pornography: An Internet Crime*. New York: Brunner-Routledge.
Wolak, J., Finkelhor, D., Mitchell, K.J. and Ybarra, M.L. (2008) 'Online "predators" and their victims: Myths, realities and implications for prevention and treatment', *American Psychologist*, 63: 111–28.

References

Abel, G.G., Becker, J.V. and Cunningham-Rathner, J. (1984) 'Complications, consent, and cognitions in sex between children and adults', *International Journal of Law and Psychiatry*, 7: 89–103.
Alison, L., Bennell, C., Mokros, A. and Ormerod, D. (2008) 'The personality paradox in offender profiling: A theoretical review of the processes involved in deriving background characteristics from crime scene actions', *Public Policy, and Law*, 8: 115–35.
Arkowitz, S. and Vess, J. (2003) 'An evaluation of the Bumby RAPE and MOLEST scales as measures of cognitive distortions with civilly committed sexual offences', *Sexual Abuse: A Journal of Research and Treatment*, 15: 237–49.
Beech, A.R., Fisher, D. and Beckett, R. (1999) *Step 3: An Evaluation of the Prison Sex Offender Treatment Programme*. London: Home Office.
Beech, A.R. and Ward, T. (2004) 'The integration of etiology and risk in sex offenders: A theoretical model', *Aggression and Violent Behaviour*, 10: 31-63
Beitchman, J., Zucker, K., Hood, J., Da Costa, G. and Akman, D. (1991) 'A review of the short-term effects of child sexual abuse', *Child Abuse and Neglect*, 15: 537–56.
Blumenthal, S., Gudjonsson, G. and Burns, J. (1999) 'Cognitive distortions and blame attribution in sex offenders against adults and children', *Child Abuse and Neglect*, 23: 129–48.

Boyd, D. (2007) 'Why Youth (Heart) Social Network Sites: The Role of Networked Publics in Teenage Social Life', in D. Buckingham (ed.), *MacArthur Foundation Series on Digital Learning – Youth, Identity, and Digital Media Volume*. Cambridge, MA: MIT Press.

Browne, A. and Finkelhor, D. (1986) 'Impact of child sexual abuse: A review of the research', *Psychological Bulletin*, 99: 66–77.

Bryce, J. (2008) *Bridging the Digital Divide: Executive Summary*. London: Orange and the Cyberspace Research Unit.

Bumby, K.M. (1996) 'Assessing the cognitive distortions of child molesters and rapists: Development and validation of the MOLEST and RAPE scales', *Sexual Abuse: A Journal of Research and Treatment*, 8: 37–54.

Burke, A., Sowerbutts, S., Blundell, S. and Sherry, M. (2001) 'Child pornography and the internet: Policing and treatment issues', *Psychiatry, Psychology and Law*, 9: 79–84.

Byron, T. (2008) *Safer Children in a Digital World: The Report of the Byron Review*. London: Department for Children, Schools and Family, and the Department for Culture, Media and Sport.

Carr, J. (2004) *Child Abuse, Child Pornography and the Internet: Executive Summary*. NCH.

CEOP (2008) *Strategic Overview 2007–2008*. London: CEOP.

Childline (2005) *Children Talking to Childline About The Internet*. London: Childline.

Daily Mail (2009) 'Generation sexting: What teenage girls really get up to on the internet should chill every parent'. Retrieved from http://www.dailymail.co.uk/femaile/article-1162777/Generation-sexting-What-teenage-girls-really-internet-chill-parent.html

Finkelhor, D. (1984) *Child Sexual Abuse: New Theory and Research*. New York: Free Press.

Finkelhor, D. and Araji, S. (1986) 'Explanations of pedophilia: A four factor model', *The Journal of Sex Research*, 22(1): 145–61.

Finkelhor, D., Mitchell, K.J. and Wolak, J. (2000) *Online Victimization: A Report on the Nation's Youth*. Alexandria, VA: National Center for Missing and Exploited Children.

Gannon, T.A. (2006) 'Increasing honest responding on cognitive distortions in child molesters: The bogus pipeline procedure', *Journal of Interpersonal Violence*, 21: 358–75.

Gannon, T. and Polaschek, D. (2005) 'Do child molesters deliberately fake good on cognitive distortion questionnaires? An information processing-based investigation', *Sexual Abuse: A Journal of Research and Treatment*, 17: 183–200.

Gillespie, A.A. (2008) *Child Exploitation and Communication Technologies*. Lyme Regis: Russell House Publishing.

Home Office (2002) 'Home Office Annual Report 2001–2'. London: Home Office.

Horley, J. (2000) 'Cognitions supportive of child molestation', *Aggression and Violent Behaviour*, 5: 551–64.

Howitt, D. (1995) *Paedophiles and Sexual Offences Against Children*. Chichester: Wiley.

Howitt, D. and Sheldon, K. (2007) 'The role of cognitive distortions in paedophilic offending: Internet and contact offenders compared', *Psychology, Crime and Law*, 13: 469–86.

Kendall-Tackett, K., Williams, L. and Finkelhor, D. (1993) 'Impact of sexual abuse on children: A review and synthesis of recent empirical studies', *Psychological Bulletin*, 113: 164–80.

Kolton, D.J.C., Boer, A. and Boer, D.P. (2001) 'A revision of the Abel and Becker Cognition Scale for intellectually disabled sexual offenders', *Sexual Abuse: A Journal of Research and Treatment*, 13: 217–19.

Livingstone, S. (2008) 'Taking risky opportunities in the creation of youthful content creation: Teenagers' use of social networking sites for intimacy, privacy and self-expression', *New Media and Society*, 10(3), 393–411.

Livingstone, S. and Bober, M. (2005) *UK Children Go Online: Final Report of Key Project Findings.* London: London School of Economics and Political Science.

Marshall, W.L., Marshall, L.E., Sachdev, S. and Kruger, R. (2003) 'Distorted attitudes and perceptions, and their relationship with self-esteem and coping in child molesters', *Sexual Abuse: A Journal of Research and Treatment*, 15: 171–81.

Medina, J. (2007) 'States weigh laws to block predators', *The New York Times*, 6 May: 29.

Middleton, D., Elliott, I.A., Mandeville-Norden, R. and Beech, A.R. (2006) 'An investigation into the applicability of the Ward and Siegert Pathways Model of child sexual abuse with Internet offenders', *Psychology, Crime and Law*, 12: 589–603.

Mitchell, K.J., Finkelhor, D. and Wolak, J. (2001) 'Risk factors for and impact of online sexual solicitation of youth', *Journal of the American Medical Association*, 285: 3011–14.

Mitchell, K., Finkelhor, D. and Wolak, J. (2003) 'Victimization of youth on the internet', *Journal of Aggression, Maltreatment and Trauma*, 8: 1–39.

Mitchell, K., Finkelhor, D. and Wolak, J. (2005) 'The internet and family and acquaintance sexual abuse', *Child Maltreatment*, 10: 49–60.

Mitchell, K., Finkelhor, D. and Wolak, J. (2007a) 'Online requests for sexual pictures from youth: Risk factors and incident characteristics', *Journal of Adolescent Health*, 41: 196–203.

Mitchell, K., Finkelhor, D. and Wolak, J. (2007b) 'Youth internet users at risk for the most serious online sexual solicitations', *American Journal of Preventive Medicine*, 32: 532–7.

Mokros, A. and Alison, L. (2002) 'Is offender profiling possible? Testing the predicted homology of crime scene actions and background characteristics in a sample of rapists', *Legal and Criminological Psychology*, 7: 25–43.

Molnar, B.E., Buka, S.L. and Kessler, R.C. (2001) 'Child sexual abuse and subsequent psychopathology: Results from the National Comorbidity Survey', *American Journal of Public Health*, 91: 753–60.

NSPCC (2009) 'Sexual abuse – calls to ChildLine during 2007/2008', *NSPCC Press Release 09, February 2009.*

O'Connell, R. (2003) *A Typology of Child Cyberexploitation and Online Grooming Practices.* Lancashire: Cyberspace Research Unit, University of Central Lancashire.

OFCOM (2008) *Social Networking: A Quantitative and Qualitative Research Report into Attitudes, Behaviours and Use.* London: OFCOM.

Quayle, E. (2007) 'Assessment Issues with Young People Who Engage in Sexually Abusive Behaviours Through the New Technologies', in M. Calder (ed.), *Working with Children and Young People Who Sexually Abuse: Taking the Field Forward.* Lyme Regis: Russell House Publishing Ltd.

Quayle, E. and Taylor, M. (2003) 'Model of problematic Internet use in people with sexual interest in children', *Cyber Psychology and Behaviour*, 6: 93–106.

Rawe, J. (2006) 'How safe is MySpace?', *Time*, 3 July. Retrieved 20 July2007, from http://www.time.com/time/magazine/article/0,9171,1207808,00.html

Roeper, R. (2006) 'Wide-open MySpace.com filled with teens, danger', *Chicago Sun-Times*, 12 April.

Sheldon, K. (2004) 'A new type of sex offender?', *Forensic Update*, October, 79.

Sheldon, K. and Howitt, D. (2005) 'A new kind of paedophile? Contact and Internet offenders against children compared', *15th European Conference on Psychology and Law*, Vilnius, Lithuania (29 June–2 July 2005).

Sheldon, K. and Howitt, D. (2007) *Sex Offenders and the Internet*. London: John Wiley and Sons.

Taylor, M. and Quayle, E. (2003) *Child Pornography: An Internet Crime*. New York: Brunner-Routledge.

TES Cymru (2005) 'Web Picture Dangers: Warning as Schoolgirls Post Indecent Photos on Internet "for a bit of fun"', 9 March.

Ward, T. and Keenan, T. (1999) 'Child molesters' implicit theories', *Journal of Interpersonal Violence*, 14: 821–83 .

Ward, T. and Siegert, R. (2002) 'Towards a comprehensive theory of child sexual abuse: a theory knitting perspective', *Psychology, Crime and Law*, 8: 319–51.

Webb, L., Craissati, J. and Keen, S. (2007) 'Characteristics of Internet Child Pornography Offenders: A Comparison with Child Molesters', *Sex Abuse*, 19: 449–65.

Withers, K. and Sheldon, R. (2008) *The Hidden Life of Youth Online*. London: Institute for Public Policy Research.

Wolak, J., Finkelhor, D. and Mitchell, K.J. (2004) 'Internet-initiated sex crimes against minors: Implications for prevention based on findings from a national study', *Journal of Adolescent Health*, 35: 424–33.

Wolak, J., Mitchell, K. and Finkelhor, D. (2003) *National Juvenile Online Victimization Study (N-JOV): Methodology Report*. Crimes against Children Research Center.

Wolak, J., Mitchell, K. and Finkelhor, D. (2006) *Online Victimization: 5 Years Later*. Alexandria, VA: National Center for Missing and Exploited Children.

Wolak, J., Finkelhor, D., Mitchell, K.J. and Ybarra, M.L. (2008) 'Online "predators" and their victims: Myths, realities, and implications for prevention and treatment', *American Psychologist*, 63: 111–28.

Chapter 17

Child pornography

Ethel Quayle

While interest in child pornography is not new, it is the case that with each technological advance we have seen an increase in the availability of such materials, and this has been most noticeable in relation to the advent of the Internet. There are historical accounts of child pornography and its distribution, which appeared to be facilitated by the popular use of photography (Taylor and Quayle 2003). The criminalisation of such material, however, made access both difficult and dangerous, although there was a period of approximately 10 years when in some European countries all pornographic materials were decriminalised. In part this appears to reflect an absence of concern with those involved in the production of the material (both children and adults) and more a concern with the consumer. In Denmark the anti-pornography laws were repealed in 1969 and Sweden then followed in 1971, and this resulted in a booming trade in child pornography, with the appearance of material in the media and in ordinary shops (Schuijer and Rossen 1992). Such decriminalisation of child pornography and its subsequent ease of both production and distribution arguably resulted in the de-pathologising of some interests and behaviours, or at least a decoupling of some of our assumptions between the nature of sexual interest in children and the notion of sexual harm (Quayle 2008). However, it is of interest that much of the commercial production of child pornography during this period involved images of children that were produced in a domestic context and sent on to magazine editors in exchange for money.

Most early studies, and virtually all legal documents, use the term child pornography, but more recently questions have been raised as to whether this term both reflects the content of what is produced, and implicitly implies consensual activity (Taylor and Quayle 2003). The term 'abusive images' is now widely used by those who advocate for children's rights in relation to sexual abuse through photography (Jones and Skogrand 2005), but this change is not straightforward. The term child pornography is consistently used in the majority of laws and policy documents internationally (Akdeniz 2008), and attempts to change terminology are thought by some to be both confusing and to not adequately capture the complex nature of the material (Lanning 2008). This is worth further consideration, as concerns about the language used are not simply a question of semantics. These tensions in terminology are reflected in this chapter.

Although it would be wrong to suggest that child pornography is a purely social construction, it is apparent that legislation in this area has led to the development of a new category of sex offender, most frequently expressed as the 'Internet offender'. Internet sex offending denotes a range of discrete but overlapping activities, all of which may involve child pornography. These include: accessing or downloading images; the trading or distribution of images; the production of images; and child solicitation, or 'grooming'. More recently, Gallagher (2007) has described additional offences, such as Internet-initiated incitement and conspiracy to commit child sexual abuse. It is of interest that all of these offences have largely become conflated in the way that we think about, and talk of, such crimes. Cassell and Cramer (2008) argue that throughout history there has been a recurring moral panic about the potential danger of communication technologies (particularly for young women) but that when investigated it is less the technology that appears to be to blame, but rather the potential sexual agency of young women, parental loss of control, and the 'specter of women who manifest technological prowess'. In a similar vein, the Internet Safety Technical Taskforce (2008) argue that although they are frequently reported in the media, US Internet sex crimes against minors have not overtaken the number of unmediated sex crimes against minors, nor have they contributed to a rise in such crimes. The report states that the increased popularity of the Internet in the United States has not been correlated with an overall increase in reported sexual offences. Evidence is cited from the US that overall, sexual offences against children have declined in the last 18 years (National Center for Missing and Exploited Children 2006), with research indicating a dramatic reduction in reports of sexual offences against children from 1992 to 2006 (Calpin 2006; Finkelhor and Jones 2008). However, seemingly at odds with this, data from the FBI (2006) indicated that between 1996 and 2006 there was a 1,789 per cent increase in the number of open cases, a 2,174 per cent increase in arrests and summons, and a 1,397 per cent increase in convictions for sex-related crimes on the Internet. While the percentages are alarming, the figures from the FBI are largely meaningless without us knowing what they represent, but they do illustrate the FBI's perception of the changing incidence of these crimes.

In contrast to the decline of reported contact sexual offences against children, public behaviour in relation to illegal or problematic Internet content has led to a substantial number of reports of child pornography. In 2006, CyberTipline (a US congressionally mandated system for reporting child crimes) received 62,365 reports of child pornography (National Center for Missing and Exploited Children 2006). The 2007 Global Internet Trend Report of INHOPE (the International Association of Internet Hotlines) indicated that during the last quarter of 2006 the hotline network processed an average of 91,000 reports per month. Approximately 35,000 of these reports were received from the public and 19,000 were determined to refer to either illegal or harmful content. INHOPE determined that 9,600 reports were related to child pornography and that this number was increasing at an average of 120 reports per month. It is unclear whether these figures represent an increasing volume of child pornography, or rather the actions of an increasingly concerned public. The reality is that we have no idea of the numbers of people who commit sexual offences related to child pornography on the Internet. We can examine conviction rates, but these reflect only the countries where possession and distribution of child pornography are both illegal and where there are either the resources or inclination to act upon detection (Quayle 2008).

In the US, Wolak *et al.* (2003) reported that law enforcement made an estimated 2,577 arrests during 12 months (starting July 1 2000) for Internet sex crimes against minors. Two-thirds of offenders who committed any of these crimes possessed child pornography. Finkelhor and Ormrod (2004) examined child pornography patterns from the FBI's National Incident-Based Reporting System (NIBRS). The data from 1997–2000 on 2,469 crime incidents involving pornography revealed that over these three years pornography offences increased by 68 per cent and juvenile victim/child exploitation pornography offences increased 200 per cent. But at the time of this report, only a small minority of all pornography offences known to the police was coded as involving a computer. Middleton *et al.* (2009) in relation to the UK, reports that for England and Wales in 1999, there were 238 convictions for publication, possession or distribution of obscene matter and indecent photographs of children. By 2005 the number had reached 1,296 which meant that convictions for Internet-related sexual offences accounted for almost one-third of all sexual offence convictions.

However, these statistics reflect only those who are caught. Other data, such as that provided by one leading UK Internet Service Provider suggested that in July 2004 they blocked more than 20,000 attempts per day to access child pornography on the Internet. More recent data from the Swedish and Norwegian blocking of access to known sites carrying child abusive images reveal as many as 15,000–18,000 daily attempts in Norway (Quayle *et al.* 2008). Such use of the WWW as a possible means of accessing child pornography was investigated by Demetriou and Silke (2003), who established a website to examine whether people who visited for the purposes of gaining access to legal material would also attempt to access illegal or pornographic material if it was offered. Over an 88-day period, 803 visitors entered the site and it was found that the majority of visitors accessed those sections purporting to offer illegal or deviant material. However, material that is produced legally can also be used in a problematic way. This was demonstrated by Lehmann *et al.* (2006) in relation to the detection and management of pornography seeking in an online clinical dermatology atlas. During the study period, one third of the search queries related to anatomical sites and over half specified children.

Moral panic?

So are the anxieties felt about the new technologies, and in particular about the use of abusive images of children, simply part of a moral panic? Mears *et al.* (2008), in a survey examining US views towards sex crimes, indicated that the public supports incarceration as an appropriate response to prosecuting child pornography offenders. The suggestion made by these authors was that Americans may support incarceration because of a belief that behaviour such as downloading abuse images will lead to a contact offence against a child. This might also be the case why convictions sometimes attract long sentences within the US, with Greenhouse (2007) giving details of a US Supreme Court decision declining to review a case in which an Arizona man was given a 200-year sentence for possessing 20 'pornographic' images of children. Yet Jenkins (2009) has argued that we see nothing constituting moral panic. It may be that while we have seen increasing anxiety about children's agency online, which result in displays of sexual behaviour or the establishment of sexual relationships, we show much greater ambivalence towards child pornography. We are concerned with the relationship between the use of images and harm against 'real' children in the offline world (largely *our* children), but we seem to demonstrate a much more complex level of interest in the photographic depiction of abusive and exploitative practices towards children.

Jenkins (2009) attributes what he calls this 'failure to launch' to several factors. He argues that one main reason is technical in that law enforcement agencies work at a technological level that is too low to comprehend trade in images as it actually is. But perhaps one factor, mentioned by Jenkins, to explain some of our ambivalence towards abusive and exploitative images of children lies in our lack of knowledge on the one hand of what these images are, and an overexposure on the other to sexualised visual materials. It is not simply that we lack concern about the illegality of images, or, as demonstrated by the 200-year sentence, the potential of such offenders to pose a further threat. Adler (2008: 3) reflects that, 'Claims about the changing nature of child pornography are difficult to verify for a number of reasons: above all, it is extremely hard, if not impossible, to measure accurately the online environment; in addition, no one outside of government can fully assess these claims because child pornography law prohibits researchers, academics, or anyone outside of law enforcement from looking at child pornography.' Yet sexualised images of children, clearly not defined in law as child pornography, are often found in contexts such as advertising (described by Rush and La Nauze 2006 as examples of corporate paedophilia). Adler's (2001) argument is that as we legislate more and more to control abusive images of children we potentially create 'a vast realm of discourse' in which the image of the child as sexual is not only preserved but multiplied. Child pornography law socially constructs the child as sexual and one result of this construction may be that more people feel sexual desire for children. We will address this further when we consider the 'creation' or 'discovery' of paedophilic interest in children.

If we look at the material found in the collections of offenders, the kinds of pictures that can be identified range from pictures of clothed children, through nakedness and explicit erotic posing to pictures of a sexual assault of the child or children in the photograph. We can make some objective sense of this by thinking of them in terms of a continuum of increased deliberate sexual victimisation (Taylor *et al.* 2001). This continuum ranges from everyday and perhaps accidental pictures involving either no overt erotic content, or minimal content (such as showing a child's underwear) at one extreme, to pictures showing actual rape and penetration of a child, or other gross acts of obscenity at the other. Taking this perspective focuses attention not on just illegality as a significant quality of pictures, but on the preferred type of pictures selected by the collector, and the value and meaning pictures have to collectors (Taylor and Quayle 2003). In trying to understand the ways in which children are victimised within the images, Taylor *et al.* (2001) generated a typology based on an analysis of publicly available images obtained from newsgroups and websites (made possible under Irish law). This 'COPINE Scale' had 10 levels ranging from indicative images to ones depicting sadism or bestiality. In 2002, in England and Wales, the Sentencing Advisory Panel (SAP) published their advice to the Court of Appeal on offences involving child pornography. The SAP believed that the nature of the material should be the key factor in deciding the level of sentence, and adapted the COPINE scale to five levels. They dropped levels 1 to 3 completely, arguing that nakedness alone was not indicative of indecency. The proposed structure was therefore that COPINE levels 5 to 6 constitute sentencing level 1 and COPINE levels 7 onwards each constitute an individual sentencing stage (Gillespie 2003). One consequence of using such a measure has been that it provides a means of communication about the images without, for most people, the images ever having been seen. It is interesting that this way of talking about child sexual abuse has also entered into ordinary discourse. While it would be carrying the argument too far to suggest that the general public talks about image level, it is apparent that the media communicates messages about child pornography in this way, and this potentially distances us from their content. A *Sunday Times* (2008) report described how 'Hart possessed 52,240 in category one, 2,419 in category two, 684 in category three, 1,445 in category four and 44 in category five' (p. 36).

In a much earlier publication, Lanning (1992) introduced an important distinction between child pornography (the sexually explicit reproduction of a child's image) and child erotica (any material, relating to children, that serves a sexual purpose for a given individual). In a similar fashion, Tate (1990: 203–17), commented on how the material ranged from 'posed pictures of naked and semi naked children, through more explicit shots of their genitalia thumbed apart to still, film and video recordings of oral, vaginal and anal sex'. While legal definitions of child pornography have to be objective and expressed in terms that allow for the proper application of due process, it becomes apparent that not all of the material that is currently circulating on the Internet would meet any legal definition of child pornography, and the definition of such images as 'abusive' is a largely subjective one. Svedin and Back (1996: 9) defined child pornography as 'a text or an image – i.e. photo, slide, film, video or computer program – that is intended to evoke a sexual feeling, fantasy or response in adults'. However, expressing criteria in terms of a capacity to generate fantasy may be problematic when objective definitions are required, as the range of materials that might evoke fantasy includes photographs that can be found in any family album or clothes catalogue.

The challenge posed by such a debate is, in the context of the huge volume of legal, but sexualised material relating to children on the Internet, as to how we might define these images, and whether we should be attempting to control their distribution. Clearly we cannot legislate against fantasy, but King (2008: 332) has argued that 'It is not clear ... that the consumer (or the rest of society) can always (or ever) be sure what category a particular image falls into, how much harm to the subject it represents, for however happy and carefree the child seems to be, we cannot know what later effects she suffered (or, indeed, what she was subjected to after or as a result of that photograph). In fact it's clear that some degree of harm is almost always done to the subject in the production and distribution of child pornography of all kinds ...'. King (2008) goes on to suggest that child pornography not only harms its immediate victims, the children whose abuse is at its centre, but also harms other children through the actions and attitudes of its consumers.

Virtual child pornography

One further challenge relates to pseudo (digitally altered) images and virtual child pornography. Gillespie (2003) has raised important issues about how different an image has to be for it to constitute a pseudo-image, possession of which in England and Wales is likely to attract a lower sentence. In the US, the constitutionality of virtual child pornography remains a critical issue. In *Ashcroft* v. *Free Speech Coalition* (2002) a majority of the Supreme Court struck down portions of the Child Pornography Prevention Act of 1996, stating that virtual child pornography created without real or identifiable minors was unconstitutionally over-broad (Quayle 2008). It might be thought that these 'pseudo-photographs' complicate our understanding of the problem and challenge our understanding of harm. Harm, however, need not always be harm towards a specific child. Most legislation against the distribution and possession of child abuse images builds on the fact that even unaware victims somehow come to harm, much in the way described by King (2008), and the increased number of abusive images in circulation may add to the likelihood that children are seen as possible objects of real abuse.

In 2003, Taylor and Quayle wrote that 'Pseudo-photographs are constructed photographs, often very cleverly done with great technical sophistication, using digital reconstruction techniques to create an image that is not a photograph of a real person, or of real events. Thus the head of a child might be placed onto the body of a woman, where the body features are manipulated to make it appear to be that of a child (breast reduced in size or eliminated, and pubic hair eliminated) ...' However, while the production of such material a few years ago might have been a technological challenge, this would not be the case today. With the advent of software packages such as Adobe Photoshop, the majority of us would be able to create quite complex digitally altered images. The prediction was made that easier and more accessible computer-aided animation and 3D computer graphics would lead to a growth in animated child pornography. This has now happened and we see evidence of wholly constructed computer images, although it is unclear as yet what impact this might have on the availability of such image distribution. One of the primary producers of such imagery is Japan where there is a huge market in *manga*, and other forms of animation, that many believe are sexually exploitative. A report in the UK's *Guardian* newspaper (*Guardian* 2008) suggested that sexually explicit comics account for a large proportion of Japan's 500 billion yen *manga* market, with many featuring schoolgirls or childlike adults being raped or engaged in sadomasochism. However, the article suggested that *manga* belonging to the popular '*lolicon*' – Japanese slang for Lolita complex – genre are likely to escape the proposed ban in Japan on the possession of child pornography, 'as MPs are concerned that outlawing them could infringe on freedom of expression and drive men who use them as an outlet for their sexual urges to commit more serious sexual offences'. However, outside of offender accounts there is little empirical research to support this while there is evidence to suggest that such *manga* is often found as part of the collections of seized images from offenders.

In countries outside of Japan there has been a bid to criminalise the possession of non-photographic visual depictions of child sexual abuse. In the UK a formal period of consultation began in relation to this in April 2007 and concluded in June of that year. Prior to this, the Criminal Law Sub Group of the Home Secretary's Task Force on Child Protection on the Internet had been considering the issues raised by computer-generated images (CGIs), drawings and cartoons which show graphic depictions of sexual abuse of children or childlike characters. The Consultation document recognised that these images do not involve harm to real children in their creation, but that the possession of such material was a cause for concern, particularly as technological advances have increased the availability of such material. In the summary of the responses to the Consultation, it was noted that many people viewed the definition of what would constitute 'pornographic' as both troublesome and opaque. There was also concern that 'stylisations of animations freely mix aspects typifying different ages', which would make the allocation of age subjective and therefore an impossible assessment of legality. Opponents of these measures, such as the American Civil Liberties Union, have argued that people's thoughts are their private thoughts, and that prohibition of pseudo-child pornography is a violation of free speech rights (Taylor and Quayle 2003). However, Oswell (2006) has presented an important argument against this stating that, although the evidential value of the virtual image is different from an actual image (and hence the forms of police investigation and legal prosecution are different), until an image can be said to correspond to an actual case of child sexual abuse, all Internet child pornography can be viewed as real. In this sense, the primary concern is not one of the effects of the image on others or one of the relations of power encoded in the image, but one of the virtual evidentiality of the image (i.e. on the image's capacity to refer to an objective reality that is both internal and external to the image).

Child pornography law

Within the last few years we have witnessed the development of supranational and international policy documents which set out to define 'child pornography' and four policy documents that are central to this issue. The European Union's Framework Decision on combating the sexual exploitation of children and child pornography entered into force in 2004 and required member states to take steps to ensure compliance by 20 January 2006. Here child pornography is defined as pornographic material that visually depicts or represents:

(i)   a real child involved or engaged in sexually explicit conduct, including lascivious exhibition of the genitals or the pubic area of a child; or

(ii)   a real person appearing to be a child involved or engaged in the conduct mentioned in (i); or

(iii) realistic images of a non-existent child involved or engaged in the conduct mentioned in (i).

As we can see, the definition in the EU Framework Decision talks about a 'real' child, 'real' person and 'realistic' images, which may prove unlikely to cover virtual images or cartoons. The Council of Europe's Cybercrime Convention (2001) came into force in July 2004, and Article 9 defines child pornography as pornographic material that visually depicts: a minor engaged in sexually explicit conduct; a person appearing to be a minor engaged in sexually explicit conduct; or realistic images representing a minor engaged in sexually explicit conduct. This relates to all people under the age of 18, but it is possible for a lower age limit of 16 to be set. The third document is the United Nation's Optional Protocol to the Convention on the Rights of the Child on the Sale of Children, Child Prostitution and Child Pornography which came into force in January 2002 and defines child pornography as 'any representation, by whatever means, of a child engaged in real or simulated explicit sexual activities or any representation of the sexual parts of a child for primarily sexual purposes'. In all three a child is defined as someone under the age of 18 years and includes both photographs of actual children as well as representations of children, which would appear to include computer-generated images. However, the issue of age is subject to several reservations and complicated by the age of sexual consent established under national law. Akdeniz (2008) draws our attention to the fact that the UN definition is broad and, as it refers to 'any representation', would also include textual material, cartoons and drawings.

The most recent relevant instrument establishing a definition of child pornography is the Council of Europe Convention on the Protection of Children against Sexual Exploitation and Sexual Abuse. While this definition is restricted to visual materials it does not require that a real child be used in their production (as is the case in the US). However, member states may opt not to criminalise the production and possession of virtual child pornography. Importantly the Convention has chosen not to criminalise the consensual production and possession of materials created by children who have reached the age of consent. However, most instruments do not directly address the issue of adolescents who make or access indecent images of children, and this in itself may prove to be problematic. Piper (2001) has argued that one of the landmark changes in terms of criminal justice policy in recent times has been the approach to juvenile crime, which in the UK led in the 1990s to the effective reduction in the age of criminal responsibility to 10 years accompanied by a series of measures that were designed to tackle youth crime. She convincingly argued that adolescents involved in criminality became less victims of social failings in need of protection but rather criminals who require the intervention of the criminal justice system (Quayle *et al.* 2008). Gillespie (2008) has argued that in the UK the criminal justice system is increasingly adopting a harsher approach to adolescents who break the law, with the law adopting very different approaches to adolescents involved in indecent images of children and those who have direct sexual contact with another adult.

ICMEC (2006) used the UN definition in its study of the184 Interpol member countries. Their results indicated that at the time of publication, 95 countries have no legislation at all that specifically addresses child pornography and 41 countries do not criminalise possession of child pornography, regardless of intent to distribute (ICMEC 2006). This report called for stiffer sentences although it does not elaborate on what these sentences might be (prison or community) and does not consider other options, such as requirement to engage with a sex offender management programme (Beech *et al.* 2008). However, in law offences related to child pornography are not all treated as the same. Akdeniz (2008) referred to this as a 'chain of liability'. At the top of the chain are those who produce abusive images or content, and these will be made up of, although not exclusively, those who will have sexually abused the children in the images. Many of these will produce images within a domestic setting where production is part of a spectrum of abusive practices. The second group that sexually exploit are those who distribute child pornography over the Internet, either commercially (for financial gain), or non-commercially, where the images themselves function as a form of currency (Taylor and Quayle 2003) or possibly as a means to raise their status in a group or to confirm their allegiance and sense of belonging to a group. The final group are those who sexually exploit the child through the possession of images downloaded from the Internet (or occasionally acquired via mobile phone). This latter group are often considered the least serious of offenders and are likely to attract a lower sentence. However, Clough (2008) has suggested that rather than being prosecuted for possession, offenders should be prosecuted for 'accessing' child pornography. If viewing the image is part of the chain of sexual exploitation set in motion by the sexual abuse committed, then it might be argued that this too should be criminalised. It would seem sensible to conclude that States should include a separate offence of 'the *intentional* viewing and accessing' of child pornography in their national body of laws (Quayle *et al.* 2008).

The children in the images

It is important to note that while child pornography on the Internet is generated in a number of ways, these photographs (and non-photographic depictions) are a permanent product of abusive practices, some of which involve a direct sexual assault on a child. As we will see, their permanence may itself be an issue for the children photographed. We can think of child pornography production coming from many sources, some of which predate the Internet. This may include: hard copy images relating to the period of decriminalisation, that have been scanned; those produced during the sexual abuse of children in domestic settings, where the child *may* know about the photography taking place; hidden, or stolen images, made, for example, by placing cameras in shower heads, or surreptitiously photographing children in swimming pools; commercial images, where the photographer may be involved in abusive practices towards the child; and self-generated material, produced by children in response to sexual demands by others, as well as through activities initiated by young people themselves. Clearly one issue here relates to confidence in the ability of professionals to identify images that are of children (as opposed to adults positioned as children). This hinges on the definition of child, which in many, but not all, jurisdictions is set at less than 18 years. A study by Cattaneo *et al.* (2008) examined some of the difficulties relating to this and noted that there is great variability in physical maturity due to biological, pathological and environmental factors. In this study photographs of 11 adult females were taken and two groups, experts and lay people, were asked to establish if each were less than 18 years and the basis for making that judgement. Their results indicated that all assessors performed poorly and the authors conclude that a more reliable categorisation might be between prepubertal and pubertal children, but this would exclude all the images of children (under the age of 18) who are sexually mature.

Schuijer and Rossen (1992) analysed the content of 'child pornography magazines and videos' that had been in circulation prior to the change of law across a number of European countries. They suggested that on the basis of the estimate of 1,065 published magazines, a conservative estimate would be the involvement of 6,000 children. Their analysis indicated that 42 per cent of the pictures were of boys, with more girls appearing in extreme forms of images. However, Australian data from Baartz (2008) describing the gender, ethnicity and age of the victims portrayed in the images examined by investigators would suggest that the children were mostly white, westernised females, aged between eight and 12 years. Asian children were the next most common ethnic group, and there was a comparative absence of indigenous Australian children. An analysis of the COPINE archive in 2003 indicated that the majority of images available were of white Caucasian and Asian children, with very few African or African-American children (Taylor and Quayle 2005). Indeed, in 2003, websites started to appear advertising specialist sites that included interracial pictures. Similarly, Carr's (2004) study, which was one of the few to analyse the images used by offenders, indicated that the vast majority of offenders selected material portraying Caucasian and Asian children.

Our lack of knowledge about children being abused through photography is reflected in the relatively small numbers who are ever identified. Where identification does take place, there is little consistent empirical data, although the National Center for Missing and Exploited Children (NCMEC) suggested that as of September 2008, 1,660 children had been identified through distributed and non-distributed images (73 per cent female and 27 per cent male). At the time of writing this chapter, this was the most complete data set of identified children available, but is based only on what has been reported to NCMEC by law enforcement (Lee 2008). The numbers for 'Gender' represent actual individual *children*, whereas the numbers for Age Category (Infant/Toddler, 6 per cent; Prepubescent, 49 per cent; Pubescent, 45 per cent) represents the percentage of identified *series*. There can be more than one child within a series so, for example, a series that has four prepubescent boys will be counted once, as the percentage represents the series, not children. The statistics for Ethnicity also represent *series* and include all the identified series in the NCMEC system, as well as some other known child sexual abuse series that are currently being investigated (Asian, 16; Biracial, 0; Black, 23; Hispanic, 19; Other, 5; Unknown, 0; and White, 1,186). It is unclear whether this data on identified children reflects the actual distribution of images currently circulating on the Internet and is certainly different in its gender distribution than is suggested by Schuijer and Rossen (1992) in relation to earlier hard copy images.

A report from Baines (2008: 34) suggests that while our knowledge of these children remains imprecise, 'In terms of content, the number of non-commercial images showing babies or toddlers is on the increase: victims in commercial images also are increasingly young, with 80 per cent estimated to be less than 10 years old. Moreover, a number of investigations by UK and overseas law enforcement agencies have highlighted the fact that there are many series of images in which the victims appear to have been abused a number of years earlier but where the images have only just come to light. This is particularly true for images of boys and where the material has been seized from a contact sexual abuser – in turn suggesting that offenders who have previously been content to keep a record of the abuse for their own personal gratification may have been detected after succumbing to the urge to share this material on the Internet. In recent years law enforcement has also seen the emergence of images – albeit so far a relatively small number – containing victims of non-white origin, including those of South American and Southeast Asian origin. This proliferation of images from a variety of source countries points to the role of the Internet in facilitating truly global communications and networking across obvious language and cultural barriers.'

Clearly children within the images do not necessarily come from countries where Internet access is widely available. There have been reports of children exploited through the production of child pornography in Mexico (Azaola 2000), South Asia (Huda 2006) and India (Kacker *et al.* 2007). What is of concern about the production of such images is that we have little knowledge of how they have become part of abusive practices against children, and no knowledge as to how they were used. We do not know if these photographs were sold on, whether they became part of commercial sexual exploitation (through the sale of DVDs) or whether their images will ever find their way onto the Internet (Quayle *et al.* 2008).

The consequences for the children within the images

There have been few studies of children victimised through the production of child pornography, and the information we have largely relates to periods that precede the wide availability of the Internet. Indeed it might be argued that where the child (or their caregivers) does not know about the images, there can be no consequences (except where images are discovered on the Internet or as part of a police investigation). Renold and Creighton (2003) listed four studies, all of which explored victimisation, one of which was by Svedin and Back (1996) drawn from a group of children exposed to both the production of pornography and intra- and extra-familial abuse. All four of these studies are broadly similar in the accounts that they give of the symptoms evidenced by these children and it is difficult to disentangle the consequences of the abuse per se from the consequences of being photographed. Söderström (2006) described differences in the process of disclosure, evidenced in his work with children that have had images of their abuse distributed via the new technologies. He suggests that the child's cognitive perception of the abuse is made more difficult due to a need to defend him/herself from facing the fact that images were taken and that the picture-taking in itself is an issue almost separate from the abuse experience. The fact that there are images of the abuse takes away the child's ability to control the disclosure of the abuse as part of the therapeutic process.

Svedin and Back (2003) reported on 30 children who had been abused and photographed in an attempt to understand what limits disclosure. The study highlighted the shame of the children, and that this shame also contributed to the continuation of the relationship with the perpetrator. Of the interviewed children, only two of them talked spontaneously, and there were five others who eventually gave a fairly complete account without being shown the pictures or the investigator saying that he/she knew what had happened (from the seized material). Five children denied that anything had occurred. All the children's accounts were fragmentary, and the children showed great difficulty in talking about their contact with the suspected perpetrator.

Consumers of abusive images

There have been several attempts to generate a more differentiated view of the activities engaged in on the Internet that are sexual in their orientation and which might cause harm to children. These have been largely conceptualised as typologies of offending behaviour, as they describe not only the activities themselves but suggest underlying motivations for offending. Several of these typologies built on earlier work that predated the Internet, such as that by Hartman et al. (1984). Alexy et al. (2005) described a typology based on the distinction between those who use the Internet as a way of furthering contact offences against children and those who use the Internet to access abusive images. These authors generated three types of offender: traders, travellers and trader-travellers. Traders were described as people who both collect and trade abusive images of children on the Internet and therefore provide a market for the further abuse of children. Travellers use the Internet to gain access to children whom they coerce into meeting them for sexual purposes. The third category, trader-travellers, are those who do both. Krone (2004) generated a more comprehensive typology along a continuum of increasing seriousness of the offence. This included a range of offences from those that did not directly involve a child to offences involving direct contact with children, and from online engagement to physical abuse. Krone's (2004) typology generated nine types of offender classes.

In a similar way, Lanning (2001) talked about 'computer offenders' who use this medium to sexually exploit and sexually abuse children. He suggested that they fall into three broad categories: situational, preferential and miscellaneous. Situational offenders include: adolescents or impulsive or curious adults with a newly found access to a wide range of pornography or sexual opportunities; morally indiscriminate people motivated by power or anger and who have a history of varied violent offences; and profiteer offenders who aim to profit from the lucrative child pornography market by involving children in sexual activity. Beech *et al.* (2008) have been critical of Lanning's (2001) typology in that while it is extensive and takes into account the many reasons for which an individual might decide to use the Internet for sexual purposes, some of these types appear to overlap and are not discrete categories. Even though Lanning and Krone both talk about those who sexually abuse and those who exploit that abuse, they make no specific distinction between the groups, which somewhat limits the usability of the proposed typologies. What is also obvious is that Lanning's typology tells us a lot about the motivation of people who offend, and how this information might be used evidentially by law enforcement, but tells us little about the offence from a victim perspective. It is also apparent that offenders collect a wide range of images, and while the primary function is largely in the service of sexual arousal, there are other functions such as social activity, collecting behaviour and meeting a set of (largely) emotionally avoidant needs (Middleton *et al.* 2006; Quayle and Taylor 2002; Sheldon and Howitt 2008). While these may not have been the initiating factors in the offending process, they may be factors that maintain the behaviour.

In trying to make sense of offending on the Internet comparisons have been made with offenders who have committed a contact offence against a child in the offline world. At present, there tends to be an assumption that in fact they are one and the same, and as Internet sex offenders are such a heterogeneous population (aside from gender and racial group which we will go on to consider) this is often going to be the case. Clearly sex offenders who have both committed a contact offence with a child or children and who then use child abuse images on the Internet are likely to have a lot in common with those who have sexually offended against a child in the offline environment. However, as yet there is surprisingly little data to support this. Seto *et al.* (2006) investigated whether being charged with a child pornography offence was a valid diagnostic indicator of paedophilia, as represented by an index of phallometrically assessed sexual arousal to children. Their results indicated that child pornography offenders had almost three times the odds of being identified as a paedophile phallometrically as offenders against children. Seto *et al.* (2006) suggested that child pornography offending is a stronger diagnostic indicator of paedophilia than is sexual offending against child victims. The results of this study pose a considerable challenge to us all.

Webb *et al.* (2007) compared 90 Internet offenders with 120 child molesters from probation caseloads across the Greater London (UK) area. Both groups had experienced substantial levels of childhood difficulties, although child molesters were more likely to have been physically abused. A significantly higher number of Internet offenders had been in contact with the mental health services as adults, and had had significantly fewer live-in relationships. On the Hare Psychopathy Checklist, child molesters scored higher than Internet offenders, although the latter were reported as having significantly more problems with 'sexual self-regulation' than child molesters. In this study, 65 per cent of Internet offenders had had one life event or more in the 12 months prior to their arrest (related to financial and social issues, and personal health and sexual difficulties). Both groups presented with a more schizoid, avoidant and dependent profile, which the authors felt was suggestive of individuals who either retreat from interpersonal and social situations, sometimes fearing rejection and cutting themselves off emotionally, or individuals who place excessive reliance on their relationships with others in order to be able to cope.

Sheldon and Howitt (2007) attempted an examination of how far Internet offenders match conceptions of contact offenders. In this study 16 Internet sex offenders, 25 contact offenders and 10 mixed offenders (those who had committed online as well as contact offences) were compared on a range of questionnaires exploring childhood and adult attachment, dispositional coping strategies, sexual fantasies and cognitive distortions. Comparing the populations, contact offenders were characterised by adverse childhoods (including sexual abuse); lengthy criminal records, and the use of emotionally oriented coping strategies. Internet sex offenders were more likely to be professionally employed; have more years in education; few criminal convictions; report some childhood difficulties and heterosexual sexualised play; high levels of paedophile fantasies and cognitive distortions but few criminal convictions of any kind. In this group paedophilic fantasies were related to sex play experiences and close themes between early childhood sexual experience and later adult abusive behaviour were evident. In relation to a separate population and within a psychodynamic framework, Wood (2007) has suggested that one feature of virtual sexual activity is the creation of a scenario loaded with meaning, which she described as a 'compelling scenario'. This often seems to encapsulate specific traumatic experiences and key object relationships from childhood and adolescence. This seems to have resonances with Sheldon and Howitt's (2007) study.

Sheldon and Howitt (2008), using a 52-item Sexual Fantasy Inventory, suggest that the findings represent a dilemma for the fantasy literature, as in this study contact offending was associated with suppressed levels of girl (paedophilic) fantasy and brings into question any simple, direct model linking sexual fantasy to contact offending and contradicts the sexual preference hypothesis. This group of contact offenders appeared to have difficulty generating fantasy, and their fantasies had more confrontational non-contact content than did those experienced by Internet sex offenders (such as exposing their genitals to unsuspecting girls, where an important part of the fantasy was the response of the other person). Of relevance to this is Howitt's (2004) suggestion in relation to the need to commit a contact offence that the explanation might be that further offending may be a stimulus to fantasy rather than a consequence. It would be tempting to speculate that for Internet sex offenders the fantasy is itself sufficient, but as yet there is little evidence to support this although in Seto et al.'s (2006) study their non-contact offenders responded sexually much more to visual images than did contact offenders.

A further study comparing Internet sex offenders with non-Internet sex offenders was published by Bates and Metcalf (2007) using data generated by the Thames Valley Programme in the UK. The two groups were compared using a battery of psychometric tests employed by the programme (Beech 1998). Seventy-eight men were assessed, half of whom had a conviction related to a contact offence and half who had committed an Internet sex offence. The overall rate of psychometrically derived 'high deviancy' was calculated by combining all of the differently weighted questionnaire scores. Their results suggested that overall rates of 'psychometric deviancy' were similar between the two groups (22.2 per cent of Internet sex offenders and 23.1 per cent of contact offenders). However, there were differences in that using the Paulhus' Balanced Inventory of Desirable Responding (BIDR) contact offenders scored more highly on the self-deception sub-scale, while Internet sex offenders evidenced much higher scores on the Impression Management sub-scale, which may be suggestive of Internet sex offenders presenting themselves in an unrealistically positive way and casting doubt on the validity of the psychometric test results for this group. It is, however, difficult to interpret the results presented within the study as no standard deviations are given and it is unclear whether this represents highly distorted scores for some offenders and not others. Their overall psychometric scores suggested that Internet sex offenders showed higher self-esteem than contact offenders, but worse emotional loneliness. It would appear, however, that the levels of deviance shown by almost one quarter of Internet sex offenders derived from the socio-affective, rather than offence-specific, category, but the largest difference was seen with the Impression Management Score.

In a recent study a data set consisting of 505 adult male Internet offenders and 526 adult male contact sexual offenders was compared. Each was allocated to one of two groups (Internet versus contact offender) based on their current index offence which was analysed by Elliott et al. (2009) across a number of measures including: offence-related beliefs and attitudes; social adequacy and interpersonal functioning; ability to effectively manage emotions and behaviours; and socially desirable responding. They found that contact offenders were characterised by a greater number of victim empathy distortions and cognitive distortions than Internet offenders and a greater bias towards favourable self-description. In contrast, Internet offenders were characterised by a greater ability to identify with fictional characters. A subsequent statistical model indicated that an increase in scores on scales of fantasy, under-assertiveness, and motor impulsivity were found to be predictive of an Internet offence type. This is interesting given that Middleton *et al.* (2009), in their study of convicted Internet sex offenders on the i-SOTP, found a slight increase in the scores on the fantasy sub-scale from pre to post treatment and concluded that, 'This scale assesses the degree to which offenders overidentify with fictional characters and it may be that these results indicate that this is a particularly difficult trait to change in those who seek pseudo-intimacy through online interactions' (p. 14).

One area that is puzzling in relation to this population is the demographic consistencies between study samples of Internet sex offenders, the most notable of which relate to gender and ethnicity. Wolak *et al.* (2003, 2005), in their study of Internet crimes against minors, reported that 99 per cent of their sample was male. This is similar to the findings of other studies (Baartz 2008; Bates and Metcalf 2007; Finkelhor and Ormrod 2004; Seto and Eke 2005; Sullivan 2007; Webb *et al.* 2007). However the majority of offenders are not only male but they are white Caucasians (O'Brien and Webster 2007; Sullivan 2007; Wolak *et al.* 2003, 2005). Webb *et al.* (2007) indicated that their 90 Internet-related offenders were predominantly white, which appeared different from their child molester sample that came from a more mixed ethnic group. Within a recent Australian sample the majority of Internet sex offenders were identified as Caucasian (86 per cent) with minimal representation in the Asian, Mediterranean and Aboriginal ethnic groups (Baartz 2008). Coward *et al.* (2009) in their analysis of an ongoing research project examined 405 cases made up of 277 sex offenders with convictions for contact sex offences and no arrest or charge for any Internet sex offence who had access to the Internet and 128 individuals charged or arrested for an Internet sex offence. Ninety-two per cent of the Internet sex offenders were Caucasian males, as compared to 73 per cent in the comparison group (which had a higher proportion of African-Americans and Hispanics).

This raises an interesting issue about sexually abusive practices and ethnicity, and whether these offender characteristics are as a result of socio-demographic patterns of Internet use, or whether they reflect differences in ethnicity and pornography use. Buzzell (2005) reported descriptive data taken from the US General Social Survey from 1973 onwards. They operationalised three technological contexts (film, theatre or VCR and websites) to describe general pornography use and the demographics of people who use it. Website access to pornography was predominantly male and declined with age, but 'More non-whites than whites have seen an X-rated film in a theater or on a VCR compared to film or website access … Use of website pornography follows the same pattern except that its use is less likely to be reported by non-white populations. Close to 20 per cent of the non-white portion of the sample reports use of pornography' (p. 41). It is unknown whether this is an example of the digital divide and whether this might change in the future as computer ownership, Internet access and skills training become less of a white, male preserve.

Risk

The question might reasonably be asked, 'Risk of what?': of becoming an Internet sex offender; the future commission of a similar, Internet-related sex offence; escalation to a further category of Internet sex offending; or the likelihood of an Internet sex offender committing a contact sexual offence against a child? To date there are few studies to inform our understanding of risk with Internet sex offenders, and this is compounded by the different kinds of populations used (e.g. prison versus community), the time frame for the data collection (more recent accounts would suggest a greater availability of illegal images of children, through, for example peer-to-peer networks), the ways in which the data are gathered (telephone interviews, self-report questionnaires, reconviction rates) and the lack of longitudinal data (Quayle 2009). In their meta-analysis of 82 recidivism studies, Hanson and Morton-Bourgon (2005) suggested that 'For those involved in applied risk assessments with sexual offenders, the review confirms sexual deviancy and antisocial orientation as major predictors of sexual recidivism and extends the range of relevant variables to include some potentially changeable characteristics: sexual preoccupations, lifestyle instability/ impulsivity, pro offending attitudes, and intimacy deficits. Readers will notice, however, that the predictive accuracy of most of the characteristics was small. Consequently, prudent evaluators need to consider a range of potential risk factors in an overall evaluation' (p. 1159). Conroy (2006), in the context of risk management of sex offenders, draws our attention to the fact that a high risk of sexually reoffending is associated with a range of factors. Harris (2006) using the meta-analysis by Hanson and Morton-Bourgon (2005) summarised these as: the presence of sexual deviancy as measured by both phallometric assessment and deviant sexual preferences, measured by standardised tools, with sexual interest in children as a strong predictive factor in child molesters, although this is not the case with rape interest for rapists, and the presence of an antisocial lifestyle and orientation, such as rule violation, poor employment history and reckless, impulsive behaviour.

This raises a further challenge as to how we conceptualise deviance in the context of Internet sex offenders. Could one way of conceptualising deviance be through the images collected by the offender? It is apparent from our earlier discussion of image level that all child abuse images are not equal. Not only is there the obvious variation that relates to age and gender of the child(ren), but there is variation as to who else is in the image and what is enacted with the child(ren). It might be argued that viewing any sexualised images of children is an indicator of deviance, but as our international definition of child is anyone under the age of 18, this would suggest that viewing images of a sexually mature 17-year-old would be seen as deviant in the same way as viewing a three-year-old child who is tied up and being hurt. While several authors have remarked on the importance of classification of Internet sex offenders by their 'cyber actions' and by the features and characteristics of their viewing behaviour (e.g. Robertiello and Terry 2007), to date there have been very few studies that have examined image content as part of the offending process (Baartz 2008; Carr 2004; Sullivan 2007). Coward *et al.*

(2009) in their comparative study examined self-reports of pornography use and found that there were no group differences in more 'conventional' forms of pornography but that there were highly significant differences in more atypical or 'deviant' pornography. These categories included material defined as: hard core; anal sex; lesbian sex; same sex; bondage/sadism; animal sex, and sexual 'themes'. In relation to viewing different types of child pornography, Internet sex offenders showed significantly higher use across all age groups of children. Glasgow (2007) has started to look at preferred content and this may open up a whole new way of thinking about risk in relation to deviancy. His prototype procedure (ISOPS) postulates that downloading pornographic files involves a dynamic relationship between available stimulus materials and sexual interest, mediated by sexual and masturbatory fantasy. He argues that files sought, stored for later use, and accessed offline are likely to more closely reflect interests than all files downloaded or browsed.

Let us return briefly to Adler's (2001) argument that the proliferation of child pornography law may (along with other factors) increase the sexual attraction felt by some people towards children. Adler (2008) argues convincingly that 'Pornography has the force of technology on its side'. However, neither the availability nor the use of abusive images of children has its origin with the Internet and there are both historical and contemporaneous accounts of child pornography use that predate it (e.g. Lanning 2001). Nevertheless, several studies (for example Galbreath *et al.* 2002; Quayle *et al.* 2000; Wilson and Jones 2008) have suggested that clinicians are encountering cases where the presence of the Internet itself seems to have been the primary impetus for paraphilic behaviour, and Wood (2007) presents an argument that the Internet may 'fan the flames' of something that might otherwise have remained smouldering within the psyche. From the number of reports to Hotlines it must be assumed that a percentage of people are either accidentally (or purposefully) exposed to abusive images, and potentially this will include a proportionately larger number of young people. Can we assume that exposure alone may influence paraphilic interest, or that it will be only influential where there is a pre-existing interest that has not been given expression? If it is the former this would give considerable rise to concern about the increasing number of people who as part of their work (e.g. police, forensic analysts etc.) are required to view images. (In this context, Wolak and Mitchell (2009) have explored the emotional impact of viewing child pornography.) One study that may be of relevance is that of Paul and Linz (2008) who examined the effects of exposure on viewer cognitions and attitudes towards deviant sexual behaviour. They used a lexical decision-making task and exposed subjects to sexually explicit depictions of females who appear to be minors (which they called 'barely legal pornography'). Their results suggest a complex relationship between viewing and attitudes, but the authors conclude that 'Findings from this study indicate that exposure to virtual child pornography, in the form of barely legal sexually explicit depictions, did result in a cognitive effect. Exposure to sexually explicit depictions featuring underage-looking models results in viewers being more likely to associate sex and sexuality to subsequent nonsexual depictions of minors' (p. 45). We do not, of course, know whether such changes would ever impact on behaviour.

To date, we have tantalising fragments of information about this population of largely white males who use the Internet to produce, trade and access abusive images of children. At least a proportion of these share many of the characteristics of contact sex offenders against children, but in many of the studies reviewed there are a percentage (in some more than others) who do not. A study by Middleton (2008) of 213 Internet offenders and 191 contact offenders, which built on an earlier data set (Middleton *et al.* 2006), examined the applicability of the pathways model of child sexual abuse with Internet offenders. This model identifies five aetiological pathways, each with primary psychological deficits, that interact to create a vulnerability to sexually offending behaviour (Ward and Siegert 2002). Middleton found that there were a number of similarities between the two groups in that the largest clusters for both Internet and contact offenders were *intimacy deficits* and *emotional dysregulation.* However, he concluded that '… almost half of the coded sample could not be assigned to any of the five aetiological pathways outlined by Ward and Siegert (2002). These individuals recorded no problems with intimacy or dealing with negative emotions, no distortions in their sexual scripts, and no anti-social cognitions, regarding the appropriateness of sexual contact with children, and yet have been prosecuted for using the Internet to access abusive images of children. This appears to suggest that there is a population of Internet offenders who do not share the psychological vulnerabilities typically displayed by sex offenders' (p. 211). How do we make sense of why these people use sexualised images of mainly white or Asian children?

Intervention

Middleton (2009) describes how in 2006 a treatment programme for Internet-related sexual offending (the i-SOTP) was given accreditation for use in the community by the National Probation Service (England and Wales). His paper reports on the clinical impact as assessed following completion of psychometric assessments pre- and post-treatment by a sample of 264 convicted offenders. The study grouped key treatment targets into two main categories. These were described as addressing socio-affective functioning (such as self-esteem issues and emotional loneliness problems) and changing pro-offending attitudes (which include victim empathy deficits and cognitive distortions that relate to attitudes and beliefs that minimise and justify offending behaviour). In 11 of the 12 measures incorporated into the psychometric battery, offenders were assessed to have changed post-treatment in the desired direction. Middleton's (2009) results indicated that the offenders' level of self-esteem increased over time, and that they were better able to accept responsibility for their behaviour following the completion of the programme. In addition, improvements were recorded in respect of self-management issues such as the control of impulsive behaviour as well as levels of both over- and under-assertiveness. There was a slight increase in the fantasy sub-scale of the Interpersonal Reactivity Inventory (Davis 1983), and as previously discussed, this may further underlie the importance of, and difficulty in changing, fantasy responding in this population.

Leclerc *et al.* (2009) use a rational choice perspective to examine the modus operandi of sexual offenders against children. Although this study does not specifically examine the Internet as a vehicle for offending it does consider the role of pornography, stating that in the case of sexual offending against children pornography presents a possible strategy and facilitator for offenders to commit their crimes. They suggest a 'Crime Opportunity Structure' which consists of three components: victim characteristics or situation; location; and the facilitators of crime, which would include the strategies used by the offender. Leclerc *et al.* (2009) suggest that these components interact with each other to create opportunities for offending against children. Such situational approaches to sexual offending (Wortley and Smallbone 2006) move the focus away from the intra-psychic qualities of the individual back to the environment. Within this framework, Taylor and Quayle (2006, in press) have attempted to address how particular qualities of Internet processes may contribute to the criminal context, drawing on the perspective of Rational Choice Theory (Cornish and Clarke 1986). Rational Choice Theory emphasises the importance of the situational context facing the offender in the period immediately before and at the time of offending, in terms of the factors that might influence decision processes. This is not to attribute the cause of offending to the Internet, but it does suggest that the structure of the Internet as we experience it has qualities that may influence how those forces that change and modify our behaviour impinge on us. One way forward is to ground our analysis in the situational context of the individual when faced with critical choices. By adopting a crime-specific analysis we can then identify features that both sustain and direct the inappropriate behaviour of accessing abuse images of children.

Conclusion

Some final thoughts in relation to child pornography and the Internet. To date, the offender literature that relates to these forms of crime makes distinctions between online and offline activity and between Internet and contact offences. This becomes more problematic when we try and address abusive practices that result in, for example, sexual behaviour with a child mediated through a webcam where no physical contact takes place and where the two are geographically disparate. The literature that reflects the use of technology by young people appears very different and acknowledges a world mediated by, rather than separate from, technology. Slane (2007) has suggested that '... claims for the independence of cyberspace sound quaint and idealistic now, largely because they are based on a false dichotomy between virtual and physical phenomena. Physical and virtual are not opposed; rather, the virtual complicates the physical, and vice versa' (p. 97). This is most obviously seen in the phenomenon of abusive images. Both producer and consumer clearly have a corporate reality, but this can be expanded to multiple representations in the virtual environment, all of which may mirror or obscure the physical existence of the individual. In a similar way, while the people using computer- mediated communication are located in a physical space, proximity to those communicated with does not limit the speed or ease of exchange of information, including images, and as Slane (2007) points out, it is possible to be 'in' multiple places at a time, '... by being both in front of the computer and "in" an online community, or by opening extra windows on your desktop' (p. 94). Increasingly the technologically enabled distribution of abusive images not only captures the abuse or exploitation of a child or children at that snapshot of time, or over a period of time, but offers such abuse up to an endless audience of voyeurs, never changing or degrading over time.

Further reading

Akdeniz, Y. (2008) *Internet Child Pornography and the Law. National and International Responses* (Aldershot: Ashgate) is an interesting review of the international legislation related to child pornography, including the United Nations and Council of Europe Frameworks. For a good, recent review of the literature related to child pornography with an emphasis on young people, see Quayle, E., Lööf, L. and Palmer, T. (2008) *Child Pornography and Sexual Exploitation of Children Online* (Bangkok: ECPAT International). It is written with a broad audience in mind so an attempt has been made to reduce the amount of jargon.

Wolak, J., Finkelhor, D., Mitchell, K.J. and Ybarra, M.L. (2008) 'Online 'predators' and their victims: myths, realities, and implications for prevention and treatment', *American Psychologist*, 63(2): 111–28, is not about child pornography but about online sexual exploitation. However, it is a good and balanced review of the literature that provides a context for thinking about exploitative practices. Wortley, R. and Smallbone, S. (2006) 'Child pornography on the Internet, *COPS: Problem-Oriented Guides For Police*, US Department of Justice, is a good overview of some of the evidential issues that relate to child pornography which also provides information for police services on how to audit their own practice. It is available online at http://Www.Ncjrs.Gov/App/Publications/ Abstract.Aspx?ID_236113

Taylor, M and Quayle, E. (2003) *Child Pornography: An Internet Crime* (Brighton: Routledge) is another useful resource. Whilst published some time ago, it is still the only book that explores some aspects of behaviours that relate to child pornography, such as collecting. Beech, A.R., Elliott, I.A., Birgden, A. and Findlater, D. (2008) 'The Internet and child sexual offending: A criminological review', in *Aggression and Violent Behavior*, 13, 216–28 is an excellent review of the literature related to child pornography placed within a criminological framework.

References

Adler, A. (2001) 'The perverse law of child pornography', *Columbia Law Review*, 209: 1–101.

Adler, A. (2008) All porn all the time. *31 NYU Rev. L and Soc. Change 695*.

Akdeniz, Y. (2008) *Internet Child Pornography and the Law. National and International Responses*. Aldershot: Ashgate.

Alexy, E.M., Burgess, A.W. and Baker, T. (2005) 'Internet offenders: Traders, travelers and combination tradertravelers', *Journal of Interpersonal Violence*, 20: 804–12.

Ashcroft v. Free Speech Coalition. 535 US 224 2002.

Azaola, E. (2000) *Boy and girl victims of sexual exploitation in Mexico*. UNICEF-DIF. Available from: www.oas.org/atip/country%20specific/AZAOLA%20Mexico%20 Child%20Sex%20Exploitation.pdf

Baartz, D. (2008) *Australians, the Internet and technology-enabled child sex abuse: A statistical profile*. Canberra: Australian Federal Police.

Baines, V. (2008) *Online Child Sexual Abuse: The Law Enforcement Response*. Bangkok: ECPAT International.

Bates, A. and Metcalf, C. (2007) 'A Psychometric Comparison of Internet and Non-Internet Sex Offenders from a Community Treatment Sample', *Journal of Sexual Aggression*, 13(1): 11–20.

Beech, A.R. (1998) 'A psychometric typology of child abusers', *International Journal of Therapy and Comparative Criminology*, 42: 319–39.

Beech, A.R., Elliott, I.A., Birgden, A. and Findlater, D. (2008) 'The Internet and child sexual offending: A criminological review', *Aggression and Violent Behavior*, 13: 216–28.

Buzzell, T. (2005) 'Demographic characteristics of persons using pornography in three technological contexts', *Sexuality and Culture*, 9(1): 28–48.

Calpin, C.M. (2006) *Child Maltreatment*. US Department of Health and Human Services. Available online at http://www.acf.hhs.gov/programs/cb/pubs/cm06/cm06.pdf

Carr, A. (2004) *Internet Traders of Child Pornography and Other Censorship Offenders in New Zealand*. New Zealand: Department of Internal Affairs.

Cassell, J. and Cramer. M. (2008) 'High Tech or High Risk: Moral Panics about Girls Online', in T. McPherson (ed.), *Digital Youth, Innovation, and the Unexpected*. The John D. and Catherine T. MacArthur Foundation Series on Digital Media and Learning. Cambridge, MA: The MIT Press, 53–76.

Cattaneo, C., Ritz-Timme, S., Gabriel, P., Gibelli, D., Giudici, E., Poppa, P., Nohrden, D., Assmann, S., Schmitt, R., and Grandi, G. (2008) 'The difficult issue of age assessment on pedo-pornographic material', *Forensic Science International*, 183(1–3): 10e21–e24.

Clough, J. (2008) 'Now you see it, now you don't: Digital images and the meaning of "possession"', *Criminal Law Forum*, 19: 205–39.

Conroy, M.A. (2006) 'Risk management of sex offenders: A model for community intervention', *Journal of Psychiatry and Law*, 34: 5–23.

Cornish, D.B. and Clarke, R.V. (1986) *The Reasoning Criminal*. New York: Springer-Verlag.

Coward, I.A., Gabriel, A.M., Schuler, A. and Prentky, R.A. (2009) (March 5–7) *Child Internet victimization: Project development and preliminary results*. Paper presented at the Annual Conference of the American Psychology-Law Society, San Antonio.

Davis, M.H. (1983) 'Measuring individual differences in empathy: Evidence for a multiple dimensional approach', *Journal of Personality and Social Psychology*, 44: 113–26.

Demetriou, C. and Silke, A. (2003) 'A criminological Internet "sting". Experimental evidence of illegal and deviant visits to a website trap', *The British Journal of Criminology*, 43: 213–22.

Elliott, I.A., Beech, A.R., Mandeville-Norden, R. and Hayes, E. (2009) 'Psychological Profiles of Internet Sexual Offenders Comparisons With Contact Sexual Offenders', *Sexual Abuse: A Journal of Research and Treatment*, 21(1): 76–92.

FBI (2006) Innocent Images National Initiative. Available online at http://www.fbi. gov/publications/innocent.htm

Finkelhor, D. and Jones, L. (2008) *Updated Trends in Child Maltreatment, 2006*. Crimes Against Children Research Center. Available online at http://www.unh.edu/ccrc/ Trends/index.html

Finkelhor, D. and Ormrod, R. (2004) *Child pornography: patterns from the NIBRS.* Washington, DC: US Department of Justice Programs, Office of Juvenile Justice and Delinquency Prevention.

Galbreath, N.W., Berlin, F.S. and Sawyer, D. (2002) 'Paraphilias and the Internet', in A. Cooper (ed.), *Sex and the Internet: A guidebook for clinicians.* New York: Brunner-Routledge, 187–205.

Gallagher, G. (2007) 'Internet-initiated incitement and conspiracy to commit child sexual abuse (CSA): The typology, extent and nature of known cases', *Journal of Sexual Aggression*, 13(2): 101–19.

Gillespie, A.A. (2003) 'Sentences for offences involving child pornography', *Criminal Law Review*, 80–92.

Gillespie, A. (2008) Reader in Law, Leicester de Montfort Law School. Personal communication by email, 12 October 2008.

Glasgow, D. (2007) *ISOPS: A prototype procedure for the assessment of Internet pornography users.* Presentation made at the Tools To Take Home Conference, Birmingham 2007.

Greenhouse, L. (2007) 'Justices decline case on 200-year sentence for man who possessed child pornography', *The New York Times*, 27 February: A13.

Guardian (2008) (10 March) Available from: www.guardian.co.uk/world/2008/mar/10/japan

Hanson, R.K and Morton-Bourgon, K.E. (2005) 'The characteristics of persistent sexual offenders: A meta-analysis of recidivism studies', *Journal of Consulting and Clinical Psychology*, 73(6), 1154-1163.

Harris, A.J. (2006) 'Risk assessment and sex offender community supervision: A context specific framework', *Federal Probation*, 70(2): 36–43.

Hartman, C.R., Burgess, A.W. and Lanning, K.V. (1984) 'Typology of collectors', in A.W. Burgess and M.L. Clark (eds), *Child Pornography and Sex Rings.* Toronto: Lexington Books, 93–109.

Howitt, D. (2004) 'What is The Role of Fantasy in Sex Offending?', *Criminal Behaviour and Mental Health*, 14: 182–8.

Huda, S. (2006) 'Sex trafficking in South Asia', *International Journal of Gynecology and Obstetrics*, 94: 374–81.

ICMEC (2006) *Child pornography: Model legislation and global review.* Available online at http://www.icmec.org/en_X1/pdf/ModelLegislationFINAL.pdf

INHOPE (2007) *Global Internet Trend Report.* Accessed on 15 October 2008 from www.inhope.org

ISTTF (2008) *Enhancing Child Safety and Online Technologies: Final Report of the Internet Safety Technical Task Force To the Multi-State Working Group on Social Networking of State Attorneys General of the United States.* Harvard University: The Berkman Center for Internet and Society.

Jenkins, P. (2009) 'Failure to launch: Why do some social issues fail to detonate moral panics?', *British Journal of Criminology*, 49: 35–47.

Jones, V. and Skogrand, E. (2005) *Position Paper Regarding Online Images of Sexual Abuse and other Internet-related Sexual Exploitation of Children.* Copenhagen: Save the Children Europe Group.

Kacker, L., Varadan, S. and Kumar, P. (2007) *Study on child abuse India.* New Delhi, India: Ministry of Women and Child Development.

King, P.J. (2008) 'No plaything: Ethical issues concerning child pornography', *Ethic Theory Moral Practice*, 11: 327–45.

Krone, T. (2004) 'A typology of online child pornography offending', *Trends and Issues in Crime and Criminal Justice*, 279: 1–6.

Lanning, K.V. (1992) *Child Molesters: A Behavioral Analysis* (3rd edn). Alexandria: National Center for Missing and Exploited Children.

Lanning, K.V. (2001) *Child Molesters: Behavioral Analysis* (4th edn). Alexandria, VA: National Center for Missing and Exploited Children.

Lanning, K.V. (2008) *Child Pornography*. Paper presented at the Child Pornography Roundtable, Washington, DC, February 2008. Alexandria: National Center for Missing and Exploited Children, Washington, D.C. February 2008.

Leclerc, B., Proulx, J. and Beauregard, E. (2009) 'Examining the modus operandi of sexual offenders against children and its practical implications', *Aggression and Violent Behavior*, 14(1): 5–12.

Lee, J. (2008) Project Specialist, Child Victim Identification Program, National Center for Missing and Exploited Children. Personal communication by email, 10 September 2008.

Lehmann, C.U., Cohen, B.A. and Kim, G.R. (2006) 'Detection and management of pornography-seeking in an online clinical dermatology atlas', *Journal of the American Academy of Dermatology*, 54(6): 1123–37.

Mears, D.P., Mancini, C., Gertz, M. and Bratton, J. (2008) 'Sex crimes, children and pornography. Public views and public policy', *Crime and Delinquency*, 54(4): 532–59.

Middleton, D. (2008) 'Internet Sexual Offending', in A.R. Beech, L.A. Craig and K.D. Browne (eds), *Assessment and Treatment of Sex Offenders: A Handbook*. Oxford: Wiley Blackwell.

Middleton, D., Elliot, I.A., Mandeville-Norden, R. and Beech, A. (2006) 'The Pathways Model and Internet Offenders: An Investigation into the Applicability of the Ward and Siegert Pathways Model of Child Sexual Abuse with Internet Offenders', *Psychology, Crime and Law*, 12(6): 589–603.

Middleton, D., Mandeville-Norden, R. and Hayes, E. (2009) 'Does treatment work with Internet sex offenders? Emerging findings from thenInternet Sex Offender Treatment Programme (i-SOTP)', *Journal of Sexual Aggression*, 15(1): 5–19.

National Center for Missing and Exploited Children (2006) *CyberTipline Annual Report Totals*. Available from http://www.cybertipline.com/en_US/documents/CyberTiplineReportTotals.pdf

O'Brien, M.D. and Webster, S.D. (2007) 'The construction and preliminary validation of the Internet Behaviours and Attitudes Questionnaire (IBAQ)', *Sex Abuse*, 19: 237–56.

Oswell, D. (2006) 'When images matter: Internet child pornography, forms of observation and an ethics of the virtual', *Information, Communication and Society*, 9(2): 244–65.

Paul, B. and Linz, D.G. (2008) 'The effects of exposure to virtual child pornography on viewer cognitions and attitudes toward deviant sexual behavior', *Communication Research*, 35(1): 3–38.

Piper, C. (2001) 'Who are these youths? Language in the service of policy', *Youth Justice*, 1: 30–9.

Quayle, E. (2008) 'Internet Offending', in D.R. Laws and W. O'Donohue (eds), *Sexual Deviance*. New York: Guilford Press, 439–58.

Quayle, E. (2009) 'Assessment of Internet Sexual Abuse', in M. Calder (ed.), *Sexual Abuse Assessments*. Lyme Regis: Russell House Publishing.

Quayle, E. and Taylor, M. (2002) 'Child Pornography and the Internet: Perpetuating a Cycle of Abuse', *Deviant Behavior*, 23(4): 331–62.

Quayle, E., Holland, G, Linehan, C. and Taylor, M. (2000) 'The Internet and offending behaviour: A case study', *The Journal of Sexual Aggression*, 6(1/2): 78–96.

Quayle, E., Lööf, L. and Palmer, T. (2008) *Child Pornography and Sexual Exploitation of Children Online*. Bangkok: ECPAT International.

Renold, E. and Creighton, S.J. (2003) *Images of Abuse: A Review of the Evidence on Child Pornography*. London: NSPCC.

Robertiello, G. and Terry, K.J (2007) 'Can we profile sex offenders? A review of sex offender typologies', *Aggression and Violent Behavior*, 12: 508–18.

Rush, E. and La Nauze, A. (2006) *Corporate Paedophilia: Sexualisation of Children in Australia*. The Australia Institute, Discussion Paper Number 90.

Schuijer, J. and Rossen, B. (1992) 'The Trade in Child Pornography', *IPT forensics*, 4. Accessed on 8 July 2002 from: http://www.ipt-forensics.com/journal/volume4/j4_2_1.htm

Seto, M.C. and Eke, A. (2005) 'The Criminal Histories and Later Offending of Child Pornography Offenders', *Sexual Abuse: A Journal of Research and Treatment*, 17(2): 201–10.

Seto, M.C., Cantor, J.M. and Blanchard, R. (2006) 'Child Pornography Offences are a Valid Diagnostic Indicator of Pedophilia', *Journal of Abnormal Psychology*, 115: 610–15.

Sheldon, K. and Howitt, D. (2007) *Sex Offenders and the Internet*. Chichester: John Wiley.

Sheldon, K. and Howitt, D. (2008) 'Sexual fantasy in paedophile offenders: Can any model explain satisfactorily new findings from a study of Internet and contact sexual offenders?', *Legal and Criminological Psychology*, 13: 137–58.

Slane, A. (2007) 'Democracy, social space and the Internet', *University of Toronto Law Journal*, 57: 81–104.

Söderström, B. (2006) 'Experiences from and questions raised in clinical practice', in *Children and Young Persons with Abusive and Violent Experiences Connected to Cyberspace*. Stockholm: Swedish Children's Welfare Foundation.

Sullivan, C. (2007) *Internet Traders of Child Pornography: Profiling Research*. New Zealand: Censorship Compliance Unit.

Sunday Times (2008) 'The paedophile vicar of Beguildy', 28 December, available online from http://www.timesonline.co.uk/tol/news/uk/crime/article5394488.ece

Svedin, C.G. and Back, K. (1996) *Children who Don't Speak Out*. Stockholm: Save the Children Sweden.

Svedin, C.G. and Back, K. (2003) *Why Didn't They Tell Us? Sexual Abuse in Child Pornography*. Stockholm : Save the Children Sweden.

Tate, T. (1990) *Child Pornography*. St. Ives, UK: Methuen.

Taylor, M. and Quayle, E. (2003) *Child Pornography: An Internet Crime*. Brighton: Routledge.

Taylor, M. and Quayle, E. (2005) 'Abusive images of children', in S. Cooper, A. Giardino, V. Vieth and N. Kellogg (eds), *Medical, Legal and Social Science Aspects of Child Sexual Exploitation*. St Louis: GW Medical Publishing.

Taylor, M. and Quayle, E. (2006) 'The Internet and abuse images of children: Search, precriminal situations and opportunity', in R. Wortley and S. Smallbone (eds), *Situational Prevention of Child Sexual Abuse*. Crime Prevention Studies (19). Monsey, NY: Criminal Justice Press/Willan Publishing.

Taylor, M. and Quayle, E. (in press) 'Criminogenic qualities of the Internet in the collection and distribution of Abuse Images of children', *Irish Journal of Psychology*.

Taylor, M., Holland, G. and Quayle, E. (2001) 'Typology of Paedophile Picture Collections', *The Police Journal*, 74(2): 97–107.

Ward, T., and Siegert, R.J. (2002) 'Toward a comprehensive theory of child sexual abuse: A theory knitting perspective', *Psychology, Crime and Law*, 8: 319–51.

Webb, L., Craissati, J. and Keen, S. (2007) 'Characteristics of Internet child pornography offenders: A comparison with child molesters', *Sex Abuse*, 19: 449–65.

Wilson, D. and Jones, T. (2008) '"In My Own World": A Case Study of a Paedophile's Thinking and Doing and His Use of the Internet', *The Howard Journal*, 47(2): 107–20.

Wolak, J., Finkelhor, D. and Mitchell, K.J. (2003) *Child-Pornography Possessors Arrested in Internet-Related Crimes: Findings from the National Juvenile Online Victimization Study.* Washington, DC: National Center for Missing and Exploited Children.

Wolak, J., Finkelhor, D. and Mitchell, K.J. (2005) *Child-Pornography Possessors Arrested in Internet-Related Crimes: Findings from the National Juvenile Online Victimization Study.* Washington, DC: National Center for Missing and Exploited Children.

Wolak, J. and Mitchell, K. (2009) *Work-Related Exposure to Child Pornography in ICAC Task Forces and Affiliated Agencies: Reactions and Responses to Possible Stresses.* Washington: OJJDP.

Wood, H. (2007) 'Compulsive use of virtual sex and Internet pornography: addiction or perversion?', in S. Ruszczynski and D. Morgan (eds), *Clinical Lectures on Violence, Delinquency and Perversion.* London: Karnac.

Wortley, R. and Smallbone, S. (eds) (2006) *Situational prevention of child sexual abuse.* Crime Prevention Studies (19). Monsey, NY: Criminal Justice Press/Willan Publishing.

Chapter 18

Harm, suicide and homicide in cyberspace: assessing causality and control

Maggie Wykes

As with every new medium, from the production of print cartoons to computer games, the Internet is frequently seen as causal of harm. News about the Net features regularly in the mainstream media of newspapers and television, very often negatively associated with crime and harm. Such concerns evolved as the Internet spread. Once commercialised in the early 1990s, fears about its potential for crime, deviance and harm grew as rapidly as the new cyber-communications systems themselves. Alongside such fears, calls for censorship, control and monitoring led to a whole range of interventions by states, police, service providers, business, lobby groups and vigilantes.

By 1999 the United Nations was seeking global vigilance (BBC 16 June 1999) for cyber-paedophiles grooming children in chat rooms. By 2002 concerns were being voiced that young girls were being encouraged to diet dangerously by pro-anorexic websites such as Blue Dragonfly (Wykes and Gunter 2005) resulting in many ISPs removing them from servers and schools and universities blocking access. In Japan, in 2005: 'The number of Japanese killing themselves in groups after meeting through the Internet – strangers afraid to die alone – soared to a record 91 last year, nearly double that of 2004' (*Times of India* 9 February 2006) leading to police calls for monitoring and tracking in chat rooms. In 2009 the Obscene Publications Act was under revision in the UK to include materials on the Internet (MOJ 19 January 2009) after a sadistic murder was reported as mimicking cyber-pornography (Rice and Wilks 2008). In each of these cases the medium, the Internet, seemed to attract as much blame as those inflicting harm on self or others, and as much, if not more, effort and debate seemed to arise around control and censorship of cyberspace than went into catching and controlling sexually abusive or violent men or supporting and nurturing the suicidal and self-destructive.

This chapter considers whether such calls for control should take precedence over the freedom of expression that has characterised the 'consensual hallucination' (Gibson 1984: 67) of cyberspace since its creation. Indeed as the American Supreme Court declared in *Reno* v. *ACLU*, the Internet is a free-speech zone protected by the First Amendment 1791, because 'the interest in encouraging freedom of expression in a democratic society outweighs any theoretical but unproven benefit of censorship' (ACLU 27 June 1997). In Europe the 1948 Universal Declaration of Human Rights, signed by 48 countries, included the right to free speech and is now part of the European Convention of Human Rights. Article 10 states: 'This right shall include freedom to hold opinions and to receive and impart information and ideas without reference by public authority and regardless of frontiers.' Nonetheless the calls for control and censorship of media of all kinds continue and now specifically the target is the Internet. The argument framed in these calls is always related to harm caused by cyber-representations and communications and in terms of harm, the most extreme harm is clearly to cause death. So this chapter will consider whether any lethal potential of cyberspace should take precedence over the importance of freedom of expression for truth, democracy and individual autonomy (Mill 1859).[1] The focus therefore is evidence of suicide and homicide where media accounts clearly attribute blame on cyberspace for extreme, actual identifiable harm and whether such cases justify the censorship of communications' freedom.

Suicide

In the UK, the 1961 Suicide Act abrogated the previous crime of suicide but criminalised the aiding and abetting of suicide. The act declares: 'A person who aids, abets, counsels or procures the suicide of another, or an attempt by another to commit suicide, shall be liable on conviction on indictment to imprisonment for a term not exceeding fourteen years' and it is this aspect where the Internet is attributed with blame despite the fact that 'aiding or encouraging suicide is illegal – but only if the offender meets the victim face to face' (*Daily Telegraph* 1 August 2008b). In early 2008, the deaths of 13 young people from Bridgend, a small town in Wales, brought to public attention fears that a 'suicide chain' through Internet chat rooms had linked the victims online. Since the deaths (now standing at 25) in Bridgend: 'The Ministry of Justice is examining whether more legislation is needed to control assisted suicide websites' (*ibid.*) despite the fact that police eventually ruled out an 'Internet pact' between the youngsters.

Clearly there is an anomaly in the Bridgend cases that defies explanation. An area that might normally see two or three young suicides in a year saw 25 in the two years prior to March 2009, men and women, aged from 15 to 28, and all by hanging, constituting the largest known cluster of young suicides on record (Cadwalladr, *The Observer* 1 March 2009). When the story broke after the thirteenth death, the social networking site Bebo was blamed as many of the dead (but not all) had spaces there. Those spaces rapidly became romanticised, commemorative 'cyber-memorials'. First headlines described an Internet death cult and this was what framed mainstream media reports, served as an explanation for the deaths and the reason to control cyberspace to protect the vulnerable. Headlines announced: 'Police have private concerns that youngsters may consider it fashionable to have an Internet memorial site and are killing themselves for reasons of prestige' (*Daily Mail* 23 January

2008) suggesting some kind of motive linked to transcendence, attributed to the infinite nature of cybersites which offer eternal youth and publicity. The mainstream press ignored the first 12 suicides until the story of Natasha Randall, the thirteenth death, was linked to the social networking site Bebo, with the Daily Mail claiming unequivocally that she was 'a wild child who surfed her way to suicide and "virtual immortality"' (*Daily Mail* 23 January 2008). Suddenly the suicides of thirteen young people, previously not national news, became the most newsworthy story around and the mainstream media invaded Bridgend and filled their pages with dire warnings about the dark side of cyberspace and poignant stories and pictures of the dead and their friends and families.

As the media feeding frenzy continued, so did the suicides, with names and faces – unusually for suicides – emblazoned across front pages and television screens until the mainstream media too were implicated in the continuing deaths. Journalists' stereotyping took over and the deaths were clustered in Bridgend (not true as they were actually spread across Glamorgan) and were motivated by celebrity in the online and offline media supported by a chat room cult (despite the fact that the first 12 deaths achieved no notoriety and some of the suicidal had no Net access at all). What probably occurred in Glamorgan was an example of suicidal contagion whereby one death tips another person into suicidal depression and/or makes suicide appear a solution, in a kind of domino effect. Certainly the deaths were alarming the coroner prior to any publicity or link to online sites because many of the young people actually, not virtually, knew each other. The mainstream media, factual and fictional, have been implicated in such contagion (Biddle *et al.* 2008: 1) but mostly in relation to the method used. So contagion does not explain the numbers of attempts at suicide but might explain the choice of hanging as a method. It might also explain the unusual phenomenon of young women using hanging in Glamorgan when pills and alcohol are the more usual choice for women, with women 'three times less likely to succeed' (Cadwalladr op. cit.) than men. The choice of hanging itself may explain the sheer numbers of actual deaths as opposed to the more usual failed attempts, particularly in relation to women. However, such information about methods is not posted on social network sites but available by searching via Google and Yahoo.

The most popular social networking websites provided not only information about the deaths but also evaluation of methods of suicide. This included for instance detailed information about speed, certainty, and the likely amount of pain associated with methods (Biddle *et al.* 2008: 3). However, an almost equal number of sites counsel against suicide. Biddle *et al.* found that:

> In England rates of suicide among young (15–34-year-old) men and women, the age groups who make most use of the Internet, have declined since the mid 1990s, a time when the use of the Internet expanded rapidly. So cases of Internet-induced suicide may be offset by potential beneficial effects or other suicide prevention strategies. (Biddle *et al.* 2008: 4)

Biddle *et al.*'s work suggests little change in the understanding of the relationship between the Internet and suicide since psychiatrist Susan Thompson (1999) wrote of the mimicking of successful suicide methods, the high rate of Net use of the most suicidal 'young' group, and the number of sites accurately detailing the fatal dose of commonly available substances and clustering of suicides following media coverage. Thompson also suggested that the Internet could be used to intervene in suicide attempts because those intending to self-harm very often declare their intentions in 'public'. Of course, this would not be without ethical difficulties.

Such a public declaration happened in the UK when Kevin Whitrick hanged himself in front of a webcam in March 2007. After he had stated his intention, others in the Patlak chat room goaded him into tying a rope to a beam and killing himself. Only afterwards did others in the chat room try to alert police but ultimately no prosecutions were possible under the 1961 act as there was no physical presence. In a typical example of technological determinism, the newspapers focused more heavily on the technology than on the behaviour of the human beings who found his suicide entertaining. In the US a case where cyber-bullying led to a young girl's suicide did result in action when the local town passed a by-law to allow fines to be imposed for Internet harassment. *The Times* relates the story:

> A mother who helped arrange a cruel Internet hoax that apparently drove a 13-year-old girl to suicide has escaped conviction on charges that could have put her in prison for 20 years. Lori Drew, 49, from Missouri, was instead convicted of only three misdemeanour offences of accessing a computer without authorisation. Each is punishable by up to a year in prison and a $100,000 fine.
>
> Prosecutors, who described the trial as the first 'cyber-bullying' case, said that Ms Drew and two others, her assistant, Ashley Grills, 18, and her daughter, Sarah, 13, created a profile of a fictitious 16-year-old boy on MySpace, the social networking website, and sent flirtatious messages from him to a teenage neighbour, Megan Meier. They named the boy Josh Evans and posted a photograph of him on his fake profile page, in which he appeared bare-chested and with tousled brown hair. Ms Drew then had their fictitious boy 'dump' the girl by saying: 'The world would be a better place without you.' Megan promptly hanged herself with a belt in her bedroom closet. (*The Times*, 20 November 2008)

Effectively what Lori Drew wrote was not illegal but the case provoked outrage in the US where the constitution protects freedom of speech and Drew could only be charged with what was widely viewed as a minor offence under the Computer Fraud and Abuse Act, not with assisting suicide or even homicide. The case led to calls for tighter control of online harassment with pro-freedom groups immediately pointing out the constitutional and ethical ramifications. Drew was eventually convicted of a misdemeanour for violating the service provider's code of conduct, making criminal what would previously have been a civil offence. She was effectively convicted of hacking but the case is still worrying US civil libertarians because of the onus of responsibility it places on users of sites like MySpace.

Technological determinism has been a feature of both these cases. The Net is a scapegoat for deeply unpleasant human activity with online bullying now being reported as more insidious and disturbing than face-to-face bullying. The problem is surely the bullying not the medium. Yet a similar case emerged in the UK where after a teenager's suicide an 'inquest, at Leeds coroner's court, heard how Stephanie had been bullied via text messages and on the MSN Messenger service on her home computer ... Her parents said she had also been looking at suicide websites' (*Daily Telegraph* 24 April 2008a). In both this and the US case there had been prior depression, treatment, suicide attempts and suicide threats which apparently were not Web related, yet it was the technology that was blamed.

In relation to suicide, moreover, there are other issues than attributing cause, including who has rights over an individual's body. That those who are not suicidal find suicide disturbing, distressing or distasteful is not enough moral reason to intervene. Moreover, the Internet can offer support and succour for those in despair and ultimately the possibility of catharsis and diversion from actual harm through communality of experience that the Internet might offer. Failing that, might it not be better to be able to die alongside or among others and with as little pain as possible, if suicide is inevitable? This seems most evident in Japan where suicide carries less stigma than in Judaeo-Christian cultures. There:

> Many [committing suicide] die in groups often by carbon monoxide poisoning in sealed vehicles in secluded and scenic places having met each other only hours before, following initial contact via the Net. (Jewkes 2007: 2)

Even so, 'people who kill themselves online account for a tiny proportion of the 30,000 Japanese who commit suicide each year' (McMurray 2007).

The cases that have attributed blame to the Internet for suicide actually reveal that if people are determined to kill themselves they try to find the most effective way; that there are conflicting messages about moral choices and personal liberty; difficult reflections to be made about causality and collusion; but more than anything people, not technologies or media, are responsible both for themselves and others. Suicide is human and should not be used as an excuse to control information and expression and monitor communications to suit political, commercial or religious agenda.

Some 'suicide' though is not self-inflicted but depends on the actions of another, the aiding and abetting of death, and here the role of the Internet is also often blamed, leading to efforts at censorship. Sometimes those who wish to die are unable or unwilling to carry out the act themselves. In the first case this is generally due to disabling illness; in the second it may be fear of failure or more extreme requirements of the experience of death. In each case the Net has sometimes been implicated.

Assisted suicide

In the first instance, voluntary euthanasia is the killing of a patient at their request when medical opinion is that it is in the patient's interest to die. Where the patient is incapacitated or fearful of pain or failure this might involve assistance from doctors, family or friends but is in any form a crime in the UK but not in all jurisdictions. In Switzerland much more liberal laws enabled the clinic Dignitas to open in 1998 to assist suicides. Similarly, in the US, Oregon has legalised euthanasia for a decade: 'Washington's Death With Dignity Act will take effect March 5. Washington voters approved Initiative 1000 to legalize the law in November. Washington would be the second state after Oregon to allow what opponents call "physician-assisted suicide"' (Seattlepi.com 9 January 2009). Holland legalised voluntary euthanasia in 1984 and 'Belgium has also legalized euthanasia under strict conditions, while France has passed a right-to-do law that empowers the terminally ill to refuse life-extending treatments but does not legalize euthanasia' (*Pravda* 27 January 1999) but elsewhere the arguments and criminalisation continue with the Council of Europe rejecting calls for the introduction of euthanasia across the community in 2005.

What the Internet has enabled is a massive exchange of information and argument on a previously little-publicised issue. It has thrown up anomalies in legislation and provided the desperate with information about where and how they might die in peace and security. In Britain the debates are about active or passive 'abetting', deriving from the case of the 1989 Hillsborough football disaster victim Anthony Bland who had feeding tubes withdrawn to allow him to die in 1993. Assisted suicide involving the administration of drugs has been sought by terminally ill or severely disabled British persons at the Swiss Dignitas clinic, in each case with an accompanying debate about the role of those who accompany loved ones to their death, given the British law. As yet no one has been convicted under the 1961 Suicide Act. Nonetheless Multiple sclerosis sufferer Debbie Purdy:

> Argued in the High Court that the lack of clarification on the law was a breach of her human rights. But two High Court judges ruled they had not been infringed and existing guidelines were adequate ... Ms Purdy is still considering travelling to Switzerland to take a lethal dose of barbiturates prescribed by Dignitas doctors. She wants her husband at her side, but fears he may be prosecuted on his return to Britain. (BBC News 3 February 2009)

The WWW hosts a video of Craig Ewart's assisted death at Dignitas (Youtube Ewart) which has had more than 235,000 hits and it is this kind of representation that has turned the many anti-euthanasia movements' attention towards the Net. In 2008, the Australian 'Federal Government is planning to make Internet censorship compulsory for all Australians and could ban controversial websites on euthanasia or anorexia' (Dudley-Nicholson 2008). Alongside states, religious organisations such as US Right to Life and UK Pro-life Alliance actively use the Net to campaign against both euthanasia and sites offering information about it while pro-choice and voluntary euthanasia groups do the opposite and use the Net to actively promote legislative change (Dignity in Dying). Currently the electronic battle to prevent promotion of euthanasia seems to be being won with Canada recently considering prohibition similar to that in Australia. The criticism of this move in Canadian newspapers is apposite for this chapter:

> First to go, reportedly, are websites counselling euthanasia or eating disorders, though it seems hard to imagine the government stopping there, and the plan has drawn natural comparisons between Internet controls in China, Iran and North Korea. But then, it also bears some resemblance to the UK's recently revealed plan to monitor – and catalogue – all Britons' e-mail and web browsing in the name of fighting terror. The sun, it seems, never sets on the British Empire's impulse to censor. So much for Churchill's famous command that 'freedom of speech and thought should reign.' (McParland, *National Post*, 30 October 2008)

These debates are examples of the remaining power of religious groups over states and the fear felt by both of the media's capability, now globally, electronic and interactive, to undermine that power. The overt arguments put by censorious lobby groups are about the sanctity of human life and whether the individual or state/church should have authority over the individual's own body, but they disguise a covert struggle for control of information.

Sui-homicide

The second area of assisted suicide to see the Net feature as causal is 'sui-homicide', meaning that one party wishes to die at the hands of another who does not die[2] and where the motives are not ill health. One of the most dramatic and contentious of these cases was that of a cannibal who advertised in a homosexual chat room for a victim who would like to be killed and eaten and received many replies from volunteers. The case saw the Internet clearly blamed and raised many complex issues about sado-masochism, consent and suicide:

> Mr Meiwes met the man he was ultimately to eat, 43-year-old Bernd-Jurgen Brandes, in early 2001, after advertising on websites for 'young, well-built men aged 18 to 30 to slaughter'. Mr Meiwes told investigators he took Mr Brandes back to his home, where Mr Brandes agreed to have his penis cut off, which Mr Meiwes then flambéed and served up to eat together. (Murphy 2004)

Meiwes cruised chat rooms and websites looking for like-minded people and information on cannibalism. 'Meiwes started chatting to like-minded cannibals on sites with names like Gourmet and Eaten Up … The first meal he prepared was a steak from Brandes's thigh, flavoured with garlic and Muscat wine and served with Brussels sprouts and deep-fried potato balls'

(Lewis 2003). Recipes for cannibals are available at www.churchofeuthanasia. org/e-sermons/butcher.html. These websites are fetishistic but Meiwes himself stressed that his fascination with eating flesh began at 12 years of age before the Net existed. Although it might have been unlikely that the two men could have met prior to cyber-connectivity, this in no way implies the sui-homicide might not have happened (indeed it may even have been a worse crime) without a consenting victim. Yet the furore that followed the case determinedly called for control of such sites with headlines like 'Yes, we can clean up the Web' (Verity n.d.). The Catholic *Tablet* featured the case in an article headed 'Evil in the virtual Eden' and argued for control on the grounds that Christianity claims: 'all human beings are to a greater or lesser extent drawn towards evil, and once we succumb it is hard to break free' (Curti n.d.). After the Meiwes case, calls for censorship went beyond the Net to cover mainstream films like *The Silence of the Lambs* and *Hannibal*. Films have been made about these bizarre events and in one case Meiwes himself successfully prevented a film about him being shown on the grounds of intellectual property and infringement of personal privacy. A song about Meiwes by German band Rammstein also provoked censorship: 'The controversy over Mein Teil prompted MTV Germany to restrict the airing of the music video to after 11 PM' (Facebook 30 November 2008).

Yet cannabalism hasn't been caused by any form of mass media. It has a complex history deeply embedded in many cultures not least the Judaeo-Christian consumption of the symbolic body and blood of Christ at communion services. It is not therefore a Net-effect, nor even illegal in many countries. Ironically Meiwes was eventually apprehended because of his Net presence 'Police tracked down Meiwes and arrested him last December after a student in Austria alerted them to an advertisement Meiwes placed on the Internet seeking a man willing to be killed and eaten' (Kassel 2003). Arguably if the Net had not been present he may have continued killing. In other words the Internet may have prevented further crimes rather than caused one.

The Meiwes case also raised issues of legislation as cannibalism is not against the law in Germany nor in many other countries. Meiwes was eventually charged with murder for 'sexual satisfaction', a charge that was problematised because the victim had volunteered to be killed in a form of suicide and, again, aiding suicide is not against the law in some countries.[3] He was sentenced to eight and a half years. Meiwes became vegetarian in prison, involved with green politics and wrote a book. This one case neatly illustrates four areas of *edge crime* – cannibalism, sado-masochism, assisted suicide and self-harm/suicide, all of which were mobilised to call for further criminalisation of consensual behaviours and further controls of the media, particularly the Internet for its role in promoting deviance.[4] Yet I could find no other instance of a case of full sui-homicide to suggest any copycat effect of the Meiwes case; only one of a failed attempt in Manchester in 2004, described in Jewkes (2007: 3). Google turned up 107,000 hits for Meiwes but none for copycat crimes. One case dubbed a 'copycat' featured no willingness to be killed by the victim: 'On two previous occasions they had played at sadomasochistic games on Herr Meyer's roof terrace. This time Herr Meyer, apparently in a fit of sexual abandonment, stabbed Herr Ritzkowsky with a screwdriver' (Boyes 2004). Meiwes was one unique case and one death; not a sound basis for further criminalisation of consensual adult behaviour nor censorship of the Internet and other media. It was technically homicide of a willing victim and was probably unique: *a single emotive crime.*

Homicide

> It is always unwise to legislate in response to a single emotive crime, and the current government consultation owes rather too much momentum to the brutal murder of Jane Longhurst, the Sussex teacher strangled two years ago. Her killer, Graham Coutts, was a regular visitor to such charming websites as Necrobabes, Death by Asphyxia and Hanging Bitches, and the day before the murder he spent about 90 minutes exploring images of necrophilia and asphyxial sex. Jane's mother, Liz Longhurst, believes that the Internet 'normalised' Coutts's disturbing sexual fantasies. (Rowan 2005)

Refreshingly this article does state clearly 'the Internet needs to be understood simply as another communication channel for those depraved, flawed sexual beings called adults' (*ibid.*). It also makes the key point that once there is real crime there are laws already in place to deal with them. Coutts was successfully prosecuted and sentenced but it was the Net that was blamed for exciting his sexual violence. Little was said of the prior real friendship between the killer and victim, nor that Coutts had a pregnant partner, nor that the meeting which led to Longhurst's death was arranged by phone not online. Most significant of all:

> Coutts was referred to consultant psychiatrist Dr Larry Culliford in December 1991. 'He was aroused by the idea of strangling women,' said Dr Culliford. 'Since the age of 15 these were daily, enjoyable thoughts, occurring during sexual arousal.' (*Courtnews* n.d.)

In 1991 at the time of referral Coutts would have been 24 years old and few would have had access to the embryonic, non-commercialised Internet; when he was 15 the WWW did not exist. Coutts' history indicates a threatening sexual profile pre-dating any Internet activity and suggests that the Net simply provided a source of already familiar pornography; it may even be that such material provided cathartic experiences ameliorating his dangerous predilections. However offensive such material might be 'we know very little about the relationship between pornography (of any sort) and actual sexual activity' (Taylor and Quayle 2003: 75) and certainly not enough to attribute responsibility for extreme sexual violence to a whole communications medium to justify censorship.

Although it is understandable that Jane Longhurst's mother might want to blame the Net for her daughter's brutal death, more often than not existing pressure groups use such extreme cases to further long-term goals by emphasising the most tenuous of links to the Internet. The high media profile given to cases of extreme sexual violence is due to their compliance with news values (Galtung and Ruge 1965; Chibnall 1977; Wykes 2001; Jewkes 2004). Not only is such crime rare and very negative (very few of us experience or witness sexual violence first hand; only 1 per cent of recorded crimes are sexual offences in the UK (Crime in England and Wales 2006–2007) but the sexual element adds both titillation and space for moral innuendo. Any link to the Net adds further negative news value to events because the Internet is the latest incantation of the media as 'dangerous'. As previously discussed in Chapter 11: 'It is the space where cyber-paeds prey in chat rooms; al-Qaeda encrypt missions, recruit martyrs and hide funds; drugs are traded and funds for terror are raised; youth is corrupted and the country's moral backbone eroded while the very basis of national security is under threat 24/7'.

Yet even the tangential links made between the Net and homicide in the Longhurst case are barely evident in other homicides. An Internet search for 'cyber' and 'murder' produced three million sites but most were referring to games. Very few killings were identifiable that had any cyber element described and there was one case in Japan of the 'murder' of an avatar (virtual husband) in the game *Maple Life*: 'The woman was charged with illegal access onto a computer and manipulating electronic data' (Sky News 23 October 2008). *Wired* had a report in 1998 titled 'Killed by the Internet' where a con man Chris Marquis was tracked down on the Web and Use-net by a man he had defrauded who planted a bomb that killed him (December 1998). In Greenwhich, Connecticut, 25-year-old Dos Reis was sentenced for the murder of a 13-year-old girl he met on the Internet. CBS reported: 'Help To Halt Online Predators. Internet Murder: Tips Every Parent Should Know' (Neal 2003). The murder took place in a shopping mall after sex in a car and the girl's guardian went on to warn 'parents to pay attention to the people with whom their children communicate on the computer' (*ibid.*) Blaming the Internet for children's naivety would be like blaming the parks for dirty old men in raincoats years ago, but it isn't only children who are naive. In Britain, Clare Wood was killed and burnt in Manchester with the chief suspect a man with a history of meeting women through online dating. A previous girlfriend claimed she had tried to warn the murdered woman about George Appleton's violence: 'I told her what he had done, to run a mile, but she said he'd told her about his past, she believed he had changed' (*Daily Mirror* 14 February 2009) . He was dubbed the 'Facebook fugitive' and found hanged a few days later near the murder scene (*Yorkshire Evening Post* 12 February 2009). Police warned women to take care using social networking sites but in this case the site was also where the ex-girlfriend met Clare Wood before warning her of the danger. In the US MSN online chat material was transcribed in an Ontario court trying a teenage girl with the murder of a rival. The chat included the defendant saying: 'I'm gonna f---in' stab her if I want to' (*Network National Post* 9 March 2009) in the months before Stefanie Rengel was stabbed and left to die. But in this case Facebook seems to provide evidence to convict rather than in any way being viewed as contributory; even the British case suggested a valuable use of the Internet to warn the possible victim was ignored. In Britian, police claimed the stalker who killed the celebrity Jill Dando used the Internet, although there was no evidence

(Wykes 2007) while Romei (1999) noted a fatal shooting in Australia after a young man traced his victim's contact and identity details online. Perhaps surprisingly, this handful of Net-related 'death' cases spans 10 years and took some searching to uncover. There may well be many more but finding so few with some effort indicates no great prevalence of Net-related homicide, nor much presence of it online to cause further harm. Indeed, there are several cases where the Internet aided detection and prosecution of homicides with the technology depicted as a valuable tool rather than a terminating one. For example, in a case in Kansas the suspect's computer gave up forensic evidence of a murder he committed that was vital for conviction: 'Murray conducted computer searches in the weeks before the slaying to solicit information about killing someone "quietly", building a bomb, using poison and which countries permitted criminal suspects to be extradited' (Carpenter 2004).

Clearly there are terrible murders which may be recorded either in the process of making extreme pornography or by passers-by on a mobile phone and placed on websites but to blame the medium that enables these to be displayed as the cause of the crime is tenuous to the point of incredulity. Moreover there are terrestrial laws in place to deal with such crime and, if anything, public accessibility to such images might improve detection and prosecution of perpetrators. Indeed, not only does there seem to be little evidence of any direct causality attributable to the Internet in homicide cases but if anything the reverse seems likely. Blaming any medium can never prevent the crime attributed to it, and it detracts from dealing with real crime and absolves the criminal from responsibility. Indeed for all human activity:

> There are two major difficulties with drawing direct causal links between media images and forms of social behaviour. The first is that they're unprovable (which results in people falling back on unhelpful appeals to 'common sense', and ignoring that correlation is not the same thing as causality). The second is that making such links draws attention away from the real causal factors of the behaviour in question, factors whose roots lie deep in the socialisation process (or lack of it) and which raise uncomfortable questions about the kind of society in which we live. (Petley 2009)

These, then, are not arguments suggesting that there is any merit in some of the aesthetically disgusting, morally and politically repugnant misogynistic material available in cyberspace and terrestrial media, but it is an argument that such material cannot turn a 'good' man 'bad' (and it *is* men who engage in sexually violent and violent crime)[5] any more than material informing schoolchildren about homosexuality is going to turn heterosexual youngsters 'queer' as was feared by the supporters of Clause 28 in the UK in the 1980s. The clause banned the depiction of so-called pretend families in schools and remains in place. 'The logic offered was that access to positive representations of gayness in childhood might increase the numbers of practising homosexuals (Hansard 18 December 1986, cited in Wykes 2001: ch. 7). This is clearly nonsense but is indicative of a fear of freedom of expression by the state and morally conservative groups. Clause 28 remains in place, supported by homophobic faith groups whom successive governments of England and Wales have feared offending. The Muslim Council of Britain argued strongly to retain Clause 28 in 2000: 'It is not without reason that both the Bible and the Qur'an, for example, strongly condemn homosexuality as a grave transgression' (Muslim Council of Britain 26 January 2000). The fear is simple: freedom of expression allows challenge to convention and orthodoxy and so undermines conservative authority groups. As a consequence extreme representations are used by such groups to argue for controls to such challenges regardless of the evidence of causal effect. That conservatism is evident in the make-up of most pro-censorship organisations.

Censorship and control

Suicide, assisted suicide and homicide are all indicative of dreadful harms, notably the death itself and its impact on others. However, a further more insidious harm has been introduced amidst claims that Internet communications must be censored and controlled to prevent such deaths. Extreme cases are being used systematically by a range of groups to call for curtailments of freedom of speech that threaten to impose enormous restrictions on liberty, expression and rights to privacy and autonomy. Suicide and homicide have been added to already mobilised campaigns to censor and curtail pornography (Chinese government), paedophile activity (Internet Watch Foundation); identity theft (Stop ID theft) and terrorism (Serious Organised Crimes Agency) online, despite the lack of any independent, empirical research that demonstrates that the Internet has caused more harm in any of these areas. The range of groups seeking censorship on the grounds of criminal and/or moral causality is expansive from the Chinese state via specialised policing units, commercial organisations, religious bodies and vigilantes. Every report of the Internet in relation to harm seems to fuel a renewed frenzy of effort, including legislative reactions, aimed at the medium rather than the perpetrators of harm, despite technical and jurisdictional challenges to controlling cyberspace (Klang and Murray (eds) 2005: 99–125; Yar 2006: 139–53; Wall 2007: 157–206). One direct result of coverage of suicide is that:

> The UK Government announced in September 2008 that it intends to update the Suicide Act 1961 to make clearer how the law on aiding suicide applies to online activities. This followed increasing public debate about the activities of suicide websites. After conducting a review of the Act, the UK Government has decided to modernise the statutory language so that it is easier for ISPs and users to understand ... The government observes that UK ISPs already remove illegal material when notified. However, the government hopes that the simplified wording of the Suicide Act will make it easier for them to remove offending sites. (Williamson 2008)

The implication is clearly that if ISPs don't self-censor, they will be prosecuted for aiding and abetting suicide. The organisation Carenotkilling supports this change with reference to Bridgend and the Internet but counsels against modifying the Act to free those who escort loved ones to Dignitas from the threat of prosecution. Carenotkilling is supported by religious groups such as the Christian Medical Fellowship and the Catholic Bishops Conference. What is ignored is that suicide rates have dropped significantly as Internet penetration has grown. In the US it dropped from 12.3 per 100,000 in 1980 to 9.7 in 2003 among 15–24-year-olds (Suicide.org) and 'Suicide rates in those aged 10–19 in the UK declined by 28 per cent in the seven year period from 1997–2003' according to an article in the *Journal of Child Psychology and Psychiatry* (Manchester University 2008). So media coverage seems to have impelled pressure from interest groups which has forced policy responses that will in turn control cyberspace, despite the lack of any evidence (indeed the evidence seems largely to contradict the claims that the Internet is causing suicide).

The lack of knowability, measurability and manageability of cyberspace alongside its constant association in the news media with extreme crime and depravity, have underwritten moves for control in a series of accounts that have mobilised the concept of threat and the accompanying fear of the unknown. These actions have much broader implications than the motive of the prevention of serious harm and include a series of changed laws, and laws applied differently than intended, all of which curtail cyber-communications and/or enable it to be surveilled. These include in the UK alone: Regulation of Investigatory Powers Act 2000 (enabling data interception and retention); Sexual Offences Act 2003 (covers using the Net to groom a child with intent to commit an act even when the act does not occur; creating/downloading indecent images/pseudo-photographs of children); Anti-Terrorism, Crime and Security Act 2001 (allows electronic surveillance in order to prevent, detect or prosecute the perpetrators of terrorism); Coroners and Justice 2009 revision (will allow the removal of suicide material from sites and/or prosecution and 'people's personal information to be shared between government departments, individuals or private companies without their consent' – Liberty 6 March 2009); Terrorism Act 2006 (criminalises posting pro-terrorist ideas online); Electronic Commerce Directive (Terrorism Act 2006) Regulations 2007 (threatens any provider of 'information society services' who hosts terror material within the European Economic Area with up to two years in prison and/or fines for hosting extreme material).

Groups fighting for freedom of speech in cyberspace such as Electronic Frontier Australia, Liberty UK and Electronic Freedom Foundation have collated and explored legislative shifts worldwide and their implications. All are concerned that the implications for such increases in efforts at censorship and control under the spurious cloak of preventing harm are manifold for our personal and democratic freedom to profess and discuss as a matter of ethical doctrine any conviction, any doctrine, however immoral it may be considered (Mill 1859).

Freedom

The term 'freedom' itself is not unambiguous. It is a term too readily used in the West to imply freedom to act, but the origins of the concept probably lie more authentically with the idea of freedom 'from' rather than freedom 'to'. In *On Liberty* (1859) Mill argued that only through freedom of speech could there be the possibility of truth and knowledge, which any form of censorship might exclude. Freedom is thus freedom from lies, bias and ignorance. Freedom of expression is not equal to freedom of action, although Mill also advocated this for individuals 'so long as it is at their own risk and peril' (Mill cited in Weckert 2000: 106). Further, when the sole person/s being harmed is/are the person/s expressing the desire for that harm there are no grounds to restrict either the expression or ensuing acts so long as those involved are consenting adults (Warburton 2001). This for Mill was about human dignity; about giving individuals autonomy over their beliefs, about democratic debate and engagement where 'the only purpose power can rightfully be exercised over any member of a civilised community, against his will, is to prevent harm to others' (cited *ibid.*: 45), meaning the threat or realisation of actual physical harm without their consent.

Consent is key to Mill's harm principle where harm is taken as physical injury not displeasure, offence or anxiety. In a contemporary context of cyber-expression defining both consent and harm are contentious. Consent depends on agreed definitions of adulthood. Simply, there is no single, uniform legal definition of 'child' (Eneman 2005: 29) so any universal model of consent is impossible. Moreover, terrestrial legislation already exists, albeit culturally variably, to prosecute those who inflict non-consensual harm, and in many instances and cultures even consensual harm between adults.[6] So the consent argument cannot apply to cyberspace which is an expressive, representational medium not an actual, physical interaction. Nor is it feasible to ask consent to a topic of discursive interaction without a priori representing it, thus confounding the possibility of consent.

Harm in Mill's terms requires physical evidence of injury to an individual/s (or the clear direct, threat of that) and ignores psychological or emotional damage now commonly accepted as harm in modern Western communities; indeed Mill specifically excluded non-physical responses to acts or words. Not only might it be important to consider non-physical harm effects per se, however much more difficult it might be to identify these at all, let alone as caused by the Internet, but critics of the harm principle also argue strongly that there is a causal or at least probable relationship between language and acts. The problem is demonstrating this effect and showing that it is directly due to the speech act/image encountered. For example in the debate over the self-harm (often slow suicide) that is anorexia there were calls in the UK to censor women's magazines and ban very slender catwalk models (Wykes and Gunter 2005) when obviously 'a well adjusted woman does not starve herself to death just because she sees a picture of a skinny model' (Cartner-Morley, *Guardian* 31 May 2000). If that were the case obesity would hardly be the massive problem it now is in Britain and the US given the lack of other than young, slender images of women in our media of all kinds. So pictures of skinny models are not per se harmful but they do reflect socio-cultural gender values about appropriate femininity that need to be challenged and changed and to do that requires free debate and argument. Importantly, to protect the freedom to do just that, to argue against prejudice, abuse, terror and violence also means protecting the freedom to articulate these and believing that justice, truth and human reason can prevail through argument. 'A commitment to freedom of expression means protecting expression for reasons more basic than our agreement with its message, for reasons independent of its content' (Moon 2008: 25).

Views of media as affecting harmfully demand intervention to pre-empt probable cause and oppose such a liberal perspective, but that in turn raises complex questions of who should pre-empt and what set of 'true' beliefs should protect us. Moreover, such views focus more on the mediated speech act than the actor. So, in many ways such debates are diversionary, as it should be remembered that media cannot 'act' nor can cyberspace, they are merely vehicles and places for expression. Furthermore they are not vehicles or places inhabited by human agents but communications systems and culture that are the result of human action. Agency is human. If that agency is actually harmful then laws exist or can be created to deal with it by prevention, deterrence or punishment. Mill's point was simple. Humans must be free to reflect, criticise and strive for knowledge or there is no autonomy and thereby no responsibility for agency; without responsibility for and autonomy over agency informed by critical reflection there is no human dignity nor respect and therefore little possibility of minimising harm.

Rather than recognising freedom of expression as potentially in this way minimising harm, the arguments for censorship presume representation is a probable cause of harm with audiences mere passive absorbers of messages who are easily turned from good to bad or sane to mad by a word or image. This, in itself, is manifestly untrue:

> People do not go into cinemas angels and come out to slash their mothers-in-law. There are other causes of evil and the fascination with blaming film simply detracts from the research that should go into the genuine causes of violence. (Winner, *Guardian* 9 July 2000)

Yet even if there were such direct effects, again the cyber-context defies any uniform agreements about control and censorship. Even if these were practicable technically and economically, which was deemed highly unlikely even by the late 1990s (Newey 1999), who might censor, on behalf of whom and according to what principles and at what cost? In the transglobal, multi-cultural, multifaith, internal, ephemeral, borderless and lawless interactivity of cyberspace who should have power of veto, if anyone?

Milton recognised the dangers of constraints on expression even in the relatively knowable and manageable, narrowly British, mass-media-free context of the seventeenth century. He urged for a constitution guaranteeing the freedom of the press and supported Cromwell's unrealised struggle to fully separate church and state in the interregnum that freed parliament from the crown (1649–1660). In Areopagitica (1644) he warned of the dangers of imposed homogeneity for a nation's unity and stressed the need to know all points of view in the search for knowledge. He remains beloved by British journalists and was much quoted during 2008, the four hundredth anniversary of his birth. For journalist Simon Jenkins, Milton 'was the articulate champion of Europe's first modern revolution, whose liberties can never be considered secure as long as rulers such as Tony Blair and George Bush plead absolutism or divinity as components of their authority' (Jenkins 2008). Milton clearly identified the problem of giving the power to censor to church, crown or state and set in place the concept of freedom of speech, first promulgated by the British Magna Carta in 1215. That concept re-emerged to underpin the French and American Revolutions and remains key to the US constitution, yet in Britain there was no such formal adoption. Indeed, in his novel of 1948, George Orwell could envisage a totalitarian *1984* where surveillance and control of dissenting ideas prevail:

> A Party Member lives from birth to death under the eye of the Thought Police. Even when he is alone he can never be sure that he is alone. Wherever he may be, asleep or awake, working or resting, in his bath or in bed, he can be inspected without warning and without knowing that he is being inspected. (Orwell 1989 edn: 219)

In the US, Noam Chomsky continued, 40 years later, to struggle against the control of the media, seeing an alignment of commerce and government 'able to filter out the news fit to print, marginalise dissent and allow the government and other dominant interests to get their message across' (Herman and Chomsky 1988: 2). Most recently there is renewed struggle for freedom of information and expression based in the UK. It launched with a convention on Modern Liberty in 2009 focusing closely on the legislative changes discussed in this chapter and their impact as in 'everybody's communications data, everybody's phone records, everybody's text messages, everybody's Internet use, airline bookings, financial records, biometric data – all of it – may be integrated by the state and accessed at will' (Mcdonald 28 February 2009). In the same month a new Centre for Freedom of the Media was launched, 'bringing together journalists, experts and scholars of the media, with public figures and the newsmakers themselves to research and evaluate the role of free and independent news media in building and maintaining political and civil freedom' (Centre for Freedom of the Media). Two of the Centre's key aims are to study 'the effects of laws and regulation/deregulation, and the new media landscape opened up by fast-changing and new technologies' (*ibid.*). Not least worrying is that such new laws and regulation (and the zealous application of older forms) seem to have clear associations with the supposed harmful effect of those new media technologies, while *incidentally* instigating control, censorship and surveillance.

Conclusion

The problem as ever with arguments about media effects lies in demonstrating a causal link. Mimicry is not one. There is no reason to believe that any violence to self or others that is carried out in the style of a mediated event would not have happened anyway. Even if it could be shown that, for example, suicides had increased significantly in areas with heavy Internet penetration (of which I could find no evidence, rather the opposite) other variables would need eliminating before the Internet could be blamed. It may be that the Internet is a source of information about effective methods of suicide leading to more successful attempts but to intervene in someone's free choice to end their life by curtailing that information contravenes any idea of autonomy or self-determination and raises a plethora of other moral and philosophical arguments. In terms of assisted suicide or euthanasia the arguments demanding restriction of information about suicide for the terminally ill or severely disabled derive directly from fundamentalist religious groups, proselytising belief not fact. Sui-homicide seems so rare and so extreme as to qualify as an aberrance and certainly no basis for regulating a mass media system to prevent 'copycat' acts. Connections between homicide and the Internet seem tenuous with at best the Internet providing a sounding board for already planned acts or a library resource for methods. If anything homicide seems more likely to be detected or convicted by Net-evidence than in any way caused by cyberculture.

It is difficult to argue that there should be no control other than parental and personal placed over Internet content that describes or even promotes violence to self or others, especially at a time of economic and social flux on a global scale when the 'best lack all conviction and the worst are full of passionate intensity' (Yeats 1921) but the alternative is to endorse censorship and then the questions who by, how and at what cost invite unacceptable answers. The arguments that the Internet has lethal potential are actually just that, theoretical arguments, not grounded by evidence nor even by reason, but by religious belief, moral repugnance, ignorance, conservatism, nationalism and fear. The fear is that a little understood and largely chaotic medium might enable those who deviate, in practice and/or belief, from dominant groups, to communicate their ideas, uncontrolled by the *filters* Chomsky (Herman and Chomsky 1988) noted, to anyone, anywhere, any time. The fear works two ways: it is actually fear by those who have power that such communication might challenge the authority, or even existence, of state, church or capital, but that fear is sold to the public very differently as threatening families, children and the vulnerable. What appears to be about protecting the vulnerable in practice assumes consent but actually also enables the securing and shoring up of the powerful. It is based on a model of people as mere puppets and dupes susceptible to online rant and rhetoric to the point where they will kill or seriously harm themselves or others. It is a model that demeans humanity and reduces individuals to an absorbent mass unable and unwilling to think critically and judge wisely.

There is no denying some ideas are abhorrent and some representations repugnant to witness but they are part of human culture and to better understand, and so try to change, humanity it is important to know all of it. By preventing access to some ideas we risk losing access to others. Knowledge becomes partial, choice is reduced and power consolidated as it is only the powerful who can try to control the publication of and access to information. Controls given consensus because they address fear of harm at an individual level easily transfer to controls to address fear of loss of power and authority at institutional and national level. So debate and dialogue, whether between just different or potentially dangerous ideas, is closed down, on the grounds of spurious connections being drawn between the Internet and harm. Suicide and homicide are used discursively within a broader demonisation of the Internet as dangerous that is seeking consensus to curtail and censor freedom of expression, and thereby democracy is also curtailed and censored.

Notes

1 This chapter is indebted to some inspirational work from students of LAW 378 Internet Crime 2008–2009 at Sheffield University, especially Nicole Bailey, Linsey Goucher and Rebecca Griffiths.
2 There is another phenomenon of homicide followed by the suicide of the killer but no evidence that I could find of the Internet being implicated. Most commonly the killer murders his own children and/or ex-partner after the collapse of a relationship (see http://www.suicideinfo.ca/csp/assets/alert48.pdf)
3 Switzerland offers assisted suicide in terminal illness through the organisation Dignitas. The Netherlands and Belgium have legalised euthanasia, while Sweden, Finland and Norway don't always prosecute physicians who help terminally ill patients to die. (http://www.edstrong.blog-city.com/read/941538.htm) 7 January 2005
4 The many sites advocating self-harm from cutting to starving that display scarred and emaciated bodies with pride alongside supportive chat rooms and advice on how to hurt yourself better, raise questions about the role of the law in relation to the self and rights over the body (Wykes and Gunter 2005).
5 Evidence shows violent and sexual crimes are overwhelmingly committed by men not just in the UK and US but globally (see Wykes and Welsh 2009: chs 8 and 9).
6 In the UK: 'In law, you cannot, as a rule, consent to an assault. There are exceptions. For example, you can consent to a medical practitioner touching and possibly injuring your body; you can consent to an opponent hitting or injuring you in sports such as rugby or boxing; you can consent to tattoos or piercings if they are for ornamental purposes. You can also use consent as a defence against a charge of what is called Common Assault.' (http://www.spannertrust.org/documents/spannerhistory.asp discusses the Spanner Case).

Further reading

There is a large range of further reading in the chapter's References but the following might offer good background material for readers:

Yar, M. (2006) *Cybercrime and Society* (London: Sage) is a comprehensive and clear overview of cybercrime. Anyone concerned to understand better the importance of freedom of expression should read Newey, A. 'Freedom of Expression: censorship in private hands', in Liberty (ed.) (1999) *Liberating Cyberspace. Civil Liberties, Human rights and the Internet* (London: Pluto) and dip into the origins of many of these debates in Mill, J.S. (1859) *On Liberty* (London: J.W. Parker). The website for Liberty (www.

liberty.org.uk) is an excellent contemporary source of articles around the role of the media, controls, censorship, privacy and freedom. An alternative account of cyber suicide and homicide is available in Jewkes, Y. (2007) '"Killed by the Internet": cyber homicides, cyber suicides and cyber sex crimes', in Jewkes, Y. (ed.) (2007) *Crime online* (Cullompton: Willan Publishing). Journalism, news values and arguments about media effects are covered in Wykes, M. (2001) *News, Crime and Culture* (London: Pluto); Jewkes, Y. (2004) *Media and Crime* (London: Sage); and Chibnall, S. (1977) *Law and Order News* (London: Tavistock).

References

ACLU (27 June 1997) http://www.aclu.org/privacy/speech/15493prs19970627.html

BBC (1999) 'Sci/Tech Unesco steps up fight against Internet Paedophiles', 16 June, available at http://news.bbc.co.uk/1/hi/sci/tech/370327.stm

Berlin, I. (1969) *Four Essays on Liberty*. Oxford: Oxford University Press.

Biddle, L., Donovan, J., Hawton, K., Navneet, K. and Gunnell, D. (2008) 'Suicide and the Internet', *British Medical Journal*, 336: 800–2 at www.bmj.com/cgi/content/full/336/7648/800

Boyes, R. (2004) 'Human body parts in fridge spark fear of cannibal copycat', *Timesonline*, 8 October, available at http://www.timesonline.co.uk/tol/news/world/article491839.ece

Cadwalladr, C. (2009) 'How Bridgend was damned by distortion', *The Observer*, 1 March, available at http://www.guardian.co.uk/lifeandstyle/2009/mar/01/bridgend-wales-youth-suicide-media-ethics

Carenotkilling http://www.carenotkilling.org.uk/?show=673

Carpenter, T. (2004) 'Ex-wife died of brutal beating, coroner testifies', *Topeka Capital-Journal* 7 December, available at http:findarticles.com/p/articles/mi-qn4179/is-20041207/ai-nl1822099

Cartner-Morley, J. (2000) *Guardian*, 31 May.

Centre for Freedom of the Media (CFOM) http://www.cfom.org.uk/index.html

Chibnall, S. (1977) *Law and Order News*. London: Tavistock.

Chinese government http://www.topnews.in/china-aims-put-stop-online-porn-closing-1250-websites-2114754

Courtnews (n.d.) http://www.courtnewsuk.co.uk/c_sex_killers/a_graham_coutts/crime_vaults/

Crime in England and Wales 2006–2007 http://www.homeoffice.gov.uk/rds/pdfs07/crime0607summ.pdf

Curti, E. (n.d.) 'Evil in the virtual Eden', *The Tablet*, available at http://www.thetablet.co.uk/article2692

Daily Mirror (2009) http://www.mirror.co.uk/news/top-stories/2009/02/14/facebook-killer-s-ex-warned-clare-wood-of-stalker-danger-115875-21121969/

Daily Telegraph (2008a) 'Girl killed herself after bullying on internet', available at http://www.telegraph.co.uk/news/uknews/1902956/Girl-killed-herself-after-bullying-on-internet.htm

Daily Telegraph (2008b) 'Suicide websites "to be blocked"', 1 August, available at http://www.telegraph.co.uk/news/2483310/Suicide-websites-to-be-blocked-html

Dignity in Dying http://www.dignityindying.org.uk/

Dudley-Nicholson, J. (2008) 'Australia's compulsory internet filtering "costly, ineffective"', *The Courier-Mail*, 29 October, available at http://www.news.com.au.technology/story/0,25642,24569656-5014239,00.html

Electronic Frontier Australia http://www.efa.org.au/Issues/Censor/cens3.html

Electronic Frontier Foundation http://www.eff.org/

Eneman, Marie (2005) 'The New Face of Child Pornography', in M. Klang and A. Murray (eds), *Human Rights in the Digital Age*. London: Glasshouse Press.

Facebook 'Mein Teil' video clip, available at http://youtube.com/watch?v=lk06_ll_vgo&feature=related Quote from Facebook (30 November 2008) available at http://www.facebook.com/topic.php?uid=5836432901&topic=146076

Galtung, J. and Ruge, M. (1965) 'Structuring and selecting news', in S. Cohen and J. Young (1982 edn) *The Manufacture of News: Deviance, Social Problems and the Mass Media*. London: Constable.

Gibson, W. (1984) *Neuromancer*. London: HarperCollins.

Herman, E. and Chomsky, N. (1988) *Manufacturing Consent*. USA: Pantheon.

Jenkins, S. (2008) 'Milton the poet was a bore and a prig. But on liberty he was majestic', *Guardian*, 12 December, available at http://www.guardian.co.uk/commentisfree/2088/dec/12/john-milton-free-speech-poetry

Jewkes, Y. (2004) *Media and Crime*. London: Sage.

Jewkes, Y. (2007) '"Killed by the Internet": cyber-homicides, cyber suicides and cyber sex crimes', in Y. Jewkes (ed.) *Crime on-line*. Cullompton: Willan Publishing.

Kassel, A.P. (2003) 'Gentleman cannibal describes "mercy killing"', *Taipei Times*, 5 December, available at http://www.taipeitimes.com/News/world/archives/2003/12/05/2003078413

Klang, M. and Murray, A. (2005) *Human Rights in the Digital Age*. London: Glasshouse Press.

Lewis, J. (2003) 'It's a web of weirdos', *The Daily Telegraph*, 2 August, available at http://www.telegraph.co.uk/comment/personal-view/3594572/Its-a-web-of-weirdos.html

Liberty http://www.liberty-human-rights.org.uk/

Liberty (6 March 2009) http://www.liberty-human-rights.org.uk/news-and-events/1-press-releases/2009/06-03-09-coroners-and-justice-bill-could-allow-black-listing-databases.shtml

Mcdonald, K. (28 February 2009) http://www.modernliberty.net/read/transcripts/citizens-and-the-state-the-crisis-of-liberty

McMurray, J. (2007) 'Japan's cyber-suicide trend takes bizarre twist', *Guardian*, 11 October, available at http://www.guardian.co.uk/world/2007/oct/11/japan/justinmcmurry

McParland, K. (2008) 'Kevin Libin: Canada's approach to web censorship – first let the flowers grow, then lop them off', *The National Post*, 30 October, available at http://network.nationalpost.com/np/blogs/fullcomment/archive/2008/10/30/kevin-libin-australian-internet.aspx

Manchester University (2008) 'UK teen suicide rates on the decline', 23 October, available at http://www.manchester.ac.uk/aboutus/news/display/?id=4091

Mill, J.S. (1859) *On Liberty*. London: J.W. Parker.

Milton, J. (1644) *Areopagitica* (pamplet and speech for the liberty of unlicensed printing to the Parliament of England).

Modern Liberty http://www.modernliberty.net/

MOJ (2009) http://www.justice.gov.uk/docs/circular-criminal-justice-01-2009.pdf

Moon, R. (2008) *Report to the Canadian Human Rights Commission concerning section 13 of the Canadaian Human rights Act and the Regulation of Hate Speech on the Internet*. Canadian Human Rights Commission, available at www.chrc-ccdp.ca/pdf/moon report en.pdf

Murphy, C. (2004) 'Cannibalism: A modern taboo', BBC News, 5 July, available at http://news.bbc.co.uk/2/hi/europe/3254074.stm

Muslim Council of Britain (2000) http://www.mcb.org.uk/media/archive/news260100.html

Neal, R. (2003) 'Help To Halt Online Predators', CBS, 7 May, available at http://www.cbsnews.com/stories/2003/05/07/earlyshow/living/parenting/main552841.shtml

Network National Post (2009) http://network.nationalpost.com/np/blogs/tornto/archive/2009/03/09/murder-accused

Newey, A. (1999) 'Freedom of Expression: censorship in private hands', in Liberty (ed.), *Liberating Cyberspace. Civil Liberties, Human rights and the Internet.* London: Pluto.

News.co.au (2008) http://www.news.com.au/technology/story/0,25642,24569656-5014239,00.html

Orwell, G. (1989 edn) *1984.* London: Penguin.

Outlaw (2008) http://www.out-law.com/page-9292

Petley, J. (2009) *Media Watch*, at http://www.mediawatchwatch.org.uk/2009/03/06/beyer-out-of-his-depth-at-the-guardian/

Pravda (1999) 'European human rights body speaks against euthanasia', 27 January, available at http://newsfromrussia.com/world/2005/04/27/59458.html

Rice, D. and Wilks, A. (2008) 'Revealed: The ultra-violent sex movies being made in Milton Keynes', *Daily Mail*, 23 January, available at http://www.dailymail.co.uk/news/article-510641/Revealed-The-ultra-violent-sex-movies-Milton-Keynes.html

Romei, S. (1999) 'net firms lead killer to victim', in *The Australian*, 4–5 December: 19–22.

Rowan, D. (2005) 'Censor the internet? Try catching the wind', *The Times*, 31 August, available at http://www.timesonline.co.uk/tol/comment/columnists/guest_contributors/article560684.ece

Seattlepi.com (2009) http://seattlepi.nwsource.com/local/395517_deathdignity10.html

Sky News (2008) 'Jilted Woman "Murdered Avatar"', 23 October, available at http://news.sky.com/skynews/Home/World-News/Japan-Woman-Arrested-For-Destroying-Online-Avatar-After-Virtual-Husband-Divorced-Her/Article/200810415127170

SOCA (Serious Organised Crime Agency) www.soca.gov.uk

Suicide.org http://www.suicide.org/international-suicide-statistics.html

Taylor, M. and Quayle, E. (2003) *Child Pornography: An Internet Crime.* London: Routledge.

The Times (2008) 'First cyber-bullying trials hears how Megan Meier, 13, killed herself after oneline taunts', 20 November, available at http://www.timesonline.co.uk/tol/news/world/us_and_americas/article5196441.ece

Thompson, S. (1999) 'The Internet and its potential influence on suicide', *Psychiatric Bulletin*, 23: 449–451.

Times of India (2006) 'JAPAN: Japan's Internet suicides soar to 91 in 2005', 9 February, available at http://www.asiamedia.ucla.edu/edu/article.asp?parentid=38921

Verity, E. (n.d.) 'Yes, we can clean up the Web', *Mail online*, available at http://www.dailymail.co.uk/news/article-207850/Yes-clean-Web.htm

Wall, D. (2007) *Cyber-crime.* Cambridge: Polity.

Warburton, N. (2001) *Freedom: an Introduction with Readings.* London: Routledge.

Weckert, J. (2000) 'What is so bad about Internet content regulation', *Ethics and Information Technology* (electronic), 2: 105–11.

Williamson, R. (2008) 'UK Government to clarify the law on suicide websites', *Bird and Bird*, 3 December, available at http://mail.twobirds.com/ve/ZZx9058V00t869174R27Z9/stype=print

Winner, M. (2000) *Guardian*, 9 July.

Wired (1998) http://www.wired.com/wired/archive/6.12/murder.html?pg=5&topic=&topic_set=

Wykes, M. (2001) *News, Crime and Culture.* London: Pluto.

Wykes, M. (2007) 'Constructing crime: stalking, celebrity, cyber and media', in Y. Jewkes (ed.), *Crime on-line*. Cullompton: Willan Publishing, 128–43.

Wykes, M. and Gunter, B. (2005) *The Media and Body Image*. London: Sage.

Wykes, M. and Welsh, K. (2009) *Violence, Gender and Justice*. London: Sage.

Yar, M. (2006) *Cybercrime and Society*. London: Sage.

Yeats, W.B. (1921) 'The Second Coming', in G. Macbeth (ed.) (1979) *Poetry 1900–1975*. Harlow: Longman.

Yorkshire Evening Post (2009) (12 February) http://www.yorkshireeveningpost.co.uk/news/Murder-hunt-finds-man-hanging.4975447.jp

YouTube (Ewart) http://www.youtube.com/watch?v=XlD7mjLEjB8

Part III

Internet Law and Regulation

Yvonne Jewkes and Majid Yar

In Part III of the Handbook, the contributors consider the ways in which legal and regulatory frameworks have developed in response to Internet crime problems. Martin Wasik (Chapter 19) concentrates on the UK in order to trace the emergence of laws focused upon computer misuse, culminating in the passing of the landmark Computer Misuse Act (CMA) of 1990. He points out that, prior to the 1980s, computers were largely specialist technological devices used for a narrowly defined range of commercial and scientific applications. There was, during this period, little or no sense that computer use entailed specific problems of security or criminal conduct, and this was mirrored in the conspicuous absence of laws related to computerised systems. The 1980s constituted a watershed in both respects, as the development of low-cost and increasingly powerful semi-conductor technology fuelled a massive computer boom. Increasingly sophisticated devices, offering an ever-widening array of applications, became more and more commonplace in both the home and workplace. In tandem with these changes, business users of computer systems began to report incidences of misuse, often perpetrated by technologically literate employees, while popular press reportage presented dramatic tales about the risks presented by computer 'hacking'. Yet, as Wasik argues, the legal establishment in the UK was profoundly divided over the need for any additional legal innovations to address computer-related offences, with some going so far as to dismiss wholesale the idea that computer crimes represented anything new or distinctive. The 'sceptics' claimed that computer-related offences could be adequately prosecuted under existing laws covering criminal damage, theft, fraud, and suchlike. This view was sustained, at least initially, by the Law Commissions of Scotland and of England. However, the pressure for change built inexorably as a number of criminal convictions for computer-related offences were quashed upon appeal, highlighting clearly the gaps and ambiguities in existing criminal law when applied to the domain of computers. The Law Commission of England was charged with producing a report on the matter, and its recommendations were subsequently used as the basis of the provisions of the 1990 Act. The Act made it a criminal offence to attempt 'unauthorised access' to a computer system, whether undertaken as an end in itself or with intent to commit a further offence. It also prohibited the unauthorised modification of a computer system, such that this would interfere with its normal operation. Taken together, these provisions effectively covered a wide range of computer-related offences, including those commonly adduced by terms such as 'hacking', 'viruses', 'malware' and 'denial of service attacks'. In this way, the CMA effectively anticipated many of the high-profile computer crime problems that came to the forefront as the networked technologies of the Internet and World Wide Web rose to prominence in the course of the 1990s.

Building on the developments explored by Wasik in the first chapter of this Part of the Handbook, Lilian Edwards, Judith Rauhofer and Majid Yar trace and evaluate further legal innovations in the UK, discussing primarily offences occurring in the online environment (Chapter 20). They address both substantive laws aimed at curtailing online offences, and laws that regulate the policing of computer-related crimes. With respect to the former, they focus upon two areas that have arguably generated the most intense concern, namely pornography/obscenity and terrorism-related offences. As noted elsewhere in the Handbook, pornography (especially child pornography) is often identified by legislators, users and law enforcement officials as one of the most urgent and serious crime problems of the Internet era (see Chapters 16 and 17 by Bryce and Quayle, this volume). Edwards *et al.* examine how the circulation of obscene materials (primarily visual depictions in the form of photographs and video recordings) stimulated the extension and amendment of existing criminal law provisions so as to include those stored and transmitted in electronic form via networked computers. However, the ability of computer technologies to manipulate existing imagery, or to generate wholly new images in digital form, has called forth measures that go beyond those established in previously existing obscenity laws. Most notably, there have been controversial steps to prohibit production, circulation and/or possession of electronically manipulated 'pseudo-photographs' depicting child sex, and to similarly prohibit computer-generated drawings and animations whose representational content is deemed akin to that of obscene visual recordings of actual persons. Recently, legal steps have also shifted away from child sex abuse imagery to include sexualised representations of adults, where those images are deemed to be of an 'extreme' or 'violent' nature.

The second area of online offending addressed here, that of terrorism, has also moved front and centre in recent years, especially in the wake of the New York, London and Madrid terrorist attacks. Starting with the Terrorism Act of 2000, the UK has seen the introduction of a number of legislative initiatives that seek, among other things, to criminalise the use of electronic communication technologies for the purpose of furthering terrorist activity. Some of these measures have proven controversial, such as the broad-brush prohibitions on the 'encouragement' and 'glorification' of terrorism, as well as those on the possession of materials deemed likely to be 'of use' for those planning terrorist attacks. The final area addressed in the chapter is that of interception and retention of electronic communications, especially the measures introduced under the Regulation of Investigatory Powers Act

(RIPA) 2000. Again, controversy has been ignited in that its critics claim the Act removes the electronic interception from judicial authorisation or review, compels communications providers (such as ISPs) to cooperate with such orders, and has excessively broad grounds upon which a warrant for interception can be issued. Thus across a range of areas, legal developments around Internet crime and regulation have served as lightning-rods for human rights campaigners and civil libertarians who fear the wholesale loss of rights and freedoms.

Moving from the UK to the US context, Susan Brenner (Chapter 21) examines the wide-ranging provisions in American Federal law that have sought to address computer- and Internet-related offences. The first major legislative provision in this area was the Computer Fraud and Abuse Act (CFAA) of 1986, which contained provisions akin to those adopted four years later in the UK's CMA 1990. However, Brenner notes that both defects in the original formulation of the law, and the limited range of offences initially covered, resulted in numerous subsequent amendments over the following decades. In addition to the CFAA, further Federal laws have been introduced covering areas such as electronic identity theft (see also Smith, Chapter 14); copyright and digital file-sharing (see also Wall and Yar, Chapter 13); child protection and child pornography (see Chapters by Bryce and Quayle, 16 and 17 respectively); and privacy rights (see also McGuire, Chapter 23). Taken together, the US has some of the most expansive and rigorous laws targeting online offences, and has served very much as a global leader in driving legal change in this area.

In Chapter 22, Katherine Williams shifts the focus from national arenas to developments in Internet law on the transnational scale. The need for common legal frameworks and standardisation is especially acute with respect to the Internet, since its global nature typically means that offences involve offenders and victims that may well be situated in different jurisdictional territories and subject to divergent legal frameworks. Williams emphasises an important distinction between regulation, voluntary coordination and law as modes of supranational control. The first uses the architecture and rules of the Internet to shape, control and standardise its operation – what Laurence Lessig dubs the 'code' of cyberspace. The second relies on common agreements and voluntary concords around best practice for enhancing Internet security. The third-level domain, that of law, operates both on the national level and on the international level proper through legal instruments such as binding conventions and treaties. International legal agreements may emerge on a piecemeal basis as a response to particular crime problems – for example, the TRIPS agreement established under the auspices of the World Trade Organisation, which seeks to curtail (among other things) the kinds of copyright violations that are enabled by unauthorised file-sharing on the Internet. However, the past decade has also seen a more strategically coordinated and wide-ranging effort to internationalise legal provisions (including the establishment of criminal sanctions) with respect to Internet crime in its broad scope. Most significant here has been the Council of Europe's Cybercrime Convention, which was finalised in 2001, and involved participation not only from the CoE's member states but also other major economic and political powers such as the United States, Japan and Canada. The Convention makes provision for the standardisation and harmonisation of national laws related to Internet offences, enhancing the powers of law enforcement agencies, and for international cooperation in matters of enforcement and mutual assistance. The Convention covers a broad range of offences, including hacking and disruption, fraud and forgery, child pornography, racist and xenophobic content, and intellectual property offences. However, the Convention has been criticised on grounds that it emphasises the economic interests of companies and governments above those of individual users, and that its provisions for the extension of prohibitions and enforcement powers takes no cognisance of privacy rights or data protection issues.

Issues of privacy and user freedom take centre stage in Michael McGuire's contribution about 'Online Surveillance and Personal Liberty' (Chapter 23). His starting point is, firstly, a profound scepticism about claims that online surveillance and micro-monitoring of user activities are necessitated by the supposedly unprecedented nature of Internet crime threats. He views such claims as 'overhyped' and excessive in character, and as serving to justify ever more invasive control and monitoring. Secondly, he argues that the practices of Internet surveillance should not be viewed in isolation, but must be understood as part of an ever-expanding 'assemblage' of surveillance that spans 'virtual' and 'terrestrial' domains. McGuire notes that Internet-related surveillance in fact takes two distinctive forms: firstly surveillance *of* users' online activities and interactions (such as the tracking of sites visited, materials downloaded, and the content of email communications), and secondly surveillance that *uses* the Internet to collected data about users' wider personal characteristics and offline life-worlds. McGuire goes on to map in detail the scope and scale of contemporary surveillance practices, pinpointing the key roles played both by government agencies and corporate interests. He concludes that the current trends inexorably lead to a profound imbalance, with Internet users being subjected to ever more invasive forms of monitoring while those responsible for such practices evade meaningful accountability and checks.

Chapter 19

The emergence of computer law

Martin Wasik

Introduction

The purpose of this chapter is to trace the developments that led to the modern law on computer misuse in the United Kingdom. For these purposes I take the 'modern law' to start with the Computer Misuse Act 1990, so this chapter is mainly concerned with the decade which ended with the passing of that Act. The 1980s was the period during which I first became interested in this subject, and it is instructive now to look back on that time with the benefit of knowledge of the many subsequent changes.

In the 1960s and 1970s computers were generally perceived to be specialised instruments with limited usefulness, primarily to improve upon manual record-keeping functions. The development of semi-conductor technology and the growth of microelectronics changed all that. For most practical purposes, the 1980s was a time before the development of the Internet, and certainly before the emergence of the World Wide Web. Computerisation was, however, gathering pace within industry, and to a lesser extent among home users in the UK. The transfer of funds electronically within the banking system developed at the very end of the 1970s, for example. Lawyers and policy-makers looked to the United States, where developments were a few years in advance of our own. At this time of growth practical measures for computer security were rather basic and, for many users, non-existent. It was a time of development and experimentation in computing and, above all, a period of expansion. Computing moved rapidly away from the province of a few highly trained individuals to that of the ordinary office and home user. In 1984, nine per cent of households in the United Kingdom were recorded as possessing a home computer, the first year in which such a statistic was collected. This figure had risen to 17 per cent by 1986 (Central Statistical Office (CSO) 1986: 6.14). The Big Bang in the City (introduction of online trading) took place in 1986. The arrival of the 'information society' was heralded (Williams 1988). Until the mid 1980s there was little sense of urgency about the issue of computer security, despite the introduction of 'computer crime' statutes in the

United States (American Bar Association (ABA) 1984), and the more frequent appearance of stories in the press about computer misuse, primarily hacking, viruses and exotic-sounding forms of fraud made newly possible by the wider availability of computing technology and the technological innocence of the new users. The press was suddenly full of stories about deviant teenage hackers who possessed incredible abilities,[1] and about the risks of addiction to computers (Shotton 1989). There was a basis of truth in these stories, but overlaid with journalistic scaremongering. Tapper commented in 1987 that computers 'seem to inspire in otherwise rational human beings feelings of such distrust, suspicion and awe as to subvert all sensible judgment' (Tapper 1987).

Much of the available early literature on the risks of computer misuse was limited in its value. Some of the 'surveys' of computer crime were very dubious, with skewed questions and an unscientific mix of concern ratings and opinion polls (Wasik 1985). An early writer achieving prominence in the UK was Wong, who compiled 'casebooks' of computer crimes (Wong 1983; Wong and Farquhar 1987). His publications followed the style of early American writings on the subject, published from the early 1970s, which were a mixture of press stories, more or less well-documented accounts from industry, and the very occasional matter which had come to court. Sometimes the same incident, differing in important details, could be found in several sources. The emphasis was often on the sensational, on the magnitude of potential risks, and on the youthful 'computer geniuses' who could target vital computer systems, apparently at will. These books may have served as useful warnings to the unwary, but little serious attempt was made to quantify the scale of the problem. Some of the early American work, completed under the auspices of the Stanford Research Institute, was heavily criticised by academic writers (see Taber 1980).

Despite the shortcomings of the early casebooks, however, they did serve to warn users and policymakers of how badly things could go wrong if computer security was ignored or mishandled. They also exposed the emerging problem that, with more and more firms adopting IT, separate IT departments were being established as a substitute for more general computer knowledge within the organisation (British Institute of Management (BIM) 1988). Senior management failed to keep pace with events, and a form of 'security blindness' could quickly develop, allowing younger, more technologically savvy employees to misuse the computer system for their own ends. Stories of using the office computer for other purposes, such as game playing, or running a private business in work time, became rife. Among the more carefully researched publications were those of the Audit Inspectorate (which later became the Audit Commission), which was responsible for an important series of surveys of business users (Audit Inspectorate 1981; Audit Commission 1984, 1987). These pioneering victim surveys proved valuable in gaining a better understanding of the fact that generally rather mundane frauds were being given the mysterious mantle of 'computer fraud'. The reports also highlighted the fact that it was basic security lapses, rather than advanced technological knowledge on the part of the fraudster, which lay at the heart of nearly all the offences. They also demonstrated the reluctance of companies to report their losses, through embarrassment, fear of adverse publicity, or a general belief that law enforcement would not be equipped to deal with such cases, or would assign a low priority to any investigation. More considered academic reflections in the field of computers and the law were first provided by Tapper (1983, 1989), although his main focus was on evidential issues rather than substantive criminal law. Technical questions of whether computer-generated statements were original evidence or hearsay occupied attention for a while, but these were soon resolved by statute.

While there was some awareness of the legislative developments in the United States and the creation of computer crime statutes, there was a period of reluctance to accept that such legislation was really necessary. Prominent among the American writings, and still worth looking at today, were those by Parker (Parker et al. 1973; Parker 1976, 1983), Taber (1979, 1980), BloomBecker (1985, 1986) and Bequai (1987). In the UK there was a commonly held view that 'computer crime' was largely old wine in new bottles. Tapper commented that in enacting computer crime statutes the state legislatures in the United States had simply 'succumbed to fashionable pressure' (Tapper 1987: 5). New methods of committing old familiar crimes might require some police and prosecution ingenuity, and some judicial development of the law where necessary, but nothing more. While it was coming to be accepted in criminal law circles that machines could not be 'deceived', and so the deception-based offences in the Theft Acts 1868 and 1978 might not work in a computer context, it was also argued that this apparent loophole could usually be avoided by charging theft instead or, if all else failed, abstracting electricity.

Those of us who became interested in this topic during the 1980s faced the dual objection that, first, the subject was too newsworthy and 'popular' to be worthy of legal academic attention and, second, that our interest was helping to elevate a matter of marginal legal interest into something much more than it actually deserved. Indeed, some writers chose to debunk the whole concept of 'computer crime'. My own book on the subject opens with two competing quotations, the first of which suggests that 'computer-related crime will soon become one of the most important areas of legal study', and the second of which is Ingraham's famous remark that 'The first myth about computer crime is that it exists ...' (Ingraham 1980). Of course, debunking the whole subject in this way was quite easy to do. The peripheral involvement of a computer in some aspect of an offence might, according to some definitions, make it a computer crime. This led to wrangling over definition. Some definitions were so wide as to imbue a number of perfectly ordinary criminal offences with the exotic title of computer crime. The compendious computer crime statutes in the United States were wide enough to include criminal damage to a computer, theft of computer hardware components and even hitting someone with a computer. The way out of the definitional stop lay in eschewing the concept of 'computer crime' altogether, and preferring instead to use 'computer misuse', thereby problematising the question whether such misuse was genuinely new in legal terms and was of sufficient interest and sufficient importance to warrant criminalisation.[2] As the Law Commission observed later, to describe peripheral behaviour as 'computer crime' was surely to prejudge the conduct in question.

Early cases

The early cases, by and large, supported the view of the sceptics that tried and trusted criminal laws could deal with the threats of the emerging computer age. The first identified threat was damage, whether to the physical computer itself, and tangible assets associated with it, such as disks and tapes, or damage to or interference with programs or data stored on the disks or tapes. Damage to tangible assets certainly created no new problems since it was clearly covered by the Criminal Damage Act 1971. The difficulty lay in intangibles, since section 10(1) of the Act stated (and still states) that 'In this Act "property" means property of a tangible nature, whether real or personal, including money ...' During the early 1980s there was a developing unreported 'case law' of magnets being used to erase data, and manipulation of data via unauthorised access, whether remotely or not. The reported instances were generally small-scale, much more in the nature of 'nuisance' or 'pranks', rather than serious crime, but it was not difficult to envisage more significant harm being caused. In a case in 1986 the defendant pleaded guilty to reprogramming his ex-employer's computer so as to display a farewell message.[3] He was conditionally discharged and ordered to pay £1,000 compensation to the firm, the estimated cost of remedying the problem.

The case of *Cox* v. *Riley*[4] in 1986 was, however, the first occasion on which the criminal damage issue was tested in court. The defendant was employed to work on a machine that cut window frames. The machine was operated by insertion of a printed circuit card that enabled the operator to specify one of 16 different window frame profiles. The defendant deliberately erased all of the programs from the card. This rendered the machine all but useless. The defendant was convicted of criminal damage by the magistrates, and the conviction was upheld by the Divisional Court. The judges in the higher court were 'emphatic' that the 1971 Act covered this behaviour relying, in the main, on nineteenth-century cases! This was criminal damage, the judges said, because there had been damage to a tangible medium (the machine, and/or the card)[5] and labour and expense were required to remedy what the defendant had done.

Criminal damage was shown to work in other cases, too. Cases of remote hacking, where the hacker had left messages, or had corrupted data could, it seemed, also be dealt with through the 1971 Act. Indeed, the initial view of the Law Commission was that *Cox* v. *Riley* solved the problem. In their Working Paper, published in 1988, they said that 'The law of criminal damage now seems to extend to persons who damage a computer system, without the need for any further reform of the law.'[6] The Scottish Law Commission agreed[7] that existing laws would cover the ground, particularly since north of the border they had in the prosecution's locker a common law offence of 'malicious mischief', which is capable of operating very widely indeed.[8] The provisional approach of the Commissions was always rather optimistic, however. One scenario that could not be catered for by using criminal damage laws had already arisen in the 1984 Canadian case of *Turner*,[9] where a hacker had gained access to a computer system and inserted a locking device that prevented legitimate users from gaining access to it. This kind of case later became known as a 'denial of service' attack. Surely, denying someone access to their own property, such as by locking it away in a drawer, or by deliberately blocking their car in a car park, cannot constitute criminal damage.[10] Even in this context, some commentators believed that the criminal damage laws would work, as long as the property under consideration was described with sufficient generality in the charge (Brown 1986; Temby and McElwaine 1987), and the Scottish Commission stuck to its ground, saying that it had heard no convincing evidence that 'denial of service' attacks were a real problem, or were likely to become so in the future. Eventually, however, the Law Commission in England changed its mind and decided that a new offence, broad enough to cover denial of service attacks without the need to prove damage to a physical target, was indeed necessary. This, in due course, formed the basis of section 3 of the Computer Misuse Act 1990.

Gold and Schifreen

The key event during the 1980s was the prosecution and eventual quashing of the convictions of the Prestel hackers Gold and Schifreen by the House of Lords. With the benefit of hindsight the case seems now even more important than it did at the time. The defendants in *Gold and Schifreen*[11] were a freelance computer journalist and an accountant. By taking advantage of some slack security procedures they were able to gain unauthorised access to material contained in the Prestel computer system, a public information service, and to user files containing all the identification numbers and passwords of subscribers. According to the various accounts of the background to the case Schifreen, who was a subscriber to Prestel, came across a supposedly secure identification code when testing new computer equipment and used it to access the system. By keying in a simple set of numbers (eight 2's) and a very obvious password (1234) he gained access to the account of a British Telecommunications employee, which contained confidential numbers of Prestel computers not available to the public. By using those numbers he was accepted as an authorised user of the passwords. Schifreen passed on the computer information to Gold, who also accessed the computer. They altered files. They also found codes belonging to the Duke of Edinburgh, among others, and used the Duke's number to access his private electronic mailbox, leaving the message 'Good afternoon, HRH Duke of Edinburgh'. The identities of the hackers soon became well known. Indeed Gold and Schifreen spoke of their exploits on a BBC television programme during 1984 and were interviewed by the computer news magazines. Schifreen gave a demonstration of the method of computer access to one reporter after which, apparently, he encouraged the reporter to inform British Telecommunications of the security lapse. Even after Prestel had been informed the defendants continued with their unauthorised accessing of the system. Clearly, they did not expect to be prosecuted but, in the event, they were charged in March 1985 with the offence of forgery. Section 1 of the Forgery and Counterfeiting Act 1981 provides:

> A person is guilty of forgery if he makes a false instrument which is, and which he knows or believes to be, false, with the intention that he or another shall use it to induce somebody to accept it as genuine, and by reason of so accepting it to do or not to do some act to his own or any other person's prejudice.

An 'instrument' is defined by section 8(1) to be, *inter alia*

> (d) any disk, tape, sound track or other device on or in which information is recorded or stored.

The defendants were charged with a total of nine counts under this section, five against Schifreen and four against Gold. They were convicted at trial in 1986 at Southwark Crown Court on all counts, in six cases on majority verdicts. Gold was fined £600 and Schifreen was fined £750, with costs of £1,000 each. They appealed and their convictions were overturned by the Court of Appeal in the summer of 1987. On appeal Lord Lane CJ said that to secure a conviction the prosecution had to prove that the defendants had 'made a false instrument', and the prosecution had focused on the idea that the user segment of the computer received the password entered by the defendants and retained it for a brief period required to verify it against user files held in the computer memory. For that brief moment, it was said, the user segment became a false instrument made by the defendants. The argument was rejected by the Court of Appeal on the basis that the Act was not designed to deal with a situation where information was held fleetingly and then expunged. Such a process was not one to which the words 'recorded or stored' in section 8(1)(d) could properly be applied.

A further appeal by the prosecution was heard by the House of Lords in April 1988, nearly two years after the original trial. At the time there was genuine uncertainty among commentators over which way the House would rule on the case. The Law Commission called a pause in its work on computer misuse to see how matters would pan out. It was thought by some that, if the House upheld the conviction, this would clearly demonstrate that existing criminal laws, with a little creative interpretation, could be used effectively in new circumstances. There were other examples to show that the House could change the law to fit novel circumstances.[12] In the event, however, the House agreed with the Court of Appeal that the prosecution had been an ill-judged attempt to force the facts of the case into the language of an Act not designed to fit them. Lord Brandon noted that the hackers had intended to demonstrate their skill rather than to gain any benefit, and also said that it had not occurred to the defendants that their actions were capable of being offences under the Act. The last point is strictly irrelevant, since the defendant's failure to appreciate the illegality of his act cannot normally amount to a criminal law defence.

The various published commentaries on the case are illustrative of the division of views about the eventual outcome of the case. One of the leading commentators on computer law, Professor Tapper, was a stern critic of the decision, arguing that the House of Lords should have been prepared to extend the meaning of words in the 1981 statute to meet the challenge of developing technology (Tapper 1989: 292). On the other hand, Professor Smith was against the criminal law being developed in such a piecemeal way, and said that extension of the law must be for Parliament, and not for the judges (Smith 1987). After the dismissal of the prosecution appeal the Home Office said that it was awaiting the outcome of the Law Commission's Report before making a decision on whether legislation was needed and, if so, what form it should take. The Law Commission itself had interrupted its work on the computer misuse project to see what the House of Lords would decide. Once the House dismissed the appeal, the pressure was on to produce firm proposals to fill the gaps.

Comparative surveys

The 1980s were a time for serious researchers to start to take stock of developments across different jurisdictions. Mention has already been made of the computer crime statutes rushed into law in the United States in the early 1980s.[13] The two main federal statutes were the Counterfeit Access Device and Computer Fraud and Abuse Act 1984, which criminalised unauthorised computer access, obtaining private financial information, and abusing federal government computers (see Tompkins and Mar 1985), and the less well known Small Business Computer Security and Education Act of the same year, which set up schemes to provide small businesses with information about management of computer technology, computer crime and security. The first state to enact computer crime legislation was Florida, followed by California and then a flood of others. By the mid 1980s 'about thirty states ha[d] enacted a quite comprehensive computer crimes or computer frauds statute that embraces most if not all of the activities which have become a cause for concern ...' (George 1985: 402). In general terms, such statutes followed a similar pattern, seeking first to define terms such as 'computer', 'computer program', 'computer software', 'data', and so on, then to criminalise 'computer trespass' or unauthorised access to a computer, an offence attracting higher penalties where there was a proven intent to defraud, steal, cause damage, or plant misleading information. Some though not all state legislation extended further, to denial of access attacks, to extortion, or to physical injury consequent upon invasion of a computer system, and even occasionally (though a clear duplication of earlier law) to theft of computers, peripherals and software.

In Europe important comparative surveys were published by the Organisation for Economic Co-operation and Development (OECD 1986), and by Ulrich Sieber for the Council of Europe, published from 1980 onwards, but especially his *International Handbook* (Sieber 1986) and *Information Technology Crime* (Sieber 1994). The 1986 work provides a comprehensive account of

European development in the threat and legal response to computer misuse during the time period with which we are concerned. His categorisation of 'the phenomena of computer crime' was three-fold: Part A: *Computer-related Economic Crimes*, comprising (i) fraud by computer manipulation, (ii) computer espionage and software piracy, (iii) computer sabotage, (iv) theft of services, and (v) unauthorised access and hacking; Part B: *Computer-related Infringements of Privacy*, comprising (i) incorrect use of data, including manipulation and erasure by unauthorised persons, (ii) illegal collection and storage of data, (iii) illegal disclosure and misuse of data, (iv) infringement of privacy laws; and a more tentative Part C: *Further Abuses*, comprising (i) offences against state and political interests and (ii) extension of offences against personal integrity. These various subheadings are explored in detail in Sieber's book, which also contains chapters on computer security measures and the emergent difficulties in effective prosecution of computer crime. The issues contained within Part B were, for the most part, the province of developing data protection laws, which were regulatory in scope and style, with criminal sanctions (essentially fines) being reserved for commercial-scale infringement or persistent breach of the rules. The issues mentioned in Part A are described by Sieber as 'the main field of computer crime today' (Sieber 1986: 3). It will be seen that the focus is on computer misuse as an *economic crime*, reflecting the fact that, during the 1980s, the main concern was the exposure of business, commerce and government to fraud via computer misuse. In contrast to the popular image of lone sophisticated hacker, however, Sieber confirmed that most manipulations of computer systems were in fact carried out by employees of victimised companies, and that such perpetrators did not generally have specialist skills, but were taking advantage of basic lapses in security. It is striking that in these compendious works there is no mention of child pornography, a phenomenon that came about only with widespread home access to computers and the development of the Internet.

The Law Commission Report

The first step on the road to legislative reform in this area came with the publication of the Scottish Law Commission's work.[14] Substantial and procedural law in Scotland is different in many respects from the law that pertains in England and Wales. Scots law continues to be based on cases rather than legislation, and the case law provides a greater flexibility for judicial interpretation and development of the law. In the 1980s there was still a clear acceptance of the position that the judges in Scotland could develop the substantive law to meet emergent new threats to public order. This tradition (alongside the availability in Scotland of broadly drawn common law offences such as 'breach of the peace' and 'malicious mischief') provided the background to a working paper that was sceptical of the need for any change at all to meet the challenges to criminal law presented by new technologies.

The English Law Commission, meanwhile, was working on its own proposals, and a Working Paper was issued for consultation in 1988, followed by their Report in October 1989. The Working Paper[15] took a similar line to the Scottish body, in that it regarded existing criminal offences for the most part as suitable to deal with computer misuse. Although the Scottish Report did propose a new hacking offence, at least where there was a proved nefarious intent, the Law Commission said in its Consultation Paper that it had 'not yet even reached any provisional conclusion' on that matter.[16] There are clear differences between the Law Commission's consultation document and its Report. Following the crucial decision in *Gold and Schifreen*, it proposed the creation of three new offences to cater for specific aspects of computer misuse. The Commission obviously had second thoughts, following the responses to its Working Paper, and after taking soundings from computer and software manufacturers, computer users in commerce, industry and the banking and financial sectors.[17] An 'impressive majority' of the more than one hundred respondents to the Working Paper had argued for the introduction of a hacking offence.[18] Although the Commission wrote its Report five years or more before the development of the Internet, it had been made aware by its advisors of the increasing risks of 'online' offending. It was now persuaded on the evidence 'that hacking by unauthorised entry or attempted entry is sufficiently widespread to be a matter of major and legitimate concern'.[19] The Commission now thought that it was worth taking steps to legislate to deal with the problem of 'deceiving a machine', but by amending the Theft Acts rather than by creating a separate offence.[20] Finally, the Commission accepted that the existing authorities on the offence of criminal damage 'cannot be relied on with sufficient confidence' to rule out the need for a new offence of unauthorised destruction or alteration of data or programs held in a computer.[21] The Commission went for a pair of tiered offences to cater for unauthorised access, a 'basic' offence, and an offence requiring proof of an ulterior intent, which would attract a higher penalty. Use of a computer for an unauthorised purpose was, however, best seen as an internal disciplinary matter and should not, therefore, be criminalised.

The Commission was, after the House of Lords' decision, under time pressure from government to produce the report, with a view to legislation being introduced in the next parliamentary session. For that reason the Commission chose to save time by attaching no draft bill to its report. Such are the vagaries of the legislative process, however, that a change of personnel following a government reshuffle meant that computer misuse was dropped from the timetable. No mention was made of it in the Queen's speech in November 1989. Its omission attracted almost as much media interest as some of the measures actually included. It later emerged that government support was to be given to a Private Member's Bill sponsored by Michael Colvin MP, the terms of which were closely in accord with the Law Commission's proposals. Another Private Member's Bill had been sponsored[22] by Emma Nicholson MP in April 1989, but was withdrawn when the government promised support for Mr Colvin's Bill. Private Member's Bills rarely become law, but this one received a swift and favourable passage through Parliament in spring 1990, and came into force, somewhat amended, on 29 August 1990.

The Computer Misuse Act 1990

The Act[23] gave effect, with some modifications, to the changes to the substantive law recommended by the English Law Commission in Law Com. No. 186. It also incorporated jurisdictional changes that were in line with those drawn up by the Commission in a separate report on fraud offences.[24]

Section 1 of the Act provided[25] that:

(1) A person is guilty of an offence if –
    (a) he causes a computer to perform any function with intent to secure access to any program or data held in any computer, or to enable any such access to be secured;
    (b) the access he intends to secure is unauthorised; and
    (c) he knows at the time when he causes the computer to perform the function that that is the case.

(2) The intent that a person has to have to commit an offence under this section need not be directed at
    (a) any particular program or data;
    (b) a program or data of any particular kind; or
    (c) a program or data held in any particular computer.

The section created a summary offence – that is, one that could be tried only in a magistrates' court. The maximum penalty, therefore, was one of six months' imprisonment, a fine not exceeding level 5 (£5,000), or both. The Law Commission's intention was that the basic hacking offence should carry a 'comparatively moderate penalty',[26] with more serious offences where an ulterior intent could be proved attracting a higher tariff. A number of implications follow from the offence being summary only. The first is that, normally, summary offences must be prosecuted within six months of the offence being committed.[27] There is special provision in section 11 of the Act, which allows a prosecution to be brought within six months of the date on which there was sufficient evidence before a prosecutor to warrant proceedings being taken.[28] In any event, no prosecution can be brought more than 3 years after commission of the offence.[29] A second implication of this being a summary offence is that there can in law be no charge in respect of an attempt to commit it.

The conduct prohibited by the section is to 'cause a computer to perform any function'. This is meant to exclude mere physical contact with a computer[30] and the scrutiny of data displayed on the screen. Reading confidential information so displayed, or more sophisticated forms of electronic 'computer eavesdropping' do not fall within the section.[31] The Law Commission was not persuaded that computer eavesdropping was a significant problem, although it was accepted that the technical position might change in the future and the matter should be kept under review. On the other hand the section does not require that the defendant should succeed in, or complete, the unauthorised access. An attempt to do so, which was thwarted by computer security measures in place, would still amount to the *actus reus* of the offence.[32] The offence is deliberately drafted so as to include such conduct, which might normally be said to fall within the scope of an attempted crime.[33] The broad drafting, therefore, largely compensates for the inability of the prosecution to charge an attempt. It is perfectly clear from the words 'any computer' in section 1(1) that the offence is not restricted to a case in which the defendant has used one computer to gain unauthorised access remotely to another computer. Direct access by the defendant to the target computer is also covered. This was also clearly the intention of the Law Commission: 'It is in our view important to ensure ... [that the offence] is directed at unauthorised users ... whether outsiders or insiders.'[34] Following a subsequent misapplication of the law, this issue had to be clarified by the Court of Appeal soon after the Act came into force.[35]

The access to the program or data that the defendant intends to secure must be 'unauthorised' access. By section 17(5) of the Act, access is to be regarded as unauthorised if the person making the access 'is not himself entitled to control access of the kind in question to the program or data, and he does not have consent to access by him of the kind in question to the program or data from any person who is so entitled'. As the Law Commission recognised, this is unlikely to be an issue with a remote hacker, but could be more complex where the access is by an insider. The prosecution have to prove that the access was unauthorised, and the Law Commission observed that it was good management practice for there to be clarity within an organisation over which person has authority to control the access which is in issue.[36] During the passage of the Bill through Parliament an amendment was moved which would have restricted the offence to cases in which the defendant had bypassed computer security measures in place. Had no such measures been put in place then the defendant would not be guilty. The amendment was rejected, partly because of the uncertainty of what might be needed to constitute 'security measures', and partly because the criminal law does not normally provide a defence simply because the victim has failed to take proper care of his belongings.

In *DPP* v. *Bignell*,[37] the Divisional Court held that an offence under section 1 of the Act was not committed where police officers, for private purposes, instructed a computer operator to extract details of two cars from a police computer. The Court came to that view because the officers were themselves entitled to access the computer, but only for legitimate police purposes. In the case Astill J said that the Computer Misuse Act was designed to criminalise 'breaking into computer systems', and that such conduct was absent in this case. The judge also noted that such behaviour fell within the Data Protection Act 1984, s.5(2)(b) and should have been prosecuted under that subsection.[38] This decision is regarded by many commentators as incorrect, since on an ordinary construction of language, authorising a person's access for one (legitimate) purpose ought not to be regarded as authorising his access for another (non-legitimate) purpose.[39] The reasoning in *Bignell* is undermined to some extent by a later decision of the House of Lords[40] but even so their Lordships in the latter case thought that the decision in *Bignell* was 'probably right'.

As far as the *mens rea* of the offence under section 1 is concerned, there are two separate aspects. The first feature is the need for the prosecution to prove the 'intent to secure access to any program or data held in any computer'.

The main point here is that 'recklessness' on the part of the defendant is not enough – 'intent' has to be shown. The Law Commission was clear that 'recklessness' should not be enough – the offence should aim to deal with 'deliberate activities' only.[41] Miss Nicholson's Bill, had it become law, would have extended to recklessness as well as intent. The second feature is that the defendant must 'know', at the time he causes the computer to perform the function, that the access he intends to secure is unauthorised.

Section 2 of the Act provided that:

(1) A person is guilty of an offence under this section if he commits an offence under section 1 above ('the unauthorised access offence') with intent –

    (a) to commit an offence to which this section applies; or

    (b) to facilitate the commission of such an offence (whether by himself or by any other person);

and the offence he intends to commit or facilitate is referred to below in this section as the further offence.

(2) [omitted]

(3) It is immaterial for the purposes of this section whether the further offence is to be committed on the same occasion as the unauthorised access offence or on any future occasion.

(4) A person may be guilty of an offence under this section even though the facts are such that the commission of the further offence is impossible.

This section creates an offence that can be tried either in the magistrates' court (maximum penalty six months' imprisonment, a fine not exceeding the statutory maximum, or both) or on indictment in the Crown Court, where the maximum penalty is five years' imprisonment. If a prosecution is brought under section 2 and the prosecution is unable to prove the intention to commit the further offence, a conviction under section 1 is possible. It would seem that this applies even if the prosecution under section 2 was brought outside the time limit applicable to section 1, but if a court was of the view that a prosecution had been brought purely for the purpose of circumventing the time limit, the prosecution would be struck out as an abuse of the process of the court.

The prosecution has to prove the defendant's intention to commit or facilitate the commission of the further offence. It does not have to be proved that the further offence was committed, or even that the defendant came close to committing it. Indeed, even if the offence intended was factually impossible to commit (such as where a targeted bank account actually had no funds in it) the offence under section 2 can be made out. This follows from section 2(4), which incorporates a rule analogous to that in the general law of attempt.[42] The further offence must be an offence punishable with a term of imprisonment of at least five years.[43] The offence can be committed in a wide range of factual situations, the most likely perhaps being the gaining of unauthorised access in order to commit theft or fraud (including the electronic diversion of funds). It would also include the gaining of unauthorised access in order to discover confidential information with which to commit blackmail at some future date, or the unauthorised access to electronic patient records with a view to altering them to put patients at risk of death or physical injury.

Section 3 of the Act provided that:

(1) A person is guilty of an offence if –
    (a) he does any act which causes an unauthorised modification of the contents of any computer; and
    (b) at the time when he does the act he has the requisite intent and the requisite knowledge.

(2) For the purposes of subsection (1)(b) above the requisite intent is an intent to cause a modification of the contents of any computer and by so doing –
    (a) to impair the operation of any computer;
    (b) to prevent or hinder access to any program or data held in any computer; or
    (c) to impair the operation of any such program or the reliability of any such data.

(3) The intent need not be directed at –
    (a) any particular computer;
    (b) any particular program or data or a program or data of any particular kind;
or
    (c) any particular modification or a modification of any particular kind.

(4) For the purposes of subsection (1)(b) above the requisite knowledge is knowledge that any modification he intends to cause is unauthorised.

(5) It is immaterial for the purposes of this section whether an unauthorised modification or any intended effect of it of a kind mentioned in subsection (2) above is, or is intended to be, permanent or merely temporary.

(6) For the purposes of the Criminal Damage Act 1971 a modification of the contents of a computer shall not be regarded as damaging any computer or computer storage medium unless its effect on that computer or computer storage medium impairs its physical condition.

This section creates an offence that can be tried either in the magistrates' court (maximum penalty six months' imprisonment, a fine not exceeding the statutory maximum, or both) or on indictment in the Crown Court, where the maximum penalty is five years' imprisonment.

The section needs to be read in the context of section 17 of the Act (the definitional section) from which it can be seen that a wide range of different forms of conduct is included within its scope. It covers all cases involving deliberate alteration or erasure of any program or data held on a computer (section 17(7)(a)) where the defendant intended thereby to impair a computer's operation, hinder access to computer material by a legitimate user, or impair the operation or reliability of computer-held material, and where he knew that the intended modification was unauthorised. It also clearly extends to a case where the defendant intentionally introduces a computer virus or worm program where such a program uses up all spare capacity thereby impairing its operation. Section 3(6) deals with the relationship between this offence and criminal damage. It is clear that the scope of the 1971 Act in relation to 'computer' cases is confined to circumstances where the physical condition of the computer or computer storage medium has been impaired.[44] The intended effect is that, if the facts of *Cox* v. *Riley* were to recur, the defendant would not now be guilty of criminal damage but would be guilty of the offence under section 3. It might have been better if the 1971 Act had been amended accordingly to make this clear, not least because the 1971 Act offence has a higher maximum penalty.

The passage of the Computer Misuse Act 1990 marked a watershed in this area of legal development. There were several comments in Parliament, during the passage of the Bill, to the effect that the rapid pace of technological change, together with the ingenuity of the criminal, would mean that the Act was likely to be the first, rather than the last, legislative word on the subject. The Law Commission could not have foreseen the pace of technological change over subsequent years. In light of the development of the Internet, the Commission's reliance on unauthorised access to 'the contents of any computer' look rather dated, and redolent of the idea that computer hacking was really just an electronic version of burglary, with trespass followed by theft. There have been relatively few prosecutions under the 1990 Act, and even fewer appellate cases. Occasionally first instance decisions have gone off-track, but these have usually been rectified on appeal. All this can be seen as a mark of success, especially bearing in mind the Law Commission's observation that the main justification in criminalising hacking was to change the climate of opinion, rather than to achieve large numbers of convictions.[45] Despite the misgivings of some, there was no change to the Act for over 10 years. Following reform proposals in 2002 and then 2005 (twice), changes were eventually made to the Act by the Police and Justice Act 2006 (which came into effect in October 2008). The details of these developments lie outside the scope of this chapter.[46] In brief, however, they are two-fold. One aspect relates to concern over the perceived limitation of section 3 of the Act in catering for 'denial of service attacks'.[47] It is worth noting, however, that in the one decided case on this issue under the Act, *DPP* v. *Lennon*,[48] an error in the magistrates' court was successfully appealed, so that the defendant then pleaded guilty. The other aspect relates simply to an increase in maximum penalties under the Act, which is best seen as part of the modern trend for the legislature to increase penalties across the board, rather than as some inherent defect in the Act. In sum, these changes amount to 'tidying up' rather than root and branch reform. It seems likely that the 1990 Act will be with us for some time to come.

Notes

1 See H. Cornwall, *Datatheft* (1987), a popular account of the activities of 'phone phreakers' and hackers.

2 According to Tapper, 'Definitional problems like this are central to the whole debate about "computer crime"' (Tapper 1987: 6).

3 *Talboys, The Times*, 29 May 1986.

4 (1986) 83 Cr App R 54.

5 Precisely what was damaged is a matter of some debate: see Wasik (1986).

6 Law Commission, Working Paper No. 110, *Computer Misuse* (1988), para. 3.68.

7 Scottish Law Commission, Consultative Memorandum No. 68, *Computer Crime* (1986), para. 3.72.

8 See, for example *HMA* v. *Wilson* (1984) SLT 117.

9 (1984) 13 CCC(3d) 430.

10 Some jurisdictions have an offence of 'criminal mischief' to deal with such cases, but the offence tends to be vaguely defined (Wasik 1988).

11 [1988] 2 WLR 984. The account of this case draws upon my earlier work, Wasik (1991: 71 *et seq.*).

12 The classic case is *Shaw* v. *DPP* [1962] AC 220, in which the House of Lords confirmed the existence of a hitherto unknown common law offence, conspiracy to corrupt public morals. See also the later case of *R* v. *R* [1992] 1 AC 599, where the House of Lords effectively abolished a very long-standing exemption, that a man could not be guilty of rape of his wife. This latter case has been described as 'an illegitimate usurpation of legislative powers by the judiciary' (Feldman 2004: paras 25, 105).

13 Valuable summaries include George (1985); Thackeray (1985).

14 Scottish Law Commission (1986) and Scottish Law Commission (1987).

15 Law Commission (1988). For a sceptical commentary see Wasik (1989).

16 para 6.2.

17 N. McEwan (2008), 'The Computer Misuse Act 1990: Lessons from the Past and Predictions for its Future', *Criminal Law Review*, 955: 966, refers to these as 'secret soundings ... not available for wider, public scrutiny', but this seems overstated. The Commission was surely entitled to change its mind, especially following *Gold and Schifreen*.

18 Law Commission, Report No. 186, *Computer Misuse*, Cm 819, 1989, para. 1.9.

19 Law Com. No. 186, para. 1.29.

20 In the event, such legislation did not take place, but the introduction of the Fraud Act 2006 has largely removed the problem.

21 Law Com. No. 186, para. 2.30.

22 See Wasik (1991: App. 2).

23 The relevant Parliamentary Debates can be found at *Hansard* HC vol. 166, cols 1134–84; vol. 171, cols 1287–339 and HL vol. 519, cols 230–47. The Bill was considered in Standing Committee C from 14 March to 28 March 1990.

24 Law Commission, *Jurisdiction over Offences of Fraud and Dishonesty with a Foreign Element* (1989) Law Com. No. 180.

25 It should be noted that this section has been amended by the Police and Justice Act 2006 and the Serious Crime Act 2007.

26 Law Com. No. 186, para. 3.10.

27 Magistrates' Courts Act 1980, s.127.

28 See *Morgans* v. *DPP* [1999] 1 WLR 968.

29 Computer Misuse Act 1990, s.11.

30 Law Com. No. 186, para. 3.23.

31 See Law Com. 186, para. 3.25.
32 This was the Law Commission's intention: see Law Com. No. 186, para. 3.16.
33 Law Com. No. 186, para. 3.19.
34 Law Com. No. 186, para. 3.5.
35 *Attorney General's Reference (No. 1 of 1991)* [1993] QB 94, dealing with the unreported trial of Sean Cropp.
36 Law Com. No. 186, para. 3.37.
37 [1998] 1 Cr App R 1.
38 See now Data Protection Act 1998, s.55 and *Rooney* [2006] EWCA Crim 3525.
39 The burglary case of *Jones* [1976] 1 WLR 672 might provide an analogy, where a householder left the house key with the defendant to keep an eye on the property when they were on holiday, but the defendant used the key to access the property to commit theft.
40 *Bow Street Metropolitan Stipendiary Magistrate,* ex parte *Government of the United States* [2000] 1 Cr App R 61.
41 Law Com. No. 186, para. 3.27.
42 Criminal Attempts Act 1981, s.1(2), as applied in *Shivpuri* [1987] AC 1.
43 Computer Misuse Act 1990, s.2(2).
44 According to Law Com. No. 186, para. 3.78, 'the new offence should deal with all computer interference cases'.
45 Law Com. No. 186, para. 2.23.
46 For discussion see Walden (2007); McEwan (2008).
47 All Party Internet Group Report, *Revision of the Computer Misuse Act*, 2004.
48 [2006] EWHC 1201.

Further reading

This chapter has been concerned with legal developments over a particular time frame. The main publications relevant to that time are Martin Wasik, *Crime and the Computer* (1991) Oxford: Clarendon Press, which provides an overview of change in the UK during the 1980s, leading up to the passage of the Computer Misuse Act 1990; and, for a comparative Europe-wide assessment, see Ulrich Sieber, *The International Handbook on Computer Crime* (1986) John Wiley and Sons. The Law Commission Working Paper No. 110 on *Computer Misuse* (1988) and Report No. 186, on *Computer Misuse* (1989), still repay careful study. The *Computer Law and Security Report* (editor Steven Saxby, of Southampton University) was an important pioneer journal in this field. Of more general popular interest are D.B. Parker, *Crime by Computer* (1976) New York: Scribner; S. Levy, *Hackers: Heroes of the Computer Revolution* (1984) New York: Doubleday; H. Cornwall, *The Hacker's Handbook* (1986) London: Century Hutchinson; and the same author's *Datatheft* (1987) London: Heinemann. Finally, there is the classic account of hacker detection, C. Stoll, *The Cuckoo's Egg* (1990) London: The Bodley Head.

References

American Bar Association Task Force on Computer Crime (1984) *Report on Computer Crime.*
Audit Commission (1987) *Survey of Computer Fraud and Abuse.* London: HMSO.
Audit Commission for Local Authorities in England and Wales (1984) *Survey of Computer Fraud.* London: HMSO.

Audit Inspectorate (1981) *Computer Fraud Survey.* London: Department of the Environment.

Bequai, A. (1987) *Technocrimes.* Lexington, Massachusetts: D.C. Heath.

BloomBecker, J.J. (1985) 'Computer crime update: the view as we exit 1984', *Western New England Law Review*, 7: 627.

BloomBecker, J.J. (1986) *Computer Crime, Computer Security, Computer Ethics.* Los Angeles: National Centre for Computer Crime Data.

British Institute of Management (1988) *Managers and IT Competence.* London: BIM.

Brown, R.A. (1986) 'Computer-related crime under Commonwealth law, and the Draft Federal Criminal Code', *Criminal Law Journal*, 10(377): 386.

Central Statistical Office (1986 and 1989) *Social Trends.* Table 6.14.

Cornwell, H. (1986) *The Hacker's Handbook.* London: Century Hutchinson.

Cornwell, H. (1987) *Datatheft.* London: Heinemann.

Feldman, D. (ed.) (2004) *English Public Law.* Oxford: Oxford University Press.

George, Jr, B.J. (1985) 'Contemporary legislation governing computer crimes', *Criminal Law Bulletin*, 21(5): 389–412.

Ingraham, D. (1980) 'On charging computer crime', *Computer Law Journal*, 2: 429.

Kelman, A. and Sizer, R. (1982) *The Computer in Court.* Aldershot: Gower.

Law Commission (1988) Working Paper No. 110. *Computer Misuse*, para. 3.68.

Law Commission (1989) Report No. 186. *Computer Misuse*, Cm 819, para. 1.9.

McEwan, N. (2008) 'The Computer Misuse Act 1990: Lessons from the Past and Predictions for its Future', *Criminal Law Review*, 955: 966.

Organisation for Economic Co-operation and Development (OECD) (1986) *Computer-related Crime: Analysis of Legal Policy.* Paris: OECD.

Parker, D.B. (1976) *Crime by Computer.* New York: Scribner.

Parker, D.B. (1983) *Fighting Computer Crime.* New York: Scribner.

Parker, D.B. *et al.* (1973) *Computer Abuse.* Stanford: Stanford Research Institute.

Scottish Law Commission (1986) *Computer Crime.* Consultative Memorandum No. 68, para. 3.72.

Scottish Law Commission (1987) *Report on Computer Crime.* Law Commission No. 106.

Shotton, M. (1989) *Computer Addiction: A Study of Computer Dependency.* London: Taylor and Francis.

Sieber, U. (1986) *The International Handbook on Computer Crime.* London: John Wiley and Sons.

Sieber, U. (ed.) (1994) *Information Technology Crime.* Verlag KG: Carl Heymanns.

Smith, T. (1987) 'Computer crime: A reply', *Yearbook of Law, Computers and Technology*, 3: 204.

Taber, J.K. (1979) 'On computer crime', *Computer and Law Journal*, 1: 517.

Taber, J.K. (1980) 'A survey of computer crime studies', *Computer and Law Journal*, 2: 275.

Tapper, C. (1983) *Computer Law* (3rd edn). London: Longman.

Tapper, C. (1987) 'Computer crime: Scotch mist?', *Criminal Law Review*, 4.

Tapper, C. (1989) *Computer Law* (4th edn). London: Longman.

Temby, I. and McElwaine, S. (1987) 'Technocrime: an Australian overview', *Criminal Law Journal*, 11: 245.

Thackeray, G. (1985) 'Computer-related crimes: An outline', *Jurimetrics Journal*, 301–18.

Tompkins, J.R. and Mar, L.A. (1985) 'The 1984 Federal Computer Crime statute: A partial answer to a pervasive problem', *Computer and Law Journal*, 6: 459.

Walden, I. (2007) *Computer Crimes and Digital Investigations.* Oxford: Oxford University Press.

Wasik. M. (1985) 'Surveying computer crime', *Computer Law and Practice*,1: 110.

Wasik, M. (1986) 'Criminal damage and the computerised saw', *New Law Journal*, 136: 763.

Wasik, M. (1988) 'Criminal damage/criminal mischief', *Anglo-American Law Review*, 17: 37.

Wasik, M. (1989) 'Law reform proposals on computer misuse', *Criminal Law Review*, 257.

Wasik, M. (1991) *Crime and the Computer*. Oxford: Clarendon Press.

Williams, F. (1988) 'The information society as a subject of study', in F. Williams (ed.), *Measuring the Information Society*. Newbury Park: Sage Publications.

Wong, K. (1983) *Computer Crime Casebook*. BIS Applied Systems.

Wong, K. and Farquhar, B. (1987) *Computer-related Fraud Casebook*. BIS Applied Systems.

Chapter 20

Recent developments in UK cybercrime law

Lilian Edwards, Judith Rauhofer and Majid Yar

Introduction

This chapter attempts briefly to look at significant recent developments in the legal regulation of cybercrime and cybersecurity in the UK. The UK is, it should be noted, made up of several legal systems (notably the criminal law of England and Wales, Scotland, and Northern Ireland are all very different) and we will for the most part concentrate on the law of England and Wales.

Cybercrime regulation has been a very live issue in recent years in the UK, driven both by the speed of evolution of technologies used to perpetuate crimes, and by the all-absorbing fear of, and attempts to prevent in future, terrorist attacks, post 9/11 in the USA and 7/7 in the UK. The uptake in popular access to broadband, and the declining costs of electronic cross-border communication and transactions, have also facilitated and expanded perpetration of a number of previously 'ordinary' crimes, such as financial fraud, credit card fraud, commercial white-collar crime and ID theft. In this chapter, however, we will focus on only two key issues where the Internet element of the crime has arguably become crucial: control of child pornography and adult obscenity online; and terrorist-related activity online. Another key Internet area where the law has been active in recent years is the extension of the existing hacking laws in the Computer Misuse Act 1990 to cover the attacks on cybersecurity known as 'denial of service' (or Distributed Denial of Service – DDOS – see Chapters 9 and 10 by Furnell and Denning this volume)

Secondly, we also look at key developments in UK regulation of *policing* of crime via interception and retention of electronic communications, which now extends not only to phone and mobile communications, as in the past, but also to email, and may in future extend to logs of web traffic, instant messaging (IM) and even activity on social networking sites such as Facebook. The law in this latter area has been heavily driven not only by UK policymakers, but also by EU law and policy developments; and we refer as appropriate therefore to some EU legal sources. The law is stated as of 1 April 2009.

Pornography and obscenity[1]

Obscenity

In the UK, a considerable amount of laws already existed to deal with obscene material, before the arrival of the Internet. In England and Wales, the main pieces of general obscenity legislation are the Obscene Publications Acts 1959 and 1964, which make it an offence to publish an obscene article, or to have an obscene article for publication for gain.[2] These Acts, it should be noted, did not criminalise the mere private *possession* of obscene material, merely its *distribution*. An 'article' is defined to include matter which may be looked at as well as read, and sound records and any film or other record of a picture or pictures.[3] An article is 'obscene' if its effect is 'such as to tend to deprave and corrupt persons who are likely ... to read, see or hear' it.[4] In practice, ever since the Williams Committee[5] reported on the operation of the Acts in 1976 following the unsuccessful prosecution of the paperback *Inside Linda Lovelace*, the 1959 Act has almost never been used to prosecute books or textual matter. Its substantial use is to restrain the circulation of obscene pictures, films and videos rather than the written word, and more particularly, the circulation of hardcore pornography.[6]

In terms of computer pornography, the 1959 Act was amended by the Criminal Justice and Public Order Act 1994 so that an 'article' included a computer disc, and 'publication' included the electronic transmission of material from one computer to another.[7] Thus the downloading of pornography from the Internet to, say, a laptop, without any physical medium as intermediary such as a disc or a printout is clearly caught. In Scotland, similar prosecutions can be brought under the Civic Government (Sc) Act 1982, s.51, which broadly covers the publication, sale or distribution of 'obscene material', which is defined to include *inter alia* a computer disc and any kind of recording of a visual image.[8] Prosecutions can also be brought in Scotland under certain common law offences.

Child pornography

The 1959 Act embodies the traditional liberal approach that it is acceptable to possess obscene material in *private*, so long as there is no attempt to publish, distribute or show it to others, particularly for gain. However in the case of *child* pornography, which in its nature features images of the criminal sexual abuse of children, Parliament has taken the view since 1988 that the phenomenon is so heinous that possession *as well as* circulation should be criminalised. Indeed child pornography has become such a key problem that a special body, the Child Exploitation and Online Protection Centre has been created to lead law enforcement efforts in this area.[9] The primary Acts here are the Protection of Children Act 1978 (POCA) (which does not apply in Scotland or Northern Ireland), and more recently, the Criminal Justice Act 1988 (CJA 1988 – which in various provisions has effect throughout the UK),[10] the latter of which makes it an offence for a person to have any indecent photograph of a child in his *possession*,[11] on top of the pre-existing offences of taking, distributing, showing or publishing such a photograph.[12] A child is defined as a person under 18.[13] The Protection of Children Act was also amended to encompass new technologies of digital manipulation in 1994 so that a new offence was added of 'making' an indecent photograph or 'pseudo-photograph' (discussed further below).

In 1995, the UK police used these new possession offences to organise their first major crackdown on international Internet paedophile rings, in an operation known as Operation Starburst. Nine UK men were arrested (alongside numerous foreign nationals abroad) and at least two convicted of possession offences under s.160 of the 1988 Act. Subsequent operations have followed, such as Operation Cathedral in 1998, which resulted in nine people being charged with various offences[14] and Operation Ore, a huge international operation carried out alongside the FBI from 2003 on, which involved the investigation of around 6,500 British suspects. As of June 2005 it was reported that the investigation had thus far resulted in 1,670 prosecutions, 1,451 convictions and 500 cautions. Akdeniz (2007) notes that this was the biggest Internet child pornography operation of recent times, producing a huge spike in the UK statistics.[15]

Adaptability of existing legislation to the Internet: pseudo-photographs and 'making'

Questions have arisen however as to whether these existing rules are sufficiently flexible when applied to the novel environment of the Internet and electronic publishing. A good recent example of the problems that can arise can be taken from English case law relating to the Protection of Children Act 1978. In R v. *Fellows and Arnold*[16] the Court of Appeal had to consider whether the Act applied in a case involving the use of a computer by two paedophiles. Images of child pornography were maintained on an electronic database and access was allowed to other paedophiles by issue of a password that allowed the images to be viewed and downloaded. The main issue for the court was whether the images stored in the computer memory could be defined as 'photographs' in terms of the 1978 Act. At the time of the alleged offences, the Act merely defined a photograph as 'including' an indecent film, a copy of an indecent photograph or film and an indecent photograph comprised in a film.[17] The photos in this case had never been printed out by the accused, but merely stored on the computer hard disc and shown on the monitor screen, and similarly made available to others. Taking a purposive approach to the statute, the court found that a visual image stored electronically on disc was not a photograph itself, but *was* a 'copy of a photograph', which fell within the definition quoted above. Furthermore, the court went on to find that knowingly holding such images on computer disc where they could be found and accessed by others, had elements of 'active participation' such that the offence of distributing or showing such photographs to others could be held to have been committed by the maintainers of the database.

The 1978 Act was in fact amended subsequent to the events of the *Fellows* case by the Criminal Justice and Public Order Act 1994, which extended the definition of a 'photograph' to include 'pseudo-photographs' which are defined as any 'image, whether made by computer graphics or otherwise howsoever, which appears to be a photograph'.[18] As we shall see below, the concept of a criminally indecent image may yet be extended further.

Possession, caching and mens rea

In *Atkins* v. *DPP; Goodland* v. *DPP*,[19] the Queens Bench Division found themselves asked to consider two interesting questions relating to Internet pornography. First, did having indecent photographs stored on the *cache* of a computer system belonging to a certain person constitute 'possession' by that person for the purpose of s.160(1) of the Criminal Justice Act 1988? And secondly, did the downloading (saving) of indecent photographs to a particular *drive* on that computer system, from the Internet, constitute the separate offence of the 'making'[20] of an indecent photograph under s.1(1) of the Protection of Children Act? The Queen's Bench found on appeal that possession was not an offence of strict liability; rather it did involve the need for some kind of knowledge of the existence and effect of the cache. '[T]here was no intention to criminalize unknowing possession of photographs.' Thus a person who knows that computers are usually set up to automatically cache images browsed, may reasonably expect consequences if he looks at indecent photos on the Net; whereas a person who knows nothing of caches or that his computer has one, will not. Accordingly in this case the possession offence was struck down.[21]

In contrast however, the Queen's Bench found that the accused *had* 'made' indecent photos by saving images *deliberately* to a particular drive of the computer. The natural and ordinary meaning of the word 'to make' was 'to cause to exist; to produce by action, to bring about'; so this was sufficient to include both the saving and the printing off of an image from the Internet. However, the court emphasised that if an image was automatically and inadvertently saved to a cache, this would not be 'making', since it, along with other offences under s.1(1) of the 1978 Act such as taking or permitting to be taken an indecent photo of a child, were serious offences (commanding higher sentences than mere possession) which could not be committed unintentionally. Similarly it has been agreed that if someone opens an attachment not knowing it contains an image of child abuse, then there is no *mens rea* for either a possession or 'making' offence.[22] There is also no liability where an attachment containing illegal images is sent unsolicited to a party so long as having opened it they do not retain it for longer than a reasonable time.[23]

Deleted images and legitimate reason defence

A key problem for investigations is that a person knowingly in possession of illegal images of child abuse is very likely to delete them from his hard disc before the police get there if he possibly can. Can an offence of 'possession' then still be charged? The matter is complicated by the fact that modern forensics can frequently retrieve deleted images, to a greater or lesser extent, even where an 'ordinary' non-expert user could not himself still gain access. Are these retrieved images still in 'possession'? In the Court of Appeal case of *Porter*,[24] the court held that possession in the context of photographs referred to a defendant's 'control or custody' of the images. If images had been deleted, then possession would depend on whether the accused had the specialist knowledge and software to be able to retrieve them; that is, it was a question of fact whether he had actual control over them. This is apparently a subjective test, not a question of what knowledge or facilities the reasonable man (or the reasonable pornographer?) would have.[25] In this particular case, Porter's appeal was successful.

A final and rather desperate defence open to the accused pornographer is to plead that they had a legitimate reason for having the images in their possession.[26] While the courts are likely to be sceptical of such claims,[27] they can exceptionally succeed.[28]

How far do you go?

When the Internet was first born, many cyber 'libertarians' alleged that it was a place beyond ordinary territorial laws, where norms such as free speech, beloved of 'netizens', took clear precedence over national laws imposing censorship. A decade and more since the Internet opened up to ordinary domestic use, the issue now is perhaps how many *more* restrictions on content can be imposed on Internet content, which would be regarded as contravening civil liberties if applied to traditional media like newspapers and TV. Four recent developments show how, in the UK at least, it is increasingly easy to justify measures against the Internet, given the 'moral panic' it arouses, which may nonetheless not be consistent with our past stance on freedom of expression in the media.

Extreme pornography[29]

As noted above, the classic liberal position on pornographic and obscene material has been that it is legitimate to possess such materials for one's own private use, but not to distribute or sell them where they may harm or offend others. Child pornography is acknowledged to represent a different class of threat since its very existence means (bar the issue of 'virtual' porn) that a criminal offence has already been perpetrated, as children cannot legally give consent to sexual activity.

In 2006,[30] however, the UK government pushed this bright line further by consulting on the prohibition of what is grouped together as 'extreme pornography'; images depicting material which is 'extremely offensive to the vast majority of people and [...] should have no place in our society'.[31] Although some of this material will, like child porn, intrinsically involve illegal acts, e.g. genuine 'snuff' movies, some will not (e.g. simulated snuff movies). A further motivation for introduction of a possession offence is apparent in Home Office statements, namely that these images are so appalling they should simply not be allowed to be owned in our society, as well as circulated. Since distributors and publishers will usually be based abroad, possession offences are arguably the only way to clamp down on circulation in the UK. The proposals, now enshrined in the Criminal Justice and Immigration Act 2008, ss 63–67, thus represent a considerable conservative shift in UK policy on censorship.

Under the 2008 rules, it is an offence to be in possession of an 'extreme pornographic image'.[32] 'Pornographic' means that the image must reasonably have been assumed to have been produced solely or principally for the purpose of sexual arousal.[33] An image includes a still or moving image, and also data that is capable of conversion into an image.[34]

'Extreme' means that an image[35]

(a) Portrays in an explicit and realistic way an act threatening a person's life or resulting in serious injury to the anus, breast or genitals ('snuff' or violent sexual porn); or an act involving sexual intercourse with a human corpse (necrophiliac porn); or sex with an animal (bestial porn); and

(b) The image is also grossly offensive, disgusting or otherwise of an obscene character.

In relation to (a), a reasonable person must think the person or animal was real. So in the example above of a simulated snuff movie, unless the reasonable person would think it was a genuine snuff movie – that is, that a real woman was actually killed – it would not qualify as 'extreme porn'. This provides a defence for ordinary entertainment films (and animations, and games) that commonly depict simulated killings and violence. As with possession of child porn, defences do exist for the accused who unknowingly comes into possession of extreme porn.[36] (Note however that everyone is presumed to know the *law*.) A defence is also available where the 'extreme image' depicts what is in reality consensual sexual behaviour, and the act is one to which consent can be given (e.g. not underage sex).[37] This should protect those making 'home tapes' of their own bondage or 'S and M' activities, as evidence of consent should be readily available from the involved parties. Penalties of up to three years' imprisonment can be imposed if a prosecution is successful.[38]

Are the new rules objectionable in a free speech society, as the likes of Amnesty International, Justice and Backlash have argued? Most ordinary folk, to be honest, probably welcome these rules unreservedly. Government advocates have pointed out that the Internet has provided easy distribution to children and adults alike of material which would never have 'cleared customs' in the past or even been made available via licensed sex shops and therefore exceptional laws are necessary. More worryingly perhaps, several tabloids have pursued the line that laws are required because real-world crimes can be inspired by consumption of extreme Internet content. The UK law itself is well known to have been inspired by the 2003 rape and murder of Jane Longhurst, whose killer was reportedly surfing the web for necrophiliac and similar sex images hours before the murder. There is no real empirical proof, though, that Internet violence generally inspires real life violence, and the argument that what you read or see directly inspires criminal behaviour has on the whole been regarded as 'not proven' for decades in UK censorship of 'offline' materials.[39]

Cartoon or computer-generated pornography

The free speech arguments may seem abstract and pious when compared to the reality reported by hardened police officers of video streaming unstoppably into the UK from abroad via P2P (peer-to-peer communication) and IM servers, depicting (in reality or simulation) the rape and murder of women for male sexual gratification. Few would argue that stopping distribution of such material is not a good thing. On the other hand it might be said that we have already slid a yard or two down that much-predicted slippery slope since the extreme porn law was passed in 2008.[40] The government's latest proposal, announced in 2007, is that possession of drawings and computer-generated images of child sexual abuse should be criminalised.[41]

These proposals seem partly inspired by claims that paedophiles are circumventing the law by using computer technology to manipulate real photos or videos of abuse into drawings or cartoons, and partly by fears of the rising popularity of Japanese *manga* and *anime* type cartoons and films which often depict extreme sex and violence, and perhaps crucially, also often involve young women of indeterminate age, for example dressed in school uniform, and with few signs of post-pubescence. In either case, it is quite possible that the law already allows many such materials to be deemed criminal images of child abuse (see discussion of 'pseudo-photographs' in *Fellows and Arnold* and the subsequent legislation, above)[42] and that adequate distribution (if not possession) laws already exist. Questions must then arise as to whether yet more laws serve more than a PR function. Advocates of the new laws will, however, respond that 'virtual' porn feeds a criminal need for child pornography which may lead on to actual abuse, even if no actual children are harmed in the making of the materials; and that circulation of such materials implies a general societal acceptability of such images which must be contradicted.

Alternately, if these laws do truly set out to create a new domain of content illegal to possess, does it encroach beyond images into the hitherto largely untouched world of text? Cartoons after all contain words as well as pictures, and comic books regularly win literary awards these days as well as being 'for kids'. If manga are criminalised today, will ultraviolent but artistically well-regarded graphic novels such as Frank Miller's *Sin City* be next? It is interesting to contrast the US position, where the Supreme Court specifically ruled some while back that rules prohibiting computer-generated or 'virtual' pornography were impermissibly wide according to the First Amendment.[43] Given the above, the overall trajectory seems to be away from a clear bright line that only Internet child porn should be illegal to possess, towards an approach that 'unwelcome' material previously tolerated as legal in a liberal society so long as used in private, should also be criminalised in the name of the children. See, for example, hints in the recent Byron Review, commissioned by the government as a high-profile examination of the safety of children online[44] that a more interventionist approach may yet be necessary.

Grooming and moderation

An increasing worry in recent years for law enforcement agencies has been 'cyber-solicitation' or 'grooming': i.e. the use of Internet chat rooms and social networking sites such as Facebook and Bebo by paedophiles, to lure children into a relationship which may progress to extensive correspondence and the creation of trust, meetings in person, cyber-sex and actual sexual abuse. The Sexual Offences Act 2003 thus created a number of new offences designed to cover this lacuna, including arranging or facilitating the commission of a child sex offence (s.15) and meeting a child following sexual grooming (s.17).

Again as with the other new offences described above, although the intent is clearly honourable, questions arise as to whether the new laws exceed the boundaries of civil liberties. Grooming involves in essence meeting a child with the intent to commit a sexual offence; but no such offence might ever in fact be committed. It is conceivable that an *attempted* grooming offence might be charged even where no actual meeting had taken place, so the *actus reus* would simply be online conversations. In the worst-case scenario, the conversations might not even be with a real child but with a police investigator posing as a child.

Finally, as of January 2009, it is illegal to moderate a 'public interactive communication service which is likely to be used wholly or mainly by children' – such as a kids' chat room, or perhaps a service like Bebo – without being vetted as fit to work with children and registered with the Independent Safeguarding Authority.[45]

Filtering, the IWF and enforcement

It is all very well to have a pile of new laws criminalising extreme porn, and in the world of child pornography, to set up new bodies like the Child Exploitation and Online Protection Centre (CEOP) that pledge in a soundbite-friendly way to 'do something about it'. Enforcing national laws remains, however, an extraordinarily difficult matter in a world where illegal content arrives via the Internet, rather than as in the 'old days', via physical borders with their accompanying custom stops and police searches. Add to this the newer developments that illegal content also now arrives via hard-to-detect peer-to-peer communication (P2P), not just the Web, that some P2P content is also encrypted, and that websites hosting child porn are now almost exclusively outside UK jurisdiction[46] and increasingly hard to close down even via international cooperation (for example if hosted in 'law havens' like Russia) and it becomes easy to see why legal enforcement in this area is increasingly focused on persuading ISPs to take on the role of banning access to content labelled illegal in the UK (also known as filtering). Filtering via non-transparent ISP industry cooperation is emerging as a clear goal of the current government (as it also is in Australia[47] and other jurisdictions) and may soon take precedence over old-fashioned law enforcement goals, such as closing down sources of porn at source, or even prosecuting individual users of child porn.

Accordingly, in 2007, the Home Office took the decision that all UK ISPs should operate a filtering 'blacklist' of known child pornography sites, maintained by a quasi-industry, non-governmental body known as the IWF or Internet Watch Foundation. The then Home Office minister Vernon Coaker issued a press release that all UK ISPs were to agree to sign up to the IWF 'blocklist' by the end of 2007, or the government would be forced to legislate. Most fell into line, although a few smaller ISPs (such as well-respected Zen Internet) refused to comply. In 2009, the NSPCC called for these ISPs to come into line, but although no positive response came from the ISPs themselves, in the process it emerged that only around 700,000 UK users had access to a non-filtered Internet, a tiny percentage.[48] Thus without much public debate and no primary or even secondary legislation, the UK has effectively created a powerful and mostly unknown system of covert online censorship, operating without judicial or parliamentary oversight.[49] It is still possible, though, that the government may yet legislate to make the obligation to take the IWF blacklist into 'hard law' and perhaps this would now be for the best, since it might at least bring in a greater degree of transparency and oversight. Civil liberties experts have considerable worries that the IWF blocklist, though well intended, may be used as an infrastructure for covert state or privatised censorship of content *other* than child pornography. This serious concern is discussed in detail by Edwards (2009).

Terrorism and the Internet

Legislative innovation in relation to Internet terrorism is nowadays associated with reactive measures instituted in the wake of the September 11 attacks in New York and Washington, and the 7 July 2005 bombings in London. While there have indeed been concerted post-9/11 and 7/7 efforts to both extend the scope of anti-terrorism legislation, and include Internet-based activities within such legislation, concerns about online terrorist activity in fact pre-date these attacks. As Denning (Chapter 10) notes, the term 'cyber-terrorism' was first coined in the 1980s, and bespoke an increasing awareness of how societal dependence upon networked computer systems created vulnerabilities that could be exploited by those sub-state and non-state actors seeking to use violence in pursuit of political ends. Generally, the conjunction between the 'Internet' and 'terrorism' has been framed in two distinctive ways. Firstly, there is the concern with the ways in which terrorist organisations may use Internet-based communications to support conventional 'terrestrial' operations. Such uses may include utilising electronic communications to coordinate and organise attacks; to disseminate know-how and expertise (for example in relation to bomb-making and other 'tools' of attack); to disseminate propaganda and recruit supporters; to issue threats and warnings that will create public fear and anxiety; and to raise funds and launder money. Secondly, there is the concern with the ways in which 'terrorists' may resort to attacks upon electronic targets, for example through the dissemination of malicious software (such as viruses), denial-of-service attacks, website defacement, or disrupting computer systems that control 'critical infrastructure' such as power, water supply, transport, and emergency services.[50] Both varieties of Internet-related terrorist activity are addressed in UK legislation introduced over the past decade.

Part I, Section 1 of the Terrorism Act 2000 defines terrorism in an extremely broad manner:

> In this Act 'terrorism' means the use or threat of action where –
> (a) the action falls within subsection (2),
> (b) the use or threat is designed to influence the government or to intimidate the public or a section of the public, and
> (c) the use or threat is made for the purpose of advancing a political, religious or ideological cause.

Thus communications with a 'threatening' content, even in the absence of any act of violence, are criminalised under the Act. This includes communications effected via the Internet or other networked electronic communication technologies. The Act further defined terrorism, under subsection (2), as an action that:

> (a) involves serious violence against a person,
> (b) involves serious damage to property,
> (c) endangers a person's life, other than that of the person committing the action,
> (d) creates a serious risk to the health or safety of the public or a section of the public, or
> (e) is designed seriously to interfere with or seriously to disrupt an electronic system.

Thus under (e) we see included under the definition of terrorism acts that disrupt the operation of the Internet and sites or services made available through it.

Offences relevant to Internet-based activity under the Act include, firstly, inviting support for a proscribed organisation (Part II, Section 12); the possession or solicitation of money or property that is used, or may be reasonably suspected to be used, for the purposes of terrorism as defined in Part I, Section 1 of the Act (Part III, Sections 15 and 16); collection or making a 'record of information of a kind likely to be useful to a person committing or preparing an act of terrorism', including (most importantly for the present discussion) a 'record' in 'electronic' form (Part VI, Section 58); and inciting 'another person to commit an act of terrorism wholly or partly outside the United Kingdom' (Part VI, Section 59). Under the above provisions, conviction can result in a custodial sentence of up to 10 years.

The provisions of the Terrorism Act 2000 have been successfully used to pursue prosecutions of Internet-based activities. For example, in 2007 three men were found guilty of inciting persons to commit acts of terrorism outside the UK, using the Internet to do so. One of the defendants, Younes Tsouli, hosted an online chat site that all three used to post messages advocating the use of grenades and car bombs to make attacks in the United States. The three were convicted between them to a total of 24 years' imprisonment with Tsouli receiving the maximum available penalty of 10 years.[51] Also in 2007, 23-year-old Samina Malik was found guilty (under Section 58) of possessing materials useful for the commission of terrorism; these included 'The Al-Qaeda Manual' and 'The Mujahideen Poisons Handbook' which she had downloaded from the Internet.[52] However, the conviction was overturned in the court of Appeal in 2008, on the grounds that the jury may have been confused or swayed by documents submitted in evidence that did not in fact relate to the offences under Section 68 with which Malik had been charged.

The Anti-Terrorism, Crime and Security Act of 2001 includes some significant further powers for the investigation of terrorist offences. Most relevant to the present discussion are the provisions of Part II (Sections 102–107). Part II implements some aspects of the European Convention on Cybercrime (see Williams, this volume), making it possible for the state to arrange for the voluntary retention of communications data by service providers (such as ISPs) (which may then be accessed by law enforcement agencies under the RIPA 2000 – see next section). The Terrorism Act of 2006 built further upon the provisions of the 2000 Act. One of the most controversial features of the Act is the prohibition (under Part I, Section 1) of the 'encouragement of terrorism'. 'Encouragement' includes here any statement that:

(a) glorifies the commission or preparation (whether in the past, in the future or generally) of such acts or offences;

Thus a statement need not exhort others to future acts to fall foul of this prohibition, but will also be defined as encouragement if it 'glorifies', celebrates or endorses a past act defined as 'terrorism'. Part I, Section 3 explicitly includes within the scope of the 'encouragement' provisions statements or representation published or circulated via the Internet. An offence under this law is punishable by up to seven years' imprisonment. The ban on 'glorification' has been widely criticised for its potential to erode freedom of expression and the breadth of its definition that could easily include a wide range of fictional or factual portrayals of political action. Particularly worrying here has been the extent to which measures of both the 2000 Act (on 'possession') and 2006 Act (on 'glorification') have created a climate in which panic sets in about potential breaches. One case in point is that of Rizwaan Sabir, a PhD student at Nottingham University, who asked a clerical assistant to download and print an al-Qaeda manual (from the website of the US Department of Justice) that he needed for his research. The university informed the police and Sabir was detained and questioned for seven days,[53] and then released without charge. Commentators, including human rights lawyers, have expressed grave concerns about the university's actions and expressed the view that the legislation has created a climate of fear that encourages unwarranted constraints upon freedom of inquiry.

Interception and retention of electronic communications: the law enforcement perspective[54]

A key shift in the balance between privacy and security is perceived to have taken place since 9/11 and 7/7 'in favour of law enforcement'.[55] Much of the anti-terrorism legislation adopted in the wake of the attacks in the US, London and Madrid relies heavily on surveillance techniques that amount to severe privacy intrusions. At the same time a paradigm shift seems to have taken place in how the state and the public perceive the role of law enforcement agencies (LEAs) and intelligence services. Rather than investigating and prosecuting crimes already committed, LEAs in their new role will focus, rather in the way depicted in the movie *Minority Report*,[56] on the prevention of crimes that may be committed in the future. Easy access to information about all citizens (rather than just those under concrete suspicion) is deemed to be necessary for the 'profiling' and categorising that underpin this preventative approach, and the facilitation of that access constitutes one of the cornerstones of the new policy. Hence since 2000 a series of new laws has been passed by New Labour, often against considerable political, public and non-governmental organisations (NGO) resistance, which have added up to a code of practice for intercepting electronic communications online in real time, and also require telcos and ISPs to retain records of electronic communications so these too can be examined as necessary by LEAs within certain time periods. The process is ongoing and its latest fruit, the government's Interception Modernisation Programme (see below) was only opened up for consultation in April 2009 as this chapter was in progress.

The Regulation of Investigatory Powers Act 2000:

(i) Interception of communications in real time

Part I, Chapter I of RIPA, which deals with the interception of communications, came into force on 2 October 2000.[57] In principle, interception of private communications is illegal. RIPA includes a general offence of unauthorised interception of 'any communication in the course of its transmission' whether by means of, among other things, a public[58] or a private[59] telecommunications system. Interceptions are deemed lawful only where they take place with the consent of both the sender and the recipient of the communication[60] or where they are carried out by the communications service provider for purposes connected with the provision or operation of that service or for the purpose of the provider's compliance with his legal and regulatory obligations.[61]

However, RIPA then goes on to give the government power both to intercept with a warrant issued by the executive *not* the judiciary (cf US control of 'wiretapping' by courts), and demands that ISPs maintain real time interception capability to facilitate this. Interception involves the delivery of the *content* of communications to third parties and should thus be distinguished from retention of 'communications data' – traffic and locational data – discussed below. Overall, the interception provisions contained in Part I, Chapter I, RIPA have been condemned by human rights campaigners, not only for their lack of judicial authorisation or oversight, but also for the expansiveness of the grounds on which a warrant may be based, the lack of protection of legally privileged material,[62] and the broadness of the exceptions to the warrant requirement.[63]

Interception warrants

Section 4, RIPA provides a defence to the section 1 tort of unlawful interception if interceptions are carried out on the basis of a warrant issued by the Secretary of State. The Secretary of State may issue a warrant, if he believes that it is necessary for certain purposes specified in section 5(3) RIPA (the 'RIPA purposes') and that the interception authorised by the warrant is proportionate[64] to its aim.[65] Interceptions under Part I, Chapter I, RIPA are governed by a Code of Practice issued by the Home Office in 2002[66] that provides guidance on the procedures that must be followed before interception of communications can take place under those provisions.

Interception capability

Section 12, RIPA allows the Secretary of State to impose an obligation on public telecommunications providers to maintain an 'interception capability'. This provision was the subject of substantial controversy when the RIP Bill was first discussed as ISPs, in particular, feared that the cost of installing such capabilities (which cost, at the time, they were expected to bear) would stifle development of their fledgling industry. In the face of threats by many of the larger providers that they would move their services to more business friendly jurisdictions, the government eventually agreed to guarantee that providers would receive 'a fair contribution towards the costs incurred'.[67] Bizarrely, intercept evidence may not actually be used in criminal proceedings, mainly to protect the secrecy of the interception process itself.[68]

Oversight

Oversight of RIPA activities is not by the ordinary courts. Instead it falls to a judicially qualified Commissioner and a Tribunal.[69] The Interception of Communications Commissioner is responsible for reviewing the granting and exercise of interception warrants although not all authorisations will be subject to scrutiny. Instead, the Commissioner will randomly select a number of warrants each year and report any errors found in an annual report. Complementing the activities of the Commissioners, Part IV of RIPA establishes the Investigatory Powers Tribunal as a means of receiving complaints under section 7(1)(a) of the Human Rights Act 1998 (HRA) and providing redress to individuals. However, these oversight arrangements provide only a minimal standard of compliance with the requirements of Article 8, European Convention on Human Rights (ECHR), particularly as regards the focus on retrospective review and the lack of independent judicial authorisation of activities. In particular, the requirement – as a condition precedent to the issuance of a warrant – of the 'belief' of the Secretary of State that an interception is necessary, is, in the view of the authors, overly subjective, especially in the light of the constraint – emphasised by the European Court of Human Rights in *Klass* v. *Germany* – that covert surveillance measures should only be permitted to the extent that they are 'strictly necessary for safeguarding the democratic institutions'.[70]

Interception under non-RIPA powers

The scope to avoid RIPA safeguards (such as they are) on uncontrolled interception has also been expanded by a recent High Court decision, *R (on the application of NTL Group Ltd)* v. *Ipswich Crown Court*.[71] In this, the Court confirmed the right of the police to require telecommunications provider NTL to take steps to intercept email not on the basis of a warrant under section 5, RIPA but under wider police powers to obtain evidence in a criminal investigation contained in section 9 of the Police and Criminal Evidence Act 1984 (PACE). The decision has been criticised,[72] however, on the grounds that the carve-out in section 1, RIPA on which the Court relied, specifically refers to 'any stored communication'.

Encryption and access to encrypted information

Even if content is intercepted in real time using RIPA, it will be useless if it is encrypted. Accordingly, s.49(2) in Part III of RIPA grants certain persons listed in Schedule 2 to RIPA the right to serve notice on any person believed, on reasonable grounds, to be in possession of an encryption key, to disclose that key. The key must be capable of decrypting 'protected information' obtained through seizure or interception.[73] The imposition of a disclosure requirement must be necessary in the interests of national security, for the purpose of preventing or detecting crime or in the interests of the economic well-being of the United Kingdom.[74] As with the conditions for obtaining an interception warrant under Part I, Chapter I, RIPA, the imposition of the disclosure requirement must be proportionate to the aim it seeks to achieve and it must not be reasonably practicable to gain access to the protected information in an intelligible form without imposing such a disclosure requirement.

Section 50 deals with the effects of a notice that has been served on a person who is also in possession of the information to be decrypted. In this case, in essence the possessor is given the option of disclosing the encryption key *or* producing decrypted text (thus avoiding possible future compromises of privacy). However, under section 50(3), the person serving the section 49 notice can still request the disclosure of the key, if the notice states that it can only be complied with by the disclosure of the key itself. Section 50 could therefore be said to drive a coach and horses through the safeguards it itself provides for user privacy.[75] That risk has only partially been addressed through the introduction of section 51, RIPA, which provides that only senior officers of the relevant agency have the right to give such a direction under section 50(3) RIPA and for limited purposes.

A person who fails to comply with a section 49 notice is liable to a fine or imprisonment of up to two years.[76] Controversially, section 53(2) includes a reversal of the burden of proof. Where the requester can show that the recipient of the notice was in possession of the requested key at any time before the notice was served, it will be assumed that he is still in possession of that key unless he can prove 'that the key was not in his possession after the giving of the notice and before the time by which he was required to disclose it'.

Although section 53(3) provides that the recipient of a notice shall be taken to have shown that he was not in possession of a key at a particular time 'if sufficient evidence of that fact is adduced to raise an issue with respect to it, and the contrary is not proved beyond a reasonable doubt', it has been argued that this presumption of continued ownership may still be in breach of rights concerning the burden of proof. At the same time, the requirement to disclose a key that may later be used to decrypt information potentially incriminating the key holder may also violate the privilege from self-incrimination under Article 6 ECHR.[77]

Finally, section 54, RIPA imposes an obligation of secrecy on any recipient of a section 49 notice and any person who becomes aware of it or its contents. Failure to comply with this tipping-off ban is an offence carrying a maximum penalty of five years' imprisonment, a sentence somewhat longer than that for failure to comply with a section 49 notice (up to two years' imprisonment).

Retention of data concerning electronic communications

In principle, retention of any data which identifies living persons ('personal data') for any longer than is necessary to fulfil the purposes for which the data was collected, is to be frowned upon and is contrary to accepted principles of data protection and user privacy. This is as true of 'communications data' in RIPA as the content of communications. 'Communications data' – which describes *inter alia* when a communication is made, who the sender and recipient were, duration of communication, where the communicators were when a mobile phone is used, etc. – can be as highly privacy invasive as the actual content of a communication and this should arguably also be deleted as soon as not needed. Furthermore, there is generally no good commercial reason for a telco or ISP to retain data about customer communications after a few months when the chance of complaints about billing or quality of service has passed. Therefore, early deleting of such data was the norm before 2000.

This became a concern to law enforcement, who saw considerable potential utility in being able to search through records of communications to establish for example the network of a suspected terrorist's contacts, or to disprove alibis. Thus in the context of fears about terrorism after 9/11, and under considerable governmental pressure, a voluntary retention period for data was adopted by the ISP and telecommunications industry in the UK under the powers of Part II of the Anti-Terrorism Crime and Securities Act 2001 (ATCSA) in December 2003.[78] It stipulated a voluntary retention period of six months for most Internet and email-related data with the exception of Web server logs (records of what websites and pages had been visited) which needed only to be retained for a maximum of four days.[79] If the voluntary code were to prove ineffective at any time, the Secretary of State had the right to impose mandatory data retention requirements[80] by order.[81]

In fact events took another direction, in the shape of pan-European involvement and the controversial passing of the EC Data Retention Directive in 2006. The Data Retention Directive (DRD) applies throughout the EU and provides for a retention period for data of six months to 24 months,[82] with an option for individual member states to introduce longer periods where they face 'particular circumstances warranting an extension for a limited period'.[83] Retained data will be available for the purposes of the investigation, detection and prosecution of serious crime.[84] The definition of 'serious crime' is left to the national law of the member states. Data required to be retained includes records of communications data relating to fixed-line phone calls, mobile phone calls, texts and emails but not Web server logs as that was felt to be too intrusive.

The UK initially implemented the Directive for fixed-line and mobile telephony services on 1 October 2007, and only adopted rules that included the more difficult case of 'Internet data' – mainly emails and Voice over Internet Protocol (VoIP) telephony – in 2009. After a brief consultation period, a period of 12 months was fixed for retention of all communications data[85] – making the period of retention for data about emails sent and received twice as long as previously under the Voluntary Code. The Data Retention (EC Directive) Regulations 2009 (2009 Regulations), which came into force on 6 April 2009, now contain all the relevant UK rules implementing the DRD. (The Voluntary Code continues to exist though its future is uncertain.)

In the meantime the DRD remains unpopular in many EU nations as an unjustified and disproportionate intrusion into personal privacy, and has already come under legal challenge. In February 2009, the European Court of Justice (ECJ) dismissed[86] an action filed by the Irish government,[87] which had challenged the legal basis for the Directive, arguing that it was a matter relating to criminal justice rather than the internal market. However, a substantive appeal to the ECJ on the grounds that the DRD does not match up to the requirements of Article 8 of the ECHR on the right to private life remains more than likely. What impact a successful challenge to the DRD would have on UK internal implementation would be interesting, given that the UK government has already signalled its plans to go beyond EU requirements in the field of data retention.[88]

Access to data retained under RIPA

Once data is retained about communications, the key question becomes, who can access that data and under what grounds? Since RIPA was ostensibly designed mainly to help LEAs in the fight against crime and terrorism, it might have been thought that only such LEAs would have automatic access to data retained (no judicial or even executive warrants are required in this part of the Act). However, this is not the case. In fact, under section 25(2) of RIPA, a huge array of 'relevant public authorities' have the right to obtain and disclose communications data retained by telcos and ISPs. The list now includes not just the obvious policing authorities and local councils, but also such wide-ranging bodies as the Financial Services Authority, the DTI (now Department for Business, Innovation and Skills (BIS)), the National Health Service, the Department of Health, the Home Office, Local Authorities, the Charity Commission and the Gaming Board for Great Britain – and may yet be expanded further. Restricted access is also provided to certain individuals working for, among others, the Foods Standards Agency, the Environment Agency and the Health and Safety Executive.[89]

Section 22(2) of RIPA lists the *purposes* for which these bodies may validly obtain access to communications data, and they are also considerably wider than just to investigate and prevent serious crime or terrorism. The very wide list of public authorities that were granted access to communications data under s.25 of RIPA, combined with the extensive list of RIPA purposes for which such access may be sought, has prompted claims that this legislation may also not be compatible with the individual's right to privacy under Article 8, ECHR. Certainly, the grounds for *access* set out in s.25 of RIPA are far wider than the grounds for which communications data can be *retained* under the DRD in the first place. Article 1(1) of the DRD clearly states that retained data should only 'be available for the purposes of the investigation, detection and prosecution of serious crime'. By contrast, RIPA powers of access to data have recently been used by local authorities for purposes as trivial as for prosecuting individuals for minor offences such as fly-tipping and dog fouling.[90] An enquiry has now been commenced into whether RIPA powers are being misused.[91] Associated worries are that granting access to such a large list of public bodies means that inevitably unauthorised privacy invasions will occur, as has often been the case in the UK public sector lately.

What next? The Interception Modernisation Programme

In May 2008, the government proposed a 'Bill on communications data retention for the prevention and detection of crime and the protection of national security' as part of its draft legislative programme for 2008/09.[92] The announcement and managed leaks from government sources prompted fears that the intent was to set up a national super-database 'holding details of every phone call, e-mail and time spent on the internet',[93] meaning that rather than individual telcos and ISPs storing their own data and granting access to them to public authorities, they would instead have to hand over that data to the government for it to be stored and accessed centrally. One argument in favour of the plan is that it would make it simpler and swifter for LEAs to retrieve the information instead of having to approach hundreds of different service providers. However, against this, the scope for abuse and data breaches by insecurity or negligence will also undoubtedly be greater if the data is held on one centralised database, particularly in light of the government's less than exemplary record at maintaining the integrity of such databases.[94] Mirroring those fears, the UK Information Commissioner's Office (ICO) issued a statement in response to the Government's plans, in which it expressed its concern:

> If the intention is to bring all mobile and internet records together under one system, this would give us serious concerns and may well be a step too far. We are not aware of any justification for the state to hold every UK citizen's phone and internet records. We have real doubts that

such a measure can be justified, or is proportionate or desirable. Such a measure would require wider public discussion. Proper safeguards would be needed to ensure that the data is only used for the proper purpose of detecting crime.[95]

The ICO pointed out that 'holding large collections of data is always risky'[96] and that 'the more data that is collected and stored, the bigger the problem when the data is lost, traded or stolen'.[97] Rather than creating a new additional system to house all communications data, the ICO offered to advise how existing systems can be improved, should they indeed be found wanting.[98]

In response to the public outcry following its announcement, the government withdrew its plans for a Communications Data Bill. Instead it promised that plans for the storage of and access to retained communications data would be discussed as part of its 'Interception Modernisation Programme' (IMP), a cross-governmental programme designed 'to maintain the UK's lawful intercept and communications data capabilities in the changing communications environment'[99] and to ensure the continued ability of LEAs to intercept and monitor communications in the face of changes in communications technology. The consultation was eventually published on 27 April 2009.[100] Among other things, it includes proposals, previously reiterated by the government,[101] to include new forms of communication, for example social networking sites and instant messaging (IM), which are not covered by the retention requirement under the DRD. Although the government appears to have retrenched – albeit reluctantly – on the question of a central super-database,[102] the consultation does however signal the government's plans still to move ahead with Deep Packet Inspection (DPI), a form of computer network packet filtering that examines the data (content) part of a packet as it passes an inspection point, which may represent a serious change in the accepted balance between citizen privacy and state security.

Conclusions

This chapter has reviewed some of the most significant recent developments in law in England and Wales as it relates to Internet crime. These provisions both create new categories of criminal offence and establish new powers for the police and other responsible agencies for the purposes of investigating and prosecuting online offences. Two main areas of offending have been covered here, namely online obscenity and terrorism-related offences. With respect to obscenity, much of the legislation under consideration has sought to extend provisions of existing obscenity laws to the emergent online environment, including matters such as the storage and transmission of obscene images in electronic form, and the use of Internet forums for 'virtual' child sex abuse and 'grooming'. Specific issues have been raised by, for example, computer-generated images and animated representation of sexual acts involving children. Most recently, and more controversially, measures have been introduced to prohibit possession of 'extreme violent pornography', seemingly inspired by the view that possession and consumption of such images demonstrably inspired actual offences of sexual violence. In the area of terrorist offences, laws have sought not only to extend to the Internet prohibitions on preparing and funding terrorist acts, but have also sought to include within the scope of terrorist activities actions that seek to disrupt the functioning of electronic systems such as the Internet. They have also included within the scope of 'terrorism' various forms of expression that might be deemed to variously 'incite', 'encourage' or 'glorify' terrorism (broadly defined), irrespective of any involvement in the perpetration of actual attacks on persons or property. Such measures have inevitably raised doubts both about the vague framing terms such as 'encourage' and 'glorify', as well as the potential chilling effects on the free expression of political opinion. Finally, we have reviewed the extension of police and investigatory powers with respect to computer and Internet-related crimes. While such provisions are undoubtedly needed so as to enable the investigation and prosecution of computer-related offences, concerns nevertheless remain over the extent of regulatory safeguards and the incremental extension of surveillance over citizens' online activities.

Notes

1 The issues in this section are discussed in greater detail in Edwards (2009).

2 1959 Act, section 2(1) and 1964 Act, s.1(2).

3 1959 Act, section 1(2).

4 1959 Act, s.1(1).

5 Committee on Obscenity and Film Censorship, HMSO, 1979, Cmnd 7772.

6 See Robertson and Nicol (1992: ch. 3). But see prosecution raised of obscene textual story posted online about the pop band Girls Aloud, reported 6 October 2008 – this was the first such prosecution in the UK under the Obscene Publications Act since an unsuccessful case in 1991. However, the case was effectively dropped by the prosecution when it came to trial. See http://www.out-law.com/page-10132

7 See Schedule 9, para. 3.

8 1982 Act, section 51(8).

9 See CEOP website at http://www.ceop.gov.uk/

10 In Scotland, the Criminal Justice Act 1988 inserted a s.52A into the Civic Government (Sc) Act 1982 which provides the simple possession offence for Scotland in s.52A (1). Other offences relating to child pornography are found in s.52 of the 1982 Act.

11 1988 Act, s.160 (England) and 161 (Scotland).

12 Protection of Children Act 1984, s.1.

13 Sexual Offences Act 2003, s.45, amending the POCA 1978, s.7(6).

14 See NCIS report *Project Trawler: Crime on the Information Highways*, June 1999, pp. 16–17. Contact details can be found at http://www.ncis.co.uk

15 See Akdeniz (2007).

16 [1997] 2 All ER 548. See also Cobley (1997).

17 See 1978 Act, s.7(2).

18 1994 Act, s.84(7). The 1994 Act also amended the definition of a photograph in the Civic Government (Sc) Act ss.52 and 52A. Note that despite the apparent width of the definition, it is limited by context – in *Atkins* v. *DPP: Goodland* v. *DPP* (2000) 2 Cr App R 248 (discussed further below) the court held that an

image which obviously consisted of pieces of two photographs physically joined together could not be said to 'appear to be' a photograph, and so did not qualify as a 'pseudo-photograph'.

19 [2000] All ER 425.

20 The offence of 'making' an indecent photograph was added both to the 1978 Act and the equivalent Scottish legislation by the Criminal Justice and Public Order Act 1994, at the same time that the concept of a 'pseudo-photograph' was also introduced to the legislation. The argument that the offence of 'making' was thus referrable *only* to 'pseudo-photographs' and not to other types of indecent photographs was however explicitly rejected in *Atkins*.

21 Similarly in *Collier* [2004] EWCA Crim 1411, it was held that if a man knows he has indecent photos in his possession (in this case on tangible media such as CD-ROMs), but he proves he did *not* know there were indecent sexual images of *children* among them, then again he is not knowingly in possession of child pornography and should be acquitted.

22 *Smith and Jayson* [2002] EWCA Crim 683.

23 See Criminal Justice Act 1988, s.160(2)(c) and discussion in *Humphreys* [2006] EWCA Crim 640; see also discussion in Akdeniz (2007).

24 [2006] EWCA Crim 560.

25 See Akdeniz (2007: 6).

26 See Criminal Justice Act 1988, s.160(2)(a); there is an equivalent defence in Scots law, see the successful plea in *R* v. *Whitelaw*, Paisley Sheriff Court, reported *Scotsman*, 6 February 2003.

27 See *Wrigley*, CA, Case No. 99/01497/Z5, 26 May 2000. The defendant, a graduate of Keele University, claimed he was conducting genuine academic research which required him to pose as a paedophile online; however, the court pointed out that he had not discussed this research with any of his tutors nor had he revealed the items in his possession on his initial arrest.

28 See *Whitelaw*, above.

29 The extreme pornography rules described below apply only in England and Wales. However, Scotland unveiled proposals in September 2008 for an even more stringent regime of their own: see http://www.theregister.co.uk/2008/09/30/scotland_extreme_pr0n_law/

30 Home Office (2006).

31 Statement by Home Office minister Paul Goggins, reported by OUT-Law, 30 August 2005.

32 Criminal Justice and Immigration Act 2008, s.63(1).

33 *Ibid.*, s.63(3).

34 *Ibid.*, s.63(8).

35 *Ibid.*, s.63(6) and (7).

36 CJIA 2008, s.65.

37 *Ibid.*, s.66.

38 *Ibid.*, 67.

39 See the explicit admission in the 2007 consultation on cartoon depictions of child sex (see note 41 below) at para. 72, that there is no known evidence that links fantasy images of child sexual abuse and the commission of offences against children.

40 See *The Register's* comment of 28 May 2008 at http://www.theregister.co.uk/2008/05/28/government_outlaws_pictures/ 'First they came for the child pornographers ... It may not have quite the same resonance as Pastor Niemuller's oft-quoted aphorism. But the reality behind this particular slippery slope is just as sinister.'

41 See Home Office (2007) and Ministry of Justice press release, 28 May 2008. Proposed legislation was introduced in the Coroners and Justice Bill 2009, still in Parliament as of 1 April 2009.

42 See note 16 above.

43 See *Ashcroft* v. *Free Speech Coalition* 534 US 234, 122 S Ct 1389.

44 Byron (2008).

45 See Safeguarding Vulnerable Groups Act 2006, Schedule 3.

46 See Internet Watch Foundation Annual Report (2009), launched April 2009, at p. 7, which reports that although over 25,000 reports of illegal images of child sexual abuse online were received in 2008, fewer than 1 per cent of the domains hosting illegal content were within the UK (and this has been the case since 2003).

47 See Ozimek (2008).

48 See Williams (2009). The article notes that EU supranational legislation might require the government to finally pass hard legislation in this area.

49 See public concerns which were aroused during the 'IWF v. Wikipedia' incident in December 2008: see discussion on Edwards' blog, at http://blogscript.blogspot.com/2008/12/iwf-v-wikipedia-and-rest-of-world.html

50 These variants of Internet-related activity are discussed in detail in Yar (2006: ch. 3).

51 'Men Jailed For Inciting Terrorism on the Internet', at http://www.out-law.com/page-8241

52 'Lyrical Terrorist' found guilty, at http://news.bbc.co.uk/1/hi/uk/7084801.stm

53 Edgar (2008).

54 The issues in this section are discussed in greater detail in Rauhofer (2009a and b).

55 Benjamin (2007).

56 Steven Spielberg (2002).

57 The Regulation of Investigatory Powers Act 2000 (Commencement No. 1 and Transitional Provisions) Order 2000 (SI 2000/2543).

58 S. 1(1)(a) RIPA.

59 S. 1(2) RIPA.

60 S. 3(1) RIPA.

61 S. 3(3) RIPA.

62 See the House of Lords ruling *In Re McE and ors* [2009] UKHL 15 at http://www.bailii.org/uk/cases/UKHL/2009/15.html

63 See, for example, Akdeniz (2000); Crossman *et al.* (2007), the Liberty Report.

64 The proportionality requirement was included in order to make RIPA compliant with the Human Rights Act 1998 (HRA) and in light of the increased relevance of the concept in European Court of Human Rights (ECtHR) case law.

65 S. 5(2)(b) RIPA.

66 The Code of Practice was adopted under s.71 RIPA through The Regulation of Investigatory Powers (Interception of Communications: Code of Practice) Order 2002 (SI 2002/1693).

67 S. 14(1) RIPA.

68 S. 17 RIPA.

69 Ss. 57 and 65 RIPA.

70 [1978] 2 EHRR 214.

71 [2003] QB 131 (QBD (Admin)). This decision has also been confirmed in *R* v. *Allsopp* [2005] EWCA Crim 703, [2005] All ER (D) 310 (Mar).

72 See, for example, Lundie (2003) 'High Court confirms police powers to intercept emails (Case comment)'.

73 S. 49(1) RIPA.

74 S. 49(3) RIPA.
75 S. 10 ECB.
76 S. 53(5) RIPA.
77 See, for example, Akdeniz (2000: 87).
78 The Retention of Communications Data (Code of Practice Order 2003 (SI 2003/3175)).
79 See Annex A of the Code.
80 S. 104(1) ATCSA.
81 S. 104(8) ATCSA.
82 Article 6 Data Retention Directive.
83 Article 12(1) Data Retention Directive.
84 Article 1(1) Data Retention Directive.
85 Regulation 5, 2009 Regulations.
86 *Ireland* v. *European Parliament and Council of the European Union*, Case C-301/06, 10 February 2009.
87 Action brought on 6 July 2006 – *Ireland* v. *Council of the European Union*, European Parliament (Case C-301/06), OJ C 237/5.
88 See discussion of the Intercept Modernisation Programme, below.
89 In July 2006, the Home Office added even more public authorities to the list through the Regulation of Investigatory Powers (Communications Data) (Additional Functions and Amendment) Order 2006 (2006 Order), SI 2006/1878.
90 See, for example, BBC News Online, 'Spy law "used in dog fouling war"', 27 April 2008, available at http://news.bbc.co.uk/1/hi/uk/7369543.stm
91 The Home Secretary announced plans to publish a consultation early in 2009 on a number of proposed changes to RIPA, including 'revisions to the codes of practice that come under the Act; which public authorities can use RIPA powers; raising the bar for how those powers are authorised, and who authorises their use': see Home Secretary's speech: 'Protecting rights, protecting society', available at http://press.homeoffice.gov.uk/Speeches/home-wsec-protecting-rights (last accessed 20 July 2009).
92 'Preparing Britain for the Future: The Government's Draft Legislative Programme 2008/09', Cm 7372, May 2008, available at http://www.official-documents.gov.uk/document/cm73/7372/7372.pdf (last accessed on 15 July 2008).
93 '"Big Brother" database for phones and e-mails', *Times Online*, 20 May 2008, available at http://business.timesonline.co.uk/tol/business/industry_sectors/telecoms/article3965033.ece (last accessed on 15 July 2008).
94 For a more detailed description of recent scandals involving the handling of personal data by government agencies see, Edwards (2009: ch. 14).
95 Statement by Jonathan Bamford, Assistant Information Commissioner, on the proposed Government database, 19 May 2008, available at http://www.ico.gov.uk/upload/documents/pressreleases/2008/proposed_government_database.pdf (last accessed on 15 July 2008).
96 *Ibid.*
97 *Ibid.*
98 *Ibid.*
99 Written answer submitted to the Earl of Northesk by Lord West of Spithead, the Parliamentary Under-Secretary (Security and Counter-terrorism), Home Office on 8 July 2008.
100 Available at
http://www.homeoffice.gov.uk/documents/cons-2009-communications-data
101 Meeting of the Fourth Delegated Legislation Committee, Hansard, Monday 16 March 2009, available at http://www.publications.parliament.uk/pa/cm/

cmtoday/cmstand/output/deleg/dg04090316-01.htm (last accessed on 1 April 2009).

102 See pp. 4 and 25 of the Consultation Paper, note 100 above.

Further reading

Up-to-date coverage of many of the important recent developments in Internet law can be found in Lilian Edwards and Charlotte Waelde's (2009) *Law and the Internet* (3rd edn), Oxford: Hart Publishing. Issues relating to the legal prohibition of child pornography are given a detailed treatment in Ethel Quayle and Max Taylor's (2003) *Child Pornography: An Internet Crime*, London: Routledge, in Quayle's chapter in this volume, and in Suzanne Ost's (2009) *Child Pornography and Sexual Grooming: Legal and Societal Responses*, Cambridge: Cambridge University Press. For more on 'cyber-terrorism', see the contrasting perspectives offered by Dorothy Denning and Maggie Wykes in their respective contributions to this Handbook, and also Majid Yar's *Cybercrime and Society* (2006), Sage Publications. Issues relating to data interception, policing and surveillance are further explored in contributions by both McGuire and Walden in the present volume.

References

Akdeniz, Y. (2000) 'Regulation of Investigatory Powers Act 2000: Part 1: BigBrother. gov.uk: state surveillance in the age of information and rights', *Criminal Law Review*, 73: 79.

Akdeniz, Y. (2007) 'Possession and dispossession: a critical assessment of defences in possession of indecent photographs of children cases', *Criminal Law Review*, 274.

Benjamin, V.O. (2007) 'Interceptions of Internet communications and the right to privacy: an evaluation of some provisions of the Regulation of Investigatory Powers Act against the jurisprudence of the European Court of Human Rights', *European Human Rights Law Review*, 6: 637.

Byron, T. (2008) *Safer Children in a Digital World: the Report of the Byron Review*. London: the Home Office.

Cobley, (1997) 'Child Pornography on the Internet', 2 Communications Law 30.

Crossman, G., Kitchin, H., Kuna, R., Skrein, M. and Russell, J. (2000) 'Overlooked: Surveillance and personal privacy in modern Britain'. Liberty Report, available at http://www.liberty-human-rights.org.uk/issues/3-privacy/pdfs/liberty-privacy-report.pdf (last accessed 20 July 2009).

Edgar, D. (2008) 'This muddled terror law limits free speech and wrecks innocent lives', at http://www.guardian.co.uk/commentisfree/2008/jul/22/terrorism.uksecurity

Edwards, L. (2009) 'Pornography, Censorship and the Internet', in L. Edwards and C. Waelde (eds), *Law and the Internet* (3rd edn). Oxford: Hart Publishing.

Edwards, L. and Waelde, C. (2009) *Law and the Internet* (3rd edn). Oxford: Hart Publishing.

Home Office (2006) *Consultation on the possession of extreme pornographic materials*, available at http://www.homeoffice.gov.uk/documents/cons-extreme-porn-3008051/

Home Office (2007) *Consultation on the possession of non photographic visual depictions of child sexual abuse*, available at http://www.homeoffice.gov.uk/documents/cons-2007-depiction-sex-abuse?view=Binary

Internet Watch Foundation (2009) Annual Report 2008. Available at http://www.iwf. org.uk/documents/20090423iwfar2008pdfversion.pdf

Lundie, A. (2003) 'High Court confirms police powers to intercept emails (Case comment)', 9 (1) *Computer and Telecommunications Law Review*, 10: 11.

NCIS (1999) *Project Trawler: Crime on the Information Highways*, June: pp. 16–17. Available at http://www.ncis.co.uk

Ozimek, J. (2008) 'Is the Internet going down down under?', *The Register*, 5 November, at http://www.theregister.co.uk/2008/11/05/aussie_internet/

Rauhofer, J. (2009a) 'Privacy and surveillance: Legal and Socioeconomic Aspects of State Intrusion into Electronic Communications', in L. Edwards and C. Waelde (eds), *Law and the Internet* (3rd edn). Oxford: Hart Publishing.

Rauhofer, J. (2009b) 'The Retention of Communications Data in Europe and the UK', in L. Edwards and C. Waelde (eds), *Law and the Internet* (3rd edn). Oxford: Hart Publishing.

Robertson and Nicol (1992) *Media Law* (3rd edn). London: Penguin.

Williams, C. (2009) 'UK gov to get power to force ISPs to block porn', *The Register*, 2 April at http://www.theregister.co.uk/2009/04/02/eu_filtering_framework/

Yar, M. (2006) *Cybercrime and Society*. London: Sage Publications.

Chapter 21

Recent developments in US Internet law

Susan W. Brenner

This chapter reviews recent developments in United States law governing the use of the Internet. It focuses exclusively on US federal law for two reasons: one is that it tends to be the most influential in the US and elsewhere; the other is that the Internet law of the 50 US states is too idiosyncratic to cover in a single chapter.

Computer Fraud and Abuse Act

What is now the Computer Fraud and Abuse Act was originally adopted in 1984 as the Counterfeit Access Device and Computer Fraud and Abuse Act of 1984 (Decker 2008). The original Act criminalised a narrow range of activities, such as knowingly accessing a computer without authorisation or by exceeding authorised access in order to obtain federal government information (Decker 2008). It quickly became apparent that the original Act suffered from a number of defects, such as a failure to define essential terms and a failure to encompass computer crime directed at computers other than those used by or on behalf of the federal government (Decker 2008).

In 1986, the Act was revised and renamed the Computer Fraud and Abuse Act (CFAA), codified as 18 US Code s.1030. This revision added definitions of terms used in the statute, restructured the crimes it created and expanded it to include other crimes (Decker 2008). The CFAA was revised four more times between 1986 and 2002 (Ohm 2008).

Perhaps the most important of these revisions came in 1996, when Congress expanded the statute's focus. Until then, the CFAA was directed at criminal activity targeting 'federal interest computers', i.e. computers used by or on behalf of a financial institution or the US government (Decker 2008). The 1996 revision replaced 'federal interest computer' with 'protected computer' (Decker 2008).

Section 1030(e)(2) of the CFAA currently defines a 'protected computer' as a computer that is (i) used exclusively by a financial institution or the federal government; (ii) is used nonexclusively by either if the CFAA violation affects that use; or (iii) is used in interstate or foreign commerce or communication. The latter category includes computers located outside the United States if they are used in a manner that affects interstate or foreign commerce or communication of the United States (United States Department of Justice 2007). The USA Patriot Act of 2001 added this language in order to establish extraterritorial jurisdiction over the s.1030(a) offences. The statute, as amended, can be used to prosecute someone who uses a computer in another country to attack computers in the United States (as long as the attack constitutes a crime under the CFAA) (United States Department of Justice 2007). The CFAA was amended again in 2008: The Identity Theft Enforcement and Restitution Act of 2008 made several important alterations in the statute (Identity Theft 2008). The revisions went into effect on 26 September 2008.

The Identity Theft Enforcement and Restitution Act added a conspiracy provision: Section 1030(b) now makes it a crime to conspire to commit any of the offences created by the CFAA (Identity Theft 2008). Prior to the adoption of this legislation, conspiring to violate the CFAA was prosecuted under 18 US Code s.371, which makes it a crime to conspire to 'commit any offence against the United States, or to defraud the United States' (*United States* v. *Pok Seong Kwong* 2007). Congress apparently believed it was appropriate to give the CFAA its own conspiracy provision. This amendment is not, however, likely to be particularly significant. The only difference between the s.371 conspiracy offence and the new s.1030(b) conspiracy offence is that the former requires the government to prove the defendant or a fellow conspirator committed an overt act in furtherance of the conspiracy, while the latter does not. The requirement of proving an overt act is not, however, particularly onerous, since it does not have to be unlawful in and of itself; prosecutors often rely on relatively trivial conduct to satisfy this requirement (Bierschbach and Stein 2007).

The Identity Theft Enforcement and Restitution Act substantially rewrote the CFAA's extortion provision: 18 US Code s.1030(a)(7). Prior to the revision, s.1030(a)(7) made it a federal crime for someone acting 'with intent to extort from any person any money or other thing of value' to transmit 'in interstate or foreign commerce' a communication containing a 'threat to cause damage to a protected computer' (United States Department of Justice 2007). The gravamen of that crime, therefore, was sending a threat to interfere 'in any way with the normal operation' of a computer or computer system, 'including denying access to authorised users, erasing or corrupting data or programs, slowing down the operation of the computer or system, or encrypting data and demanding money for the decryption key' (United States Department of Justice 2007). The problem was that this provision was too narrow; it did not, for example, encompass threats 'to the business that owns the computer system, such as threats to reveal flaws in the network, or reveal that the network has been hacked' (United States Department of Justice 2007).

A case that illustrated the problems with this version of the statute was Myron Tereshchuk's attempt to extort $17 million from MicroPatent, a company that distributes patent and trademark information (US Department of Justice 2004). According to the indictment, Tereshchuk hacked into MicroPatent's computer network and obtained confidential proprietary information (US Department of Justice (2004). He then used alias email accounts to send the company a series of emails in which he demanded that MicroPatent pay him $17 million or he would release the information publicly (US Department of Justice 2004). In a generic sense, Tereshchuk was clearly engaging in extortion, but the method he used did not fit within the language of s.1030(a)(7) as it existed when he engaged in his extortion attempt.

The revised statute makes it a crime for someone, acting 'with the intent to extort from any person any money or other thing of value,' to transmit a communication in interstate or foreign commerce that contains any of the following: (i) a threat to damage a protected computer; (ii) a threat to obtain information from a protected computer without being authorised to do so or by exceeding one's authorisation to access the computer or a threat to impair the confidentiality of information obtained from a computer 'without authorisation or by exceeding authorised access'; or (iii) a demand or request for 'money or other thing of value in relation to damage to a protected computer' when 'such damage was caused to facilitate the extortion'.

The revised version of s.1030(a)(7) would apparently encompass Tereshchuk's attempt to commit extortion. Section s.1030(a)(7) now encompasses threats based on compromising the confidentiality of information improperly obtained from a computer, which are precisely the type of threats Tereshchuk was charged with transmitting. To the extent the revised statute fails to reach certain types of activity, the perpetrators may be liable to prosecution under the Hobbs Act, 18 US Code s.1951. Section 1951(a) makes it a federal crime to obstruct, delay or affect commerce by engaging in extortion. Section 1951(b)(2) defines 'extortion' as obtaining property 'from another, with his consent, induced by wrongful use of actual or threatened force, violence, or fear'. Since Tereshchuk sought to induce MicroPatent to surrender property – money – by inducing fear that he would release confidential proprietary information, his conduct would fall under this provision (which is apparently what he was prosecuted under). The US Department of Justice has noted that the Hobbs Act can be used when a prosecution under s.1030(a)(7) is not possible (United States Department of Justice 2007). Perhaps the most important change the Identity Theft Enforcement and Restitution Act of 2008 made to s.1030 was a modification to the provision that defines the most commonly used of the CFAA crimes: 18 US Code s.1030(a)(5).

Section 1030(a)(5) creates three crimes, all of which target activity that is directed at a computer or computer network. Section 1030(a)(5) makes it a crime to do any of the following: (i) knowingly cause the transmission of a program, information, code or command and intentionally damage a computer; (ii) intentionally access a computer without authorisation and recklessly cause damage; or (iii) intentionally access a computer without authorisation and thereby cause damage and loss. The Identity Theft Enforcement and Restitution Act added 'and loss' to the third offence; prior to this amendment, the offence paralleled the second offence, making it a crime to access a computer without authorisation and cause damage (only). (Identity Theft 2008).

Section 1030(e)(8) of the CFAA defines 'damage' as impairing 'the integrity or availability of data, a program, a system, or information'. Section 1030(e)(11) defines 'loss' as 'any reasonable cost' to a victim, which includes 'the cost of responding to an offence, conducting a damage assessment, and restoring the system or data 'to its condition prior to the offence'; loss also includes 'any revenue lost, cost incurred, or other consequential damages incurred because of interruption of service'.

Until the adoption of the Identity Theft Enforcement and Restitution Act, the then s.1030(a)(5)(B) imposed damage requirements that acted as a jurisdictional prerequisite for the commencement of a prosecution under s.1030(a)(5). Under that version of the statute, a prosecution for committing any of the three s.1030(a)(5) crimes could not be brought unless the conduct at issue caused (or for attempt charges, would have caused) one of the following: loss to one or more persons aggregating at least $5,000 in a one-year period or one of the following: the modification or impairment of the medical examination, diagnosis, treatment or care of one or more individuals; physical injury to any person; a threat to public health or safety or damage to a computer system used by a government entity in connection with law enforcement, national defence or national security (Prosecuting Computer Crimes 2007). The Identity Theft Enforcement and Restitution Act moved these requirements to s.1030(c)(4)(A), where they serve as factors to be considered in sentencing someone for committing a s.1030(a)(5)(B) offence.

What is the significance of that change? To understand the import of this modification to s.1030(a)(5), it is necessary to understand why the $5,000 element was included in the prior version of the statute. When Congress transformed the Counterfeit Access Device and Computer Fraud and Abuse Act of 1984 into the Computer Fraud and Abuse Act of 1986, it created the 'new subsection 1030(a)(5) to 'penalise those who intentionally alter, damage, or destroy certain computerised data belonging to another' (United States Senate Report 1986). Congress also included a jurisdictional damage requirement to limit the applicability of this provision. The new s.1030(a)(5):

> penalize(d) alteration, damage or destruction in two circumstances. The first is those which cause a loss to the victim or victims totaling $1,000 or more in any single year period. The [Senate Judiciary] Committee believes this threshold is necessary to prevent the bringing of felony-level charges against every individual who modified another's computer data. Some modifications or alterations, while constituting 'damage' in a sense, do not warrant felony-level punishment, particularly when almost no effort or expense is required to restore the affected data to its original condition. The $1,000 valuation has been reasonably calculated by the Committee to preclude felony punishment in those cases, while preserving the option of felony punishment in cases involving more serious alteration, damage, or destruction. [The second circumstance encompassed by a violation of s.1030(a)(5) was altering, damaging or deleting data relating to medical care and treatment.] The Senate Judiciary Committee's report noted that if the $1,000 damage requirement could not be shown in a given case, it might be possible to prosecute the offender for a misdemeanor violation under another subsection of the CFAA. (United States Senate Report 1986)

In 1996, Congress increased the s.1030(a)(5) damage requirement from $1,000 to $5,000, apparently to ensure that the statute's definition of significant financial loss reflected the increased importance of computers in the US economy (Skibell 2003). In 2001, the USA PATRIOT Act kept the $5,000 damage requirement and added the other requirements described above, i.e. the modification or impairment of medical data, physical injury to a person, a threat to public health or safety or damage to a computer used by a government entity in the administration of justice, national defence or national security (USA PATRIOT Act 2001). The three s.1030(a)(5) crimes were moved to new s.1030(a)(5)(A) and the jurisdictional damage requirements were codified in the new s.1030(a)(5)(B) (Prosecuting Computer Crimes 2007). As the Department of Justice explained, s.1030(a)(5)(A) 'prohibit[ed] certain acts when accompanied by particular mental states, while section 1030(a)(5)(B) require[d] the government to prove that a specific kind of harm resulted from those actions. A violation occurs only where an act [met] the elements of both subsections' (Prosecuting Computer Crimes 2007).

The Identity Theft Enforcement and Restitution Act deleted s.1030(a)(5)(B) and moved its damage requirements to s.1030(c), where its requirements become factors to be considered in sentencing someone for violating what is now s.1030(a)(5)(B). The current s.1030(a)(5)(B) offence consists of intentionally accessing a computer without being authorised to do so and, 'as a result of such conduct,' recklessly causing damage, as defined earlier.

Why did Congress eliminate the jurisdictional elements from the s.1030(a)(5) offences? There had been earlier efforts to eliminate the jurisdictional limitations – particularly the $5,000 damage requirement – but until 2008 Congress declined to do so. In 2000, Senator Patrick Leahy explained why he was opposed to doing this:

> [Senate Bill 2448] would have eliminated the $5,000 jurisdictional threshold and thereby criminalised a variety of minor computer abuses, regardless of whether any significant harm results. As America Online correctly noted in a June, 2000 letter, 'eliminating the $5,000 threshold for … would risk criminalising a wide range of essentially benign conduct. …' Similarly, the Internet Alliance commented in a June, 2000 letter that '[c]omplete abolition of the limit will lead to needless federal prosecution of often trivial offences that can be reached under state law. …'
> In my view, … [o]ur federal laws do not need to reach each and every minor, inadvertent and harmless computer abuse – after all, each of the 50 states has its own computer crime laws. Rather, our federal laws need to reach those offences for which federal jurisdiction is appropriate. (Leahy 2000)

Congress's view obviously changed, no doubt in part because of the increase in cybercrime. The jurisdictional requirements formerly included in s.1030(a)(5)(B) barred prosecutors from bringing charges in instances involving otherwise egregious conduct that did not demonstrably inflict any of the varieties of 'harm' codified in that subsection. One author, for example, noted that while 'spyware may "damage" a computer by altering data, the damage is unlikely to meet the requisite $5,000 damage threshold necessary for federal criminal jurisdiction' (Hoffstadt 2007). Congress presumably decided that eliminating the jurisdictional requirements frees federal prosecutors to use s.1030(a)(5) in appropriate instances and assumed they would exercise their prosecutorial discretion to avoid abusing the power this gives them.

Copyright

This section examines developments in two areas of US copyright law: The Digital Millennium Copyright Act and file-sharing in violation of general federal copyright law. The discussion below examines two cases that respectively clarified the requirements for bringing a suit under either theory.

Digital Millennium Copyright Act

Perhaps the most notable development in this area was the US Court of Appeals for the Federal Circuit's adding a new limitation to the scope of the Digital Millennium Copyright Act (DMCA) (Argento 2008).

The Federal Circuit imposed the requirement in *Chamberlain Group, Inc.* v. *Skylink Technologies, Inc.* Chamberlain sued Skylink for trafficking in violation of 17 US Code s.1201(a)(2). The case involved technology used in garage door openers:

> This dispute involves Chamberlain's Security+ line of GDOs and Skylink's Model 39 universal transmitter. Chamberlain's Security+ GDOs incorporate a copyrighted 'rolling code' computer program that constantly changes the transmitter signal needed to open the garage door. Skylink's Model 39 transmitter, which does not incorporate rolling code, nevertheless allows users to operate Security+ openers. Chamberlain … contends that because of this property of the Model 39, Skylink is in violation of the anti-trafficking clause of the DMCA's anticircumvention provisions, specifically s.1201(a)(2). (Chamberlain 2004)

Skylink moved for summary judgement on Chamberlain's DMCA claim, and won; the federal district court granted summary judgement and dismissed the suit. Chamberlain appealed to the Federal Circuit (Chamberlain 2004).

In deciding whether the district court acted correctly, the Federal Circuit began its analysis by noting that the circumvention prohibited by the DMCA '*is not* a new form of infringement but rather a new violation prohibiting actions or products that facilitate infringement' (Chamberlain 2004). The court found it 'significant that virtually every clause of s.1201 [of the DMCA] that mentions "access" links "access" to "protection"' (Chamberlain 2004). That was significant because Chamberlain argued that the court should interpret the DMCA as if Congress had created a new protection for copyrighted material without any reference to the protections copyright owners already have under other law or the rights the Copyright Act gives the public.

Chamberlain has not alleged that Skylink's Model 39 infringes its copyrights, nor has it alleged that the Model 39 contributes to third-party infringement of its copyrights. Chamberlain's allegation is considerably more straightforward: The only way for the Model 39 to interoperate with a Security+ GDO is by 'accessing' copyrighted software. Skylink has therefore committed a per se violation of the DMCA. (Chamberlain 2004)

The Federal Circuit disagreed, concluding that Congress 'could not have intended such a broad reading of the DMCA' (Chamberlain 2004). It found Chamberlain's interpretation of the DMCA ignored the 'significant differences between' those whose 'products enable copying and those, like Skylink, whose products enable only legitimate uses of copyrighted software' (Chamberlain 2004).

The Federal Circuit therefore rejected Chamberlain's argument that the DMCA creates a new property right for copyright owners, holding instead that it 'prohibits only forms of access that bear a reasonable relationship to the protections the Copyright Act otherwise affords copyright owners' (Chamberlain 2004). The court held that one claiming a DMCA trafficking violation under s.1201(a)(2) must prove:

(1) ownership of a valid *copyright* on a work, (2) effectively controlled by a *technological measure*, which has been circumvented, (3) that third parties can now access (4) *without authorisation*, in a manner that (5) infringes or facilitates infringing a right *protected* by the Copyright Act, because of a product that (6) the defendant either (i) *designed or produced* primarily for circumvention; (ii) made available despite only *limited commercial significance* other than circumvention; or (iii) *marketed* for use in circumvention of the controlling technological measure. A plaintiff incapable of establishing any one of elements (1) through (5) will have failed to prove a prima facie case. A plaintiff capable of proving elements (1) through (5) need prove only one of (6)(i), (ii), or (iii) to shift the burden back to the defendant. (Chamberlain 2004)

The Federal Circuit affirmed the lower court's grant of summary judgement for Skylink because it found Chamberlain had not established the

fifth element of its claim, the critical nexus between access and protection. Chamberlain neither alleged copyright infringement nor explained how the access provided by the Model 39 transmitter facilitates the infringement of any right that the Copyright Act protects. There can therefore be no reasonable relationship between the access that homeowners gain to Chamberlain's copyrighted software when using Skylink's Model 39 transmitter and the protections that the Copyright Act grants to Chamberlain. The Copyright Act authorised Chamberlain's customers to use the copy of Chamberlain's copyrighted software embedded in the GDOs that they purchased. Chamberlain's customers are therefore immune from s.1201(a)(1) circumvention liability. In the absence of allegations of either copyright infringement or s.1201(a)(1) circumvention, Skylink cannot be liable for s.1201(a)(2) trafficking. (Chamberlain 2004)

In the wake of the Chamberlain decision, commentators have concluded that the Federal Circuit interpretation of the DMCA maintains its effectiveness while mitigating the stifling effects that would have resulted from its accepting Chamberlain's proposed interpretation of the statute (Argento 2008). Some have noted, though, that the Federal Circuit's interpretation seems in certain respects to be inconsistent with the language of the DMCA. As one commentator pointed out, there would seem to be no reason for Congress to have included defences such as fair use and interoperability in the DMCA unless it created a 'new right above and beyond infringement' (Argento 2008).

Despite this and other questions about its conclusions, the Federal Circuit's imposition of the 'reasonable relationship' requirement is likely to persist. The Federal Circuit has reaffirmed its commitment to the requirement in two subsequent decisions, one of which was issued in 2008 (Argento 2008; Blueport 2008). And since the Federal Circuit has exclusive jurisdiction over copyright appeals from federal district courts, the 'reasonable relationship' requirement will persist as long as this court finds it appropriate (28 US Code s.1295).

Copyright Act

Capitol Records, Inc. v. *Thomas* is one of many lawsuits brought by or on behalf of companies that own or control the copyrights in recorded music. As one source noted, by the beginning of 2008 the Recording Industry Association of America had sued over 20,000 individuals for direct infringement resulting from their use of peer-to-peer file-sharing software like Limewire or Kazaa (Tratos 2008). The suits are part of an RIAA strategy that consists of filing infringement suits against users of peer-to-peer software that seek outrageous damages, offering to settle the suit for a minimal amount (usually $3,000) and then either settling (which is the usual outcome) or taking the case to trial (Tratos 2008).

In the *Thomas* case, six record companies sued Jammie Thomas claiming that she had infringed their copyrighted 'sound recordings pursuant to the Copyright Act ... by illegally downloading and distributing the recordings via the online peer-to-peer file-sharing application known as Kazaa' (Capitol Records 2008). Thomas refused to settle and the case went to trial; the jury found Thomas had wilfully infringed on 'all 24' of the plaintiffs' sound recordings and awarded them statutory damages of $9,250 for each infringement (Capitol Records 2008). The total damage award was $222,000.

Thomas filed a motion for a new trial, arguing that the award of damages was excessive and violated the due process clause of the United States Constitution. The district court judge *sua sponte* raised another issue: whether he erred 'in instructing the jury that making sound recordings available for distribution on a peer-to-peer network, regardless of whether actual distribution was shown, qualified as distribution under the Copyright Act' (Capitol Records 2008).

In analysing the latter issue, the federal judge began by noting that the applicable statutory provision – 17 US Code s.106(3) – gives a copyright owner the exclusive right 'to distribute copies ... of the copyrighted work to the public by sale or other transfer of ownership, or by rental, lease, or lending' (Capitol Records 2008). The question was whether putting songs on a peer-to-peer network qualified as distribution.

Since the Copyright Act does not define the term 'distribute', the federal judge turned to other sources. He first found that the plain language of the statute did not resolve the issue because s.106(3) merely 'explains the manners in which distribution can be effected ... [It] does not state that an offer to do any of these acts constitutes distribution' (Capitol Records 2008).

The judge then considered the plaintiffs' argument that under the Copyright Act, 'distribution' is synonymous with the term 'publication'. Section 101 of the Copyright Act defines 'publication' as 'the distribution of copies ... of a work to the public by sale or other transfer of ownership, or by rental, lease, or lending'. Section 101 also states that 'offering to distribute copies ... for purposes of further distribution, public performance, or public display, constitutes publication'. Notwithstanding this, the judge found that publication and distribution are not synonymous under the Copyright Act:

> [S]imply because all distributions within the meaning of s.106(3) are publications does not mean that all publications within the meaning of s.101 are distributions. The statutory definition of publication is broader than the term distribution as used in s.106(3). A publication can occur by ... the 'distribution of copies ... of a work to the public by sale or other transfer of ownership, or by rental, lease or lending' s.101. This portion of the definition of publication defines a distribution as set forth in s.106(3). However, a publication may also occur by 'offering to distribute copies ... to a group of persons for purposes of further distribution, public performance, or public display' s.101. While a publication effected by distributing copies ... of the work is a distribution, a publication effected by merely offering to distribute copies ... to the public is merely an offer of distribution, not an actual distribution. (Capitol Records 2008)

The *Thomas* judge then addressed the plaintiffs' argument that s.106(3) of the Copyright Act creates 'two separate rights – the right to "do" distribution and the right to "authorize" distribution. Therefore, making sound recordings available on Kazaa violates the copyright owner's exclusive right to authorize distribution' (Capitol Records 2008).

The judge disagreed. He found that the 'the authorization clause merely provides a statutory foundation for secondary liability, not a means of expanding the scope of direct infringement liability' (Capitol Records 2008).

Finally, the judge in the *Thomas* case relied on a decision from the US Court of Appeals for the Eighth Circuit: in *National Car Rental System, Inc. v. Computer Associates International, Inc.*, the Eighth Circuit held that 'infringement of [the distribution right] requires an actual dissemination of ... copies' (National Car

Rental 1993). Since Eighth Circuit precedent is binding on the District Court for the District of Minnesota, the *Thomas* judge applied this principle to the case before him and held that distribution requires the actual dissemination of copies of a copyrighted work (Capitol Records 2008). He noted, though, that his holding does not leave

> copyright holders without redress ... A person who makes an unauthorised copy ... of a copyrighted work for the purposes of uploading it onto a peer-to-peer network, absent a defence such as fair use, violates the reproduction right. 17 USC s.106(a). That person might also be liable for indirect infringement to the extent that her conduct caused others to engage in unauthorised reproduction, adaptation, public distribution, public performance, or public display of another's ... work. (Capitol Records 2008)

Since the judge had instructed the jury erroneously on what they had to find to conclude that Thomas engaged in distribution in violation of s.106(3), the court ordered a new trial.

Many saw the judge's decision as a blow to the RIAA and its file-sharing suits. The *Thomas* case was the first, and so far only, of these suits to go to trial; the jury's verdict was seen as a victory for the RIAA, but now that verdict has been set aside. At this writing, the RIAA is attempting to appeal the district court's decision setting aside the verdict to the Eighth Circuit Court of Appeals, in hopes of getting the decision reversed. Thomas, on the other hand, is pressing for a new trial, perhaps hoping she will prevail when the jury is given a different instruction on the distribution issue.

Even if it stands, the *Thomas* court's decision still leaves the RIAA with alternative claims it can pursue against someone like Thomas (Kravets 2008). And the RIAA can usually show actual distribution because its hired investigators always download music from a targeted individual's peer-to-peer sharing folder (Kravets 2008). In the *Thomas* case, the judge rejected Ms Thomas's argument that distribution to 'an investigator acting as an agent for the copyright owner cannot constitute infringement' (Capitol Records 2008).

What is perhaps most interesting about the *Thomas* court's opinion is the plea the judge added at the end:

> The Court would be remiss if it did not take this opportunity to implore Congress to amend the Copyright Act to address liability and damages in peer-to-peer network cases such as the one currently before this Court ... The defendant is an individual, a consumer ... She sought no profit from her acts. The myriad of copyright cases cited by Plaintiffs and the Government, in which courts upheld large statutory damages awards far above the minimum, have limited relevance in this case. All of the cited cases involve corporate or business defendants and seek to deter future illegal commercial conduct. The parties point to no case in which large statutory damages were applied to a party who did not infringe in search of commercial gain.

The statutory damages awarded against Thomas are not a deterrent against those who pirate music in order to profit. Thomas's conduct was motivated by her desire to obtain the copyrighted music for her own use. The Court does not condone Thomas's actions, but it would be a farce to say that a single mother's acts of using Kazaa are the equivalent, for example, to the acts of global financial firms illegally infringing on copyrights in order to profit in the securities market. (Capitol Records 2008)

While the judge said he did not discount the plaintiff's claim that, 'cumulatively, illegal downloading has far-reaching effects on their businesses', he also said the damages awarded against Ms Thomas were disproportionate: 'Thomas allegedly infringed on the copyrights of 24 songs – the equivalent of approximately three CDs, costing less than $54, and yet the total damages awarded is $222,000 – more than five hundred times the cost of buying 24 separate CDs and more than four thousand times the cost of three CDs' (Capitol Records 2008). He then reiterated his call for Congress to take steps to mitigate the unfairness inherent in suits like the one brought against Ms Thomas.

Other federal district courts have issued rulings that indicate they, too, are far from comfortable with the liability and penalties copyright law can impose on individuals like Ms Thomas. Congress, however, seems unlikely to address this issue for at least two reasons. One is that it has long been sympathetic to the RIAA's and the Motion Picture Association of America's concerns about file-sharing. In 2008, it included a provision in funding for higher education legislation that requires universities and colleges receiving federal funds to develop plants to prevent copyright violations by their students (Bangeman 2008). The other reason Congress is not likely to take up this issue is the fact that it has many other far more pressing concerns to deal with for at least the foreseeable future.

Child Online Protection Act

In *Ashcroft* v. *American Civil Liberties Union*, the US Supreme Court upheld the Third Circuit Court of Appeals affirming a district court decision that enjoining enforcement of the Child Online Protection Act (COPA) on the grounds that it violated the First Amendment (Ashcroft 2004).

The Court began its analysis by noting that the Child Online Protection Act is Congress' 'second attempt ... to make the Internet safe for minors by criminalising certain Internet speech' (Ashcroft 2004). The first was the Communications Decency Act of 1996 (CDA), which the Court held unconstitutional in *Reno* v. *American Civil Liberties Union*. The Court held that the CDA was unconstitutional because it was not 'narrowly tailored to serve a compelling governmental interest and because less restrictive alternatives were available' (Reno 1997).

COPA, successor to the CDA, makes it a crime knowingly and for 'commercial purposes to post material that is 'harmful to minors' (47 US Code s.231(a)(1)).

The statute defines material that is 'harmful to minors' as encompassing material that (i) is obscene, (ii) panders to the 'prurient interest', (iii) depicts, describes or represents, 'in a manner patently offensive to minors', an actual or simulated sexual act, exhibition of the genitals or the female breast, or (iv) taken as a whole, lacks serious literary, artistic, political, or scientific value for minors (47 US Code s.231(e)(6)). A 'minor' is defined as someone under 17 years of age, and one acts with 'commercial purposes' if they are 'engaged in the business of making such communications' (Ashcroft 2004).

The Supreme Court noted that while the COPA defines all of the above content as criminal, it creates an affirmative defence (Ashcroft 2004). The affirmative defence lets one who has put material harmful to minors online for commercial purposes 'escape conviction under the statute' by showing that they restricted access to material harmful to minors by using credit cards, access codes, digital certificates or 'other reasonable measures that are feasible under available technology' (47 US Code s.231(c)(1)).

The American Civil Liberties Union and a group of Internet content providers sued to bar enforcement of COPA, arguing that it violated the First Amendment because there were other, less restrictive alternatives that could achieve the goal of restricting minors' access to 'harmful materials' (Ashcroft 2004). The district court granted an injunction barring enforcement because it found that blocking or filtering technologies 'may be at least as successful as COPA would be in restricting minors' access to harmful material online without imposing the burden on constitutionally protected speech that COPA imposes on adult users or Web site operators' (Ashcroft 2004).

The Supreme Court agreed. It began its analysis of COPA by noting that statutes which suppress a large amount of speech that adults have a constitutional right to receive and send to each other is unconstitutional if less restrictive alternatives would be at least as effective in achieving the purpose the legislation was enacted to achieve (Ashcroft 2004). It also noted that when plaintiffs challenge the enforcement of such a content-based restriction, the burden is on the government to prove that the proposed alternatives 'will not be as effective as the challenged statute' in achieving the relevant goal(s) (Ashcroft 2004).

The Supreme Court then agreed with the district court that filtering technologies are an alternative that is less restrictive than COPA and that is likely to be even more effective as a means of restricting children's access to the material targeted by COPA (Ashcroft 2004). The Court noted that a Congressional Commission assigned to investigate this issue 'unambiguously found that filters are more effective than age-verification requirements' (Ashcroft 2004). It also noted that filters are 'not a perfect solution to the problem of children gaining access to harmful-to-minors materials' because they can block 'some materials that are not harmful to minors and fail to catch some that are' (Ashcroft 2004). The Supreme Court found, though, that '[w]hatever the deficiencies' of filters are, they were not dispositive of the issue before it because the government did not produce evidence 'proving that existing technologies are less effective than the restrictions in COPA' (Ashcroft 2004). The Court therefore upheld the issuance of the injunction and remanded the case for further proceedings below (Ashcroft 2004).

In so doing, it noted that it was not holding that Congress 'is incapable of enacting any regulation of the Internet designed to prevent minors from gaining access to harmful materials' (Ashcroft 2004). It also noted that its ruling did not prevent the government from producing evidence in an attempt to convince the district court that 'COPA is the least restrictive alternative available to accomplish Congress' goal' (Ashcroft 2004). The Supreme Court found that this possibility survived because the parties had not 'devoted their attention to the question whether further evidence might be introduced on the relative effectiveness of alternatives to the statute' because they had been concentrating on the constitutional issue (Ashcroft 2004).

In 2007, after further proceedings, the district court held that COPA violates the First Amendment because (i) it is not narrowly tailored to the compelling interest of protecting minors, (ii) the government did not show it is the least restrictive and most effective alternative and (iii) it is impermissibly vague and overbroad (*American Civil Liberties Union* v. *Gonzales* 2007). The district court therefore permanently enjoined the Attorney General and his officers, agents, employees and attorneys 'from enforcing or prosecuting matters premised upon COPA at any time for any conduct' (*American Civil Liberties Union* v. *Gonzales* 2007). In 2008, the Third Circuit Court of Appeals, having found the district court's reasoning to be sound, affirmed its order enjoining enforcement of COPA (*American Civil Liberties Union* v. *Mukasey* 2008).

At the end of October 2008, the US Department of Justice filed a petition asking the Supreme Court to review the decisions below. If the Court grants review, it is likely to affirm those decisions.

Child pornography

In 1996 Congress, concerned about the increased proliferation of child pornography, adopted the Child Pornography Protection Act (CPPA), which was codified as 18 US Code s.s.2251–2260. Much of the impetus for the CPPA came from the increased use of computer technology and the Internet; Congress found that both made it much easier to create and to distribute child pornography (Child Pornography Protection Act 1996).

Congress first outlawed child pornography in 1977 (Protection of Children Against Sexual Exploitation Act 1977). The 1977 enactment focused on the use of 'real' children in the production of child pornography (Free Speech Coalition 1999). By the end of the twentieth century, it had become apparent that computer technology could allow the creation of 'virtual' child pornography, i.e. child pornography the production of which did not involve the use of 'real' children.

The CPPA was adopted to bring federal legislation outlawing child pornography up to date, to allow it to deal with the enforcement problems that had arisen due to the emergence of computer-generated child pornography. To this end, it introduced a new definition of child pornography: Section 2256(8) of Title 18 defines 'child pornography' in part as 'any visual depiction' that 'is, or appears to be, of a minor engaging in sexually explicit conduct'. In *Ashcroft* v. *Free Speech Coalition*, the Supreme Court held that this definition of child pornography violated the First Amendment because it criminalised the creation, possession and distribution of material the production of which did not involve 'real' children (*Ashcroft* v. *Free Speech Coalition* 2002). The *Ashcroft* Court explained that child pornography involving the use of 'real' children can be banned because its creation necessarily involves the victimisation of children (*Ashcroft* v. *Free Speech Coalition* 2002). The Court explained that virtual child pornography cannot be criminalised because it is speech and because the creation of this speech does not involve the victimisation of a real human being (*Ashcroft* v. *Free Speech Coalition* 2002).

The *Ashcroft* Court also struck down another section of the CPPA. Section 2256(8)(D) criminalised the possession and distribution of material that had been 'pandered' as child pornography – that is, as pornography involving 'real' children – regardless of whether it actually was child pornography. The *Ashcroft* Court held that this provision was also unconstitutional because it meant someone could be prosecuted for possessing 'unobjectionable material that someone else had pandered' as child pornography (*United States* v. *Williams* 2008).

Congress responded by adopting the Prosecutorial Remedies and Other Tools to end the Exploitation of Children Today Act (PROTECT Act), which did a number of things. The sections below examine its more important provisions.

Definition of child pornography

The PROTECT Act replaced the definition struck down by the *Ashcroft* court with a new one (Feldmeier 2003). The definition currently found in s.2256(8)(B) defines child pornography as 'any visual depiction, including any photograph, film, video, picture, or computer or computer-generated image or picture ... of sexually explicit conduct' in which: (i) the production of such visual depiction involves the use of a minor engaging in sexually explicit conduct; (ii) the visual depiction is a 'digital image, computer image, or computer-generated image that is, or is indistinguishable from, that of a minor engaging in sexually explicit conduct'; or (iii) the depiction 'has been created, adapted, or modified to appear that an identifiable minor is engaging in sexually explicit conduct.' Section 2256(11) explains that 'indistinguishable' means virtually indistinguishable, in that the depiction is such that an ordinary person viewing the depiction would conclude that the depiction is of an actual minor engaged in sexually explicit conduct'. Section 2256(11) notes that this definition of indistinguishable 'does not apply to depictions that are drawings, cartoons, sculptures, or paintings depicting minors or adults'.

Congress took this approach – instead of simply defining child pornography as material the production of which does involve the use of real children – in an effort to alleviate the prosecution's burden of proof in a child pornography case (Feldmeier 2003). Prosecutors claimed it would be extraordinarily difficult for them to prove that the person in an image was a child, instead of a youthful-looking adult (Feldmeier 2003).

In adopting the new definition of child pornography, Congress sought to accommodate the *Ashcroft* holding and the concerns of prosecutors (Feldmeier

2003). Under the law as it currently exists, the prosecution has the burden of proving that the depiction of a child in an image is indistinguishable from that of a real child (Feldmeier 2003). This creates a rebuttable presumption that the image does, in fact, depict a real child (Feldmeier 2003). The defendant can then rebut that presumption by showing that the 'alleged child pornography was not produced using any actual minor or minors' (18 US Code s.2252A(c)). Section 2252A(c) of Title 18 of the US Code creates this alternative as a way of letting defendants raise the issue of virtual child pornography as a defence in a child pornography prosecution.

So far, no federal court has ruled on the constitutionality of the s.2252(c) affirmative defence. The *Ashcroft* Court found that the prior version of the defence was inadequate given the definition of child pornography contained in the statute then in effect: 'Even if an affirmative defence can save a statute from First Amendment challenge, here the defence is incomplete and insufficient' (*Ashcroft* v. *Free Speech Coalition* 2002). The Court declined, however, to decide if the state can impose the burden of rebutting a presumption that material is child pornography on a defendant (*Ashcroft* v. *Free Speech Coalition* 2002). Many believe that the affirmative defence codified in s.2252A(c) is unconstitutional insofar as it relieves the prosecution of the burden of proving beyond a reasonable doubt that the material which forms the basis of a prosecution is, in fact, 'real' child pornography (Feldmeier 2003).

Pandering

The PROTECT Act added a new pandering provision to Title 18 of the US Code (PROTECT Act 2003). The new section – 18 US Code s.2252A(a)(3)(B) – makes it a crime 'knowingly' to promote, distribute or solicit in interstate or foreign commerce by any means, including by computer, 'material or purported material in a manner that reflects the belief, or that is intended to cause another to believe, that the material' either is or contains one of the following: 'an obscene visual depiction of a minor engaging in sexually explicit conduct' or 'a visual depiction of an actual minor engaging in sexually explicit conduct'. As the Supreme Court later noted, the 'express findings' for the legislation that added this offence 'indicate that Congress was concerned that limiting the child-pornography prohibition to material that could be *proved* to feature actual children ... would enable many child pornographers to evade conviction' (*United States* v. *Williams* 2008).

In 2004, Michael Williams was charged with violating this section based on his sending an undercover officer a message stating that he had pictures of men molesting his four-year-old daughter (*United States* v. *Williams* 2008). He pleaded guilty but reserved the right to challenge the constitutionality of the statute on appeal to the Eleventh Circuit Court of Appeals; after that court reversed his conviction on the s.2252A(a)(3)(B) charge, the Supreme Court granted *certiorari* to hear the case.

The Supreme Court reversed the Eleventh Circuit's decision. The Court held that 'offers to provide or requests to obtain child pornography are categorically excluded' from the protections of the First Amendment (*United States* v. *Williams* 2008).

The Eleventh Circuit believed it a constitutional difficulty that no child pornography need exist to trigger the statute. In its view, the fact that the statute could punish a 'braggart, exaggerator, or outright liar' rendered it unconstitutional ... That seems to us a strange constitutional calculus. Although we have held that the government can ban both fraudulent offers ... and offers to provide illegal products, the Eleventh Circuit would forbid the government from punishing fraudulent offers to provide illegal products. We see no logic in that position; if anything, such statements are doubly excluded from the First Amendment. (*United States* v. *Williams* 2008)

According to the Supreme Court, the statute is in effect an inchoate crime provision – like attempt and conspiracy provisions – and, like other inchoate crimes, it imposes liability even when the commission of the actual crime is impossible (*United States* v. *Williams* 2008).

Obscene child pornography

The PROTECT Act created a new child pornography crime: producing, receiving, possessing or manufacturing obscene child pornography (PROTECT Act 2003). Obscene child pornography is defined as 'a visual depiction of any kind, including a drawing, cartoon, sculpture, or painting' that depicts (i) a minor engaging in sexually explicit conduct and is obscene; or (ii) 'an image that is, or appears to be, of a minor engaging in graphic bestiality, sadistic or masochistic abuse, or sexual intercourse and lacks serious literary, artistic, political, or scientific value' (18 US Code s.1466A). The latter part of the statute is intended to implement the US Supreme Court's standard for determining what is, and is not, obscene: in *Miller* v. *California*. In the *Miller* case, the Court held that to be constitutional under the First Amendment, obscenity statutes must 'be limited to works which, taken as a whole, appeal to the prurient interest in sex, which portray sexual conduct in a patently offensive way, and which, taken as a whole, do not have serious literary, artistic, political, or scientific value' (Miller 1973).

In 2008, a federal district court held that part of s.1466A is unconstitutional because it is 'not subject to a limiting construction that would avoid the constitutional problem of prohibiting images that neither involve the use of actual minors or constitute obscenity' (*United States* v. *Handley* 2008). This court held that the first option noted above – that the material depicts a minor engaging in sexually explicit conduct – is constitutionally sound, but the second is not; it found that the second is over-broad because, as noted above, it does not contain terms that would narrow its scope to satisfy the requirements of the First Amendment (*United States* v. *Handley* 2008).

Privacy

In the United States, the primary guarantees of privacy in the face of government action are two constitutional provisions: the Fourth and Fifth Amendments. There have been several interesting developments in this area over the last year or two, all of which have taken the form of decisions by the lower federal courts. The Supreme Court has not so far taken any cases involving digital privacy, but it will certainly have to do so at some point. Until then, the lower courts' decisions are the only source of authority.

Fourth Amendment

The Fourth Amendment creates a right to be free from 'unreasonable' searches and seizures (US Constitution, Amendment iv). To be 'reasonable', a search or seizure must be conducted either pursuant to a lawfully authorised search or arrest warrant or pursuant to one of the exceptions the US Supreme Court has recognised to the warrant requirement (Annual Review of Criminal Procedure 2008). A 'search' constitutes an intrusion on an individual's reasonable expectation of privacy (Katz 1967). A 'seizure' constitutes an interference with someone's possession and use of their property (Soldal 1992). The sections below review how the Supreme Court has applied the Fourth Amendment to areas in which technology and privacy intersect.

Wiretapping: content of communications

In 1928, the Supreme Court held that wiretapping – intercepting the content of telephone calls – did not violate the Fourth Amendment (Olmstead 1928). The Olmstead Court reached this result because it construed the Fourth Amendment in light of the law, and technology, that existed when it was written, instead of in terms of the goals it was intended to achieve. The majority of the *Olmstead* ruling held that wiretapping was not a search because the tap was outside Olmstead's home, so the officers did not trespass inside his house; they also held it was not a seizure because no tangible property was taken from Olmstead (Olmstead 1928).

In 1967, the Supreme Court reversed Olmstead and held that FBI agents violated the Fourth Amendment by installing an 'electronic listening and recording device' on the outside of a telephone booth to record calls being made by Charles Katz (Katz 1967). In so doing, the Court announced a new standard for applying the Fourth Amendment's privacy protections: '[T]he Fourth Amendment protects people, not places. What a person knowingly exposes to the public, even in his own home or office, is not a subject of Fourth Amendment protection ... But what he seeks to preserve as private, even in an area accessible to the public, may be constitutionally protected' (Katz 1967). In a concurring opinion, Justice Harlan articulated the standard that has been used to implement the *Katz* holding:

> [T]here is a twofold requirement, first that a person has exhibited an actual (subjective) expectation of privacy and, second, that the expectation be one that society is prepared to recognise as 'reasonable.' Thus a man's home is ... a place where he expects privacy ... On the other hand, conversations in the open would not be protected against being overheard, for the expectation of privacy under the circumstances would be unreasonable. (Katz 1967)

Katz is still the standard the Supreme Court uses to determine when the conduct of law enforcement officers violates a reasonable expectation of privacy and therefore constitutes a 'search' under the Fourth Amendment.

In the context of intercepting the contents of telephone calls, emails and other electronic communications, the default standard is no longer the *Katz* decision, as such. In 1968, Congress enacted a statutory scheme – popularly known as 'Title III' – which implements the requirements of the *Katz* decision and adds certain requirements (Decker 2008). The original version of Title III only applied to telephone calls, but it has been amended to include emails and other electronic communications within its protections (Decker 2008). It is, therefore, clear that law enforcement officers must obtain a Title III order – the equivalent of a search warrant – to lawfully intercept the contents of telephone or electronic communications (Decker 2008).

Wiretapping: traffic data

Katz dealt only with the *contents* of a telephone call. In a subsequent decision, the Supreme Court dealt with the related issue of whether the transmittal information – the traffic data – generated by a telephone call is private under the Fourth Amendment.

The case was *Smith* v. *Maryland*, and the issue was 'whether the installation and use of a pen register – which captures the numbers dialed on a telephone – is a "search" under the Fourth Amendment' (Smith 1979). Police suspected Smith of being engaged in criminal activity; to confirm their suspicions, they had the phone company install 'a pen register at its central offices to record the numbers dialed from the telephone at [his] home ... The police did not get a warrant or court order before having the pen register installed' (Smith 1979). The pen register confirmed that Smith was committing a crime; prior to trial, Smith moved to suppress the evidence obtained by the pen register, arguing that its installation and use was a warrantless search in violation of the Fourth Amendment. He analogises the use of the pen register to the use of the wiretap in Katz, but the Supreme Court did not agree.

The *Smith* Court began by noting that the standard used to implement *Katz* is the two-pronged test Justice Harlan enunciated in his concurring opinion: (i) whether the individual has exhibited a subjective expectation of privacy in the thing, place or endeavour; and (ii) whether society is prepared to regard the individual's subjective expectation of privacy as reasonable. The Court found *Smith* met neither criterion:

> Since the pen register was installed on telephone company property at the telephone company's central offices, petitioner ... cannot claim that his 'property' was invaded or that police intruded into a 'constitutionally protected area.' Petitioner's claim ... is that, notwithstanding the absence of a trespass, the State ... infringed a 'legitimate expectation of privacy'.... [A] pen register differs ... from the listening device employed in *Katz*, for pen registers do not acquire the *contents* of communications ... (Smith 1979)

The Supreme Court therefore held that Smith did not have a cognisable Fourth Amendment expectation of privacy in the numbers he dialled from his home phone.

The *Smith* Court's decision created a dichotomy: under *Katz*, the contents of communications *are* protected by the Fourth Amendment, at least while they are in transmission. But under *Smith*, the data generated by and used in the process of transmitting communications is not protected because the user of the telephone, email or other communication service knowingly shares that data with the service provider.

The installation and use of technology that captures traffic data is now governed by a statutory scheme analogous to the Title III scheme noted above. The problem courts are now grappling with is that the distinction between content data and traffic data is no longer as clear as it once was.

Nowhere is this as evident as it is with post-cut-through dialled digits, or PCTDD. As a federal district court explained:

> Post-cut-through dialed digits are ... 'numbers dialed from a telephone after the call is initially setup or 'cut-through.' ... In most instances, any digit dialed after the first ten is a PCTDD. 'Sometimes these digits transmit real information, such as bank account numbers, Social Security numbers, prescription numbers, and the like.' ... In such circumstances, PCTDD contain the 'contents of communication' ... At other times, PCTDD are other telephone numbers, as when a party places a credit card call by first dialing the long distance carrier access number and then the phone number of the intended party, ... or when an extension number is dialed. (In re US for Orders 2007)

In several reported cases, federal law enforcement agents have asked federal district courts to give them access to all the PCTDD acquired by the installation of a pen register. Courts have, so far, refused to do so, on the grounds that granting such a request would violate the *Katz* holding (and Title III) by allowing the government to use a pen register to obtain at least some of the contents of a communication. These courts have suggested that to obtain PCTDD, law enforcement officers must use a Title III order, the equivalent of a search warrant.

At the end of 2008, however, a federal district court in New York reversed the decision from which the quoted material above comes and ordered the installation of pen registers on the target 'wireless telephones' (in re US 2008). This court reversed the earlier decision because the government offered an alternative it had earlier claimed was not available: in the prior PCTDD cases, the government claimed it could not use a pen register to collect the calling information (the telephone traffic data) to which it was legitimately entitled to under *Smith* without also collecting PCTDD data that constituted the contents of a communication, as well.

In those cases, the government claimed there was 'no technology' that could filter content PCTDD from non-content PCTDD. In the most recent case, the government told the federal district court that the law enforcement agency seeking the use of the pen registers would 'configure its computers so as to immediately delete all PCTDD' collected (in re US 2008). The district court reversed the earlier order denying the government's request for the use of pen registers because it found that the government's deleting PCTDD eliminated the *Katz* problem, i.e. the fact that the pen registers would capture content as well as traffic data.

It will be interesting to see how courts deal with this complex issue in the future. The latest court to address this issue accepted the government's solution, but it does not completely resolve the problem: even under this solution, law enforcement officers are capturing content-PCTDD; if the agents were so inclined, they could keep, decode and use the data.

Technology not in general public use

The Supreme Court's 2001 decision in *Kyllo* v. *United States* is its most recent parsing of the *Katz* standard. The issue in *Kyllo* was whether 'the use of a thermal-imaging device aimed at a private home from a public street to detect relative amounts of heat within the home constitutes a 'search' within the meaning of the Fourth Amendment' (Kyllo 2001).

Federal agents who suspected Danny Kyllo was growing marijuana in his home used a thermal imager to detect heat signatures in his home and garage: 'The scan … was performed from … across the street from the … house … . [It] showed that the roof over the garage and a side wall of petitioner's home were relatively hot compared to the rest of the home and substantially warmer than neighboring homes' (Kyllo 2001). The agents used this information from the thermal detector to obtain a warrant to search Kyllo's home, where they found a marijuana-growing operation. When he was indicted, Kyllo moved to suppress the results of the thermal imaging, arguing that the scan was a warrantless search conducted in violation of the Fourth Amendment (Kyllo 2001).

The Supreme Court agreed, holding that the Fourth Amendment is to be construed 'in a manner which will conserve public interests as well as the interests and rights of individual citizens' (Kyllo 2001). Its holding provides some guidance as to how the *Katz* test is to be applied when the use of new technology is at issue: 'Where … the Government uses a device that is not in general public use, to explore details of the home that would previously have been unknowable without physical intrusion, the surveillance is a "search" and is presumptively unreasonable without a warrant' (Kyllo 2001).

So far, most of the reported *Kyllo* cases deal with whether or not the use of a trained drug detection dog is a search, but there is one case that at least implicitly applies *Kyllo* to computer forensic technology. The case is *United States* v. *Crist*, and the issue arose from Crist's motion to suppress evidence seized from his computer.

Here is a summary of what led Crist to file that motion: Crist rented a house in Camp Hill but was late with rental payments. After he fell two months behind, his landlord hired Jeremy and Kirk Sell to move Crist's stuff out of the house. Crist had made arrangements to move some of his things and most of his furniture, but had not moved everything by the time the Sells showed up at his house. According to the court, '[s]cattered throughout the nearly vacant rooms were Crist's possessions, including a keyboard, a PlayStation gaming console, and a personal computer. After taking photographs ... the Sells began removing Crist's possessions and placing them on the curb for trash pickup' (*United States* v. *Crist* 2008).

A few days later, Jeremy called his friend Seth Hipple, whom he know was looking for a computer; Jeremy told Hipple he put Crist's computer out for trash pickup so Hipple showed up and took it (*United States* v. *Crist* 2008). Later, Crist came to his house and discovered the Sells removing his things. He looked for his computer and then asked them where it was (*United States* v. *Crist* 2008). When the Sells said they did not know, Crist called the police 'to complain of the theft of his computer, and Officer Adam Shope took a report' (*United States* v. *Crist* 2008).

Hipple took the computer home and, while working with it, found 'video files depicting children performing sexual acts' (*United States* v. *Crist* 2008). He deleted the files and called the police; when an officer arrived, Hipple said he found the computer and discovered child pornography on it (*United States* v. *Crist* 2008). The officer took the computer, which was sent to an analyst at the Pennsylvania Attorney General's office to be forensically examined (*United States* v. *Crist* 2008). A special agent with the AG Office's computer forensics department conducted an examination of the computer. He began by creating an MD5 hash value of the hard drive, which is a

> unique alphanumeric representation of the data ... When creating the hash value, Agent Buckwash used a 'software write protect' ... to ensure that 'nothing can be written to that hard drive.' ... After that, he created an image, or exact copy, of all the data on Crist's hard drive.
>
> Buckwash then opened up the image ... in a software program called EnCase ... He explained that EnCase does not access the hard drive ... through the computer's operating system. Rather, EnCase ... . reads every file – bit by bit, cluster by cluster – and creates an index of the files contained on the hard drive ...
>
> Once in EnCase, Buckwash ran a 'hash value and signature analysis on all of the files on the hard drive' ... to 'fingerprint' each file ... [H]e compared those hash values to the hash values of files ... known or suspected to contain child pornography. [He] discovered five videos containing known child pornography ... [and] 171 videos containing suspected child pornography ...
>
> Afterward, Buckwash 'switch[ed] over to a gallery view ... ,' and was able to 'mark every picture [he] believe[d] is notable, whether it be child pornography or ... something specific.' Ultimately, he discovered almost 1600 images of child pornography or suspected child pornography.
>
> Finally, [he] conducted an internet history examination by reviewing files known as 'index [dot] dat' files, which ... amount to a history of websites the computer user has visited. After extracting the ... files, [he] used ... NetAnalysis, which 'allows you to sort for suspected child pornography.' (*United States* v. *Crist* 2008)

Crist was indicted for possessing child pornography and moved to suppress the evidence obtained from his computer. The motion raised two issues:

(i) whether Agent Buckwash's examination exceeded the scope of Hipple's search of the computer; and (ii) whether the use of EnCase was a Fourth Amendment 'search' (*United States* v. *Crist* 2008).

The significance of the first issue derives from the fact that the Fourth Amendment only applies to actions by law enforcement officers. Hipple's looking through Crist's computer was not a Fourth Amendment search because he was acting on his own, not as an agent of the police (*United States* v. *Crist* 2008). The police could therefore look at everything he had seen – without getting a search warrant – and not violate the Fourth Amendment. Crist, though, claimed Buckwash's EnCase examination both exceeded the scope of Hipple's private search and itself constituted a 'search' under the Fourth Amendment (*United States* v. *Crist* 2008).

The prosecution argued (i) that because Hipple had been 'into' Crist's computer, Crist no longer had a Fourth Amendment expectation of privacy in the computer and (ii) that the EnCase examination was not a search because 'Buckwash never "accessed the computer" ', but 'simply ran hash values on it (*United States* v. *Crist* 2008). The court rejected the first argument, relying on a Court of Appeals case which held that simply because private citizens examined some disks belonging to the suspect did not mean he lost his Fourth Amendment expectation of privacy in the disks they did not examine.

That left the second issue: whether the EnCase examination was a Fourth Amendment search. If it was, it was unconstitutional because it clearly exceeded the scope of what Hipple had done (*United States* v. *Crist* 2008). The district court held it was a search:

> To derive the hash values ... the Government ... removed the hard drive from the computer, created a duplicate image ... and applied the EnCase program to each compartment, disk, file, folder, and bit. By subjecting the entire computer to a hash value analysis every file, internet history, picture, and 'buddy list' became available for Government review. Such examination constitutes a search.
>
> Moreover, the EnCase analysis is a search different in character from the one conducted by Hipple, and thus it cannot be defended on the grounds that it did not exceed the private party search ... [T]he rationale ... is that the private search was so complete, no privacy interest remained. That is certainly not the case here.
>
> Hipple opened 'a couple of videos' and deleted them, a far different scenario from the search in *Jacobsen*, wherein the opening of a package ... necessarily obviated any expectation of privacy. Here, the Hipple private search represented a discrete intrusion into a vast store of unknown electronic information. While Crist's privacy interest was lost as to the 'couple of videos' opened by Hipple, it is no foregone conclusion that his privacy interest was compromised as to all the computer's remaining contents.
>
> ... [T]he *Runyan* court found that no privacy interest remained in a disk once some of its contents had been viewed. As to the unopened disks, the court found privacy rights intact, and held unlawful a warrantless search of such disks. Where, as here, substantial privacy rights remained

after the private search and the government actors had reason to know the EnCase program would likely reveal more information than they had learned from Hipple's brief search ... the scope of the private search was exceeded ... (*United States* v. *Crist* 2008)

The court therefore ordered the evidence obtained through the forensic examination of Crist's computer to be suppressed.

While the *Crist* court did not specifically rely on *Kyllo* in reaching its conclusion, the *Kyllo* principle – that law enforcement's using technology not available to the general public constitutes a search – certainly influenced the result. The *Crist* court was careful to explain that the agent's EnCase analysis differed in scope and technique from the search conducted by the private citizens, differences that are a direct function of the agent's using the EnCase software.

The proposition that *Kyllo* influenced the *Crist* court's holding is also derivable from an opinion issued by a federal court of appeals. In *United States* v. *Andrus*, the defendant argued that a law enforcement agent's using EnCase to access password-protected files on the hard drive of his computer was a *Kyllo* search (*United States* v. *Andrus* 2007). Andrus claimed the agent erred in not determining whether the files were password-protected before he used EnCase to access them; his argument, essentially, was that by password protecting his files he had put them beyond the reach of the average citizen, therefore establishing a Fourth Amendment reasonable expectation of privacy in the files (*United States* v. *Andrus* 2007). He lost, because the Court of Appeals held that he had not shown that the use of password protection is so common in US society that officers should know to ask about it before using EnCase (*United States* v. *Andrus* 2007).

Andrus apparently thought he was raising a *Kyllo* argument, at least implicitly because the Court of Appeals did something unusual: after it rejected his appeal, it issued an opinion denying his request for rehearing; in the opinion, it found that the *Kyllo* issue had not explicitly been presented in the original appeal (*Andrus* 2). The court of appeals also noted, in this opinion, that its earlier decision had not reached the issue of whether EnCase software can be used to bypass password protection on computer files and whether *Kyllo* applies to the use of such technology (*Andrus* 2).

It is clear, from these cases, that the issue of whether *Kyllo* applies to the use of EnCase and similar technologies will be addressed by both state and federal courts in the near future.

Fifth Amendment and encryption

The Fifth Amendment states that no one can be 'compelled to be a witness against himself' (US Constitution, Amendment v). This creates what is known as the privilege against self-incrimination. It applies when someone is compelled to give testimony that incriminates him or her (*United States* v. *Hubbell* 2000).

The Fifth Amendment privilege only comes into play when all three elements are present. The first is compulsion; the Fifth Amendment does not protect communications that are made voluntarily; voluntary statements waive the privilege (*United States* v. *Mandujano* 1976). Compulsion usually takes the form of a subpoena enforceable by civil contempt sanctions (Hubbell 2000). The compulsion must seek to extort 'testimony' – oral or written communications – from an individual because the Fifth Amendment privilege does not encompass physical evidence *per se* (Hubbell 2000). But the act of producing physical evidence (documents, videotapes, etc.) in response to government compulsion can itself be a testimonial act encompassed by the privilege (Hubbell 2000).

To be 'testimonial,' the act of producing evidence must establish that the evidence exists, that it is within the control of the person being compelled to produce it and that the evidence produced is 'authentic', i.e. is the evidence sought by the subpoena (Hubbell 2000). Finally, the compelled testimony must be 'incriminating'; the Supreme Court has held that the privilege 'not only extends to answers that would in themselves support a conviction under a ... criminal statute but likewise embraces those which would furnish a link in the chain of evidence needed to prosecute the claimant for a crime' (Hoffman 1951).

Communications that are posted online – in whatever form – will be outside the privilege because the poster was not 'compelled' to post them, i.e. was not 'compelled' to testify. This is true regardless of whether the comments are posted in public areas such as websites or newsgroups or in private conversations in a chat room. Someone in a chat room chatting with an undercover officer is under no compulsion to have that conversation; indeed, she cannot be under any official compulsion because she is not aware she is speaking to an agent of the state. Compulsion is therefore quite lacking as to the content of communications posted online.

One area in which the Fifth Amendment can come into play involves the use of encryption. Encryption can be used to protect the contents of online communications or data files stored in a computer or on other storage media. If files are encrypted with an essentially unbreakable encryption algorithm, the only way law enforcement can access the content of those files is with the key that can be used to decrypt the files (*In re Boucher* 2007).

What if the owner of the files refuses to give up the key to law enforcement? In answering this question, the first issue that arises is whether the law enforcement request constitutes compulsion. If a grand jury issues a subpoena to the owner directing him to produce the key to the grand jury, this could implicate the privilege against self-incrimination. The subpoena establishes compulsion; and it is reasonable to assume, if only for the purposes of analysis, that the contents of the encrypted files will incriminate their owner. The critical question, therefore, is whether or not the subpoena compels the production of incriminating *testimony*.

Answering this question requires considering two different scenarios: in the first, the owner of the files has committed the key to memory, so to 'produce' the key to the grand jury he would have to appear before the grand jury and tell them what the key is. In the second scenario, the owner of the files has recorded the key somewhere, in a diary, let us say; to 'produce' this key to the grand jury he would have to give the grand jury the entry in the diary.

If the owner of the files committed the key to memory, then he can claim the Fifth Amendment privilege and refuse to recite it before the grand jury as long as the contents of the files would incriminate him. Reciting the key to the grand jury constitutes a factual assertion: the owner is being asked 'What is the key needed to encrypt these files?' If he answers, he would be responding with a factual assertion in the form of 'The key needed to encrypt these files is ...' This establishes testimony. And although the key itself may not be incriminating, it becomes a link in the chain of evidence needed to prosecute him if the contents of the files are incriminating, since the government cannot access the contents of those files unless he 'testifies' as to the key. But while the privilege would protect someone from being compelled to recite a memorised encryption key, the government could override the claim of the privilege by granting the person immunity for the act of producing the key (Hubbell 2000).

This scenario essentially occurred in a federal case from Vermont (Boucher 2007). Boucher was entering the United States from Canada; a Customs Officer took his laptop, turned it on and saw file names that seemed to indicate the files contained child pornography (Boucher 2007). Since the officer could not open the files, he asked Boucher for assistance; Boucher did 'something' to the laptop out of the officer's sight. After the officer looked a little more, he turned the laptop off; when he tried to turn it on, he discovered that the hard drive was now encrypted (Boucher 2007).

A grand jury subpoenaed Boucher and ordered him to produce the encryption key for the laptop. The opinion indicates the government wanted Boucher to give it the key, which implies that he had it memorised and would have been able to tell them what it was. Boucher moved to quash the subpoena, claiming it required him to give testimony that incriminated him; Boucher argued that his act of producing the key constituted testimony that was incriminating and was compelled, because it would be given under the subpoena (Boucher 2007).

The federal court agreed; it found the act of producing the encryption key was testimonial under the standard outlined above: 'Entering a password into the computer implicitly communicates facts. By entering the password Boucher would be disclosing the fact that he knows the password and has control over the files on drive Z. The procedure is equivalent to asking Boucher, "Do you know the password to the laptop?" ' (Boucher 2007). The court therefore granted Boucher's motion to quash the subpoena, which presumably means the government cannot proceed with a prosecution based on the contents of the laptop (if, indeed, they include child pornography). Giving Boucher immunity was obviously not an option the government could pursue because immunity would prevent the government from using (i) the password and (ii) anything derived from his producing the password (i.e. the contents of the laptop) against him.

There are, so far, no cases addressing the second scenario. For this scenario, assume the encryption key is recorded as a diary entry. The key itself is not testimony; it is an artefact, not a communication. But if the owner delivers the key to the grand jury, it can be used to 'produce' the contents of the encrypted files; as in the *Boucher* case, the government has the file but their content is inaccessible without the key. The issue therefore is whether the owner's act of giving the entry containing the key to the grand jury is a testimonial act of production encompassed by the privilege against self-incrimination. If providing the key is testimony, then the owner – like Boucher – can claim the privilege because the elements of compulsion and incrimination are present; if the act of providing the key is not testimonial, then the owner cannot claim the privilege. Basically, the question is whether this scenario differs in any material respect from the *Boucher* scenario. Logically, it should not.

The problem is that while the Supreme Court has not addressed this situation, it has suggested that the act of producing the key to a strongbox containing incriminating documents is not 'testimony' within the scope of the Fifth Amendment privilege, but the act of reciting the combination to a wall safe containing such documents is (Hubbell 2000). The distinction the Court draws is whether the act in question requires an individual to express 'the contents of his own mind' (Doe 1988). In dicta (i.e. language that was not part of the holding of a case), the Court has indicted that handing over a tangible key is a purely physical act like the other acts it has found not to be testimonial, but reciting a combination does require the person to use his or her mind to make a factual assertion, e.g., 'the combination to the safe is ... ' That premise, of course, is consistent with the holding in the *Boucher* case.

The Supreme Court's dicta can be construed as indicating that when the encryption key in this second scenario was recorded, it assumed tangible form and became an artefact like the key to a strongbox. Under this theory, since the key has an independent, external existence, the owner of the files can give the key to the grand jury without having to communicate the contents of his own mind, which would eliminate his ability to claim the privilege against self-incrimination. While this analysis can be derived from comments in various Supreme Court opinions, it seems both inappropriate and inconsistent with prior cases applying the 'act of producing evidence as testimony' principle. Courts have held, for example, that producing a gun in response to a court order was encompassed by this principle, which meant the owner of the gun could take the Fifth Amendment and refuse to comply with the order (*People v. Havrish* 2007). If the act of producing guns and other tangible items can be testimonial under the Fifth Amendment, then there is no reason why the act of producing an encryption key that has been recorded or otherwise reduced to tangible form should not also be protected.

Further reading

In the US, most of what has been, and is being, written about cybercrime appears in articles published in law reviews. There is, so far, no law review that specialises in cybercrime, but the Journals of Law and Technology published (often online) by a number of US law schools sometimes publish articles in this area. The best way to locate those articles would be simply to run a Google search for the topic cybercrime and a Journal of Law and Technology (also known as JOLT). There are few books in this area, probably because the field is still relatively new; another factor may be the fact that US law is changing rapidly, so books are not the ideal way to address these issues. *Cybercrime: The Investigation, Prosecution and Defence of a Computer-Related Crime* (2006) edited by Ralph Clifford (Columbia Academic Press) is an excellent survey of both US law and practice. Brenner's *Cyber Threats: Emerging Fault Lines in the Nation-*

State (2009) (Oxford: Oxford University Press) surveys how the US generally deals with the challenges of cybercrime.

References

17 US Code s.101.

17 US Code s.106.

17 US Code s.1201.

18 US Code s.371.

18 US Code s.1030.

18 US Code s.1466A.

18 US Code s.1951.

18 US Code s.2256.

18 US Code s.2252A.

18 US Code s.2256.

28 US Code s.1295.

47 US Code s.231.

American Civil Liberties Union v. Gonzales (2007) US District Court for the Eastern District of Pennsylvania, 478 F.Supp.2d 775.

American Civil Liberties Union v. Mukasey (2008) US Court of Appeals for the Third Circuit, 534 F.3d 181.

Annual Review of Criminal Procedure (2008) 'Warrantless Searches and Seizures,' *Georgetown Law Journal*, 37: 39–132.

Argento, Z. (2008) 'Interpreting Chamberlain's "Reasonable Relation" between Access and Infringement in the Digital Millennium Copyright Act', *Boston College Intellectual Property and Technology Forum*, 102902.

Ashcroft v. American Civil Liberties Union (2004) US Supreme Court, 542 US 656.

Ashcroft v. Free Speech Coalition (2002) US Supreme Court, 535 US 234.

Bangeman, E. (2008) 'Tennessee Anti-P2P Law to Cost Colleges over $13 Million', *Ars Technica*, November 18.

Bierschbach, R. and Stein, A. (2007) 'Mediating Rules in Criminal Law', *Virginia Law Review*, 93: 1197–1258.

Blueport Co., LLC v. United States (2008) US Court of Appeals for the Federal Circuit, 533 F.3d 1374.

Capitol Records, Inc. v. Thomas (2008) US District Court for the District of Minnesota, 2008 WL 4405282.

Chamberlain Group, Inc. v. Skylink Technologies, Inc. (2004) US Court of Appeals for the Federal Circuit, 381 F.3d 1178.

Child Pornography Protection Act (1996) Pub. L. 104-208, Div. A, Title I, s.101(a) [Title I, s.121, 110 Stat. 3009.

Decker, C. (2008) 'Cyber Crime 2.0: An Argument to Update the United States Criminal Code to Reflect the Changing Nature of Cyber Crime', *Southern California Law Review*, 81: 959–1016.

Doe v. United States (1988) US Supreme Court, 487 US 201.

Eltringham, S. (ed.) (1997) 'Prosecuting Computer Crimes', US Department of Justice, http://www.usdoj.gov/criminal/cybercrime/ccmanual/index.html.

Feldmeier, J. (2003) 'Close Enough for Government Work: An Examination of Congressional Efforts to Reduce the Government's Burden of Proof in Child Pornography Cases', *Northern Kentucky Law Review*, 30: 205–28.

Free Speech Coalition v. Reno (1999) US Court of Appeals for the Ninth Circuit, 298 F.3d 1083.

Hoffman v. United States (1951) US Supreme Court, 341 US 479.

Hoffstadt, B. (2007) 'The Voyeuristic Hacker,' *Journal of Internet Law*, 11: 1–20.

Identity Theft Enforcement and Restitution Act of 2008, Pub. L. 110-326, Title II, ss.203–208, 122 Stat. 3561 (2008).

In re Boucher (2007) US District Court for the District of Vermont, 2007 WL 4246473.

In re US (2008) US District Court for the Eastern District of New York, 2008 WL 5082506.

In re US for Orders (2007) US District Court for the Eastern District of New York, 515 F.Supp.2d 325.

Katz v. United States (1967) US Supreme Court, 389 US 347.

Kravets, D. (2008) 'Thomas Mistrial Decision Bolsters RIAA Litigation', *Wired*, 25 September.

Kyllo v. United States (2001) US Supreme Court, 533 US 27.

Leahy, P. (2000) 'Statement of Senator Leahy at Markup of Hatch-Leahy-Schumer Substitute Amendment to S. 2448', US Senator Patrick Leahy, http://leahy.senate. gov/press/200010/001005.html

Miller v. California (1973) US Supreme Court, 413 US 15.

National Car Rental System, Inc. v. Computer Associates International, Inc. (1993) US Court of Appeals for the Eighth Circuit, 991 F.2d 426.

Ohm, P. (2008) 'The Myth of the Superuser: Fear, Risk, and Harm Onine', *UC Davis Law Review*, 41: 1327–1402.

Olmstead v. United States (1928) US Supreme Court, 277 US 438.

People v. Havrish (2007) Court of Appeals of New York, 8 NY3d 389, 866 NE2d 1009.

Prosecutorial Remedies and Other Tools to end the Exploitation of Children Today Act of 2003 (2003) Pub.L. 108–21, Title I, s.103, Title V, ss.502–507, 510, 117 Stat. 650.

Protection of Children Against Sexual Exploitation Act (1977) Pub. L. 95–225, s.2(a), 92 Stat. 7.

Reno v. American Civil Liberties Union (1997) US Supreme Court, 521 US 844.

Skibell, R. (2003) 'Cybercrimes & Misdemeanors: A Re-evaluation of the Computer Fraud and Abuse Act', *Berkeley Technology Law Journal*, 18: 909–44.

Smith v. Maryland (1979) US Supreme Court, 442 US 735.

Soldal v. Cook County (1992) US Supreme Court, 506 US 56.

Tratos, M. (2008) 'Entertainment on the Internet: The Evolution of Entertainment Production, Distribution Ownership, and Control in the Digital Age', Practicing Law Institute, 930: 259–77.

USA PATRIOT Act (2001) Pub. L. 107–56, Title V, s.506(a), Title VIII, s.814, 115 Stat. 366, 382.

United States Department of Justice (2004) 'Press Release – Wi-Fi Hacker Pleads Guilty to Attempted $17,000,000 Extortion', http://www.usdoj.gov/criminal/cybercrime/ tereshchukPlea.htm.

United States Department of Justice (2007) 'Prosecuting Computer Crimes', http:// www.cybercrime.gov/ccmanual/index.html

United States Senate Report No. 99–432 (1986) 'The Computer Fraud and Abuse Ac of 1986', 1986 US Code Congressional and Administrative News, pp. 2479–96.

United States v. Andrus (2007) US Court of Appeals for the Tenth Circuit, 483 F.3d 711.

United States v. Andrus (2007) US Court of Appeals for the Tenth Circuit, 499 F.3d 1162 (Andrus 2).

United States v. Crist (2008) US District Court for the Middle District of Pennsylvania, 2008 WL 4682806.

United States v. Handley (2008) US District Court for the Southern District of Iowa, 564 F. Supp.2d 996.

United States v. Hubbell (2000) US Supreme Court, 530 US 27.

United States v. Jacobsen (1984) US Supreme Court, 466 US 109.

United States v. Mandujano (1976) US Supreme Court, 425 US 564.

United States v. Pok Seong Kwong (2007) US Court of Appeals for the Fifth Circuit, 237 Fed. Appx. 966.

United States v. Williams (2008) US Supreme Court, 128 S.Ct. 1830.

Chapter 22

Transnational developments in Internet law

Katherine S. Williams

Introduction

Information, communication and communication technologies might be said to form the basis of modern life. They lie at the core of social relations, business relations and power relations in the modern era. World politics can no longer simply deal with international relations nor just with nation states; it has to take note of information, information pathways and the spread of information infrastructures and of the uses made of these by businesses and other non-state actors. Some refer to this as the information revolution and, in a particularly insightful discussion, Toffler (1980) called it the 'Third Wave' of the evolution of human societies. The first wave was a move from hunter-gatherer to agricultural societies; the second moved from agricultural to industrial societies; and the current third wave sees us transferring from industrial to information societies. Toffler predicted that this third 'revolution' towards an information society or information age would be as fundamental in changing our society as were the first two. The general acceptance is that this information 'revolution' and the proliferation and diffusion of international communication technologies has spearheaded the globalisation of modern life in both space and time and has had impacts across all aspects of modern life: social, educational, entertainment, economic, cultural, political, diplomatic, military, criminal and terrorist. If this is true it means that power and politics encompass more than nation states and their needs and struggles (Luke 2001: 113). Real power changes can take place over the Internet or in the media; the Internet means that the power to inform, persuade, debate, witness, discuss, slander, disseminate misinformation or disinformation, carry out propaganda attacks can be done by anyone, anywhere, any time, and can reach millions of others. If this is truly the information age it means that real power is more democratic; it also means that discovering truth is more possible but also more complex and time-consuming. It is easier to motivate and move people to act, on truth or on supposed truths. The information era has democratised power and international relations.

Those are the positive elements, but there are also negative factors. The Internet has had global effects on criminality; ordinary criminal offences may be committed through use of the Internet, there are new ways of offending, and the Internet itself might be the object of offending. It has also opened up new ways of mass offending. The use of computers and particularly the Internet for criminal and deviant acts by individuals, corporations and states are well known. Criminals no longer need physical proximity between them and their victim and an offence can be committed against a system or computer without being aware of its physical location. Many offences can be committed by one person simultaneously against a number of victims in diverse locations at set times when the offender has an alibi. Physical elements such as time and place may therefore be distorted, as might identity. Impersonation is possible, there is no need for physical similarities and one can 'move around' almost invisibly. It can be useful to some dangerous groups such as paedophiles and terrorist organisations (see Chapters 10, 16 and 17). It has also opened up possibilities for extension of state control or state harm (McGuire 2007). In this chapter these extreme offences will be briefly considered to test the effectiveness of international controls.

Whatever deviance or offending is undertaken its consequences can be more far-reaching than before because it is not geographically or temporally restricted by state boundaries; this alters the nature of interactions and of deviance but does not necessarily render them completely different (McGuire 2007). The new behaviours test and stretch existing legal concepts, regulatory frameworks and social 'norms' or expectations. Much has been written about its global nature and the claimed impossibility of regulation or control whether by laws or otherwise by single sovereign states (see, for example, Brenner 2004, 2007: 14, and Chapter 21 of this volume) and this has led to calls for a need to grant national systems functionality across international boundaries and for international or multinational systems (though these claims are questioned: Goldsmith and Wu 2006; McGuire 2007). This chapter will focus on the international aspects of control – legal and regulatory – and on the call for governments and states to recognise the need for a comprehensive new policy and new institutional structure to deal with the threats and vulnerabilities associated with this globally interconnected information system and thereby ensure public safety and economic and social stability. It will consider first the regulatory aspects, then the more legal controls and finally assess these as well as questioning what they might achieve and whose ends they serve.

The presumed ideal running through this chapter is that one should aim to preserve as much free expression and other individual rights as possible while also preventing computers and the Internet from being used to harm and destroy individuals, their rights or their communities/societies. Sometimes aspects of this ideal conflict and each individual will need to assess how it ought to be resolved; here the resolutions of the international community will be laid out for consideration and assessment.

Regulation versus law

The Internet is not controlled by vertical hierarchies but rather by loose social networks which are lateral systems having no permanent identity; they decentralise power, so empowering individual members and having positive democratic outcomes. All these positive aspects of networks also open them up to those intent on exploitation and domination. The question is how to control the negative while not stifling the positive. The temptation is to tame the technology, to shoehorn it into the present hierarchical systems of control, particularly the legal and commercial power of states. However, many of the differences between negative behaviours online and in the real world suggest that the pure model of national legal constraint will fail. In this climate a more international framework is likely to arise; at the moment this has largely tended to support the national constraints, facilitating cross-border investigations etc. (see discussion below) though there are some differences.

In particular it is generally accepted that control of cyberspace cannot be achieved through law alone, rather it must include four means: law; 'code' (meaning computer code) and Internet governance (Lessig 2006); the market; and norms of behaviour. Only two aspects act strongly at an international level – Internet governance and law – and these will form the core of the consideration in the rest of this chapter. Some of the international legal instruments call upon states to use regulation through the market and through norms of behaviour.

Regulation by code and Internet governance

Whilst regulation by code is not exclusively an international method of control it is clear that it operates across international boundaries. Here the basic architecture of the Internet provides the tools whereby it might be controlled or regulated. Underlying the operation of computer interaction, especially the Internet, is the code, the facility and rules by which the computers interconnect. From early on, the desire was to keep governments and therefore legal controls away from the basic governance of the Internet so, it was hoped, preserving free expression and privacy. This required regulation based on the technical requirements necessary to guarantee person-to-person communication (P2P) backed up with self-regulation and private sector leadership. The ideal was to deliver effective regulation from the building blocks of the Internet, from within its most basic and crucial aspects, and by this means guarantee that everything else would necessarily be controlled. To act outside the code would not be possible as it would break out of the system itself, rather like not being able to drive too fast because a car engine is not built to go above a certain speed or because speed cameras as you enter an area affect the operation of an engine preventing it speeding. Therefore in the 1990s Internet governance became linked to governance without governments and involved the technical management of the Internet in governing aspects like domain names, IP addresses, Internet protocols and the root server system. This bottom up governance, excluding governments, was seen to be the best way to protect individual freedoms such as freedom of expression, to ensure speedy access by users and to guarantee flexibility for the introduction of new innovations in an area where new Internet services and applications were rapidly appearing.

In 1999 Lessig noted the success of this form of governance for the first 20 years of the Internet and delineated code as being the means by which or the place where our ideals and values would be protected or destroyed. He noted that people write code and in so doing decide which values to respect and which will be broken. Code, like law, is artificially constructed and whilst many applaud the way in which it protects both individual rights of access to the Internet and freedom of expression, some see these as negative and as destructive of social values where they interfere with competing ideals such as protection from racial hatred or the desire to preserve a particular social, political or religious order or state. For Lessig (1999, 2006) the test is to keep the code free and serving pubic interests of openness and neutrality, especially as to content. Many others, especially some governments want to tame the Internet and the information it delivers. Private interests and individuals would also like to control the physical and code elements, to exploit it for personal gain. Fortunately, in its early years the Internet was run for public benefit, the good of the many. The question is, will that remain and how will it be protected?

Interestingly, although design of the Internet was funded by US government resources, the US Government did not interfere in its construction, its governance nor in which values were protected. However, the private initiatives involved have been US and those working on the code embraced US values and the architecture they constructed tends to prioritise these; elements like free expression, free access to information and privacy are given central places. By the mid 1990s the influence of the Internet on social, commercial and political life was clear, and some states wanted greater influence over the system; the US favoured continued distance from government influences and, under its influence, a new non-profit-making private corporation was set up, the Internet Corporation for Assigned Names and Numbers (ICANN). It had a memorandum of understanding intended to guarantee that the market and private forces, not governments, would lead the development of the Internet – there were four aspects of this: security and stability of the Internet; competition in the domain name server (DNS) market; bottom-up policy development; and global representation; it was only the last that included governmental input, which was in the form of advice only and could be ignored. The advice came from the international Governmental Advisory Committee (GAC). The hope was that ICANN could protect the Internet from interference, that it could remain governed by and for the imperatives of the information era: absolute access to information, freedom of expression and privacy. However, any outside control was always bound to have some effect. The question was how much the new 'improved' regulation would alter the Internet.

To begin with it was fairly minimal, especially as state control was only advisory. There were some worrying changes, for example in 2000 after intervention from the UN World Intellectual Property Organisation (WIPO), the architecture of the Net started to be used to protect intellectual property rights over privacy and over free access to all media, by protecting well-known names and trademarks and allowing intellectual property right holders access to registration contact details of those who violate their rights. Then, following the terrorist attacks on 11 September 2001 the whole mood of the administration and control underlying code altered, and GAC began to insist on some control to turn the Internet from an ideal of a democratic domain into a more secure zone; they insisted on cybersecurity and so ICANN had to justify any decision to ignore GAC advice.

Despite this closer control many governments remained dissatisfied, especially as GAC only included 100 states whereas the Internet is truly global. In 2003 the UN called a World Summit on the Information Society (WSIS) to consider the global digital divide between rich and poor countries and to ensure that 50 per cent of the world's population was connected by 2015 (for more information see http://www.itu.int/wsis/index.html). At this summit some states called for greater governmental control of the Internet while others saw this as a threat to individual rights, to economic interests, and as something which would result in slowdown of the system and a threat to the integration of future advances. In the end the WSIS envisaged a 'people-centred, inclusive and development-oriented Information Society where everyone can create, access, utilise and share information and knowledge, enabling individuals, communities and peoples to achieve their full potential' (WSIS 2003: principle 1). There were also suggestions for greater involvement of civil society (Civil Society 2003) and to ensure respect for human rights and communication rights. Out of the summit the Working Group on Internet Governance (WGIG) was established to provide recommendations. WGIG was a multi-stakeholder partnership of governments, the private sector and civil society (including technical and academic members) where each participant was equal and was intended to develop an inclusive model of governance. It defined Internet governance as 'the development and application by governments, the private sector and civil society, in their respective roles, of shared principles, norms, rules, decision-making procedures, and programmes that shape the evolution and use of the Internet' (WGIG 2005) and suggested that the multi-agency approach should be expanded and strengthened. However, they could not agree on a final model and instead suggested a number of possibilities, each of which involved a lessening of US control, something the US were reluctant to agree to, wishing to retain oversight over some aspects while recognising that other nations had an interest in their own country code Top Level Domain (ccTLD). After discussing this at the WSIS meeting in Tunis in 2005 some common, though rather vague, ground was found. Firstly, they agreed on some basic principles of Internet governance such as multi-stakeholder involvement, security and stability of the Internet, national control (sovereignty) over ccTLD domain name space, and that the role for each government in Internet governance should be equal. Secondly, they resolved to establish a multi-stakeholder discussion group which would not have decision-making capacity: an Internet Governance Forum (IGF). Finally, they decided to begin enhanced cooperation among 'relevant organisations' (including governmental and non-governmental bodies). Some interpreted this enhanced negotiation as a better flow of information while others saw it as a process to move towards a cooperative model for the management of critical aspects of the Internet. One thing which is clear from Tunis is that this cooperation should not interfere with day-to-day technical and operational matters but rather relates to international public policy issues (Tunis 2005: paragraph 69); there is however no indication of where one ends and the other begins.

Following Tunis a system was put in place called the Joint Project Agreement (JPA) which gave ICANN some independence from the US government. This has led to better relations and greater consultation between ICANN and other governments and agencies, a broadening of the membership of the ICANN board and a closer relationship between ICANN and GAC. Despite strong attempts these moves and others have led to confidence that a bottom-up process of development will still work and deliver Internet governance fit for the future. However, formal intergovernmental negotiations are less positive and there is still little formal agreement on how this should interact with the day-to-day functioning of the Net.

There are other problems: Lessig (and others whose ideal is absolute freedom and delivering open public networks) warn that the changes in ICANN board membership have instated individuals with a more closed perspective and are delivering a network more likely to serve big commercial interests and governments rather than individuals and the public. This is happening while the system retains the appearance of protecting free access and freedom of expression; it is portrayed as corrosion from within (see Murray 2007: ch. 4). However, it seems likely that ICANN's days are numbered. Whether it will be replaced by a system that serves the commercial community and protects elements such as trademarks and intellectual property, or one that serves the wider Internet community, and how much governmental control comes to the fore, are the questions as yet unresolved. The first will lead to a closed and controlled market, the second to greater freedom of expression. The effect of governmental control will differ depending on which governments take precedence; within states governmental control is, in some parts of the world, overtaking the international protections and standards.

From this it is clear that 'code' and 'government without governance' has so far generally served the Internet and its users well. It has given the widest possible access to the information age and protected individuals from the worst excesses of political/religious/and even economic control. However, it is also clear that states are becoming increasingly mindful of the power of the Internet and the need to control and/or harness that to their own ends. In some states this has led to massive interference with access to the Internet, in others it has meant that there are calls to curb access to protect certain political ideals or values such as protecting children from harms caused by viewing certain information or harm caused by hate messages (personal, political or other). Most states recognise that controls of these sorts through code may be unacceptable or unattainable and therefore turn to legal means.

Control through the persuasive intervention of international governmental organisations

The international community is powerless to encroach on national sovereignty by imposing international action and many international instruments wish to respect this sovereignty so fall shy of legal rules and instead set out ideals, leaving states to decide how to realise them. This is control through persuasion, and generally the international community persuades states to alter their internal laws in order to achieve the ideals. Here two such endeavours will be considered. The first is that set out by the Organisation for Economic Cooperation and Development (OECD), an international organisation of 30 countries (mostly developed nations) drawn together to preserve the ideals of representative democracy and the free market economy. As seen below the OECD uses education and persuasion to try to move states to take measures, often protective but non-controlling, to safeguard its citizens from harm. The second is that attempted by the European Union (EU), a political and economic union of 27 member states whose core function is to unify legal rules so as to deliver a single market guaranteeing free movement of people, goods, services and capital. The EU uses two measures, the first is persuasive and asks states to set in place similar safeguards to those suggested by the OECD, and the second moves to a more legal level and is used particularly where the free market may be thought to be in danger.

OECD guidelines for the security of information systems

Since 1986 the OECD has also been active in the area of computer security. In the 1980s it identified a range of activities relating to companies that it considered should attract criminal sanctions in order to protect commerce and economic stability. In 1992 it published its first Guidelines for the Security of Information Systems and this was updated in 2002. This calls on all users to take responsibility for developing and maintaining computer security, as it is only if everyone takes responsibility that the OECD believes we can approach a culture of security and make the Internet as safe an environment as possible. It recognises that different users engage at different levels and that this should be reflected in the level of responsibility they should be expected to embrace. Individual end users are therefore given advice on matters such as ensuring virus-checking software is installed on their computers and is kept up to date. Governments, on the other hand, are called upon to take active measures to ensure greater security and these are expanded on in the Implementation Plan (OECD 2003). The first raft of measures calls on governments to put in place a national policy concerning information security and ensure that they deliver cross-border cooperation so that a global culture of security can become a reality (they might do this through ratifying the Council of Europe's Cybercrime Convention). It also expects nation states to support other participants in civil society in their efforts to address security by, for example, raising awareness of law and policy in this area and both raising awareness of and facilitating the adoption of relevant responses by users and providers of services. It also suggests that governments take internal initiatives to combat cybercrimes by:

- enacting a comprehensive set of substantive criminal, procedural and mutual assistance legal measures to combat cybercrime and ensure cross-border cooperation. These should be at least as comprehensive as, and consistent with, the Convention on Cybercrime (2001);

- identifying national cybercrime units and international high-technology assistance points of contact and creating such capabilities to the extent they do not already exist;

- establishing institutions that exchange threat and vulnerability assessments such as national CERTs (Computer Emergency Response Teams); and

- developing closer cooperation between government and business in the fields of information security and fighting cybercrime.

The OECD therefore seeks to persuade states of the importance of making provision in this area without requiring it. Whilst it recognises a prominent place for legal regulation and international legal structures and cooperation on enforcement, it only views this as one tool in the building of a secure system and seeks a more all-encompassing regime. In 2005 it prepared a report on how member states had chosen to deal with computer security which provided a rich information resource on national approaches to the problem. The report calls on all computer users to play a part and places on an equal footing legal and self-regulatory systems as well as individual vigilance in the building of a secure community; truly an all-inclusive culture of security.

European Union framework decision on attacks against information systems

The European Union was fairly quick to recognise the importance of the information society and its potential for opening up new services and markets that could be exploited by its business base and enjoyed by its citizens. They also recognised early on the potential dangers which might arise from exploitation of this technology and therefore the need for a legal framework to regulate it and allow it to be fully exploited without any fetters on competition or any dangers to trade and industry or even to individuals.

One of their earliest moves was the Commissions Communication on *Illegal and Harmful Content on the Internet* (COM (96), 487 final) that purported to be a protection for the individual and for the promotion of democracy. However, it became embroiled in EU politics, and subject to the competing pulls of free expression, the legal structure of the internal market, competition rules and rules concerning free services. Consequently it became more an instrument to ensure that the Internet provided the conditions necessary for commercial growth both of the Internet itself and of legitimate industries, services and businesses that relied on it. It focused on the tightening up of legal aspects so that it would provide the certainty necessary for business to grow.

However, the desire to protect individuals has never died and whilst not intervening too greatly the EU has recognised the need for some protection of individuals such as in the area of protecting young people (Green Paper 1996). This led to the first legal protection of minors and human dignity in Council Recommendation 98/560/EC (1998) which promoted a national framework expecting member states to pass laws to ensure the widest possible level of freedom of expression while also protecting the consumer and ensuring that content did not breach basic standards of human dignity nor impair the development of minors. Due to rapid changes in technology and the media this was updated in Council Recommendation 2006/952/EC (2006) which called states to take further action. Member states are expected to ensure:

1 that individuals and businesses enjoy a right of reply across all media, including the largely unregulated online media;

2 that measures exist to enable young people to make responsible and safe use of audiovisual and online information services (by, for example, improving parental awareness and training teachers and others as to the means of ensuring safe use by young people);

3 that they work to promote a responsible attitude on the part of the information services industry, professionals, intermediaries and users by encouraging industry to avoid all discrimination, encouraging widespread and simple public reporting of illegal content or use of the Internet; and draw up a code of conduct to be followed by the audiovisual and online information services industry and professionals and a Kitemark or quality label to show users whether a service has complied with the right standards.

The Council also expects the industry to take positive measures to protect young people, including the exchange of best practice across the industries and member states and the adoption of EU-agreed symbols and warning messages; the use of filters to prevent material which offends human dignity being carried over the Internet; an accepted content labelling system for all television and online services; and the adoption of both protection against discrimination online and the active promotion of equal potential of for example men and women. Finally, the Commission recognised it should take a positive responsibility to protect both minors and human dignity so agreed to: support the establishment of a second-level domain name which would only host sites which guaranteed respect for dignity and protection of young people; introduce a free phone number with information about these issues; and support the exchange of information and best practice across the industry so facilitating the creation of codes of conduct and a system of self-regulation.

More widely there are a few other protections for individuals. As did the US the EU chose to lay legal responsibility for illegal content with those who create and choose to distribute it rather than with those who provide the connectivity of service, Internet service providers (ISPs). However, whilst promoting the possibility of self-regulation it envisaged the need for an underlying system allowing the competent authorities (often the police) to intervene in protecting the consumer from illegal or harmful content, though this aspect has always been problematic and the line between the illegal and the otherwise somewhat harmful has never been clear. It has therefore left the door open to the imposition of different levels of moral regulation by each member state as was accepted in the case of *R* v. *Henn and Darby* (Case 34/79 [1979] ECR 3795, Decision of the Court of Justice). Many saw this as moving away from democracy and guarantees of free expression. Furthermore whilst such a compromise might be operable in the offline community it contravenes the borderless nature of online information services and so arguably is in breach of the free market in this area and thereby is seen as contravening the democratic and free basis of the Internet.

In each of the above the EU relies on persuasion and setting of standards it hopes that states will respect, or allowing states to set boundaries of decency which might reflect their own national standards but be different from those in other states. These are very mild international actions and serve to suggest a harmonised approach but not to harmonise control at either a national or international level. However, in its protection of the market it has sometimes strived to go further, setting standards for control.

By 1999 the Commission of the European Union had come to recognise that information systems (including personal computers, personal digital organisers, mobile telephones, intranets, extranets and the networks, servers and other infrastructure of the Internet) and communications networks had become a central element in the lives both of its citizens and of businesses in member states and that these systems were becoming increasingly difficult to separate and delineate. They wanted citizens and businesses to enjoy the clear benefits offered by these new technologies but were increasingly aware of problems arising out of these media; problems which could arise from anywhere in the world and jeopardise information security (the ability of systems to confidently resist accidental events or malicious actions). In response to the need for a competitive 'knowledge-based economy' that would deliver growth and job creation, the Commission (eEurope 1999) designed an action plan to help Europe to exploit the full potential of the new technologies while avoiding their most damaging elements. The Commission believed this would also help to protect the environment and improve people's quality of life. This resulted in the adoption of the European Union Framework Decision on Attacks Against Information Systems (EU Council Framework Decision 2005/222/JHA of 24 February 2005) that aims to strengthen criminal judicial cooperation on attacks against information systems. This is achieved through the development of effective tools and procedures. The Decision applies to criminal offences committed intentionally and involving: illegal access to information systems (such as hacking); illegal data interference; and illegal system interference which includes the intentional serious hindering or interruption of the functioning of an information system by whatever means (for example, a denial of service attack) which can cause hundreds of millions of pounds worth of damage as well as damaging the reputation of legitimate enterprises, undermining confidence in the systems. It covers all forms of malicious software that might be used to modify or destroy data (such as viruses, logic bombs, Trojan horses and worms). The Framework Decision includes malicious interception of communications, something that breaks confidentiality and privacy and undermines reliability, malicious misrepresentation such as identity theft or spoofing and aiding, abetting and attempting to commit these offences.

It further calls on states to lay down effective and deterrent punishments (it includes ideas such as the temporary or permanent disqualification from online activity) and requires states to view substantial losses caused by a criminal organisation as an aggravating circumstance. Jurisdiction can be taken for acts on a member state's territory or by one of its nationals, where more than one state could take jurisdiction they are expected to cooperate in one action. As with the Cybercrime Convention they are required to exchange and share relevant information and evidence and to establish 24-hour contact availability. In fact, in many ways, the Framework Decision mirrors the Cybercrime Convention, lending weight to the need for member states to alter their national laws to bring them in line with the Convention and so ratify it.

The EU seems to have a rather schizophrenic approach to Internet regulation and be undecided about the proper balance between the promotion of responsible and focused self-regulation guided by EU pronouncements and the desire on the part of the EU and member states to take control and impose regulation from above. The tension is most strongly felt where the Internet is seen to threaten or prejudice free-market competition, one of the guiding principles of the EU. This tension is replicated at the broader international level.

International law

Generally criminal laws and their enforcement, including the investigation and criminal court procedures, are all set at a national level. Assuming that national authorities use their laws to uphold their international obligations such as areas protected by United Nations rights treaties and similar fundamental documents, international treaties generally leave the limits of the criminal law and enforcement regulations for national sovereignty. Whilst a few crimes such as murder are recognised by almost all states, most criminal law is very culturally specific. Even where a crime, such as murder, is almost universally recognised and controlled the exact definition is culturally defined; so, for example, in some states euthanasia is always murder, in others it might be excused or even legalised in defined cases. Therefore, most criminal laws are jurisdictional and in most cases all elements of the offence are committed in one state so that territorial differences only rarely become inconvenient and often extradition is sufficient to deal with them, or they are dealt with via international agreements concerning respect for foreign judgements (including enforcements of criminal punishments). There is therefore (except in the area of war or large-scale human rights atrocities) rarely any need for international criminal laws. However, the global nature of the Internet has caused this accepted status quo to be questioned and the call has been for both harmonisation of the criminal law through the passing of internationally accepted substantive criminal laws and agreements on policing global Internet use for criminal activities. In Internet offending where the laws and their enforcement are territorial but the offences or the means of committing them may be spread over and have effects in many territories the problems begin to arise and the cracks in a territorially based legal and enforcement system are clear; it provides a perfect scenario for would-be offenders to take advantage, often with impunity. The offenders can avail themselves of the borderless advantages of the Internet while enforcement agencies are hampered by the need to respect each other's sovereignty. In this area national laws controlling computer security might be thought to be a waste of time and in many respects they are. They do not provide real security but rather serve national interests; they give an appearance of computer security so businesses might believe that they are less likely to suffer from such criminal attacks and feel safe setting up within that territory but they often fail to provide real security for computer users, whether they are individuals or companies, especially against concerted and planned acts of computer offending. If criminal controls are to succeed then they need to apply across national boundaries, preferably having global application. This has led to calls for bilateral, multilateral and international cooperation in defining crimes and in the pooling of investigative and enforcement techniques, the claim is that without these international mechanisms control of crimes committed through and on this medium will be impossible.

Piecemeal control through individual crimes

Many international controls are piecemeal and some arise out of international interventions to control non-Internet behaviours. Here, rather than tackling Internet crime as a whole, the international legal community moves to deal with one aspect or type of problem. Problems chosen are generally those with most significance for the political systems involved. One such area (and the only one considered here) is piracy; it is of focal importance to the economic well-being of Western states. Control in this area grows out of non-Internet crime. From the 1970s the global problems of counterfeit goods and piracy started to be recognised and GATT (General Agreement on Tariffs and Trade) opened international negotiations for the control of this area. In 1994 this culminated in the TRIPS (Trade Related Aspects of Intellectual Property Rights) Agreement which, in artice 61, included provision for the implementation of criminal procedures and penalties in cases of trademark counterfeiting or copyright piracy on a commercial scale. At that time the use of computers and the Internet in this trade was not of central concern but this has altered and the potential for the Internet to facilitate this market is now recognised, as is the desire to control it. In 2008 DLA Piper, using data from online intellectual property specialist Commercial Security International, estimated that the online market for counterfeit goods in the UK was £800m. A French court recently ruled that eBay had to pay LVMH (Hermes) €38.6m for having such lax regulation of their site that it effectively allowed its use to trade in counterfeit goods (Aziz 2008). If this situation is upheld on appeal auction websites and possibly even Internet service providers (ISPs) may cease to escape liability. These are only examples from the counterfeit market; when one factors in the downloading of audio and visual materials in breach of copyright the losses are enormous and almost impossible to quantify. In this climate TRIPS has continued to work on and tighten up this area but the most recent moves come from negotiations between a small number of states (in plurilateral negotiations between the US, the EU, Australia, Canada, Japan, Korea, Mexico, New Zealand and Switzerland) on the Anti-Counterfeiting Trade Agreement (ACTA). This is intended to sit alongside the TRIPS Agreement to create a new layer of intellectual property protections and set higher standards for enforcement which states can choose to opt into if they want to tackle the modern trends in intellectual property theft in the global economy which the participating nations consider pose serious and significant threats to the world economy. ACTA propose three categories of provision: international cooperation on enforcement; best enforcement practices; and the legal framework for enforcement (IP Justice White Paper on the Proposed Anti-Counterfeiting Trade Agreement (ACTA) 2008). Rather than criminalising ISPs ACTA proposes to remove their liability if they cooperate with right holders in the removal of infringing materials (through take-down or blocking facilities) and in facilitating right holders to determine the true name and contact details of infringers. This presents a pragmatic solution, setting minimum standards to be met by ISPs and others but where the first intent is to secure compliance; and by holding enforcement measures in the wings if they fail to comply, it gives them time to self-regulate with a clear message that failure may be followed by legally enforced compliance. Presumably the idea is that this will encourage international electronic safeguards as a standard feature, so offering global protection even if not all states are signatories. However, it poses a threat to free expression and to what some argue is the ideal of free use of the Internet. It also opens the door for similar use of the threat against ISPs to force further infringements of expression without necessarily full legal power behind it. This might result in a control of the Internet which impacts on free expression worldwide. For example, in some European states such as Germany there are very strict laws concerning the sale of items to do with the Holocaust or to publicise certain views about whether it occurred or not. If ISPs are required to respect these for material sent to German addresses (something it is technically possible to require) they might decide that it is cheaper to restrict these materials for all Internet users and so curtail access to materials and goods which are perfectly legal in other states (as has already happened). Reliance on this type of regulation might therefore endanger free expression.

Furthermore, the type of action taken here only protects against a very narrow band of unacceptable activity, in this case that which threatens legitimate businesses who may have invested time and money into the development of new products and services. However, the harms from the Internet are potentially much wider than this and the international community needs to consider how to deal with borderless criminal activity that can have almost limitless damaging effects. The Council of Europe has been the major contributor to this area of international law.

Council of Europe Cybercrime Convention

In the mid 1990s the G8 was reviewing high-tech crimes and was urging the need for a concerted effort at preventing cybercrime. Trade and national and international economic stability required an electronic environment free from miscreants of all sorts, so enhancing consumer and business confidence in electronic trade. In 1997 the Council of Europe began its negotiation on the cybercrime convention and the G8 agreed that one treaty, negotiated at the Council of Europe (COE), would be most beneficial. In return the Council of Europe opened its negotiations to non-member states such as Canada, Japan, South Africa and the US.

The COE was no stranger to the ills posed by computer-related activities such as hacking, fraud and pirated software. As far back as 1989 it had begun to work in these areas with Recommendation No. R (89) 9 concerning substantive law which resulted in some harmonisation of national concepts regarding certain forms of computer misuse. In 1995 this was followed by Recommendation No. R (95) 13 concerning problems of procedural law connected with information technology. Whilst these instruments elicited some positive responses by member states, for example by passing specific legislation criminalising certain types of computer-related behaviour such as hacking, manipulation of computer-held material, and distribution of programs that impede the operation of a computer, they failed to deliver true security at an international level. This failure arose partly because they were regionally limited to Europe, partly due to the lack of international investigation and enforcement procedures and partly because the global effects of computer technology in the guise of the Internet, the subsequent creation of a global village and recognition of this as a highly lucrative trade route were not then foreseen. Therefore further international plans that would harmonise the laws in respect of computer-directed criminal activities and give a minimum level of protection from mischief mongers was attractive.

The negotiations on the Cybercrime Convention were conducted by the Experts on Crime in Cyber-space (PC-CY); by 1999 they had clearly mapped out most of the aspects which would make up the final treaty but it was not finalised until 2001. It is groundbreaking, being the first multilateral international treaty that is designed to address computer-related crime. The aim of the Convention was firstly to establish a common criminal policy through harmonisation of national legislation (articles 2–13), secondly to enhance law enforcement and prosecution powers (articles 14–22) and finally to improve international cooperation, especially in relation to enforcement and mutual assistance (articles 23–35). Through this three-pronged approach it aims to resolve the major impediments to legal control: disparate substantive laws, lack of harmonised investigative and enforcement powers, and lack of state cooperation. To dismantle these impediments the Convention first sets out a harmonisation in the understanding of the terminology and here links the definition of 'computer system' to the function of processing, so including telecommunications systems and permitting room for future technological advances. It then moves on to the three substantive areas of its operation.

Firstly, in Section 1 of Chapter II, it sets out to harmonise four areas of substantive law and connected provisions. Here the core aim is to ensure that ratifying states pass laws to criminalise:

activities which threaten confidentiality, integrity and availability of computer data and systems (articles 2–6). For example, hacking (including the production, sale, or distribution of hacking tools), systems interferences that compromise network, computer or data integrity and availability (such as, unauthorised and intentional damage or alteration of data, suppression of or hindering of computer systems) and illegal or unauthorised interception of computer data;

the use of computers to commit certain traditional crimes such as computer related forgery and fraud (articles 7 and 8);

child pornography (article 9); and

intellectual property violations, it expands criminal liability for copyright offences (article 10).

Whilst potentially this offers some protection to everyone (including individuals) in application it protects mainly economic interests of businesses, organisations and governments. Importantly it does not generally seek to interfere with free speech or with most content-related activities; the only exception to this is in the area of child pornography. Later, in 2003, racist and xenophobic content were added under the Additional Protocol to the Convention on Cybercrime, concerning the Criminalisation of acts of a Racist and Xenophobic Nature Committed through Computer Systems 2003.

The Convention, in Article 12, recommends that legal persons (companies) also be made liable for any of the above criminal offences committed for their benefit (even if they do not actually benefit). The limiting factor is that they will only be liable for the actions of key personnel within their organisation, or those ordered by such key personnel even if carried out by others (corporate liability). Article 11 also includes aiding and abetting in any of the crimes listed and Article 13 sets out sanctions that should be proportionate and should both punish and deter. States are also required to take jurisdiction over all such offences committed on their territories, on registered ships or aircraft or by their nationals abroad.

Secondly, Section 2 of Chapter II provides for a minimum level of domestic criminal law powers and procedures that are necessary to ensure all member states are able to investigate and prosecute people who use computer systems to violate these substantive laws. This includes powers necessary for detecting, investigating, and prosecuting computer crimes such as the preservation of computer-stored data and electronic communications (Article 16), system search and seizure of data, preservation and disclosure of traffic data and authorised real-time interception of data including the power to compel ISPs to monitor a person's activities online in real time. It also provides for trans-border access to stored computer data and permits the use and transfer of evidence that is in electronic form and relates to any offence. This is a very wide provision and in the era of mobile phones with Internet capabilities it might become one of the most used provisions and yet it is not limited to Internet crime. This access to and transfer of evidence applies to electronic evidence in any crime, it is not confined to computer-related crimes. This is particularly surprising as there is no requirement that the act be an offence in the state where the search for data is taking place. There have been attacks on these sections of the Convention (see TreatyWatch 2009). In particular the data retention and preservation sections are seen as being too invasive of the privacy of Internet users, possibly even infringing Internet expression in anonymous postings (Aldesco 2002: 110) and of not being proportionate to the requirements of effective investigation of the offences. The US approach to use just data preservation, if used carefully, seems less likely to breach privacy than is the system of data retention that tends to be used in Europe (Rowland and MacDonald 2005).

The investigative and enforcement powers are therefore very broad so the lack of references to concepts such as privacy and data protection are particularly unacceptable. Where international treaties provide for powers to be given to state agencies they usually provide for the protection of privacy (see the Interpol, Europol and Schengen agreements), in a treaty concerning data one would also expect to see personal data protected and respected but this treaty has no provisions to protect these citizen rights. Whilst there is an exemption in the case of political offences this term is not defined (what is political in one state may not be in another) and this exemption is not available in the case of real-time data monitoring. Even more surprisingly there is no requirement for judicial oversight of cases of assistance; a law enforcement agency can take the decision alone (of course, many states may have provision for judicial oversight in their national laws). This omission is even more surprising as there is no requirement that instances of assistance be publicised *ex post facto*; there are, therefore, no oversight or other checks and balances over its use.

Finally, Chapter III encompasses agreement on cooperation in the enforcement measures, catching offenders and making them liable for their activities; this may have been the major impetus behind the Convention. It requires states to provide a fast, effective and broad regime of international cooperation to facilitate the investigation and court proceedings in respect of offences and offenders related to computer systems and data and for the collection of evidence in electronic form concerning any criminal offence including trans-border access to stored data on remote computers where they do not require aid. This means that law enforcement agencies will have to assist police from other participating countries to cooperate with their mutual assistance requests. The Convention considers cybercrime to be extraditable offences and calls on states to set up a round-the-clock contact network to provide immediate assistance with cross-border investigations such as asking a foreign law enforcement agency to collect computer-based evidence for use in another country.

Under Article 15 and the preamble parties to the convention must guarantee the conditions and safeguards necessary to protect human rights and the principle of proportionality. Here it also explicitly recognises the right of everyone to freedom of thought, freedom of expression including the right to both impart and receive information and the need to respect individuals and their rights more generally. However, it is in the low priority given to individual rights that the Convention is most vulnerable to attack and shows that it has been more a vehicle for protection of states, often richer states, economic and commercial interests than to protect individuals. This was seen in the way in which copyright infringement was included in the Convention. There was strong lobbying from both organisations and weaker and less rich nations to either exclude this area completely, as it is already included under the TRIPS Agreement (see above) and did not need to be repeated here. Furthermore the way in which it is included here expands liability for intellectual property as it fails to take account of public interest in the use of such material for criticism and scholarly analysis and it promotes it to an offence for which one can be extradited. However, richer nations are very interested in the protection of copyright to defend their economic interests and those of major commerce, and saw its inclusion here as a way of tying more nations to being bound to protect copyright. If states wanted to enjoy the benefits of information security they would also have to protect against copyright infringement; it was getting wider agreement to the criminal aspects of TRIPS by the back door. It was also a way of enhancing the requirement to cooperate in the enforcement of copyright infringement; the enforcement and cooperation elements of the Cybercrime Convention are superior to those in TRIPS and it was a way of increasing the likelihood of catching and convicting these offenders, again serving economic interests. Less wealthy nations may want information security, be willing to protect against computer crime and cooperate in their enforcement; they may well be unwilling to agree to cooperation in the area of intellectual property. Its inclusion may therefore jeopardise the *raison d'etrê* of the Convention: computer security. Furthermore, in negotiating for the Cybercrime Convention there was pressure to make room within copyright crime for a defence of providing for the needs of those with disabilities, increasing access for the visually impaired by means of large-print digital copies of books; in rejecting this it showed that the commercial interests were more important than those of individuals and actively providing for equality.

The final example of the link of the Convention with commerce and power rather than individual interests comes in discussion of the protection against child pornography. There was discussion of requiring ISPs to take responsibility for sites carrying this content and criminalising them for lapses in their responsibility. ISP lobby groups and some larger states lobbied hard against this outcome which might have protected children but would have proved expensive to implement and might have had negative impact on freedom of expression in the banning of material in case it infringed child pornography standards; it might even have breached the US First Amendment. This last was also a reason for the exclusion of more content-based offences from the Convention and the need for the 2003 Protocol to cover racism and xenophobia; its inclusion within the original Convention would have precluded US ratification because it would have been a breach of First Amendment rights. The protection against child pornography is generally welcomed but many consider that it goes too far because it includes 'realistic images representing a minor engaged in sexually explicit conduct' (article 9(2)(c)). This wide provision protects the dignity of all children not to be depicted as sexual objects, it also conveys the contempt which is felt for child pornography and those who enjoy viewing it; finally it removes the need for prosecutors to prove that the images depict the violation of actual children. However, in a number of states it might be seen as too invasive of free expression, for example, according to *Ashcroft* v. *Free Speech Coalition* it breached the US First Amendment guaranteeing free expression. To overcome this the US Congress enacted the PROTECT Act to include a limited version of the ban which covers images which are indistinguishable from real images of young people actually engaging in sexually explicit behaviour (this was necessary in order to permit the US to ratify the Convention). Others states may well limit it in similar ways.

The link of the Convention with commerce and power relations is seen when one considers what it was intended to accomplish – to persuade more states to make provision against cybercrime. Some states still have little or no criminal protection or enforcement procedures in this area. Twenty-three states have now ratified it, including the USA where it came into force in 2007 (it is the only non-member state of the Council of Europe to have ratified and had to overcome a number of possible First Amendment issues in order to facilitate its ratification). A further 23 have signed but not yet ratified, including the UK. The UK's failure to ratify is surprising. It was prominent in negotiating the Convention and moved to criminalise the use of computers both to commit offences and to cause harm to other computers. Within the time period for which it has been open for signature and ratification 23 is a substantial number, with only four member states of the Council of Europe having failed to sign, and many of those who have signed actively preparing to ratify. This level of ratifications, especially that of the US, indicates the importance of international agreement and cooperation to the effective control of cybercrime; without it national laws and enforcement procedures can only achieve limited success. However, 23 states is a small minority of nations and a long way from delivering global security. For those who believe strongly in the need for legal control of the Internet it is a form of failure.

The Convention is wide-ranging and ambitious: unifying criminal laws; unifying powers of investigation and enforcements; and delivering interstate cooperation. If globally accepted and ratified it would guarantee a powerful level of computer security. However, this potential may also be limiting its implementation because in order to ratify states have to alter their substantive criminal laws, alter their investigative powers and procedures and implement practical measures to guarantee cooperation. All of this may preclude ratification; for some states the expense may be prohibitive, for others the provisions may violate ideals of free expression, citizens' rights or other basic ideals. Therefore its strength in its potential to deliver computer security may also have been its most limiting factor and have prevented wider ratification.

Cyber-terrorism and Cyberwar

In the risk-obsessed modern era it seems necessary to deal with the most worrying international threats posed by computers and the Internet: their use in terror attacks or acts of war. It was the occurrence of the 9/11 attacks that moved the international community to agree on a more cooperative approach to governance of the system; one answerable to governments and which often worries individuals and governments. With our reliance on these technologies to deliver basic necessities of life – safety-critical systems – many believe we are vulnerable to rogue attacks, generally referred to as cyber-terrorism and cyberwarfare. However, one needs to study whether such attacks are likely; each will be studied in turn.

In line with almost all other groups most terrorist organisations use the Internet for their purposes (see Denning, Chapter 10). Some illegal purposes fall short of cyber-terrorism; for example hacking into sites (covered under the Cybercrime Convention), commiting traditional crimes, sometimes for money or to obtain funds and other backing for their causes (covered in the Cybercrime Convention or under general criminal laws), or disseminating illegal content (covered under the Council of Europe Convention on the Prevention of Terrorism 2005). These acts, whilst illegal, fall short of 'cyber-terrorism' as defined by Denning:

> premeditated, politically motivated attacks by subnational groups or clandestine agents against information, computer systems, computer programs, and data that result in violence against non-combatant targets. (Denning 1999: 2, 27)

She expands on this in her evidence to the House Armed Services Committee in May 2000:

> Cyberterrorism is the convergence of cyberspace and terrorism. It refers to unlawful attacks and threats of attacks against computers, networks and the information stored therein when done to intimidate or coerce a government or its people in furtherance of political or social objectives. Further, to qualify as cyberterrorism, an attack should result in violence against persons or property, or at least cause enough harm to generate fear. Attacks that lead to death or bodily injury, explosions, or severe economic loss would be examples. Serious attacks against critical infrastructures could be acts of cyberterrorism, depending on their impact. Attacks that disrupt nonessential services or that are mainly a costly nuisance would not.

Such action might be attractive to terrorist groups as it is cheaper, can be conducted remotely and anonymously, the number of targets is very large, one attack could affect many people and, if large-scale, it would be likely to attract attention. However, it takes technical knowledge and it would be difficult to achieve levels of damage similar to physical attacks, it would also be possible for states and/or commercial organisations to claim it was the result of a system failure and hide the intent and so bury the message. Despite all of this, attacks of this ilk are unlikely, though the possibility of such attacks needs to be taken seriously as the effects would be devastating (Denning 2001, and Chapter 10; Weimann 2004, 2006).

> It seems fair to say that the current threat posed by cyberterrorism has been exaggerated. No single instance of cyberterrorism has yet been recorded; U.S. defense and intelligence computer systems are air-gapped and thus isolated from the Internet; the systems run by private companies are more vulnerable to attack but also more resilient than is often supposed; the vast majority of cyberattacks are launched by hackers

with few, if any, political goals and no desire to cause the mayhem and carnage of which terrorists dream. (Weimann 2004: 10–11)

However, using the broader definition suggested by the Committee of Experts on Terrorism (CODEXTER 2007) the threat becomes more likely:

Cybercrime and use of Internet for terrorist purposes include several elements:

a. Attacks via the Internet that cause damage not only to essential electronic communication systems and IT infrastructure, but also to other infrastructures, systems, and legal interests, including human life;

b. Dissemination of illegal content, including threatening terrorist attacks; inciting, advertising, and glorifying terrorism; fundraising for and financing of terrorism; training for terrorism; recruiting for terrorism; as well as

c. Other logistical uses of IT systems by terrorists, such as internal communication, information acquisition and target analysis.

With this definition terrorist attacks are far more likely (Council of Europe 2007) and CODEXTER considered that this threat deserved both to be taken seriously and tackled (see also Sieber 2006; Council of Europe 2007). They looked for 'the existence of "terrorist-specific" gaps in "computer-specific" conventions and "computer-specific" gaps in "terrorist-specific" conventions' CODEXTER (Committee of Experts on Terrorism 2007: 2) and found none. Their conclusion was that it was necessary to encourage wider ratification of both the Cybercrime Convention and the Council of Europe Convention on the Prevention of Terrorism (2005) in order to deliver the highest possible level of protection against such threats; the recommendations were accepted by the Cybercrime Convention Committee (2008). If they are right then the key to preventing or dealing with such attacks is wide international ratification of the two treaties. Whilst CODEXTER is confident that these treaties are capable of delivering security from cybercrime this will only happen if they are ratified and implemented.

The second problem is cyberwar, cyber conflict at the level of nation states. This is something that may concern states but not something to which they wish to draw attention – they pose the risk. As with cyber-terrorism the concept is capable of a number of interpretations:

Collecting information – clearly in the information age war will change and the side with the best intelligence may win, even if they have only a small force. Information can redistribute power and break down borders, can make the weak strong and the strong weak. Therefore cyber espionage is bound to play a large part in future international relations.

Distributing information – states are constantly collecting, storing, processing, communicating and presenting information more carefully and in more intelligent ways and information is one of the most important strategic resources and weapons, to be used as a propaganda tool.

Distorting information – states can bend information to their own end, altering power within other states or trying to destabilise a state or a non-state organisation.

Vandalism – it might involve disrupting or destabilising an adversary's information or communication systems through large-scale denial of service attacks.

Military communication – much military communication is now high tech, and can be intercepted and altered.

Attacking resources necessary to life – using computers or the Internet to attack power, water, fuel, communication, transport etc. This action is intended to kill or instil fear in ordinary citizens.

Just as with cyber-terrorism not all of these should be classed as true cyberwar, some are merely necessary ills of the information age just as toxic waste products were the necessary result of the industrial age. Others are devious distortions of the use of information. Only a few might be classed as true cyberwar, actions such as cyber vandalism and attacking resources necessary to life: premeditated attacks on states against information, computer systems, computer programs, and data that result in violence against non-combatant targets (Denning 1999: 2, 27). Is this extreme sort of cyber-conflict at the level of nation states likely to occur? At the moment probably the danger is low because where states have greatest capacity (rich Western states) they claim to be against its use; where states are felt to be more inclined to use it they lack the capacity for a large-scale attack (Denning 2007).

From this it appears that whilst the most serious attacks (cyber-terrorism and cyberwar) are unlikely, the only way of tackling one if it happened would be through use of the international conventions. Furthermore, the way to catch and prosecute any acts against users, commerce, governments or individuals that fall short of this would be through the international conventions. Of course, where states are the transgressors even the conventions may be unable to help; their control may be through threat of international condemnation. However, the conventions, and the real threat of prosecution might deter some would-be offenders, especially in less serious cases, and lesser attacks could be, and have been, very damaging to information security and their prevention and control is hampered without international cooperation. From this perspective, whilst the conventions cannot resolve all problems, they are important but will only be effective if they are widely ratified and implemented. In effect an individual bent on dissemination of criminal materials such as hate messages or child pornography or who wants to destroy an Internet or to cause terror only needs one state to be outside the Convention, they only need one safe haven for it to lose its power to deliver legal control. Of course, most of the power of the Convention will come from its ability to dissuade most people and to catch most offenders, and that will only happen with wide ratification of the Convention. No law ever prevents all crime or catches all criminals.

Conclusion

International intervention to control the Internet is progressing at a number of levels and it is likely that it will become more rather than less regulated and some of the ideals of free access to information, free expression and privacy will slowly be eroded. At a level of code this is beginning as one gets more state intervention in its control, through the intervention of both commerce and international politics. Though if it follows the first principle of the WSIS 'people-centred, inclusive and development-oriented Information Society where everyone can create, access, utilize and share information and knowledge, enabling individuals, communities and peoples to achieve their full potential' (WSIS 2003) this may be kept to a minimum. At a legal level these two are also in play, drawing the international community towards conventions that tackle substantive law, instigate similar investigative and other techniques necessary to enforcement of these and deliver trans-border cooperation. Again it has often been the desire to protect commerce or commercial interests that has led to these moves. However, since 2001 security has also been a central concern. In the future the need to raise revenue may lead the way to more intrusive policies. As Internet commerce increases there is a fear that many transactions are escaping local sales taxes such as VAT. Governments are becoming more concerned about these issues and are searching for ways to ensure revenues are forthcoming (Siliafis 2009). Some have suggested that the way forward may be via geo-identification whereby taxing of online transactions might be achieved by tracing the IP address and matching it with an actual place, so that tax authorities (or sellers acting as the tax collectors) will be able more easily to identify where consumption takes place (Svantesson 2007a, 2007b). The technology is largely available, the only obstacle is the issue of privacy but this may not survive the desire to secure revenue.

Much of the present regulation and legal intervention both at national and international levels are thought necessary because most people and the state accept that computer technology has opened up new areas of activity requiring new modes of control. However, some, such as McGuire (2007), suggest that this preoccupation distorts the area allowing attention to be diverted from the harms posed by states and corporations and permits them to weave a legal and regulatory straitjacket extending the 'control society' but not protecting the users. Murray (2007: chs 8–9) portrays the incursions into regulatory interventions, particularly by organisations such as ICANN, as being destabilising rather than stabilising, claiming that problems with the system have only been exacerbated as each new level of regulation is added. So the intervention of the UN through WIPO led to a distorted protection for intellectual property over other interests, similarly WSIS has and continues to cause other distortions, such as those based on differences between governments or states. Part of the problem is that these regulatory frameworks are pulling the architecture of the Internet in different directions, there are political, ideological and commercial differences being played out and any rules or regulations are the result of compromise and always distorting. Design of Internet architecture is no longer ruled by the needs of dissemination of information alone, but each intervention is distorting. The architecture is one area where the international control of the Internet and therefore the power (which is information) is being played out and controlled. Users, in sufficient numbers, may be able to pull the system into line to deliver the ideal of a 'people-centred, inclusive and development-oriented Information Society where everyone can create, access, utilize and share information and knowledge, enabling individuals, communities and peoples to achieve their full potential' (WSIS 2003: principle 1).

For McGuire the focus should be on the changes to social interaction that are made possible via the Internet rather than the preoccupation with breaking the barriers normally formed by space and time. Whilst the technological advances do extend and complicate these dimensions, they do not break or irrevocably alter them; the core remains constant. Therefore he suggests that technology does not produce new crimes but merely '... expands *already extant* deviant possibilities' (McGuire 2007: 7), and he recognises three main categories of deviant behaviour: undesired entry into spaces; undesired entries that result in damage or other harmful impacts; and undesired entries that result in permanent destruction. Whilst not ignoring the victimisation many people suffer he questions the levels of harm claimed by governments and businesses (with vested interests) as being caused by the Internet and instead suggests that the harms of control are as bad, if not worse. He also notes that the controls do not usually prevent harms (in the broad sense outlined by Hillyard *et al.* 2004) caused by states, and sometimes fail to prevent those caused by businesses; in fact the controls sometimes prevent these entities from taking responsibility for harms they cause (p. 4). Here he is looking at harms, so deviance, not legal parameters, and the real changes appear only with the 'fusion of deviance and control' and it is this that results in truly different dimensions of harm. He prioritises Feinberg's (1984) limitation of choices as the most destructive form of harm but McGuire considers a spatial ordering where the worst breaches occur on or close to the body and then move out from there, and the least problematic occur in global space. From this it is clear that many of the controls, particularly legal controls, are seen to be wrongly focused and may be more destructive than helpful, some aspects may cause or facilitate more harm rather than delivering security, especially for individuals.

There are other possible problems. Many of the most problematic harms for individuals, hacking and other access to computers, might be addressed through better systems design, both protective hardware and more secure software. However, the existence of international and national criminal laws to curb cybercrime may result in corporations being less inclined to build more secure systems. One of the elements that might best protect individuals is situational crime prevention: systems that are harder to break into, both physically and electronically.

International efforts to deliver security on the Net may, at their worst, be more destructive than the ills they are trying to address. At best they are ineffective: in the case of code because increasingly it fails to focus on the end users; in the case of law because insufficient states sign up to and implement the international protections and those protections are focused on the wrong goals.

Further reading

There is an enormous amount of literature concerning transnational developments in Internet law though most of it appears merely as adjuncts to discussions of national controls. In order to cover all aspects one needs to read a number of sources. The material concerning code and its control is discussed at length in Lawrence Lessig's *CODE: Version 2* (2006), Basic Books. A more concise though equally useful consideration of this can be found in Andrew D. Murray, *The Regulation of Cyberspace* (2007), Routledge–Cavendish, in which Chapter 4 is of particular interest, setting the scene and analysing some of the modern moves to control in this area. Some of the other chapters also usefully deal with specific aspects of legal controls, especially that pertaining to the control of content. For European and international legal controls the best sources are the original legal documents and explanations produced by the organisations themselves (see the References for many references to these). There is also a very useful synopsis to be found on pages 477–87 of D. Rowland and E. Macdonald, *Information Technology Law* (2005), Cavendish and a clear discussion of the international tensions and how these are being played out in this area by Wolfgang Kleinwachter (2007) *Internet Governance and Governments: Enhanced Cooperation or Enhanced Confrontation?* Comms. L. 12(4): 111–18. A more analytical and critical account of the need for controls at all is found in Michael McGuire's (2007) *Hypercrime: The New Geometry of Harm*, Abingdon: Routledge-Cavendish, where he takes a critical stance on the whole area of control of cybercrime but also of the concept of cybercrime at all. He looks rather at harm from the perspective of individuals in time and space and questions certain central tenets of control generally, but particularly of control in a system not tied by either time or place. As such it provides an interesting antidote to the more common texts in the area, sets an innovative perspective to our thinking on both crime and control in the modern era.

References

Aldesco, A.I. (2002) 'The Demise of Anonymity; A Constitutional Challenge to the Convention on Cybercrime', *Loy. LA. Ent. L. Rev.* 23: 81, as referenced in D. Rowland and E. Macdonald (2005) *Information Technology Law.* London: Cavendish.

Aziz, K. (2008) 'eBay Liable for Counterfeits', *Intellectual Property Newsletter*, 31(7): 3. See also http://www.reuters.com/article/marketsNews/idINL2910194320080630?rpc=44 (last accessed 20 February 2009).

Brenner, S.W. (2004) 'Towards a Criminal Law for Cyberspace – Distributed Security', *Boston University Journal of Science and Technology Law*, 10(2): 8–34.

Brenner, S. (2007) 'Cybercrime: Re-thinking Crime Control Strategies', in Y. Jewkes (ed.), *Crime Online.* Cullompton: Willan Publishing.

Civil Society (2003) *Shaping Information Societies for Human Needs*, at http://www.itu.int/wsis/docs/geneva/civil-society-declaration.pdf

CODEXTER (2007) *Opinion of the Committee of Experts on Terrorism (CODEXTER) for the Attention of the Committee of Ministry on Cyberterrorism and Use of Internet for Terrorist*

Purposes. Found at http://www.coe.int/t/e/legal_affairs/legal_co-operation/fight_against_terrorism/4_Theme_Files/Cyberterrorism%20opinion%20E(last accessed 9 July 2009).

Commission of the European Communities (1996) *Illegal and Harmful Content on the Internet* COM(96)487final. Found at http://www.drugtext.org/library/legal/eu/eucnet1.htm(last accessed 9 July 2009).

Council of Europe (2007) *Cyberterrorism: the use of the Internet for terrorist purposes.* Strasbourg: Council of Europe.

Council Recommendation 2006/952/EC (2006) *Protection of minors and human dignity in audiovisual and information services (2006 recommendation).* Official Journal L 378 of 27.12.2006. A Summary is found at http://europa.eu/scadplus/leg/en/lvb/l24030a.htm (last accessed 20 February 2009).

Council Recommendation 98/560/EC (1998) *Protection of minors and human dignity in audiovisual and information services.* Official Journal L 270 of 7 October 1998.

Cybercrime Convention Committee (2008) document T-CY (2008) INF 02 E, at: http://www.coe.int/t/dg1/legalcooperation/economiccrime/MoneyLaundering/Projects/MOLICO/AC/Output1.1/Anti-corruption%20Action%20Plan_2007-2009_eng.PDF

Denning, D.E. (1999) *Activism, Hacktivism, and Cyberterrorism: The Internet as a Tool for Influencing Foreign Policy.* Washington, DC: Nautilus.

Denning, D.E. (2001) *Is Cyber Terror Next?* New York: US Social Science Research Council, at http://www.ssrc.org/sept11/essays/denning.htm

Denning, D.E. (2007) 'Assessing the CNO Threat of Foreign Countries', in J. Arquilla and D. Borer (eds), *Information Strategy and Warfare.* London: Routledge.

DLA Piper Report (2008) reported at http://www.vnunet.com/vnunet/news/2220773/online-counterfeitgoods-market-800m (last accessed 20 February 2009) http://www.computing.co.uk/computing/news/2220722/auction-sites-hotspot-fake (last accessed 20 February 2009) http://www.silicon.com/retailandleisure/0,3800011842,39262810,00.htm (last accessed 20 February 2009).

eEurope (1999) 'An information society for all', at http://ec.europa.eu/archives/ISPO/eif/InternetPoliciesSite/Crime/CrimeCommEN.html (last accessed 20 February 2009) and the summary found at http://europa.eu/scadplus/leg/en/lvb/l24221.htm (last accessed 20 February 2009).

European Union Council Framework Decision 2005/222/JHA of 24 February 2005 on attacks against information systems, at: http://register.consilium.eu.int/pdf/en/04/st15/st15010.en04.pdf or http://eur-lex.europa.eu/LexUriServ/site/en/oj/2005/l_069/l_06920050316en00670071.pdf (last accessed 20 February 2009) and the summary can be found at http://europa.eu/scadplus/leg/en/lvb/l33193.htm (last accessed 20 February 2009).

Feinberg, J. (1984) *Harm to Self.* Oxford: Oxford University Press.

Goldsmith, J. and Wu, T. (2006) *Who Controls the Internet?: Illusions of a Borderless World.* Oxford: Oxford University Press.

Green Paper (1996) on *Protection of Minors and Human Dignity in Audiovisual and Information Services,* COM (1996) 483 Final.

Hillyard, P., Pantazis, C., Tombs, S. And Gordon, D. (2004) *Beyond Criminology: Taking Harm Seriously.* London: Pluto Press.

IP Justice White Paper on the Proposed Anti-Counterfeiting Trade Agreement (ACTA), 25 March 2008, at http://ipjustice.org/wp/2008/03/25/ipj-white-paper-acta-2008/ (last accessed 20 February 2009); further details are also available at Public Knowledge, *Anti-Counterfeiting Trade Agreement,* at http://www.publicknowledge.org/issues/acta (last accessed 20 February 2009).

Lessig, L. (1999) *Code and Other Laws of Cyberspace.* New York: Basic Books.

Lessig, L. (2006) *CODE: Version 2.* New York: Basic Books.

Luke, T.W. (2001) 'Cyberspace as Meta-Nation: The Net Effects of Online EPublicanism', *Alternatives,* 26(2): 113–142.

McGuire, M. (2007) *Hypercrime: The New Geometry of Harm.* Abingdon: Routledge-Cavendish.

Murray, A.D. (2007) *The Regulation of Cyberspace: Control in the Online Environment.* Abingdon: Routledge-Cavendish. A GlassHouse Book.

OECD (2002) OECD *Guidelines for the Security of Information Systems: Towards a Culture of Security,* at http://www.oecd.org/dataoecd/16/22/15582260.pdf (last accessed 20 February 2009).

OECD (2003) *Implementation Plan for the OECD Guidelines for the Security of Information Systems and Networks: Towards a Culture of Security,* at http://www.oecd.org/dataoecd/23/11/31670189.pdf (last accessed 20 February 2009).

OECD (2005) *The Promotion of a Culture of Security for Information Systems and Networks in OECD Countries.* OECD: Working Party on Information Security and Privacy, at http://www.oecd.org/dataoecd/16/27/35884541.pdf (last accessed 20 February 2009).

Rowland, D. and MacDonald E. (2005) *Information Technology Law.* London: Cavendish.

Sieber, U. (2006) 'International Cooperation against Terrorist Use of the Internet', *Revue internationale de droit pénal,* 77(3–4): 395–449.

Siliafis, K. (2009) 'International initiatives on e-commerce taxation; different jurisdictions, different rules? Are these different initiatives pointing to the same direction or do they seem miles apart?' Paper delivered to the 24th BILETA Annual Conference, Winchester.

Svantesson, D. (2007a) 'E-Commerce Tax: How The Taxman Brought Geography To The "Borderless" Internet', *Revenue Law Journal,* 17(1): Article 11.

Svantesson, D. (2007b) 'Protecting Privacy on the "Borderless" Internet – Some Thoughts on Extraterritoriality and Transborder Data Flow', *Bond Law Review,* 19(1): Article 7.

Toffler, Alvin (1980) *The Third Wave.* London: Pan Books.

TreatyWatch (2009) http://www.treatywatch.org/ (last accessed 20 February 2009).

Tunis (2005) *Tunis Agenda for the Information Society,* November 18, 2005, Part II, Internet Governance, at http://www.itu.int/wsis/documents/doc_multi.asp?lang=en&id=2267 I 0

Weimann, G. (2004) *Cyberterrorism: How Real Is the Threat?* Special Report No 119 to the United States Institute of Peace, at http://www.usip.org/pubs/specialreports/sr119.html (last accessed 20 February 2009).

Weimann, G. (2006) *Terror on the Internet: The New Arena, the New Challenges.* New York: United States Institute of Peace Press.

WGIG (2005) *Final Report of the Working Group on Internet Governance,* Geneva, July 2005, at http://www.wgig.org/WGIG-Report.html (last accessed 20 February 2009).

WSIS (2003) *Declaration of Principles,* Geneva 12 December 2003.

Chapter 23

Online surveillance and personal liberty

Michael McGuire

Introduction

Claims that the advent of the Internet has produced an 'unregulable' wild zone – 'the vacuum of a lawless space' as it has recently been maintained (Espiner 2008) – seem increasingly misjudged. Whilst retaining its emancipatory potentials, a narrow range of interests have succeeded in transforming the Internet into one of the most effective tools for monitoring (and thereby controlling) behaviour ever created. As the new order of mandatory visibility takes shape online, criminologists face several challenges in theorising the seemingly contradictory dynamic of enhancements and diminutions to freedom the Internet offers.

Not only do the continuities of online surveillance with those directed at more intimate proximities rule out loose talk about the monitoring of a 'virtual', or a 'cyber' space, they make it difficult to draw lines or to say how a piece of surveillance conducted on the Internet is functionally independent of that conducted via a CCTV system, or a mobile phone network. Instead we must consider Internet surveillance as one part of an assemblage of controls (cf. Deleuze and Guatarri 1988), something facilitated by the spatial compression and enhanced networking of social interaction I have elsewhere referred to in terms of a process of 'hyperspatialisation' (McGuire 2007). It is a key challenge then to define how (if at all) Internet surveillance is *different* from other components of this control assemblage, with its 'multiple connections across myriad technologies and practices' (Haggerty and Ericson 2000: 610) and second, how it complements them.

A further challenge relates to how an account of online surveillance can be developed which is appropriately criminological. The bare fact is that the 'obvious need' invoked by the control elite to watch and record social interaction on (or off) line has meant that many forms of Internet surveillance are legally sanctioned. And without any tangible crimes, what remains? In this chapter I aim to highlight those aspects of online surveillance that ought to be of concern – not just to criminologists, but to all of us. To do this I will need to clarify three key aspects of online surveillance:

(i)   who is doing it;
(ii) the ends at which it is directed;
(iii) how they are doing it.

Having considered these I then turn to the issue of legalities. What kind of agents use the Internet to monitor others? To what degree and what kinds of sanctions (or lack of them) result from excesses here? Questions relating to how equitably the capacity to observe is now being distributed then arise and highlight the role of criminal law, both in reinforcing imbalances in transparency and the ways in which it might be developed to redress them.

In 2005, Google users found that they were suddenly able to access over 1,000 surveillance cameras around the world that had been linked to the Internet (Poulsen 2005). Clearly *access* to the Internet had provided them with an opportunity to scrutinise the diverse environments these cameras were trained upon, from office and restaurant interiors to Japanese barnyards. But Internet interactions were not themselves the surveillance target. The proposed creation of a UK database retaining details of all emails sent over the Internet (Travis and Norton-Taylor 2008; Williams 2008a) raises similar ambiguities. Does this count as an example of 'online surveillance' when the database would also include phone call and text-messaging data? Connections between different forms of networked communication produce one set of dilemmas about where online surveillance begins or ends. Convergences between such technologies (where a mobile phone becomes more like a computer, and vice versa) produce another. An initial distinction seems therefore to be essential if we are to make sense of the complex relationships between Internet and communications surveillance in general:

(i)   Surveillance *of* Internet interaction: that is, surveillance directed at the way individuals communicate or behave using the Internet. I will refer to this throughout as *Type I Internet surveillance*;

(ii) Surveillance that *uses* the Internet: that is, surveillance where the Internet is used only as a tool for accessing the growing diversity of data sources about individuals. I will refer to this throughout as *Type II Internet surveillance*.

Though both activities can be thought of as 'surveillance involving the Internet' it is clear that there are important differences. Type I surveillance involves only the content of social interactions which have been spatially extended by the Internet, while Type II surveillance provides access to a wider spectrum of information about individuals' lives and worlds. Whilst my focus will be largely restricted to Type I approaches in this chapter, any serious consideration of the role of the Internet within contemporary surveillant assemblages can scarcely ignore the latter. Indeed, if 'the Internet' is taken to refer not just to the World Wide Web but the growing global communication network in its entirety, then Type II monitoring arguably becomes the variety of more fundamental interest.

The who, why and wherefore of online surveillance (I): agents

It would be overly simplistic to assume that it is 'criminals' and the way that they engage in Internet surveillance that constitute the chief objects of criminological interest. For it is important to distinguish uses of the Internet by criminals to acquire information of value to them and uses of the internet *for criminal ends*, such as theft, even though the two activities may often be related. Many forms of Internet crime, such as phishing, are not exclusively surveillance activities but old-fashioned deceptions where information acquisition plays a subordinate role. And very often access to the personal details which facilitate criminal behaviours like phishing have not arisen from primary acts of surveillance but from secondary acquisitions, such as the theft of poorly guarded data. The growth in criminal trading of personal data (one recent report (Casciani 2008) suggested names, addresses, passport numbers and credit card numbers could be bought for around £80 in some online marketplaces) is more often facilitated by careless handling of such information rather than by specific acts of surveillance. Thus, whilst traditional criminals do now engage in surveillance-like activities in order to collect data which may further their goals, it would be misleading to single them out as the primary agents – either of Type I or Type II surveillance. There are other social actors more deeply steeped in Internet surveillance than the criminal fraternity.

A less obvious set of candidates – one which provides a telling indication of the pluralisation of surveillance – is produced by the penetration of such activities into our private lives and relationships – even the family itself. It is not just that family and domestic life has become increasingly porous to *outside* eyes; family members have themselves become active and willing participants in the use of the Internet for surveillance purposes. Parents spy on children, children spy on each other, while husbands covertly scrutinise their wives. One recent study in the UK (OII 2008) indicated that within nearly half of relationships – around 44 per cent of couples – at least one partner admitted to monitoring the other partner's Internet activities. As the table below suggests, the variety of ways in which this occurred is evidence of the growing sophistication of surveillance skills such actors can call upon.

But partner snooping is just one manifestation of the growth in interfamilial spying. Other recent research (Garlik 2008) has suggested that over 70 per cent of parents may now be covertly observing what their children do online. Twenty-five per cent confessed to secretly logging on to their child's social networking page with another 25 per cent admitting that they had even created their own social networking persona in order to be able to monitor what their children are doing (*ibid.*). In the US figures were higher, with around 45 per cent of parents admitting to installing software to monitor their children's behaviour and 53 per cent using filtering software to control what they can access (Lenhart and Madden 2007). In addition the Internet

Table 23.1 Monitoring of partner's Internet activities by UK couples

Internet monitoring activity	% engaged in it
Read their spouse's emails	20%
Read their SMS	20%
Checked browser history	13%
Read instant messaging tags	5%
Used monitoring software	2%
Pretended to be another person	1%

Source: OII 2008

tended to be the most regulated form of media in the home, with parents significantly more likely to place restrictions on its use compared to television or games consoles (*ibid.*). But Type I surveillance – observing children's online behaviours – is only the beginning. As we will see in the following section, parental surveillance also involves Type II behaviours where the Internet is one of a range of networked technologies used to effect more sophisticated monitoring of their children.

Type I and II forms of Internet surveillance have also begun to affect our broader social lives. In particular it has become relatively commonplace for friends and associates to use the Internet in order to acquire covert information about each other. The phenomenon of what has been termed 'lateral surveillance' (cf. Andrejevic 2005) begins to order social life according the logics of visibility – even where this amounts to no more than checking up on what old friends, lovers or peers are up to. Thus, the role of search engines extends beyond introducing the term 'googling' into the English language. It marks a social as well as a linguistic shift, with research in the US (Madden *et al.* 2007) indicating that a majority of respondents (53 per cent) now admit to using search engines to find out about friends, colleagues, prospective dates and so on. For the most part search engines are involved in innocent snooping, with the majority of searches (72 per cent) used to obtain simple contact details, rather than intimate personal information (*ibid.*). However, around a third of searches were directed at public record information, personal information or, perhaps more worryingly, for photographs or images of targeted individuals. Where this, on occasions, begins to merge into more overtly criminal stalking behaviours, it seems to be former partners rather than casual acquaintances that pose the greater risk here – with the lack of evidence for any major upturn in 'stranger' based killings or rapes between 1993 – 2008 (McGuire 2007) counting as one corroboration for this.

Nor is 'googling' restricted to the surveillance of others. In a strange reflection of the narcissism that seems to go with cultures of high visibility (Lasch 1991), many of us now spend an inordinate amount of time monitoring ourselves. In 2007 47 per cent of respondents confessed to engaging in this – a figure which has more than doubled over the past five years (Madden *et al.* 2007). Our apparent willingness to post significant amounts of personal information online – most obviously in the form of the detailed profiles seen on social networking sites – emphasises the influence of a society of 'spectacles' (Debord 1994) in rendering such transparency more desirable. In such a context peer surveillance seems almost natural. Whilst certain protections (such as setting one's profile to 'private') prevent complete transparency, these are not too hard to circumvent if you know someone reasonably well. Guessing a password, or accessing a computer that has been left unattended are among the low-tech options. The tendency of social networking sites to leave personal data accessible, even after users have deleted their accounts (a situation currently under investigation by the Information Commissioner) makes this method of peer surveillance even easier (Vallance 2008). The counter-surveillance tools that emerge in response are a further indication of the emerging distortions within social life. Software such as like Blockstatus.com or Sitemeter.com can indicate who has blocked or deleted you on Instant Messenger programs like MSN, how many visitors there have been to a personal webpage and, in some cases, even their URL or web address. Other more devious social outcomes of enhanced transparency include websites designed to help us evade scrutiny from partners, friends or employers by creating fake alibis or background noises (Nugent and Hall 2004).

While increasing online surveillance among family members or peers indicates a widening distribution of the new logics of visibility, the resources available to governments or businesses to scrutinise behaviour online continue to outstrip the capacities of private individuals. Recent research by the US National Association of Colleges and Employers (NACE), indicated that more than a quarter of potential employers in the USA had 'googled' their job candidates or had examined their profiles on social networking websites for useful information (NACE 2006). Even where there is no financial stake in choosing the right candidate the Internet is often now used to assess the professional worth of individuals, with 'respectable' institutions such as universities equally happy to conduct surveillance activities on candidates, by examining their social networking pages (Shepherd and Shariatmadari 2008).

But whilst the phenomenon of workplace surveillance is hardly 'new' news, the Internet certainly provides employers with new opportunities for engaging in it. Recent figures (Proofpoint 2007) suggest that in the US over a third of companies regularly audit outbound email – a rise of around 7 per cent from 2006 whilst almost the same amount (32.1 per cent) employ staff to read or analyse emails sent by staff. More than one in six companies surveyed (16.9 per cent) employed staff whose *primary or exclusive* job function was to monitor communications. Automated surveillance was even more extensive – around 60 per cent of companies used software for monitoring content in webmail or intended to do so within the next 12 months. Other research from the American Management Association (AMA 2005) suggests that monitoring of employees' Internet activities may be even higher – with around 76 per cent of employers monitoring usage, and 55 per cent examining employee email messages. In the UK anything between 50–75 per cent of workplaces use some form of electronic or IT monitoring of their employees (McGovern et al. 2007) – even though there is evidence that such actions are counterproductive. For example, it may block research which is often of direct financial benefit to the company (Carvel 2008).

These totalising logics of scrutiny find their fullest expression where government acts as the main agent of Internet surveillance. Indeed such surveillance seems increasingly driven more by the rationale of 'because we can' than any coherent need. Government online surveillance takes both active and passive forms. On the one hand 'monitoring in advance' occurs where Internet communications deemed 'undesirable' are filtered or blocked. In contrast to the less subtle and more widely reported attempts to block content elsewhere (RSF 2003), justifications for filtering in Europe, North America and other democratic countries have been based on 'socially acceptable' reasons such as security or the need to block child abuse images. A failure to consult or to engage with the public about decisions being taken on their behalf has been a recurrent theme. One of the more controversial examples in the UK has been the use by British Telecom of the 'Cleanfeed' software since its filters are not determined by public agreement or parliamentary decision, but entirely on the advice of the (self-appointed) Internet Watch Foundation (IWF). Recent attempts by the IWF to block images of a child that featured on an album cover by the German rock group Scorpions are indicative of the ill-informed censorship that results from this lack of public accountability. Not only were their actions pointless (the images had already been in the public domain for over 30 years), but excessive – whole pages of Wikipedia were blocked to UK users as a result (BBC 2008). Similar assumptions and pressures have been evident in the USA where the Children's Internet Protection Act (CIPA) of 2000 has compelled public schools and libraries to use Internet filtering technology or lose funding for information technology support if they fail to comply. But filtering of political Internet content is also on the increase in supposedly 'open' societies. In Switzerland, for example, ISPs were ordered to block access to websites critical of Swiss courts (Ramachander 2008) while the UK Government has proposed blocking Islamic websites it judges to be 'extreme' (*Daily Express* 2008) – based on criteria it, not the public, determines.

'Active' forms of Internet surveillance by governments are even more symptomatic of the totalising attitudes at work within this constituency. For this is no longer surveillance focused upon targeted, or intelligence-driven data acquisition but a generalised scrutiny of any kind of communications – the so-called 'vacuum cleaner approach' (cf. McCullagh 2006). The notorious FBI Carnivore system (EPIC 2006), designed to monitor email addresses and web pages browsed by surveillance targets, once described as 'the most intrusive web-based technology ever developed' (Ventura *et al.* 2005), has now been absorbed into the still more extensive DCS (Digital Collection System) network. Carnivore had already touched on numerous legally contentious areas – such as failing to acquire necessary wiretap warrants (a fact quickly remedied by the 2001 PATRIOT Act). But its form of Internet surveillance was still, in principle, restricted to the acquisition of communication addresses, rather than content. By contrast the DCSnet can now record and store all Internet interactions, irrespective of their content or whether these relate to investigations of criminal or terrorist activity (Singel 2007). Given access to this widened pool of data it was almost inevitable that the FBI would attempt to pass it on to the National Security Analysis Center so that it could be 'mined' in order to predict, not who is, but who 'might' be a terrorist.

However, the possibility that innocent citizens could be implicated in terrorism investigations in the absence of any concrete evidence linking them to radical groups was a step too far for Congress. It has (so far) denied funding for the data mining software (Rood 2008) though the DCSnet remains fully active.

Similar government attitudes have also prevailed in the UK. Powers acquired under the Regulation of Investigatory Powers Act (RIPA) requiring all ISPs to install 'black box' software to enable interception of communications by police and security agencies have been extended by the 2001 Anti-Terrorism Crime and Security Act (ATCS) which orders the retention of Net data for up to six years. The Communications Data Bill proposes a further widening of scrutiny by creating an 'uberdatabase' where every phone call, email, and Internet browsing session conducted by UK citizens would be stored – again irrespective of its innocence. Under the proposals, even the simple act of purchasing a mobile phone would require a passport to be presented and the purchaser's details to be entered onto a national database (Leppard 2008). In the face of widespread outrage the UK Government has sought to play down some aspects of the bill (Williams 2008a) though they have also signalled that the resulting database would be run by a private company, ignoring warnings from figures across the political spectrum (not least the former Director of Public Prosecutions) that this would further stimulate the growth of an 'information honey pot' irresistible to both criminals and terrorists (Travis and Norton-Taylor 2008). And this of course is just what we know of the UK government's enthusiasm for the total surveillance of electronic communications. Other governmental agencies such as the GCHQ monitoring body augment these capacities – most obviously by extending communications surveillance beyond national boundaries. In conjunction with the US National Security Agency (NSA), GCHQ operates the shadowy Echelon project where email data and other communications material is siphoned as a matter of routine – again with little or no outside scrutiny (Campbell 2000; Bamford 2002).

The prominent role of 'big government' within Internet surveillance is hardly surprising. More disturbing has been the increase in Type I and Type II surveillance activities by *local* governments and associated agencies. In the UK the RIPA and ATCS legalisations granted local authorities significant new rights to examine communications data and they have been happy to exploit these new powers. Between March 2007 and March 2008 permission for 9,535 'directed surveillance authorisations' was given, with 1,707 specific requests for communications data from over 150 local authorities (Hope 2008). In the USA a similar devolution of surveillance activities has been occurring, with both States and local authorities taking on rights to scrutiny from the Federal government that, in many cases, go beyond those of the higher authority. As Kennedy and Swire (2004) point out, weaker controls have led to the majority of wiretaps now occurring here, again with less than transparent rationales in many cases. The use in 2005 of Maryland's State's terrorism surveillance programme (Harwood 2008) to track two Dominican nuns who had protested against the Afghan war is typical.

The pathological eagerness of governments to use electronic networks to acquire information (any information) is matched only by the other main agent of Internet surveillance – the commercial world. As we would expect, their surveillance activities are often conducted in collusion with governments – for example much of the filtering software discussed above is managed by private companies. Likewise, commercial connections between local government and private sector mean that data obtained through government activities is often sold onto the private sector without permission (the sale of court data to marketing companies by the North Carolina State government (Bergstein 2004) is one recent example). But the private sector is also a significant independent agent of Internet surveillance. Central to this is its control of the very technologies that make online interaction possible. Not only has provision of Internet access itself provided new business opportunities, software such as the search engine has created some of the world's fastest growing businesses, with Google especially prominent here. Significantly, a large part of their business is closely linked to surveillance and Google is now reckoned to hold more personal data about individuals than almost any other agency (Conti 2008). In a recent report (PI 2007), Privacy International placed Google at the bottom of its rankings for respecting privacy, below other online service companies such as Amazon, Yahoo and even Microsoft and many of its practices fail to respect EU data protection law (cf. EC 2008). The expansion of Google's data-acquisition structure into areas such as communications, social networking, financial management and even remote software provision by way of 'over two dozen interconnected products and services' (Zimmer 2008) can only increase their capacity for scrutiny. The creation of Google accounts that require personal details in order to register enhances this capacity still further.

Many Internet Service Providers (ISPs) were initially reluctant policemen and complained about the monitoring requirements placed on them by legislation such as RIPA. Changes in these attitudes have not only arisen from government pressure to monitor more extensively (government recommendations that UK ISPs will be required to collect information on file sharers (Digital Britain 2009) is the latest example of such pressures); enhanced surveillance by ISPs is also motivated by self-interest. The emergence of 'bandwidth hungry' applications like BitTorrent mean that ISPs begin to get 'less for their money' as more and more space is taken up by customers who download films and other large files but who are unwilling to pay for the network upgrades required to produce faster speeds. 'Monetising' users in the style of Google, by trading in their personal data, is one solution. The likely result of all this, as some have argued, is 'a coming storm of unprecedented and invasive ISP surveillance' (Ohm 2008: 1).

Beyond the companies who engage in surveillance as part of providing Internet services lies a multitude of further commercial organisations seeking to profit from the information they can acquire from Internet users. Data brokers such as Choicepoint or LexisNexis now hold millions of files, often acquired from publicly accessible data and are regularly consulted by employers, credit reference groups and law enforcement agencies. Such companies are instrumental in the blurring between Internet surveillance and surveillance throughout other networks and engage in both Type I and II varieties of surveillance. In turn, data they gather can be used by companies such as Zabasearch which enables Internet users to search for information about individuals' criminal history, credit ratings and birthdates or 'Wink.com' which provides 'people-search engines' making it easier to retrieve personal pages from social networking profiles and elsewhere.

Companies with more traditional business interests, from advertisers to supermarkets to media groups have also been swept up in the proliferation of online surveillance practices. Whilst traditional advertising faces threats from new media, the capacity provided by the Internet to record 'point and click' behaviours provides it with new opportunities. The UK has seen a particularly rapid growth in this sector, with expansion at around 40 per cent per annum and users bombarded by new techniques, many involving informal surveillance (Story and Pfanner 2006). Retailing businesses have also found surveillance to be commercially attractive in tracking consumer behaviour. The Internet plays a special role here, both in stimulating the shift to online shopping and in enabling far easier monitoring of shoppers' preferences and habits. Requirements to give up personal details to use commercial sites, the locating of monitoring software on home computers (the notorious 'cookies') which maintains surveillance even after sites have been left, or the proactive pursuit of consumers by observing where and what they click upon are developments which have transformed the commercial world into as active a participant in online surveillance as governments. And, like data-brokers, stores are increasingly aware that once they have such information it becomes another way in which profits can be made, by trading it with other commercial agents interested in acquiring such data. As a result, companies like Acerno in the US have acquired information on over 140 million online shoppers (Hansell 2008). Thus, in spite of its undoubted convenience, shopping online involves a treble cost to users. Personal data must be surrendered in order to participate; it must be handed over free (while granting stores the right to profit from it) and finally, users may then be exposed to the usual dangers that come with the creation of large databases. To date the record of businesses in protecting personal information has been as wanting as that of governments. Online shopping sites regularly fail standard security tests – for example many sites use email addresses as passwords and around 60 per cent respond to forgotten password requests with email addresses – thereby permitting fraudsters to verify whether an email address is registered on various e-commerce sites (Bradbury 2008). Sending unencrypted passwords over open networks is clearly a bad idea but less than 14 per cent of e-commerce sites were found to use a 'second-tier' form of security such as a password. Even fewer were PCI-DSS compliant – the security standard now used by credit card firms (*ibid*.). Significant rises in 'card not present fraud' (up by 37 per cent in the UK between 2006–7, (APACS 2008)) is a predictable outcome.

The who, why and wherefore of online surveillance (II): targets and techniques

To classify the targets of online surveillance under the broad category of 'data' or even 'information' would clearly be rather general. The rich variety of what is sought can be better grasped by dividing targets into two broad categories: 'static' data in the form of personal information, and 'dynamic' data in the form of communications and behaviours. Table 23.2 below provides a quick overview of (some of) the continuities between the targets and techniques of online surveillance that will be discussed in this section.

The increased attraction of personal information as a target is very much related to its intrinsic social 'value' which like other value abstractions such as stocks, bonds or futures, can be bought, sold and traded in (cf. McGuire 2007: ch. 3). The value of personal information has also been enhanced by decisions on the part of the State and commerce (never formally stated) to use this as a *security* device – a sort of guarantee of authenticity, fixed by identity cards, password details and so on. As part of this process, personal information is transformed into a kind of 'key' that provides access to property – a development clearly not unrelated to the increased criminal interest in it. Acquiring such data as means to unlock doors to electronic value/wealth is made a good deal easier by the actions of databrokers like governments – both in *creating* this new norm and in the incompetent management of it.

Internet surveillance can also be directed at 'dynamic' targets such as conversations and other social interactions. While conversations are clearly of interest to almost all the agents mentioned in the previous section, they are especially so for governments – from remote monitoring of conversations

Table 23.2 Overview of continuities between the targets and techniques of online surveillance

Surveillance target		Examples	Surveillance techniques (selected)	
			Automated	Non-automated
Static	Personal data	Bank account or financial data, addresses, password data, date of birth etc.	Cookies Keystroke software Spyware Tracking or 'web' bugs	Wiretapping Data trading Requirement to provide data for access to services
Dynamic	Communications	Conversations, interactions, messages	Browser records Download histories	Phishing Accessing PCs directly
	Behaviour	1. opinions, intentions, preferences 2. previous history 3. spatial locations and movements	Copyright bots Interception software for email, IRC or VoIP data Software filters	Monitoring by using false identities

between suspected terrorists, through to software-enabled detection of censored words and phrases. Initially, message exchange and communication via the Internet was fairly rudimentary compared to telephone communications. Interactions were text-based using media such as bulletin boards or email, though these were not in real time. The advent of IRC (Internet Relay Chat) from around 1988 remedied this and the emergence of chat rooms supporting communities of various kinds enriched the surveillance potentials of online conversation (cf. Smith and Kollock 1999). In turn, under the cover of National Science Foundation grants, the CIA has funded several projects centred upon automated monitoring and profiling of chat room communications (McCullagh 2004). Internet eavesdropping can also be conducted in 'low-tech' ways, most obviously by the assumption of false identities – for example police impersonation of children in chat rooms to snare suspected paedophiles. It has even become de rigueur for marriage guidance sites to direct their clients towards surveillance of conversation conducted in chat rooms (Save Your Marriage 2008).

Monitoring email conversations has been a more straightforward operation, and can also be conducted in 'low' as well as 'high-tech' ways – for example by looking over someone's shoulder or accessing the computer used to send the mails. More comprehensive surveillance programmes such as Carnivore or the DCSNet are now able to intercept mobile phone text messages as well as emails. But email is not always the most useful kind of surveillance target – messages can be obscure or deliberately coded. Thus the advent of VoIP (voice over internet protocol) systems such as Skype, which have made real-time Internet voice communication into a reality, also makes listening in more attractive. Such systems seemed, at first, likely to pose problems for surveillance in that the digital technologies involved in VoIP are different from that used on telephone exchanges, thereby ruling out older wiretapping methods. But whilst some policing agencies complained that the digital encryption methods used on Skype made tapping impossible, reports that a fugitive executive was tracked down following phone calls made on Skype suggest otherwise (Leyden 2008). Methods for monitoring VoIP conversations have been discussed in specialist papers (see for example Wang *et al.* 2005) and it seems indubitable that the DCSnet discussed in the previous section is capable of enabling such monitoring. Such capacities also now extend across national borders. Early in 2008 a system used by Chinese security services for tracking Skype text conversations was uncovered, purely accidentally, by Canadian activists and computer security experts (Markoff 2008). The tracking system was directed at customers of Tom-Skype, a joint venture between a Chinese company and Skype and was activated when key words or phrases like 'democracy' or 'Tibet' appeared in text conversations.

Complementing conversations as a target is a second category of dynamic surveillance – that involving our behaviours. Monitoring behaviour is often far more revealing a medium than conversation, for the extension of the body by communications technologies leaves continuous traces where 'habits, routines, rhythms and flows are digitised for the purposes of control' (Elmer 2004: 47). Digital traces of our intentions, beliefs and attitudes are left by the websites we visit, the search terms we use and the objects we download or purchase.

For governments, such information can be usefully combined with details of conversations or other data, for the purposes of criminal investigation – for example where child pornography sites have been visited, or material downloaded which indicates criminal intent. However, such patterns need not always correlate precisely with out intentions, and can often be highly ambiguous and legally questionable. Take, for example, Section 58 of the Terrorism Act 2000 that makes it a crime to have materials 'likely to be useful to a person committing or preparing an act of terrorism'. The behaviour of Samina Malik in downloading Jihadi manuals or writing poetry in praise of martyrdom under the pen name of the 'lyrical terrorist' might, at another point in history, have been read as nothing other than a form (however dubious) of artistic exploration and expression (Taylor 2007). But in the climate of a feverish war against terrorism, these Internet behaviours were more than sufficient to secure a conviction against her. The CPS strenuously denied she was prosecuted for 'writing poetry' but free speech advocates pointed out that there was no attempt to secure a conviction on the more serious grounds of intention or incitement to commit a terrorist act (*ibid.*). Similar ambiguities arose with the arrest of a Nottingham University student who downloaded an al-Qaeda training manual as part of research for his dissertation on Islamic terrorism, along with a member of staff who had assisted him (Ozimek 2008). The fact that this research was being conducted for a Masters in International Security and had been sanctioned by his tutor, or that the manual was listed on the Politics reading list made little difference to the interpretation of his behaviour.

Though government monitoring of Internet activity for reasons other than national security or for fighting crime would appear to preclude detailed monitoring of our habits and patterns of behaviour, no such constraints apply to monitoring of behaviour by the commercial sector. Not only is it more easily justified in terms of 'commercial imperatives', it is sanctioned by a range of legal structures we will consider in the following section. Thus, advertisers can legitimately target Internet users by the use of a significant variety of surveillance techniques. They can leave 'cookie' software on personal computers which report whenever a particular site is visited. They can use 'web' or 'tracking' bugs delivered by spam email or web pages to deliver messages about who has read the mail, or looked at the page (cf. Bennett 2001). Or they can simply monitor users' 'click-on' behaviours to track how and where they browse. Companies such as DoubleClick based their entire business upon the use of commercial surveillance software such as DART (Dynamic Advertising, Reporting, and Targeting). Concern from privacy advocates had already led to the intervention of the Federal Trade Commission that prevented DoubleClick combining data on customers' online behaviours with data on other purchases. So, when in 2007 Google purchased DoubleClick, there were numerous (ultimately unsuccessful) protests against this further inflation in Google's data acquisition capacity (Olsen 2007). Meanwhile, the Webwise software developed by Phorm, discussed in the previous section, goes even further. Used by ISPs such as BT and Virgin Media, Webwise does not just record the URL of every page visited, but also Internet searches, Web-based email, the content of forms completed online and posts on blogs or forums. The unprecedented potential behavioural data this generates, together with Phorm's failure to seek user consent during the initial trials has generated a number of legal challenges that will be discussed shortly.

In addition to their commercial appeal, online behaviours are also a surveillance target for the purposes of commercial *enforcement* – protecting copyright, profits and so on. In this way commerce further transforms the Internet into a disciplinary mechanism directed at commercial rivals and employees as well as customers. Policing tools like the so called 'copyright bot' (a program which traverses the Web searching for illegally downloaded music, films, software or other content) are now so widely used that Viacom has demanded websites like YouTube be prevented from including *any* content which is invisible to these bots – even the 'private' videos which make up so much of the content there (Doctorow 2007). Companies are equally prepared to use the Internet (or related communications devices such as camera phones) to protect their products against spying by commercial rivals – or to conduct such spying activities themselves. And whilst corporate espionage has been around for as long as there have been commercial rivals to steal information from, the Internet and associated devices have provided a new set of opportunities to engage in it. Recent research by PricewaterhouseCoopers suggests that corporate espionage now costs the world's 1,000 largest firms in excess of $45 billion annually, a figure that had doubled between 1990 and 2000 – precisely when the Internet spread across the world (Whittle 2008). Attention is more often directed at corporate spying at the international level with regular warnings from Western security agencies of China's growing involvement here. In 2007 MI5 alerted over 300 British banks and accountancy firms to the possibility of Chinese electronic espionage. Oil, engineering, aviation and IT firms are among the many other sectors that have been reportedly targeted (Blakely *et al.* 2007). Finally, as we also saw earlier, employee behaviours are also a target for online surveillance by commerce – from their Web browsing habits to their personal communications.

The capacity for remote monitoring of behaviours provided via the Internet and related technologies extends also to our spatial movements and habits – a further sign of the hyperspatial character of contemporary social interaction. Online crime maps, detailing spatial distributions of offences (cf. Home Office 2009) are only one, more familiar instance of this trend. A panoply of interconnected devices – from RFID (Radio Frequency Identification), to GPS (Global Positioning Systems) or webcams, combine to blur the line in this context between Type I and Type II Internet surveillance. As 'ubiquitous' computing becomes ever more the norm, the likelihood of everyone everywhere at any time being accessible to Internet surveillance also becomes more likely. The drive to include RFID devices in clothing or in the wider environment is already well underway (Crace 2007), while wireless Internet, combined with GPS and mobile phone technologies, increasingly mean that parents can connect to the Internet and monitor where there children are, what they are doing, how long they are doing it and with whom.

Commerce has a particular interest in tracking technologies, with systems such as the BehaviourIQ suite (used by Tesco and other retailers) enabling stores to conduct sophisticated Type II monitoring of almost every pattern of behaviour customers exhibit – especially their movements (*Economist* 2007). A variant on this are technologies that fix upon customers' mobile phone signals to track their movements. Already in use in several shopping malls around the UK, technologies like these – for example the Path Intelligence system in use in Portsmouth – has been investigated by the Information Commissioner's Office (ICO) which noted that, whilst it is acceptable where phone owners were not identified, there were clear dangers of it being used in conjunction with other sources of personal information to provide more detailed surveillance profiles for stores to use (Richards 2008). Whether it is tracking one's girlfriend through her mobile phone (Outlaw 2006), observing fellow students move around a university (Bloom 2008), or utilising travel 'smart cards' like London's Oyster Card (BBC 2006b) to record an individual's movements, networked technologies are coming together to create the ultimate scenario – an individual transparent not just in term of personal details, opinions, attitudes or behaviour but also in terms of where they are and what they are doing – any time, any place.

The legalities of online surveillance: liberty, rights and criminality

The erosion of seemingly stable social boundaries produced by hyperspatialising technologies like the Internet is now creating a new order of transparency where visibility becomes all but compulsive and invisibility a mark of status. Yet in spite of the concerted resistance of what have been termed 'privacy advocates' (Bennett 2008) regulatory responses to this have been largely inadequate. The (inevitable) result has been to promote, almost under our noses, a new control elite able to accumulate information at the margins of (and sometimes beyond) existing legal constraints. It is here that criminologists can make a distinctive contribution, by setting out standards of actual, or possible criminality that have so far been conspicuously lacking.

Fundamental to the development of an adequate regulatory framework is a proper recognition of the imbalances in visibility that have been noted. It is not just that agents such as the State and commercial sectors have acquired grossly disproportionate *resources* to monitor citizens, but that they have granted themselves *rights* to do so – rights skewed heavily in their favour. Such imbalances are further reified by the neo-feudalist economy of personal information that emerges in tandem. For whilst such information is arguably as much the 'property' of an individual as any material object like a house, citizens must defer the rights of ownership over it in order to be able to gain access to the membership rights of contemporary consumerism. In what has been called 'the commodification of the self' (Haggerty and Ericson 2000: 617) personal information can be bought and sold in ways that exclude the owner, not just from a share in the profits, but from any part in the transaction.

There appear to be three clear relations between current legal realities and surveillance, online or otherwise:

(i)   where surveillance practices are protected and permitted by legislation;
(ii) where surveillance practices are neither legislated for nor against – the 'grey area'. Many practices here rely on misleading or deceptive ways of monitoring;
(iii) where surveillance practices occur which are specifically illegal.

In effect, this taxonomy provides a way in which the new elite of the control society can be defined – as those who do not just have greater access to invisibility, but who have a monopoly on (i), are better able to deploy (ii) to their advantage and rarely face prosecution for activities related to (iii).

UK law manifests these asymmetries quite clearly, granting major rights of online surveillance to government and commerce while providing few reciprocal rights of scrutiny for its citizens. Thus, the limited protections offered by legislation such as the Freedom of Information Act (FIA) contain numerous exemptions (not least its failure to extend to the private sector), ambiguous wording (the decision to release information for public scrutiny depends heavily upon how 'in the public interest' is defined) and few mechanisms for enforcement (cf. Cornford 2001). Protections against communications intrusion are largely covered by the Data Protection Acts (DPA), the Environmental Information Regulations (EIR), and the Privacy and Electronic Communications Regulations (PECR). But, like FIA, they tend to be ring-fenced with exceptions – for example, whilst PECR requires (in Regulation 7) that communications data be erased when no longer required for the purposes of transmitting a communication this is subject to the qualification that it can be used for 'marketing or value added services' (supposedly with consent), 'customer services', or 'marketing of electronic communications services fraud prevention'. Vague wording is also a feature of the Data Protection Acts (1984 and 1998) – for example, the stipulation that '... data should not be kept longer than is necessary for the purposes for which it is processed' is hardly very transparent. Similarly, infringements of the Act rarely result in criminal sanctions – despite what has been described as 'systemic failures in the government's handling of private data' (Ferguson 2007). The creation of the Information Commissioners Office (ICO) was meant to have helped in enforcing these provisions but, given that the office has few real powers to intervene, its role has, so far, been largely symbolic. As the British Computer Society point out in their critique of the ICO's Data Protection Strategy (BCS 2007: 5) the ICO needs to do a lot more than 'promote good practice' in defending data security or communications privacy in general.

Even where the ICO has been presented with clear evidence of potentially serious data breaches it has shown a marked reluctance to act. For example when, in 2008, a man managed to purchase a computer on eBay which happened to contain millions of Royal Bank of Scotland and NatWest customer details (including mothers' maiden names, addresses and scans of signatures), his attempts to report this to the ICO were rebuffed. Instead their best suggestion was to return the computer to the original owner so that they could 'deal with it' (Oates 2008). Proposals which would allow the ICO to make spot checks on government and public sectors to see if they are complying with Data Protection legislation remain on the drawing board at present (Outlaw 2008) and even were they to be implemented would be hugely inadequate since they omit private sector organisations – even though figures from the US suggested that, in 2008, over 80 per cent of data breaches occurred here, from financial services to (private) medical and healthcare companies (ITRC 2008).[1] A three-year investigation by the European Commission into the inadequate protection of data in the UK (Dyer 2007) and the lack of powers possessed by the ICO are indicative of concerns about its effectiveness. Suggestions that the Commission may take the UK to court for failing to properly protect UK citizens' data further reinforces the impression of a jurisdiction which fails to protect its citizens while constantly reinforcing its own rights of scrutiny. The free hand given to Phorm's Webwise monitoring software is typical. Phorm's particular method of scrutinising individuals' personal data, and of redirecting users (without their consent) to its website resulted in a number of legal challenges on the basis that such actions contravene RIPA (BBC 2008). Yet in spite of these potential violations, the UK criminal justice system was reluctant to intervene. The City of London Police (who had received formal complaints about Phorm's actions) justified their decision not to prosecute on the grounds that the case would be 'too complex' and that there was 'no criminal intent' on the part of Phorm (Hanff 2008). Whether 'complexity' or 'lack of criminal intent' would prevent child pornography or manslaughter cases coming before a court is clearly an interesting legal question. In June of 2008 the EU Commission wrote to the UK government to inquire why they had taken no action against Phorm under the PECR legislation. The UK government failed to respond to the EU query by the prescribed deadline and when, eventually, it did bother its formulaic response made no mention of the key issue – that BT, the UK's biggest telecommunications provider, had allowed many thousands of its customers' Internet behaviours to be secretly monitored without their consent (Williams 2008b).[2]

The European Courts have in certain cases proved to be a useful brake upon the erosion of privacy by the UK government. The European Convention on Civil Rights (subsequently ratified into UK law within the Human Rights Act of 1998) has, in Article 8, created a general right of privacy where none previously existed. On the other hand the Convention also sanctions interventions by the State or commerce into private communications where this is for some 'legitimate' objective, a qualification that, as we have seen, licenses a wide range of asymmetric snooping activities. European standards of online privacy have also been somewhat undermined by the controversial Data Retention Directive of 2006, which required member states to retain data for between six months to two years (EPIC 2007). However, within individual European jurisdictions some signs of a greater commitment to citizens' privacy have emerged. In Germany for example, the Constitutional Court has specifically curtailed the rights of intelligence agencies to collect data secretly from suspects' computer hard drives unless human lives or state property are in danger. And not only must law enforcement agencies obtain a judge's permission before secretly placing spyware on a suspect's computer, personal data may also not be collected during an investigation (Deutsche Welle 2008). At the same time security agencies in Europe have often deemed themselves to be above the law when it comes to conducting online surveillance. Complaints by German Police that VoIP calls on the Skype network were 'too hard to decipher' were used to justify attempts to plant 'remote forensic software' – malware to the rest of us – on personal computers (Leyden 2008). Swiss police have also considered planting software (trojans) onto individuals' private computers to listen in on VoIP communications, irrespective of whether such actions would be legal, or whether any evidence gathered would be submissible to a court (Leyden 2006).

Whilst the US has, in principle, more legislative safeguards in place it has also led the way on the new order of telecommunications surveillance. The ratification of the Communications Assistance for Law Enforcement Act (CALEA) legislation in the mid 1990s, which compelled telephone companies to specifically design their systems so as to make wiretapping easier, set the tone. Though CALEA was not at this point applicable to Internet data or communications a 2004 application from the Department of Justice (in conjunction with the Federal Bureau of Investigation (FBI) and Drug Enforcement Administration (DEA)) to extend CALEA to the Internet and VoIP communications was ratified by the Federal Communications Commission who took the view that, since broadband has effectively replaced local telephone exchanges, the legislation would cover them anyway. The supposed 'lawlessness' of the Internet has served as a recurring justification for the need to extend surveillance and endorsed numerous legal fudges or asymmetric forms of protections. For example, whilst the 'full pipe' recording of every kind of Internet communication which DCSnet facilitates appears to be in contravention of Federal law and possibly the Constitution, because surveillance occurs via 'digital code' agents are (arguably) permitted to retain data beyond usual time limits. Whilst the Federal government has methodically extended its right to eavesdrop – not least in authorising the NSA to engage in wiretapping ordinary Americans (Risen and Lichtblau 2005), legal challenges by civil liberties groups such as the American Civil Liberties Union (ACLU) have been ultimately blocked by the Court of Appeals which refused to rule on the legality of the operations (ACLU 2008). Threats from the Senate judiciary committee to hold the Bush administration in contempt of court for ignoring subpoenas requiring documentation about the warrantless wiretap program made little impact, while attempts to hold the private companies which had colluded in this surveillance to legal account have proved equally unsuccessful. Electronic Frontier Foundation (EFF) lawsuits against the telephone company AT&T in 2006 have been met by new legislation that gives telecommunications firms unprecedented legal immunity from any kind of action based on their collaboration in spying (Eggen and Kane 2008). And hopes that the Obama administration might be more liberal on Internet eavesdropping may need to be tempered by the fact that Vice President Biden was one of the leading figures in drafting CALEA (McCullagh 2008).

Legal anomalies also reinforce the business sector's use of the Internet as a surveillance tool. The 'right' to leave cookies on users hard drives, or the virtual carte blanche granted to data brokers to buy and sell information obtained or traded online is usually justified by the ever flexible ethical principle of 'business pragmatics'. For example, though the US Privacy and Electronic Communications (PEC) regulations require that cookies can only be used where a visitor to the site 'consents' to them, because they provide a useful (and rapid) way in which sites recognise users, cookies end up with a 'de facto' legitimation. For, provided there is a cookie policy accessible from everywhere on the site then they remain within the letter of the law, though not perhaps within the spirit of more egalitarian transparencies.

The onus placed upon consumers to explicitly 'refuse' surveillance practices on the Internet and elsewhere is an increasingly common pattern in which the grey legal areas denoted by (ii) above are exploited. One of the most pernicious instances of what Gary Marx has, in another context (2006), called 'soft surveillance' or 'mandatory volunteerism' has been the deceptive use of opt-in clauses (where users must consciously un-tick a box if they are to opt out) regarding use of personal information. In one of the worst recent examples of this, the 2007 privacy policy of Rupert Murdoch's Sky corporation required customers to actively telephone a special number if they did not want Sky to 'share information ... held by the Sky group about you ... with other companies outside the group, including for sales, marketing and market research purposes by such companies' (Jones 2007). Though this was a clear and cynical exploitation of consumer ignorance, Sky faced no legal comeback. Predictably the UK ICO had little power to deal with it other than to 'seek reassurances' from Sky that they would desist from the practice. Facebook has also used the concealed opt-in strategy to expose its users to surveillance for commercial benefit. The 'Beacon' software platform, which fed details of members' actions on third party sites to advertisers operated, at first, on an automatic 'opt-in' basis. Only after it received over 50,000 protests from users did it allow them to opt out of having their Internet activities circulated in this way (Story and Stone 2007). Attempts by Facebook to utilise 'opinion polls' posted on its site – which detail members' attitudes towards everything from politics to their favourite films – and sell these as market research tools to corporations (again without permission) are their latest twist on the mandatory opt-in tactic (Wray 2009).

The contempt with which commerce tends to hold the law regarding personal data often extends beyond exploitation of these grey areas into specific infringements of legal requirements on privacy. In 2006, what was described as one of 'the largest deliberate breach(es) of privacy in Internet history' took place when it was discovered that the company Gratis Internet had been using fake Internet surveys which promised free iPods to collect, and then sell on data about millions of customers – in spite of clauses on their website which stated specifically that 'we will never give out, sell or lend your name or information to anyone' (Levine 2006). This pattern of deception also extends to more familiar companies such as Tower Records, Victoria's Secret, and eBay (among others) who have all been involved in similar breaches or laxity with customer information (cf. Outlaw 2004).

In the workplace, companies are notoriously reluctant to observe international standards on privacy such as the International Labour Organisation's (ILO) code of practice, in spite of medical evidence suggesting that the monitoring of employees can damage their health – in particular illnesses brought on by increased stress levels. Research has indicated (McGovern et al. 2007) that feelings of exhaustion and anxiety related to work were 7.5 per cent higher among the 23 per cent of UK employees where IT systems are used to check the quality of work produced than in other groups, a figure even higher in call centres – where workplace surveillance is often draconian. But companies' 'need' to monitor employees almost always takes precedence over employees needs, whether for health or privacy, so that the kind of successful legal challenge made by a secretary from Wales over the long-term surveillance of her personal communications is rare (Liberty 2007).

If we contrast the laxity of controls over Internet surveillance by the State and commerce with what applies to the rest of us the realities of the emerging order of invisibility fall very clearly into focus. Take for example the UK Computer Misuse Act of 1990. Rather than this serving as a considered response by government to the emerging information economy it was little more than a device to secure the punishment of two hackers who had been unsuccessfully prosecuted for managing to penetrate the (then rather primitive) BT Prestel system (cf. Higney 2006). The hamfistedness of the resulting legislation has been manifested most recently in the 2005 case of a systems penetration expert called Dan Cuthbert who was convicted of unauthorised access to the tsunami charity website run by the Disasters Emergency Committee (DEC), a site actually managed by BT (cf. Sommer 2005). After making a contribution to the fund Cuthbert became concerned at the way the site was responding – not least given he had just supplied credit card details and other personal information. Suspecting a possible phishing site (and there had been a number of news stories of fake tsunami charity sites used to defraud donors) he used his expertise to test whether the site was fraudulent. However, BT's intrusion detection system was activated leading to Cuthbert's arrest and ultimate conviction under the Computer Misuse Act. Little or no consideration was given in the case to his intentions – the mere act of asymmetric scrutiny was enough to secure him a criminal record.

The 2000 Terrorism Act further strengthened Government powers to exclude access to computer systems by making certain acts of hacking into potential terrorist offences, though the way this was defined was sufficiently vague as to render many forms of intrusion as 'terrorist'. Even where access is obtained to networks which results in no damage and which exposes security flaws there has been little sign that governments are willing to entertain anything other than a one-directional form of surveillance. The collusion between the UK and US governments during the long-running saga over the British computer expert Gary MacKinnon is indicative of such presumptions. Having detected machines used by the US military which lacked adequate password or firewall protection, MacKinnon was able to hack into them in order (he imagined) to inspect covert files relating to UFOs. In spite of a diagnosis of Asperger's Syndrome his final appeal to the House of Lords was rejected leaving him facing extradition to the US and a lengthy prison sentence for so-called 'cyberterrorist' offences (Hancock 2009). Similar patterns occur in almost every context where citizens attempt to claim reciprocal rights of scrutiny. Whether it is leaking Government secrets or simply reading partners emails (cf. Calman 2005), some form of legal sanction can usually be made to apply. It is hard therefore to escape the conclusion that there is one governing rationale that has come to characterise the regulation of surveillance in the Internet age – we can look at you, but you cannot look at us.

Winning and losing the privacy war – encryption, disguise and the law

The imbalances in the way contemporary rights of invisibility are distributed are nowhere emphasised more starkly than in the legalities surrounding attempts to *hide* or *disguise* our online interactions from scrutiny. Most of us take it for granted that when we close our front curtains we do not just signal a *desire* for privacy, but that the law will protect us where this desire is not respected. The new offence of voyeurism for example, which was created under the Sexual Offences Act 2003, was specifically designed to prohibit 'peeping tom' style behaviours and a number of convictions have followed from individuals who have violated privacy – even CCTV operators who used their cameras to spy on private sexual behaviours have been prosecuted (cf. BBC 2006a). But where online or electronic communication occurs any assumption of a 'right' to privacy seems increasingly untenable. For every program designed to 'close the curtains' by blocking intrusive monitoring software, legal alternatives for getting around this seem to exist. Indeed, just to use Internet communications at all is to have to accede to conditions of service that permit some form of monitoring.

Gary Marx (2003) has considered certain strategies that might be used to evade surveillance but when it comes to the Internet, the only real way to be sure of retaining privacy is to bypass it altogether. For example, so-called 'darknets' – closed networks used for file-sharing (see Biddle *et al.* 2002) – might provide some degree of private networked interaction. However, for those who wish to continue using the Internet proper, three alternatives seem to remain. One is the attempt to remove the digital traces of one's interactions altogether. Hiding what one has been up to from parents, lovers and so on would seem to be effected relatively straightforwardly – for example by deleting files, or copies of sites visited from the browser history. However, it is also a fact of life in the information age that, short of complete destruction of the data source altogether, nothing is ever really deleted, for there will always be some form of forensic process which can recover the data from a PC or elsewhere. The remaining alternatives centre upon attempts to acquire a kind of artificial invisibility, in terms of *disguise*. For this to be effective it needs to involve more than the adoption of online pseudo-identities. Instead it is the communication itself that needs to be obscured. The use of a so-called 'proxy' server, where websites are accessed from one's computer by the use of an intermediary or 'proxy' computer (see Frontline 2007 for some details) offers some protection by hiding the origin of a communication. Otherwise disguise needs to centre upon the message itself, utilising some process of encoding or encryption. And here we touch upon the underlying political economy of online communication again, for there is no more stark sign of the asymmetries within information societies than the ongoing struggle to control the practice of encryption. Simple codings of communications (reversing the alphabet, substituting letters etc.) are not illegal, since such codes can easily be cracked by security agencies, or indeed anyone with a little understanding of cryptography. Legal problems arise where more powerful forms of encryption are used. Governments increasingly demand access to any very powerful 'key' used to encrypt communications, in effect denying citizens another kind of right to online privacy. For example, in the UK the RIPA legislation contained a clause which permitted police to demand encryption keys and though this clause wasn't technically implemented until 2007, police have wasted no time is utilising its powers. In 2007 a group of animal rights activists became some of the first UK citizens to be issued with an S49 notice demanding they provide access to data encrypted on their hard drives 'in an intelligible form' or (under an S51 notice) that they hand over the keys to it (Ward 2007).

In the USA battles to control encryption have been more intense and have been conducted across a variety of fronts. In the 1990s attempts were made by the NSA to impose the use of the so-called 'clipper chip' encryption system on telecommunications companies. Since government agencies would hold the encryption key to the chip 'in escrow', adoption of the clipper chip would have given them the capacity to decrypt any message or communication over the Internet, at least in the US. But the endeavour proved to be a rare setback in the drive towards enforced visibility. Not only were there numerous technical flaws with the system, but the commercial world also quickly realised that introducing it would put them at a commercial disadvantage. Their protests were probably more influential than those of civil liberties groups like the EFF in forcing the US government to abandon this tack. As a result, other tactics for the control of encryption have been pursued. One strategy has been to impose export restrictions on encryption software. Since any software of a certain encryption strength (greater than 40 bits) is classified as 'munitions', special licences must be obtained for export. A related tactic has been to pursue legal action against anyone who publishes encryption algorithms or software. The publication of a basic encryption software program by maths professor Daniel Bernstein in the early 1990s led to a long legal battle with the US government (cf. McCullagh 2003). Indeed even the inventor of the PGP (pretty good privacy) encryption system – now an Internet standard – was initially prosecuted once it began to be used outside the US (and could be classified as an 'export'). A third approach towards controlling encryption, one also pursued in the UK, has been the on-off pressure placed on legislators to pass laws that restrict its use – for example the attempt (ultimately rejected) in the 2003 Domestic Security Enhancement Act (dubbed Patriot II) to make use of encryption a felony where the encryption had been used to 'commit a crime' (in practice opening the way to a general control of encryption).

As it stands, encryption presents an intriguing subject for the student of the legal background to compulsory visibility. Though the cards are seemingly all in governmental hands, attempting to control encryption, as legislators have found, is hampered by some basic pragmatics – not least the fact that such attempts risk damaging the commercial interests of European and American IT companies. There are in any case already numerous, freely available encryption programs which, unless encryption as a whole is to be criminalised, will always make attempts to control it unrealistic. Indeed, even where encryption is used there are some obvious ways around it – for example Federal agents were able to circumvent attempts by a Mafia boss to code communications by installing a keylogging system that read his password every time it was typed in (*USA Today* 2003). Given prevailing attitudes it should not be too surprising that legislation requiring those who *manage* our personal information to encrypt it for our security has been far less forthcoming. Recent provisions passed in Nevada and other US States compelling businesses or government agencies to use encryption when sending personal data may be a sign of change, though – in failing to define what is meant by 'electronic transmission' and omitting to set out any penalties for the misdemeanour (Marks 2008) – the legislation is hardly robust. Meanwhile, the UK has no such legislation in place, nor is there any sign that there will be in the near future.

Conclusions and futures

The realities of Internet surveillance present a clear indication of how little the new social order of life in a hyperspace – a multiply connected world where interaction is indifferent to spatio-temporal distance – is understood. Whilst certain parties continue to acquire hugely disproportionate rights to engage in practices which would be illegal previously, for most of us the debate remains sufficiently abstract for there to be little interest in resisting this. Whilst the value of abstracted property, such as digital copyright or electronic money, has been recognised quickly enough, the value of *information* – especially that involving our personal lives – remains unclear to most of us. Trends in our relationship to communications technology – for example the shift to 'ubiquitous computing' – is likely to make the matter still more pressing. In a world where even the clothes we wear may contain RFID locator tags, personal transparency becomes pervasive. Internet surveillance may only be a tip of a very large iceberg, but it provides a telling indicator of the security or commercial 'imperatives' that, so far, have been successful in tipping the balance of visibility towards citizens and away from more privileged agents.

Note

1 Figures released by the ICO (ICO 2008) appear to show the opposite, with over two thirds of UK public bodies implicated in data breaches in 2008. But given that the private sector regularly hides, or fails to report, data breaches these figures are likely to be incomplete.
2 In July 2009 BT quietly dropped Phorms Webwise tracking software following a long protest campaign and the threat of legal action. They were quickly followed by other ISPs such as TalkTalk and Virgin Media.

Further reading

Whilst surveillance in general now has an extensive literature, detailed studies of Internet surveillance itself are rather more lacking. Partly because, as argued here, it is not always easy to separate Internet specific forms of surveillance from the wider project of tapping communications networks. David Lyon's (2002) 'Surveillance in cyberspace: the Internet, personal data, and social control' provides a brief introduction to the topic. For a discussion of some of the legal issues, Diffie, W. and Landau, S. (2001) *Privacy on the Line: The Politics of Wiretapping and Encryption* is worth consulting – though this is largely concerned with regulation in the USA. A more up-to-date discussion by the same authors, with a specific focus upon Internet surveillance, can be found in their *Scientific American* article 'Internet Eavesdropping: A Brave New World of Wiretapping' (September 2008). Dwayne Winseck's (2002) 'Netscapes of Power' highlights the continuities between market power, corporate interest and the asymmetric forms of surveillance which new communications networks facilitate. For a useful overview of questions relating to privacy online see Solove *et al.* (2006) *Privacy, Information, and Technology* (though note again a focus upon the US legal system). Akdeniz *et al.* (1997) 'Cryptography and Liberty' discusses the development of cryptography regulation in the UK context. Recent literature on Internet cryptography is rather lacking though Smith's (1999) *Internet Cryptography* is still relevant in terms of the broad concepts, though somewhat technical. Vincent (1998) *The Culture of Secrecy: Britain, 1832–1998* (Oxford University Press) provides a fascinating historical background to all forms of surveillance in the UK and highlights the particular culture of obsessive secrecy and intrusion which typifies communications policy and regulation there.

References

ACLU (2008) '*ACLU v. NSA*: The Challenge to Illegal Spying', American Civil Liberties Union, see: http://www.aclu.org/safefree/nsaspying/index.html

Akdeniz, Y. *et al.* (1997) 'Cryptography and Liberty: Can the Trusted Third Parties be Trusted? A Critique of the Recent UK Proposals', *Journal of Information, Law and Technology*.

American Management Association (2005) '2005 Electronic Monitoring and Surveillance Study', see http://www.amanet.org/press/amanews/ems05.htm

Andrejevic, M. (2005) 'The Work of Watching One Another: Lateral Surveillance, Risk, and Governance', *Surveillance and Society*, 2(4): 429–97, available at: http://www.surveillance-and-society.org/articles2(4)/lateral.pdf

APACS (2008) 'Card Fraud Facts and Figures', APACS Key Facts, see: http://www.apacs.org.uk/resources_publications/card_fraud_facts_and_figures.html

Bamford, J. (2002) *Body Of Secrets: How America's NSA and Britain's GCHQ Eavesdrop On The World*. London: Arrow Books.

BBC (2006a) 'Peeping Tom CCTV workers jailed', 13 January, see: http://news.bbc.co.uk/1/hi/england/merseyside/4609746.stm

BBC (2006b) 'Oyster data is "new police tool"', 13 March, see: http://news.bbc.co.uk/1/hi/england/london/4800490.stm

BBC (2008) 'Wikipedia child image censored', 8 December, see http://news.bbc.co.uk/1/hi/uk/7770456.stm

BCS (2007) 'BCS Response to the ICO's Data Protection Strategy Consultation Draft', *British Computer Society*, available at: http://www.bcs.org/upload/pdf/ico-dp-response.pdf

Bennett, C. (2001) 'Cookies, web bugs, webcams and cue cats: patterns of surveillance on the world wide web', *Ethics and Information Technology*, 3: 197–210.

Bennett, C. (2008) *The Privacy Advocates: Resisting the Spread of Surveillance*. Cambridge, Massachusetts: MIT Press.

Bergstein, B. (2004) 'Database Technology Helps Lawyers Scoop up Clients', *USA Today*, 28 March.

Biddle, P., England, P., Peinado, M. and Willman, B. (2002) 'The Darknet and the Future of Content Distribution', paper presented at ACM Workshop on Digital Rights Management, 18 November, available at: http://www.bearcave.com/misl/misl_tech/msdrm/darknet.htm

Blakely, R. *et al.* (2007) 'MI5 alert on China's cyberspace spy threat', *The Times*, 01 December, see: http://business.timesonline.co.uk/tol/business/industry_sectors/technology/article2980250.ece

Bloom, J. (2008) 'Tracking technology in the corridors of learning', *Guardian*, 13 March, see: http://www.guardian.co.uk/technology/2008/mar/13/research.privacy

Bradbury, D. (2008) 'Is online shopping ever secure?', *Guardian*, 10 April, see: http://www.guardian.co.uk/technology/2008/apr/10/ecommerce.hacking

Calman, C. (2005) 'Spy Vs. Spouse: Regulating Surveillance Software On Shared Marital Computers', *Columbia Law Review*, 105(7): 2097–134 see: http://www.columbialawreview.org/assets/pdfs/105/7/Calman-Web.pdf

Campbell, D. (2000) 'Inside Echelon', *Telepolis*, see: http://www.heise.de/tp/r4/artikel/6/6929/1.html

Carvel, J. (2008) 'Most employers restrict staff time on internet, says survey', *Guardian*, 2 December, see: http://www.guardian.co.uk/technology/2008/dec/02/workplace-internet-monitoring-blocked-access

Casciani, D. (2008) 'UK identities sold for £80 online', BBC, 17 November, see: http://news.bbc.co.uk/1/hi/uk/7732569.stm

Conti, G. (2008) *Googling Security: How Much Does Google Know About You?* eBook edition : Addison Wesley Professional.

Cornford, T. (2001) 'The Freedom of Information Act 2000: Genuine or Sham?', *Web Journal Current Legal Issues*, available at: http://webjcli.ncl.ac.uk/2001/issue3/cornford3.html

Crace, J. (2007) 'Walk on the wired side: jacket that lets parents keep track of children', *Guardian*, 23 October.

Daily Express (2008) 'Smith bid to close terror websites', 17 January.

Debord, G. (1994) *Society of the Spectacle*. New York: Zone Books.

Deleuze, G. and Guatarri, F. (1988) *A Thousand Plateaux Capitalism and Schizophrenia*, trans. B. Massumi. London: Athlone.

Deutsche Welle (2008) 'Germany's Highest Court Restricts Internet Surveillance', *Deutsche Welle*, 27 February see http://www.dwworld.de/dw/article/0,2144,3152627,00.html

Diffie, W. and Landau, S. (2001) *Privacy on the Line: The Politics of Wiretapping and Encryption*: Cambridge, Massachusetts: MIT Press.

Diffie, W. and Landau, S. (2008) 'Internet Eavesdropping: A Brave New World of Wiretapping', *Scientific American* (September).

Digital Britain (2009) Interim Report, BERR and DCMS, see: http://www.culture.gov.uk/what_we_do/broadcasting/5631.aspx

Doctorow, C. (2007) 'Why a rights robocop will never work', *Guardian*, 30 October.

Dyer, C. (2007) 'Europe's concern over UK data protection "defects" revealed', *Guardian*, 1 October see: http://www.guardian.co.uk/uk/2007/oct/01/eu.humanrights

EC (2008) 'Opinion on data protection issues related to search engines', EC Article 29 Data protection Working Party, 4 April, see: http://ec.europa.eu/justice_home/fsj/privacy/workinggroup/index_en.htm

Economist (2007) 'Watching as you Shop', *The Economist*, 6 December, see: http://www.economist.com/displaystory.cfm?story_id=10202778

EFF (2007) 'FOIA Litigation: Electronic Surveillance Systems', *Electronic Freedom Foundation*, see: http://www.eff.org/issues/foia/061708CKK

Eggen, D. and Kane, P. (2008) 'Surveillance Bill Offers Protection To Telecom Firms', *Washington Post*, 20 June, see: http://www.washingtonpost.com/wp-dyn/content/article/2008/06/19/AR2008061901545_pf.html

Elmer, G. (2004) *Profiling Machines*. Cambridge, Massachusetts: MIT Press.

EPIC (2006) 'EPIC Carnivore Page', see http://epic.org/privacy/carnivore/

EPIC (2007) 'Data Retention', see: http://epic.org/privacy/intl/data_retention.html

Espiner, T. (2008) 'Ashdown: Internet is a "lawless space"', *ZdNet* 27 November, see: http://news.zdnet.co.uk/security/0,1000000189,39564639,00.htm

Ferguson, T. (2007) 'MPs condemn government's data failures', *ZdNet* 19 December, see: http://news.zdnet.co.uk/security/0,1000000189,39291620,00.htm

Frontline (2007) 'Circumvention of Internet censorship and filtering', see: http://www.frontlinedefenders.org/manual/en/esecman/chapter2_6.html

Garlik (2008) 'Parents snooping on social networks', http://www.garlik.com/news.php – Press Release.

Haggerty, K. and Ericson, R. (2000) 'The Surveillant Assemblage', *British Journal of Sociology*, 51(4): 605–22.

Hancock, S. (2009) 'Clock ticking for hacker McKinnon', BBC, 15 January, see: http://news.bbc.co.uk/1/hi/uk/7831481.stm

Hanff, A. (2008) 'City of London Police – Too complex to spend public money'. No DPI, see: https://nodpi.org/2008/09/22/city-of-london-police-to-complex-to-spend-public-money/

Hansell, S. (2008) 'What Online Stores Sell: Data About You', *New York Times*, 24 October see: http://bits.blogs.nytimes.com/2008/10/24/what-online-stores-sell-data-about-you/

Harwood, C. (2008) 'Criminalising dissent', *Guardian*, 15 October, see: http://www.guardian.co.uk/commentisfree/cifamerica/2008/oct/15/terrorism-civil-liberties-surveillance

Higney, F. (2006) 'Interview with Robert Schifreen', LITF bulletin 1, available at: http://www.legalitforum.com/ipi/legalitforumv2/index.jsp?pageid=litf_bulletin_015

Home Office (2009) 'Crime maps online across England and Wales', Press Release, 6 January, see: http://press.homeoffice.gov.uk/press-releases/online-crime-maps

Hope, C. (2008) 'Local authorities launched 10,000 snooping operations last year', *Daily Telegraph*, 27 July see: http://www.telegraph.co.uk/news/uknews/2446314/Local-authorities-launched-10,000-snooping-operations-last-year.html

ICO (2008) 'Privacy watchdog calls on CEOs to take responsibility for data protection safeguards', Press Release, 29 October.

ITRC (2008) '2008 Data Breach Stats', Identity Theft Resource Centre, available at: http://www.idtheftcenter.org/BreachPDF/ITRC_Breach_Stats_Report_2008_final.pdf

Jones, R. (2007) 'Are your personal details being broadcast far and wide by Sky?', *Guardian*, 8 December, see: http://www.guardian.co.uk/money/2007/dec/08/personaldetails

Kennedy, C.H. and Swire, P. (2004) 'State Wiretaps and Electronic Surveillance After September 11', *Hastings Law Journal*, available at: SSRN: http://ssrn.com/abstract=416586

Lasch, C. (1991) *The Culture of Narcissism* (revised edition). New York: W.W. Norton and Company.

Lenhart, A. and Madden, M. (2007) 'Teens, Privacy and Online Social Networks', *Pew Internet and American Life Project*, see: http://www.pewinternet.org/pdfs/PIP_Teens_Privacy_SNS_Report_Final.pdf

Leppard D. (2008) 'Passports will be needed to buy mobile phones', *Sunday Times*, 19 October see: http://www.timesonline.co.uk/tol/news/politics/article4969312.ece

Leyden, J. (2006) 'Swiss gov "mulls" spyware to tap VoIP calls', *The Register*, 10 October, see: http://www.theregister.co.uk/2006/10/10/swiss_voip_wiretap_plan/

Leyden, J. (2008) 'Skype Trojan wiretap plan leaks onto the net', *The Register*, 29 January, see: http://www.theregister.co.uk/2008/01/29/skype_trojan/

Levine, G. (2006) 'Spitzer Sues Gratis Over E-Mail Data Sale', *Forbes*, 23 March, see: http://www.forbes.com/2006/03/23/spitzer-gratis-email-cx_gl_0323autofacescan10.html

Liberty (2007) 'Court rules spying on employee's personal communications is illegal', Liberty press release 3 April see: http://www.liberty-human-rights.org.uk/news-and-events/1-press-releases/2007/employee-spying.shtml

Lyon, D. (2002) 'Surveillance in cyberspace: the Internet, personal data, and social control', *Queens Magazine* (September).

Madden, M. *et al.* (2007) 'Digital Footprints', *Pew Internet and American Life Project*, see: http://www.pewinternet.org/pdfs/PIP_Digital_Footprints.pdf

Markoff, J. (2008) 'Surveillance of Skype Messages Found in China', *New York Times*, 1 October, see: http://www.nytimes.com/2008/10/02/technology/internet/02skype.html?pagewanted=1and_r=1

Marks, H. (2008) 'Nevada Law Requires Encryption', *Information Week*, 13 October.

Marx, G. (2003) 'A Tack in the Shoe: Neutralizing and Resisting the New Surveillance', *Journal of Social Issues*, 59(2): 369–90.

Marx, G. (2006) 'Soft Surveillance: The Growth of Mandatory Volunteerism in Collecting Personal Information – "Hey Buddy Can You Spare a DNA?"', in T. Monahan, (ed.), *Surveillance and Security: Technological Politics and Power in Everyday Life*. Cullompton: Willan Publishing.

McCullagh, D. (2003) 'US "will not enforce" encryption laws', *CNet*, 16 October, see: http://news.zdnet.co.uk/security/0,1000000189,39117187,00.htm?r=2

McCullagh, D. (2004) 'Security officials to spy on chat rooms', *CNet*, 24 November, see: http://news.cnet.com/2100-7348_3-5466140.html

McCullagh, D. (2007) 'FBI turns to broad new wiretap method', *ZDNet*, 30 January, see: http://news.zdnet.com/2100-9595_22-151059.html

McCullagh, D. (2008) 'Joe Biden's pro-RIAA, pro-FBI tech voting record', *CNet*, 23 August, see: http://news.cnet.com/8301-13578_3-10024163-38.html

McGovern, P., Hill, S., Mills, C. and White, M. (2007) *Market, Class, and Employment*. Oxford: Oxford University Press.

McGuire, M. (2007) *Hypercrime: The new geometry of harm*. Abingdon: Routledge.

NACE (2006) 'More Than One Quarter of Organizations Have Googled Job Candidate Profiles', *National Association of Colleges and Employers*, Press Release, 11 July see: http://www.naceweb.org/press/display.asp?year=andprid=240

Nugent, H. and Hall, A. (2004) 'Now sex cheats can buy an alibi for £800 a day', *The Times*, 30 August.

Oates, J. (2008) 'Data watchdogs did not want to see eBay bank server: watching the watchmen', *The Register*, 28 August, see: http://www.theregister.co.uk/2008/08/28/data_bank_details/

Ohm, P. (2008) 'The rise and fall of invasive ISP surveillance', available at: http://ssrn.com/abstract=1261344

OII (2008) 'Me, My Spouse and the Internet: Meeting, Dating and Marriage in the Digital Age', *Oxford Internet Surveys*, at http://www.oii.ox.ac.uk/research/project.cfm?id=47

O'Keefe, K. and Seltzer, W. (2008) 'USA and Canada: Filtering Report' Open Net Initiative Document, available at: http://opennet.net/research/regions/namerica

Olsen, S. (2007) 'Privacy concerns dog Google-DoubleClick deal', *CNet*, 17 April, see: http://news.cnet.com/Privacy-concerns-dog-Google-DoubleClick-deal/2100-1024_3-6177029.html

Outlaw (2004) 'Tower Records settles web site security charges', *OUT-LAW News*, 23 April, see: http://www.out-law.com/page-4481

Outlaw (2006) 'Mobile phone tracking, girlfriend stalking and the law', *The Register*, 2 February, see: http://www.theregister.co.uk/2006/02/02/mobile-phone_tracking/

Outlaw (2008) 'ICO to get powers to audit public bodies without consent', *Outlaw*, 25 November, see: http://www.out-law.com/page-9618

Ozimek, J. (2008) 'The New Order: When reading is a crime', *The Register*, 30 May, see: http://www.theregister.co.uk/2008/05/30/student_arrested_downloading_book/

PI (2007) 'A Race to the Bottom: Privacy Ranking of Internet Service Companies', *Privacy International Interim Report*, see: http://www.privacyinternational.org/article.shtml?cmd per cent5B347 per cent5D=x-347-553961

Poulsen, K. (2005) 'Google exposes web-surveillance cams', *The Register*, 8 January, see: http://www.theregister.co.uk/2005/01/08/web_surveillance_cams_open_to_all/

Proofpoint (2007) 'Outbound Email and Content Security in Today's Enterprise', available at: http://www.proofpoint.com/id/outbound/index.php

Ramachander, S. (2008) 'Europe: Filtering Report' Open Net Initiative Document, available at: http://opennet.net/research/regions/europe#footnote27_tsbwmmt

Richards, J. (2008) 'Shops track customers by mobile phone', *The Times*, 16 May, see: http://technology.timesonline.co.uk/tol/news/tech_and_web/article3945496.ece

Risen, J. and Lichtblau, E. (2005) 'Bush Lets U.S. Spy on Callers Without Courts', *New York Times*, 16 December.

Rood, J. (2008) 'FBI Data-Mining Plan Hits Roadblock in Congress', *ABC*, 26 June, see: http://abcnews.go.com/Blotter/Story?id=5255140andpage=1

RSF (2003) 'The Internet under Surveillance' Reporters Without Borders Report, available at http://www.rsf.org/IMG/pdf/doc-2236.pdf

Save Your Marriage (2008) 'How to Find Out if Your Spouse is a Chat Room Cheat', see http://saveyourmarriage.co.uk/how-to-find-out-if-your-spouse-is-a-chat-room-cheat/

Shepherd and Shariatmadari (2008) 'Would-be students checked on Facebook' *Guardian*, 11 January, see: http://www.guardian.co.uk/uk/2008/jan/11/accesstouniversity.highereducation

Singel, R. (2007) 'Point, Click ... Eavesdrop: How the FBI Wiretap Net Operates', *Wired*, 29 August, see: http://www.wired.com/politics/security/news/2007/08/wiretap?currentPage=all

Smith. M and Kollock, P. (1999) *Communities in Cyberspace*. London: Routledge.

Smith, R. (1999) *Internet Cryptography*. London: Addison-Wesley.

Solove, D. *et al.* (2006) *Privacy, Information, and Technology*. New York: Aspen.

Sommer, P. (2005) 'Computer Misuse Prosecutions', *Computers and Law*, 16(5), Society for Computers and Law, available at: http://www.scl.org/editorial.asp?i=1098

Story, L. and Pfanner, E (2006) 'The Future of Web Ads Is in Britain', *New York Times*, 4 December see: http://www.nytimes.com/2006/12/04/technology/04adcol.html?_r=2andadxnnl=1andoref=sloginandadxnnlx=1230579609-GrleK7YHrV+FCsYhUWz4WA

Story, L. and Stone, B. (2007) 'Facebook Retreats on Online Tracking', *New York Times*, 30 November, see: http://www.nytimes.com/2007/11/30/technology/30face.html

Taylor, J. (2007) 'Suspended sentence for the "lyrical terrorist"', *Independent*, 7 December.

Travis, A. and Norton-Taylor, R. (2008) 'Private firm may track all email and calls', *Guardian*, 31 December, see: http://www.guardian.co.uk/uk/2008/dec/31/privacy-civil-liberties

USA Today (2003) 'Proposed encryption laws could prove draconian, many fear', *USA Today*, 31 March.

Vallance, C. (2008) 'Facebook faces privacy questions', *BBC*, 18 January, see: http://news.bbc.co.uk/1/hi/technology/7196803.stm

Ventura, H., Miller, J.M. and Deflem, M. (2005) 'Governmentality and the War on Terror: FBI Project Carnivore and the Diffusion of Disciplinary Power', *Critical Criminology*, 13(1): 55–70.

Vincent, D. (1998) *The Culture of Secrecy: Britain, 1832–1998*. Oxford: Oxford University Press.

Wang, X., Chen, S. and Jijodia, S. (2005) 'Tracking Anonymous PeertoPeer VoIP Calls on the Internet', *CCS'05*, 7–11 November, available at: http://ise.gmu.edu/per cent7exwangc/Publications/CCS05-VoIPTracking.pdf

Ward, M. (2007) 'Campaigners hit by decryption law', *BBC*, 20 November, see: http://news.bbc.co.uk/1/hi/technology/7102180.stm

Whittle, S. (2008) 'Countering Corporate Espionage', *ZdNet*, 7 January, see: http://resources.zdnet.co.uk/articles/0,1000001991,39291900-1,00.htm

Williams, C. (2008a) 'UK.gov "to drop" überdatabase from snoop Bill', *The Register,* 25 September see: http://www.theregister.co.uk/2008/09/25/interception_modernisation_bill/ –

Williams, C. (2008b) 'BT's secret Phorm trials: UK.gov responds', *The Register*, 16 September, see: http://www.theregister.co.uk/2008/09/16/phorm_eu_berr/

Winseck, D. (2002) 'Netscapes of Power', in D. Lyon (ed.), *Surveillance as Social Sorting: Privacy, Risk and Automated Discrimination*. London: Routledge, 176–98.

Wray, R. (2009) 'Facebook aims to market its user data bank to businesses', *Guardian*, 1 February, see: http://www.guardian.co.uk/business/2009/feb/01/facebook-seeks-to-exploit-user-information

Zimmer, M. (2008) 'The Gaze of the Perfect Search Engine: Google as an Infrastructure of Dataveillance', in M. Zimmer and A. Spink (eds), *Web Search*. Springer-Verlag: 77–99.

Part IV

Policing the Internet

Yvonne Jewkes and Majid Yar

Having considered the history of the Internet and evolution of cybercrime, the different forms that Internet-related offending can take, and the legislation that has been introduced in response to it, Part IV of the *Handbook of Internet Crime* moves on to look at the policing, investigation, regulation and punishment of the problem. 'Policing' is used here in its broadest sense. As we shall see, much policing of cyberspace is not concerned with 'the police' at all, but rather with non-police regulatory bodies (Internet Service Providers, global interest groups and hotline providers, private security firms set up specifically to protect business interests, and so on).

However, it is with 'the police', as we traditionally know them, that we start our discussion. Yvonne Jewkes (Chapter 24) explores the challenges faced by public law enforcement agencies when confronting Internet crime. First she offers an overview of the types of crime commonly perpetrated in cyberspace and the difficulties faced by the police in tackling them. Some of these offences are the subjects of other contributions (pornography, child sexual abuse, electronic theft of intellectual property rights, identity theft and hacking), though they are not discussed specifically in relation to policing. Other issues – cyber-bullying, hate crime, fraud and crimes facilitated by online auction sites such as eBay – are not covered in detail elsewhere in the volume. Jewkes discusses the various policing initiatives set up to investigate cybercrime, some of which have already failed and been dissolved; others are showing more signs of success. She is somewhat critical of the police's ability and willingness to investigate cybercrime, noting that the problems of cooperation and law enforcement across geographical boundaries and legal jurisdictions are exacerbated by a very traditional occupational culture, resistance among individual police officers who do not see cybercrime as 'proper' police work, and inadequate resources to make an impact on the range of criminal activities discussed in this *Handbook*.

As already mentioned, one of the distinctive features of Internet policing and crime prevention has been the involvement of a wide array of private actors. Attempts to police the Internet by non-state or quasi-public actors have emerged hand-in-hand with the proliferation of online crime problems and have intensified public awareness and concern over such crimes. For example, commercial computer- and information-security companies perform numerous 'policing' functions for profit, and organisations representing the interests of businesses (such as copyright holders in the entertainment industry) undertake investigations, intelligence gathering, and initiate legal actions. These developments are all discussed by Majid Yar in Chapter 25. Yar's analysis is set within the context of significant shifts in the provision of policing, which have seen both a commodification of crime control and a 'responsibilisation' of individuals for their own protection and security. Computer users thus become 'consumers' of security goods and services, rather than 'citizens' who have a right to expect protection from the state as part of a social contract. Like contributors to Part I of this volume (see Chapters 3 and 4 by Sandywell and Miller respectively) Yar situates developments in Internet policing within the context of systemic political-economic changes and the transition to a neo-liberal mode of capitalism.

In Chapter 26 Matthew Williams takes up the theme of responsibilisation and further reminds us that, alongside the public police, commercial providers, and private interest groups, ordinary citizens themselves are involved in the day-to-day policing of online environments. Williams's focus is on Internet social spaces – social networking sites, role-playing games and the kinds of graphic virtual worlds populated by avatars – and his themes are community, identity and morality. According to Williams, user groups in these social spaces frequently have sought to institute their own systems of (formal and informal) social control and sanctions in order to address transgressive behaviour, rather than refer such problems to public agencies as a matter of course. This may be understood variously as 'good citizenship' or as 'vigilantism', and raises important questions about power and freedoms in the management of the online environment. Drawing on his own research Williams observes that virtual world citizens prefer the use of vigilante justice, peer pressure, shaming and ostracism to maintain order as opposed to formal mechanisms of control by 'official' regulatory bodies.

In the penultimate chapter of the *Handbook,* Janet Chan, Gerard Goggin and Jasmine Bruce turn our attention away from the criminality and regulatory issues connected with the Internet and focus on how new technologies have been used by practitioners, organisations and consumers of criminal justice knowledge. They describe the extent to which Internet technologies have transformed the nature and impact of 'mass media' and public communication, noting that a new space has been created for information generation and retrieval, reports and commentaries, interactive discussions, as well as the transmission of ideas. All these developments, they say, have important consequences for the nature and communication of knowledge about crime and justice. In a detailed discussion informed by their own empirical research, Chan, Goggin and Bruce demonstrate how the Internet has affected the way creators of criminal justice knowledge do their work and how the technology is used by organisations such as the police, the courts, and the criminal justice policy community, i.e. government agencies, citizen groups, and other stakeholders. The consequences of this new mode of communication on public attitudes to crime and punishment and its potential as a deliberative space for engendering informed and durable public judgements on law and order issues are highlighted by the authors.

Far from simply presenting a range of new crime problems, the Internet and related technologies can, then, be viewed as a valuable new tool in combating 'conventional' crime. Recent developments include the establishment of online mechanisms for victims and witnesses to report crimes, and websites enabling 'whistle-blowers' to anonymously confide details of corporate wrongdoing. However, one of the most far-reaching and fascinating examples of the capacity and effectiveness of Internet technologies to assist with crime detection and resolution must surely be that of computer forensics. Forensic investigations and data recovery are central to the study of cybercrimes and criminal justice but there is little criminological literature on the subject. Ian Walden (Chapter 28) provides our final contribution, discussing the forensic tools used by investigators to conduct examinations of suspects' computers, and considering the gathering and presentation of evidence in preparation for criminal cases. As Walden explains, the science of cyber-forensics is fraught with difficulty. Data in a networked environment is often intangible and transient, and (echoing Jewkes's point in Chapter 24), lack of adequate training of law enforcement officers, prosecutors and the judiciary only exacerbates these difficulties. As he says, seizing systems and data has become a relatively pedestrian exercise, but accessing and analysing it within the time and resource constraints imposed by legal procedure presents a significant challenge.

Walden not only provides an overview of the technical elements of cyber-forensic investigations but also situates them within a moral and legal framework, i.e. against the rights of the perpetrator, the victim, and others caught up in the investigative process. He reminds us, then, of the point made in the Introduction to Part I of this volume, that the Internet should not be viewed simply as a communications technology, but also as a set of socially, politically and culturally embedded practices that have influenced the contours and textures of everyday life and profoundly reshaped the ways in which crime is conducted and justice carried out. Quite simply, for many of us life is unimaginable without the Internet. It affects almost every aspect of the ways in which we work, play and interact with others, and it continuously challenges our moral boundaries. It is debatable whether academic criminology has yet addressed the subject of Internet crime with anything like sufficient commitment or enthusiasm, but the Editors hope that the *Handbook of Internet Crime* will make a useful contribution to this emerging field.

Chapter 24

Public policing and Internet crime

Yvonne Jewkes

Introduction

One of the fastest moving areas of criminality is cybercrime. As technology becomes more sophisticated, more affordable and more mobile, the opportunities for those with access to the Internet to use it for nefarious purposes have increased exponentially. The Internet's anonymity can engender feelings of invincibility, infallibility and acceptability. In addition, its sheer pervasiveness has made numerous offences – from illegal sharing of music to buying and selling stolen and counterfeit goods on Internet auction sites such as eBay – commonly practised and widely tolerated. The inherent characteristics of the Internet make policing cybercrime immensely difficult and, as we shall see, there have been a number of unsuccessful attempts in recent years to set up policing bodies that are capable of tackling the various offences committed in cyberspace. Added to the secrecy afforded by the virtual realm, and its unbounded scope, the police face further difficulties in terms of cooperation and law enforcement across geographical boundaries and legal jurisdictions. A very traditional occupational culture, resistance among individual police officers who do not see cybercrime as 'proper' police work, and inadequate resources to make an impact on an ever expanding range of criminal activities are also major obstacles to tackling cybercrime. All these factors are severe impediments to the police and will be discussed in this chapter. Following an overview of the types of crime commonly perpetrated in cyberspace, and the difficulties faced by the police in tackling them, the chapter will discuss the various policing initiatives set up to investigate cybercrime and bring offenders to justice, concluding with observations on their success and likely directions for the future.

Obstacles to policing cybercrime

The focus throughout this chapter is on 'Internet crimes'; offences that take place via the network that supports email and the World Wide Web. Broadly speaking, cybercrimes can be classified in two categories: crimes that cannot be committed in any other way or against any other type of victim (in other words, where the computer is the target of the offence; for example, unauthorised access to systems, tampering with programs and data, planting of viruses and so on); and familiar or conventional crimes that are facilitated by computer and information technologies ('cyber' versions of fraud, identity theft, stalking, and so on). In some cases, criminal activities may encompass both categories. For example, acts of terrorism can involve qualitatively new offences enabled by computer technologies or, alternatively, may integrate cyberspace into more traditional activities such as planning, intelligence, logistics, finance and so on. Additionally, there are a number of activities that are not necessarily illegal but may constitute what most people would consider harmful to some users (such as some forms of pornography, gambling, unsolicited email, unregulated sales of medicines and prescription drugs and so on). Finally there are activities that may occupy a grey area between social harms and illegal acts, depending on their severity and the legal jurisdiction in which they take place; cyber-bullying and online hate crimes may fall into this category.

Global statistics, though unreliable, indicate that cybercrime is dramatically increasing in number and severity but that successful policing of the problem remains inadequate; indeed, it is estimated that still only 10 per cent of computer-related crime is reported and fewer than two per cent of cases result in a successful prosecution (www.intergov.org; see also discussion in Wall 2007: 17–20). The reasons for the under-reporting of cybercrime are complex, but there are two predominant explanations for its low visibility. First, there may be a failure on the part of some victims of cybercrime to recognise that a crime has taken place, or alternatively that an act to which they have been subjected is illegal. Offences may be carried out over a relatively long period of time before the victim realises that something is amiss and, in some cases, crimes and their perpetrators remain unknown and their effects are not felt. Thus, although the notion of any crimes being 'victimless' has been vigorously challenged, especially in the criminological literature on white-collar crime, locating cyber-victimisation can be problematic because victims can remain as anonymous as offenders. Identifying victimisation is further problematised in cases of virus propagation because the numbers of victims affected may be simply too large and dispersed to identify, and because viruses can continue to create new victims long after the virus was generated and – hypothetically speaking, given the rarity of successful investigations and prosecutions – long after the offender has been caught and punished (Jewkes and Yar 2008). Interestingly, in the case of viruses, low-level victimisation can be extremely widespread as warnings are often issued before the virus is released, causing millions of computer users to change or modify their online activity. Usually described in apocalyptic terms (and frequently by companies selling anti-virus software), these programs may cause a degree of panic even when, as with the much-publicised Conficker virus unleashed on 1 April 2009, it is not immediately clear what damage it can do.

The second factor in the under-reporting of cybercrime is the reluctance on the part of some victims to involve the police. Both private individuals and businesses may be unwilling to admit their victimisation for fear of adverse publicity or damage to their reputation, or they may simply be apathetic. Like the more general category of white-collar crime, cybercrime seems remote and intangible, especially when compared to offences such as interpersonal violence, street crime, domestic burglary, car theft and sexual assault. The following section provides an outline of some of the crimes unique to, or significantly enhanced by, computer technologies, together with a brief consideration of policing strategies relating to the offences.

Pornography

The most high-profile form of 'policing' aimed at the Internet to date has been targeted at pornography, especially material which exploits children. While the trade in abusive images of children has dominated debates about the potentially subversive role of the Internet, the issue of pornography generally (i.e. the kind of 'adult' pornography that in pre-Internet times was to be found on the top shelves of newsagents) is rather more ambiguous. It is a subject that provokes fear and fascination in equal measure and, while online pornography was the force that propelled the rapid growth of the Internet and demonstrated its commercial potential, equally it was pornography that precipitated the establishment of some of the most high-profile organisations which police the Net. 'Adult' cyberporn has democratised sexual gratification and provided greater freedom of access to women, as well as its traditional customers, men (Jewkes and Sharp 2003), yet at the same time it has reignited debates about the exploitation of women and the relationship between pornography and rape (Aitkenhead 2003). Justice Secretary Jack Straw has announced his intention to make owning, downloading or viewing bestiality, necrophilia or severe sexual violence illegal via an amendment to the Criminal Justice and Immigration Act 2008. This move was prompted by the case of Jane Longhurst, who was sexually assaulted and murdered by Graham Coutts, an acquaintance who reportedly was addicted to sites that encouraged deviant sexual practices including necrophilia and asphyxiation. However, the government's bid to prevent people viewing images of rape and sexual violence has divided opinion among feminists with some commentators arguing that such legislation might be a smokescreen and could even be counterproductive. For example, Laura Schwarz of political activist network Feminist Fightback argues that 'to focus on porn as the primary cause of violence against women is not only reductive and simplistic but politically dangerous. It prevents a more in depth analysis of the causes of sexual violence and ignores other forms of violence – police violence, state violence or the violence of the capitalist system'. Avedon Carol, of Feminists Against Censorship (FAC) goes further, arguing, 'this legislation only has value in a police state because it does not do anything to prevent violence against women. It suppresses sexuality, which can only create more problems later' (*New Statesman*, 28 October 2008).

Given the current political and moral climate in which prurience and censorship are framing the output of traditional broadcast media to a level not seen for many years, and where government control over individuals' lives is increasing unabated, it is easy to be cynical about attempts at legislative control. For the police, it is very difficult to enforce laws against activities that take place in private. Despite the alarmism over the tragic case of Jane Longhurst, reported incidents involving adult victims are extremely rare. Moreover, the difficulties in policing the sheer volume of pornographic material generated and circulated globally on the Internet are compounded by different moral codes and divergent legal responses in different countries. Diversity of definition is brought most sharply into focus in relation to communications between countries with a tradition of freedom of speech and those that are more repressive. For example, material that is considered mildly pornographic in the UK and Ireland may not be censured (or indeed, censored) at all in Sweden or the Netherlands but may be subject to much stricter regulation in the Middle East.

Sexual crimes involving children and adolescents

As the preceding discussion highlights, while debates about the role of pornography in sexually motivated crimes remain contested, the last 20 years have witnessed a shift in cultural attitudes, partly due to the greater freedom of access to pornography offered by the Internet. Law enforcement reflects this changing technological and cultural landscape and, while the production and distribution of sexually explicit images of adults no longer constitute a policing priority, the launch of the Child Exploitation and Online Protection (CEOP) Centre in 2006 underlines the UK police's commitment to stemming the global Internet trade in child pornography. One of their achievements has been to develop a proactive strategy based on specialist intelligence and technical expertise. This approach has involved undercover officers posing as children on fake websites and in chat rooms to lure paedophiles; employing powerful face recognition software to match images and trace abusers, victims and locations; establishing a permanent presence in countries with problems such as sex tourism and assisting local police to identify offenders; and working in partnership with the computer industry to develop new products and services that prevent children from being exposed to abuse.

More broadly, the facility to report sexual abuse on individual police force websites might encourage victims to report offences. Currently, each of the 43 forces in England and Wales has its own individual site which are almost exclusively 'first generation' sites; that is, sites primarily designed as a public relations tool to promote that force and to disseminate public information, as opposed to 'second generation' interactive or transactional sites, or 'third generation' sites which adjust dynamically to individual user requirements. The lack of interaction between the public and police is, according to one police superintendent, a missed opportunity: '[I]t is not just information that twenty-first century citizens want from the police via the Internet. They also want to use everyday police services, just as they could if they called a police officer to their home address or visited a police station ... there is a significant demand for interactive online police services that the police service are not yet satisfying' (www.e-policingreport.com).

While there is a danger that the police could become the victims of information overload, there is no doubt that computer technologies could improve the accessibility of police services and alleviate some of the stigma sometimes experienced by victims when reporting offences, especially those of a sexual nature. This is a major issue in relation to child abuse where the perpetrators of such crimes often remain protected by the fear and shame felt by their victims. It may take years for allegations to come to light (if they ever do) and, given the likely numbers of Internet child porn sites, promises that the law will eventually hunt down offenders seem optimistic. In support of police initiatives, however, it can be noted that the arrest and conviction of music mogul Jonathan King in 2001 for sexual assaults on children going back to the 1970s was precipitated by an email sent to police investigators by one of King's victims. The Child Exploitation and Online Protection Centre are now claiming similar success, having set up a website allowing victims of paedophiles to report their experiences. The initiative led to their first successful prosecution in June 2006 when a Nottinghamshire man who had groomed several young girls in chat rooms was sentenced to nine years in prison. Equally, however, it must be remembered that victims are getting younger, partly because very young children (in some cases babies and children of pre-speech age) cannot tell anyone what they have been subjected to. For example, one of the victims of an eight-man paedophile ring convicted in May 2009 was just three months old. This was the culmination of an 18-month international police operation codenamed Algebra, during which a total of 125,000 still and video images that were shared among the eight men were discovered, together with a log of chat room conversations revealing the extent of abuse perpetrated mostly on the children of unsuspecting 'friends'. Algebra also uncovered a further 70 suspects in 16 regions of Britain and action against another 35 suspected child abusers involved in this particular paedophile ring is ongoing.

The use of the Internet for facilitating online abuse of children remains one of the most feared phenomena of the late-modern age. The predatory paedophile is the bogeyman of our time, although opinion is divided about whether the inherent properties of the Internet encourage individuals who would not otherwise commit such offences, or whether it has simply made easier (and, in some senses, easier to detect) crimes that previously were occurring anyway (see Quayle, Chapter 17). In January 2009 a report was published in the United States which appeared to contradict what we know – or think we know – about the problem of child sexual abuse, particularly online 'grooming' of children by adults. The 278-page document, compiled by the Berkman Center for Internet and Society at Harvard University, reported on the findings of the Internet Safety Technical Task Force, a group made up of 49 attorneys-general and representatives of ISPs and social networking sites. The taskforce were charged with examining the problem of sexual solicitation of children online, and their conclusion was that there is not a significant problem and that the reality of online grooming runs counter to popular perceptions of the dangers reinforced by depictions in the media (http://cyber.law.harvard.edu/research). The report's finding that the Internet is not an especially dangerous place for children coincided with police appeals for sightings of a 15-year-old girl from the north of England who had disappeared with a 49-year-old man with whom she had been communicating on Facebook for six months (see Jewkes, forthcoming).

One of the most disturbing trends of recent years is the willingness of children to engage in criminal and deviant activities in cyberspace, both putting themselves at risk of victimisation in ways that they would not consider doing in a non-virtual environment and engaging in more extreme 'offending' behaviours than they would in the 'real' world. To take an example of each of these scenarios from police forces in the UK: Kent police report that predatory adults are taking advantage of the willingness of young people to experiment with their sexuality over the Net predominantly by engaging in sexually explicit chat, but also by exposing their bodies in front of a webcam, sometimes in response to threats from an adult who has groomed them (http://tinyurl.com/agfq2j). Devon and Cornwall police have discovered that the Internet has facilitated children's criminal and deviant activity, particularly in relation to aggressive, and sexually aggressive, behaviours. They report that children as young as 10 are posing as predatory paedophiles on Internet networking sites to frighten other children they have fallen out with (*Guardian* 9 January 2009).

Cyber-bullying

Kent Constabulary report that 94 per cent of young people go online from home and many have multiple points of access, including from their mobile phone. In addition, 22 per cent of students report having their own webcam. Outside the home, free Wi-Fi zones in coffee shops, university libraries and other public spaces are becoming increasingly widespread. It is perhaps unsurprising, given this private and public penetration of digital technology, that in a 2002 survey, 25 per cent of young people between the ages of 11 and 19 years reported that they had been threatened or bullied via their computers or mobile telephones, including death threats (http://tinyurl.com/oabfem).

The ubiquity of social networking sites and mobile phones with built-in camera and Internet access has led to numerous cases where crimes have been filmed while they are being committed and immediately circulated. Alongside regular reports of 'happy slapping' (where an unsuspecting victim is assaulted while someone else films the attack on a mobile phone camera) several cases of murder and manslaughter of strangers by young people have been recorded, including the beating to death of a 38-year-old man by three male youths and a 14-year-old girl who reportedly approached their victim at random and announced, 'We're filming a documentary about happy slapping' before punching and kicking him to death (http://news.bbc.co.uk/2/hi/uk_news/4478318.stm).

The popularity of mobile digital technologies that can send text and images instantly has also led to many cases of what has been termed 'sexual bullying' (http://www.guardian.co.uk/world/2007/nov/30/gender.pupilbehaviour). For example, in 2007 a 16-year-old schoolboy was charged with sexually assaulting a 14-year-old girl, and another was charged for filming the attack and distributing the pictures on his mobile phone. Another relatively new phenomenon is 'sexting', where an individual sends nude or suggestive photos of themselves over their mobile phone. In 2008, 18-year-old Jessica Logan committed suicide following months of taunting and bullying after nude images of herself that she had sent to her boyfriend were circulated, first across her Cincinnati high school and subsequently far beyond. In the United States, a survey carried out by the National Campaign to Prevent Teen and Unplanned Pregnancy found that one in five teenagers had sent or posted online nude or semi-nude pictures of themselves and 39 per cent had sent or posted sexually suggestive messages (http://uk.reuters.com). So widely reported has 'sexting' been (including stories of young celebrities who have found their 'private' photos posted online) that Australia's state government of New South Wales launched an education campaign in May 2009 to try to educate young people about the dangers of the practice and warn them of the consequences which can include bullying, harassment, sexual assault and, in the case of Jessica Logan, suicide.

In some instances, then, 'bullying' moves into much darker territory. One of the most notorious cases of abuse filmed and photographed on phones and circulated via the worldwide web was that of the bullying and torture by American Military Police personnel of inmates detained in Baghdad's Abu Ghraib. Few readers of this chapter will be unaware of the iconic image of a hooded man connected to electrical wires, or that of Private Lynndie England posing in front of a line of naked men, cigarette dangling from mouth, finger pointing towards the genitals of the naked victims, although these were by no means the most brutal examples of abuse, many of which were simply too sexually explicit and disturbing to be reproduced in the mainstream media and some of which were never released because the US government feared that they would damage America's image abroad. According to Mark Hamm, based on the evidence of the 16,000 photographs compiled by the United States Army's Criminal Investigation Division, the abuse took place in response to instruction from top US officials to 'take off the gloves' in prisoner interrogations (Hamm 2007). It is not too fanciful to conclude that this abuse of Iraqis at the hands of untrained US interrogators and authorised at the highest level, might have remained undisclosed were it not for mobile digital technology.

Hate crime

The promotion of many forms of hatred and extremism is widespread and the Internet is a relatively cheap and accessible means of connecting similarly minded people across the world, informing them of events, changes in ideology and discussions of tactics, and coalescing their belief systems. The Net is a sophisticated tool for recruitment and unification, providing links between hate movements that were previously diverse and fractured, and facilitating the creation of a collective identity and empowering sense of community (Perry 2001: 177). At the same time, it facilitates a phenomenon called 'leaderless resistance' which consists of small guerrilla cells capable of striking autonomously (Levin 2002: 964).

Various groups on the political far right – neo-Nazis, skinheads and groups with ties to the Ku Klux Klan – use the Net to target a youthful and impressionable audience with racist, anti-Semitic and homophobic propaganda with little fear of the kind of legal sanction that might accompany the circulation of such material in more 'traditional' forms (Whine 1997; Zickmund 2000). One of the main problems for police and prosecutors is that there can be a grey area between the communication of threats and the circulation of ideas (Levin 2002). Although Germany and many other European countries have criminalised the publication and distribution of hate propaganda, the Internet remains largely unregulated and there is little the police can do unless a specific crime is reported. Moreover, the constitutional protection afforded to 'free speech' in the USA makes it difficult to challenge the global dissemination of messages of hate. In February 1998, student Richard Machado became the first person to be convicted in the States of 'hate crime' after he sent racist, threatening emails to approximately 60 mostly Asian students at the University of California, Irvine (UCI). The law under which he was prosecuted was that of violating students' right to attend a public college, for which he received a one-year prison sentence (Levin 2002).

A study by UK-based Internet security company SurfControl claims that the number of 'hate and violence' sites increased 300 per cent over a four-year period between 2000 and 2004 (The Register 2004). This rapid, continued growth makes policing difficult enough but, in addition, many cybercrimes, including the perpetration of hate crimes, may involve a considerable physical distance between offender and victim. The fact that each may reside in different countries, or even different continents, means that the coordination required between different police authorities (which may necessitate individual officers making trips around the world to liaise with their overseas counterparts) can be an expensive undertaking. In these times of fiscal constraint and public demands for more localised community policing programmes, chief constables are arguably unlikely to direct precious resources into a type of crime that is costly, difficult to investigate and low down on most people's priorities for their police service.

The use of the Internet to promote hatred is not confined to racially motivated attacks. In July 2001 the ISP, Demon, won a change to the injunction protecting the killers of two-year-old James Bulger when they were released from custody and given new identities. The original form of the injunction, designed to prevent the mass media from publishing or broadcasting details of the offenders or their whereabouts, was deemed 'inappropriate' for the Internet because of the risks of a service provider inadvertently providing access to material about the pair and consequently being found in contempt of court. ISPs are now compelled to take all reasonable measures to prevent this from happening. A similar order was imposed on behalf of Maxine Carr following her release from prison in 2005 (the first time a lifetime injunction to protect identity has been awarded to someone not convicted of murder). Her QC made the case for his client's anonymity on the basis of serious threats and allegations made in Internet chat rooms and their linking to unfounded press reports about her (*Guardian* 25 February 2005).

However, a more recent case demonstrates how unregulatable the Internet can be. In November 2008 the case of 'Baby P', a two-year-old tortured and killed by his mother's boyfriend, shocked the British public. Breaching two separate legal orders, several Internet sites revealed the child's identity and posted photographs of his mother and stepfather along with their names, address, and other personal details. Several social networking sites had to take swift action to remove pages with the mother's profile on after online vigilantes began a campaign calling for violent retribution against them, and the court trial itself had to be postponed for several months (with the cause of the delay being cited as 'legal reasons').

Electronic theft and intellectual property rights

One of the most obvious consequences of the new information and communications revolution is its creation and distribution of unimaginably more information-based products that force us to re-evaluate traditionally held ideas about crime and criminality. For example, theft has commonly involved one person taking something belonging to another person without his or her permission – the result being that the first party no longer has possession of the property taken. Investigation of this type of offence is usually relatively straightforward in so far as it involves property that is tangible, visible and atom based (Goodman 1997). But in a virtual context, it is quite possible for one person to take something that belongs to another person without permission and make a perfect copy of the item, the result being that the original owner still has the property even though the thief now has a version as well (Goodman 1997; Yar 2008a). Such acts challenge conventional and legal definitions of offences and render traditional copyright laws irrelevant (see Wall and Yar, Chapter 13). They also make it almost impossible for the police to justify diverting scarce resources into investigating piracy, even if they had the expertise.

Electronic reproduction of data can take many forms. One of the most common is 'peer-to-peer' file sharing, which has arguably returned to the Internet a sense of the liberal, collective ethos and benign anarchy that characterised its early days in the 1960s and 1970s. But for the film and music industries who are losing millions of dollars in lost sales, this form of digital piracy taking place the world over is every bit as unlawful as the knowing and criminal use of the Internet to market or distribute copyrighted software (Yar 2005). Historically the industry has been slow to respond to the problem of file sharing, and broadband technology has made it even quicker and easier to download music and movies illegally. However, some CDs are now being manufactured in such a way as to make it impossible to play them (and copy them) on a PC. Meanwhile, the Record Industry Association of America (RIAA) is taking legal action against individuals it alleges offer file-swapping services on university campuses, and the Movie Picture Association of America is attempting to close down sites that distribute films online. But many believe that big corporations are being forced into playing cat-and-mouse games they can't possibly hope to win because – as the RIAA's infamous closure of Napster demonstrated – when the illegal business of one outfit is terminated, numerous others will appear in its wake.

Most recently, legal controversy has arisen around the Sweden-based website Pirate Bay, which is a forum for people to post music, movies, computer games and other forms of electronic media. Pirate Bay directs searchers to media files available across the Internet, but does not store or offer any content itself, thus circumventing anti-piracy laws. While its operators claim they are acting within the law, copyright holders claim it is a major source for piracy; a belief upheld in law in 2009 when Pirate Bay's four owners were found guilty of breaking copyright law and each sentenced to a year in jail and ordered to pay £2.4 million in damages. The four men remain defiant, however; one of them, Peter Sunde, said in a Twitter posting that the case is 'just theatre for the media' and that nothing will happen to the site. As this volume goes to press the founders of Pirate Bay face a further prosecution in Italy and could face substantial fines over and above the ones already brought in Sweden (http://www.guardian.co.uk/technology/blog/2009/may/04/pirate-bay-italy). However, as the first police raid occurred in 2006 during which officers shut down the website and confiscated its servers – and since then the police estimate that Pirate Bay has received around £46,000 a month from advertisers, in addition to several sizeable donations – the men behind the site may be justified in their bravado.

Invasion of privacy and theft of identity

The entitlement to security of person is regarded as a fundamental human right, yet the scope and pervasiveness of digital technologies open up new areas of social vulnerability. Invasion of privacy takes many forms from 'spamming' to online defamation, stalking and violence. Spamming has thus far been considered little more than an extension of conventional junk mail, although it is increasingly being recognised as an insidious and frequently illegal activity. It can encompass electronic chain letters, links to pornographic sites, scams claiming that there are extensive funds – for example, from over-invoiced business contracts or a deceased relative's will – available for immediate transfer into the target's bank account, fraudulent pyramid investment schemes, phoney cancer cures and bogus test kits for anthrax. One increasingly prevalent crime, originating particularly in countries in West Africa, and targeting women in Europe and the US, is online dating scams, whereby fraudsters post bogus photographs and establish relationships with vulnerable victims (sometimes over several months) before persuading them to send them money. In addition, the past few years has seen a massive rise in incidents of so-called 'phishing', in which communications purporting to come from legitimate organisations such as banks and building societies target Internet users, inducing them to voluntarily surrender sensitive financial information that can then be used to defraud them. The extent of such fraud solicitation has reached such levels that the EU has recently launched the Consumer Protection Cooperation Network in an attempt to tackle cross-border Internet scams (Espiner 2007).

The law also offers protection to individuals whose reputation is slurred by defamatory Internet content. Teachers and lecturers seem particularly vulnerable to such attacks. In 2000, Demon paid over £230,000 to a British university lecturer who claimed that the ISP had failed to remove two anonymous Internet postings defaming him, while in America a 'teacher review' site set up by students at the City College of San Francisco resulted in one teacher filing a lawsuit against the site, denouncing it as a 'disgusting, lie-filled, destructive force' (Curzon-Brown 2000: 91). Teachers themselves have to be cautious; in 2006, a former Conservative Party politician successfully sued Tracy Williams, a college lecturer, who had accused him of being a 'Nazi' in an online discussion forum relating to the Iraq war; Williams was ordered to pay a total of £17,200 in damages and costs (Gibson 2006).

The current ubiquity of social networking sites further blurs the boundaries between private and public identities, as some students have discovered when fined by their universities for 'breaking the rules' on post-exam celebrations and posting photographic 'evidence' on their sites. In addition, staff at some universities have checked personal profiles on such sites to make decisions about whether or not to admit individual students. However, the dangers of assuming that one's 'private' identities are protected in cyberspace were most graphically illustrated in the case of Amanda Knox and Raffaele Sollecito, accused of the sexual assault and murder of Leeds University student, Meredith Kercher, in Perugia, Italy in November 2007. Before the couple were even arrested and formally charged, the press reproduced text and images from their MySpace pages (including pictures of them individually posing with weapons) and linked this content to the police allegations against them.

Another cybercrime related to privacy is the theft of personal identity, a practice that has dramatically increased in the last few years. In 2007, the US Federal Trade Commission reported that 8.3 million Americans had been victims of identity theft over a 12-month period. Meanwhile, the UK credit-checking agency Experian reported a 69 per cent increase in identity theft over the same period. According to UK government figures, identity theft now costs the British economy £1.7 billion per annum (Home Office 2006). Identity theft encompasses a full range of offences from the appropriation and use of credit card numbers to the wholesale adoption of someone else's persona. It can be mundane and opportunistic; for example, many identity thieves rummage through dustbins for discarded credit card statements or pick up receipts left at bank ATMs. However, more high-tech versions include hacking into an individual's personal computer in order to steal his or her bank and credit card details, using software programs designed to work out or randomly generate PIN numbers, and 'skimming' credit cards in shops and restaurants to produce a near perfect copy of the original card. Apart from financial fraud, identity theft has come to be viewed as an important 'precursor' enabling a range of further offences, including illegal immigration and human trafficking using stolen identities (see http://www.met.police.uk/op_maxim/). Concern over the growth of identity theft has inspired initiatives such as the UK government's Identity Fraud Steering Committee, which brings together police, government and financial bodies in an attempt to develop a coordinated response. Meanwhile financial services providers such as banks and credit card companies now routinely offer customers 'identity theft insurance' intended to protect individuals against the consequences of having their identity stolen and used to defraud them. Police responses have included the London Metropolitan Police's Economic and Specialist Crime Command that now investigates identity theft alongside other financial crimes.

Fraud

Identity theft clearly can be a prelude to fraud, but fraud can be perpetrated via the Internet without recourse to stealing someone else's bank account details, credit card number, or other aspects of their documentary identities. A growing number of criminal offences are facilitated via eBay, the immensely popular online auction site. In the UK eBay's Head of Law Enforcement, Steve Edwards, has been emphatic in his defence of the site, claiming that it does not encourage criminal activity and that when crimes *are* perpetrated, eBay is quick to respond. In a press release put out jointly by eBay and the Metropolitan Police, Garreth Griffith, head of Trust and Safety at eBay.co.uk asserts:

> eBay is committed to keeping criminals off our site. We have long sent out the message that eBay is the worst place to sell stolen items because of the open and transparent nature of the site's operation: we can see what criminals are doing and we have their contact details. (http://www. outofyourhands.com/eBAy_partners_with_police_forces.pdf)

Yet such sentiments paint only a partial picture. Offences facilitated by eBay include the sale of knives and other weapons, metabolic steroids, hardcore pornography and abusive images of children. In addition the site has been used for selling goods that are counterfeit, breach intellectual copyright laws or are knowingly stolen, faulty or damaged. In a landmark legal ruling in 2008 a French court ordered eBay to pay €19.28m to Louis Vuitton Malletier and €17.3m to its sister company Christian Dior Couture for damage to their brand images and for causing 'moral harm'. The parent company LVMH demanded damages over two issues: first it argued that eBay had committed 'serious errors' by not doing enough to prevent the sales of fake goods in 2006, including Louis Vuitton bags and Christian Dior products; it also argued that eBay had allowed unauthorised sales of perfume brands owned by the group. Their view is that, whether the perfumes are real or fake, an offence has been committed because the sale of real goods and perfumes on eBay violates the company's authorised distribution network which only allowed sales through specialist dealers (*Guardian* 1 July 2008).[1]

While these kinds of offences can cost luxury brand companies millions, more pervasive in terms of perpetration and victimisation are offences involving handling stolen goods, financial fraud, obtaining property by deception or instances where sellers simply fail to provide goods to buyers. According to newspaper reports, the police in England and Wales investigate one alleged eBay scam every hour, some of which have moved beyond the cyber-realm and precipitated 'real world' crimes including burglary, assault, possession of firearms offences, civil disputes, harassment and an arson attack (*Daily Mail* 8 October 2008). Users of the auction website reported an estimated total of more than 8,000 crimes in 2007 prompting eBay to respond by offering training to 2,000 police officers to tackle suspected Internet fraud. Cases that came to court in 2007 included that of a woman in South Wales who made more than £13,000 from photographs bearing forged signatures of celebrities and was given a 42-week suspended jail term, and a man from Yorkshire who was given a 26-week suspended sentence and 180 hours' community service after selling £40,000 worth of fake Take That tickets to 270 victims on eBay (*Daily Mail* 8 October 2008).

Information security, personal security and cyber-trespass

Collectively known as 'hackers', individuals who seek to infiltrate computerised information systems can be driven by a wide range of motives including a relatively benign belief in freedom of access to information for all or even, simply, a desire for mastery for its own sake (Taylor 2003). But it is those who perpetrate acts of vandalism, incapacitation, espionage or terrorism (who more accurately should be termed 'crackers') that receive most attention. Three acts of trespass commonly occur in cyberspace. First is the deliberate planting of viruses which either act immediately to disable systems ('denial-of-service' attacks) or are 'sleeping viruses' to be activated or neutralised at a later date when ransom negotiations have taken place or when the virus originator has long since disappeared from the organisation targeted. An example of the former was the denial-of-service attack targeting eBay, Yahoo, Amazon and CNN, among others, which effectively shut down their websites for hours at an estimated cost of $1.2 billion. The culprit was found to be a 15-year-old hacker from Montreal, dubbed Mafiaboy, who eventually served an eight-month sentence in a Canadian detention centre. An example of a sleeping virus concerned the case of Timothy Lloyd, a senior programmer for defence contractor Omega Engineering, manufacturers of sophisticated measurement and control systems for, among others, NASA and the US Navy. Anticipating his imminent dismissal, Lloyd exacted his revenge by planting a software time bomb that was detonated 20 days after he left the company, deleting critical computer programs at a cost of over $10 million to the company and 80 job losses. The second form of cyber-trespass concerns the deliberate manipulation or defacement of presentational data, e.g. home pages. Such website defacements were occurring at a rate of over 5,000 per week at the start of 2008 (Zone-H.org 2008). One case involved the identification by Italian police of six members of a hacker group (aged 15–23) who attacked over 600 websites in 62 countries, replacing official home pages with anti-globalisation slogans. The case was notable for the number and significance of the targets, which included the Pentagon, NASA, the Chinese government, US law courts, universities, media organisations, ISPs, political parties and celebrities.

Thirdly, trespass can involve acts of extortion, spying or terrorism whereby computer systems are infiltrated and access gained to companies' classified information, or systems of the armed forces, police, defence or intelligence agencies. The scope and anonymity afforded by the Internet – together with the fact that increasingly money only exists in electronic form – are attracting organised gangsters to turn to computer fraud. In an article entitled 'Hacker hit men for hire', *Business Week Online* reports that Internet mercenaries are now offering their services in destroying 'your Web enemy' (Blank 2001). In countries where wages are low and opportunities are limited but computer literacy is advanced, the Internet has spawned an enterprise culture involving the sale of various services. For the right price, Internet outlaws will steal information from a rival company, obtain credit card details of thousands of customers at a time in order to hold a business to ransom or bombard the chosen target with tens of thousands of emails in a single day thus jamming computer networks and disrupting normal business. In 2007, transatlantic fashion retailer TK Maxx was targeted by hackers who stole the details of 45.7 million customer credit cards, thought to be the largest such theft of its kind to date (Clark 2007).

The penetration of any security system may be damaging enough, but the risk of harm increases exponentially with the size of organisation targeted. Among the potential consequences of deliberate acts of sabotage are the capacity to disrupt or damage water, gas and electricity supplies, close all international communications, manipulate air traffic control or military systems, hack into a hospital's computer system and alter details of medical conditions and treatments, tamper with National Insurance numbers or tax codes and paralyse financial systems. Although 'cyberhomicide' has not yet been reported many of these activities suggest that it may only be a matter of time (Goodman and Brenner 2002). Nevertheless, most commentators believe that, while these kinds of possibilities are terrifying to contemplate, the likelihood of such calamitous events occurring through human error is far greater than the chance of malicious hackers, mercenaries or terrorists bringing down a country's infrastructure. To illustrate the vulnerability of supposedly secure systems to human frailties, in the last three years dozens of stories have been reported in the media concerning laptops, computer discs and memory sticks containing personal data, details of financial transactions, or sensitive material that have been lost or mislaid. The UK's HM Revenue and Customs alone have admitted to seven serious incidents of data loss, including two mislaid CDs containing the personal and financial details of 25m people; among them, 350 individuals in the police's witness protection scheme who had been given new identities to ensure their safety.

Like many of the other cybercrimes mentioned in this section offences relating to security are notoriously difficult to police and the problem may be wider than simply a reluctance to investigate. While technophobia may be no more prevalent within the police than it is in the public at large (itself a point of debate for many commentators), a lack of computer savvy *is* a serious problem for the police and is compounded by insufficient training on either computer usage or computer crime (Goodman 1997; Hyde 1999; Woods 2002; Jewkes and Andrews 2005; Wall 2007). Although the police are routinely trained in the use of criminal database systems, the skills required are rudimentary and they do not prepare officers for tackling serious cybercrimes of the kind described here.

Specialist units for policing cybercrime

Cybercrimes pose significant challenges for the police service. Although many are familiar offences, their context and scope, and the technical expertise required to investigate them, have compelled the police to examine their capacity to respond. As other chapters in this volume have described (see especially Chapter 25), much of the monitoring, regulation, protection and enforcement related to cybercrimes is not the responsibility of state-controlled public police forces at all. Governments, the police, Internet service providers (ISPs) and Internet users all broadly agree that the latter two groups – ISPs and users – must bear the primary responsibility for cleaning up cyberspace. In addition there are a growing number of interest groups – such as Women Halting Online Abuse (WHOA), Internet Hotline Providers in Europe (INHOPE) and Cyberangels – who support a particular cause or aspect of regulation. There also exist numerous organisations that support specific business interests, such as the Business Software Alliance (BSA) that represents many of the big software companies and works closely with law enforcement agencies to enforce copyright laws and investigate cases of software theft. Finally, in recent years there has been a proliferation of private security firms set up to protect corporate data for commercial businesses who place a premium on discretion and privacy when it comes to their computerised records and data systems. These developments may be symptomatic of a situation in which the scope, scale and structure of the Internet outstrips the capacity of any single enforcement or regulatory body (Wall 2007: 167–77; Yar 2008b).

The police themselves are becoming part of a more diverse assortment of bodies with policing functions, and the array of activities we term 'policing' is becoming increasingly diffuse within and between nation states (Reiner 2000). Just as the policing of terrestrial space has demanded a 'joined-up approach' between individual citizens, private sector agencies and the police, so too has the policing of cyberspace become a pluralistic endeavour. In some countries 'policing' functions have been awarded to other state-funded organisations. For example, in New Zealand, the Censorship Compliance Unit (CCU) within the Government's Department of Internal Affairs has responsibility for regulating and detecting some cyber offences. Because the CCU investigates a relatively narrow range of offences, including the policing of Internet child pornography, it has developed a proactive strategy based on specialist intelligence and technical expertise and claims higher success rates than comparable police units (Jewkes and Andrews 2007).

So, when commentators talk of 'cybercops', they may be referring to a wide range of different bodies or strategies encompassing those whose primary aim is to 'protect', for example, authorities who use encryption and digital 'fingerprinting' techniques to protect copyrighted material, to those whose primary aim is to 'enforce'. The international police coordination body, Interpol, and its European equivalent, Europol, also support cross-border investigation and act as conduits for the pooling of intelligence and expert knowledge. However, although Interpol and Europol have put themselves forward as the most effective organisations to establish a global cyberpolice force, in reality such a move is some way off. Cooperation between member states is undoubtedly desirable, but in reality it is hard to achieve and investigations can be held up for months while law enforcement agents from different countries struggle to find compatible modus operandi.

The names and precise operational remits of specialist units dealing with cybercrime vary, then, from force to force (and in some forces will differ from the examples given below). In the main, however, they fall into four categories. First, there are scientific support units or forensic investigation units which carry out forensic examinations of seized computer equipment and data recovery, as well as investigating cases involving DNA, fingerprints and so on. Secondly, there are departments that gather intelligence on major crimes, usually in support of a force CID or fraud squad. Variously called (among other names) the 'Force Intelligence Bureau', 'Crime Squad', 'Specialist Investigations Department', or 'Intelligence and Specialist Operations', personnel in these units tend to work on major, cross-boundary investigations such as terrorism and fraud, and they gather intelligence on persistent, known, 'career' offenders. The third group of specialist units are those with a broader remit to investigate offences committed against computer systems as well as to investigate traditional crimes that have a 'high-tech' element. These include force high-tech crime units, computer crime units or telecoms and computer crime units. Finally, there are units that deal with obscene images of children and/or investigate paedophile networks. These include child protection units or child protection and investigation units, paedophile units, abusive images units, obscene publications units and vice squads. The names of these departments indicate some of their differing functions but, while all may have a duty to investigate sexual images of children on the Net, not all of them will include within their remits the safeguarding of children in chat rooms or the more general welfare of children in the community. One of the most high-profile units dealing with children's welfare is the Metropolitan Police's Paedophile Unit based at New Scotland Yard. It is charged with carrying out proactive and reactive operations against those who manufacture and distribute paedophile material, including via the Internet. But it also carries out operations against high-risk predatory paedophiles operating within the 'real' (as opposed to virtual) community and is part of a wider group, the Child Abuse Investigation Command which has a far wider range of responsibilities in relation to child welfare than only computer-related offences and, in addition to the Paedophile Unit, incorporates 27 child protection teams and four major investigation teams who work in partnership with professional agencies such as social services, and health and education authorities.

Most forces have at least one specialist unit which falls into one of the four categories outlined above, although in some forces one department will be responsible for all the offences mentioned, albeit in conjunction with officers from other, more 'traditional' departments such as CID or special branch. The picture is further complicated by the fact that some police forces have complex structures, with departments containing numerous specialist units with overlapping responsibilities. An example is Hampshire Constabulary whose CID contains the Specialist Investigations Department, which includes a Financial Investigation Unit, Fraud Squad, Computer Crime Unit, Child Protection Unit and Paedophile Unit. Kent Constabulary, on the other hand, has a Central Operations Unit that incorporates Intelligence and Specialist Operations, Major, Serious and Organised Crime, Forensic Investigation,

Tactical Operations and Special Branch, any or all of which might be called upon to investigate cybercrime.

Since the turn of the millennium several new initiatives have been introduced in an attempt to effectively police cybercrime. At a national level, several initiatives have been tried, although many commentators believe them to have been rather half-hearted. In January 2000, the Home Office assigned what we now know to be a woefully inadequate £337,000 to the National Criminal Intelligence Service (NCIS) to target fraud, money laundering, pornography, cyber-stalking, email viruses, paedophilia and hacking. The following year the National Hi-Tech Crime Unit (NHTCU) was established. Made up of a team comprising representatives from the National Crime Squad, the National Criminal Intelligence Service, HM Customs and Excise, the Ministry of Defence and seconded police officers, this was one of the first casualties of the sheer volume of information generated about cybercrime. Five years later, in 2006, the NHTCU was absorbed into the new Serious and Organised Crime Agency (SOCA) which, as the name suggests, has a very broad remit, but includes the investigation of 'cyber' offences such as online frauds and scams. In the same year the Child Exploitation and Online Protection (CEOP) Centre was launched which, in addition to investigating cases in the ways outlined earlier, has a remit to educate young people and their parents about the dangers of online activities (http://www.ceop.gov.uk). The latest policing cybercrime initiative came into operation in 2009. Based in the Metropolitan Police Service, the Police Central e-crime Unit (PCeU) provides specialist officer training and coordinates cross-force initiatives in support of the new National Fraud Reporting Centre (NFRC) and the National Fraud Intelligence Bureau (NFIB). PCeU was created in response to calls by the Association of Chief Police Officers (ACPO) for increasing capacity and capability within the police service to get to grips with modern forms of Internet crime and is jointly funded by Government (to the tune of £3.5 million and the Met (£3.9 million), though it will also seek support from industry partners (http://press.homeoffice.gov.uk/press-releases/new-specialist-ecrime-unit). Meanwhile, the European Union has established its own agency to tackle cybercrime, ENISA (the European Network and Information Security Agency). Operational since May 2005, it aims to 'enhance the capability of the European Union, the EU Member States and the business community to prevent, address and respond to network and information security problems' (ENISA 2008). Yet, with a paltry budget of 6.9 million Euros for 2007 (about £5 million), it remains to be seen how much impact it can have upon computer crime across the 27 member states (Jewkes and Yar 2008).

The establishment of initiatives such as NHTCU, SOCA, CEOP, PCeU and ENISA may seem attractive to those who are alarmed by recent moral panics concerning the apparent expansion and increased visibility of cybercrimes and may, superficially at least, appear to fulfil prophesies of international law enforcement agencies patrolling the electronic beat and hunting down paedophiles, pornographers and criminal masterminds. But as the NHTCU's brief life demonstrated, expectations of these kinds of organisations can be wildly ambitious and unrealistic, at least within the context of the finite resources within which they must operate. The sheer size and scope of the Internet, the volume of electronic traffic it facilitates, the varying legal responses to cybercrime in different countries and other inter-jurisdictional difficulties combine to ensure that the police feel they remain in a perpetual game of 'catch-up' with the vast numbers of criminally minded individuals who lurk in the shadowy corners of cyberspace. For example, the fact that ENISA's 'mission' places it at a considerable remove from the day-to-day operational business of policing should come as little surprise, as it is perhaps a recognition of the overwhelming nature of the demands faced by any supposed 'Internet police'.

Policing cybercrime: emerging trends and challenges for the future

There are clearly no easy solutions to the problems of policing and prosecuting cybercrimes but, as an initial step forward, progress could arguably be made in three areas. The first is legislation (see also chapters in Part III). An area of legislation that requires continued attention in the UK and elsewhere is the modernisation of substantive *and* procedural laws so that not only is there international agreement on what constitutes criminal activity in cyberspace but there is also an adequate legal framework in place for its investigation. Significant strides have been made in this area, with legislation such as the Regulation of Investigatory Powers Act (RIPA) in 2000, the Terrorism Act (2000), the Anti-Terrorism, Crime and Security Act (2001), and the Terrorism Act (2006) enhancing the capacity of authorities to collect and use electronic communications data. At the international level, the ratification of the European Convention on Cybercrime has laid the groundwork for harmonising legal definitions and sanctions regarding such offences (as of January 2008, the Convention has been signed by all EU member states, 39 member states of the Council of Europe, along with the United States, Canada and Japan).

While governments need to review existing laws, they also need to avoid drafting hasty and ill-thought-out legislation on the back of media campaigns and public anxiety. One law, brought into force in 2004, criminalises the 'grooming' of children for purposes of sexual abuse, which has caused concern among civil liberties groups because it is designed to target adults who meet a child after contact has been made on the Internet but *before* any offence has taken place. This raises the question of whether *thinking* about sexual acts is the same as committing them and – even if a case reaches court – proving intent is notoriously difficult for the police and prosecutors. Similarly, concerns have been raised about the erosion of privacy rights and the lack of judicial review in measures for Internet surveillance included in the raft of recent anti-terrorism legislation.

Secondly, in addition to reviewing and updating their legal statutes which will help the police build a case for prosecution when cybercrimes are committed, governments must also do more to prevent such offences occurring in the first place. Their collective failure to do so is part of a wider neglect of the potential scope and costs of cybercrime and the harm that it can cause. Thus far, governments have been considerably more adept at introducing *reactive* measures (those that provide for the prosecution of offences after they occur) than pioneering *preventive* initiatives. Somewhat belatedly in March 2003 the UK Department of Trade and Industry announced a new 'Foresight' project on Cyber Trust and Crime Prevention. In a statement, John Denham, then Minister for Crime Reduction and Policing, claimed that the initiative would 'help ensure that technology is used to benefit society and ... police officers have the latest tools and technology to protect and police our communities and to minimise criminal misuse' (www.foresight.gov.uk). Many critics will be wary of a government initiative designed, as its press release states, to ensure that 'long term financial information is held in a consistent and compatible format that allows its retrieval in 20 years or more'. And while few would question the need for the police or Customs and Excise to 'protect and detect in the virtual world as in the real' (www.foresight.gov.uk), especially in their efforts to counter terrorist and cyber-terrorist threats, more may be troubled by the use of technology to hold sensitive or confidential information about individual citizens.

Thirdly, greater attention needs to be paid to the information and computer literacy skills of police officers at all levels of command and in national, regional *and* local contexts. The raising of competence levels may seem a completely different issue from that of policing cybercrime but, for many critics, the problems are interrelated. If the police are to be considered competent in tackling cybercrime, they must present an image of a technologically savvy force of cybercops, rather than a disunited band of 'technoplods' struggling to play catch-up with organised criminals and computer-literate deviants. The imperative on the 43 forces of England and Wales to get up to speed in their approach to cybercrime has been brought dramatically into focus by what must be seen as the ultimate failure of the NHTCU initiative. This case illustrates that police forces that assume cybercrime is not part of their remit cannot necessarily rely upon some national-level agency to intervene and relieve them of the burden of cyber-policing. Goodman (1997) calls for police managers to think strategically about computer crime in terms of recruitment, education, training and allocation of resources, and advises that officers should be encouraged to think about how technology might help them improve operations. He also suggests that computer science graduates should be targeted in police recruitment campaigns and further implies that the appointment of officers with qualifications in computing and related areas will help to change the culture of an institution in urgent need of modernisation. Unfortunately, at the present time, the police cannot easily offer attractive salaries to recruit skilled staff in what is a very competitive market, and the costs of ongoing training in a fast-moving, constantly evolving technological environment may be prohibitive (Jewkes and Andrews 2005). However, if these three areas – legal, governmental and occupational – are not tackled, the police will continue to find themselves playing catch-up in cyberspace.

Note

1 Thanks to James Treadwell for drawing my attention to this story.

Further reading

There is still relatively little written about policing cybercrime compared with other areas of criminality. As the references indicate, much of the most useful material is to be found on the Internet, and it is worth visiting police websites to monitor the progress of individual forces' e-policing strategies and their approaches to crimes involving computers. Among scholarly discussions of cybercrime, including its policing, the editors of this volume have published several; see Y. Jewkes (ed.) (2007) *Crime Online* (Willan Publishing); Y. Jewkes (ed.) (2003) *Dot.cons: Crime, Deviance and Identity on the Internet* (Willan Publishing), M. Yar (2006) *Cybercrime and Society* (Sage); and our co-authored chapter on 'Policing cybercrime: emerging trends and future challenges' in T. Newburn's *Handbook of Policing* (2008, Willan Publishing). A contribution specifically about policing abusive images of children is Jewkes, Y. and Andrews, C. (2005) 'Policing the filth: the problems of investigating online child pornography in England and Wales', *Policing and Society* 15(1): 42–62.

References

Aitkenhead, D. (2003) 'Net porn', *Observer Review*, 30 March: 1.

Akdeniz, Y. (2003) 'Regulation of child pornography on the Internet' (www.cyberrights. org/reports/child.htm).

Bell, J. (2003) 'I cannot admit what I am to myself', *Guardian*, 23 January (www. guardian.co.uk).

Blank, D. (2001) 'Hacker hit men for hire' (www.businessweek.com).

Budd,T., Sharp, C. and Mayhew, P. (2005) *Offending in England and Wales: First Results from the 2003 Crime and Justice Survey*, Home Office Research Study 275. London: HMSO.

Clark (2007) 'TK Maxx hit by theft of 46m credit card details', 30 March, http://www. guardian.co.uk/money/2007/mar/30/business.retail

Crank, J.P. (1998) *Understanding Police Culture*. Cincinnati, OH: Anderson.

Cullen, D. (2003) 'Child porn list leaked to Sunday Times' (www.theregister.co.uk).

Curzon-Brown, D. (2000) 'The teacher review debate part II: the dark side of the Internet', in D. Gauntlett (ed.), *Web.studies: Rewiring Media Studies for the Digital Age*. London: Arnold, 91–4.

ENISA (2008) 'ENISA Mission', http://www.enisa.europa.eu/pages/01_01.htm

Espiner, T. (2007) 'EU To Launch Scam Crackdown', 26 February, http://news.zdnet. co.uk/security/0,1000000189,39286068,00.htm

Foresight (2000) *Turning the Corner. Report of the Crime Prevention Panel*. London: Department of Trade and Industry (www.foresight.gov.uk).

Gibson, G. (2006) 'Warning to chatroom users after libel award for man labelled a Nazi', 23 March, at http://www.guardian.co.uk/media/2006/mar/23/digitalmedia. law

Goodman, M. (1997) 'Why the police don't care about cybercrime', *Harvard Journal of Law and Technology*, 10: 465–94.

Goodman, M. and Brenner, S. (2002) 'The emerging consensus on criminal conduct in cyberspace', *International Journal of Law and Information Technology*, 10(2): 139–223.

Hamm, M. (2007) '"High crimes and misdemeanors": George W. Bush and the sins of Abu Ghraib', *Crime, Media, Culture: An International Journal*, 3(3): 259–84.

HMIC (2001) *Open All Hours: A Thematic Inspection Report on the Role of Police Visibility and Accessibility in Public Reassurance*. London: Home Office.

Home Office (2006) Updated Estimate of the Cost of Identity Fraud to the UK Economy', at http://www.identity-theft.org.uk/ID per cent20fraud per cent20table. pdf

Hyde, S. (1999) 'A few coppers change', *Journal of Information, Law and Technology* (available at http://elj.warwick.ac.uk/jilt/99-2/hyde.html).

Jenkins, P. (2001) *Beyond Tolerance: Child Pornography on the Internet.* New York, NY: New York University Press.

Jenkins, P. (2003) 'Cut child porn link to abusers', *Guardian*, 23 January (www.guardian. co.uk).

Jewkes, Y. (forthcoming) 'Much ado about nothing? Representations and realities of online soliciting of children', in *Journal of Sexual Aggression* special issue.

Jewkes, Y. and Andrews, C. (2005) 'Policing the filth: the problems of investigating online child pornography in England and Wales', *Policing and Society*, 15(1): 42–62.

Jewkes, Y. and Andrews, C. (2007) 'Internet child pornography: international responses', in Y. Jewkes (ed.), *Crime Online.* Cullompton: Willan Publishing.

Jewkes, Y. and Sharp, K. (2003) 'Crime, deviance and the disembodied self: transcending the dangers of corporeality', in Y. Jewkes (ed.), *Dot.cons: Crime, Deviance and Identity on the Internet.* Cullompton: Willan Publishing, 36–52.

Jewkes, Y. and Yar, M. (2008) 'Policing cybercrime in the twenty-first century', in T. Newburn (ed.), *Handbook of Policing* (2nd edn). Cullompton: Willan Publishing.

Levin, B. (2002) 'Cyberhate: A legal and historical analysis of extremists' use of computer networks in America', *American Behavioural Scientist*, 45(6): 958–88.

Perry, B. (2001) *In the Name of Hate: Understanding Hate Crimes.* New York, NY: Routledge.

Reiner, R. (2000) *The Politics of the Police* (3rd edn). Oxford: Oxford University Press.

Silverman, J. and Wilson, D. (2002) *Innocence Betrayed: Paedophilia, the Media and Society.* Cambridge: Polity Press.

Taylor, P.A. (2003) 'Maestros or misogynists? Gender and the social construction of hacking', in Y. Jewkes (ed.), *Dot.cons: Crime, Deviance and Identity on the Internet.* Cullompton: Willan Publishing, 126–46.

The Register (2004) 'Hate Websites Continue to Flourish', 10 May, at http://www. theregister.co.uk/2004/05/10/hate_websites_flourish/

Wall, D. (2007) *Cybercrime.* Cambridge: Polity.

Whine, M. (1997) 'The far right on the Internet', in B. Loader (ed.), *The Governance of Cyberspace: Politics, Technology and Global Restructuring.* London: Routledge, 209–27.

Woods, P. (2002) *E-Policing* (www.e-policingreport.com).

Yar, M. (2005) 'The Global "Epidemic" of Movie "Piracy": Crime-Wave or Social Construction?', *Media, Culture and Society*, 27(5): 677–96.

Yar, M. (2006) *Cybercrime and Society.* London: Sage.

Yar, M. (2008a) 'The rhetorics and myths of anti-piracy campaigns: criminalization, moral pedagogy and capitalist property relations in the classroom', *New Media and Society*, 10(2): 457–75.

Yar, M. (2008b) 'The Computer Crime Control Industry: The Emerging Market in Information Security', in K. Franko-Aas (ed.), *Technologies of Insecurity: Surveillance and Securitization of Everyday Life.* London: Routledge.

Zickmund, S. (2000) 'Approaches to the radical other: the discursive culture of cyberhate', in D. Bell and B.M. Kennedy (eds), *The Cybercultures Reader.* London: Routledge, 237–53.

Zone-H.org (2008) 'Last week's Attacks', 10 February, http://www.zone-h.org/

Chapter 25

The private policing of Internet crime

Majid Yar

Introduction

Discussions about the policing of Internet crime have identified the manifold problems and limitations encountered by public agencies when attempting to regulate and monitor the online environment. Factors including the transnational scale of the Internet, the sheer scope and variety of online offences, and the lack of resources and technical expertise among criminal justice agencies, have left the police struggling to provide an adequate response to online crime problems (see Jewkes, Chapter 24; also Jewkes and Yar 2008). Almost inevitably in such a situation, a range of private (non-state) organisations, communities and individuals have emerged to take on a significant part of the responsibility for policing the Internet. A range of other significant factors has also acted to reinforce to prominence of private initiatives in this domain. Firstly, from its inception the culture of the Internet has tended to favour self-regulation among users, not least because of a commitment to preserving the Internet as a space of open communication free from state censorship and interference. Consequently, user communities have sought to institute their own systems (formal and informal) of social control and sanctions in order to address transgressive behaviour, rather than refer such problems to public agencies as a matter of course. Secondly, recent decades have witnessed a more general trend towards the pluralisation, multi-lateralisation and privatisation of policing across all societal domains. The private policing of the Internet can be viewed as a specific instance of these more general developments (Yar 2008). All of these aforementioned factors will be discussed in detail below.

The regulatory architecture and culture of the Internet

The distinctive regulatory architecture of the Internet has taken the form of a complex amalgam of dispersed mechanisms. From a legal perspective, constitutional limitations (as in the USA) and statutory measures have been introduced over the years to control Internet content (Biegel 2003). However, such formal measures are only one small part of the overall apparatus that regulates Internet activity. The piecemeal nature of its regulatory architecture reflects the overall manner of the Internet's development, viz. as a distributed network that has grown from the 'bottom up' through users instituting themselves as 'nodes' that connect to the Net, rather than a 'top-down' initiative whose topography and membership is prescribed in advance (Castells 2002). The preference for a self-regulatory system was instituted in the early years of the Internet. For example, it was the Clinton administration that, in 1998, created ICANN (the Internet Corporation for Assigned Names and Numbers) to take responsibility for the management of Internet Domain Names and IP addresses, as well as promoting the operational stability of the Internet (Mueller 1999; ICANN 2008). ICANN is a not-for-profit corporation comprising a wide range of 'stakeholders' including government representatives, business organisations, independent consultants and academics, and seeks to develop its policies 'through bottom-up, consensus-based processes'. While critical questions have been asked about the extent to which ICANN is able to be truly independent of governmental influence (Kleinwaechter 2003), the pluralistic nature of its composition is testimony to the multi-party character of Internet regulation. Moreover, ICANN's remit is fairly limited, being restricted to formal and structural aspects of the Internet as an operating environment, and it takes no responsibility for managing or arbitrating on the substantive *content* of websites.

The regulation, policing or control over Internet content (including the prohibition or removal of content) is a deeply contested issue among stakeholders and users. As noted in the Introduction, the culture of early Internet activists was deeply imbued with both a 'counter-cultural' commitment to the maximisation of free speech and open communication, and a corresponding suspicion of both governmental control and the motivations of powerful corporations (Yar 2006: 23). Many of these activists expressed fears that the Internet would progressively fall under the sway of state censorship (something that, alas, has been borne out by increasing state efforts worldwide to block access to politically inconvenient content through use of blocking and filtering technologies – see Deibert *et al.* (2007). The defence of free speech, and of the open exchange of knowledge and ideas, has been ardently pursued by a number of organisations. For example, the Electronic Frontier Foundation (EFF) was established in 1990 by a coalition of 'lawyers, policy analysts, activists, and technologists' in order to defend free speech online and combat attempts at censorship by mounting legal challenges against both the US government and large corporations (see http://www.eff.org; see also Gelman and McCandlish (1998) for an example of the EFF's public role). Similarly, the Electronic Privacy Information Centre (EPIC) was set up in 1994 with a view to protecting users' privacy and defending their civil liberties in the online environment (see http://epic.org; see also EPIC 2007). However, as we shall see below, the rise of various Internet-based crime problems has stimulated the growth of a wide range of extra-state organisations and alliances aimed at monitoring the Internet for objectionable content and activities, and pursuing the prohibition and removal of such material.

Policing of Internet content by non-state actors

Attempts to police the Internet by non-state or quasi-public actors have emerged hand-in-hand with the proliferation of online crime problems and intensified public awareness and concern over such crimes. Considerable attention has come to be devoted to monitoring the Internet for content that may variously be seen as illegal or improper (such as child pornography, hate speech and illegitimate and unlicensed copyrighted content). For example, the Internet Watch Foundation (IWF) was established in the UK in 1996 by an association of Internet Service Providers (ISPs), with government backing, although it operates as a self-regulating charitable trust; its membership has subsequently expanded to include operators of mobile telecommunications services, content providers, filtering companies, search engine providers and financial companies (see http://www.iwf.org.uk). Its initial brief was to combat child pornographic material (or, as they prefer it, 'child sexual abuse images'), its brief was later expanded to cover both criminally obscene (but non-child-oriented) content and instances of hate speech (material inciting racial hatred). The IWF operates a 'hotline' to which interested parties (be they representatives of organisations or individual members of the Internet-using public) can report illegal content. The IWF produces a 'blacklist' of websites or pages it deems to contravene relevant UK laws on child sex abuse, obscenity and race hatred, and this list is used by many ISPs to block access to, or remove from the Web, offending content. As a result of its operations the IWF claims to have reduced the proportion of child pornographic content that is hosted in the UK from 18 per cent of the worldwide total in 1997 to less that 1 per cent by 2003. Other organisations pursuing similar roles include Women Halting Online Abuse (WHOA – founded in 1997 to combat Internet-based abuse and harassment); the Internet Hotline Providers in Europe (INHOPE – founded in 1999); Cyberangels (an Internet safety education programme initiated in 1995 as a spin-off from the US-based 'Guardian Angels' movement famous for citizen action against street crime); and ASACP (Association of Sites Advocating Child Protection – an alliance of US-based adult pornographic content providers which undertakes measures such as: self-regulation through approved membership and certification of legitimate adult sites; informing member providers about child protection laws; engaging in educational and outreach activities directed toward government and the public; and providing a hotline through which both adult content providers and consumers can report child pornography identified on the Internet (ASACP 2005)).

However, the role of organisations such as the IWF remains controversial. As I write this, there has emerged a dispute in the UK following a decision by the IWF that a page on the free online encyclopaedia 'Wikipedia' contravened child pornography laws. The IWF then arranged to have access to said page blocked for those accessing the Internet using UK-based ISPs. The page in question dealt with the veteran German rock band The Scorpions, and featured the cover of an album, *Virgin Killer*, with a photograph of a naked pre-pubescent girl (BBC News 2008a). Critics of the IWF's actions objected on a number of grounds: firstly, because by denying users access to the offending page, the IWF were effectively blocking access to its non-illegal text content as well as its potentially (yet unproven) illegal imagery; secondly, the block on this one page had knock-on effects for UK users of Wikipedia, and for some time they were unable to edit any of the encyclopedia's pages (Wikipedia 2008); thirdly, it has been argued that the album in question has been freely available across Europe for some 30 years since its initial release (in 1976), and during that time no legal challenge has been presented to it on the grounds of its illegality. Consequently, the IWF has acted as 'police, judge and jury' in bypassing due legal process and deciding unilaterally to censor Internet content. Some 24 hours later, the IWF retracted its ban, stating that 'in light of the length of time the image has existed and its wide availability, the decision has been taken to remove this webpage from our [black]list.' (BBC News 2008b – UK-based readers can now view the offending image and judge for themselves, at: http://en.wikipedia.org/wiki/Virgin_Killer). Critics may be less than reassured by these developments, as the IWF's volte-face may be seen as something only forced upon them by public outcry and negative media coverage (Richmond 2008). Moreover, it raises wider issues around the private policing of the Internet insofar as such organisations are not inherently publicly accountable via democratic mechanisms, as would be the policing decisions of public agencies. To surrender judgements about what comprises the public interest to private and unaccountable groups may be seen as a dangerous development that needs to be curtailed if the freedom of online expression is to be effectively safeguarded.

Paralleling the emergence of organisations that police the Web for images of child sexual abuse, recent years have also seen the establishment of groups addressing hate speech online, and in the context of post-9/11 concerns about terrorism, groups that monitor the Internet for extremist Islamic sites that advocate terrorists attacks. For example, the Jewish human rights organisation The Simon Wiesenthal Centre has now been active for a number years in monitoring the Internet for anti-Semitic hate websites and moving to have them shut down (see http://www.wiesenthal.com). Similar activities are undertaken by the Anti-Defamation League (see http://www.adl.org/); the Arab-American Anti-Discrimination Committee (ADC); and The Southern Poverty Law Centre (which monitors and exposes online hate speech by far right groups through its *Intelligence Report*, as well as offering hate speech education and training). Such groups work through a variety of strategies, ranging from exposing instances of online hate speech, through pressuring ISPs to remove such content, to mounting legal challenges against those who post such material online. However, such efforts are often frustrated by problems of cross-national legal pluralism, i.e. the different legal definitions and prohibitions about what counts as hateful speech in different jurisdictions. This problem is particularly apparent when dealing with the USA and Europe; much of what is prohibited as hate speech under European anti-discrimination laws is protected free speech in the United States. Consequently, the producers of hateful speech can exploit these legal differences to have their websites hosted in countries where it is afforded constitutional protection, bypassing the more stringent anti-hate laws in Europe (Yar 2006: 104–5; see also Whine 2000 and Barnett 2007).

A third area that has seen an upsurge of non-state policing activity is that undertaken by groups representing the interests of commercial intellectual property (IP) rights holders, especially copyright in areas such as music, motion pictures and computer software. The proliferation of illegal file sharing and downloading of copyrighted content has provoked IP rights holders to invest in the creation of a veritable slew of organisations dedicated to policing the Internet for such violations. Examples include: the Counterfeiting Intelligence Bureau, the International Intellectual Property Alliance, the International Anti-Counterfeiting Coalition, the Alliance Against Counterfeiting and Piracy, the Coalition for Intellectual Property Rights, the Artists Coalition Against Piracy, and the Federation Against Copyright Theft, as well as numerous existing trade organisations that have established specialist groups and initiatives to combat 'piracy' (such as the Motion Picture Association, the Recording Industry Association of America, the Association of British Phonographic Industries, and the Business Software Alliance). Such organisations purport to 'lift the burden of investigation from law enforcement agencies' (AACP 2002: 2) by engaging in a range of increasingly intensive policing activities. Where public agencies have been reluctant to invest time and resources in tackling IP violations, industrial and commercial interests have 'filled the void'. In addition to intelligence gathering and undercover operations, and pursuing legal action against offenders, they have attempted to bring IP offences into the criminal justice mainstream through, for example, the appointment of specialist liaison personnel to assist and advise responsible agencies in the detection and prosecution of copyright theft (for more on these issues see Wall and Yar, Chapter 13, and Yar 2005).

The commercial provision of Internet policing

I turn now to consider a second sense in which the policing of the Internet has taken on a private form, namely the commercial (for-profit) provision of goods and services aimed at crime prevention, detection and resolution. The private sector now provides a wide range of IT security products and services on a commercial basis. These products and services are variously concerned with: safeguarding the integrity and operation of computer systems; controlling access to systems; and protecting the data content of systems from theft, unauthorised disclosure and alteration. The provision of such security measures takes an ever-expanding array of forms, including:

- security services, such as consultancy on threat analysis, systems security design and implementation, contingency planning, and disaster recovery (Nugent and Raisinghani 2002: 7);

- design and provision of software for user authentication and controlling access (e.g. password systems, smart cards, and most recently biometrics such as fingerprinting and face recognition) (Halverson 1996: 9; Wright 1998: 10; Nugent and Raisinghani 2002: 8; Smith 2006);

- design and provision of software for countering 'hacking' or unauthorised intrusion (e.g. firewalls, intrusion detection systems, early warning systems) (Grow 2004: 84; Grabosky and Smith 2001: 40);

- design and provision of software for detecting and eradicating 'malicious software' (e.g. viruses, worms and Trojan horses);

- provision of systems for safeguarding confidential, proprietary, and business-sensitive data (e.g. encryption software to enable secure financial transactions over public networks such as the Internet, and technologies preventing unauthorised copying and reproduction of copyright-protected digital content such as software, music and motion pictures) (Rassool 2003: 5–6; Vaidhyanathan 2003: 176–7);

- training for organisations and their employees in using and implementing security systems and procedures.

The overall financial scale of this industry is difficult to determine with precision, depending on how narrowly or broadly 'computer crime control' is defined. Nevertheless, we can glean some preliminary indications of its extent and growth. Research estimates placed US companies' spending on computer security at $2.8 billion in 1999, $3.4 billion in 2000, projected to rise to $9.9 billion in 2005. The global financial outlay on such products and services is placed at $27 billion (Grow 2004: 84). Overall growth in the sector has remained high (30 per cent in 2003 – Computer Weekly 2003: 1), bucking the slowdown in much of the IT sector following the bursting of the 'dot. com' bubble (Castells 2002: 105–6). The market for security software (such as firewalls, anti-virus systems and intrusion detection systems) has expanded particularly strongly, growing by 18 per cent between 2001 and 2002 (Lemos 2002), and continuing on a strong upward trend. The market for managed security services (wherein organisations outsource computer security provision to an external contractor) has also shown strong growth in the early years of the new millennium, with an estimated expansion from $720 million in 2000 to $2.2 billion in 2005 (Lemos 2002).

From an individual consumer perspective, the greatest investment in Internet policing technologies falls in the areas of preventive software. Concerns about children's access to sexually explicit and violent content have encouraged parents to purchase Internet filtering software. There now exists a wide range of commercially available filtering packages, such as *Cyber Patrol*, *X-Stop*, *Cyber Sitter*, *Net Nanny*, *Child Safe*, *Cyber Sentinel*, *Content Protect*, and *Winguardian*. Such software contains databases of adult-oriented sites, and parents can use them to 'lock' Web browsers' access to such sites; consequently, parents can allow their children to surf the Internet with the reassurance that youngsters will neither be unintentionally exposed to pornographic material, nor will they be able to access such content should they deliberately go looking for it. Serious doubts have been raised about the effectiveness of such filtering programs; on the one hand they have been found to fail to identify and block access to a considerable amount of 'undesirable' content, while on the other hand they have also been shown to 'over-filter' and thereby block access to legitimate teenage education and health information sites that inevitably use terms of a sexual nature (Hunter 1999; Greenfield *et al.* 2001; Larkin 2002; Richardson *et al.* 2002). Similarly, fears about online financial fraud, identity theft and malicious software (viruses, worms and the like) have served to stimulate a massive market for software applications that scan for and eliminate viruses, block attempts at 'phishing', and generally protect computer systems behind 'firewalls' (McGraw 2006). Almost no personal computer user is now without a package such as *Norton Internet Security, Kaspersky, Drive Sentry, McAfee Anti-Theft, Web Root, AVG*, etc. Symantec, the manufacturers of the popular *Norton* range of Internet security products, now operates in more than 40 countries and has in excess of 17,000 employees. This is just one example of the scale of the commercial sector that has emerged to privately meet the demand for Internet security and protection.

Understanding the rise of private Internet policing

The rise of this extensive privatised, market-led provision of Internet policing and computer security can be attributed to a range of factors. Firstly, as noted in the introduction, we must pay due attention to the broader shifts in the organisation of policing that have characterised Western industrial societies in recent decades. There now exists a voluminous literature dealing with recent changes in policing and crime control, and numerous attempts to situate such changes within a wider theorisation of social, political and economic transformation. We cannot here engage with the full range of such changes (such as the rise of 'actuarial justice' and 'penal expansionism'), as they have little direct relation to the issue at hand (on the former, see Feeley and Simon 1992, and on the latter Christie 2000). Nor can we evaluate the wide range of social-theoretical frameworks mobilised to explain such changes, such as the 'risk society' thesis, or the supposed transition to a 'late' or 'post' modernity (on risk see Loader and Sparks 2002: 92–95; on late modernity and crime control see Young 1999 and Garland 2001; on postmodernity and policing see Reiner 1992). Indeed, there would appear to be considerable disagreement about the scope and scale of such changes, and their wider significance. Thus, for example, Bayley and Shearing (1996) claim that there has occurred a fundamental fragmentation and pluralisation of policing, and that the current trends mark the end of the monopolistic system of public policing established in the early nineteenth century; Jones and Newburn (2002), in contrast, adopt a more gradualist approach, seeing such changes as extensions of a long-established process in which social control is 'formalised' by *both* public *and* private agencies. However, what most analysts seem to agree upon is that there *have* been significant shifts in the provision of policing and crime control, marked by its commodification in tandem with a 'responsibilisation' in which the burden of crime control is shifted towards non-state agencies and individuals (Muncie 2005: 37, 39). In this context, non-state actors are encouraged to protect themselves against the threat of criminal victimisation via market mechanisms, such that they become *consumers* of security good and services, rather than *citizens* who have a right to expect protection from the state as part of a social contract (Bowling and Foster 2002: 981–2). These trends, I suggest, typify the organisation of Internet policing. Responsibility for crime prevention falls largely (albeit not exclusively) upon the potential victims, and they are typically expected to access such provision through the purchase and contracting of security goods and services. Likewise, the provision of crime prevention and detection constitutes an ever-expanding array of market opportunities for private security providers. We must situate these developments in Internet policing within the context of systemic political-economic changes, specifically the emergence of new modes of social coordination, or governance, as part of the transition to a neo-liberal mode of capitalism.

The concept of governance has become one of the most oft-cited yet contested social scientific concepts in recent years (Lee 2003: 3). On my understanding, governance refers to a specific mode of social coordination and ordering, one which moves away from 'government' by a centralised state apparatus, and toward a more heterodox, self-organising *network* of actors situated within market and civil societal, as well as governmental and quasi-governmental, spheres (Rhodes 1997; see also Kjaer 2004; Stoker 2008). In the move to governance the state increasingly eschews the hierarchical, top-down delivery of social order, instead externalising responsibility onto extra-governmental actors, while maintaining an interest in 'steering' such activity through the formulation of policy goals and agenda-setting (Crawford 2006; also Jessop 2003, 2004). I see the emergence of this mode of social governance as integrally tied to the transition to a neo-liberal regime of capitalist accumulation and regulation (Jessop 2002). The 'failures' of Keynesian economics and state welfarism to ensure either sustained economic growth or the achievement of public welfare goals (including crime reduction), paved the way for a 'de-centring' of the state. This move found its political articulation in the rise of the New Right, with its insistence that the competitive mechanisms of the market are inherently more efficient than state bureaucracies in the delivery of social goods; that the scope of state expenditure needs to be 'rolled back' in order to reduce the burdens of taxation which inhibit economic growth; that the state provision of social goods undermines individual self-reliance and responsibility, and curtails freedom of choice. Consequently, there has emerged a range of state strategies in consonance with the neo-liberal project, including liberalisation and deregulation of markets, and privatisation of the public sector (Jessop 2002: 461). In the domain of policing and crime control, the displacement of responsibility onto extra-governmental actors (businesses, voluntary organisations, and individuals) has the advantage of externalising costs and relieving public agencies such as the police from the burden of responsibility for an ever-widening array of crime control tasks.

I suggest then that the emergence and rapid growth of the commercial sector in Internet crime control must, in the first instance, be situated within the context of the neo-liberal regime of governance. As Wall (2001: 174) notes, while the public police may resent the consolidation of the private sector in cybercrime policing, 'resource managers appear happy not to expend scarce resources on costly investigations'. The character of this tension becomes apparent if we consider the limited resources the police can make available for tackling the rapid rise in computer-related crimes. For example, the UK police's National Hi-Tech Crime Unit was established in 2001, comprising 80 dedicated officers and with a budget of £25 million; however, this amounts to less than 0.1 per cent of the total number of police, and less than 0.5 per cent of the overall expenditure on 'reduction of crime' (Wales 2001: 6; Home Office 2002). As Wall (2007: 183) observes, 'the public police mandate prioritises some offending over others', and the public and political focus upon 'street crimes' and 'conventional crimes' (crimes of violence, robbery, drug-related offences, and such like) diverts resources away from the policing of computer crime. In such a situation, the police have little choice but to accept the incursion of commercial organisations into computer crime control.

A second crucial driver in the growth of privatised Internet policing can be located in the transformation of economic activity brought about by the development of an informational economy. Recent academic discussions have identified a transformation of economic life, often associated with the emergence of 'post-industrial' capitalism (Bell 1999). Since the 1970s, Western economies have moved increasingly away from their traditional dependence upon industrial production, and economic growth has come to depend upon the creation, exploitation and consumption of information. As Castells (2002) points out, economic dependence upon information (typically in digitised and computerised form) has come to permeate economic activity, being central to a wide range of business activities – research and development; product design; coordination of manufacturing; and advertising, sales and marketing. The array of financial services and transactions essential for the working of the capitalist economy have also shifted into the electronic information communication environment; prime examples include the computerised working of contemporary trading in stocks and shares, money and futures markets, banking and insurance. From the perspective of consumers, the development of information technology has reshaped the experience of shopping, with goods and services being accessed and purchased via electronic communication, such as 'e-shopping' and online banking via the Internet. The inevitable upshot of these developments has been a great dependence upon those electronic systems that store, process and communicate information. The potential threats to these systems' integrity, be it the risk of unauthorised access, manipulation, corruption or destruction, have served to create a new market for computer and information security, as both business organisations and consumers seek to protect themselves from the vulnerabilities associated with their use of ICTs. As the UK government's Department of Trade and Industry (DTI) notes, 'Protecting information has never been more important. Organisations face a wide range of risks to their data, including virus attacks, inappropriate usage, unauthorised access and theft or systems failure' (DTI 2004: 1). They go on to note how theft of information has profound implications in terms of commercial losses (business-sensitive and proprietorial information may fall into the hands of competitors), damage to reputation and trust, and financial costs associated with potential legal action and data recovery (DTI 2004: 9). Consequently, state strategies aimed at maximising economic gains from the information economy place great emphasis upon encouraging business organisations to secure computer systems and data storage against illegal intrusion and interference.

A third and final driver behind the privatisation of Internet policing can be located at the more conjunctural level of politics. In the course of the 1990s, Western societies' use of information technologies generated in political, state-security and military arenas a heightened sense of vulnerability. The basic claim here is that Western advanced nations' social and economic stability is now crucially reliant on what has been dubbed the 'critical information infrastructure' (CII), and that serious disruption to this infrastructure could result in potentially catastrophic consequences (Cordesman and Cordesman 2001; Dunn and Wigert 2004; Dunn 2005). Thus, for example, accidental failure or deliberate sabotage of the computer systems governing financial markets could induce a massive economic crisis. Moreover, it has been noted that the complex material infrastructure of Western nations has been incrementally integrated with computerised systems, such that the basic coordination and functioning of water, power, transport and emergency services are now reliant on electronic communications (Milone 2003; Lewis 2006). The failure of these information systems could thus induce effects ranging in severity from mild inconvenience to serious loss of civilian life. Consequently, security analysts identified a growing threat from 'information warfare' – warfare conducted by targeting information rather than material or human assets. At the same time, it was held that computer-related vulnerabilities might make such warfare an appealing option for 'terrorist' actors; as one commentator has put it, a scenario in which the 'logic bomb' displaces the 'truck bomb' as a weapon of choice (Denning 2000).

Such threat assessments have stimulated extensive investment in programmes to secure information infrastructures against cyber-attack, especially in the wake of the 9/11 terrorist attacks. In 1999, the Clinton administration committed $1.46 billion for combating the threat of cyber-terrorism (Hamblen 1999; Miyawaki 1999). In 2000, they issued the first comprehensive plan for protecting the US critical information infrastructure, *Defending America's Cyberspace: National Plan for Information Systems Protection*. In the wake of 9/11, the Bush administration earmarked a further $839.3 million for cyber-security as part of the Homeland Security appropriations bill (Dunn and Wigert 2004: 201). Similarly, other nations have substantially increased the resources allocated to protecting information infrastructures in the wake of the 9/11 attacks: for example, Australia's CII protection budget was set at $2 million in May 2001, but tripled the following year to $6 million, and allocated a total of $24.9 million over four years (Dunn and Wigert 2004: 43). The rapid expansion of CII protection budgets, fuelled by a heightened sensitivity to potential terrorist attacks, has fuelled demand for computer security services, thereby driving the growth of the computer crime control industry over recent years. This upsurge in anti-terrorist computer security provision can be viewed as illustrative of a broader dynamic in which fears over crime risks (real or imagined) actively incite demand for innovation and expansion in crime control – an instance of what Hope (2006) calls 'reflexive securitization', a kind of feedback loop in which social action and reaction are shaped by assessments of 'the crime problem'.

Critical issues about private policing

In this final section, I would like to draw attention to some important problems that may follow as a consequence of the development of private policing of the Internet. Two issues in particular will be considered here, those of *accountability* and *equity*.

With respect to accountability, I have already noted that critics have raised doubts (as in the recent case of the IWF and Wikipedia) about the warrant that private actors have (or ought to have) in policing the Internet. The history of public policing in Western democracies has typically been a balancing act between upholding the authority of the police as agents of the state in enforcement of its laws, and ensuring their accountability to the public to whom they are ultimately responsible. Thus there have developed over time mechanisms to ensure that police are subject to public scrutiny and to whom they must provide justification for their decisions (be they decisions to act, or not to act, in response to particular crime problems and situations). For example, in the UK each police force is accountable to an elected Police Authority, comprising local councillors, magistrates and members of the general public. Through such mechanisms the public interest can be upheld and the public voice on policing decisions heard. However, no such mechanisms exist where private policing is concerned (Loader 1997, 2000; Loader and Walker 2004, 2006). Any individual or group can potentially set themselves up with a brief to police the Internet, according to their own interests, priorities or moral convictions (thus, as we have already seen, members of particular ethnic and religious minorities police the Internet for what they deem instances of hate speech; women's rights activists do likewise with pornography; those interested in child protection tackle child sexual abuse images; and IP rights holders search for and take action against what they deem illegal exploitation of their properties). Inevitably, conflicts can and do arise about whether the actions of such groups are actually in the wider public interest (as opposed to any given group's sectional interest), and when controversial decisions are taken (as in the IWF's decision to block access to Wikipedia) there is no direct mechanism through which they can be held accountable. Thus the proliferation of private policing brings with it a 'democratic deficit' and a potential 'legitimacy gap', insofar as private actors are considerably harder to oversee and regulate.

The second salient issue is that of equity. The principle of equity holds that freedom from criminal predation, and protection from it, is a right of all citizens. Hence the system of public policing aspires to the principle that it serves all citizens equally, and the protection offered by the police should in no way reflect individuals' social or economic standing. The sytem can and does of course fall far short of this principle in practice, favouring some sections of society over others when it comes to protection from crime, but the principle nevertheless remains a standard by which the effectiveness of public policing is judged, and serves as grounds for criticism when it falls short of its aspiration. However, the privatised (especially market-mediated) provision of policing works on a quite different principle. Since its goods and services are *commodities* that are to be purchased, the market system inevitably discriminates among its potential users (i.e. customers) according to their ability to pay for the goods and services in question (Bayley and Shearing 1996: 593–5; Burbidge 2005). Thus the Internet user who wishes to protect herself from computer viruses, the theft of sensitive personal data via hacking, and so on, will only be able to do so insofar as she can afford to buy the software that provides this protection. This situation threatens to entrench a hierarchy of inequality when it comes to protection from Internet-based crimes, with the most financially secure enjoying the greatest online security, while the economically disadvantaged come to occupy the most risk-intensive positions in the online world. This can be seen as a further extension of the problem of 'digital divides' (van Dijk and Hacker 2003; Warschauer 2004), the social exclusion from new information and communication technologies that serves only to exacerbate existing patterns of social inequality. If the most socially disadvantaged cannot make full and effective use of new communication technologies for fear of criminal victimisation, this will inevitably place them at a further social, economic and political disadvantage since the accrual of agency in all these spheres of action is increasingly mediated by electronic systems such as the Internet.

Conclusions

This chapter has explored the ways in which the policing of the Internet takes shape as a system of disparate, fragmented and private provision. We have noted the roles played both by 'third sector' (non-governmental) bodies, and the massive involvement of commercial actors who provide policing goods and services on a for-profit basis. The emergence of these trends has been linked to a range of factors, including the more general trend towards pluralisation, multilateralisation of policing, the increased economic importance of the information economy, and the political sensitivities about vulnerability arising from societal dependence on computerised systems. I have concluded by noting some of the problems that this situation creates for policing the Internet in the public interest; issues that are likely to feature significantly in critical debates about Internet policing as time goes on.

Further reading

Compared to the extensive scholarly literature on policing in general, the specific issue of Internet policing has been largely neglected. Some of the salient issues in the tensions between public and private policing of the Internet are discussed by Jewkes and Yar (2008) 'Policing Cybercrime: Emerging Trends and Future Challenges', in T. Newburn (ed.), *Handbook of Policing* (2nd edn), Willan Publishing; see also Jewkes (2003) 'Policing the net: cyber crime and cyber liberties', in Y. Jewkes (ed.), *Dot. cons: Criminal and Deviant Identities on the Internet*, Willan Publishing. One of the few examinations of the emergence of a private, for-profit sector in policing electronic information and computer crimes is my article, 'Computer Crime Control as Industry: Virtual Insecurity and the Market for Private Policing' (2008) in K.F. Aas *et al.* (eds), *Technologies of Insecurity: The Surveillance of Everyday Life* (Routledge-Cavendish). For an examination of the broader issues around the governance and regulation of the Internet, see Brian Loader (ed.) (2007) *The Governance of Cyberspace: Politics, Technology and Global Restructuring*, Routledge and Mathiason's (2008) *Internet Governance: The New Frontier of Global Institutions*, Routledge. For broader discussion of the privatisation of policing in our criminal justice systems, see Les Johnston's (1992) *The Rebirth of Private Policing*, Routledge; and for a critical discussion of these same developments, see Ian Loader and Neil Walker (2007) *Civilising Security*, Cambridge University Press.

References

AACP (Alliance Against Counterfeiting and Piracy) (2002) *Proving the Connection: Links between Intellectual Property Theft and Organised Crime*. London: AACP.

ASACP (Association of Sites Advocating Child Protection) (2005) 'Why ASACP?', at http://www.asacp.org/index.php

Barnett, B.A. (2007) *Untangling the Web of Hate: Are Online 'Hate Sites' Deserving of First Amendment Protection?* New York: Cambria Press.

Bayley, D. and Shearing, C. (1996) 'The future of policing', *Law and Society Review*, 30(3): 585–606.

Bell, D. (1999 (orig. 1973)) *The Coming of Post-Industrial Society*, (3rd edn). New York: Basic Books.

Biegel, S. (2003) *Beyond Our Control? Confronting the Limits of Our Legal System in the Age of Cyberspace*. Cambridge, Mass.: MIT Press.

Bowling, B. and Foster, J. (2002) 'Policing and the police', in M. Maguire, R. Morgan and R. Reiner (eds), *The Oxford Handbook of Criminology*. (3rd edn). Oxford: Oxford University Press.

BBC News (2008a) 'Wikipedia Child Image Censored', Monday 8 December, at http://news.bbc.co.uk/1/hi/uk/7770456.stm

BBC News (2008b) 'IWF Backs Down in Wiki Censorship', Tuesday 9 December, at http://news.bbc.co.uk/1/hi/technology/7774102.stm

Burbidge, S. (2005) 'The Governance Deficit: Reflections on the Future of Public and Private Policing in Canada', *Canadian Journal of Criminology and Criminal Justice*, 47(1): 63–86.

Castells, M. (2002) *The Internet Galaxy: Reflections on the Internet, Business, and Society*. Oxford: Oxford University Press.

Christie, N. (2000) *Crime Control as Industry*. London: Routledge.

Computer Weekly (2003) 'IDC Sees Bright Future for IT Security Services', at www.computerweekly.com/Articles/2003/04/30/194225/Idc-sees-bright-future-forit-security-services.htm

Cordesman, A.H. and Cordesman, J.G. (2001) *Cyber-threats, Information Warfare and Critical Infrastructure Protection: Defending the U.S.Homeland*. Westport: Greenwood Publishing.

Crawford, A. (2006) 'Networked governance and the post-regulatory state? Steering, rowing and anchoring the provision of policing and security', *Theoretical Criminology*, 10(4): 449–79.

Deibert, R., Palfrey, J., Rohoznski, R. and Zittrain, J. (eds) (2007) *Access Denied: The Practice and Policy of Global Internet Filtering*. Boston, MA: MIT Press.

Denning, D. (2000) *Cyberterrorism*. Testimony before the Special Oversight Panel on Terrorism Committee on Armed Services US House of Representatives, 23 May 2000.

DTI (Department of Trade and Industry) (2004) *Information Security: Hard Facts*. London: DTI.

Dunn, M. (2005) 'The socio-political dimensions of critical information infrastructure protection (CIIP)', *International Journal of Critical Infrastructures*, 1(2/3): 258–68.

Dunn, M. and Wigert, I. (2004) *International CIIP Handbook: An Inventory and Analysis of Protection Policies in Fourteen Countries*. Zurich: Swiss Federal Institute of Technology.

EPIC (Electronic Privacy Information Centre) (2007) *Privacy and Human Rights: An International Survey of Privacy Laws and Developments*. Washington, DC: EPIC.

Feeley, S. and Simon, J. (1992) 'The New Penology: Notes on the Emerging Strategy of Corrections and its Implications', *Criminology*, 30(4): 449–74.

Garland, D. (2001) *The Culture of Control: Crime and Social Order in Contemporary Society*. Oxford: Clarendon.

Gelman, R.B. and McCandlish, S. (1998) *Protecting Yourself Online: An Electronic Frontier Foundation Guide*. New York: HarperCollins.

Grabosky, P. and Smith, R. (2001) 'Telecommunication fraud in the digital age: the convergence of technologies', in D. Wall (ed.) *Crime and the Internet*. London: Routledge.

Greenfield, P., Rickwood, P. and Tran, H.C. (2001) 'Effectiveness of Internet Filtering Software Products', at http://www.acma.gov.au/webwr/aba/about/recruitment/filtereffectiveness.pdf

Grow, B. (2004) 'Software', *Business Week*, June 21: 84.

Halverson, G. (1996) 'As Internet Booms, So Do Hacker-Proofing Measures', *Christian Science Monitor*, 88(144): 9.

Hamblen, M. (1999) 'Clinton commits $1.46b to fight cyberterrorism', at http://www.cnn.com/TECH/computing/9901/26/clinton.idg

Home Office (2002) 'Home Office Annual Report 2001–2', at http://www.homeoffice.gov.uk/docs

Hope, T. (2006) 'Mass Consumption, Mass Predation – Private Versus Actors?', in R. Lévy, L. Mucchielli and R. Zaubermann (eds), *Crime et Insécurité: un Demi-Siècle de Bouleversements-Mélanges Pour et Avec Philippe Robert*. Paris: Hatmattan.

Hunter, C. (1999) 'Internet Filter Effectiveness: Testing Over and Underinclusive Blocking Decisions of Four Popular Filters', at http://www.copacommission.org/papers/filter_effect.pdf

ICANN (the Internet Corporation for Assigned Names and Numbers) (2008) See http://www.icann.org/

Jessop, B. (2002) 'Liberalism, neoliberalism, and urban governance: a state-theoretical perspective', *Antipode*, 34(4): 452–72.

Jessop, B. (2003) 'Governance and Metagovernance: On Reflexivity, Requisite Variety, and Requisite Irony', in H. Bang (ed.) *Governance as Social and Political Communication*. Manchester: Manchester University Press.

Jessop, B. (2004) 'Hollowing out the Nation-State and Multilevel Governance' in P. Kennett (ed.), *A Handbook Of Comparative Social Policy*. Cheltenham: Edward Elgar.

Jewkes, Y. (2003) 'Policing the net: cyber crime and cyber liberties', in Y. Jewkes (ed.), *Dot.cons: Criminal and Deviant Identities on the Internet*. Cullompton: Willan Publishing.

Jewkes, Y. and Yar, M. (2008) 'Policing Cybercrime: Emerging Trends and Future Challenges', in T. Newburn (ed.), *Handbook of Policing* (2nd edn). Cullompton: Willan Publishing, 580–606.

Johnston, L. (1992) *The Rebirth of Private Policing*. London: Routledge.

Jones, T. and Newburn, T. (2002), 'The transformation of policing? Understanding current trends in policing systems', *British Journal of Criminology*, 42(1): 129–46.

Kjaer, A.M. (2004) *Governance*. London: Routledge.

Kleinwaechter, W. (2003) 'From Self-Governance to Public-Private Partnership: The Changing Role of Governments in the Management of the Internet's Core Resources', *Loyola of Los Angeles Law Review*, 36(3), at http://llr.lls.edu/volumes/v36-issue3/kleinwaechter.pdf

Larkin, M. (2002) 'Pornography-Blocking Software May Also Block Health Information Sites', *The Lancet*, 360: 1946.

Lee, M. (2003) 'Conceptualizing the new governance: a new institution of social coordination'. Paper presented at the Institutional Analysis and Development Mini-Conference, 3 and 5 May 2003, Workshop in Political Theory and Policy Analysis, Indiana University, Bloomington, Indiana, USA.

Lemos, R. (2002) 'Computer-Security Industry Leads the Way to Growth', *CNET*, 2 February, at http://www.zdnet.co.uk/business/0,39020645,2103776,00.htm

Lewis, T.D. (2006) *Critical Infrastructure Protection in Homeland Security: Defending a Networked Nation*. New Jersey: Wiley-Blackwell.

Loader, B. (ed.) (2007) *The Governance of Cyberspace: Politics, Technology and Global Restructuring*. London: Routledge.

Loader, I. (1997) 'Thinking Normatively about Private Security', *Journal of Law and Society*, 24(3): 377–94.

Loader, I. (2000) 'Plural Policing and Democratic Governance', *Social and Legal Studies*, 9(3): 323–45.

Loader, I. and Sparks, R. (2002) 'Contemporary landscapes of crime, order and control: governance, risk and globalisation', in M. Maguire, R. Morgan and R. Reiner (eds), *The Oxford Handbook of Criminology* (3rd edn). Oxford: Oxford University Press.

Loader, I. And Walker, N. (2004) 'State of Denial? Rethinking the Governance of Security', *Punishment and Society*, 6(2): 221–8.

Loader, I. and Walker, N. (2006) 'Necessary Virtues: The Legitimate Place of the State in the Production of Security', in J. Wood and B. Dupont (eds), *Democracy, Society and the Governance of Security*. Cambridge: Cambridge University Press.

Loader, I. And Walker, N. (2007) *Civilising Security*. Cambridge: Cambridge University Press.

McGraw, G. (2006) 'Software Security: Building Security-In', at http://www.issa-nova.org/Documents/ArchivePresentations/Presentation-12.2006-McGraw.pdf

Mathiason, J. (2008) *Internet Governance: The New Frontier of Global Institutions*. London: Routledge.

Milone, M. (2003) 'Hacktivism: securing the national infrastructure', *Knowledge, Technology and Policy*, 16(1): 75–103.

Miyawaki, R. (1999) *The Fight Against Cyberterrorism: A Japanese View*. Washington: Centre for Strategic and International Studies.

Mueller, M. (1999) 'ICANN and Internet Governance: Sorting Though the Debris of "Self-Regulation"', *Info – The Journal of Policy, Regulation and Strategy for Telecommunications*, 1(6): 497–520.

Muncie, J. (2005) 'The Globalization of Crime Control – the Case of Youth and Juvenile Justice: Neo-Liberalism, Policy Convergence and International Conventions', *Theoretical Criminology*, 9(1): 35–64.

Newburn, Tim (2002) 'Atlantic crossings: "policy transfer" and crime control in the USA and Britain', *Punishment and Society*, 4 (2): 165–94.

Nugent, J. and Raisinghani, M. (2002) 'The Information Technology and Telecommunications Security Imperative: Important Issues and Drivers', *Journal of Electronic Commerce Research*, 3(1): 1–14.

Rassool, R.P. (2003) 'Antipiracy – Trends and Technology (A Report from the Front)', at http://www.broadcastpapers.com/asset/ IBCWidevineAntipiracy.pdf

Reiner, R. (1992) 'Policing and postmodern society', *Modern Law Review*, 55/56: 761–81.

Rhodes, R. (1997) *Understanding Governance: Policy Networks, Governance, Reflexity and Accountability*. Bristol: Open University Press.

Richardson, C.R., Resnick, P.J., Hansen, D.L., Derry, H.A. and Rideout, V.J. (2002) 'Does Pornography-Blocking Software Block Access to Health Information on the Internet?', *JAMA: Journal of the American Medical Association*, 288: 2887–94.

Richmond, S. (2008) 'The Internet Watch Foundation Must Learn from the Wikipedia Debacle', *Daily Telegraph*, Wednesday 10 December, at http://blogs.telegraph.co.uk/shane_richmond/blog/2008/12/10/the_internet_watch_foundation_must_learn_from_the_wikipedia_debacle

Smith, R. (2006) 'Biometric Solutions to Identity-Related Cybercrime', in Y. Jewkes (ed.) *Crime Online*. Cullompton: Willan Publishing.

Stoker, G. (2008) *Governance Theory and Practice: A Cross-Disciplinary Approach*. London: Palgrave Macmillan.

Vaidhyanathan, S. (2003) *Copyrights and Copywrongs: The Rise of Intellectual Property and How it Threatens Creativity*. New York: NYU Press.

van Dijk, J. and Hacker, K. (2003) 'The Digital Divide as a Complex and Dynamic Phenomenon', *The Information Society*, 19: 315–26.

Wales, E. (2001) 'Global focus on cyber-crime', *Computer Fraud and Security*, 1(6).

Wall, D.S. (2001) 'Maintaining order and law on the internet', in D. Wall (ed.), *Crime and the Internet*. London: Routledge.

Wall, D.S. (2007) *Cyber-crime: The Transformation of Crime in the Information Age*. Cambridge: Polity.

Warschauer, M. (2004) *Technology and Social Inclusion: Rethinking the Digital Divide*. Boston, Mass: MIT Press.

Whine, M. (2000) 'Far right extremists on the Internet', in D. Thomas and B. Loader (eds), *Cybercrime: Law Enforcement, Security and Surveillance in the Information Age*. London: Routledge.

Wikipedia (2008) 'Internet Watch Foundation and Wikipedia', at http://en.wikipedia.org/wiki/Internet_Watch_Foundation_and_Wikipedia

Wright, H. (1998) 'Biometrics The Next Phase in Network Security', *NZ Infotech Weekly*, September 28: 10.

Yar, M. (2005) 'The Global "Epidemic" of Movie "Piracy": Crime-Wave or Social Construction?', *Media, Culture and Society*, 27(5): 677–96.

Yar, M. (2006) *Cybercrime and Society*. London: Sage.

Yar, M. (2008) 'Computer Crime Control as Industry: Virtual Insecurity and the Market for Private Policing', in K.F. Aas, H.O. Gundhus and H.M. Lomell (eds), *Technologies of Insecurity: The Surveillance of Everyday Life*. London: Routledge-Cavendish.

Young, J. (1999) *The Exclusive Society*. London: Sage.

Chapter 26

The virtual neighbourhood watch: netizens in action

Matthew Williams

Introduction

The Internet provides a fertile ground for new social formations. Since its inception users have congregated in online spaces to interact for work and pleasure. Improvements in technology have increased the immersive affordance of online spaces. Text-only interaction has been superseded by graphically rich three-dimensional virtual worlds where users interact via avatars and purchase and build virtual property. These new online spaces are big business with increasing numbers of citizens now making a living purely from virtual world endeavours. However, as with all new technology, criminal opportunity follows. Research by Kaspersky Labs (2007) found that malicious programs (e.g. Trojans which steal password and account information) targeting virtual worlds increased by 145 per cent in 2007. Identity theft, fraud, harassment, theft of virtual objects, vandalism of virtual property, money laundering and child pornography are but a few of the deviant acts that make up the virtual world 'crimewave'. This chapter begins by charting the rise of the virtual world phenomenon while delineating the 'crime' problem that manifests inside their virtual borders. The main body of the chapter focuses on how citizens of virtual worlds have learned to govern their territories via a variety of social, technical and legal control.

Online social spaces

The Internet has become increasingly social. The expansion of the domestic Internet since the mid 1990s has seen it grow from an information sharing and retrieval tool to a fully interactive, immersive and transformative social arena. *Web1.0* technologies common on the early Internet include email, newsgroups, instant message chat (such as MSN Messenger) and websites that have no capacity for collaborative content generation (i.e. static websites meant solely for information retrieval). The leap to *Web2.0* technologies was accompanied by a sea change in web content generation and interpersonal interaction. The shift from web1.0 to web2.0 was characterised by the democratisation of web content production. Web2.0 technologies allow 'readers' of websites to easily contribute to their content. These include Wikis, blogs and social networking sites such as Facebook, MySpace, eBay and Bebo. Technology commentators have begun to talk of *Web3.0*, a label that is yet to be fully defined but is said to include technologies that provide Internet users with a more 'realistic' interactive online experience (Williams 2006). These technologies include 2D and 3D graphical spaces such as Second Life, Habbo Hotel and Active Worlds (see Figure 26.1). Users enter these worlds as *avatars*, representations of themselves in graphical form. Most of these worlds allow users to buy virtual land and to build properties. Massively Multiplayer Online Role-Playing Games (MMORPG), such as World of Warcraft and EVE Online also use similar technologies as virtual worlds allowing thousands of game players to interact and trade online. However, it would be a misnomer to claim that Web3.0 technologies were the first to offer Internet users an escape from the 'offline' world. Multi-User Domains (MUDs) and Multi-User Object Oriented Domains (MOOs) emerged just under two decades ago with the first LambdaMOO opening its virtual doors to the public in 1990. These text-based social and gaming spaces (see Figure 26.2) have been awarded much attention over the past decade by writers who focused on issues such as community, identity and morality (see Rheingold 1993; Baym 1995; Turkle 1995; Dietrich 1997; Shaw 1997; Danet 1998; Markham 1998; Reid 1999).

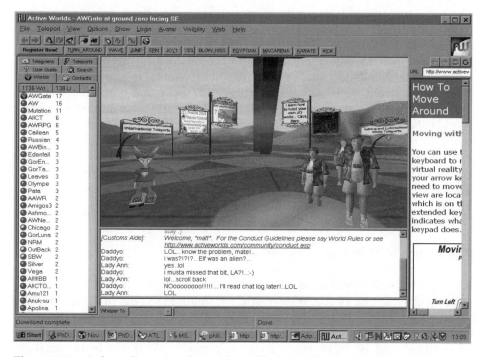

Figure 26.1　A three-dimensional virtual world such as Active Worlds

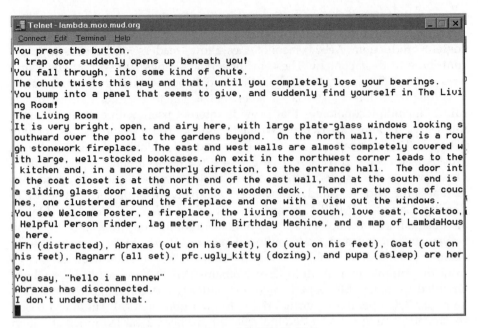

Figure 26.2 A conventional text-based MUD/MOO

Reynolds (2005) neatly delineates virtual worlds in his *Four Worlds Theory*. He identifies ludic worlds (aka game-worlds such as World of Warcraft), social worlds (such as Habbo Hotel), civic worlds (such as Second Life) and the geographic world (our offline world). He sees these worlds as being distinct from each other and uses the concept of *identity* to highlight the key differences in relation to law and morality. A fifth type of world not included in the four worlds theory are corporate worlds, which are on the increase. While the technological architecture of these worlds is common they can differ normatively. Social structures, behaviour, social and economic sanctions and regulations can differ dramatically between worlds. For example in ludic worlds the harassment and even virtual killing of others can be the norm while in civic and social worlds such actions are banned and in some cases can lead to a criminal prosecution in the 'offline' world. Due to the game-like nature of ludic worlds where the consequences of players' actions depend on alternative and specific game rules this chapter focuses on civic and social online worlds, deviance and its governance.

The nature of civic and social virtual worlds

Rheingold (1993) was one of the first writers to draw a link between the increasing social use of the Internet and the demise of community offline. The claims being made during this time of technological utopian optimism went as far as to identify the Internet as the new 'third' space – next to the home (first space) and work (second space) (Oldenburg 1999). Evidence for these claims came from an increasing Internet population who began to organise themselves into social groupings online which bore similar characteristics to *Gemeinschaft* communities. However, Rheingold's (1993) utopian perception is quite unique. Authors such as Lash (2001) and Beniger (1987) see social relations in the digital age as being thin and stretched resulting in a lack of substance and meaning. Beniger's (1987) notion of pseudo-community is a useful comparison to Rheingold's 'virtual community'. The demise of *Gemeinschaft* community, characterised by communal relationships, and the subsequent rise of *Gesellschaft* relations, typified by impersonal indirect relations, is taken as the basis of pseudo-community. In the case of Beniger's thesis mass communication replaced more intimate forms of interpersonal communication. As technology advances non-face-to-face communication becomes commonplace, which fosters interactions devoid of social cues and presence, resulting in ephemeral social relationships. On the other hand Rheingold (1993) believes the Internet has created new avenues and forms of interaction that are of substance and help form new forms of online community. This disagreement is at the core of the 'virtual community' debate and remains relevant to understanding the nature of civic and social virtual worlds and their crime and governance problems.

The most common conception of community in academic discourse is grounded in the work of Tönnies (1979). There are physical, temporal and moral dimensions to community. A common geographic territory is shared, there is a common history, a collective value system and often a shared religion and language. Using this definition several conflicts begin to become apparent. First, while the Internet can be considered a space, it is not physical. Individuals cannot physically live in cyberspace. Secondly, there are questions over the extent to which groups in cyberspace can have a shared history, value system, religion or language. Lockard (1997) is reluctant to apply the term community to online social formations due to the small bandwidth for communication. He states that communication alone cannot replace community's manifold functions. Healy (1997) argues that with such a small fraction of the world's population online, social formations do not oblige their participants to deal with diversity. In this sense online social formations are no more than voluntary associations of like-minded people, without the additional demands of offline community that help forge its very nature.

Further criticisms revolve around the technological deterministic nature of Rheingold's (1993) claims. Moreley and Robins (1995) reject Rheingold's ideas labelling them conservative and nostalgic. The idea that technological change and innovation can turn around the social and cultural decay in contemporary American societies is naive. In line with contemporary thinking about the demise of offline community and the emergence of culture at-a-distance, Wittel (2001) draws attention to the way in which much of the literature discusses the imaginary aspects of virtual community (Anderson 1983). This in itself is an indication that online social formations are not communities in the traditional sense. Further, the idea of the *'virtual* community' is flawed in its presumed dichotomy between the 'real' and the 'unreal'. Many writers have taken the presumed dichotomy of the 'real' and the 'virtual' for the basis of their analyses (see Virilio 1997; Baudrillard 1998). However, the empirical studies that exist in this area have repeatedly shown that experiences online are not considered as 'virtual' or apart from 'real' life, and that this presumed dichotomy is a false one (Markham 1998; Miller and Slater 2000).

While many authors provide strong arguments against the notion of communities online it must be stressed that most of the analysis in the early to mid 1990s of computer-mediated communication lacked empirical insight. Since the late 1990s the Internet has been considered a site of empirical enquiry. Studies of users began to highlight how the Internet is a collection of very different social spaces, all with unique characteristics that shape the way in which individuals interact. The Internet is then an umbrella term for a range of technologies that afford users different ways of interacting. Of the studies that have been conducted on virtual worlds, the majority have focused upon text-based environments, limiting the ability to form a general analysis of computer-mediated communication as a whole (for examples see Baym 1995; Danet 1998; Markham 1998). However, the analyses from these studies have been controversial in that they challenge the majority of the criticisms of online community. The idea that the Internet has 'thinned' out interaction, and that notions of history and narrative are no longer integral to sociality is being questioned.

The virtual world 'crimewave'

While it is well established that cybercrimes are now a significant component of the crime problem (see Williams 2009) researchers still know relatively little about how crime and deviance impacts upon virtual worlds. Recent empirical research into a civic virtual world found that citizens and tourists were frequently subject to an array of attacks including harassment, identity theft, trespass and vandalism (Williams 2006). These acts of in-world deviance had a deleterious impact upon community cohesion and business revenue.

Spoofing and identity theft

In Williams's (2006) study spoofing or the appropriation of another avatar's identity was a common attack. Malicious citizens of the virtual world took on the persona of others by hacking into accounts. While masquerading as an other, the perpetrator would conduct delinquent acts in an attempt to escape identification, to damage the reputation of the hijacked persona or to steal virtual property. In a 2008 study by the European Network and Information Security Agency (ENISA) 30 per cent of virtual world users reported being subject to a spoofing attack.

There are currently three common methods that facilitate spoofing. The first, Trojans, surreptitiously record computer activity, via keyloggers and screen grabbers, to identify and communicate back to the cyber criminal sensitive security information. The other two methods are phishing and pharming. Phishing attacks use both social engineering and technical subterfuge to steal world users' personal identity data and financial account credentials. Such schemes use 'spoofed' emails and in-world messages to lead world citizens to counterfeit websites designed to trick recipients into divulging personal identification data such as account usernames and passwords. Pharming removes the social engineering element with a technological fix. Usually a Trojan malware is installed on a victim's computer that automatically directs the user to the spoof website address when the original bookmark is selected.

Griefing (virtual world harassment)

Griefing within virtual worlds can be compared to Wall's (2001) conception of cyberviolence. This categorisation covers a multitude of deviant acts, both criminal and sub-criminal. It relates to the sending of unwanted emails that are obscene, threatening or abusive (Ellison and Akdeniz 1998). It may involve the posting of personal details on publicly accessible message boards resulting in unwanted forms of contact, both Internet based and in the physical world. It involves the imitation of a victim's online persona (spoofing) and the commission of deviant acts in their name, ruining online reputations and jeopardising friendships and business relationships. It also involves various forms of textual violent acts that are often sexual in nature.

The Internet allows communication with another person unconstrained by social reality, thus creating a certain psychodynamic appeal for the perpetrator who chooses to become a harasser or cyberstalker (Meloy 1998). In the majority of cases only written words are used, and other avenues of sensory perception are eliminated; one cannot see, hear, touch, smell, or emotionally sense the other person. Yet some concern surrounding harassment and cyberstalking is based on the idea that it might be a prelude to physical stalking (Reno 1999).

Griefing, while initially manifesting online, can migrate to the offline world of the victim. Name-calling in emails and chat can turn into threats literally on victims' doorsteps. Such migration occurred during Williams's (2006) research. John Robinson, also known as 'Slavemaster' within the world under study, was arrested by Kansas state police for the suspected murder of five women during June 2000. Suzette Trouten, Robinson's last victim, was a member of the world, known as Faith. She frequented Gor worlds to practise fantasy sadomasochistic rituals with other like-minded members. It was within this world that she embarked on a relationship with her eventual murderer. Following several exchanges within the world, Faith decided to forge an offline relationship with Slavemaster. This relationship led to her eventual demise. Reports during the time of the investigation stated that Robinson was known to have solicited sadomasochistic sex over the Internet several times (CNN.com 2000).

Theft

Within virtual worlds community members and players own and exchange virtual property that has actual monetary value offline. The case of the Shanghai gamers Qiu Chengwei and Zhu Caoyuan in 2005 provides a lucid example of the inadequacies of law in relation to online theft. Both were players of the online game *Legends of Mir 3* that allows thousands of users from all over the globe to participate synchronously. In this game items can be used to enhance the power and status of players. In this case Chengwei loaned his 'dragon sabre' to Caoyuan shortly after acquiring it. Caoyuan then proceeded to sell the sabre on eBay without permission for the sum of 7,200 yuan (£460). Chengwei informed the police of this theft. However, the authorities claimed it could not be reported as theft as the sabre did not physically exist. As a result of this unsatisfactory response Chengwei murdered Caoyuan in real life (BBC 2005). While some countries such as South Korea do have laws that govern the theft of virtual property many do not, noting that theft is only possible if the item is physically tangible.

Obscenity and child pornography

Paedophiles and distributors of obscene materials are known to frequent virtual worlds. Operation Starburst in July 1995 was one of the first international investigations into paedophile rings and the Internet. Resulting from the investigation nine British men were arrested (Akdeniz *et al.* 2000). Operation Starburst was the first investigation to uncover a direct link between child abuse and the use of the Internet. The Sexual Offences Act 2003 (s.15) introduced a new offence of meeting a child following sexual grooming. Online grooming (or via mobile phone and other means) with the intent to 'physically' meet a child with the intention of abusing them is now a criminal offence carrying a maximum sentence of 10 years' imprisonment. The immersive potential of virtual worlds has lead paedophiles to create virtual playgrounds where they role-play grooming activities involving child 'bot' avatars (artificial life forms). While there is no 'real' child behind the avatar, images of children can be used to make the 'bot' avatar look childlike. Debate exists on the function of these role-playing activities. Some argue these virtual playgrounds allow paedophiles to practise their grooming tactics while others claim these virtual spaces help harmlessly satisfy the needs of the paedophile.

Vandalism

The ability to build virtual objects within civic and social online worlds has opened up opportunities for vandalism. Many users of these worlds build homes, offices, shops and even cemeteries in an attempt to mimic the geographic world and establish online community. Williams's (2006) research highlighted the potential for a small group of world users to disrupt community cohesion via coordinated acts of vandalism. While the visual effects of in-world vandalism are short-lived (the original code that produced the virtual object can be easily reinstated) evidence suggests that these activities can cause psychological damage to victims. This can certainly be seen in cases where objects imbued with meaning such as virtual gravestones are vandalised (Williams 2004).

Netizens in action: controlling deviance in virtual worlds

All virtual worlds have mechanisms for regulating deviant activity. The most common are End User Licence Agreements (EULA) which specify age requirements and behavioural expectations. Generally, if any of these rules are broken a user can have their account suspended or cancelled. Other mechanisms of control include dispute resolution, in-world lawyers and virtual police services.

Williams's (2006) research provides a case example of how the regulation of deviant behaviour matured over time in a virtual world. During the early years of the world under study control came under the jurisdiction of one individual, the world administrator. This oligarchic system made one individual jury, judge, prosecutor and defender in all cases. As the population of this virtual world was small and control was effective there were few cries for a more democratic system. Yet as the world population expanded the demands on the oligarchic system increased. As a result world citizens began to self-regulate, forming vigilante groups. This style of control removed the burden on the world administrator who was only called upon to adjudicate in serious acts of deviance such as account hacking or racial/sexual harassment.

The vigilante system of control received wide support from citizens within the world. Its democratic nature and zero-tolerance approach to deviance won the favour of the majority of the population. However, the heyday of this system was short-lived given the increasing sophistication and organisation of deviant activity. The emergence of an organised vandalism group within the world called into question the adequacy of community-based methods of informal social control. A more organised response to such threats emerged in the form of the *Peacekeepers*. The role of this organisation was to patrol the various areas of the world to identify, report, record and punish instances of deviant activity. The Peacekeepers were essentially a voluntary police service organised into a police academy whose members were bestowed with additional powers to those of the general population. These powers included the ability to judge behaviour and bestow punishment without oversight. In the majority of cases punishment took the form of temporary ejection from the world. More severe forms of punishment included account suspension and ultimately cancellation – world banishment.

Tertiary online crime prevention

The ability of volunteer police services, as capable guardians (Felson 1994), to punish offenders 'on the spot' exemplifies how tertiary crime prevention has developed within virtual worlds. This form of order-maintenance policing deters and prevents recidivism by endowing virtual police services with additional powers (such as the ability to eject offenders from the environment and to lock down and remove accounts). Further, virtual police services perform a similar function to reassurance policing in offline communities – a visible virtual patrol reassures and secures citizen confidence, altering perceptions of safety (Crawford and Lister 2004). However, these efforts to formalise social control are only marginally effective at reducing instances of in-world deviance. While the virtual police services may be effective at reducing organised forms of deviant activity and associated citizen anxieties, more sporadic acts of deviance remain prevalent. Groups of online deviants are easier to identify reactively, given their collective identity and their necessary embeddedness within online social networks. In contrast, random acts of deviance by individuals are more difficult to detect.

Primary online crime prevention

Methods of spoofing, griefing and online vandalism are governed by offenders' levels of technical knowledge. A successful in-world deviant is very often an adept hacker. Hackers look for weak points or loopholes in computer code that they use to gain access to secured areas, akin to Wall's (2001) categorisation of *Cybertrespass*. It follows that a change in the architecture of a virtual world to make it more complex and secure would have the beneficial result of reducing the ability for hackers to gain access to private areas. In most virtual worlds the architecture is updated and rewritten several times a year. While this process is not a direct response to the need to reduce general online deviance, it does create a diffusion of benefits in a routine and a systematic way (Pease 1997). Advances in system technology can be considered as a form of primary crime prevention. Target hardening a virtual world's code increases the perceived effort of hacking (Clarke 1997; Newman and Clarke 2003). This primary form of virtual world crime prevention allows for a systematic eradication of deviance regardless of the level of organisation.

Dissent in virtual worlds

Williams (2006) highlights how both formal primary and tertiary methods of regulation within the virtual world under study came under significant criticism from citizens. This was party as a result of the institution of 'virtual law' that replaced the tacit understandings underpinning the vigilante justice model so favoured by citizens. In tandem with the introduction of the Peacekeepers, online community charters and bodies of law were drawn up in a response to the unprecedented deviant acts the world faced. Yet world citizens began to question the effectiveness of these new bodies of virtual law to bring about justice. The introduction of systematic modes of regulation, while at first considered a civilising advancement, proved to be far less effective at curtailing deviance than previous vigilante methods. World citizens began to express disenchantment with the institution of 'virtual law' and associated technological forms of punishment. Flaws in the system began to appear due to the failure of the techno-mediated punishments handed out by the Peacekeepers. As deviants could easily 'reincarnate' themselves and return with little opposition they could escape the most severe sanction of 'virtual death', making redundant the deterrent aims of punishment.

While each of the sanctions available to Peacekeepers (see above) had a disabling effect, the rule-breaker could easily subvert each one if persistent. Even the most severe sanction – the closure of account and contacting an ISP – was flawed due to the autonomy granted to all Internet users to reinvent themselves, allowing them to choose a different ISP and open a new account in the world under a different identity. These technological shortfalls left Peacekeepers with a limited arsenal to combat deviant activity. Not only were they ill equipped, they also faced high levels of opposition from community members who believed they were unaccountable and imposed justice in an overtly crime control fashion.

The importation of offline policing styles into the world not only introduced the benefit of more systematic regulation, but also brought with it the problems of accountability and discretion. It is no surprise to see publicly expressed concerns over the policing of virtual worlds when similar disquiet is expressed offline. Primarily there was a general hostility towards the Peacekeepers due to their influence upon the environment. Many world citizens were concerned that the presence of Peacekeepers resulted in a decline in the quality of interaction, and a subsequent decrease in community membership. Peacekeepers were seen as antagonising, often inducing the behaviour they are required to police. The overarching discontent lay with a concern over abuse of power. A large number of experienced Peacekeepers engaged in bully tactics, jeopardising any form of due process. Many world users considered the policing system to be devoid of any oversight or review, evidenced by the selective implementation of world law. This led many of them to the belief that Peacekeepers were unaccountable and 'out of control'. As a result a desire emerged among world citizens to reintroduce the more flexible distributed forms of regulation that were in play before the introduction of the Peacekeepers. This hark back to community-led vigilantism was further fuelled by the continued belief by some that offline modes of regulation remain alien to the online context.

The call for the reintroduction of vigilante-style regulation meant a reliance upon shaming to bring about social control. In many respects the advocates of the shaming process in virtual worlds reflect the empirical evidence of its success in offline contexts (Ahmed *et al.* 2001). Shame has been considered an inevitable way in which individuals regulate themselves and others. Ahmed *et al.* (2001: 315) concisely summarise the points made by many community members in stating, 'since self- and social regulation are necessary to the just and peaceful co-existence of human communities, shame is to this extent desirable.' Effective virtual world deviance reduction then lies in the balanced integration of community-led and formal modes of regulation. Such a hybrid system allows for a focus upon both the on-time offender who can be shamed and either expelled or reintegrated into the community, and more organised deviant acts that require an equally organised regulatory response.

Shaming as control in virtual worlds

Williams's (2006) finding that virtual world citizens prefer the use of vigilante justice, peer pressure and ostracism to maintain order resonates with research conducted in other online communities. Reid (1999) notes how the medieval practice of charivari in thirteenth- and fourteenth-century France has similar characteristics to modes of informal regulation within an online community named JennyMUSH. Whereas charivari involved the public ridicule and physical taunting of an individual who had transcended community rules, the mediation of deviance within online environments often involves the use of shaming via textual performances. This process finds resonance in

Braithwaite's (1989) work on shaming. Essentially the virtual offender's moral conscience is considered to be a far more effective deterrent against further deviance than any formal form of governance. Braithwaite's theory relies on the assumption that to be shamed is undesirable; so undesirable as to prevent someone from committing a crime. Shaming can also work on two levels: it can be applied directly by an audience, be it verbal or tacit communication, such as a frown, or it can be internally applied by the wrongdoer. What is important for both forms of shaming to work is the existence of a conscience. Drawing from learning theories, Braithwaite (1989) contends that we all have a learned conscience, or classical conditioning, inculcated from early childhood, which tells us the difference between right and wrong, and it is this conscience that allows us to feel the pains of shaming. To go further, Braithwaite (1989) has argued that internal shaming is far more powerful that shaming by onlookers, for two reasons. Firstly, shaming oneself has the benefit of immediacy because wrongdoers know instantly that they have done something wrong. For this reason the pains of shaming are amplified. Secondly, because shaming can be immediate, it has the power of educating the wrongdoer and reinforcing his or her classical conditioning. Here we can see clear similarities with both control and learning theories, and from this we could say Braithwaite's (1989) theory takes for granted that people are motivated to offend, and have to be pressured socially not to do so. The effectiveness of shaming is then reliant on an individual being bonded to family and wider social structures such as the community.

Braithwaite (1989) devotes considerable attention to distinguishing between shaming that is reintegrative and shaming that is not. Drawing from labelling theory, he states that shaming that is disintegrative can result in stigmatisation. Braithwaite continues to note that if shame is applied without forgiveness at a later stage then this may lead to secondary deviance, and possibly abjection in a criminal subculture. It is Braithwaite's (1989) contention that if the current 'disintegrative' shaming process in Western societies was to be replaced by 'reintegrative' practice, the result would be a reduction in recidivism. The next stage in this process is the reintegration of the wrongdoer back into the community. For reacceptance to work there can be no stigmatisation, so the disapproval must be placed on the wrongful act or the behaviour itself and not the individual as a person. This prevents any criminal label being attached to the person holistically. Once the wrongdoer has been shamed, they are forgiven and it is hoped that the severity of the shame would have re-educated them or built upon their classical conditioning, which would hopefully prevent recidivism.

Reintegrative shaming in virtual worlds

Applying such thinking to virtual worlds, there is little doubt that complex social relationships are played out within these online spaces. Markham's (1998) and Mnookin's (1996) accounts of social interaction online show how individuals developed complex interdependencies, characterised by social and emotional bonds. These online interdependent social networks provide a fertile ground for the use of shaming in Internet deviance reduction. While the constraining effects of the family are absent within virtual worlds (unless family members are also present online), the bonds to other citizens and online community are as significant as offline ties. For example strong relations within purely social worlds, such as Active Worlds and Second Life, are important to sustaining positive reputation and status. Acts of shaming online invariably draw on these ties, attempting to either humiliate the wrongdoer or draw upon their classical conditioning in an attempt to induce feelings of guilt.

The process of shaming draws upon bonds to virtual community. As Braithwaite (1989) contends, it is deterrence that is the key to crime reduction – the fear of being humiliated by your peers or being made to feel the pains of guilt. Offenders are made to feel discomfort as a result of internal guilt, triggered by a classical conditioning, which has expanded to encompass elements of the virtual world community. Virtual world citizens with attachments and commitments, and who are involved and believe in their online community, become subject to the potential pains of shaming, and as such become subjects of social control.

There is a clear desire among members of virtual worlds for the maintenance of in-world vigilante styles of regulation. The relative effectiveness of shaming in comparison to techno-mediated punishments is more than evident to community members. In many respects the advocates of the shaming process reflect the empirical evidence of its success in offline contexts (Ahmed et al. 2001). However, there are questions over the successful application of shame in *all* virtual world contexts. Given the unique characteristics of virtual worlds – anonymity, ephemerality of interaction and disinhibition – it is questionable whether vigilante-style regulation, which is dependent upon shaming (whether reintegrative or disintegrative), will be any more effective than organised forms of virtual policing.

Disintegrative shaming in virtual worlds

Evidence from some virtual worlds and other forms of online community indicate disintegration is a common outcome of the online shaming process. A common example of ritual shaming can be seen in the practice of 'toading', often found in Multi-User Domains. The process usually involves the system administrator, or the person at the peak of the community hierarchical scale, altering the appearance and/or description of the offender's persona into something shameful (commonly a toad, which can be traced back to fantasy gaming and the Dungeons and Dragons role-playing genre). A process of public ridicule then begins with the victims and other sympathetic community members venting their anger upon the offender via derisory speech. This way of controlling deviant behaviour is well established in many online communities and discussion groups (Reid 1999). Examples of shaming have been seen in the mediation of 'virtual rape'. After the failed efforts of technological mediation (e.g. exclusion from the community) in the case of Mr Bungle – a player accused of sexually violating others in multi-player game LambdaMOO – textual methods were employed which aimed to disempower his actions (Dibbell 1993). These textual performances involved the community 'shunning' the assailant and ultimately 'shaming' him; they were textually and socially performative; and they successfully secured the social ostracism of the offender. Similar instances of vigilante justice have emerged in other cases of sexual harassment online. Reid (1999) recounts an instance of 'virtual rape' in the Multi-User Domain named JennyMUSH, an environment created for the purpose of counselling women who had suffered offline sexual abuse. The harasser taunted and verbally abused several of the online visitors, while performing acts of sexual violence through text. Given the nature of the environment, the assailant's actions were considered exceptionally harmful. Members of the community were encouraged to textually harass the assailant in an attempt to deliver punishment.

The outcome of the shaming process in these examples was to ostracise the wrongdoer permanently. While some citizens of virtual worlds have adopted external disintegrative tactics in order to shame wrongdoers (Reid 1999), others draw on the internal classical conditioning, in an attempt to induce guilt and to reintegrate the offender. Part of the reason for this disparity in approach may be technological. In both the JennyMUSH and Mr Bungle examples the environments were textually mediated, allowing individuals to alter the offender's appearance via their textual performances. The graphical component of newer virtual worlds does not allow for such flexibility. Vigilante groups cannot change the appearance of a wrongdoer, making external disintegrative shaming more difficult to achieve.

A further explanation for variance in approaches to shaming relates to levels of interdependency. Not all online environments are characterised by complex social networks. Braithwaite (1989) contends that internal shaming is more effective at reducing deviance than shame applied by onlookers. The extent to which this can be said to be an accurate portrayal of the shaming process in all online environments is dependent upon the social embededness of its members. The level and complexity of interdependencies within online environments vary and are more likely to be less multifarious than those existent offline. For example, while complex social and emotional interdependencies may exist in virtual worlds, the more significant relationships evident in family networks are absent. The ephemeral nature of some online relationships has undoubtedly resulted in the use of externally imposed disintegrative shaming. Humiliation is a more effective punishment if the individual has no complex set of online interdependencies in-world. In these circumstances any appeal to the individual's classical conditioning would fail to bring about the desired shame due to a lack of in-world socialisation. The more draconian rituals of public ridicule then become the only effective way of shaming these less bonded individuals. This leaves the question of public ridicule as punishment. In the offline world the mode of punishment as spectacle (Foucault 1979) was successful in the eighteenth and nineteenth centuries due to the offender's constant residence among their community peers, allowing the shaming to have a sustained effect. Yet shaming in a virtual environment is short-lived. The purpose of public ridicule must then lie in a form of justice based on the alleviation of the feelings of those harmed. The chief concern is to protect the virtual world's integrity and to expel anyone that threatens its solidarity, while simultaneously repairing the harm done via a process of retribution. However, this process of justice may result in the opposite effect; by encouraging virtual world citizens to taunt and abuse others, derisory performances are given a free and legitimate reign, encouraging a lack of trust and interdependence. Without trust and interdependency a community becomes fragmented when members grow ever more anxious over the possibilities of victimisation and the eventual demise of their online environment.

The application of shaming within virtual worlds is complicated by the differing levels of social bond to the immediate online context. Where individuals lack complex online interdependencies it is unlikely that reintegrative shaming would be effective in reducing recidivism. Alternative disintegrative shaming tactics may be more effective in humiliating the offender, but the punishment is temporary given the ephemeral and anonymous nature of the online context. This marginal effectiveness of shaming cannot justify the use of vigilante methods alone. It seems most beneficial to combine both methods of vigilantism and organised virtual policing, relying on techno-mediated forms of punishment where social forms fall short.

'Policy Transfer' from virtual worlds

General Internet governance remains a controversial issue. However, several of the lessons learned from within virtual worlds have the potential to be transferred to other online contexts. First, Williams's (2006) finding, that heterogeneous regulatory approaches are more successful at reducing deviance and maintaining victim satisfaction, resonates with current thinking around wider Internet governance. The second finding, that technology or architecture can be an effective regulator, relates to the most current perspectives on Internet regulation. Addressing the first finding, the majority of the world citizens recognised the need for both internal and external regulation. While many ardently called for 'net federalism', claiming a distinction between 'real' and 'virtual' space, in the face of extreme deviant/criminal activity, opinions were tempered, acknowledging instead the need for a joint 'online/offline' approach to regulation. This perspective was also mirrored in citizens' attitudes towards Peacekeeper activity and jurisdiction. The disenchantment expressed over the overt crime control measures employed by the Peacekeepers highlighted the benefits, both in terms of deviance reduction and victim/community satisfaction, of a joint community-'governmental' online regulatory partnership. The combination of the mediatory techniques that once dominated the social control infrastructure and official Peacekeepers was considered to simultaneously reflect the inclusive reintegrative approach of the community while maintaining a more systematic policing service.

This first point is reflected in much of the established thinking behind Internet regulation more generally. A combined decentralised approach to Internet regulation has been advanced for three reasons. First, cyberspace is resistant to regulation by any particular sovereign (Greenleaf 1998). Its transnational nature makes it complex for one body of jurisprudence to dominate. Secondly, the manifestation of cybercrimes, especially 'indigenous' forms of online deviant activity, can escape legal rationalisation, calling for alternative methods of redress. Lastly, a growing body of 'netizens' are claiming independence from the physical world, rejecting 'terrestrial' laws, instead preferring 'decentralised emergent laws' (Johnson and Post 1996). Essentially 'cyberspace does have characteristics that distinguish it from real space, and they make it more difficult for us to develop a coherent approach to how it should (or should not) be regulated by law' (Greenleaf 1998: 600).

The second finding, that the technology or the architecture of virtual worlds is an effective regulator, resonates with the current legal scholarship of Greenleaf (1998), Hosein *et al.* (2003) and Lessig (1999). Regulation is excursed trimodally within virtual worlds – through established online values, conventions and regulations, via external bodies of applicable law and via technology. The first two modes, which might be considered socio-legal, exercised their regulation *ex post*. An offender would be punished after the deviant act had been committed. The second mode of technological regulation, which may be considered the 'nature' of virtual worlds, exercised its regulation *ex ante*. For example, alterations in code, akin to that of situational preventative methods, prevent would-be offenders from vandalising property. The 'tightening up' of code, removing loopholes and weak spots, has the systematic effect of increasing the perceived effort, increasing the perceived risks and reducing anticipated rewards of deviant activity (Clarke 1997; Newman and Clarke 2003). This was experienced on several occasions within Williams's (2006) study during system-wide architectural upgrades.

The idea that technology is a more effective regulator of cyberspace than laws, norms or markets has been advanced by Lessig (1999). It was Lessig's (1999) aim to counter the technological deterministic view that the Internet could not be regulated. Instead he subscribed to a 'digital realism' that recognised the disruptive capacity of technology within cyberspace. Rejecting Boyle's (1997) notion of an Internet Holy Trinity – that regulation was impossible due to the *technology of the medium*, the *geographical distribution of its users*, and the *nature of its content* – Lessig (1999) found that the thread that links all of the Internet's characteristics together – code or architecture – could be used to control behaviour. Much in the same way that a virtual world's architecture can restrict the behaviour of deviants, Lessig (1999) saw it performing a similar function on a much wider scale.

The effectiveness of technology as regulator can be accounted for in several ways. First, technology can disrupt human action, forcing individuals to renegotiate paths and goals (Latour 2000). Second, technology, code or architecture is malleable – it is easily shaped by actors that have access to its control. Third, the way in which technology imposes constraints on how people can behave is more pervasive and immediate than other modes of regulation. Fourth, technology is more readily and rapidly adaptive than laws, norms or markets to cyber criminal threats, allowing it to control both criminal and sub-criminal behaviour. Fifth, changes to system architecture have a preventative approach. It is far more effective to prevent an online offence as opposed to reactively identifying and apprehending an offender. Finally, it is a native form of regulation, making it less contentious. Often the origins of the technology are concealed, and hence its regulatory practice is perceived as less coercive than a state-sponsored regime. Technology is then perceived to be more benign, merely shaping – or even facilitating – individual choices

(Boyle 1997). The effectiveness of technology as a regulator then lies in its ability to alter behaviours, its ability to be shaped, its rapid adaptability, its *ex ante* approach, its wide-reaching scope, its sensitivity towards criminal and sub-criminal activity, and its less visible approach to social control.

Examples of the effectiveness of technology as a regulator could be seen in the system-wide architectural upgrades within Williams's study. However, not all uses of technology were so effective. The use of bots – software designed to automatically monitor profanity – within certain cities and towns caused a degree of contention among citizens. The bots were only programmed to identify American expletives, leaving a substantial proportion of the world's population free to break its laws. This shortfall in the technology forms the basis of Hosein *et al's*. (2003) argument which aims to complicate the role architecture or code has in regulating cyberspace. Instead of being a self-executing benign regulator, Hosein *et al.* (2003) talk of technology as a biased cultural artefact, which is embedded with subjectivity. For this reason alone, there can be no certainty that technology will produce a particular behaviour. In the case of the bots in Williams's study, the objective to reduce profanity failed because of the technology's reliance upon code writers. Hosein *et al.* (2003) continue to complicate this relationship. Instead of claiming it is the technology that determines freedom and rights, they take a non-technologically deterministic approach, arguing instead that individuals (code writers) become the alternative sovereign. Concerns are raised about the accountability of these new masked regulators, and the basis or root of their authority is questioned. They conclude by considering technology as one form of regulation that cannot be separated from other modalities. Technology, law, social norms and markets are all intricately connected, and need to remain so if regulators are to make sense of them. Online regulation should then be considered a socio-technical issue, where the nature or roots of regulation are not always made clear and are in constant flux; where its outcome is never certain, and sometimes even autonomous. Clearly further research is required to map out socio-technical relations to better understand under what set of conditions actors are able to regulate technology, and in what circumstances technology autonomously regulates behaviour.

If we are to accept that technology on its own cannot regulate, either within virtual worlds or the Internet more generally, then reactive modalities, such as community-led and formal modes of policing, are required to regulate where technology cannot. However, achieving the right balance is complex when online community members feel such strong animosity towards external state interference. Yet if our aim is to reduce all forms of online deviance/crime then a continuum of regulation is required (Bonnici and Cannataci 2003). As Grabosky and Smith (2001: 8) note, 'much computer-related illegality lies beyond the capacity of contemporary law enforcement ... security in cyberspace will depend on the efforts of a wide range of institutions.' While it is not realistic to ask for immunity from state regulation, there are clear regions where a sovereign need not become involved. A realistic expectation is that state intervention is likely to remain where economic issues or public concerns are strong motivators. In all other cases, where the cost of intervening is likely to be non-commensurate to the outcome, a sovereign will more than likely devolve regulation onto the online community members themselves (Bonnici and Cannataci 2003).

Conclusion

Virtual worlds are social microcosms in a virtual atavistic state. These online communities, in some respects, are the modern ancestors of offline communities. Many exist without regulation, while others struggle to implement nascent forms of governance. This chapter has provided an example of a virtual world that has seen dramatic system-wide shifts in regulatory practice in a relatively short space of time. What took centuries to occur in offline communities has taken less than a decade to occur online. During this relatively short period social, technological and formalised modes of behavioural control vied for supremacy. The outcome was a recognition of the need for a mixed approach to in-world control which resonates with current thinking about Internet governance more generally.

Further reading

Markham's (1998) *Life Online: Researching Real Experience in Virtual Space*, Alta Mira, provides an ethnographic study of a textual virtual world used for teaching and learning, which develops some insightful thoughts on life in virtual worlds which have stood the test of time. An excellent overview of the development of online community is provided by Baym's (1988) article, 'The Emergence of Online Community', in S. Jones (ed.), *CyberSociety 2.0*. One of the first explorations of deviance and punishment in textual virtual worlds is MacKinnon's (1997) 'Punishing the Persona: Correctional Strategies for the Virtual Offender' in S. Jones (ed) *Virtual Cultures: Identity and Communication in Cybersociety*, Sage. Mnookin (1996) 'Virtual(ly) Law: The Emergence of Law in LambdaMOO', *Journal of Computer-Mediated Communication*, 2(1), offers a detailed overview of Mr Bungle in LambdaMOO and the subsequent community reaction, and is a must read for anyone interested in the legal aspects of virtual worlds. A good overview of control practices in a variety of virtual worlds is furnished by Reid's (1999) 'Hierarchy and Power: Social Control in Cyberspace', in P. Kollock and A. Smith (eds), *Communities in Cyberspace*, Routledge. Finally, perhaps the definitive work on the emergence of virtual community is Rheingold's (1993) *The Virtual Community: Homesteading on the Electronic Frontier*, HarperCollins.

References

Ahmed, E., Harris, N., Braithwaite, J. and Braithwaite, V. (2001) *Shame Management Through Reintegration*, Cambridge: Cambridge University Press.
Akdeniz, Y., Walker, C. and Wall, D. (2000) *The Internet, Law and Society*. London: Longman.

Anderson, B. (1983) *Imagined Communities: Reflections on the Origin and Spread of Nationalism.* London: Verso.

Baudrillard, J. (1998) *Selected Writings.* Cambridge: Polity.

Baym, N. (1995) 'The Emergence of Community in Computer-Mediated Communication', in Steven Jones (ed.), *CyberSociety.* Newbury Park, CA: Sage.

BBC (2005) '"Game theft" led to fatal attack', at http://news.bbc.co.uk/1/low/technology/4397159.stm

Beniger J.R. (1987) 'Personalization of Mass Media and the Growth of Pseudo-Community', *Communication Research,* 14(3): 54–62.

Bonnici, J.P.M. and Cannataci, J.A. (2003) 'Access to Information: Controlling Access to Information as a Means of Internet Governance', *International Review of Law, Computers and Technology,* 17(1): 51–62.

Boyle, J. (1997) 'Foucault in Cyberspace: Surveillance, Sovereignty and Hard-Wired Censors', *University of Cincinnati Law Review,* 177, at http://www.law.duke.edu/boylesite/foucault.htm

Braithwaite, J. (1989) *Crime, Shame and Reintegration.* Cambridge: Cambridge University Press.

Castells, M. (2001) *The Rise of the Network Society* (2nd edn). Oxford: Blackwell.

Clarke, R.V.G. (1997) *Situational Crime Prevention: Successful Case Studies* (2nd edn). Guilderland, NY: Harrow and Heston.

CNN.com (6 August 2000) at www.cnn.com/2000/US/06/08/barrel.bodies.02/

Crawford, A. and Lister, S. (2004) 'The Patchwork Future of Reassurance Policing in England and Wales: Integrated Local Security Quilts or Frayed, Fragmented and Fragile Tangled Webs?', *Policing: An International Journal of Police Strategies and Management,* 27(3): 413–30.

Danet, B. (1998) 'Text as Mask: Gender, Play, and Performance on the Internet', in Steven Jones (ed.), *CyberSociety.* Newbury Park, CA: Sage.

Dibbell, J. (1993) 'Rape in cyberspace or how an evil clown, a Haitian trickster spirit, two wizards, and a cast of dozens turned a database into a society', *Village Voice,* 38(51): 36–42.

Dietrich, D. (1997) '(Re)-fashioning the Techno-Erotic Woman: Gender and Textuality in the Cybercultural Matrix', in Steven Jones (ed.), *Virtual Culture: Identity and Communication in Cybersociety.* London: Sage.

Ellison, L. and Akdeniz, Y. (1998) 'Cyber-stalking: the Regulation of Harassment on the Internet', *Criminal Law Review, Special Edition: Crime, Criminal Justice and the Internet*: 29–48.

ENISA (2008) 'Virtual Worlds, Real Money: Security and Privacy in Massively-Multiplayer Online Games and Social and Corporate Virtual Worlds', at www.enisa.europa.eu/doc/pdf/deliverables/enisa_pp_security_privacy_ virtualworlds.pdf

Felson, M. (1994) *Crime and Everyday Life.* Thousand Oakes, CA: Pine Forge Press.

Foucault, M. (1979) *Discipline and Punish: The Birth of the Prison.* London: Peregrine.

Grabosky, P. and Smith, R. (2001) 'Digital Crime in the Twenty-First Century', *Journal of Information Ethics,* 10: 8–26.

Greenleaf, G. (1998) 'An Endnote on Regulating Cyberspace: Architecture vs Law?', *University of New South Wales Law Journal,* 21(2): 593–22.

Healy, D. (1997) 'Cyberspace and Place: The Internet as Middle Landscape on the Electronic Frontier', in D. Porter (ed.), *Internet Culture.* New York: Routledge.

Hosein, G., Tsavios, P. and Whitley, E. (2003) 'Regulating Architecture and Architectures of Regulation: Contributions from Information Systems', *International Review of Law, Computers and Technology,* 17(1): 85–97.

Johnson, D.R. and Post, D. (1996) 'Law and Borders: The Rise of Law in Cyberspace', *Stanford Law Review,* 48: 1367–80.

Kaspersky Labs (2007) at http://www.viruslist.com/en/analysis?pubid=204791985.

Lash, S. (2001) 'Technological Forms of Life', *Theory, Culture and Society*, 18(1): 105–20.

Latour, B. (2000) 'When things strike back: A possible contribution of science studies to the social sciences' *British Journal of Sociology*, 51(1): 107–23.

Lessig, L. (1999) *Code: And Other Laws of Cyberspace*. New York: Basic Books.

Lockard, J. (1997) 'Progressive Politics, Electronic Individualism and the Myth of Virtual Community', in D. Porter (ed.), *Internet Culture*. London: Routledge.

MacKinnon, R.C. (1997) 'Punishing the Persona: Correctional Strategies for the Virtual Offender', in S. Jones (ed.), *Virtual Cultures: Identity and Communication in Cybersociety*. London: Sage.

Markham, A. (1998) *Life Online: Researching Real Experience in Virtual Space*. Walnut Creek, California: AltaMira.

Meloy, J.R. (1998) 'The Psychology of Stalking', in J.R. Meloy (ed.), *The Psychology of Stalking: Clinical and Forensic Perspectives*. London: Academic Press Ltd.

Miller, D. and Slater, D. (2000) *The Internet: An Ethnographic Approach*. Oxford: Berg.

Mnookin, J. (1996) 'Virtual(ly) Law: The Emergence of Law in LambdaMOO', *Journal of Computer-Mediated Communication*, 2(1), at http://www.ascusc.org/jcmc/vol2/issue1/lambda.html

Morely, D. and Robins, K. (1995) *Spaces of Identity: Global Media, Electronic Landscapes and Cultural Boundaries*. London: Routledge.

Newman, G. and Clarke, R.V. (2003) *Superhighway Robbery: Preventing e-commerce Crime*. Cullompton: Willan Publishing

Oldenburg, R. (1999) *The Great Good Place*. New York: Marlowe and Company.

Pease, K. (1997) 'Crime Prevention', in M. Maguire, R. Morgan and R. Reiner (eds), *The Oxford Handbook of Criminology*. Oxford: Oxford University Press.

Reid, E. (1999) 'Hierarchy and Power: Social Control in Cyberspace', in P. Kollock and A. Smith (eds), *Communities in Cyberspace*. London: Routledge.

Reno, Rt Hon. J. (1999) *Report on Cyberstalking: A New Challenge for Law Enforcement and Industry*. A Report from the Attorney General to the Vice President August 1999, at http://www.usdoj.gov/criminal/cyber-crime/cyberstalking/html

Reynolds, R. (2005) *The Four Worlds Theory* http://terranova.blogs.com/terra_nova/2005/08/the_four_worlds.html

Rheingold, H. (1993) *The Virtual Community: Homesteading on the Electronic Frontier*. New York: Harper Collins.

Shaw, D.F. (1997) 'Gay Men and Computer Mediated Communication: A Case Study of the Phish.Net Fan Community', in Steven Jones (ed.), *Virtual Culture: Identity and Communication in Cybersociety*. London: Sage.

Tönnies, F. (1979) *Gemeinschaft und Gesellschaft. Grundbegriffe der reinen Soziologie*. Darmstadt: Wissenschaftliche Buchgesellschaft.

Turkle, S. (1995) *Life on Screen: Identity in the Age of the Internet*. London: Weidenfield and Nicolson.

Virilio, P. (1997) *Open Sky*. London: Verso.

Wall, D. (2001) 'Maintaining order and law on the Internet', in D. Wall (ed.), *Crime and the Internet*. London: Routledge.

Williams, M. (2004) 'Understanding King Punisher and his Order: Vandalism in an Online Community – motives, meanings and possible solutions', *Internet Journal of Criminology*, at http://www.internetjournalofcriminology.com/Williams%20-%20Understanding%20King%20Punisher%20and%20his%20Order.pdf

Williams, M. (2006) *Virtually Criminal: Crime, Deviance and Regulation Online*. London: Routledge.

Williams, M. (2009) 'Cybercrime', in Fiona Brookman *et al.* (eds), *Handbook of Crime*. Cullompton: Willan Publishing.

Wittel, A. (2001) 'Towards a Network Sociality', *Theory Culture and Society*, 18(6): 542–562.

Chapter 27

Internet technologies and criminal justice

Janet Chan, Gerard Goggin and Jasmine Bruce

Introduction

In this chapter, we turn our attention away from the criminality and regulatory issues connected with the Internet[1] and focus on how the new technologies have been used by practitioners, organisations and consumers of criminal justice knowledge. We discuss how Internet technologies have transformed the nature of 'mass media' and public communication and the implications of this transformation on criminal justice. We are interested in the proposition that the new forms of media and new modes of public communication that centre on the Internet potentially broaden and deepen the role of citizen-consumers in shaping criminal justice policy. One consequence of this, for instance, may be that the Internet can provide alternative sources of knowledge about crime and punishment and a space for 'deliberative democracy' about criminal justice policy not totally driven by narrow law and order politics.

The chapter is organised as follows. We begin with a recap of the literature on the impact of traditional media on criminal justice, particularly the way in which 'old media' journalists, sources, police and other criminal justice practitioners generate and communicate knowledge about crime and crime control. We then discuss how Internet technologies have changed the way criminal justice knowledge is generated and communicated. We provide examples of how the Internet has been used by organisations such as the police, the courts, and the criminal justice policy community – government agencies, citizen groups, and other stakeholders. This is followed by an examination of how the Internet has transformed the mass media and public knowledge. We go on to explore how the Internet may have influenced public attitudes towards crime and punishment and its potential as a deliberative space for engendering informed and durable public judgements on law and order issues. We conclude by summarising the issues raised and posing questions for further research.

'Old media' and criminal justice

There is a significant literature on how criminal justice knowledge is constructed in traditional mass media. With the growing importance of media in contemporary societies, there has long been a recognition that the media have become a critical conduit for knowledge of criminal justice – and indeed a significant factor in how the criminal justice system is shaped and operates. The scene was set by landmark works such as Hall *et al.*'s *Policing the Crisis* (1977) and Ericson, Baranek and Chan's *Visualizing Deviance* (1987), *Negotiating Control* (1989) and *Representing Order* (1991). Since then there have been a number of studies that seek to analyse in detail how the media report and represent criminal justice (e.g. Schlesinger and Tumber 1994; Doyle 2003; Altheide 2006; see Doyle 2006 for a state-of-the-art assessment of current research on crime and the media).

Reporting crime has been an important part of the professional definition of reporters and news, and the creative, constructive role of journalists has been well recognised (Chibnall 1975). The relationships among journalists, their sources, organisations, the truth regimes and practices have received considerable research attention (Ericson 1998). The contemporary practices of media management and public relations employed by police forces, government and non-government organisations have also become an important, and much-debated, part of how criminal justice knowledge is created (Ericson *et al.* 1989).

There is a long-standing debate about how consumption of traditional media affects people's attitudes towards criminal justice – and the changing nature of media, as well as the Internet, is making this discussion even more complex. There are various approaches to understanding how the media influence attitudes. Broadly, we would agree that the media play an important role in constructing most people's social and political realities. Casey and Mohr (2005) give a new twist to a common view, in suggesting that given the public's general lack of knowledge about criminal justice matters, the media's tendency to cover newsworthy events (such as violent crimes or serious offenders) means that news stories – selective or inaccurate as they may be – are 'vivid and salient', thus capturing people's attention and enabling recall. Over a period of continual exposure to such coverage, people may develop a distorted view of crime and justice (2005: 146). Nevertheless, the link between media coverage and public attitudes is not straightforward: even analysts who take a more narrow psychological perspective note that people's opinions are shaped by a variety of intrinsic and extrinsic factors (Casey and Mohr 2005) and mediated by a range of factors such as economic conditions, ideological beliefs, and other psycho-social factors (Allen 2004: 61–2).

In sociological terms, the role of traditional media in shaping public knowledge and attitudes has often been framed in terms of agenda setting in criminal justice matters, being a primary source of knowledge about crime and punishment, participating in the constitution of social order, and acting as an agency of social control.

Agenda setting Media coverage sets the parameters for thinking about crime and punishment. The media determine what topics are covered (or not covered), how they are framed, and the frequency and duration of the coverage. Media stories on criminal justice matters have often been criticised as inaccurate, selective, exaggerated or biased and one of the primary causes of misinformed public opinion about these matters. In turn, these misinformed public views are said to have formed the basis of punitive policies and practices by policymakers and judicial officers (Casey and Mohr 2005; Beale 2006, but see Matthews 2005 for a critique of the 'punitiveness myth').

Primary source of knowledge Most people do not have first-hand knowledge of crime and punishment; the media are the primary source of information about the level and types of crime that have occurred in their communities, the way offenders have been processed in the criminal justice system, and the preventive strategies and corrective programmes that have been used to address the problems. The knowledge provided by the media is mostly about what happened (primary understanding), occasionally about why (secondary understanding), and very often about what it was like (tertiary understanding), especially among the visual media and tabloid newspapers (Ericson *et al.* 1991). Research in the UK suggests that people are more knowledgeable about criminal acts and police investigations than sentencing and punishment; very often this knowledge is gained from television dramas rather than from information programmes (Gillespie and McLaughlin 2003).

Participation in the constitution of order As both cultural agents and cultural products, the media take a central role in 'mapping [the] moral territory' of society:

> They do so by constant reference to the authorised knowers who are well placed in their respective organisations to offer the demarcations of symbolic boundaries, which in turn provide the very basis of cultural classification and order in social life. (Ericson *et al.* 1989: 60)

The media both construct and assume the existence of a kind of societal consensus about what constitutes order and justice. In the absence of direct, independent sources of knowledge about crime and punishment, the media 'fill in the void with factual detail and a consensual framework, thus giving the public both a factual basis for their commitments as well as a context in which to understand them' (Ericson *et al.* 1989: 62).

Agency of social control Apart from shaping public understanding of crime and punishment at the symbolic level through delivering certain visual or verbal messages, the media can have 'social control' effects through intentional reporting aimed at raising awareness of social problems, righting injustices, or uncovering scandals; deliberate silence (e.g. on suicides or prejudicial publicity on court cases) in the public interest; or unintended pressure their reports have on individuals or organisations (Ericson *et al.* 1989: 65–70). The media have often been implicated in the co-production of 'moral panics'

(S. Cohen 2002; see Garland 2008 for a historical and critical analysis of the concept) about particular types of crime, social group, or behaviour that are regarded as a threat to social order or security. Such panics typically generate new policies, programmes or ways of controlling the problem. Investigative journalism, which has been credited for uncovering corruption and political cover-ups, is also another way in which the media can put pressure on organisations or governments to rectify problems and institute reforms.

There is now a small but important body of work that grapples with prominent changes in media and the nature of news: the increasingly commercial nature of media; the demise or at least challenges faced by traditional news and current affairs formats; the rise of entertainment and 'infotainment', and other popular genres, and their role in providing news, current affairs and information; and tabloidisation. Beale, for instance, states a common view in suggesting that:

> media content is shaped by economic and marketing considerations that override traditional journalistic criteria for newsworthiness ... In the case of network news, this strategy results in much greater coverage of crime, especially murder, with a heavy emphasis on long-running, tabloid-style treatment of selected cases ... Newspapers also reflect a market-driven reshaping of style and content, accompanied by massive staff cuts, resulting in a continued emphasis on crime stories as a cost-effective means to grab readers' attention. (Beale 2006: 401; cf. Pfeiffer *et al.* 2005)

Others have discussed the rise of 'true-crime' television programming, and the frequent use of reconstructions and dramatisations of crime in non-fictional genres, as well as the televised justice from the O.J. Simpson trials through to *Judge Judy* and reality programmes constructed from pieces of video footage (taken from surveillance cameras, for instance) (Biressi and Nunn 2003; see also Doyle 2003). Here the developments in media are very much a by-product of the movement of 'high-tech military visualisation and computational devices into criminal justice applications' (Haggerty 2004: 494). This has led to the involvement of media in what has been called the 'control' or 'surveillance' society (Lyon 2001; Andrejevic 2004), as well as the emergence of the possibility of citizens 'watching' police and other criminal justice actors through a 'counter-law' environment of surveillance technologies (Ericson 2007). Another fascinating development in contemporary media has been the advent of competitions, voting, and opinion polls, what media scholar John Hartley (2006) has dubbed 'plebiscitary democracy'. Especially in media representation of crime and justice, the opinion poll, often conducted by, or on behalf of, the media outlet, is now commonplace. It has been argued that the construction of a 'punitive public' that dominates law and order politics is premised on a three-way, mutually constituted relationship among politicians, opinion polls and media (Casey and Mohr 2005).

Still others note the diversity of public opinion, and the need for actors in crime and justice, such as governments, for instance, to communicate proactively with the existing variety of publics (Christie 1998). There are important studies that grapple with tabloidisation, evaluating claims that it provides greater diversity of voices and perspectives about crime (or even leads to a democratisation of news) (Grochowski 2002). There is much to suggest that a clear understanding of the relationship between media consumption (of entertainment as well as news and information forms) and knowledge or feelings about crime and justice still awaits us.

So while debate continues about how criminal justice knowledge is constructed in traditional mass media, the difficulty now is that the world of media is fast changing before the analyst's eyes and ears. Implicated in the various changes to traditional media, such as the rise of infotainment, lifestyle and reality formats, is the profound changes that new technologies and media cultures are bringing. Especially important is the emergence of cross-platform, multi-modal news, across television, radio, magazines, newspapers, Internet and mobiles. The implications of the potentially rich information available via blogs, websites and data feeds from the Internet are yet to be understood (Grochowski 2006).

Use of Internet technologies

Internet technologies have transformed the nature and impact of 'mass media' and public communication. A new space has been created for information generation and retrieval, reports and commentaries, interactive discussions, as well as the transmission of ideas. Other chapters in this Handbook (Curran, Sandywell, Miller) provide an introduction to the key features of the Internet for social practice, globalisation, and everyday life. With this background in mind, we wish briefly to highlight salient features of the Internet that bear upon new modes of public communication for how criminal justice information and knowledge is shaped.

While the beginnings of the Internet lie in the post-Second-World-War years, the 'network of networks' officially launched in 1969, and technologies such as email, file transfer programs, games, Internet relay chats, newsgroups, and online communities (such as MUDs and MOOs) were developed over the next two decades. The Internet began to be widely used outside research and scientific communities from the early 1990s onwards, and, as well as email, what immediately become highly significant for media was the emergence of the World Wide Web. The Web, and Web culture, quickly established expectations that government, corporate, organisational, and other 'official' information would be quickly available via the Web. While previous research has examined the use of information technology by criminal justice practitioners such as police (see Chan et al. 2001; Chan 2001, 2003), research specifically on Internet technologies remains underdeveloped. The following are some examples of how the Internet is being used by criminal justice stakeholders, such as the police, the courts, legal practitioners, and the criminal justice policy community.

Police

Hoey (1998) has raised the spectre of the rise of the 'technocops' in the twenty-first century that replaces the 'bobby on the beat' image of traditional policing. She has suggested that 'police computer-power will continue to grow at a dramatic rate' (1998: 90). Previous researchers have discussed some of the benefits and constraints of introducing information technology (Chan 2003) and mobile phones (see Manning 2001), but few studies have looked specifically at the use and impact of Internet technologies on policing. Anecdotal evidence can be gleaned from a search on the Internet.

Around the world, police organisations are using Internet technologies to communicate with the general public in a variety of ways. The most direct and obvious way is via organisational websites. Police in the United Kingdom, for example, are using these websites to provide organisational and crime-related information, to recruit new members, to collect criminal intelligence, and to obtain feedback from citizens.[2]

One of the innovations adopted in some jurisdictions enables citizens to report minor crimes via the Internet (see, for example, London Metropolitan Police https://online.met.police.uk/report.php). Of course, not everyone will be comfortable reporting crime via the Internet. A US study by Alarid and Novak on community perceptions of different reporting methods (by phone, in person and over the Internet) found that:

> Support of Internet reporting yielded a small but significant demographic of citizens who were willing to report nonserious crimes online. Citizens who were young, higher educated, White home owners were more likely to report crimes online than citizens who had less than a high school education, were African-American or Latino, or were older. (Alarid and Novak 2008: 35)

To encourage citizens to use this facility, the Kent Police 'Report a Crime' website is presented in seven other community languages (https://reportacrime.kent.police.uk/language) and website users can view video clips in British sign language. Here the Internet technology has made it possible for many hitherto neglected language and cultural groupings to be much more visibly represented in the process of criminal justice. The obvious limits in many societies remain, however, underscored here with the injunction to 'Please use English when you are reporting a crime'.

While online reporting may potentially save citizens' time and improve police efficiency, these benefits can be limited by a number of factors (Smith 2005). First of all, not everyone in the community has access to the Internet. This differential access to technology means that a paper-based system must continue in parallel with an online system, thus limiting its potential cost savings. Online reporting may also be complicated by jurisdictional boundaries between law enforcement agencies: crime might unintentionally be reported to the wrong agency and thus requires referral or further processing. There is always the chance that online reporting might be used inappropriately, for example, the false reporting of crime (Smith 2005: 28–9). Online reporting is therefore a double-edged sword for police: it promises to free up police time to pursue other tasks but at the same time may produce additional paperwork for police. For example, online reports may have to be followed up or rewritten and end up taking police resources away from other activities such as face-to-face contact between police and community members (Smith 2005: 28–9). These are concerns that have been raised in the broader literature on policing and information technology: one of the proposed benefits of introducing computerised systems is that it would 'streamline' administrative tasks; however, such developments have in the past created additional office work for police (see Chan *et al.* 2001: 113).

Apart from online crime reporting, police have extended Crime Stoppers programmes that relied on old technologies such as telephone to the use of secure online websites for gathering information and intelligence useful for crime prevention and criminal investigation. For example, the Crime Stoppers programme in Queensland, Australia is a partnership between a community volunteer organisation and the Queensland Police Service (see http://www. police.qld.gov.au/programs/crimeStoppers/). Citizens are asked to contact Crime Stoppers to provide information on crime occurrence, suspicion of planned commission of crime, and addresses where drug production or distribution is alleged to be happening. Providers of such information are guaranteed anonymity and identity protection, with IP addresses of their computers removed by the secure servers. Crime Stoppers websites typically have a 'Most Wanted' page with photographs of alleged offenders, asking for information to help solve the crimes. The achievement of the programme is also publicised on the website. For example, the UK Crime Stoppers site states that

> It's been almost 3 years since the charity Crimestoppers launched the Most Wanted section of the website. More than 400 arrests and charges have been made as a direct result of appeals being featured on the site. 20% of these can be attributed to information received via the Crimestoppers anonymous telephone number. These arrests include crimes of murder, rape, robbery, drug smuggling and assault. (http://www.crimestoppers-uk.org/most-wanted/our-achievements)

A multifaceted evaluation of the telephone-based Crime Stoppers programme in Victoria, Australia in 2004 indicates that the programme was generally highly supported by police and citizens and regarded as cost-effective with 1.9 per cent of calls leading to arrests (Challinger 2004). We are not aware of any published evaluations of the success of the online versions of Crime Stoppers.

Recent trends suggest that police are looking for a variety of ways to incorporate Internet and mobile technology into modern policing. For example, some police forces are starting to use social networking sites like Facebook for a variety of purposes, including the dissemination of crime news, appeals for information, public relations, and a subtle surveillance of social networks. Examples of such police forces include: Manchester Police (zdnet.com.au/news/security/soa/Your-new-Facebook-friends-The-police-/0,130061744,33

9288334,00.htm), New York City Police Department, West Midlands Police (UK) and Queenstown Police in New Zealand (see http://www.facebook. com/pages/Queenstown-Police/36732244172). The effectiveness of such sites remains to be evaluated, but there is anecdotal evidence of success: for example, on 12 January 2009, New Zealand police claimed to have made their first arrest based on information given to them by members of the public who had viewed video footage of suspects on the Queenstown Police Facebook page (http://www.facebook.com/note.php?note_id=57551831768).

Police are also using other Internet applications such as YouTube for similar purposes. For example, Canadian police uploaded video footage of a suspect to YouTube in the hope that a member of the public would recognise the image (http://www.theage.com.au/news/web/police-use-youtube-as-wanted-poster/2006/12/19/1166290588975.html). Similarly, it has been reported that New South Wales Police in Australia are working on a project referred to as VIEW (Video Image Evidence on the Web). This application would enable community members to upload criminal evidence in the form of video files from their phone or computer directly to a police website (http://www.news. com.au/technology/story/0,25642,23427865-5014108,00.html).

The courts and legal practitioners

The Internet has facilitated the dissemination of legal information on an unprecedented scale. For example, the Australasian Legal Information Institute (AustLII) website (http://www.austlii.edu.au/austlii/) contains hundreds of databases on cases and legislation for all Australian as well as New Zealand jurisdictions. The website provides free access to such information and receives about 600,000 hits each day.

Other developments have seen improved access to case information on court trials and judgements. The Federal Court of Australia, for example, has a website that not only provides a searchable database of its judgments, transcripts of court hearings and videos of judgment summaries, it is also a portal for a suite of e-Court facilities. These include online search for legal information, electronic lodgement of court documents by litigants or legal representatives, a virtual courtroom which 'assists in the management of pre-trial matters by allowing directions and other orders to be made online by the relevant docket Judge', a case management tool for parties or practitioners to communicate with court staff and a link to the Commonwealth Courts Portal which provides court staff and legal practitioners with 'real-time information about cases before the courts' (see http://www.fedcourt.gov.au/ecourt/ ecourt_slide.html).

The use of live streaming and archiving of videos containing Federal Court judgement summaries in cases of public interest is a particularly important development for public awareness and understanding of the courts. Before the availability of such technologies, the public has had to rely on journalists to report on court trials. The Internet allows courts to bypass the media and publish their own sources of information. It also 'appears to overcome concerns expressed by judges about the media's lack of interest in broadcasting extended coverage other than in most sensational cases' (Stepniak and Mason 2000:

74). Providing public access to court information online does not preclude journalists from selectively reporting on sensational cases, but it does mean that the public has access to a broader spectrum of case information. The Internet has also provided a forum for the general public to discuss and debate legal cases, although there are ongoing concerns about the quality and accuracy of the information published online (see Fox *et al*. 2007: 128).

Another area where the Internet is making an impact is in relation to the influence of prejudicial publicity on criminal trial juries. The reporting of information prejudicial to the accused by traditional news sources such as newspapers and television could unduly influence the verdicts of criminal trials involving juries and hence there are *sub judice* rules, non-publication orders, and remedial measures designed to restrict such publicity (see Chesterman *et al*. 2001). With the advent of the Internet these issues of prejudicial publicity and jury decision- making are becoming increasingly difficult for courts to manage. According to the NSW Law Reform Commission:

> Prior to the Internet, potentially prejudicial publicity and commentary was relatively controllable. Publications from outside the State rarely had mass penetration and publishers were relatively accountable to the law… The increase of web-based information, entertainment and commentary, and household access to it, creates an exponential growth in problems relating to the management of criminal jury trials where there is only imperfect control of the media. (NSW Law Reform Commission 2008: 93)

The capacity of the Internet to store large quantities of material – including information not usually reported in traditional media – and the availability of search engines increase dramatically the probability of prejudicial information such as the accused person's prior convictions being available to jurors in a criminal trial (Chesterman *et al*. 2001: 202–3). Given that the Internet transcends national and jurisdictional borders, it is impossible for authorities to restrict the flow of information across jurisdictions – a highly relevant issue in the context of potentially prejudicial text published online in the United States being available to criminal juries in Canada (Young and Pritchard 2007).

Criminal justice policy communities

The ability of the Internet to reach a wide audience makes it an extremely useful instrument for consultation, public education and advocacy for criminal justice policy actions. Government organisations are making greater use of Internet technology as part of the law reform process. 'E-consultation' is the term used in the literature to refer to online forums which facilitate the involvement of community members, lobby groups and expert advisers in the policy process (Janssen and Kies 2005: 319). One recent example is the Australia Law Reform Commission's investigation into Australia's 'secrecy laws' – laws that impose duties on public servants to maintain confidentiality and secrecy of commonwealth information. Even though the Commission called for formal submissions to be made, it also created an online 'Secrecy Forum' to encourage informal discussion and debate (See http://www.alrc. gov.au/inquiries/current/secrecy/talking-secrecy/index.html).

There have been some spectacular successes in the use of Internet technology to mobilise global citizen support for major political or social movements. Avaaz.org, for example, have mounted high-profile campaigns for action on a range of global issues such as climate change, human rights abuses, food crises, democratic rights, wars and conflicts. The movement has grown in one year (since 2007) to 'over 3.2 million members in every nation of the world' (http://www.avaaz.org/en/about.php). One example of criminal justice reform involved an ad campaign to close the US military prison in Guantánamo Bay; this was supported by over 80,000 members. Another example was an online petition calling for 'meaningful dialogue between China and the Dalai Lama' following China's violent crackdown on Tibetan protests and riots in March 2008; the petition was signed by 1.5 million people (collected in three weeks) and was 'delivered privately to Chinese officials and publicly in an 84-city global Day of Action' (http://www.avaaz.org/en/report_back_2/). These campaigns are similar to those mounted by an older, also highly successful Web-based American political movement, MoveOn.org Political Action aimed to 'fight for a more progressive America and elect progressive candidates' (http://www.moveon.org/about.html). Among its campaigns was a 'virtual march' to end the genocide in Darfur which involved the support of over 100,000 'virtual marchers' (http://pol.moveon.org/darfur/). The Australian GetUp is a similar Web-based community advocacy movement designed to give 'everyday Australians opportunities to get involved and hold politicians accountable on important issues' (http://www.getup.org.au/about/). Like Avaaz, GetUp focuses on broad environmental and human rights issues. Two of its campaigns are in justice-related areas: a call for the Federal Government to put an end to mandatory detention of asylum seekers and to take a more consultative approach in its 'intervention' (into problems of child abuse) in the Northern Territory that respects human rights (http://www.getup.org.au/campaigns/).

The Internet also provides local community-based organisations with a new medium to promote prison reform. One relatively early, if obscure, website is a homespun homepage on one of the most popular, free hosted websites (Geocities). This is 'The Real Illumination on the Prison Population' (TRIPP), 'committed to exposing the disparity issues plaguing America's INjustice System and aggressively pursue elimination of a biased judicial process' (http://www.geocities.com/CapitolHill/1526/). Justice Action in Australia is a community organisation which campaigns for prison reform. Its members include 'prisoners, academics, victims of crime, ex-prisoners, lawyers and general community members'. The group's philosophy is based on the idea that 'meaningful change depends upon free exchange of information and community responsibility' (http://www.justiceaction.org.au/index.php). Community groups like Justice Action are not new in their campaign for prison reform, but the Internet enables them to take their campaign to a State, national and worldwide audience.

The Internet also provides an opportunity for other stakeholders to run more targeted campaigns. For example, a recent development in Australia has seen the NSW State government propose that some of the State's prisons be privatised. This has been met with fierce opposition from union groups representing the State's prison guards. Such tension between government and union groups is not new. What is new is how groups such as trade unions have harnessed new media to run their anti-privatisation campaign. They ask visitors to the website to sign a petition to the Minister (www.stopthecelloff. org.au). Another example is the US group Mothers Against Drunk Driving (http://www.madd.org/) which was established in 1980 with the mission to eliminate drunk driving and to support victims of drunk driving. Their website is now a sophisticated tool, that brings together typical kinds of Web-based information (available in English and Spanish), with email communication, press releases and information, registration and donation, and a blog.

Other examples from the Australian context show how alliances have formed to try to counter the rhetoric of 'law and order' politics that tends to emerge in the lead up to government elections. For example, prior to the 2003 election in New South Wales, a group calling themselves Beyond Bars was established. The group describes itself as 'a coalition of community and church organisations, activist groups, academics and individuals with an interest in social justice'. The aim of the alliance is to 'promote social justice solutions to a range of criminal justice system issues with a particular focus on finding alternatives to imprisonment'. It also aims to dispel common myths about 'law and order' by providing 'fact sheets' on a range of criminal justice issues (see http://www.beyondbars.org.au/). This is an instance where criminologists engage with the new technology and use it as a powerful tool for social change, as suggested by Barak's 'newsmaking criminology' (Barak 1988, 2007), or the related but broader project of 'public criminologies' (Chancer and McLaughlin 2007).

These examples illustrate the ways in which Internet technologies have been used by criminal justice practitioners, citizens and other stakeholders. The picture is far from complete – much more research is needed to provide a more systematic understanding of the impact of Internet technologies on criminal justice policy, administration and practice.

Internet and knowledge of criminal justice

The advent of the Web, and the ease of use of constructing webpages through coding, meant that users themselves could set up websites, gain visibility and publicity, and act as new kinds of intermediaries in the process of generating information and interpretations about criminal justice. What the rise of the Web, now taken for granted, brought about is what has been called 'disintermediation' (Flew 2005). This is the idea that public communication and media have fundamentally departed from the one-to-many broadcast model, represented by classic ideas of television, radio, or newspapers – where the media is produced by journalists, presenters and technicians, and then delivered to its audiences, who have only limited ways to interact with it. Rather the viewer, or reader, is now an actor that engages not so much in production but 'produsage' (Bruns 2008). The couch potato has become the couch commander, able to choose from a wide range of sources, and to combine and represent these in their own website, blog or RSS feed (really simple syndication web feeds that allow regular updates of websites, blogs, and so on, to be published by readers' browsers). The consumers can, more easily, go straight to the underlying sources of news and information, without relying upon the intermediaries of traditional media, such as journalists or media organisations.

Currently the fundamental concepts of news and journalism are being furiously debated. The rise of citizen journalism – in various forms – has become important, even to the day-to-day gathering of stories and content for mainstream media. Readers are invited to send in their photos and ideas and, in effect, contribute to the reporting of news. A more thoroughgoing development is the rise of open news, in which interested consumers actually construct, edit and control news sites, through the filtering, authoritative role of journalists (Bruns 2005).

Key also to how Internet technologies are transforming the nature of mass media is the new development of user-generated content. At present, a wide range of actors using the media for public communication are grappling with the dynamic, complex interplay of technologies that in one form or other allow consumers to create content themselves, and then make it available via the Internet to all kinds of audiences. Connected to the rhetorics of user-generated contents, and the rise of the consumer as producer, is the idea of social media. Social media is a rather broad and vague term for a range of new Internet technologies that work on principles of social networking and other new forms of association. Social media forms, such as Facebook, YouTube, MySpace, and user-generated content have been associated with the phenomenon dubbed 'Web 2.0'. Social networking systems – notably Facebook, LinkedIn, and earlier forms such as Orkut and Friendsters, but also now the text messaging, microblogging network Twitter – link friends and acquaintances, providing ways not only to create very large groups and networks, but new ways of presenting the self, and communicating with others. These kinds of social networking systems are creating the intimate, but large-scale media architectures that are increasingly requiring those wishing to engage with public communication to reckon with them. Politicians now, for instance, flourish their Facebook or MySpace pages, as do police forces. Another related and key Internet development is the resurgence of online worlds, and the complexity of online communities, shown in the very popular Second Life but also in massively multiplayer gaming, that underline the new questions of policing, order and criminal justice that emerge in such contexts (Wall and Williams 2007). Ironically, it has become possible for criminal justice consumers to 'disintermediate' traditional sources, and greatly augment, re-present (even mash up) and interpret criminal justice communication. The response of some institutions, notably courts, has been to seek to reassert and bolster the long-accepted principles of how citizens come to understand and participate in criminal justice.

An important debate regarding the Internet with important implications for criminal justice revolves around online news and journalism. Early research on online news sought to make sense of exactly what forms this took, and how it compared to traditional sources of news (Pavlik 2001). One enduring issue has been the debate over the quality and objectivity of online news and journalism (Ruggiero 2004). There is some evidence to suggest that there are now real difficulties in sustaining traditional models of journalism, predicated on accounts of the fourth estate and on a high-prestige view of the profession to which hard-hitting news and investigative journalism are key. Newspapers, which contain the home of such journalists, are finding it difficult to sustain their revenues. As well as the diversification of media, and pluralisation of news across Internet, mobile, television, and other platforms, the real threat is actually coming from loss of advertising revenue. The 'rivers of gold' that advertising represented for newspapers from their display and classified advertisements is rapidly moving to the online environment, especially with the combination of websites and search engines. Some analysts of online journalism, then, see it as being far more susceptible, indeed driven by market-driven trends (E. Cohen, 2002). Others take a more sanguine view, arguing that online journalism is developing its own particular models, with great potential (Matheson 2004a, b; Deuze 2007) and that consumers are increasingly turning to online sources as an integral part of their individual mix of media channels and outlets.

Impact of the Internet on public attitudes

With the advent of the Internet, there have been important changes to traditional media organisations, and these are now increasingly hybrid and cross-platform – offering a newspaper, online news, and search facility; or television, programme downloading, and chat on a website. A 2008 study by the US Pew Foundation found that consumers were increasingly combining traditional and new online sources of news on a daily basis (Pew 2008). Further alternative sources and new media forms have emerged to extend the options for citizens not only to choose their information, but also to produce media themselves, or more widely circulate their views. For these reasons, it could be argued that the agenda-setting role of traditional media has been diluted.

There is no guarantee that the presence of alternative sources would improve the quality of the information. There is, of course, a greater scope for readers to identify information that is more accurate: for example, texts of court judgements contain full and unabridged information on what the court (or, more accurately, a particular judicial officer or a panel of judges) has written about a particular case. Similarly, there is the potential for a variety of perspectives to be represented on the Internet, including views directly opposed to those presented by the traditional media, organisation spokespersons, and government officials. It could be argued that readers, however, do not necessarily try to access these alternative sources, either because of convenience or by force of habit, unless they have reasons to doubt the information provided by traditional media outlets. Further research into this is required, but it can be observed that increasingly alternative sources, from blogs, websites, or email, do circulate quite widely, and often are known by a surprising range of users. It could also be contended that the new media environment requires readers to be much more vigilant about the veracity of information accessible from the Internet. This implies that readers who are more educated or critical users of the new media are less likely to allow the media (old or new) to set limits or have undue influence on their understanding of criminal justice issues – something no different from the situation before the advent of the Internet. However, this too is questionable. For one thing, with the Internet has developed new protocols and ways of filtering, rating and evaluating information, as the debate over Wikipedia illustrates.

Although traditional media outlets are no longer the primary sources of knowledge about crime and punishment on the Internet, their ready access to official sources – for example politicians, police, prosecution authorities, courts and other government officials – means that they are well placed to provide more immediate and authoritative accounts of what happened. They generally have more resources to produce news stories in a digestible and attractive format, accompanied by video footage, and with frequent updates. They are also more likely to have 'authorised knowers' (experts, high-ranking officials, experienced journalists or commentators) that enhance the legitimacy and believability of their accounts. Similarly, organisations with resources to hire experienced writers, communications specialists, graphic artists and technicians can present their messages in a highly attractive and convincing manner. In contrast, individual bloggers or less endowed community organisations cannot compete for attention on the Internet except through skilful knowledge and deployment of Internet media strategies (as the examples of GetUp, Avaaz or Beyond Bars show), established networks, strategic indexing of contents for search engines, or posting contents that are dramatic or sensational. The consequence of this inequality of access to resources is likely to be that traditional media outlets, especially with incorporation of new Internet technologies, are well-placed to maintain their powerful position as primary sources of knowledge about crime and punishment.

To what extent does the Internet allow alternative mapping of society's moral boundaries or a breakdown of the consensual framework about criminal justice issues? Certainly the presence of a great variety of perspectives on any particular issue is made possible by the Internet. There is scope for conservative 'law and order' rhetoric to exist alongside a range of political stances from liberal democratic discourse to radical libertarian or even anarchic views. Readers are free to access a spectrum of perspectives that were not readily available before the Internet. They are also made aware of the existence of alternative frameworks and standards of morality. However, what occurs with the dominant or 'consensual framework' in particular societies regarding criminal justice attitudes is something that needs further investigation, in relation to specific contexts, and also with regard to social, historical and cultural factors at work in society that are responsible for more enduring criminal justice attitudes to be formed. It is worth recalling Ericson's summary of the institutional approach (as opposed to 'effects' and 'dominant ideology') to media, crime and justice:

> the mass media have diverse and conflicting influences; and moreover, that these influences are a function not only of mass media organisations, content, and mode of presentation, but also of the broader social networks of which they, their sources, and their readers are a part. (Ericson 1991: 221)

There is every reason to believe that the new media can have the same capacity for delivering social control effects as the old. This capacity may even have increased as accounts of social problems, injustices, scandals and so on are much more easily and quickly written, read, commented on and widely circulated on the Internet than traditional media stories. Politicians, government authorities and organisations no longer simply monitor traditional media stories for damage control purposes; instead, proactive public relations strategies are employed to manage political or organisational image, since all sources on the Internet are potential critics and destroyers of reputation.

What are the implications for criminal justice policy? While the Internet can deliver a wider range of information sources and a greater variety of perspectives on criminal justice issues, there is no guarantee that the public would be 'better informed' in the sense of understanding criminal justice issues. Efforts to 'educate' the public about criminal justice issues may be quite limited in effectiveness:

> Public education programmes rely ... on flawed, one-way exchanges between the expert and the public, insufficient to make a lasting impact on public knowledge and attitudes. (Green 2006: 132)

There is increasing recognition that to generate informed public *judgement* – as opposed to ill-informed public opinion – communication between experts and the public must be a two-way exchange, with opportunities for in-depth deliberation. While the media are effective in consciousness raising, especially in relation to high-profile criminal justice issues, they do not provide a forum for the public to debate and 'work through' the actions and consequences so that they can come to a resolution of the issues 'cognitively, emotionally, and morally' (Yankelovich 1991: 65, quoted in Green 2006: 142).

A Deliberative Polling conducted in the UK suggests that such forums can lead to a more liberal and less punitive attitude to crime and punishment (Green 2006: 134). In general, the aim is to engender public judgements that are both informed and durable. One of the promises of the Internet is that it could facilitate such deliberative spaces where large numbers of participants can take part virtually without the costs involved in face-to-face Deliberative Polling exercises. But how successful have online forums been in facilitating such in-depth and constructive deliberations? Janssen and Kies's (2005) review of the empirical research on the quality of online deliberations found enormous differences in conclusions. They criticised the methodologies used in the studies, especially the way the 'deliberative quality' of discussion was operationalised. Drawing on a number of researchers' work, they listed the characteristics of an 'ideal public sphere' for deliberative democracy; these include reciprocity, justification, reflexivity, ideal role-taking, sincerity, inclusion and exclusion equality, and autonomy from state and economic power.

As well as looking forward to future experiments in deliberative democracy and criminal justice using Internet technologies, it is interesting to consider another view of how the Internet contributes to changing public attitudes. The Internet is often decried as an unruly, emotional, vituperative and at times 'irrational', hothouse – for instance, in the way the blogosphere is derogated, as a place where abuse is the currency, rather than sincere, respectful and thoughtful exchange and turn-taking. This is reminiscent of the way that media are seen as distorting information on criminal justice, or particular developments in media (the rise of satirical, comedy news programmes, chat shows, tabloidisation, or sensational reporting) are seen as baleful influences on public attitudes. It could be argued that, actually, this is democracy in action, warts and all. And that the Internet has deepened this, leading to problematic and unhelpful tendencies, but also leading to new possibilities for positively changing public attitudes (Hermes 2006). This is the argument put, for instance, by political theorist John Keane in suggesting that the Internet is leading to a growth in 'monitory democracy' (Keane 2008), that offers new checks and balances on the exercise of power, and new possibilities for citizens to express their views, even if these are sometimes thought to be 'ill-informed'. This view on the Internet, and on the entwined changes in media, could actually offer a way forward to the impasse of debates on media, public attitudes, and public policy – responding to scholars who have noted that information is perhaps not enough, and that the emotion, sensation and passion bound up in particular media genres is also an important part for those seeking to reform policy to engage with (Daly 1995; Freiberg 2001).

Conclusion

In many respects the relationship between the Internet and criminal justice is in its infancy. As we have explored in this chapter, there are many experiments underway with the Internet's use in criminal justice knowledge, by practitioners in criminal justice, and in the dynamics of public attitude formation, but directions are not yet clear. However, in our conclusion we will offer some preliminary thoughts and voice a number of concerns.

Firstly, the Internet has demonstrably created many more sources of information, news, and entertainment for members of the public interested in criminal justice, but the implications of this remain difficult to gauge. We are doubtful, for instance, that the much vaunted 'disintermediation' is happening in the way it was predicted. To be sure, there is often a proliferation of accounts and views, but these, of course, are also mediated in some way. Alternative sources are increasingly available and availed upon by even those with only a glancing knowledge and critical insight. The task remains, and indeed is redoubled, for consumers of Internet media to pick their way deftly through a bewildering array of primary, secondary, tertiary, and mixed sources of information on criminal justice matters. Information overload is one problem, but also pressing are the problems about understanding the authors, provenance, and credibility of criminal justice texts. The old models of vetting, checking and presentation by skilled journalists and their editors are being displaced by new models of filtering, quality control and redaction, developed by communities of bloggers or open source news. Yet these emergent systems are not so well known, nor are they well integrated with the important traditions of journalism and critical commentary. There is a real need for authoritative research upon the nature of these new media worlds of criminal justice consumers, and what their implications are for understanding policy.

Secondly, while democratisation is a worthy and desirable objective, its realisation is a fraught project, especially when it comes to the Internet. The Internet has often been associated with the conferral or achievement of freedom (for instance, in particular countries where websites, blogs or mobile phones offer media options out of the reach of state or corporate control). However, there is a growing awareness that the whole of the political spectrum can avail itself of the Internet and the possibilities for greater participation and influence it can offer. This has the potential to accentuate existing tendencies in criminal justice. For instance, victim-focused accounts, law and order lobbies and advocates for more punitive approaches could further crowd out other views, not to mention evidence-based and rational approaches. Certainly there is a 'multiplication of forums' underway through the Internet that is reshaping citizenship, and in criminal justice too the challenge is to 'devise new ways of encouraging informed political engagement' (Hermes 2006: 307).

Thirdly, while not much research is available on the Internet and how it has affected public attitude formation, it is highly likely that the new technology will make it even more imperative that the media's representation of criminal justice is carefully evaluated. Existing scholarship on 'old' media shows, for instance, that: media outlets vary considerably in terms of their coverage of criminal justice issues – for instance Ericson *et al.*'s 1991 content analysis shows significant differences between quality and popular outlets, and between mediums. Further studies show that people are not passive consumers – they choose the papers they read, the TV stations they watch, and often they believe who they want to believe. Moreover, charges that the 'old media' report only violent crime, sensationalise, personalise, distort, amplify and so on ignore the fact that media stories are cultural products, not archives of 'facts'. So why would things be different with the Internet? The Internet is bringing profound transformations in traditional media enterprises, at the same time that it offers opportunities for new entrants and innovative media forms, large and small. More than anything, as it changes and complicates media production, the Internet is part of a profound change to media consumption. This is something that we need to study in depth, with great attention to the specific habits of consumers, features and characteristics of genres and programmes, and new media cultures, and also with a recognition of how various institutions and organisations pertinent to criminal justice are appropriating and shaping these technologies.

Notes

1 For our purposes, we define the Internet as technologies that revolve around the co
   Internet protocol (technically speaking the TCP/IP protocol – or transmission cont
   protocol/Internet protocol). We are especially interested in the 'public' Intern
   that is, the Internet accessible by the general public. This can be distinguished
   'intranets' and other forms of 'closed' organisational telecommunications and
   communications networks. Narrowing this down further, we are particularly
   to register and explore uses and concepts of the Internet as it is playing a p.
   media and public communication.

2 See Appendix in Hyde (1999) for a 'whistle stop tour of police websites' for
   examples of these towards the end of the twentieth century.

Further reading

There are very few research studies on the impact of the Internet on criminal justice.
However, the following provide some useful background readings: Chan, J. (2003)
'Police and New Technologies', in T. Newburn (ed.), *Handbook of Policing*. Cullompton,
Devon: Willan Publishing, pp. 655–79; Deuze, M. (2007) *Media Work*. Digital Media
and Society Series. Cambridge: Polity Press; Grochowski, T. (2006) 'Running in
Cyberspace: O.J. Simpson web sites and the (de)construction of crime knowledge',
Television and New Media, 7(4): 361–82; and finally, Grant, C. (2007) 'The Internet, New
Collectivities and Crime', in C. Grant, *Crime and Punishment in Contemporary Culture*.
London: Routledge, pp. 91–110.

References

Alarid, L.F. and Novak, K.J. (2008) 'Citizens' Views on Using Alternative Reporting
   Methods in Policing', *Criminal Justice Policy Review*, 19(1): 25–39.
Allen, R. (2004) 'What Works in Changing Public Attitudes: lessons from rethinking
   crime and punishment', *Journal for Crime, Conflict and the Media*, 1(3): 55–67.
Altheide, D. (2006) 'The Mass Media, Crime and Terrorism', *Journal of International
   Criminal Justice*, 4(2006): 982–97.
Andrejevic, M. (2004) *Reality TV: The Work of Being Watched*. Lanham, MD: Rowman
   and Littlefield.
Barak, G. (1988) 'Newsmaking Criminology: reflections on the media, intellectuals and
   crime', *Justice Quarterly*, 5(4): 565–87.
Barak, G. (2007) 'Doing Newsmaking Criminology from within the Academy',
   Theoretical Criminology, 11(2): 191–207.
Beale, S.S. (2006) 'The News Media's Influence on Criminal Justice Policy: how market-
   driven news promotes punitiveness', *William and Mary Law Review*, 48(2): 397–481.
Biressi, A. and Nunn, H. (2003) 'Crimes of violence in social/media space', *Space and
   Culture*, 6(3): 276–91.
Bruns, A. (2005) *Gatewatching: Collaborative Online News Production*. New York: Peter
   Lang.
Bruns, A. (2008) *Blogs, Wikipedia, Second Life, and Beyond: From Production to Produsage*.
   New York: Peter Lang.
Casey, S. and Mohr, P. (2005) 'Law-and-Order Politics, Public-Opinion Polls and the
   Media', *Psychiatry, Psychology and Law*, 12(1): 141–51.

Chadee, D. and Ditton, J. (2005) 'Fear of Crime and the Media: assessing the lack of relationship', *Crime, Media, Culture*, 1(3): 322–32.

Challinger, D. (2004) *Crime Stoppers in Victoria: An Evaluation*. Technical and Background Paper No.8. Canberra: Australian Institute of Criminology.

Chan, J.B.L. (1995) 'Systematically Distorted Communication? Criminological knowledge, media representation and public policy', *The Australian and New Zealand Journal of Criminology*, 28: 23–30.

Chan, J.B.L. (2001) 'The Technology Game: how information technology is transforming police practice', *Criminal Justice*, 1(2): 139–59.

Chan, J.B.L. (2003) 'Police and New Technologies', in T. Newburn (ed.), *Handbook of Policing*. Cullompton, Devon: Willan Publishing, 655–79.

Chan, J., Brereton, D., Legosz, M. and Doran, S. (2001) *E-policing: The Impact of Information Technology on Police Practices*. Brisbane: Old Criminal Justice Commission.

Chancer, L. and McLaughlin, E. (2007) 'Public Criminologies: diverse perspectives on academia and policy', *Theoretical Criminology*, 11(2): 155–73.

Chesterman, M., Chan, J. and Hampton, S. (2001) *Managing Prejudicial Publicity: An Empirical Study of Criminal Jury Trials in New South Wales*. Sydney: Law and Justice Foundation of NSW.

Chibnall, S. (1975) 'The Crime Reporter: a study in the production of commercial knowledge', *Sociology*, 9(1): 49–66.

Christie, S. (1998) 'Trial by Media: politics, policy and public opinion, the case of the ACT heroin trial', *Current Issues in Criminal Justice*, 10(1): 37–51.

Cohen, E.L. (2002) 'Online Journalism as Market-Driven Journalism', *Journalism of Broadcasting & Electronic Media*, 46(4): 532–48.

Cohen, S. (2002) *Folk Devils and Moral Panics: The Creation of the Mods and Rockers* (2nd edn). London: Routledge.

Daly, K. (1995) 'Celebrated Crime Cases and the Public's Imagination: from bad press to bad policy?', *The Australian and New Zealand Journal of Criminology*, 28: 6–22.

Deuze, M. (2007) *Media Work*. Digital Media and Society Series. Cambridge: Polity Press.

Doyle, A. (2003) *Arresting Images: Crime and Policing in Front of the Television Camera*. Toronto: University of Toronto Press.

Doyle, A. (2006) 'How Not to Think about Crime in the Media', *Canadian Journal of Criminology and Criminal Justice*, October: 867–85.

Ericson, R.V. (1991) 'Mass Media, Crime, Law, and Justice: An Institutional Approach', *British Journal of Criminology*, 31(3): 219–49.

Ericson, R.V. (1998) 'How Journalists Visualise Fact', *The Annals of the American Academy*, 560: 83–95.

Ericson, R.V. (2007) 'Rules in Policing', *Theoretical Criminology*, 11(2): 367–401.

Ericson, R.V., Baranek, P.M. and Chan, J.B.L. (1987) *Visualizing Deviance: A study of news organization*. Toronto: University of Toronto Press and Milton Keynes: Open University Press.

Ericson, R.V., Baranek, P.M. and Chan, J.B.L. (1989) *Negotiating Control: A Study of New Sources*. Toronto: University of Toronto Press and Milton Keynes: Open University Press.

Ericson, R.V., Baranek, P.M. and Chan, J.B.L. (1991) *Representing Order: Crime, Law and Justice in the News Media*. Toronto: University of Toronto Press and Milton Keynes: Open University Press.

Flew, T. (2005) *New Media: An Introduction* (3rd edn). Melbourne: Oxford University Press.

Fox, R.L., Van Sickel, R.W. and Steiger, T.L. (2007) *Tabloid Justice: Criminal justice in an age of media frenzy*. London: Lynne Rienner Publishers.

Freiberg, A. (2001) 'Affective Versus Effective Justice: Instrumentalism and Emotionalism in Criminal Justice', *Punishment and Society*, 3(2): 265–78.

Garland, D. (2008) 'On the Concept of Moral Panic', *Crime, Media, Culture*, 4(1): 9–30.

Gillespie, M. and McLaughlin, E. (2003) *Media and the Shaping of Public Knowledge and Attitudes Towards Crime and Punishment*. London: Rethinking Crime and Punishment, accessed 15 July 2009, available at http://www.rethinking.org.uk/latest/pdf/briefing4.pdf

Green, D.A. (2006) 'Public Opinion versus Public Judgment about Crime', *British Journal of Criminology*, 46(1): 131–54.

Grochowski, T. (2002) 'The "tabloid effect" in the O.J. Simpson case: the National Enquirer and the production of crime knowledge', *International Journal of Cultural Studies*, 5(3): 336–56.

Grochowski, T. (2006) 'Running in Cyberspace: O.J Simpson web sites and the (de)construction of crime knowledge', *Television and New Media*, 7(4): 361–82.

Haggerty, K.D. (2004) 'Technology and Crime Policy: a reply to Michael Jacobson', *Theoretical Criminology*, 8(4): 491–97.

Hall, S., Critcher, C., Jefferson, T., Clarke, J. and Roberts, B. (1977) *Policing the Crisis: Mugging, the State, and Law and Order*. London: Macmillan.

Hartley, J. (2006) 'Sync or Swim? Plebiscitary Sport, Synchronized Voting, and the Shift from Mars to Venus', *South Atlantic Quarterly*, 105(2): 409–28.

Hermes, J. (2006) 'Citizenship in the Age of the Internet', *European Journal of Communication*, 21(3): 295–309.

Hoey, A. (1998) 'Techno-Cops: information technology and law enforcement', *International Journal of Law and Information Technology*, 6(1): 69–90.

Hyde, S. (1999) 'A Few Coppers Change', *The Journal of Information, Law and Technology*, 2, accessed 16 January, available at http://www.law.warwick.ac.uk/jilt/99-2/hyde.html

Janssen, D. and Kies, R. (2005) 'Online Forums and Deliberative Democracy', *Acta Politica*, 40: 317–35.

Keane, J. (2008) 'Monitory Democracy: The Secret History of Democracy since 1945', lecture given to School of Journalism, Fudan University, Shanghai, 29 October, available at http://www.johnkeane.net/pdf_docs/Jk_Lecture_monitory_democracy_shanghai_2008.pdf

Lyon, D. (2001) *Surveillance Society: Monitoring Everyday Life*. Buckingham: Open University Press.

Manning, P. (2001) 'Information Technology in the Police Context: the "sailer" phone', in J. Yates and J. Van Maanen (eds), *Information Technology and Organizational Transformation: History, Rhetoric, and Practice*. Thousand Oakes: Sage Publications, pp. 205–22.

Matheson, D. (2004a) 'Negotiating Claims to Journalism: webloggers' orientation to news genres', *Convergence: The International Journal of Research into New Media Technologies*, 10(4): 33–54.

Matheson, D. (2004b) 'Weblogs and the epistemology of the news: some trends in online journalism', *New Media and Society*, 6(4): 443–68.

Matthews, R. (2005) 'The Myth of Punitiveness', *Theoretical Criminology*, 9(2): 175–201.

NSW Law Reform Commission (2008) *Jury Directions*, Consultation Paper 4. Sydney: NSW Law Reform Commission.

Pavlik, J.V. (2001) *Journalism and New Media*. New York: Columbia University Press.

Pearson, M. (2005) 'Police Digital Communications and the Media', *Australian Journalism Review*, 27(1): 105–22.

Pew (2008) *Audience Segments in a Changing News Environment: Key News Audiences now Blend Online and Traditional Sources*. Washington: The Pew Research Centre for the People and the Press.

Pfeiffer, C., Windzio, M. and Kleimann, M. (2005) 'Media Use and its Impacts of Crime Perception, Sentencing Attitudes and Crime Policy', *European Journal of Criminology*, 2(3): 259–85.

Ruggiero, T.E. (2004) 'Paradigm Repair and Changing Journalistic Perceptions of the Internet as an Objective News Source', *Convergence: The International Journal of Research into New Media Technologies*, 10(4): 92–106.

Schlesinger, P. and Tumber, H. (1994) *Reporting Crime: The Media Politics of Criminal Justice*. Oxford: Clarendon Press.

Smith, E. (2005) 'Online Crime Reporting: should law enforcement turn to the internet for savings?', *Public Management*, July: 26–30.

Stepniak, D. and Mason, P. (2000) 'Court in the Web: impact of the Internet on the cameras in court debate', *Alternative Law Journal*, 25(2): 71–4.

Wall, D.S. and Williams, M. (2007) 'Policing Diversity in the Digital Age: Maintaining Order in Virtual Communities', *Criminology and Criminal Justice*, 7(4): 391–415.

Young, M.L. and Pritchard, D. (2007) 'Cross-Border Crime Stories: American media, Canadian law, and murder in the internet age', *American Review of Canadian Studies*, 36(3): 407–26.

Chapter 28

Computer forensics and the presentation of evidence in criminal cases[1]

Ian Walden

Introduction

Digital information is the form in which the 'Information Society' carries out its activities, whether through software applications, emails, data feeds or the Web. When cybercrimes occur, the ability of law enforcement agencies (LEAs) to investigate and prosecute the perpetrators will be driven by the availability and accessibility of such data to investigators, whether in the context of intelligence gathering, evidential retrieval, analysis or presentation in court.

Any criminal investigation interferes with the rights of others, whether the person is the subject of an investigation or a related third party. In a democratic society any such interference must be justifiable and proportionate to society's need for protection. However, the growth of cybercrime raises unique issues in respect of the appropriate balance between investigatory need and Internet users' privacy rights; as well as the interests of communication service providers (CSPs), the intermediaries that build, operate and supply communication services. This chapter critically examines the manner in which a balance has been achieved between these diverse and competing interests.

The first part of this chapter deals with problems raised by data for LEAs investigating cybercrime. It is beyond the scope of this chapter to engage in a detailed examination of the full range of forensic techniques employed in a cybercrime investigation. Instead, attention is given to two key elements: identifying the suspect and obtaining data about his communication activities. The second part of the chapter examines the use of computer and network-derived forensic material as evidence in criminal proceedings.

Cyber-forensics

The investigation of cybercrime and the gathering of appropriate evidence, the science of 'forensic computing', can be extremely difficult and complex. This arises from the intangible and often transient nature of data in a networked environment. The technology renders the process of investigation and recording of data extremely vulnerable to defence claims of errors, technical malfunction, prejudicial interference or fabrication. Such claims may lead to a ruling against the admissibility of such evidence.

A lack of adequate training of law enforcement officers, prosecutors and the judiciary will often exacerbate these difficulties. Substantial efforts have been made recently to address this training need, with the establishment of specialised facilities and courses,[2] supplemented by training offered by vendors of forensic applications and services. Additionally, computer forensics has become a recognised academic discipline, leading to a range of qualifications at higher education institutions.[3]

Until recently, the practice of digital or cyber-forensics had developed rather haphazardly, often based on expediency and circumstance, reflecting the story of the information and communication technologies (ICTs) industry itself. However, attempts are being made to impose greater professionalism in the field, to better serve the needs of the market, both public and private sector, and to improve the quality of evidence being used in criminal prosecutions.[4]

The experience of law enforcement agencies has also been formalised through the issuance of guidance on the forensic treatment of computer-derived evidence. The Association of Chief Police Officers has published a 'Good Practice Guide for Computer-Based Electronic Evidence'.[5] Such guidance has become a de facto benchmark, against which the practices of law enforcement officers are likely to be evaluated. Additionally, more formal forensic standards are being developed and promulgated in the field, designed to bolster the use of digital evidence.

This section briefly considers two key challenges in a digital investigation: identifying the suspect and obtaining data relevant to the suspect's criminal activities. However, first, consideration is given to some of the problems that handling data creates for investigators, some of which the law has expressly tried to address or mitigate.

Addressing the data problems

Data raises a range of problems for investigators, many of which require both specialist technical skills and an appropriate procedural framework. The first is the 'identity problem': how do we establish an adequate forensic link between an item of data and the virtual identity of the person to whom the data relates, and then between the virtual identity and a real-world person?

A second issue is the 'location problem', although this really covers at least three distinct issues arising from where the data is found. Related to resolving the 'identity problem' is the need to identify the physical location of the suspect. In a mobile phone context, for example, cell site analysis may determine whether the suspect in possession of an identified handset was present in a locality at the relevant time. Location also has jurisdictional implications, since cyberspace activities cross state borders requiring investigators to seek data residing outside their national jurisdiction.[6]

A third aspect of the location problem arises from the fact that forensic data may also be present within a network forming part of the Internet, and may be found on terminal equipment operating at the edges of the network, such as a PC. The law sometimes treats data obtained within a network differently from that same data when it is at the edges. Data may reside on the ICTs of the victim, the suspect or some third party, such as a CSP or online service provider. The same data may be obtained via its transmission across a network, so-called intercepted data. Rules of criminal procedure address LEA access to these different sources of evidence: data 'at rest' and data 'in transmission'.

The nature of ICT makes data notoriously vulnerable to loss and modification, as well as being simultaneously surprisingly 'sticky'. These characteristics may be referred to respectively as the 'integrity problem' and the 'stickiness problem'. The former means the process of obtaining forensic data and is a significant technical challenge for investigators, since it may itself modify the source data or related metadata, such as time and date stamps, fatally undermining the evidential value of the material.

The 'stickiness' of data is attributable to the multiple copies generated by ICTs, particularly in an Internet environment. While the 'stickiness' of data generally advantages the investigator, the availability of data may not enable a successful prosecution where the defendant is unaware of its existence.[7] Conversely, the perception that ICT data is transient may advantage a defendant, where he can raise doubt about the existence of relevant forensic data. In *Caffrey*,[8] for example, defence counsel was able to create sufficient doubt as to the existence of a Trojan Horse virus on the defendant's PC at the relevant time, for the defendant to be acquitted, despite expert testimony to the contrary.

Related to 'stickiness' is the 'analysis' problem created by the volume and nature of the data that an investigator may be required to handle. Modern data media can store vast amounts of data, while networks are capable of transmitting huge bitstreams of data. While an investigator may be able to obtain and preserve such data, the ability to access, manage and analyse it for subsequent presentation in court can present significant problems, from the need to overcome protection mechanisms, to the availability of appropriate resources within time limits imposed by law.

The digitisation of information means that traditionally distinct forms of data are represented in a common language: binary machine code. This creates a 'data type' problem, where existing legal rules treat the forensic obtaining of different types of data differently, e.g. communications content and communications attributes. Determining the applicable procedural regime governing the lawful obtaining of different types of data can be a significant challenge.

An inability to address some or all of these problems can directly impact the prosecutorial process, especially evidential admissibility and the probative value of any forensic data.

Traceability

One of the classic aphorisms of the Internet age is that 'On the Internet, nobody knows you are a dog'.[9] However, in the course of an investigation, the investigator will need to identify the person carrying out the illegal activity, whether canine or not! The process of establishing a real-world person's identity from their Internet-related identity creates a significant forensic and legal hurdle.

Broadly speaking, there are two initial sources of forensic data to assist the identification process; that created by a suspect's use of communication services and the content of a person's communications activities. In the former, we seek to identify the source, and often the recipient, of a communication, based on some unique identifier. This will generally identify the equipment from which the communication originated, and may identify a specific user, such as an email address. However, where the terminal equipment is available for multiple access, proving that a specific person was using the equipment or account at the relevant time is an obvious forensic challenge and potential defence. Successfully completing this forensic trail to a real person raises substantial challenges for investigators.

In respect of communications content, investigators may be able to obtain evidence disclosed by a suspect in the course of his activities, whether knowingly, unwittingly, or inadvertently, such as 'cookies'.[10] In *Vallor*,[11] the virus writer was identified through postings made to various Internet bulletin boards about his activities, under the name of 'Gobo'. One common means of identification is through payment data, such as credit card details, used to purchase online services. In the child abuse case *Landslide*[12] and subsequent 'Operation Ore', for example, the primary source of identification evidence was credit card details registered by subscribers.

It is worth briefly examining some of the complexities that arise when an investigator needs to resolve an IP address to an individual. When utilising any Internet-based service the originator and recipient of a message require an IP address, a unique number that identifies the relevant resources. That IP address is then logically linked to the originator's pseudonym and domain name, e.g. i.n.walden@qmul.ac.uk. However, whilst the IP address is unique, the person to whom it is linked will usually vary. ISPs and corporate networks will generally, for reasons of efficiency, dynamically assign an IP address to a user each time they log on to a service.

Identification in a cyberspace environment is often therefore a four-stage process (Clayton 2005). First, it is necessary to identify the IP address(es) that need(s) to be resolved to a machine or person. The recorded source IP address may, however, have been 'spoofed', where a false source IP address is inserted in the packet headers. While 'spoofing' may be carried out at an individual user level, it may also be done on a commercial level, as a service offered to users wanting to use the Internet anonymously (a 'darknet' service).[13]

Second, one has to establish the entity, such as a CSP, to whom the IP address has been assigned. This can be relatively straightforward, for example using 'whois' software to interrogate one of the regional, national or local registry databases. However, since the registries do not have a requirement to verify such information, a large proportion of it is often inaccurate, either because false information was supplied in the first instance, or because the information is not kept up to date. An alternative is to use a 'traceroute' application to follow the route of the packets across the Internet.[14] In either case, if accurate, an IP address holder will be found. Generally, this will be a CSP or organisation, although an individual may be identifiable if he has a fixed IP address.

Where a block of IP addresses belongs to an entity, the third stage will be to approach the IP holder to match the target IP address to a specific user.[15] This may be achieved by studying one or more historic logs, recording a session's start and end, such as a Dynamic Host Configuration Protocol (DHCP) system for dynamically allocated IP addresses. This process will not be feasible where the IP holder provides an anonymous service such as a cyber café; the user has logged on to an unsecured wireless network or, most commonly, the IP holder does not maintain a complete log of IP address allocation.

The final stage is to obtain the subscriber's account details, such as home address, from the CSP's records. The existence of administrative records will depend on the nature of the connection provided, as well as the method of payment for the service. For 'free' Internet services, the key identification data may consist of the 'Calling Line Identity' (CLI) number of the user's line. As mobile telephones become a standard access device for the Internet, detailed administrative records may not exist for subscribers using 'pay as you go' services.

The above illustrates that the ability to trace a person from their IP address is dependent on the input of different entities and the existence of various logs and records. As will be discussed later, the forensic value of such logs and records has recently prompted governments to impose data retention requirements on CSPs operating at stages 3 and 4, in order to preserve the identification data, rather than depend on the vagaries of an entity's practices and procedures.

Obtaining data

The process for obtaining data generally involves a number of different stages: (a) identifying what data may be available and where it may reside; (b) preserving such data; (c) analysis of the data for intelligence and evidential purposes, and (d) legal presentation of the data and evidence derived from it. There are certain accepted rules that govern these processes. The ACPO Guide promulgates standard forensic practices for obtaining data based on four principles:

Principle 1: No action taken by law enforcement agencies or their agents should change data held on a computer or storage media which may subsequently be relied upon in court.

Principle 2: In exceptional circumstances, where a person finds it necessary to access original data held on a computer or on storage media, that person must be competent to do so and be able to give evidence explaining the relevance and the implications of their actions.

Principle 3: An audit trail or other record of all processes applied to computer based electronic evidence should be created and preserved. An independent third party should be able to examine those processes and achieve the same result.

Principle 4: The person in charge of the investigation (the case officer) has overall responsibility for ensuring that the law and these principles are adhered to.

As noted above, forensic data may be obtained during transmission, or when residing on a resource or device. This section briefly considers some of the pertinent technical features of ICT resources from which digital evidence may be obtained. It should be remembered that every incidence of cybercrime will have a unique life cycle, from first detection and reporting to any eventual proceedings.

Data may be held on a huge variety of types of media. Media vary in respect of mobility and ease of use, from fixed hard drives on computers, to tapes and removable USB flash drives. However, all such media are becoming cheaper, have greater storage capability and operate at greater speeds, all of which feeds into 'analysis' problems in terms of the volumes of data potentially involved.

Most storage media have four-way functionality, enabling data to be written to, read, modified and deleted. Digital media store data in different ways physically, such as magnetic particles and laser-created pits; as well as at a logical level, in terms of partitions, drives and sectors. The ways a device logically handles data has direct implications for subsequent forensic analysis. Microsoft's FAT and NTFS file systems and Unix's FFS system, for example, utilise space on the storage media differently, requiring the use of different analytical techniques to examine data. Under all file systems, however, data is not necessarily stored contiguously, but will often be fragmented in blocks, which are only logically associated through addressing information.

The deletion of data from digital media takes different forms. The deletion of files in standard desktop applications will generally only result in the removal of the addressing information associated with each block of data, or the files are simply treated as deleted and are renamed in another directory, such as the 'Recycle Bin'. As such, the data remains on the media, and is potentially recoverable, until it has been either overwritten by new data, or been deleted by other means. This residual physical representation of erased data is sometimes referred to as 'data remanence', and is one source of the 'stickiness' data problem.

As well as the organisation of files in terms of the characteristics of the digital media, operating systems and applications also use systems for identifying and organising data, in terms of file names, extensions, folders and directories. Such systems often maintain a range of valuable forensic details about the attributes of a data file, in terms of its size and usage. Usage data, such as the date and time at which actions were carried out,[16] is obviously an extremely valuable forensic source, but is also highly vulnerable to claims of inaccuracy, modification and interference. As such, it will often require some form of corroboration using other sources, such as a date in a digital photograph or the actual commission of the offence.

To address the 'integrity' problem, an investigator needs to obtain the data in a manner that is complete, yet minimises interference with the target data. Data may simply be printed and copied, although this may result in alterations to the metadata associated with the target data, creating evidential vulnerabilities. For most digital media, the most common technique used is that of 'imaging'.[17] Imaging involves the acquisition and creation of a complete bitstream image of the digital media, such as hard drive or smart card, in a non-invasive manner. A number of copies of the image are generally created, a master copy for evidential purposes, a copy on which analysis is carried out, and a third that is provided to the suspect for his own verification and analysis purposes. The images are widely accepted as an accurate representation of the original digital media, and the use of such images never appears to have been successfully challenged before the English courts.

One critical element of the process of forensic analysis is the capability to map the events recorded on the various devices to real time, in terms of establishing an accurate chronology of events relating to criminal conduct. Most ICTs will time record; yet such multiplicity, coupled with their susceptibility to inaccuracy, makes mapping events in cyberspace to the real world a considerable forensic challenge. This problem is obviously exacerbated by the transnational context and different time zones within which networks operate.

CSP-derived data

In a cybercrime environment, a substantial amount of evidence may be obtained from those providing communication services, i.e. CSPs. Such evidence may comprise communication content, or the attributes of a communication session, such as the duration of a call. Some such data may be considered as being 'at rest', in that it is stored by the CSP during the provision of its services; other data will be available 'in transmission' across communication networks, through a process of interception. Obtaining access to CSP-derived data is subject to a distinct regulatory framework.

One dominant feature of the modern communications environment is the proliferation of CSPs utilising alternative access and core network technologies, both wireline and wireless. As a consequence, it can be assumed that most data will be transmitted across a number of different networks owned or operated by different legal entities. As such, relevant evidence may need to be obtained from various CSPs within the communication process. Whatever the form of network, the availability of evidence for an investigation is predicated on the network having the capability to obtain and retain relevant content and communications data.

Intercept capability

The term 'intercept capability' is traditionally used to describe the capture of content and communications data, whether 'in transmission' or 'at rest', from a CSP. Under the Regulation of Investigatory Powers Act 2000 (RIPA), a person has a duty to give effect to a warrant if they provide a 'public telecommunication service' or where they 'control' a telecommunication system that is located in the UK (s.11). What constitutes 'control' over a network, system or service in a jurisdiction has become considerably more complex in a modern communications environment. The rise of Mobile Virtual Network Operators and Internet telephony are two prominent examples of market developments that can create significant problems for law enforcement in terms of operating an intercept capability. In both cases, law enforcement may address a request for data access to one CSP, only to find that fulfilment of the request can only be met by a third party provider of network infrastructure.

Compliance with a warrant is subject to a defence that the CSP is not required 'to take any steps which it is not reasonably practicable for him to take' (s.11(5)). However, this is further qualified by section 12 of the RIPA, which provides for a process whereby the Home Secretary can impose a requirement to establish and maintain a specific 'intercept capability'. The Secretary of State has the power to issue a notice to a specified CSP detailing the measures that it must implement in order to establish an interception capability and the timescales within which the requirement must be met.[18]

The costs arising from compliance may be significant, in terms of both capital (e.g. switches with intercept functionality) and operational (e.g. personnel) expenditure. Under the RIPA, the Secretary of State has a duty to ensure that a CSP 'receives such contribution as is, in the circumstances of that person's case, a fair contribution towards the costs incurred' in establishing an 'intercept capability' (s.14). Similarly, in respect of communications data, the Secretary of State has to make 'appropriate contributions towards the costs incurred' by CSPs in responding to requests for information (s.24). LEAs are also required to pay CSPs a fee each time they make a request for data. Shifting some of the financial cost on to LEAs may act as an effective restraint on the use of such techniques.

Communications content

Interception of communication content is governed in England by Part I, Chapter I of the RIPA, supplemented by a Code of Practice.[19] The Act makes it an offence to intercept a communication being transmitted over a public telecommunications system without a warrant issued by the Secretary of State; or over a private telecommunication system without the consent of the system controller (s.1). The RIPA regime is not, however, primarily designed to tackle the activities of those intercepting communications in the furtherance of their criminal activities; rather its purpose is to control the interception, surveillance and other investigative practices of LEAs consistent with the European Convention on Human Rights (ECHR). The European

Court of Human Rights (ECtHR) has repeatedly held English law to breach the Convention in respect of protecting privacy rights of individuals in such circumstances.[20]

The RIPA comprehensively details conduct in respect of an interception that has 'lawful authority'.[21] An 'interception' occurs when communication content is made available during transmission, to a person other than the sender or the intended recipient (s.2(2)). This includes any storage of the communication in the telecommunications system prior to its receipt, such as voicemail or an unread email (s.2(7)). An example of communications stored in the course of their transmission that has recently come to light is a practice referred to as the 'virtual dead drop'. Rather than send a message direct to the recipient, the sender prepares the message in his Web-based email account and saves it to the 'drafts' folder on his account. The intended recipient is then able to access the shared account, review the message and save a draft reply. By utilising a single account, the conspirators reduce the digital footprint created by communications. This is apparently a method used by those involved in the Madrid train bombings in March 2004[22] and by Kafeel Ahmed, the man who drove a car bomb into Glasgow airport.[23]

In contrast to other jurisdictions, the power to authorise communications interception resides not with the judiciary but with the executive branch of government, in the form of a Secretary of State, from the Home Office, Defence or Foreign Office.[24] An interception warrant may only be issued by a Secretary of State where he considers it necessary on the following grounds:

- in the interests of 'national security';
- for the prevention or detection of 'serious crime';
- in order to safeguard the 'economic well-being of the UK'; or
- in response to a request under mutual legal assistance procedures (s.5).

Additionally, an application for a warrant may only be made by those persons listed in the RIPA, such as the Director General of the Serious Organised Crime Agency and the Commissioner of the Metropolitan Police (s.6(2)). The conduct authorised by the warrant must be proportionate to the objective sought, including whether the information 'could reasonably be obtained by other means'.[25] Considerations of proportionality must be assessed by the Secretary of State and also inform management of the warrant's implementation.[26] The implicit assumption being that interception is an investigative technique of last resort.

The warrant must identify a particular subject or premises, against which the interception is carried out (s.8(1)). Where an individual is the subject, interception may be carried out against any communication service used by that person, such as landline, mobile and Internet account, provided such services are detailed in the warrant; in the form of 'addresses, numbers, apparatus or other factors … used for identifying the communications' to be intercepted (s. 8(2)).

A special procedure for *ex post* judicial scrutiny exists through two different mechanisms. First, the Act established the Interception of Communications Commissioner who reviews the exercise and performance of the powers and duties granted to persons under the RIPA and prepares an annual report. The Commissioner has already raised concerns about the level of resource required to operate an effective oversight regime, especially given the volumes involved with communications data.[27] Second, persons are granted a right to bring proceedings, or make a complaint to the Investigatory Powers Tribunal (s.65).[28]

Communications data

As discussed already, establishing the identity of a suspect is obviously the starting point for commencement of criminal proceedings. However, users are often not readily identifiable from the naming and addressing information processed during a communications session. The difficulties associated with this have established a perception of the Internet as a realm of anonymity, where we can engage in conduct without fear of exposure, which in itself has encouraged criminality. However, anonymity is not the default setting in cyberspace and a user's CSP will often have substantial amounts of data in relation to the provision of services that may enable identification.

It is valuable to understand the different types of data that may be generated in our modern communications environment. Broadly speaking, when a CSP provides services, it obtains data from three main sources, listed below.

- Customers and users will disclose information to the CSP.
- Data will be generated by the ICT systems and resources used by the CSP in the provision of its services.
- Data is obtained from third parties, such as other CSPs and payment providers.

Part I, Chapter II of the RIPA uses the term 'communications data' to encompass these diverse sources of forensic material; generally referred to as 'traffic data', 'usage data' and 'subscriber data' (s.21(4), (6)).

Traffic data includes the telephone number of a calling and called party, and the IP address of the sender and recipient of an Internet transmission. As noted earlier, in respect of traceability, such naming and addressing schemes may identify a person, generally the service subscriber rather than the actual user, but may only identify a CSP, IP holder or an item of terminal equipment connected to the network. Establishing the forensic link between such data and an actual person will generally require corroborative data from other sources. Traffic data also includes information about the networks themselves, including the IP addresses of the routers or 'hops' taken by message packets transmitted over the Internet. Such data can be valuable in an investigation, potentially enabling the real origin of the message to be determined where the sender has attempted to spoof his identity or 'launder' his communications through foreign networks.

Usage data would include any time and date-related data, including time/date stamps; duration data generated from recorded events, such as log-in and log-out connection data and itemised telephone call records; information about the amount of data downloaded or uploaded; information concerning connections, disconnections and reconnections; information relating to forwarding or redirection services; and information relating to the use of specific communication services subscribed to, such as instant messaging, web storage capacity or call barring services. One key forensic issue with all time data is the need to account for time zone differentials arising from the diverse location of network components, the preferred method being the use of Co-ordinated Universal Time.[29]

Subscriber data would cover user-disclosed data such as personal preferences, address information for installation and billing purposes; as well as data obtained from a third party, such as a credit reference agency for credit checks. It could include a user's login password, which would potentially enable law enforcement access to protected data. Currently, the vast majority of requests for data are made in respect of subscriber data, rather than traffic or usage data.

In 2007, over 500,000 requests for communications data were made each year by public authorities, although the vast majority came from police and other main investigative agencies.[30] However, this figure does not reflect that a single recorded request often contains requests for data on multiple persons, which would greatly inflate this number. Part I, Chapter II of the RIPA contains powers that enable LEAs to require the disclosure of 'communications data' from a 'telecommunications operator', superseding use of the existing mechanisms. The request may be made to any person who provides a 'telecommunication service', which would include both publicly and privately provisioned services, such as 'hotels, restaurants, libraries and airport lounges'.[31] However, the Government is considering extending the obligation to other types of online service providers, such as social networking sites.

Under the provisions, a 'relevant public authority' can, under an appropriate authorisation, give 'notice' to a CSP requiring access to specified communications data. A notice shall only be issued by a 'designated person' within an authority where it is considered necessary for any of the public interest grounds set out in the Act: national security; preventing or detecting crime or preventing disorder; the economic well-being of the UK; public health and safety; the collection or assessing of tax, duty, levy or related payment, and preventing death or personal injury (s.22(2)). Proportionality considerations when requesting data would include any collateral intrusion on the rights of third parties not under investigation.[32]

The list of those designated as a 'relevant public authority' under Part I, Chapter II, include numerous public bodies, ranging from local authorities, National Health Service authorities to the Food Standards Agency and the Postal Services Commission. However, the Secretary of State has the power to restrict the types of data that may be accessed by a public authority, as well as the purposes for which such data may be used (s.25).

In order to rationalise and standardise requests for communications data, a system of accredited Single Points of Contacts ('SPoCs') has been established for public authorities exercising law enforcement functions, empowered to and responsible for making requests for information to CSPs. Each authority must have a trained individual, or group of individuals, through whom requests for information must be made. The SPoCs are intended to 'help the public authority to regulate itself, by providing internal advice on quality assurance, and will also provide authentication of the public authority'.[33] The latter issue is facilitated by maintenance of a Home Office register, to which CSPs may refer when in receipt of a request for information. A CSP is only required to accept requests from appropriately registered SPoCs and an authority should not try to acquire such data in the absence of an accredited SPoC.[34]

Data retention

As already noted, the patterns created by the communications attributes of criminal and terrorist networks in cyberspace are extremely valuable to law enforcement agencies for discerning the operational nature of such networks. Such evidential data will be generated by the networks, as traffic passes into, across and out of each network, and will often be as transient as the communication session itself. To address such transience, governments have looked to the imposition of express preservation and retention obligations upon the providers of communication services.

Generally, communications data is retained by CSPs for relatively short periods of time, due both to the cost of storage and compliance with data protection rules.[35] However, a criminal investigation may require access to data generated over a considerable period of time, particularly in serious crime cases, such as terrorism or organised crime. Prior to the events of September 11 2001, the issue of data retention had been raised by LEAs, but had been rejected by Government. However, following the attacks, the Government's position on the issue fundamentally shifted and data retention provisions were incorporated as a key initiative in the Anti-Terrorism Crime and Security Act 2001 ('ATCSA'). Part II of the Act established a voluntary code of practice on the retention of communications data, with reserve powers for the Secretary of State to make it mandatory. The Secretary of State was empowered to enter into contractual agreements with individual CSPs about their data retention and retrieval practices, detailing service levels that the CSP must meet and the charges that can be levied against the requesting agencies.

The voluntary scheme has since been superseded by a mandatory regime introduced to transpose a harmonisation measure of the European Union.[36] EU action on data retention followed the 2004 Madrid bombings. The Directive imposes a mandatory minimum retention requirement of six months and a maximum of 24 months (article 6), and the UK has adopted a 12-month period.[37] In terms of costs, the Retention Directive is silent, leaving it to the discretion of member states. The UK has decided to continue with existing arrangements and contribute to any additional costs incurred.[38]

While we have no case law directly addressing the lawfulness of such universal retention under human rights law, an analogy may perhaps be drawn from *R (on the application of S) v. Chief Constable of South Yorkshire and others*.[39] In this test case, the court was asked to consider whether the continued retention of fingerprints, samples or DNA profiles under the Police and Criminal Evidence Act 1984 (PACE) section 64(1A), obtained lawfully by the police, was an interference with a person's private life, under Article 8(1) of the ECHR. The Law Lords, with one exception (Baroness Hale), held that 8(1) was not engaged by such practices; therefore it was not necessary to go on to consider whether it could then be justified under 8(2). This approach differed from that of the Court of Appeal, which had held that 8(1) was engaged, but that 8(2) provided justification.[40] However, on further appeal to the ECtHR, it was held that article 8(1) was engaged and that article 8(2) did not provide an adequate justification.[41] Considerable opposition to this Directive continues to be expressed, not least by business and national data protection authorities.[42] Large-scale data retention must itself be seen as vulnerable to abuse, a new security risk, and concerns have been voiced that such provisions breach data protection and human rights laws, as a disproportionate response to an unmeasured threat.

Suspect-derived data

In the normal chain of events, a cyber-surveillance operation will lead to the identification of one or more suspects and data concerning their illegal conduct. However, the evidential value of the forensic material generated will vary depending on the process involved. At some point in an investigation law enforcement agents will initiate a search and seizure of certain physical locations relating to the suspect to obtain further forensic material.

When carrying out a search and seizure operation, the objective is to obtain any data that may be relevant to the investigation, subject to any rules protecting certain categories of material, such as legally privileged material; and to obtain it in a manner that does not enable any material subsequently adduced as evidence to be successfully challenged. Such data may be contained in various forms of digital media and may comprise physical source documents, such as photographs, or printouts from the media. Where the digital media form part of a computing resource, the process of seizure will vary considerably according to whether the system is operating at the time, and whether it is connected to a network; since the process of closing down a system and disconnecting it from a network may have serious forensic implications.

The main statutory instrument governing seizure, PACE, expressly includes 'any information stored in any electronic form' (s.20) and 'any computer disk or other electronic storage device'.[43] A constable may also require 'any information which is stored in any electronic form and is accessible from the premises to be produced in a form in which it can be taken away …' (s.19(4)), which would enable law enforcement officers to obtain information held on remote systems under a single search warrant, since information in electronic form will be accessible from a networked computer on the searched premises.

A search and seizure warrant can generate problems where relevant material is held on a computer system being used at the time of the search, since any attempt to seize the material may result in either the loss or alteration of the evidence. Another problem for LEAs is the geographical scope of a warrant, where the seized computer is connected to a network; and the volume of data that is generally subject to seizure. The time and expense involved in sifting and scrutinising seized data can be a serious impediment to a process of investigation.

Protected data

Even when data has been lawfully obtained, investigators increasingly find that seized data, or the device on which data resides, is protected by some form of security measure, such as a password or cryptographic mechanism, which renders the data inaccessible, unintelligible or, indeed, undiscovered by investigators. In the US, for example, when the notorious hacker Kevin Mitnick was finally arrested, many of the files found on his computers were encrypted and investigators were never able to access them (US Department of Justice 1999). Protected data is increasingly becoming a standard feature of computing applications; access to such protected data is therefore seen as one of the biggest future challenges for computer forensics.

In the context of criminal procedure, access issues are not simply binary, the data being attainable or not; law enforcement agencies are also subject to temporal constraints, such as custody and prosecution time limits, which may be missed if the data cannot be accessed within a reasonable period of time.

A distinction can also be made between protection mechanisms operating at the level of the ICT resource, such as storage media or a software application, and those that operate on the data itself that is the subject of processing. A password to access a machine, device, directory or file, for example, differs in nature, and is treated differently in law, from a cryptographic technique that creates unintelligible ciphertext. The former are referred to as 'access' protections, while the latter as 'conversion' protections, although the latter is a subset of the former. Protected data should also be distinguished from techniques that can conceal data, such as steganography,[44] where investigators are not even aware of the presence of hidden information.

Protection measures applied to data may be implemented at an individual level, an organisational level, or at any combination of these or other points within the processing life cycle of data. So, for example, an LEA may obtain access to a person's email account by requesting password data under a communications data request to the CSP, either covertly or post-arrest as an alternative to obtaining cooperation from the suspect. A CSP may also be required to remove any encryption protection applied by it as part of its provision of an intercept capability.[45]

The nature of data security technologies means that investigating authorities have essentially three options in respect of gaining access to, or conversion of, protected data they have seized:

- require the person from whom the data has been obtained to access, or convert, the data into an intelligible plain-text format;
- require the person to disclose the necessary information or tools, or provide assistance to enable the authorities to access, or convert, the data into an intelligible format themselves; or

- utilise technologies and techniques that enable the data to be accessed, or converted, without the active involvement of the person from whom the data was obtained.

As coercive investigative techniques, the first two options require lawful authority, and English law contains provisions addressing both situations under the RIPA. With the latter option, the issue is primarily one of having the necessary technical resource that can be applied to the task within the relevant timescales.

As with cybercrime in general, the true scale of the protected data problem is unclear. When the Government first raised the issue in 1999, examples were given where encryption was encountered in cases involving child abuse images, attempted murder and sexual assault, fraud and financial crime and terrorism.[46] However, the Part III provisions were not brought into force until October 2007 purportedly because 'the development and adoption of encryption and other information protection technologies has been slower than was anticipated' (Home Office 2006: para. 6).

Under Part III of the RIPA, 'protected information' means:

any electronic data which, without the key to the data –
(a) cannot, or cannot readily, be accessed, or
(b) cannot, or cannot readily, be put into an intelligible form (s.56(1)).

This definition recognises the distinction between 'access' and 'conversion' protections. A 'key' comprises 'any key, code, password, algorithm or other data the use of which (with or without other keys):

(a) allows access to the electronic data, or
(b) facilitates the putting of the data into an intelligible form' (s.56(1)).

This broad formulation is intended to cover every type of information held, including data that has been memorised.[47] The key may also not be singular, but comprise multiple pieces of data, potentially held or under the control of multiple persons, every one of which may require a notice. Where a person is no longer in possession of a key, and can therefore not comply with the disclosure notice, he is under a duty to supply any information that may facilitate obtaining the key or the protected information in intelligible form (s.50(8), (9)).

Where necessary and proportionate, a person may be required by notice to disclose the 'key' that would enable investigators to render the information intelligible themselves (s.50(3)(c), 51). The Act recognises that such a requirement should only arise when 'special circumstances' are present and it is considered proportionate, bearing in mind the possibility of collateral intrusion with the rights of others. There has been substantial criticism directed at these provisions, especially from elements within the business community and ICT profession. Critics felt that the disclosure requirement undermined the deployment and reliance on the use of cryptographic techniques as a security technology; as well as damaging the UK economy by placing it in an unfavourable position vis-à-vis its trading partners.[48] As a consequence various statutory safeguards were introduced governing the handling of keys by the authorities to whom they are disclosed, breach of which may give rise to civil proceedings for recovery of any loss or damage caused.

Where a legal obligation is imposed upon a person under investigation, a failure to comply will result in sanctions. Under the RIPA, it is an offence if a person 'knowingly fails, in accordance with the notice, to make the disclosure required ...',[49] which carries a maximum two-year prison term.[50] Under the Terrorism Act 2006, this penalty was increased in 'a national security case' to five years.[51] In proceedings for the offence of non-disclosure, a person is presumed to be in possession of the relevant key, for disclosure itself or for rendering the protected information intelligible and disclosing the information, if the prosecution can show, beyond reasonable doubt, that he was in possession of it at any time before the disclosure notice was given.[52] A defendant can challenge this presumption, therefore, if they can adduce sufficient evidence to raise doubt in respect of their possession; show that it was not reasonably practicable to make the disclosure within the time limit, or it was disclosed as soon as reasonably practicable after the time limit.

Where an offence is committed through non-compliance with a lawful requirement, any penalty will need to act as an appropriate deterrent against refusal to comply. It is inevitable, however, that a person may choose not to comply with the request to disclose, thereby accepting the penalty, rather than comply and potentially expose themselves to prosecution for a more serious offence with greater penalties. Whilst such a scenario may be seen as unfortunate, it would seem to be a necessary compromise where the rights of the individual are balanced against the need to protect society.

The raising of an adverse inference against a person in criminal proceedings for a failure to supply certain information raises issues concerning the right to a fair trial, under Article 6 of the ECHR. In particular, it may be viewed as an infringement of the individual's right to silence, right not to self-incriminate. Convention jurisprudence indicates that whilst a conviction may not be based solely or mainly on a refusal to supply such information,[53] an adverse inference may in specified circumstances be drawn from such a refusal when assessing the evidence adduced by the prosecution.[54]

The English courts have had an opportunity to consider such issues in *S and A*.[55] The defendants were both arrested in connection with terrorist offences. In the case of S, he was detained in a room where an encryption key appeared to have been partially entered in the computer. With A, computer materials seized subsequent to his arrest included a computer disk that contained an encrypted area. The defendants appealed against the notices requiring that they disclose the encryption keys on grounds of self-incrimination. The court noted that the legality of this process had to be addressed in two stages. The first question was to determine whether the principle was engaged at all. Relying upon the ECtHR decision in *Saunders*,[56] the court noted that the right not to self-incriminate does not extend to material that can be lawfully obtained and has 'an existence independent of the will of the suspect'. The key was held to be such an independent fact, similar in nature to a urine sample taken from a driver suspected of driving under the influence. However, in addition, it was noted that the defendant's knowledge of the key could also be an incriminating fact. The second stage for the court, if it is assumed that the principle is engaged, is to consider whether the interference with the right consequent upon the issuance of the s.49 notice is necessary and proportionate. Here the court held that the procedural safeguards and limitations on usage detailed in the RIPA were sufficient to negate any claim of unfairness under the PACE, s.78.

The third approach is for investigators to break the protection mechanism. The totality of seized material may provide the possibility of shortcut attacks, such as keys or passwords being recovered from disk space or memory sticks, or via back doors found or built into the technology; or investigators will have to engage in brute force attacks, involving heavy computational processing. The viability of the latter course of action, converting the data into an intelligible form through utilising available techniques, will depend on a number of factors, including the strength of the security technology, the multiplicity of protection systems employed, and the period within which the data needs to be converted. One stated reason for the Government's plans under the Terrorism Bill 2006 to extend the period of detention without trial, from the then 14 days to 90 days, was to give investigators more time to work through encrypted data.

Some governments have recognised the need to establish some such 'in-house' technical capability to assist law enforcement investigations. In 2001, the UK Government established a National Technical Assistance Centre (NTAC) that is designed to provide the necessary technical expertise to law enforcement agencies, on a 24-hour basis, to try and access protected data without the involvement of the suspect; at an initial capital cost of £25 million (Home Office 2001). NTAC also provides a clearing-house for liaison with industry in seeking access to protected material, both seized and intercepted data.

Breaking the protections applied to data will utilise a variety of techniques. The use of covert surveillance techniques prior to the seizure of protected material, such as the installation of keyloggers on a suspect's machine, may become a standard technique deployed in anticipation that data is protected. In the longer term, the ability of LEAs to access protected data will depend on developments in technology, since techniques may be developed which are essentially incapable of being overcome.

Evidential issues

The next stage in the criminal justice process is the presentation of evidence obtained to a court or tribunal of fact in the course of criminal proceedings. The process is governed by set rules and procedures, from pre-trial to the hearing, designed primarily to safeguard the rights of defendants. Computer-derived evidence may present a range of issues that need to be addressed, whether by the prosecution, defence or court.

The evidence presented before the court is shaped by a number of factors. First, the nature of the offences with which the perpetrator has been charged will dictate the issues to be proved in a court of law. The choice of charge will have resource implications, which may be a determinant factor. Third, the availability of evidence obtained forensically will often dictate the charges laid against the defendant. Encrypted data, for example, may force the prosecution to proceed on the basis of charges for which the evidence is legible. Fourth, a conspiracy may involve international elements in jurisdictions with whom no suitable mutual legal assistance procedure exists, which can render evidence gathering effectively impossible.

Pre-trial disclosure

A fundamental element of an individual's right to a fair trial under article 6 of the ECHR is the principle of 'equality of arms', such that the defendant is put, as far as possible, in the same position as the state prosecutor in respect of access to legal advice and the evidence upon which he is to be tried.[57] To meet this obligation requires that the prosecution disclose to the defendant the evidence that they intend to use in the course of the prosecution.[58] While disclosure is a critical component of fairness, it is also considered to be 'one of the most abused', resulting in substantial inefficiencies in the operation of the criminal justice system and obstructing justice.[59] The difficulty of handling computer-derived material is one area where the disclosure process can struggle to function properly.

While disclosure is an element of criminal proceedings, such issues first arise in the course of an investigation, as an element of the forensic process. The principle of fairness at the heart of the prosecutor's disclosure obligation extends backwards to the investigative stage, placing a duty upon an investigator to pursue all reasonable lines of inquiry, whether supporting the case against the suspect or otherwise.[60] So, for example, if a suspect claims that a seized computer was used by more than one person, the claim must be investigated, both in terms of interviewing such other persons and the analysis carried out of the data found on the hard disk.

The prosecutor's duty continues throughout the course of the proceedings and extends both to evidence that the prosecution intend to use, as well as 'unused'[61] material that might undermine its case or assist the accused. A failure by the prosecutor to disclose aspects of his case prior to the trial may result in the evidence being held inadmissible. A failure to comply with the duty of disclosure in respect of unused material, because it is lost or destroyed, quite conceivable with computer-derived evidence, may result in the proceedings being stayed for abuse of process.[62] A failure by the defence to disclose may result in the judge or jury drawing an inference from such behaviour.[63]

The disclosure obligation has certain implications for digital investigations. First, seized data storage media may contain the equivalent of many thousands of pieces of paper. It is estimated, for example, that 27 gigabytes of data if printed would produce a stack of A4 paper 920 metres high,[64] which means producing hard copies of all material will be unfeasible. Only a small proportion may be actually used by the prosecution, but it must all be detailed in the 'disclosure schedule' and be made available to the defence. Indeed, the volume involved sometimes means that not all material is examined by investigators. In such situations, the disclosure officer may simply have to state the reasons why the material has not been examined and the fact that it is not known whether such material meets the 'undermine or assist' test.[65]

As well as seized material, there may be substantial evidence held by a victim or third party, to whom access may be needed, but which they may be unwilling or inefficient about providing. While difficulties obtaining third-party evidence may impact on the fairness of a trial, the demand for such information may also interfere with the rights of the third party, such as the privacy or confidentiality of information.[66]

Admissibility

While much time and resource may be expended during a digital investigation, the product of such forensic activity may not be permitted as evidence in any subsequent criminal proceedings. Admissibility is concerned with the ability to submit evidence into court for consideration by the judge or jury. Our interest in questions of admissibility concerns the extent to which the forensic product may be excluded from the court. Indeed, challenges to the admissibility of such evidence are a key defence strategy in cybercrime prosecutions (Smith *et al.* 2004). The more vulnerable computer- and network-derived evidence is to exclusion, the more problematic will be the prosecution of cybercrimes.

Evidential exclusions can be broadly distinguished into two categories: the first focuses on the material itself, while the second on the circumstances through which it is obtained. In the first, the unreliability of the material is the primary concern, either because the person was not witness to the facts, as in hearsay; or because the reliability of the source from which it is derived is considered vulnerable, as computers were treated in the early years. In the second, the policy concerns are the activities of the investigators in obtaining the material. This can be further subdivided into 'protective exclusions', where the objective is to protect the investigative process, which is the case with the inadmissibility of intercept product; and 'fairness exclusions', where the rights of the defendant have been, or could be, infringed were the material to be admitted. These exclusions may occur through statutory prohibition or through judicial discretion.

As well as fair trial concerns related to procedural rules governing the investigative process, the concept of a fair trial is also enshrined in human rights instruments, specifically the ECHR, Article 6, to which English courts must give consideration. In addition, a trial may be considered unfair where the investigative process involved a breach of other human rights, such as the right to privacy, at Article 8. LEAs must therefore give mind to such exclusionary rules in the course of a digital investigation, since their application may be triggered by the choice and manner in which the investigation is carried out.

The historic basis for presenting evidence in court is through the use of witnesses, persons capable of giving testimony about what they witnessed and being subjected to cross-examination by opposing counsel. As such, documentary evidence has been treated somewhat cautiously due to the perceived difficulties of challenging it. A fundamental distinction has existed in English law between the concepts of 'real' and 'hearsay' evidence. Real evidence is direct from the witness, while hearsay may be described as 'second-hand' evidence the truth of which cannot be directly testified to. Whether computer-derived evidence is real or hearsay in a particular instance will depend on the nature of the information being fed into the computer system. Where computers are operating in a mechanistic way, as automatic recording systems or simply as calculating tools, the evidence they produce is real.[67]

Due to its perceived unreliability, the law has historically excluded hearsay evidence from court. However, as documentary evidence has become the norm in most cases, legal reform has removed many of the barriers to the admissibility of hearsay evidence. The Criminal Justice Act 2003 has further enhanced the admissibility of hearsay evidence in criminal proceedings by codifying existing rules and removing the common law rule against the admissibility of hearsay evidence.[68] Where a representation is made by a machine, but depends on the accuracy of the information supplied to it by a person, then such a representation is not admissible unless the accuracy of the information can be proved; this reflects the old computer adage: 'garbage in, garbage out'.

Despite this liberalisation in respect of hearsay, the courts also retain a general discretion to exclude such evidence.[69] Given the volume of material potentially generated from digital media, both content and metadata, this discretion to exclude may prove valuable to the courts.

Until 2000, section 69 of the PACE imposed special rules governing the admissibility of evidence derived from computers in criminal proceedings. Such rules reflected a widely held view that computers 'are not infallible …occasionally malfunction … often have "bugs"' and therefore 'must be regarded as imperfect devices'.[70] However, the rules presented an increasing obstacle to the prosecution of computer-based crime and led to their eventual repeal. Nevertheless, many of the issues raised in relation to this 'old' admissibility requirement continue to be relevant in relation to the exclusion of hearsay evidence and the probative value of computer-derived evidence, especially in relation to issues of data integrity.

Under section 69, for all computer evidence it had to be shown that there were no reasonable grounds for believing that the evidence was inaccurate because of improper use of the computer; and that at all material times the computer was 'operating properly', or if not, that any improper operation did not affect the accuracy of the evidential product. To satisfy a court that these conditions had been met, it was necessary to obtain either a certificate or oral testimony from a person who occupies 'a responsible position' in relation to the operation of the computer system.[71] Therefore, the evidential burden fell on the party relying on the evidence, generally the prosecution. The broad nature of the language used presented obvious opportunities for the defence to challenge computer-derived evidence. The conditions were therefore the subject of significant consideration by the courts, requiring the court to hold a trial within a trial (voir dire).

In a networked environment, for example, did the requirement hold in respect of each and every machine involved in the processing of the evidential information? In *Cochrane*,[72] an appeal against a prosecution for theft of monies from a building society's cash machines was upheld because the Crown were unable to adduce evidence about the operation of the company's mainframe computer that had authorised the withdrawal, as well as the cash machine itself. However, identifying and certifying that all the relevant computers in an Internet environment were 'operating properly' would be impossible.[73] Generally, two broad categories of argument would be pursued by defence counsel. First, the system had faults, errors or other malfunctions that impacted on the reliability of the data produced from the system.[74] Second, that the criminal conduct itself had generated such faults, errors or malfunctions in the computer system or its data content.[75]

One category of evidence that is considered to be inadmissible is data obtained 'in transmission', through interception. The purpose of the exclusion is to protect from disclosure, forensic inquiry and defence counsel matters related to the operation of the warrant regime and the activities of the intelligence and law enforcement agencies. The exclusion is applicable in both criminal and civil proceedings; although intercept evidence *would* be admissible when it does not reveal anything about the activities of UK LEAs, such as the product of 'unofficial or private eavesdropping'[76] or foreign intercept product.[77]

Over the years, there have been calls from parliamentary committees and others for reform of the current rules, to bring the UK into line with other jurisdictions that allow the admission of intercept evidence. The Home Secretary is again currently considering a change, as opposition from the law enforcement community diminishes. Two problems for Government remain to be solved; the concern that disclosures about intelligence activities may prejudice the interests of the intelligence services, and the issue of disclosure and the potential volume of material involved.

While the previous grounds for exclusion have direct relevance to computer- and network-derived evidence, there is also a general power given to courts to exclude evidence on grounds of fairness, under s.78 of PACE. Considerations of fairness extend back to the manner in which the evidence was obtained, not just the trial itself. The sole consideration when deciding to exclude under s.78 is one of fairness; therefore, a court should not exclude simply to punish an investigating agency for its failure to comply with procedural obligation, since it already has jurisdiction to order a stay for abuse of process.

Probative value or evidential weight

Defence applications for evidential excluded will generally target either the reliability of the evidence or the process under which it was obtained. Where such applications are rejected and the evidence admitted, defence have a second opportunity to challenge the reliability of evidence during trial by casting doubt on the probative value or weight that should be given by the judge or jury to such evidence in proving all the elements of the offence. The defence objective is to raise sufficient doubt to undermine the standard of proof required of the prosecution.

What weight or value should be given to computer-derived evidence? In the absence of statutory guidance, a court may be referred to other sources of guidance that may be considered relevant to either the conditions in which the evidence was held by the forensic source or the manner in which it was obtained. ACPO Guidelines, for example, although designed to support investigators, inevitably also provide potential grounds upon which defence counsel may challenge the probative value of computer-derived evidence, where such guidance has not been followed.

In general the features that computer-derived evidence must exhibit can be drawn from the field of data security, since the features that an organisation needs to protect its data are comparable to the features that evidence should display: authenticity, integrity and accountability.

Authenticity

Authenticity is concerned with the origin of the material and can be further subdivided into two tests. The first is the need to establish a link between the material and the accused. Such evidence depends on investigators being able to address the 'identity problem'. The location of the source computer may mean that multiple users had potential access to the machine at the relevant time, which can make it difficult to show 'beyond reasonable doubt' that the accused was the person with 'his fingers on the keyboard'.

In a networked environment, where the illegal content or the act is only evidenced from remote sources, authenticity will mean establishing an adequate evidential link between the material and the virtual identity used, and then between that and the defendant. As much as machines may have multiple users, online identities may be shared, compromised or 'spoofed', where someone deliberately inserts incorrect identification details into a message.

Even when it is beyond dispute that the source computer belongs to the suspect, a second course of challenge is for the accused to deny that he was aware that such illegal or incriminating material was present on his machine; the so-called 'Trojan Horse' defence. Widespread ignorance about the manner in which computers and the Internet work, coupled with the technical reality that data can be placed surreptitiously on a remote machine, means that such claims can be a fruitful basis for disputing prosecution evidence. In *Schofields*,[78] for example, the prosecution was unable to offer evidence against the defence expert's report that a 'Trojan Horse' virus found on the machine of the accused could have placed the indecent images on the hard drive without his knowledge.[79]

A second authenticity test is to link the material to the relevant computer or system, the 'computer source' test. This is partly an extension of the person/material test, since people operate in a networked environment through computers. However, it also arises from the manner in which some environments operate. For example, what is displayed on a computer screen when a 'webpage' is downloaded over the Internet may potentially comprise a mosaic of material drawn from different computers based in different jurisdictions, the image being assembled only at the moment it is requested. Such mechanisms have apparently been used for the distribution of child abuse images.

Integrity

In terms of integrity, the concern is to show that the material is accurate and complete. This essentially reflects the 'operating properly' test that was previously an admissibility test under section 69. While the burden of proof has been shifted, the party adducing computer-derived evidence may still need to ensure that they have the necessary evidence, whether oral or documented, to be able to refute any serious challenge raised as to the integrity of evidence. For a complex system, this may require an array of witnesses with familiarity of the different components.

Accountability

Accountability is concerned with the circumstances under which evidence is obtained and subsequently handled. Computer-derived evidence is notoriously vulnerable to alteration, which extends from the manner of obtaining it, the acquisition process discussed above, to the handling of such evidence by investigators, prosecutors and expert witnesses at all stages until trial, the 'chain of custody test' (Sommer 1998). This could be particularly relevant where a digital copy of an original item of evidence was being relied upon in court.[80]

A simple example of the vulnerability of digital evidence to alteration is a document created using Microsoft Word. As well as the document, the application generates metadata about the document, for example detailing the time and date the document was created, modified and accessed. However, an investigator, when accessing such a document may inadvertently alter the document, in some way and therefore alter such metadata.[81] Alterations made to a file once it is in the possession of an investigator obviously creates a strong basis upon which to raise a challenge to the probative value of evidence. LEAs therefore need to follow procedures designed to minimise such accountability threats and ensure the provenance of any adduced evidence, including disk 'imaging' techniques and filming screen shots.

Expert witnesses

The complexities of obtaining and presenting computer-derived evidence to a court will mean that in many cases expert witnesses will be required. The expert will be required to explain to the judge and jury the evidence being adduced, since much computer-derived evidence is unintelligible to the normal person. The person will generally be concerned with the properties of the ICTs from which the evidence is derived, rather than the content of the retrieved material. An expert essentially acts as an interpreter, addressing those matters outside lay experience and knowledge. As such, the role of an expert is not simply to present facts, but also to offer opinions and interpretations on matters on which he has expertise.

Under English law, both the prosecution and defence team will need to make use of the services of 'expert witnesses', although they are both under a duty to be impartial. The prosecution expert will generally be engaged at an earlier stage in the proceedings than the defence expert, in order to carry out a range of tasks, such as assisting law enforcement at the scene of the crime. The defence expert will be looking for any flaws in the evidence itself; the procedure under which it was collected, analysed and presented; possible arguments that may be used by defence counsel, or, indeed, confirming to the instructing solicitor that the evidence does not support the defendant's contentions, which may facilitate a guilty plea.

The prosecution expert will usually draft a technical report which will then be disclosed to the defence and reviewed by their expert, who will draft a response report. Generally, although there will be areas of disagreement and challenge between the two reports, the experts will also be encouraged to identify those issues upon which there is agreement and these points will form the contents of a single report for submission to the court and consideration by the jury. This may include, for example, an agreed glossary of terms to describe various elements and operations of ICTs.

One problem with experts in the fields of computer and communications technologies is the huge range of systems and applications that may be involved and therefore the range of skills required of an expert. An expert in Unix systems, for example, may not be able to assess IP-based transmission protocols and networks. The technology is also developing so rapidly that an expert's knowledge, if he is no longer actively working in an area, may become outdated relatively rapidly. Therefore, a complex case may require the use of a series of experts. However, there is also a general absence of formalised professionalism within the field of computing, which means that it may be difficult for lawyers to assess whether an expert's skills are appropriate and sufficient for the tasks before him; let alone whether he has the necessary communication skills to present effectively in court. Expertise will generally comprise a mix of qualifications and experience.

In other evidential fields, controversy about the admissibility of expert testimony has arisen where the expertise is considered 'novel and untried', i.e. where the science underpinning the expertise is not well established.[82] While such questions about evidence in respect of the manner in which ICTs operate are unlikely to be raised, a challenge could arise where the expert utilises novel forensic techniques, such as self-authored software tools, to analyse and present conclusions about data under investigation.

Conclusion

Evidence gathering will generally require the deployment of various investigative techniques, covert and coercive. While these techniques are by no means new, their deployment within an ICT environment can challenge traditional procedural concepts. The needs of law enforcement have to be balanced against the rights of the perpetrator, the victim, and others caught up in the investigative process. In the current political environment, that complex balancing compromise has shifted decisively in favour of law enforcement. The shift has been most forcefully felt by CSPs, with ever greater obligations and demands being placed upon them.

Seizing systems and data may have become a relatively pedestrian exercise, but accessing and analysing it within the time and resource constraint imposed presents a significant and growing challenge. Choices inevitably have to be made, which can operate in favour of perpetrators of cybercrimes. Addressing the data problems created by digital investigations requires a variety of approaches, legal, procedural and technical. However, the forensic challenges increase in complexity when the computer crime involves an international dimension.

Computer-derived evidence is prevalent in the vast majority of legal proceedings today. Such evidence was initially viewed with considerable distrust by legislators, legal professionals and public alike, often born primarily out of ignorance. There remains considerable scope to challenge computer-derived evidence, based in part on the forensic processes. For law enforcement agencies it has required appropriate training and resources to ensure that such evidence can form the basis of a successful prosecution. From a defence perspective, there are concerns that the scarcity of resources in this complex area can impact on the quality of representation that defendants receive.

Notes

1 The chapter is based on material previously published in Walden (2007).
2 E.g. In July 2005, the Centrex National Specialist Law Enforcement Centre (NSLEC) and the National Centre for Applied Learning Technologies (NCALT) launched a 'High Tech Crime First Responder E-Learning Programme' for police officers and staff. See www.centrex.police.uk
3 For example, the University of Glamorgan offers a BSc or HND in Computer Forensics.
4 For example, the Council for the Registration of Forensic Practitioners, established in 2000 (www.crfp.org.uk).
5 The fourth edition, published in July 2007, is available at http://www.acpo.police.uk/asp/policies/Data/ACPO%20Guidelines%20v18.pdf
6 See generally Walden (2007) at Chapter 5.
7 E.g. *Atkins* v. *DPP*; *Goodland* v. *DPP* [2000] 2 All ER 425; [2000] 1 WLR 1427.
8 Southwark Crown Court, 17 October 2003.
9 *New Yorker* cartoon, 5 July 1993.
10 'Cookies' may be configured to include user names, passwords and other identification data.
11 [2004] 1 Cr App R (S) 319.
12 *US* v. *Reedy*, 304 F 3d 358, 60 Fed R Evid Serv 133 (5th Cir(Tex) Aug 26, 2002).
13 E.g. www.anonymizer.com
14 See http://www.webopedia.com/TERM/T/traceroute.html Traceroute data may also be misleading, see Clayton (2005: 3.5.3).
15 Determining time can itself be difficult, due to machine errors and time values (e.g. time zones and daylight saving).

16 The three primary date systems are creation date, last modified date and last accessed date.

17 See, for example, EnCase (www.encase.com) used by the majority of LEAs in the UK.

18 The Regulation of Investigatory Powers (Maintenance of Interception Capability) Order 2002 (SI No. 1931).

19 Home Office, 'Interception of Communications Code of Practice'.

20 E.g. *Malone* v. *UK* [1984] 7 EHRR 14 and *Halford* v. *UK* (1997) IRLR 471.

21 Sections 1(5)(c), 3, 4 and 5.

22 *New York Times*, 'Unsent e-mail helped plotters co-ordinate Madrid bombings', 30 April 2006, available at www.nytimes.com

23 See BBC News, 'Doctor admits car bomb charge', 11 April 2008, which states that the terrorist's brother had been alerted 'to a draft e-mail available to read online'.

24 In addition, the Northern Ireland ministers and Scottish ministers have devolved powers to issue warrants, but only in respect of 'serious crime' (s.5(3)(b)).

25 *Ibid.* s.5(2)(b) and (4).

26 Interception Code, above, note 19, at para. 2.5.

27 Report of the Interception of Communications Commissioner for 2004 (HC 549), November 2005, ('IC Report 2004'), at para. 22.

28 See www.ipt-uk.com

29 Otherwise known as 'Greenwich Mean Time'.

30 Report of the Interception of Communications Commissioner for 2007, at para. 3.7.

31 Code 2007, at paras 2.15–2.16.

32 Code 2007, at paras 2.5–2.6.

33 Statement made by Caroline Flint, Home Office Minister, at House of Commons Standing Committee on Delegated Legislation, Hansard, 4 November 2003, Col. 024.

34 Code 2007, at para. 3.15.

35 The Privacy and Electronic Communications (EC Directive) Regulations 2003 (SI No. 2426).

36 Directive 2006/24/EC on the retention of data generated or processed in connection with the provision of publicly available electronic communications services or of public communications networks and amending Directive 2002/58/EC; OJ L 105/54, 13 April 2006 ('Retention Directive').

37 The Data Retention (EC Directive) Regulations 2009, SI No. 859.

38 *Ibid.*, at 11.

39 [2004] UKHL 39.

40 (2003) 1 All ER 148.

41 *S and Marper* v. *UK*, ECtHR, 4 December 2008.

42 See, for example, the Article 29 Working Party Opinion 113/2005, 21 October 2005.

43 Serious Organised Crime and Police Act 2005 (SOCPA), s.66(3)(c).

44 Steganography is the science of concealing information in other information, from the Greek for 'covered writing'.

45 For example in compliance with a RIPA section 12 notice.

46 See DTI Consultation Document, *Building Confidence in Electronic Commerce* (URN 99/642), March 1999.

47 Part III Code, at para. 3.11.

48 For example, the *Financial Times*, Leader, 'RIP, R.I.P', 14 July 2000.

49 RIPA, s.53(1).

50 *Ibid.*, s.53(5)(a).
51 RIPA, s.53(5A), (5B).
52 *Ibid.*, s.53(2).
53 Except for a specific offence of non-disclosure.
54 See *Murray* v. *UK* (1996) 22 EHRR 29, at paras 41–58.
55 [2008] EWCA Crim 2177.
56 *Saunders* v. *UK* [1996] 23 EHRR 313, at para. 69.
57 For example, *Jespers* v. *Belgium* (1981) 27 DR 61.
58 Criminal Procedure and Investigations Act 1996.
59 Court of Appeal, 'Disclosure: A Protocol for the control and management of unused material in the Crown Court', 2006, at para. 1.
60 CPIA, s.23(1)(a). See also CPS Disclosure Manual, at para. 3.5.
61 Unused in the sense that it does not form part of the prosecution's case.
62 *R (on the application of Ebrahim)* v. *Feltham Magistrates Court* [2001] 2 Cr App R 23.
63 CPIA, s.11. See *Tibbs* [2000] 2 Cr App R 309.
64 ACPO Guide, at p. 34. Available from: http://www.acpo.police.uk/asp/policies/Data/ACPO%20Guidelines%20v18.pdf
65 *Ibid.*
66 *Alibhai and others* [2004] EWCA Crim 681.
67 For example, the *Statute of Liberty* [1968] 2 All ER 195; *Castle* v. *Cross* [1984] Crim L R 682; *Sophocleous* v. *Ringer* [1988] RTR 52.
68 Part II, Chapter 2.
69 CJA, s.126(1).
70 Steyn J., in *Minors* [1989] 1 WLR 441, 443D–E.
71 See *R* v. *Shephard* (1993) 1 All ER 225.
72 [1993] Crim LR 48.
73 See *Waddon* [2000] All ER (D) 502.
74 See *DPP* v. *McKeown and Jones* [1997] 1 WLR 295.
75 *Governor of Brixton Prison and another*, ex parte *Levin* (1996) 4 All ER 350.
76 In *Attorney-General's Reference (No. 5 of 2002) sub nom R* v. *W* (2005) 1 AC 167, at 174H.
77 See *R* v. *P and others* (2001) 2 All ER 58.
78 Reported in The Times Online, 18 April 2003.
79 This also arose in *Julian Green*, Exeter Crown Court in July 2003.
80 *Kajala* v. *Noble* (1982) 75 Cr App R 149.
81 For example, if you go to the menu, Tools, Word Count, recounting the words in a document constitutes a recorded modification.
82 For example, *Gilfoyle* [2001] 2 Cr App R 57.

Further reading

For a general treatment of the subject matter in this chapter within a broader context, see Walden, I. (2007) *Computer Crimes and Digital Investigations* (Oxford: OUP). From a US perspective, the leading text is Casey, E. (2004) *Digital Evidence and Computer Crime* (Academic Press). The leading text on English law of evidence is *Cross and Tapper on Evidence* (2007) (Oxford: OUP). For a comparative study of cybercrimes in court, see Smith, R., Grabosky, P. and Urbas, G. (2004) *Cyber Criminals on Trial*. Cambridge: Cambridge University Press.

References

Association of Chief Police Officers (ACPO) Guide: 34. Available from http://www. acpo.police.uk/asp/policies/Data/ACPO%20Guidelines%20v18.pdf

Clayton, R. (2005) 'Anonymity and Traceability in Cyberspace', University of Cambridge, November, at http://www.cl.cam.ac.uk/~rnc1/thesis.pdf, at 2.2.

Home Office (2001) 'Head of NTAC announced' (096/2001). Press Release, 30 March. London: Home Office.

Home Office (2006) *Investigation of Protected Electronic Information*. Consultation Paper, June: para. 6. London: Home Office.

Smith, R., Grabosky, P. and Urbas, G. (2004) *Cyber Criminals on Trial*. Cambridge: Cambridge University Press, 62.

Sommer, P. (1998) 'Digital footprints: Assessing computer evidence', *Criminal Law Review*, Special Edition, December.

US Department of Justice (1999) Press Release, 9 August, available at www.usdoj.gov/ criminal/cybercrime/mitnick.htm

Walden, I. (2007) *Computer Crimes and Digital Investigations*. Oxford: Oxford University Press.

Glossary

Advanced fee fraud Also known as the Nigerian Letter Scam, this fraud typically works by offering the victim large returns in return for assistance in extracting monies which are supposedly held captive in bank accounts in another country. An 'advanced fee' is requested from the victim to assist with the extraction, but he or she never gets to see a share of the (in reality non-existent) millions promised.

Anonymity The ability to engage in social action and communication without having one's identity available to others.

Anti-globalisation movement A broadly based social protest movement that emerged during the 1990s, in resistance to economic globalisation and its control by Western governments and corporations.

Avatar A computer user's representation of himself/herself or alter ego in graphical form. Users enter virtual social worlds such as Second Life as *avatars*.

Child Developmental stage in the early years of life. Who counts as a child, and which distinctive characteristics are associated with being a child (childhood) are subject to great variation across cultures and history.

Child pornography Representations featuring a child or children depicted in an explicitly sexualised manner and/or engaging in sexual activity. Such representations include records of actual child sexual abuse, as well as various images (such as drawings and animations) that have not required the participation or presence of a child for their production. A child may variously be defined for the purposes of child pornography as (a) a pre-pubescent, or (b) an individual who may have physically matured but who is still under the legal age of majority. Given legal differences across countries, any given article may or may not be deemed to be child pornography dependent on how the age of legal majority or sexual maturity are defined.

Computer forensics Specialism within forensic science that focuses upon the acquisition of legal evidence derived from computer systems and their associated media.

Control of the body An aspect of surveillance achieved via an interface of technology and corporeality that can range from direct physical contact between flesh and technological device, to more oblique or covert methods of monitoring and codifying the body.

Copyright Those property rights associated with 'original' expressions, be they in visual, spoken, written, audio or other forms. The possession of copyright over an expression entitles the holder to control its copying and distribution.

Cracking A generally derogatory term used to describe activities associated with 'hacking' in its second sense, that of unauthorised access to computer systems.

Crime Any act that contravenes law and is subject to prosecution and punishment by the state. See also **Deviance**.

Criminalisation The application of the label 'criminal' to particular behaviours or groups, this term reflects the state's power – transmitted via the media, among other institutions – to regulate, control and punish selectively.

Cybercrime Any criminal activity that takes place within or by utilising networks of electronic communication such as the Internet.

Cyberspace The interactional space or environment created by linking computers together into a communication network.

Cyberstalking Stalking that takes place via online communication mechanisms such as email, chatrooms, instant messaging, social networking sites, and discussion lists. See also **Stalking.**

Cyber-terrorism Activity that seeks to realise political ends by unlawful (and usually violent) means, and that (1) utilises electronic communication networks to further those ends (such as the dissemination of propaganda, fundraising or recruitment) and/or (2) targets computer networks and information systems for attack.

Dataveillance Surveillance that focuses not upon the visual or other tracking of the physical individual, but on collecting, collating and analysing data about the individual's activity, often in the form of electronic records.

Denial-of-service An attack on a networked computer or computers that disrupts normal operations to such an extent that legitimate users can no longer access their services.

Deviance Behaviour that may not necessarily be criminal, but which may transgress collective norms about appropriate or acceptable behaviour. While crimes are subject to formal, legal sanctions, those actions deemed deviant may be subject to informal sanctions such as social stigmatisation and denunciation.

Digital divide Patterns of socially embedded inequality that differentiate persons according to their ability to access and/or use new communication technologies. See also **Social inclusion and exclusion**.

Downloading The act of copying digital material posted or made available online into the storage medium on one's computer.

e-commerce Market economic activity undertaken via the Internet or similar electronic communication networks.

'Effects' research A tradition of research that focuses on the impact or effects of media texts, including Web-based texts, on audience attitudes or behaviours. Although media influence is a popular explanation for much crime and other behaviours, including suicide among the young, much 'effects' research has been discredited for isolating media influence from all other variables.

Encryption Techniques and tools associated with encoding or scrambling data in such as way as to render it incomprehensible to others not in possession of a 'key' that is needed to decypher the data into its original legible form.

File sharing The practice of allowing others to make copies of files stored on a computer via downloading. The practice is generally associated with the sharing of music, movies, images and software via websites dedicated to such copying.

Globalisation The social, economic, political and cultural processes in which local and national spatial limits on interaction are overcome, and thus come to span the globe.

Hacking A term with two distinctive meanings. Firstly, the act of creative problem-solving when faced with complex technical problems; and, secondly, illicit and usually illegal activities associated with unauthorised access to, or interference with, computer systems. The latter is often referred to as **Cracking.**

Hacktivism Political activism and social protest that uses hacking tools and techniques.

Hate speech Any form of speech or representation that depicts individuals or groups in a derogatory manner with reference to their 'race', ethnicity, gender, religion, sexual orientation, or physical or mental disability in such a manner as to promote or provoke hatred.

Hidden crime Criminal acts that tend to go largely unobserved, unremarked and unrecorded in official assessments and measures of criminal activity.

Identity-related crime The unauthorised appropriation and use of an individual's personal identifying details, or the alteration and/or fabrication of personal identifying information, used to commit a criminal offence.

Indecency Any form of representation, expression or action (especially of a sexual nature) which may be held to be potentially offensive to the sensibilities of some or most of a society's members. In many (though not all) Western democracies, expressions which may be considered indecent are nevertheless tolerated and not subject to strict legal prohibition.

Information society A stage of socio-economic development in which the importance previously allocated to the production of material goods and resources is superseded by the centrality of knowledge and information in economic activity.

Information warfare The use, management, manipulation and/or disruption of information flows against an opponent or enemy.

Intangible goods Goods over which an individual or other legally recognised entity (e.g. a company) has rights of possession, but which do not take a materially tangible form.

Intellectual property Property which takes the form of ideas, expressions, signs, symbols, designs, logos, and similar intangible forms.

Internet The publicly accessible network of computers that emerged in the 1970s and came to span the globe by the late 1990s.

Internet auctions Online marketplaces enabling individuals and businesses to post a wide variety of items for sale.

Legal pluralism The differences in legal regulations and prohibitions apparent across different states.

Malicious software A general term for a variety of computer codes (such as viruses, logic bombs and Trojan Horses) which are designed to disrupt or interfere with a computer's normal operation.

Moral panic An unwarranted or excessive reaction to a perceived problem of crime, deviance or social disorder, often produced by representations in the mass media.

Netizen More than just somebody who uses the Internet, a *netizen* is somebody who is a good citizen of an online community. Some *netizens* have been involved in constructing parts of the Net and forming it into a major social force. Others are simply members of mailing lists and discussion groups, sharing information and opinion.

Obscenity A notoriously slippery term used to denote representations, expressions or actions (often of a sexual nature) which are held to be generally offensive and thus unacceptable by society at large. Obscenity is almost invariably subject to legal prohibition and formal, criminal sanctions. Just what constitutes an 'obscenity' is, however, deeply contested, and subject to profound variation across cultural contexts and to change over time.

Official crime statistics Measures of the scope, scale and nature of criminal offending compiled and published by the state and allied criminal justice agencies.

Paedophilia The sexual attraction among adults towards children of either sex. The term is applied somewhat indiscriminately to denote both 'lookers' (for example, those who download abusive images of children from the Internet) and 'doers' (those who actually abuse children themselves).

Phishing The fraudulent practice of sending emails to individuals that purport to come from a legitimate Internet retailer or financial service. The aim of phishing is to persuade the victim to voluntarily disclose sensitive information, such as bank account and credit card details, which can then be exploited to defraud the individual concerned.

Piracy A popular term for copyright violations – the unauthorised copying, distribution or sale of informational goods over which some party claims to possess proprietorial rights.

Policing A wide range of activities which serve to monitor and control social behaviour. Policing may be undertaken by official state-sanctioned bodies (such as the police), by private organisations, by communities or individuals.

Pornography Visual or written representations of a sexually explicit nature, whose primary aim or use is to stimulate sexual excitement.

Privacy The right to be left alone; freedom from observation and interference from others.

Property rights Legally institutionalised rights to own and control goods.

Public opinion An aggregate measure of views or beliefs held among a specified population about a particular issue.

Recording of crime The process through which reported incidents are officially classified and recorded as instances of crimes.

Reporting of crime The process through which incidents of criminal victimisation are reported to authorities such as the police or to other organisations and bodies who monitor crime levels.

Representations of crime The constructions and depictions of crime and criminals that circulate within mass media, political discourse, and official accounts of the 'crime problem'. Such representations may purport to be either 'factual' or 'fictional' in character.

Social inclusion and exclusion The duality in which some individuals and groups are economically, politically and culturally incorporated within the social order, and others are excluded from full participation within it. See also **Digital divide.**

Social networking The practice of encountering, interacting and forming social relations with others using Internet-based sites or services designed for this purpose.

Spoofing The fraudulent practice of establishing facsimiles of legitimate websites, to which victims can be directed and where they will unknowingly surrender sensitive information such as bank details, credit card numbers and account passwords.

Stalking Repeated harassing or threatening behaviour in which an offender persistently contacts, follows, approaches, threatens or otherwise subjects a victim to unwelcome attentions. See also **Cyberstalking**.

Surveillance The systematic observation and monitoring of people and places as a tool for effecting greater control over behaviour.

Surveys of crime and victimisation An alternative to official crime statistics, criminal victimisation surveys ask members of the public about their experiences of crime, including many that, for a variety or reasons, may not have been reported to the police or other authorities.

Technological determinism This term means overstating the power of the Internet and underplaying the importance of the individual actor. Like wider debates about the effects of harmful media content, much mediated public discourse about computer-related crime is underpinned by a strong technological determinism, suggesting that there is something inherently sinister about the technology itself.

Terrorism A notoriously slippery and contested term. In its most conventional sense, it denotes the use of violence or the threat of violence in pursuit of political ends. See also **Cyber-terrorism**.

Transnational crime and policing Criminal activities that span the borders of national territories, and crime prevention and control initiatives designed to tackle or reduce such offences.

Trojan Horses Malicious software programs which are infiltrated into computers disguised as benign applications or data.

Viruses Pieces of computer code that can 'infect' computer systems causing disruption to their normal operation.

War on Terror Rhetorical and political response among Western governments in the wake of the September 11 2001 attacks, which adopts a highly aggressive and 'pro-active' stance in identifying, capturing and disabling actual, suspected and potential terrorists, along with those who are perceived to sympathise with or support their goals.

Web 2.0 A widely used but rather amorphous term that is often used to identify Web-based tools and services that enable users to collaborate and share information, with a particular focus upon 'user-generated' content.

Website defacement The activity of altering the code organising a website so as to alter the visible screen content.

World Wide Web or **WWW** A system of interlinked documents that can be accessed and navigated via the Internet using Web browser software.

Worms A computer worm is a self-replicating program. It uses a network to send copies of itself to other nodes (computers on the network) and may do so without any user intervention. Unlike a **virus** it does not need to attach itself to an existing program. Worms almost always cause at least some harm to the network, if only by consuming bandwidth, whereas viruses almost always corrupt or devour files on a targeted computer.

Index